Introduction to Research Methods and Data Analysis in Psychology

Second Edition

DARREN LANGDRIDGE

GARETH HAGGER-JOHNSON

PEARSON

Prentice Hall

Harlow, England • London • New York • Boston • San Francisco • Toronto • Sydney • Singapore • Hong Kong
Tokyo • Seoul • Taipei • New Delhi • Cape Town • Madrid • Mexico City • Amsterdam • Munich • Paris • Milan

Pearson Education Limited
Edinburgh Gate
Harlow
Essex CM20 2JE
England

and Associated Companies throughout the world

Visit us on the World Wide Web at:
www.pearsoned.co.uk

First published 2004
Second edition 2009

ISBN 978-0-13-198203-1

British Library Cataloguing-in-Publication Data
A catalogue record for this book is available from the British Library

Library of Congress Cataloging-in-Publication Data
Langdridge, Darren.
    Introduction to research methods and data analysis in psychology /
Darren Langdridge, Gareth Hagger-Johnson. -- 2nd ed.
        p. cm.
    ISBN 978-0-13-198203-1 (pbk.)
    1. Psychology--Research--Methodology. 2. Psychology--Statistical
methods. I. Hagger-Johnson, Gareth. II. Title.
    BF76.5.L33 2009
    150.72--dc22

                                                            2009003560

10 9 8 7 6 5 4 3 2 1
13 12 11 10 09

Typeset in 9.5pt Stone Serif by 30
Printed and bound by Ashford Colour Press Ltd, Gosport

The publisher's policy is to use paper manufactured from sustainable forests.

Introduction to Research Methods and
Data Analysis in Psychology

Visit the *Introduction to Research Methods and Data Analysis in Psychology*, Second Edition, Companion Website at **www.pearsoned.co.uk/langdridge** to find valuable **student** learning material including:

- Multiple choice questions to test your knowledge of key terms
- Short answer questions to give you further practice at exam-style questions
- Weblinks to useful sites to help you explore relevant topics in more depth
- Downloadable datasets and text files to accompany exercises and examples from Sections 2 and 3
- A guide with useful tips and common traps

PEARSON
Education

We work with leading authors to develop the
strongest educational materials in psychology
bringing cutting-edge thinking and best learning
practice to a global market.

Under a range of well-known imprints, including
Prentice Hall, we craft high-quality print and
electronic publications which help readers
to understand and apply their content, whether
studying or at work.

To find out more about the complete range of our
publishing, please visit us on the World Wide Web at:
www.pearsoned.co.uk

Dedication

This book is dedicated to the memory of my grandparents,
Sheila and Albert Preece, whose love and support will never
be forgotten
–D. L.

This book is dedicated to Richard Street, whose patience
and understanding make my work possible.
–G. H.-J.

Brief contents

List of figures   *xvii*
Guided tour   *xxii*
Preface   *xxiv*
Acknowledgements   *xxvi*
Publisher's acknowledgements   *xxvii*

Part 1 Introducing research methods

1	Starting out in research	3
2	Variables: definitions and measurement	40
3	Reliability, validity, sampling and groups	50
4	Collecting data 1: interviews and observation	61
5	Collecting data 2: questionnaires and psychometric tests	87
6	Collecting data 3: experimental and quasi-experimental designs	113
7	E-research	137

Part 2 Analysing quantitative data

8	Fundamentals of statistics	163
9	Entering and manipulating data	192
10	Graphical representation and descriptive statistics	210
11	Bivariate analysis 1: exploring differences between variables	230
12	Bivariate analysis 2: exploring relationships between variables	255
13	Analysis of variance (ANOVA)	271
14	Multivariate analysis of variance (MANOVA)	295
15	Regression	316
	■ Statistical test flowchart	325
16	Introducing R and R commander	328

Part 3 Analysing qualitative data

17	Fundamentals of qualitative research	361
18	Transcribing, coding and organising textual data	373

19	Phenomenological research methods	386
20	Grounded theory	405
21	Discourse analysis	418
22	Life story and narrative research	443
23	The use of computers in qualitative research	460
24	Mixed methods	474

Part 4   Ethics and reporting findings

25	The ethics and politics of psychological research	499
26	Reporting and presenting findings	512
	Appendix: Tables of critical values for statistical tests	526
	References	534
	Index	545

Contents

List of figures   *xvii*
Guided tour   *xxii*
Preface   *xxiv*
Acknowledgements   *xxvi*
Publisher's acknowledgements   *xxvii*

Part 1   Introducing research methods

1	Starting out in research	3
	Introduction	3
1.1	Why research?	4
1.2	A very brief history of science	6
1.3	Quantitative versus qualitative?	13
1.4	A brief introduction to methods in the social sciences	16
1.5	Planning research	16
	Further reading	38

2	Variables: definitions and measurement	40
	Introduction	40
2.1	Operationalising variables	41
2.2	Independent and dependent variables	42
2.3	The problem of error and confounding variables	43
2.4	Levels of measurement	45
2.5	Categorical and continuous variables	48
	Further reading	49

3	Reliability, validity, sampling and groups	50
	Introduction	50
3.1	Reliability	50
3.2	Validity	51
3.3	The role of replication in the social sciences	52
3.4	Populations and samples	53
3.5	The problem of sampling bias	53

3.6	Methods of sampling	54
3.7	Sample sizes	57
3.8	Control and placebo groups	59
	Further reading	60

4	**Collecting data 1: interviews and observation**	**61**
	Introduction	61
4.1	Interviewing	62
4.2	Types, purposes and structures of interviews	62
4.3	Interview techniques	66
4.4	Group discussions	71
4.5	Repertory grid techniques	74
4.6	Observation	75
4.7	Structured and non-participant observation	76
4.8	Participant observation	82
	Further reading	85

5	**Collecting data 2: questionnaires and psychometric tests**	**87**
	Introduction	87
5.1	Questionnaires	87
5.2	The first rule of questionnaire design: don't reinvent the wheel	88
5.3	General principles, types and structure of questionnaires	89
5.4	Writing questions and measuring attitudes	93
5.5	Psychometrics	100
5.6	Reliability	100
5.7	Validity	104
5.8	Psychometric tests	108
	Further reading	*111*

6	**Collecting data 3: experimental and quasi-experimental designs**	**113**
	Introduction	113
6.1	The role of experiments in psychology	114
6.2	Types of experiment	116
6.3	Identifying four sources of error in experiments	123
6.4	Four ways to reduce error in experiments	125
6.5	Types of experimental design	126
6.6	Running an experiment	131
6.7	Describing an experiment: a note about causality	133
6.8	Returning to the basics of design	135
	Further reading	*136*

7	E-research	137
	Introduction	137
7.1	Types of e-research	138
7.2	A warning – what is the population?	139
7.3	E-research and online topics	140
7.4	E-research and offline topics	144
7.5	Ethical issues in e-research	154
	Further reading	159
	Resources	160

Part 2 Analysing quantitive data

8	Fundamentals of statistics	163
	Introduction	163
8.1	Descriptive and inferential statistics	165
8.2	Measures of central tendency and dispersion	165
8.3	Probability	176
8.4	Levels of significance	181
8.5	The normal distribution	183
8.6	Understanding z-scores	187
8.7	Standard error	188
8.8	Parametric versus non-parametric tests	189
8.9	Statistical power	190
	Further reading	191
9	Entering and manipulating data	192
	Introduction	192
9.1	First steps with SPSS	193
9.2	The Data Editor window	196
9.3	Defining variables	197
9.4	Entering data	200
9.5	Saving and opening data files	201
9.6	Sorting and splitting files	201
9.7	Selecting cases	204
9.8	Recoding variables	206
9.9	Computing new variables	208
	Further reading	209
10	Graphical representation and descriptive statistics	210
	Introduction	210
10.1	Descriptive statistics	211
10.2	Simple and complex bar charts	216

10.3	Histograms	220
10.4	Pie charts	222
10.5	Box plots	223
10.6	Scattergrams	225
10.7	Editing charts	229

11	**Bivariate analysis 1: exploring differences between variables**	**230**
	Introduction	230
11.1	Theoretical issues in inferential statistics	230
11.2	Introducing the *t*-test	232
11.3	Calculating an independent groups *t*-test	235
11.4	Calculating a related *t*-test	241
11.5	Introducing non-parametric tests of difference	245
11.6	Calculating a Mann–Whitney *U*-test	246
11.7	Calculating a Wilcoxon test	250

12	**Bivariate analysis 2: exploring relationships between variables**	**255**
	Introduction	255
12.1	Introducing chi-square	256
12.2	Calculating chi-square	258
12.3	Introducing correlation coefficients	263
12.4	Calculating correlation coefficients	265

13	**Analysis of variance (ANOVA)**	**271**
	Introduction	271
13.1	Terminology and techniques	272
13.2	Calculating a one-way ANOVA	275
13.3	Calculating a two-way ANOVA	286
13.4	Calculating a mixed design ANOVA	290
13.5	Non-parametric alternative: Kruskal–Wallis and Friedman	293

14	**Multivariate analysis of variance (MANOVA)**	**295**
	Introduction	295
14.1	When would you use MANOVA?	296
14.2	Introduction to MANOVA	298
14.3	Calculating a MANOVA	299
14.4	Running a discriminant function analysis	309
	Further reading	315

15	Regression	316
	Introduction	316
15.1	Terminology and techniques	317
15.2	Calculating multiple regression using SPSS	321
	Further reading on statistics	324
	■ *Statistical test flowcharts*	325

16	Introducing R and R commander	328
	Introduction	328
16.1	What is R?	328
16.2	Installing new R libraries	332
16.3	The R commander	333
16.4	Importing data into R	338
16.5	Getting started with R code	339
16.6	Making comments	340
16.7	Basic R commands	340
16.8	Vectors	341
16.9	Large and small numbers	342
16.10	Save your code	342
16.11	Creating and saving a data frame	343
16.12	Graphs	343
16.13	Independent *t*-test	345
16.14	Related *t*-test	346
16.15	Mann–Whitney test	347
16.16	Wilcoxon test	347
16.17	Chi square	347
16.18	Correlation and linear regression	348
16.19	Multiple regression	349
16.20	One-way ANOVA	350
16.21	Two-way ANOVA	352
16.22	Repeated measures ANOVA	354
16.23	Reshaping wide format data into long format	355
	Further R resources	357
	Further reading	357

Part 3   Analysing qualitative data

17	Fundamentals of qualitative research	361
	Introduction	361
17.1	Philosophical underpinnings: the old paradigm	362
17.2	Philosophical underpinnings: the new paradigm	365
17.3	Revisiting the qualitative versus quantitative debate	367
17.4	Limitations of the new paradigm for the social sciences	368
17.5	Varieties of qualitative methods and analysis	369
	Further reading	372

18   Transcribing, coding and organising textual data   373
        Introduction   373
18.1   Purposes and principles of transcription   374
18.2   Systems of transcription   376
18.3   Transcription as analysis   377
18.4   Coding qualitative data   378
18.5   Thematic analysis   382
18.6   Organising and presenting the analysis of textual data   383
        Further reading   385

19   Phenomenological research methods   386
        Introduction   386
19.1   The fundamentals of phenomenology: philosophical issues   387
19.2   The fundamentals of phenomenology: methodological issues   389
19.3   Searching for meaning: phenomenological psychology and the
        Duquesne School   392
19.4   Searching for meaning: interpretative phenomenological analysis (IPA)   397
19.5   Strengths, limitations and debates   401
        Further reading   404

20   Grounded theory   405
        Introduction   405
20.1   Introducing grounded theory   406
20.2   Collecting data   406
20.3   The dynamic nature of meaning making   407
20.4   Coding   409
20.5   Memo writing   412
20.6   Theory development   412
20.7   Strengths, limitations and debates   414
        Further reading   417

21   Discourse analysis   418
        Introduction   418
21.1   The turn to language   419
21.2   Approaches to the study of discourse   421
21.3   Discursive psychology   422
21.4   Foucauldian discourse analysis   432
21.5   Strengths, limitations and debates   439
        Further reading   442

22	**Life story and narrative research**	**443**
	Introduction	443
22.1	The turn to narrative	444
22.2	Selecting informants	445
22.3	Collecting data	447
22.4	Triangulation	451
22.5	Analysing life story data	451
22.6	Writing a life story	454
22.7	Narrative practice and form	456
22.8	Strengths, limitations and debates	457
	Further reading	459
23	**The use of computers in qualitative research**	**460**
	Introduction	460
23.1	Use of computers in qualitative research	461
23.2	Qualitative analysis software	462
23.3	Introducing NVivo	463
23.4	Getting started with NVivo 2.0	464
23.5	NVivo version 8.0	469
23.6	Controversies and debates	473
	Further reading	473
24	**Mixed methods**	**474**
	Introduction	474
24.1	Similarities between methods	475
24.2	Four models of (sequenced) mixed methods	477
24.3	Four models of triangulated methods	483
24.4	Blended or 'hybrid' methods	486
24.5	Q method	487
24.6	Other hybrid methods	493
24.7	A final comment	493
	Further reading	494
	Resources: Q method	495

Part 4   Ethics and reporting findings

25	**The ethics and politics of psychological research**	**499**
	Introduction	499
25.1	Ethical fundamentals	500
25.2	Confidentiality and anonymity	502
25.3	Deception	502
25.4	Discomfort and harm	503

25.5   Consent   504
25.6   Non-participation and withdrawal   504
25.7   Research with (non-human) animals   506
25.8   Equal opportunities   508
25.9   Politics and psychological research   509
25.10   Evaluation research   510
25.11   The need for balance   510
        Further reading   *511*

26   Reporting and presenting findings   512
        Introduction   512
26.1   The standard scientific report style   512
26.2   Writing up qualitative research   519
26.3   Writing skills   522
26.4   Presenting research – writing for publication   524
        Further reading   525

        Appendix: Tables of critical values for statistical tests   526
        References   534
        Index   545

Supporting resources

Visit **www.pearsoned.co.uk/langdridge** to find valuable online resources

Companion Website for students
- Multiple choice questions to test your knowledge of key terms
- Short answer questions to give you further practice at exam-style questions
- Weblinks to useful sites to help you explore relevant topics in more depth
- Downloadable datasets and text files to accompany exercises and examples from Sections 2 and 3
- A guide with useful tips and common traps

For instructors
- A set of PowerPoint slide lectures for each chapter
- Classroom activities to help students engage with key topics

Also: The Companion Website provides the following features:
- Search tool to help locate specific items of content
- E-mail results and profile tools to send results of quizzes to instructors
- Online help and support to assist with website usage and troubleshooting

For more information please contact your local Pearson Education sales representative or visit **www.pearsoned.co.uk/langdridge**

List of figures

1.1	The hypothetico-deductive approach	12
1.2	Location of the PsycINFO database in Ovid	27
1.3	Open selected resources button	27
1.4	Search Tools tab	27
1.5	Map Term dialogue box	28
1.6	Mapping Display	28
1.7	Search History	29
1.8	Two search histories	29
1.9	Combining two search histories	29
1.10	Search results display	30
6.1	A parallel groups design	128
6.2	A factorial design	128
6.3	A crossover design	129
6.4	A Latin square design	131
8.1	Example of normal distribution curve overlaid on histogram	184
8.2	The normal distribution curve	186
8.3	Standard deviations and the normal distribution	186
8.4	Area enclosed by the mean and $z = 1.0$	187
9.1	Windows Start Screen	194
9.2	Initial SPSS dialogue box	195
9.3	The Data Editor window	196
9.4	Switching between views	197
9.5	The Variable View window	197
9.6	The Data View window	201
9.7	Sorting data	202
9.8	The Variable Picker button	203
9.9	Selecting cases 1	204
9.10	Selecting cases 2	205
9.11	Recoding into different variables	207
9.12	Recoding old into new values	207
9.13	Computing new variables	209
10.1	Obtaining frequencies output	212
10.2	Frequencies dialogue box	212
10.3	Frequencies: Statistics dialogue box	213
10.4	The Viewer window	214
10.5	Statistics output table for age	214
10.6	Explore dialogue box	216

10.7	Obtaining the Chart Builder	217
10.8	Chart Builder dialogue box	217
10.9	Simple Bar button	218
10.10	Simple Bar dialogue box (1)	218
10.11	Simple Bar dialogue box (2)	219
10.12	Output for simple bar chart	219
10.13	Simple Histogram button	220
10.14	Simple Histogram dialogue box	221
10.15	Output for simple histogram	221
10.16	Pie Chart button	222
10.17	Output for pie chart	223
10.18	Simple Boxplot button	224
10.19	Output for simple boxplot	225
10.20	Simple Scatter dialogue box	226
10.21	Output for simple scatter (1)	227
10.22	Output for simple scatter (2)	227
10.23	Add Fit Line at Total button	228
10.24	Chart Editor	228
10.25	Chart Editor button	229
11.1	Observed difference in means on the sampling distribution of means	234
11.2	Data entered correctly for an independent groups t-test	238
11.3	Independent-Samples T-test dialogue box	239
11.4	Group statistics output table	240
11.5	Independent samples t-test output table	240
11.6	Data entered correctly for a related t-test	243
11.7	Paired-Samples T-test dialogue box	244
11.8	Paired samples statistics output table	244
11.9	Paired samples correlations output table	245
11.10	Paired samples t-test output table	245
11.11	Non-parametric independent samples dialogue box	249
11.12	Rank output table for the Mann–Whitney test	250
11.13	Statistics output table for the Mann–Whitney test	250
11.14	Related-Samples dialogue box	253
11.15	Rank output table for the Wilcoxon test	254
11.16	Statistics output table for the Wilcoxon test	254
12.1	Chi-square test dialogue box	261
12.2	Case processing output table	262
12.3	Cross-tabulation output table	262
12.4	Chi-square statistics output table	263
12.5	Linear and non-linear relationships	265
12.6	Correlation dialogue box	269
12.7	Pearson correlation coefficient output	270
12.8	Spearman correlation coefficient output	270
13.1	Data being used for independent ANOVA computations	276
13.2	Data being used for repeated measures ANOVA computations	277

13.3	Univariate ANOVA dialogue box	278
13.4	Univariate: Options ANOVA dialogue box	279
13.5	Univariate: Post Hoc ANOVA dialogue box	279
13.6	ANOVA descriptive statistics output table	280
13.7	ANOVA test output table	281
13.8	ANOVA multiple comparisons table	281
13.9	Defining factors dialogue box	283
13.10	Repeated Measures ANOVA dialogue box	283
13.11	ANOVA descriptive statistics output table	284
13.12	Table of Mauchly's test of sphericity	284
13.13	Table of within-subjects effects	285
13.14	Related *t*-test output	285
13.15	Univariate ANOVA dialogue box for two-way ANOVA	287
13.16	Univariate ANOVA profile plots box for two-way ANOVA	287
13.17	ANOVA descriptive statistics output table	288
13.18	ANOVA test output table	289
13.19	ANOVA multiple comparisons table	289
13.20	Interaction graph	290
13.21	ANOVA descriptive statistics output table	292
13.22	Mauchly's test of sphericity	292
13.23	Tests of within-subjects effects table	292
13.24	Tests of within-subjects contrasts table	292
13.25	Between-subjects effects table	293
14.1	Data being used for the MANOVA	300
14.2	Obtaining MANOVA	301
14.3	General linear model: Multivariate dialogue box (1)	301
14.4	General linear model: Multivariate dialogue box (2)	302
14.5	Multivariate: Contrasts dialogue box	302
14.6	Descriptive statistics	303
14.7	Box's test	304
14.8	Multivariate tests	304
14.9	Levene's test	305
14.10	Tests of between-subjects effects	306
14.11	Contrast results	307
14.12	MANOVA plot for PCS	308
14.13	MANOVA plot for MCS	309
14.14	Obtaining discriminant function analysis	310
14.15	Discriminant function analysis dialogue box	311
14.16	Classify dialogue box	311
14.17	Eigenvalues output	312
14.18	Wilks' Lambda output	312
14.19	Structure matrix output	313
14.20	Combined groups plot	314
15.1	Linear Regression dialogue box	322
15.2	Regression summary output table	323

15.3	Regression ANOVA output table	323
15.4	Regression coefficients output table	323
16.1	Finding the appropriate platform on the R website	330
16.2	Downloading the R program file from the R website	330
16.3	Starting R in the Windows Start menu	331
16.4	Setting the CRAN mirror	331
16.5	Setting the working directory	332
16.6	Installing the Rcmdr library	334
16.7	Starting Rcmdr	335
16.8	Importing a data file	335
16.9	Naming the data file, specifying a missing data indicator, and specifying the field separator	336
16.10	Specifying which variables are categorical	336
16.11	Summarising continuous variables	337
16.12	Summarising categorical variables	337
16.13	Saving your work	342
16.14	A boxplot produced in R	350
16.15	A graphical representation of a Tukey post-hoc test	351
16.16	A line graph and bar graph of the same data, shown together	353
16.17	Example of the wide format data	354
16.18	Example of the long format data	355
23.1	The Launch Pad	465
23.2	The Project Pad	465
23.3	Document Explorer	466
23.4	An example document imported into NVivo	466
23.5	Example of In-Vivo coding	467
23.6	The Coder	468
23.7	Options window produced when creating a document	469
23.8	NVivo Workspace	470
23.9	The Navigation View	471
23.10	The List View	471
23.11	The Detail View pane	472
24.1	The model of preparation (adapted from Mayring, 2001)	478
24.2	The model of generalisation (adapted from Mayring, 2001)	479
24.3	The model of profoundisation (adapted from Mayring, 2001)	480
24.4	The model of triangulation (adapted from Mayring, 2001)	481
24.5	A framework for thinking about models of triangulation	483
24.6	Q-grid for 49 Q statements, showing layout and numerical values assigned to each position	488
24.7	Flash Q: the initial sort	491
24.8	Flash Q: moving the cards into a forced normal distribution	492

Guided tour

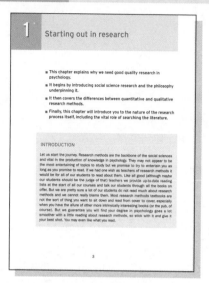

A chapter **Introduction** briefly outlines what the chapter will cover, and how it will do so.

Study boxes give examples of the application of research methods and data analysis with classic and cutting-edge research in psychology.

Activity boxes aid learning by giving simple, quick activities that students can do to help them apply a concept themselves. They also give hints and tips to show how this learning can be taken further.

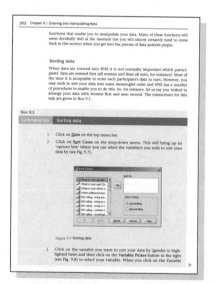

Command boxes offer detailed instructions of how to carry out statistical analysis using the latest version of SPSS and are linked to SPSS files available from the website.

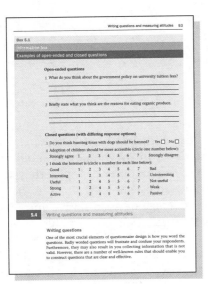

An **Information box** provides the would-be researchers with examples and tips to help them plan research, avoid common mistakes, and ensure a successful project.

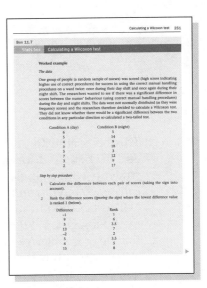

A **Stats box** presents the hand workings of common statistical calculations.

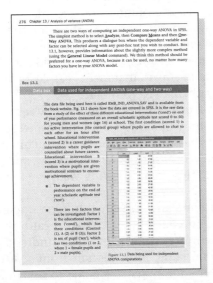

A **Data box** gives further detail on the data used within examples.

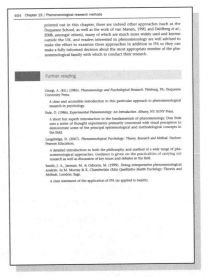

At the end of each chapter, annotated **Further reading** directs students towards helpful books and websites that will give them a deeper understanding of what they've learnt.

Preface

This book aims to present a comprehensive introduction to research methods and data analysis for undergraduate students in psychology. It should provide students with a single textbook to cover the majority of topics they will typically encounter in an undergraduate course in psychology.

This book is unusual because of the coverage of quantitative and qualitative methodologies. While there are many books that aim to introduce either quantitative or qualitative methods, there are very few books that address both. It is also worth noting that those books that do claim to cover both quantitative and qualitative approaches invariably fail to provide sufficient depth on one or the other for most undergraduate courses in psychology.

In addition, this book introduces students to the range of research methods used in psychology using topical real-life examples wherever possible. Considerable coverage is given on the analysis of data from both quantitative (by hand and using SPSS for Windows version 16.0) and qualitative perspectives. The material on the analysis of data is predominantly non-mathematical with formulae kept to a minimum. Increasing numbers of students in psychology lack any formal mathematical training and often find the mathematical presentation of data analysis highly alienating. While it is recognised that some key concepts require the use of basic mathematics, the widespread use of computer packages for the analysis of data means that students can learn statistics 'by doing', not simply by following mathematical formulae.

The book also includes activity boxes (which can be used by lecturers or tutors for class/laboratory activities), study boxes (detailing published research) and information boxes. It is thought that this organisational structure should best facilitate student learning, and the use of the book in classroom and laboratory activities by university lecturers. The accompanying website (see below) provides easy access to these sources.

The principal market will be first, second and possibly third year undergraduates on psychology degrees. Students on courses in sociology, health sciences, applied and generic social sciences, cultural studies, business studies and the humanities may also find this book of value. Professionals from a variety of other disciplines wanting a simple yet comprehensive guide to psychological research methods and data analysis may also find this text of use.

Structure of the book

The book consists of four parts:

■ **Part 1** provides information on research methods. This includes details of the philosophy underpinning the discipline and the distinction between quantitative and qualitative methods. There is detailed advice on searching and reviewing the literature along with information on a number of key issues including the need for accuracy in measuring variables, reliability, validity, sampling and much more. This section also provides coverage on the range of methods used by psychologists to collect data with guidance on interviews, observation, experiments, questionnaires and psychometric tests. There is also a chapter providing advice on conducting 'e-research'.

- **Part 2** provides coverage of the quantitative analysis of data and introduces the reader to the use of SPSS for Windows (version 16.0). This section begins with coverage of the fundamentals of statistics and then moves progressively through the most commonly used statistical tests in psychological research today. Information is provided on the calculation of these statistics by hand and using SPSS. For the really keen, there is an introduction to a piece of new (and free) statistics software called 'R'. At the end of Chapter 15 there is a statistical flowchart designed to guide the reader through the selection of appropriate statistical tests.

- **Part 3** covers qualitative methods of analysis and introduces the reader to phenomenological approaches, grounded theory, discourse analysis and life story/narrative research. The section begins by providing further discussion of the philosophical issues underpinning qualitative and quantitative research. Information is provided on transcription and coding before moving on to cover each of the major approaches to qualitative research in use today. There is also coverage of the use of computers in qualitative analysis and also a chapter on mixed methods.

- **Part 4** covers the important issues of ethics and politics along with information and guidance on reporting and presenting your findings.

Although the book is designed to be read from Chapter 1 through to Chapter 26, the interested reader should be able to dip into any of the chapters without too much difficulty. Most chapters do not rely on others for understanding, but readers new to research methods are advised to progress through the book from Chapter 1 to Chapter 26 to maximise understanding.

Supplementary material

Additional student and lecturer material for this book is provided on an accompanying website (www.pearsoned.co.uk/langdridge). The following student/ lecturer items are available:
- PowerPoint presentation lectures for each chapter;
- Activity boxes as printable handouts for laboratory classes;
- interactive tests to facilitate student learning;
- list of web links;
- information about updates and amendments;
- downloadable text and data files for Parts 2 and 3.

Acknowledgements

I would like to take this opportunity to thank Graham Gibbs, Dallas Cliff and Sue Frost for all the support given to me during my time at the University of Huddersfield when the first edition of this book was written. Thanks also to Trevor Butt, Donna Gornall and Rudy Van Kemenade for feedback on chapters in the first edition.

Darren Langdridge

I am grateful to Darren Shickle and other colleagues in the Academic Unit of Public Health, Leeds Institute of Health Sciences, for their support. I would also like to thank Martha Whiteman and Tony Coxon for their ongoing advice and encouragement. For regular snippets of useful knowledge, I am indebted to Andrew Wawrzyniak, Jeremy Miles and Andy Fugard.

Gareth Hagger-Johnson

Publisher's acknowledgements

We are grateful to the following for permission to reproduce copyright material:

Figures and tables

Figures 1.2, 1.3, 1.4, 1.5, 1.6, 1.7, 1.8, 1.9, 1.10 from OvidSP, July 2008, Ovid Technologies, Inc., Courtesy of Ovid Technologies, Inc.; Figure 9.1 and other Microsoft products screenshots reprinted with permission from Microsoft Corporation; Figure 9.2 and other SPSS software screenshots from Vijan, S., 14 August 2003, Director of Professional Services, SPSS (UK) Ltd, www.spss.com/uk, Screenshots presented with permission of SPSS (UK) Ltd; Figures 16.9, 16.10, 16.11, 16.12 showing R Commander from Fox, J., 27 October 2008, Courtesy of John Fox; Figures 23.1, 23.2, 23.3, 23.4, 23.5, 23.6, 23.7, 23.8, 23.9, 23.10, 23.11 showing NVivo software from QSR International Pty Ltd., www.qsrinternational.com, Courtesy of QSR International Pty Ltd; Figure on page 438 from Didgeridoo Records flyer distributed in Songbird (CD) by Eva Cassidy, Beyond the Sea Limited, Special thanks to Martin Jennings; Tables A4 and A5: adapted *An Introduction to Statistics in Psychology*, Pearson Education (Howitt, D. and Cramer, D. 2000).

Text

Box on page 434 adapted from *Discourse Dynamics: Critical Analysis for Social and Individual Psychology*, Routledge (Parker, I. 1992) pp. 6–22.; Box on page 506 adapted from *Guidelines for Psychologists Working with-Animals* (2007) © The British Psychological Society, Reproduced with permission.

In some instances we have been unable to trace the owners of copyright material, and we would appreciate any information that would enable us to do so.

Introducing research methods

1 Starting out in research

2 Variables: definitions and measurement

3 Reliability, validity, sampling and groups

4 Collecting data 1: interviews and observation

5 Collecting data 2: questionnaires and psychometric tests

6 Collecting data 3: experimental and quasi-experimental designs

7 E-research

1 Starting out in research

- This chapter explains why we need good quality research in psychology.
- It begins by introducing social science research and the philosophy underpinning it.
- It then covers the differences between quantitative and qualitative research methods.
- Finally, this chapter will introduce you to the nature of the research process itself, including the vital role of searching the literature.

INTRODUCTION

Let us start the journey. Research methods are the backbone of the social sciences and vital in the production of knowledge in psychology. They may not appear to be the most entertaining of topics to study but we promise to try to entertain you as long as you promise to read. If we had one wish as teachers of research methods it would be for all of our students to read about them. Like all good (although maybe our students should be the judge of that) teachers we provide up-to-date reading lists at the start of all our courses and talk our students through all the books on offer. But we are pretty sure a lot of our students do not read much about research methods and we cannot really blame them. Most research methods textbooks are not the sort of thing you want to sit down and read from cover to cover, especially when you have the allure of other more intrinsically interesting books (or the pub, of course). But we guarantee you will find your degree in psychology goes a lot smoother with a little reading about research methods, so stick with it and give it your best shot. You may even like what you read.

1.1   Why research?

We will start by explaining just what research methods are and why you need to complete several years of courses on research methods and data analysis during a degree in any social science, but most especially in psychology. In short, research is the systematic study of some topic in order to find answers to questions. In psychology these questions are invariably (though not exclusively) about people – while in chemistry, for example, they are about chemical things. The important issue at stake here is what evidence we can provide for the questions we ask and answers we give. So, if we want to know whether there is a difference between men and women in driving ability and, most particularly, whether women are safer drivers, we would want to provide evidence for any claims we make. Every day we see, hear and read things based on so-called 'common sense':

■ Watching sex on television is harmful to children (or violence on television produces a more violent society).

■ Children living with single parents do less well in school than children living with two parents.

■ Women are more naturally caring and therefore make better parents than men.

■ Men are better at mathematics than women.

However, these beliefs are often based on prejudice, speculation or just simply misinformation. Unless we have evidence, from good quality research (and it is very important that the research is good quality), we cannot make any reliable claims (for or against) these statements. As good psychological researchers we want better than that. Why else do we study this subject? We want to be able to contribute to debates such as these, understand more about human nature and provide evidence that either supports or challenges statements such as these. And this is why we need to know about methods of research and data analysis. Only through knowledge of research methods can we carry out good quality research that elevates our findings above the opinion and speculation that we encounter on an almost daily basis on TV, in the papers or in everyday conversation.

We need think only of some classic psychological findings to realise the value of good quality research. The studies by Solomon Asch (1951, 1952, 1956) on group conformity are a good example (see Box 1.1).

Box 1.1	Study box

Asch, S. E. (1956). Studies of independence and conformity: I. A minority of one against a unanimous majority. *Psychological Monographs*, **70** (9) (whole issue, no. 416).

Asch recruited participants for a study on 'visual perception'. If you were a participant you would find yourself seated in the second to last row in a laboratory (with only one person behind you) and six to eight people in front of you. You would not realise that the other participants (who are all confederates, that is, people working with the experimenter) forced you into this seating position. You are asked to judge the lengths of vertical lines drawn on a board at the front of the room. There is one standard line and three comparison lines. All the people in the room are asked to call out which line is the same length as the standard line. The answer is very obvious as one line is the same length and the other two lines are either much shorter or longer than the standard line. Answers are called out person by person from front to back along the rows. In the first test everyone announces the correct answer and calls out the letter attached to the line that matches the length of the standard line shown on the board. Then the experimenter puts up a board with another standard line and three comparison lines (again with one obvious match). Once again, one by one, the participants (starting at the front) call out the correct answer. However, in the third round of the test with yet another board (once again with an obvious line match), the first participant calls out the wrong line letter, and so does the next person and the next (six people in total) until it is your turn. Of course you think you would give the correct answer regardless of what everyone else said as it was obvious what was the correct answer. Well, it is not that simple. Asch found that one in three people went along with the group and gave the wrong answer when it came to their turn to call out the letter of the matching line. Asch knew that the choice was obvious because he repeated the experiment with participants writing their answers privately on paper and the judgements were almost totally error free (less than 1 per cent of mistakes). It was obvious to Asch that the participant went along with the group because of the effect of group pressure and the desire to conform. This finding was found time and time again as Asch and others replicated the experiment and it has established itself as an extremely strong and stable psychological finding about human nature.

The Asch studies used an innovative experimental method to manipulate the participants and demonstrate a particular aspect of human behaviour. The thing to remember from this example is that the fascinating findings obtained about conformity and group pressure only happened through appropriate knowledge and use of research methods. Without an understanding of research methods we would not be able to carry out studies like this and make claims about human nature that are any better than 'common sense', and psychology would be a much more limited discipline.

1.2	A very brief history of science

First we must begin by stating that this will be a very (!) brief history of psychological research (if you want to explore the history of psychology and the social sciences in more detail look at the Further reading section at the end of the chapter for some suggested reading material). We will move rapidly (and superficially) through a great deal of history in order to show how current debates about particular approaches to research methods came about. We will also introduce you to several new ideas, which should enable you to understand more about the nature of psychological research today (and the structure of this book).

The beginnings of science

Social research as we know it today emerged out of a scientific age. Very early thinkers (before the sixteenth century) who wrote about human nature tended to speculate at a very general level about the nature of humanity and/or rely on their status as an 'authority' for justification of their arguments. Often these speculations were sophisticated and insightful but they were rarely based on evidence collected in a systematic manner. However, Francis Bacon (1561–1626) and Isaac Newton (1642–1727), working in the physical sciences (what we now tend to understand as biology, chemistry and physics), clearly and widely demonstrated the value of empirical work in making claims about the world. That is, work based on experience – invariably through observation of or experimentation with the natural world rather than theory or speculation. It is important to note that early scientists such as these still thought they were studying processes created by God, albeit in scientific ways. This scientific approach emerged as a force to be reckoned with, as it enabled technological innovations that had practical and beneficial impact on life at that time.

It is perhaps not surprising given the success of the physical sciences that many of the early figures in the social sciences wanted to position their work within the realm of science, for with science came credibility and respectability. So, for instance, Sigmund Freud (1856–1939) proclaimed his work to be the scientific study of human nature. At that time it was widely believed that the same scientific methods were applicable to both the physical and the social sciences and indeed this belief continues to this day among many psychologists. Freud, one of the early psychological theorists and founder of psychoanalytic theory, used clinical case studies based on therapeutic interviews with his patients to generate data and then theories (we talk more about these particular methods in Chapter 4). His theories about human nature came from close observation of his patients and led to an enormous body of work which still influences the discipline today. Psychoanalytic theory has, however, been subject to considerable criticism for not being scientific at all despite the claims of its founder to the contrary. The over-reliance on clinical case study to provide data has led to charges of bias in the data collected. But perhaps the most significant criticism that is levelled at psychoanalytic theory concerns the perceived lack of concrete testable statements about the theory. Instead, critics have argued that psychoanalytic theory is not scientific at all, for (1) there is little possibility of testing the imprecise statements that stem from theory, and (2) even when evidence provides a challenge to the statement it is not rejected but merely modified to fit the evidence. We will come back to some of these issues later when discussing the work of the philosopher Karl Popper, who strongly argued against psychoanalysis as a science (and also again in Chapter 17 when introducing qualitative methods).

Later psychological theorists have tended, often as a reaction against psychoanalysis, to embrace (what they believed to be) scientific methods more strongly (often more strongly than theorists in the natural sciences!). For instance, behaviourism emerged as the dominant approach to psychology in the middle of the twentieth century. Behaviourists concentrated on only that which was directly observable and dismissed research into the workings of the mind (like psychoanalysis and what we now call cognitive psychology) as unscientific. They believed that only through study of directly observable events could psychology be a truly scientific discipline. In their defence, this is not an untenable position. There are good philosophical arguments that lend support to this position. Needless to say, many others disagreed with this position. Cognitive psychologists believed that it was possible, and indeed scientific, to study the workings of the mind. This position became more and more influential and in the early 1980s cognitive psychology became the dominant theoretical approach in the discipline. At the same time, interest in behaviourism lessened. Although interest in behaviourism still continues to this day, it is no longer the dominant approach to psychological research that it once was. More recently, we can see other movements in the discipline that provide radical challenges to the dominant cognitivism. These approaches do not necessarily seek to be scientific at all and provide an alternative to more 'traditional' scientific psychological research. We will talk more about these recent developments later in this chapter and then again in Part 3 when we introduce the range of qualitative research methods within psychology that have assumed increasing importance in recent years.

So what is science?

This is not as simple a question as it seems. Although many people believe there is a single approach to method that we call science, the truth is that the criteria for scientific knowledge are controversial and subject to considerable debate. The desire to clearly explicate the scientific method exists because it is believed by many that only through use of the scientific method can we be confident in the quality of the knowledge we obtain about the world.

Perhaps the easiest way to answer the question posed at the start of this section is to contrast knowledge about the world obtained through science (or scientific investigation) with ordinary everyday (or 'common-sense') knowledge. Chalmers (1999: 1) starts his excellent discussion of the philosophy of science through an examination of the widely held 'common-sense' view of science:

When it is claimed that science is special because it is based on the facts, the facts are presumed to be claims about the world that can be directly established by a careful, unprejudiced use of the senses. Science is to be based on what we can see, hear and touch rather than personal opinions or speculative imaginings. If observation of the world is carried out in a careful, unprejudiced way then the facts established in this way will constitute a secure, objective basis for science.

This mistaken view still remains a widely held view about the nature of science. It is this understanding of science, in various guises, that has been taken up by many social scientists and most particularly psychologists. As you can see, the two factors that mark out science from everyday knowledge in this formulation are that we (1) acquire information about the world through experience and (2) that the information we acquire in this way is objective. The first claim, that science should be based on empirical evidence (evidence acquired through experience, observation, experimentation and so on), is less controversial for psychologists as many (but not all) would support this position. Without empirical data derived from good quality research many psychologists believe we would have no findings and therefore no evidence to enable us to make claims about human nature.[1] However, even this first issue is not as straightforward as it seems, for many 'mature sciences' such as physics do not simply rely on the collection of data for their advancement. Indeed, some of the most important and exciting work in physics is theoretical and not empirical at all. The second statement, that science (and therefore psychology if it claims to be a science) must be objective, is even more controversial. Many psychologists would support this claim and believe strongly that one of the central purposes of research methods is to enable us to collect empirical data that are objective and free from bias. These people believe that this approach enables psychologists to make stronger claims about human nature than those based on subjective information derived through everyday experience. While many, if not all, psychologists would wish for their research to be privileged above common sense, not all believe that we can claim the work we do is objective. Instead these psychologists argue that a more useful (and better/more accurate/realistic) understanding of the nature of the discipline comes about when we do in fact explicitly recognise the subjective nature of the research process. We will come

---

[1] It is important to clarify what we mean by empirical (and empiricist) here. In a very strict sense empiricism is based on the assumption that all knowledge claims about the world must be derived through direct experience of the world (through our five senses). Very few people would subscribe to this very strict definition today as it is generally believed that direct experience does not provide incontrovertible access to truths about the world. However, modern-day adherents of empiricism believe that gathering data (often through experimentation using instruments and tests rather than through direct experience) does move us closer to the truth than theoretical argument alone. Willig (2001) clearly and importantly marks out the difference between the terms **empiricism** and **empirical** as follows: 'While "empiricist" refers to the attitude that all knowledge claims must be grounded in data, "empirical" is a descriptive term referring to research involving the collection and analysis of data' (p. 4). And psychology is very much an empirical discipline.

back to these issues in more detail later when we discuss the differences between **quantitative** and **qualitative research** in the social sciences.

Induction

Induction is the process by which scientists decide on the basis of multiple observations or experiments that some theory is true or not. If we observe natural phenomena, such as the effect of a Bunsen burner flame on a chemical element like sodium, we can conclude, on the basis of multiple observations, a general principle: that all sodium glows orange when heated with a flame. The common nature of induction is that through a finite number of observations (or experiments) we generate a general conclusion for all such future observations (or experiments). A great deal of science relies on this principle. Drug efficacy and safety provide one obvious example. On the basis of repeated drug trials we learn which drugs are effective in treating which conditions and we also learn which drugs are safe for us to consume and which are not. Because we have repeatedly found a drug to work (and be safe) in these trials, we conclude that it will always act in this way in the future.

However, there is a problem with the method of induction that has challenged philosophers of science for many years. The problem is a simple one to pose but a very difficult one to answer (if it is possible to answer at all): how can a finite number of observations about some event in the past (such as the effect of a flame on sodium or a drug in treating some illness) *guarantee* that we will always see this same effect in the future? Firstly, we can never be certain that we have considered the full range of relevant conditions, and secondly, there is no certainty that the course of nature will not change. We cannot know with certainty that in the future sodium will always glow orange or the drug will work in the same way. Think of it like this. We set you the task of observing and describing the bird that we commonly know as the swan. You go out and about the lakes in the United Kingdom and observe a common pattern. The swan is a large white bird. Observation after observation demonstrates that the swan is always large and white when an adult. Therefore, you conclude, on the basis of your multiple observations, that *all* swans are large white birds. You have used induction from a finite number of cases to make a general theory (or in science, law) about the natural world. However, the next summer you go on holiday to Australia and discover a black swan on your first visit to a lake. This one observation immediately overturns your general theory of swans despite the very large number of observations you had in support of your theory. The problem is that we can never guarantee that our general conclusion formed from a number of observations (even if the number of observations is very large) will always follow in the future. This is, of course, a major problem for all scientific research that relies on an inductive approach to theory generation.

Popper and the need for falsifiability

Sir Karl Popper (1902–1994) responded to the problem of induction with what he believed to be the solution for scientific research. His arguments remain extremely influential in science and the philosophy of science today. Popper (1963) argued that science does not rely on induction in the first place. He thought that science started with theories (or in his words 'conjectures') which it sought to test. These initial theories were intuitive and lacking supporting evidence. Scientists seek to test their theories (or conjectures) through observation or experimentation to ascertain whether they stand up to the test. If they do not stand up to the test we must reject the theory or conjecture and start again with an alternative. If the theory or conjecture does work when tested then scientists are able to continue to uphold the theory (not as a statement of truth about the world but as an undefeated theory). In this form, Popper essentially argues that we learn from our mistakes. Science understood in this way does not therefore rely on induction. For Popper it is the *falsifiability* of conjectures that matters when making scientific inferences and not repeated positive tests of a conjecture. Evidence in support of a conjecture, from a finite number of observations – an inductive approach – is not important. What is important is that science forms clearly testable conjectures or theories which it then seeks to refute. Science is simply a series of 'conjectures and refutations' (the title of Popper's 1963 book on the topic).

But what separates science from non-science for Popper? If we do not search for evidence supporting a theory but only evidence designed to refute a theory, what makes physics a science and astrology a non-science? Popper termed this the 'problem of demarcation'. He believed that the key issue that separates science from non-science is that scientific conjectures are *at least falsifiable*. That is, they are always framed as clear and explicit statements that can be tested and refuted if the evidence from empirical research fails to support them. In contrast, disciplines that are not scientific, such as astrology, do not provide clear and explicit conjectures that can be refuted. Their conjectures are so imprecise that no evidence can ever serve to disprove the theory. Popper used the criterion of falsifiability to separate science from non-science and marked out psychoanalysis as a 'pseudo-science' despite its claims to be scientific (see Box 1.2).

Box 1.2

Activity box   Science and pseudo-science

- In pairs spend some time thinking of a couple of key conjectures (or theories) put forward by astrology or psychoanalysis. Write these down as clearly and explicitly as possible.
- Now plan a study to test the conjectures you have written.
  - Can these conjectures be falsified by your study? Does this differ from conjectures put forward in chemistry, physics or biology? Why?
  - How do you think astrologers or psychoanalysts would respond to and explain your findings if the conjectures were falsified? Do you think chemists, physicists or biologists would react differently? Why?

The failings of falsification and Bayesianism

Although Popper's ideas remain influential in science today, they have been subjected to considerable criticism. The principal criticism is an obvious one. While Popper has produced a sophisticated understanding of science that enables us to separate science from pseudo-science, he has not actually dealt with the problem of induction at all. He has not given us a way of understanding *positive* scientific knowledge, only *negative* scientific knowledge. And for most scientists it is *positive* scientific knowledge that is the most important. Popper shows us that a single negative example can disprove a theory but provides no mechanism for judging whether a theory is right or not. We treat and cure illnesses because we know that certain causes (such as a drug) always (as far as we can tell) have certain effects (such as a cure for illness). We need to know why we should prefer one theory to another and for that we need some criteria for judging the quality of theories on the basis of how much evidence we have in support of them. Popper seems to have ignored what is arguably most important for science.

So, how are we going to resolve the problem of induction? For if we believe in positive science and the benefits of past observations (or experiments) in predicting future effects we need to deal with the problem of induction. One possible (although not perfect) solution has been proposed by the Bayesians (named after Thomas Bayes, 1701–1761). Bayesians are philosophers who argue that our beliefs (including scientific beliefs) come in degrees. So, for example, we may believe that there is a 50 per cent chance (or 0.5 degree likelihood) of rain tomorrow and only a 10 per cent chance (or 0.1 degree likelihood) of snow. That is, we express the likelihood of future events on the basis of past knowledge. These degrees of belief are the extent to which events are subjectively probable (and we will talk about probability much more in later chapters on statistics).

The essence of Bayesianism is that it does not matter what degree of probability you assign to some event in the first place (for instance, when you propose a conjecture or theory) as long as you revise your probability prediction in a rational way when faced with evidence in support of or against your conjecture. With this principle in mind we can see a way through the problem of induction. For, although we still cannot state with absolute certainty that sodium will always glow orange when subjected to a flame or a particular drug will always cure an illness, we can state that it is very likely that they will act in these ways in the future because we have so much evidence in support of these conjectures from past observations. It is highly probable that sodium will burn orange and we would be very surprised if it did not. The Bayesian approach to probability enables us to revise our conjectures on the basis of empirical evidence and be confident (or not) to different degrees in the strength of our conjectures on the basis of past evidence. This clearly enables us to say something about our knowledge of the world on the basis of positive evidence supporting our theories.

Like all philosophical principles the Bayesian approach has been the subject of considerable criticism. In essence, the criticism concerns the subjective nature of the judgements being made about probability and inherent difficulties in deciding between two competing positions. However, even accepting this difficulty, we think it serves as a useful way of understanding the nature of particular approaches to the generation of social scientific knowledge. If you want to read more about this approach and the debates surrounding it, see Chalmers (1999).

The hypothetico-deductive method

The approach most commonly understood as the principal scientific method within the social sciences is known as the **hypothetico-deductive** method. This is often, mistakenly, contrasted with the method of induction. In fact this approach must be seen in relation to an inductive approach rather than in opposition to it. The hypothetico-deductive approach first entails the researcher producing **hypotheses** (or specific predictions) to be tested. These predictions are subject to some empirical test and deductions made from the results of the test. Most often the hypotheses to be tested stem from **theories** about the object of study. Theories are systems of ideas or statements that explain some phenomena. They are generally derived from previous inductive research (series of observations for instance) or through intuition and reasoning. Through empirical tests of the hypotheses we can find evidence that supports or challenges our theory. If there is evidence to challenge the hypothesis it is rejected and the theory must be abandoned or amended to account for the data. If the test produces evidence in support of our hypothesis we can say we have support for our hypothesis and therefore our theory (see Fig. 1.1).

The hypothetico-deductive approach continues in a cyclical fashion, with hypotheses generated from theories being tested empirically and this evidence providing support for or challenges to the theory that generated the hypotheses. On this basis, increasing knowledge is gathered about the object of study and theories are developed and modified to account for the empirical data we have about the world. Much, though not all, research in psychology follows this hypothetico-deductive approach. This has prompted criticism from some

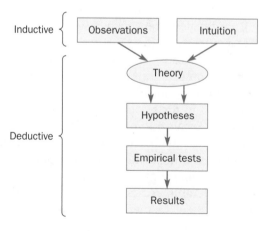

Figure 1.1 The hypothetico-deductive approach

people who believe that psychology has moved too quickly to model itself on a particular, rather restricted, view of the natural sciences. This move is considered a problem, for many people believe that the discipline has not yet built a sufficiently strong base of knowledge discerned from inductive research to produce generally accepted systems of ideas, or **paradigms**, that can be tested (Kuhn, 1970). It is, arguably though probably, the case that psychology needs both inductive and deductive approaches to research.

1.3	Quantitative versus qualitative?

Although the preceding discussion of philosophy was necessary and important, the distinction between types of research that you will most often encounter on a regular basis in psychology is that between **quantitative** and **qualitative** research. The reason for needing to engage with the difficult philosophy so early on is because it provides the backdrop necessary for understanding the essential differences between quantitative and qualitative research and it is vital for psychologists to understand the differences between these two types of research. At a very simple level, quantitative research is that which involves numbers and qualitative research is that which does not. However, there is more to this important distinction than these simple principles and we address this in more detail below.

Quantitative research

Quantitative research (and therefore quantitative research methods) is research that concerns the quantity or measurement of some phenomenon. What this means is that quantitative research is concerned with quantifying (measuring and counting) phenomena. This is still the dominant analytic approach used in psychology in the United Kingdom, continental Europe, Australasia and the United States today. As stated in the previous section, quantitative research tends to subscribe to a particular empirical approach to knowledge, believing that if we measure things accurately enough we can make claims, with some degree of certainty, about the object of study. Quantitative research also tends to use the hypothetico-deductive approach to knowledge acquisition. See Box 1.3 for a good example of quantitative research.

| Box 1.3 | Study box |

Loftus, E. F. & Palmer, J. C. (1973). Reconstruction of automobile destruction: An example of the interaction between language and memory. *Journal of Verbal Learning and Verbal Behavior*, **13**, 585-9.

Elizabeth Loftus and colleagues have conducted numerous experiments on eyewitness testimony over the years. In this study Loftus & Palmer showed their participants a short film of a traffic accident in the laboratory. Participants were given questionnaires about what they had just witnessed. Unknown to the participants the questionnaires they completed were worded differently depending on which condition they were assigned to (all watched the same film). In one condition participants were asked the question 'How fast were the cars going when they *hit* each other?' and in the other condition they were asked the question 'How fast were the cars going when they *smashed* into each other?'

Those asked the latter question (with the prime word 'smashed') gave consistently higher speed estimates for the cars than those asked the former question (with the prime word 'hit'). Furthermore, when participants were questioned one week later about whether they remembered seeing any broken glass in the film those asked the question with 'smashed' were twice as likely to recall broken glass as those asked the question with 'hit'. In fact, the film showed no broken glass. This, and many later studies, demonstrate the effect of what we now call 'leading questions' on memory and recall and has had very important implications for the way people are questioned in the criminal justice system.

Quantitative research also tends to be characterised by a number of other qualities. Firstly, quantitative research is often conducted in controlled settings, such as psychology laboratories, in an attempt to produce findings that are as objective and unaffected by external influences as possible. Quantitative research also tends to focus more on behaviour than qualitative research (which tends to focus more on meanings). Quantitative research also tends to be concerned with prediction rather than 'mere' description (the remit of much qualitative research). Finally, quantitative research tends to involve the use of experimental methods and/or the use of structured questionnaires or observation, often conducted with large numbers of participants. As we are sure you will have noticed, we have avoided saying that quantitative research *always* subscribes to one particular philosophical

Advantages	Disadvantages
■ Precise (in terms of measurement) ■ Controlled (in terms of design) ■ Makes claims about causation ■ Has predictive power (can generalise to other settings on the basis of some finding in a particular setting) ■ Is the dominant approach in psychology	■ May grossly oversimplify the complexity of human nature ■ May fail to recognise or be explicit about the subjective nature of social science research ■ May fail to recognise the individuality and autonomous nature of human beings

position or method. Like much in life, and certainly like much in the social sciences, things are not so clear-cut. For there will always be research that crosses and challenges these traditional divisions (see Chapter 24 on mixed methods).

Qualitative research

Qualitative research (and therefore qualitative research methods) is research that is concerned with the quality or qualities of some phenomenon. Unlike quantitative research, qualitative research is principally concerned with text and meaning. Unlike many quantitative researchers, qualitative researchers predominantly reject the idea that there is a simple relationship between our perception of the world and the world itself. There is also a greater focus on an inductive,[2] rather than hypothetico-deductive, approach to research. However, much qualitative research in psychology is still empirical though often based on the collection of data from a relatively small number of individuals. In general, then, qualitative researchers do not believe that there exist 'definable and quantifiable "social facts"' (Rist, 1975: 18). That is, there are not truths about the world that are waiting to be discovered through more and more sophisticated methods of investigation and measurement. Qualitative research often involves the collection of text-based data through, for instance, small numbers of semi-structured or unstructured interviews. This text then forms the basis of the material for analysis. We will talk about the nature of qualitative research much more in Part 3 where we will also introduce some of the (many) different approaches to this increasingly important type of research.

Advantages	Disadvantages
■ Recognises the subjective experience of participants	■ Cannot apply traditional notions of validity and reliability (see Chapter 3) on the data
■ Often produces unexpected insights about human nature through an open-ended approach to research	■ It is often not appropriate or even possible to make generalisations or predictions
■ Enables an 'insider' perspective on different social worlds	■ Needs justification for it is still not a widely and consistently accepted approach to psychological research
■ Generally does not impose a particular way of 'seeing' on the participants	■ Lack of replicability

2 Strictly speaking, no approach can be purely inductive for we always set out to study *something*. So, for instance, if we set out to study the qualities of dogs we must first find a number of dogs to study. There is always a theoretical backdrop to the questions we ask, no matter how much we try to approach the objects of study without preconceptions. However, qualitative researchers would argue that their approaches attempt to be inductive through explicitly recognising this issue and attempting to understand the qualities of phenomena 'in their appearing' rather than from a particular theoretical perspective (with all sorts of assumptions and expectations that that entails).

1.4	A brief introduction to methods in the social sciences

Now that we have covered the important background to social science research through a quick excursion into philosophy, we will briefly give you a taste of the variety of research methods and forms of data analysis available to researchers in psychology. As you probably know already, psychology is an extremely broad and disparate discipline. In reality there are many 'psychologies' rather than one psychology. At their heart all forms of psychology are interested in understanding more about people and human nature and sometimes animals and animal nature, but tackle this question in radically different ways. So, in biological psychology we see a concern with understanding the biological processes (most often, within the brain) underpinning human behaviour. In social psychology we see a concern with understanding the person (or groups of people) in relation to other people and the wider world more generally. Not surprisingly, these different forms of psychology require quite different methods of research and data analysis.

We have already outlined the basic distinction between quantitative and qualitative research methods (and previously explained the philosophical principles upon which this distinction is based). Quantitative methods of data collection include experiments, structured interviewing, structured observation and the use of structured questionnaires. Interviews, observations and questionnaires are structured, as opposed to unstructured or semi-structured, in that they consist of a predetermined structure (so a set list of questions in an interview or questionnaire or a predetermined list of things to observe). We talk more about these methods in Chapters 4, 5 and 6. Qualitative methods of data collection include unstructured and semi-structured interviews, participant observation (where you observe while taking part in the setting you are observing) and occasionally use of semi-structured questionnaires. Quantitative methods of analysis are principally concerned with the analysis of numerical data and this is where the use of statistics is encountered (Chapters 8 to 16). Qualitative methods are quite varied but principally concerned with the analysis of text and include approaches such as phenomenological/thematic analysis, grounded theory and discourse analysis (Chapters 17–22).

1.5	Planning research

At last we can move on to a little more about the practicalities of carrying out research and tackle a few of the key aspects of psychological research. The sooner you can carry out your own research the better, for it is only through doing this that you can truly understand what the excitement of research is all about. Some of what is written below, with the notable exception of the material on searching and reviewing the literature below, relates to *quantitative* research rather than *qualitative* research. We will cover the planning and process of qualitative research specifically in Part 3.

The 'explosion' of psychological literature

A new psychology article is now published, on average, every 15 minutes (Adair & Vohra, 2003)! The increasingly fast pace of research in psychology means that we cannot possibly read all of the relevant articles, even within specific topic areas. With the best will in the world, we have to make a conscious decision *not* to read a good proportion of the available literature. Four problems have been created, which apply to academics and students alike:

1 How can we access the growing literature?
2 How can we stay up to date with the literature?
3 How can we read all of the relevant literature?
4 How can we cite literature appropriately and selectively?

We cannot control which literature our institutions have access to, but we can develop some practical strategies for finding, reading and citing research effectively. By effective, we mean methods that are the best use of your time. That is, to find a manageable number of relevant articles quickly, read them, and summarise their content. By relevant, we mean relevant *to* your research question (see below). Some of the more traditional strategies are increasingly less effective. For example, we could only read textbooks, but these provide second-hand accounts of a field, and tend to date quickly. Psychology research moves fast. We could read **narrative review** articles. These are written accounts of the literature, similar to an essay, but without a systematic strategy for deciding which research articles should be included (**systematic reviews** are described below). Narrative reviews would not provide the substantive detail that research papers offer. Narrative reviews can be biased by what the author of the review decided was important to include. In the two sections that follow, we provide some practical strategies for searching the literature in two scenarios. The first part of this section describes how to search the literature (**searching for reading**). The second describes how to write about the literature in the form of a literature review (**searching for writing**), which is also mentioned again in Chapter 26.

Searching for reading

The term 'literature review' can sometimes refer to the broad and 'light' reading of a wide body of literature(s) in a fairly general topic area. This is a worthwhile activity, but is better described as browsing or skimming. Browsing and skimming are valuable activities that have their place in the student toolbox, but have their limits. They do not provide a summary of the body of work that surrounds a specific topic or research question. We need to read existing work before starting our own research, and that means selecting relevant articles to read. A literature review can be formally defined as 'the comprehensive study and interpretation of literature that relates to a particular topic' (Aveyard, 2007: 5). The term 'comprehensive' may seem at odds with the term 'particular'. Reading comprehensively requires a deep approach, whereas focusing on one topic may seem like a surface approach. This is not the case. By focusing on one topic, it is possible to read comprehensively *within* that topic. There are at least seven reasons why this kind of literature review is an important part of the research process. It will enable you to:

■ improve your knowledge and understanding;

■ keep abreast of new developments;

■ find out what research has been conducted before;

■ identify gaps in the literature;

■ find validated and reliable scales or tests;

■ find examples of appropriate research designs;

■ avoid committing a jingle or jangle fallacy (discussed below), and to clarify terminology.

It is not sufficient simply to browse the literature in order to understand a topic. There is simply too much information. If you are planning your own research, you will normally want to find relevant existing research before you begin. To do that, you need to design a research question, before searching the literature with that question in mind. This will help you find out what has been done before.

Jingles and jangles

You may think that there is no existing psychological literature for a topic you have decided to study. This is highly unlikely. Psychological terms tend to suffer from the **jingle** and **jangle** fallacies. Terms which are different, but given the same name, are jingles (e.g. some researchers use the term **short term memory** instead of **working memory**). Jangles are terms that are the same, but are given new words (e.g. **sociability** is more or less the same as **extraversion**). A plethora of different terms to describe personality traits appeared in the literature during the twentieth century. It took several decades for researchers to agree on a common language to describe them (see Chapter 5): the big five model. Eventually, this made the literature much easier to read! When embarking on new research, you are most likely to commit a jangle fallacy. It is all too easy to assume that your topic is a new one, and proceed straight into research without a thorough review of the literature. Researchers frequently declare that they have discovered a new construct or psychological mechanism that is simply old wine in new bottles. It often turns out that there is already a great deal of research in the published literature, described using different names.

Narrow your focus

Searching the literature depends on having a focus for the search. Usually this is in the form of a research question (or questions) that is guiding your investigation. You may have been assigned a topic, or a choice of topics, as part of your course. If you are lucky, you will have the freedom to choose what topic you study. You may have been inspired to conduct a project through reading an article or book on the topic. This is very often the starting point for any search of the literature as you can identify the sources given in the study in the reference list (the list at the end of a journal article, book or book chapter) listing the exact source of information being used in support of an argument (see Chapter 26 on report writing for more on the practicalities of referencing sources). Simply by looking at the sources listed in the reference list you may begin to gather a body of evidence. However, this is not a systematic strategy for searching the literature. You may miss newer research, and relying on other researchers' reference lists can provide a biased picture of the literature. Once you have chosen a topic, or been assigned a topic, we recommend designing a research question and then searching electronic databases. These methods are both described below.

Designing a research question

It is worth spending some time designing a good research question before you approach the literature. This is easier said than done. You may find that you struggle to design a research question because you don't know enough about the literature. This can leave you in a 'catch 22' situation. You may be able to get guidance from a supervisor, or use a pre-specified list of ideas (see Box 1.4). If not, there is no easy solution, but remember that you can modify your search question. The trick is not to spend too long reading the literature without a specific aim. Learning what *not* to read is an important skill. In the health sciences, and frequently in psychology, the PICO model can be used to create a clearly defined research question (adapted from Lewis & Roberts, 2008):

- Patient/Population/Problem. This will determine the sampling frame (described in Chapter 2). For example, we might restrict the search to elderly people, or to adolescents.
- Intervention. The treatment or condition which participants were assigned to.
- Comparison/Control. This is usually a control group, or a group not receiving a treatment. In psychology, it is usually another 'level' of the condition which participants were assigned to (the other level of the independent variable, a term defined in Chapter 8).
- Outcome. This is the dependent variable. We want to know if the independent variable (the treatment) influences the dependent variable (the outcome).

PICO can be modified for psychology research by replacing 'intervention' with the independent variable (e.g. the effect of the manipulation in the experiment) in a study design. In Chapter 6, we will describe the various kinds of experimental designs and the terms 'independent' and 'dependent' variable more fully. Part 3 of this book describes how to generate qualitative research questions.

As an example, we were interested in what research had been published into the effect of jogging on depression in adults. Using the PICO model, the research question can be defined in the following way:

- Population: adults.
- Intervention: jogging.
- Control: no jogging.
- Outcome: depression.

The research question is, therefore, 'In adults, does jogging reduce depression?' Because the intervention is not being compared with a different kind of treatment, in this example we can ignore the 'control' part of the PICO model. It is likely that many studies will include a control condition, 'no jogging', but we will need to read the literature before making assumptions about what kinds of studies have been conducted (see below).

Selecting databases

There are specialist databases for psychology which will enable you to identify appropriate material to read and then if it is relevant include in your review (e.g. PsycINFO). By learning to use these databases you will have a vast amount of information at your fingertips. We strongly recommend searching more than one database for relevant articles. It is not sufficient to rely on PsycINFO, because it does not provide coverage of many journals that could be relevant. A considerable amount of qualitative research is published in sociology journals, many of which are not included in PsycINFO. No single database provides complete coverage of all relevant journals. One of the strengths of psychology as a discipline is that none of its topics are studied exclusively by psychologists. Important research can be found in sociological, medical and biological journals, for example. Normally, at least three databases should be searched. For example, you may search PsycINFO, then Medline, then EMBASE. There will almost certainly be duplicates (articles that appear in more than one database), but you are less likely to exclude important articles.

Databases should not be confused with interfaces. Interfaces are software that allow you to search databases, using an Internet browser. The interfaces and databases available to you will depend on what is available at your library. This table shows some of the most popular interfaces and the databases they cover. The interfaces available to you may vary, and so may the databases available

	Interfaces		
	Ovid	Web of Knowledge	PubMed
Databases			
PsycINFO	Y	N	N
Medline	Y	Y	Y
EMBASE	Y	N	N
Science Citation Index	N	Y	N
Social Science Citation Index	N	Y	N
Arts & Humanities Citation Index	N	Y	N

within each interface. For advice, contact your library or information services support team. The table on page 20 provides an approximate guide to which databases are indexed by three popular interfaces. It illustrates the importance of using more than one interface and database. Psychology research can be found in any of the 18 boxes that follow! To get a good picture of the literature, you need to look through more than one 'window'.

Designing search terms

Search terms are the words you will use when searching databases. It is important that you include synonyms (different words for the same concept), especially if there are lots of jangles for the phenomenon you are interested in. If you have a supervisor who is familiar with the subject area, they may be able to help you identify appropriate search terms. For example, if you are interested in the relationship between emotion and the stress hormone cortisol, a psychologist familiar with the area would know that the term 'HPA axis' should also be included. If your research is in the area of health, the PubMed and Ovid interfaces can help you identify synonyms and related terms (see below).

Controlled vocabulary

Some databases, such as Medline, require a **controlled vocabulary** approach. When several different terms are available that describe a similar thing, it will encourage you to select a single heading for these terms. This helps keep the medical literature controlled, avoiding terms that are jingles and jangles of each other. **MeSH headings** (**Me**dical **S**ubject **H**eadings) are useful if your research involves health, but are not available in all databases. We find PubMed's MeSH facility quite useful as a starting point (see www.ncbi.nlm.nih.gov/sites/entrez?db=mesh). For example, we looked for synonyms for 'fish oils' and found the terms 'cod liver oil', 'fatty acids, omega-3', 'docosahexaenoic acids' and 'eicosapentaenoic acid'. These are all included by the MeSH heading 'Fish Oils' [Mesh]. It even provided a definition: 'Oils high in unsaturated fats extracted from the bodies of fish or fish parts, especially the livers. Those from the liver are usually high in vitamin A. The oils are used as dietary supplements, in soaps and detergents, as protective coatings, and as a base for other food products such as vegetable shortenings.' When we entered 'working memory', we learned that this term is covered by 'Memory, Short-Term' [Mesh]. In PsycINFO, the 'Map Term' feature can be used in a similar way (see Box 1.5).

Link key words together

Key words and phrases should be linked together into a **search string**. Phrases are often identified using inverted commas (e.g. 'working memory'). This means that the terms 'working' and 'memory' will not be treated as separate terms, but as a single term. Different databases have different methods for linking key terms together. Some interfaces (e.g. Web of Knowledge) use **Boolean operators**: the words **AND**, **NOT** and **OR**. When combined to form a search string, they tell the database how to combine your key words. **AND** will narrow a search, reducing the number of articles retrieved. This is a good way to focus your search, and shows that you have a well-designed research question (e.g. fish oil **AND** working memory. The keyword **NOT** will also narrow your search, by excluding irrelevant papers (e.g. cows **NOT** beef). The **NOT** operator should be used carefully, because it can exclude many articles that could be relevant. The keyword **OR** will expand your search, by including either of the terms (e.g. fish oil **OR** omega-3). Some interfaces (e.g. Ovid) link key words and phrases in a different way. In Ovid, each search string is stored separately and then combined using **AND** or **OR**. (see Box 1.5 for an example).

Truncation symbols and wildcards

Truncation symbols are used when the suffix of the word is allowed to vary. For example, 'memor*' would retrieve the terms 'memory', 'memorize', 'memorization'. These vary, depending on the database and interface. Usually the symbol is an asterisk (*) but sometimes an exclamation mark (!), question mark (?) or dollar symbol ($) is used.

  Wildcards are symbols that represent *any* letter. There are two types of wildcard. A question mark can be used to identify *one or more* letters. For example, behavi?r would retrieve behavior (sic) and behaviour. A hash can be used to identify *one letter only*. For example, organi#e would retrieve organize and organise.

Box 1.4

Activity box   **Searching the literature**

The purpose of this literature review protocol (Lewis & Roberts, 2008) is to illustrate how you can search the literature in an organised way. The table below can be modified to suit your needs. A blank version is available to download from the book website. You can print this and use a separate copy for each search that you perform. Remember to pick a topic for review that is neither too broad nor too narrow (approximately 10–15 articles maximum). If your topic is too broad:

- focus on a narrower population;
- focus on a more specific intervention;
- focus on a more specific outcome;
- consider using the NOT operator to make your search string more precise.

We have not provided instructions on how to use every database. However, you may find the instructions for using PsycINFO useful (see Box 1.5). If you are new to literature searching, don't worry about the level of detail

▶

Box 1.4 *Continued*

included here. Focus on steps 1 to 5. We have included later steps so that you are aware of the need to look at different sources in your future study.

1.	My research question is:							
	Population or Problem		Intervention or Independent variable		Control (if relevant)		Outcome or Dependent variable	
2.	adults	AND	jogging	AND	[keyword]	AND	depression	
3.	OR		OR		OR		OR	
4.	[keyword]		running		[keyword]		major depression	
		Date:	Search string used:	Enter number of articles:	Comments:			
5.	PsycINFO							
6.	Medline							
7.	EMBASE							
8.	Science Citation Index							
9.	Social Science Citation Index							
10.	Arts & Humanities Citation Index							
11.	Other databases?							
12.	Unpublished research?							
13.	Grey literature?							
14.	Other strategies?							
15.	Create single list		Filename: (e.g. Endnote or Reference Manager)					
16.	How many duplicate articles?							
17.	Create final list (duplicates removed)		Filename:					
	For each article from your final list, make notes under the following headlines:							
	Unique ID number	Available?	Retrieved?	Where stored?	Have I read it yet?	My thoughts and comments		
e.g.	ID1	Yes	Yes	In my cognitive psychology folder	Yes	Enjoyed this one. Lots of strengths to mention in my literature review		

Note: The numbered steps in the table correspond to the numbered steps in the text that follows

Box 1.4 *Continued*

1 Design a specific research question. Use the PICO model if appropriate. Express this clearly at the top of the literature search table. A poorly designed research question will make it much more difficult to search the literature. The PICO model will not be appropriate for qualitative searches where it is necessary to work more flexibly to identify appropriate sources.

2 Enter the keywords for each part of the research question, combining the terms using AND.

3 Use the controlled vocabulary feature (e.g. in MeSH or PsycINFO) to identify synonyms or other appropriate search terms.

4 Under each keyword, enter synonyms or other appropriate keywords for each part of the research question, combining them with the search terms above using OR. You have now created a search string.

5 to 10. For each database, starting with PsycINFO, modify the search string as appropriate for that database. Most databases will contain help files or instructions, and your library website may contain useful resources to help you. Make a note under each heading for:

   a the date of the search;

   b the exact search string you used;

   c the number of articles;

   d any comments about the search (e.g. ways in which the search string needed to be modified for this database).

This may seem like a lot of detail, but it can be extremely useful later in the research process. It is likely to save time in the long run. If you are writing a literature review, it is essential to report your search strategy in detail. Readers should be able to reproduce the search that you performed.

11 Decide what other databases you want to include, if any. For example:

   ■ Cochrane Database of Systematic Reviews (produced by the Cochrane collaboration: www.cochrange.org/reviews);

   ■ CINAHL – Cumulative Index to Nursing Allied Health (www.wales.nhs.uk/sites3/docmetadata.cfm?orgid=520&id=96462);

   ■ Biological Abstracts (may be available to you using Ovid).

12 Decide what unpublished sources you want to include. For example:

   ■ ISI Conference Proceedings (http://wok.mimas.as.uk/)

   ■ ProQuest Digital Dissertations (http://proquest.umi.com/login)

   ■ Zetoc Conference Proceedings (http://zetoc.mimas.ac.uk/)

   ■ UK Clinical Research Portfolio Database (http://public.ukcrn.org.uk/search/)

Box 1.4 *Continued*

13 Grey literature refers to work that is published, but has not been peer reviewed for an academic journal. For example, it may include government policy documents or a research report produced by the voluntary or community sector. Small-scale evaluations and audits can be classed as grey literature.

- Grey Net (www.greynet.org)
- Open-SIGLE (http://opensigle.inist.fr/)

Do not assume that grey literature has a lower quality than academic research published in journals. Research can be produced outside the academic sector and be high in quality.

14 Other strategies can be useful for finding relevant literature. Try the following:

- Hand search in journals that are appropriate for your topic. For example, if you are interested in the effect of emotions on memory, then flicking through the journal *Cognition and Emotion* could help you find relevant articles. This can often be particularly helpful when searching for qualitative articles as they are often (though by no means always) published in specialist journals (such as *Qualitative Research in Psychology*; *Discourse & Society*; *Journal of Phenomenological Psychology*; and so on).
- Asking fellow students or colleagues what they have read. Very often, the best articles that we have read are those recommended to us by colleagues. These articles are not always detected by an electronic literature search. Word of mouth is a valuable search tool.
- Exploring a social bookmarking tool, such as *CiteULike* (www.citeulike.org).
- Asking an expert in the field. Consider asking someone in your department who is knowledgeable in the topic area what key readings they would recommend. Do not, however, send e-mails to academics asking for help with your literature review. It is fair to ask for a pointer in the right direction, but not to ask for help with search strategies. If you do, you are very unlikely to receive a reply!

15 Compile your results into a single list, and save this. Many interfaces will let you export the results from searches into bibliographic software, such as *Endnote* or *Reference Manager*, which help you organise your references.

16 Identify which articles are duplicates (the same article retrieved by more than one database) and remove them.

17 Create a final list, with duplicate articles removed. This is the list you will use. Make sure that each article has a unique number that you can use to identify it.

▶

Box 1.4 *Continued*

Decide which articles you want to retrieve for reading. Carefully make notes that tell you whether you have retrieved an article, and where it is. Some articles may not be available because your library does not have access to the journal. Interlibrary loans can be useful, but you may be charged for this service. Seek advice from your library or information support team for guidance. Consider excluding the article from your review if you cannot get access to it.

Consider using social bookmarking to store and share your references (e.g. on CiteULike, **www.citeulike.org**).

Make a **mind map** of the literature you have selected. Mind maps are creative diagrams where you organise your thoughts and ideas by association, rather than logic. You can draw arrows, make connections between concepts, and learn about which areas you need to consider in more detail. Mind mapping can help you connect the themes, findings, strengths and weaknesses of each article. All you need is a blank sheet of paper, but you may want to consider downloading a free mind mapping tool, such as Freemind (**www.freemind.org**).

Searching the World Wide Web (WWW)

You may also find it useful to look for information on the Web but you will need to be very careful about the quality of the material you find there. It is (mostly) not **peer reviewed**, meaning that the quality of the research has not been approved by other academics as suitable for publication in a journal. Whilst there is clearly well researched and documented information on the Web, there is also a lot of rubbish. Deciding what is sound and what is not is no easy task and you would be well advised to focus your search – initially at least – on academic books and journals that can be found through university libraries. There is a stronger likelihood that the information in these sources will be the result of good quality research and theorising, though it is by no means certain even here. One of the key transferable skills that all psychologists should be able to demonstrate is a critical scepticism about knowledge claims. Your training in research methods – and this book – will help you develop that invaluable skill.

Box 1.5

Command box   **Searching PsychINFO using the OVID interface**

This box illustrates how to perform a basic search of the PsychINFO database, using the Ovid interface. The databases and interfaces available to you may vary.

1   Open the Ovid interface. Seek advice from your library or information support team on whether this interface is available to you (if not, there may be other interfaces available).

▶

Box 1.5 *Continued*

2   Select **PsycINFO** for the range of dates you would like to restrict your search to (we have selected the year 2002 onwards for this example, see Fig. 1.2). Click on the **Open selected resources** button (Fig. 1.3) to open the database interface.

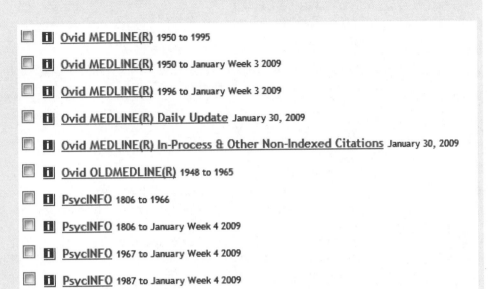

Figure 1.2 Location of the PsycINFO database in Ovid*

Figure 1.3 Open selected resources button*

3   Click on the **Search Tools** tab (see Fig 1.4) which will switch to the **Search tools** function. The **Map Term** option is selected by default. Enter the keyword you would like to map (e.g. jogging) and then click on **Search** (see Fig. 1.5).

Figure 1.4 Search Tools tab*

* Screenshots courtesy of Ovid Technologies, Inc.

Box 1.5 *Continued*

Figure 1.5 Map Term dialogue box*

4   A list of mapped terms is displayed. In our example, we have chosen a *specific* search strategy, and want to focus on jogging (not general terms such as **Exercise**). The appropriate term for this database has been identified as **Running**. Tick this box and then click on **Continue** (see Fig. 1.6). The **Explode** option should be ticked by default. Explode means that any subheadings under the heading you have selected will be included in the search.

Figure 1.6 Mapping Display*

5   The appropriate search string (set of search terms) has been sent to the **Search History** box (see Fig. 1.7). We can see that the string **/exp Running** has retrieved 255 articles. '/exp' means that the term has been explored. If you repeat this search, you may find that more articles have been published on this topic since we performed our search.

* Screenshots courtesy of Ovid Technologies, Inc

Box 1.5 *Continued*

Figure 1.7 Search History*

6   Repeat steps 3 to 5 for the outcome variable we are interested in (depression). Here, several different kinds of depression are listed. We decided to focus our search on the subject heading **Major Depression**. This retrieved 26,845 articles.

7   If necessary, repeat steps 3 to 5 for other keywords (e.g. the population group you are interested in, any other variables which are relevant). In our example, it would not be appropriate to specify such a broad population group as adults. We can always exclude articles that do not describe adults, later on.

8   Combine the two separate searches using the Boolean operator **AND**. In Ovid, this can be performed automatically. Tick the two boxes for each search you have performed. Next to **Combine searches with:**, click on **And** (see Fig. 1.8).

Figure 1.8 Two search histories*

9   The two strings have been combined (exp Running/ AND exp MAJOR DEPRESSION/), and three articles have been retrieved (see Fig. 1.9). Click on **DISPLAY** to see their details.

Figure 1.9 Combining two search histories*

* Screenshots courtesy of Ovid Technologies, Inc

Box 1.5 *Continued*

10   The list you have created is displayed in a new window (see Fig. 1.10). You can store your list by clicking on **Email** or **Save**. Consult your library or information support team if you want to use software to store your results. Some universities make **Endnote** or **Reference Manager** available for students.

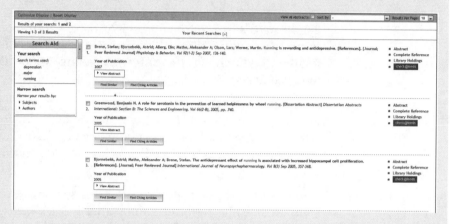

Figure 1.10 Search results display*

Reading review articles

Review articles are secondary accounts of the existing literature on a topic. Obviously, it is a good idea to read review articles if you want to find out more about an area. Using the word 'review' in a search can identify review articles. Finding review articles is a useful scoping exercise, performed before you conduct your own search of the literature. Review articles come in two forms: narrative and systematic.

Reading narrative reviews

These are verbal descriptions of the literature, as interpreted by a researcher. Their length can vary – anything from 2,500 words to 10,000 words. As such, a narrative review is a secondary account of the available research. Narrative reviews are a good way to sensitise yourself to recent developments in a particular area. However, they may date quickly. Many journals now exist that are devoted to the publication of review articles: for example, *Annual Review of Psychology* is a very good place to start. The *Trends* journals are useful summaries

---

* Screenshot courtesy of Ovid Technologies, Inc

of recent developments in a field (e.g. *Trends in Cognitive Sciences*). Other journals carry reviews alongside original research articles. For example, *Personality and Individual Differences* publishes a small number of review articles.

Reading systematic reviews

Systematic reviews are reviews where the authors declare a pre-specified search strategy. Inclusion and exclusion criteria are agreed in advance, to avoid possible bias that may occur in a narrative review. Without a search strategy, the danger of narrative reviews is that the author can present their personal interpretation of the literature. This can be a good thing, but it means that studies with particular findings or views can be excluded. Some authors begin with a systematic review, and then switch to a narrative review if the strategy does not produce enough results (e.g. Shenkin, Starr & Deary, 2004). Narrative reviews and systematic reviews can both be considered pieces of research in their own right. The discussion section at the end will often provide clues about hot topics for future research in the area – perfect when deciding what research question you can ask in your own research.

Meta analysis

It is sometimes useful to combine the results from several different research studies. This can be used to produce a single estimate of the findings across the whole literature. The results of different research studies can vary, so it is important to consider the totality of evidence, rather than looking at individual studies. Meta analysis is often a supplement to systematic reviews. Usually, the meta analysis will be performed on a selection of studies which were included within a systematic review. Not all systematic reviews are suitable for meta analysis, because the studies may be too different to make meaningful comparisons. This is called the **apples and oranges problem**. Despite this weakness, meta analyses are an efficient way to learn about the existing research in your topic area, if one has been conducted.

Overviews

Believe it or not, there are now systematic reviews of systematic reviews! In the Cochrane collaboration (see http://thecochranelibrary.com), these are called **overviews**. There aren't too many at the moment, but if the current rate of 'explosion' continues in psychology, we will increasingly rely on systematic reviews and on overviews to critically appraise the literature. You may find one or two relevant overviews in your area.

Writing your review

Many psychology students are asked to *write* a literature review. This is a written account of many of the processes described above. As such, it requires more than reading. You have to evaluate, or critically appraise, the literature. A written literature review can take several different forms:

- a separate piece of work, assessed separately;
- a preliminary exercise that will form the basis of a research project;
- a section of a larger piece of written work, such as a report or dissertation.

The section below outlines the processes involved in writing a literature review, which are similar in all three cases. The level of detail you are expected to include will vary, depending on your task. But what is a written literature review exactly? Well, a written literature review critically summarises and evaluates existing research findings (see Box 1.6). Reviews should highlight relationships between different material in the form of similarities and differences. It should also show how previous material relates to original research. It is useful to ask the following questions when writing a review:

- What do we already know?
- What are the main concepts?
- What are the relationships between these concepts?
- What are the existing theories?
- Where are the gaps in existing understanding?
- What views need to be tested further?
- What evidence is lacking?
- Why study the research problem?
- What contribution will the present study make?
- What research designs or methods are appropriate/inappropriate and why?

The purpose of writing a review is usually to demonstrate that you can evaluate, not simply re-describe, the literature. The person reading your review will want to see that you can:

- identify a clear research question (e.g. in the PICO format), not too broad and not too narrow;
- search several databases;
- select relevant readings;
- critically appraise evidence;
- balance conflicting evidence;
- focus on a specific topic;
- cite references appropriately;
- identify gaps in existing research and hot topics for future research.

If a review has already been conducted, this does not mean that you cannot produce one yourself. In fact, you may find that you interpret the literature in a different way. However, it does mean that you have to read the literature yourself. You cannot rely on existing reviews if you are writing about primary research.

Many students assume that they cannot criticise published work, because if it has been published, it has nothing wrong with it. This is not the case. You may be surprised at the range in quality of published research. Put simply, some articles are better than others. This is why we have to appraise the literature, rather than simply absorb and describe it. In the chapter on ethics and politics of research, we alert you to some of the reasons that research does and does not get published. Bad papers can be published and good papers can go unpublished! Systematic reviews (described previously) try to include unpublished research, for this reason. Further tips on writing a good literature review are given in Box 1.7.

Box 1.6

Information box

Critical appraisal

What does it mean to critically appraise the literature? It involves giving considered and justified examination of the methods, findings and interpretations of the data. When critically evaluating a piece of research you need to go beyond description by giving opinions (based on psychological knowledge and not your own personal opinions) and evaluations. It is important that you do not take everything at face value and instead you must question and explore the literature. This can be done by relating different types of material to each other, looking for similarities, differences and contradictions. You should also be explicit about underlying theories and values in the work you are reviewing.

- Give considered justified examination of the methods, findings and interpretation.
- Go beyond description by giving opinions (based on psychological knowledge and not your own opinions) and evaluations.
- Do not take everything at face value – question and explore the literature.
- Relate different types of material to each other – look for similarities, differences and contradictions.
- Be explicit about underlying theories and values in the work you are reviewing.

Choosing a topic to write about

You may have been assigned a research topic or research question to review. If not, and you have a choice, pick a topic that interests you or one which you think is important. Start with a general area. For example:

- mental health;
- cognition;
- emotion;
- development.

Next, narrow the topic. You cannot conduct a literature review of the areas listed above, because they are too broad. Refine your topic by specifying the constructs you are interested in, within the topic area. For example:

- depression;
- attention;
- sadness;
- stress.

These constructs are still too broad to conduct a literature review. Using the PICO model (if appropriate), you can combine these constructs with an intervention to create a research question. For example, 'in adults, does running reduce depression?' Alternatively, you can narrow the focus by combining two or more constructs together:

- depression and personality traits;
- attention and mood;
- sadness and lifestyle choices;
- stress and social phobia.

To refine even further, you may want to restrict the topic to a particular population:

- depression and theory of mind in children;
- attention and mood in adolescents;
- sadness and lifestyle choices in adults;
- stress and social phobia in the elderly.

Use the literature searching techniques described above to find out how many articles you are likely to find. If it is the first literature review you have conducted, aim for a maximum of 10 to 20 articles. You need to be able to read the articles in depth, without going too narrow. Some topics will not have enough published articles to justify a review (e.g. 'Synaesthesia in people with Down's syndrome', 'Extraversion in tree lizards'). If you are conducting a review for a large piece of work (e.g. a dissertation), you will need to read more.

Box 1.7

Writing a good review

If you are required to write a literature review as a form of assessment, please consult the guidelines you have been given. The form of a written literature review can vary. Some may require specific features, such as an abstract, word count, structured headings, and particular styles of referencing.

Remember the purpose

- What questions are you trying to answer?

Read with a purpose

- What sort of literature is appropriate?
- What ideas or information is important?
- Do not try to read everything.
- Read critically.
- Keep organised notes and bibliographic information.
- Draw a mind map.

Write with a purpose

- Start writing as soon as you can.
- Look at previous reviews for ideas about structure and style.
- Write a plan.
- Decide what you are going to say before you decide how to say it.
- Write critically.
- Do not use other researchers' reference lists when making citations. If you need to, you must cite these appropriately as secondary sources (e.g. Smith, 1990, cited in MacDonald, 2000).

Organising ideas

- Structure in a logical way – generally *not* by author – tell a story as you would in an essay.
- Group similar information together.
- Show the relationship between the work of different researchers, highlighting similarities and differences.
- Indicate the position of the work in the history of the research area.
- Start general and move to more specific issues.
- Include enough description to let the reader know what you are talking about.
- Describe your search strategy in detail.

Theory

Following a review of the literature you will encounter theories or ideas designed to explain or further understand the topic you are interested in. This is the starting point for the hypothetico-deductive research process (although you may occasionally start with an unsupported conjecture instead) and much quantitative research in psychology. In general, a theory may be characterised as *abstract* or *specific*. Abstract theories are general theories that may be applied to a number of particular topics or settings, while specific theories are, as the name suggests, specific to a particular setting or topic. The theory being investigated in a particular study informs the formation of the hypothesis (or hypotheses) to be tested.

Variables

Variables are identified events that change in value. We devote all of the next chapter to defining and measuring variables in quantitative research so we will not dwell on it too long here. In brief, variables are the things that vary (or alter) so we can make comparisons. So, we might want to look at whether women are better drivers than men. But how do we define the concept of 'a better driver'? We need to specify what our variable is here – is it fewer crashes? Or fewer people injured or killed? Or some other measure of being a good driver? As we are sure you can imagine, there are very many different ways of measuring the concept of 'being a good driver'. It is vital that we are clear and explicit about what we mean when carrying out studies in psychology, for other researchers must be able to see exactly what we have done when we report our findings (so they know what we have done and can try to replicate our study if they wish). In addition, it is only through explicit definitions of variables and accurate measurement that we can be sure we are all measuring the same thing.

Hypotheses

A hypothesis is a specific statement concerning a limited element of a theory. It needs to be highly specific and unambiguous so that it can be appropriately tested and either supported or refuted (e.g. Alcohol consumption is the strongest predictor of condom non-use among young people). We talk more about hypotheses in the following chapters. We say we **operationalise** concepts when we develop specific ways of measuring something. This essentially entails the translation of psychological concepts into specific variables that can then be incorporated into hypotheses to be tested empirically. For instance, how do we measure alcohol consumption and condom non-use among young people? In order to answer this question we need to operationalise the concepts of alcohol consumption and condom use such that we could produce a hypothesis to test.

Sampling

A sample is very simply the group of people we are studying in our research. It is rare to be able to study everyone in the population of interest to us. It would not really be feasible to survey every man and woman driver in the country to find out who has fewest crashes or the best attitude towards driving. What we need to do instead is take a smaller number of people from our population of interest (in this case male and female drivers) and study them. In quantitative research we will then tend to make claims about the whole population on the basis of what we find out from our sample (you would rarely do this in qualitative research). Just think of opinion polls (or surveys) to get a good grasp of the idea here. The researchers in the opinion poll agency send out questionnaires (or more often these days use the telephone or e-mail) to question a number of people believed to be representative of some population (Labour Party members or young people, for instance). Then, on the basis of the responses given by the people in the sample, claims are made about the views of the whole population. The danger, of course, is that we may have a sample that is *not* **representative** of the population as a whole and whose responses therefore are very different from the majority of people in the population. We need an appropriate sample that is representative in some way of our population, and there are a number of techniques to help us do this (this is covered in detail in Chapter 3).

Design

The design of a study is the overall structure of the research. So, do we need to conduct a survey using a questionnaire or carry out an experiment? Is it best to carry out an observation or use a case study method? The decision about which design we use is dependent on a number of factors but most importantly on the type of question we wish to seek answers to. If we want to understand what being a single parent means to young women it is probably a bad idea to choose an experimental design. Instead, we should seek to use a design that emphasises meaning and the subjective experiences of our participants (such as a phenomenological investigation – a qualitative approach). Conversely, we may want to know very simply whether women believe they are better drivers than men. In this case we might be advised to use a questionnaire survey and ask the opinions of a large number of women so that we can make claims about women in general. While the design of any study should be principally informed by the research questions (or hypotheses), this is not the only consideration that impacts on design. Another factor that is important is the researcher's belief about research (and also their ability to use different methods). Some qualitative psychologists believe that quantitative (positivist) research using, for instance, experiments or questionnaire surveys is fundamentally flawed and therefore pointless. Similarly, some quantitative psychologists believe that qualitative research with small numbers of participants is fruitless. These debates are ongoing and are unlikely to be resolved in the very near future. We will discuss such debates a little more in Part 3 when we cover qualitative methods in more detail. Another constraint on the design you may use concerns your available resources. If you do not have access to the population of interest or cannot afford to survey 10,000 people then you will have to adapt your design accordingly. We do not live in a world of infinite resources and research must be 'real world' (Robson, 2002).

Analysis

Your chosen design will affect the type of analysis that is appropriate. If you have a qualitative case study design you will want to analyse your data using an appropriate qualitative method. Conversely a large-scale survey or experiment may call for the use of statistical analysis. A quick word of warning for when you conduct your own research: remember to think about the method of analysis early on when planning your research. Do not leave this to the end after you have collected your data, for you may find yourself in the unenviable position of being unable to analyse your data in the way you wished. We have had to 'rescue' a number of research projects where students had not thought carefully about the particular statistics that they wished to use in advance of distributing their questionnaires. You can carry out some forms of analysis only if you have collected the right sort of data in the right way (this is covered in relation to quantitative research in the next chapter and in relation to qualitative research in Part 3).

Findings

Once you have analysed your data you will produce findings based on your interpretation of your data and results. Your findings will feed back to your theory by providing support for or evidence against the theory. This may lead to a rejection of or, more likely, reformulation of the theory. What is often important in making this judgement is whether your findings can be replicated. **Replication** is very important in all scientific enquiry as we can only be confident in our findings if they are found again when another person repeats the study (exactly) with another sample of participants.

Further reading

Butler, G. & McManus, F. (2000). *Psychology: A Very Short Introduction*. Oxford: Oxford University Press.

As you might expect from its title, this book is very short. However, it provides concise accounts of the history of psychology and its current sub-disciplines. There are several other books in the *Very Short Introduction* series that you may find relevant.

Chalmers, A. F. (1999). *What Is This Thing Called Science?* 3rd edn. Milton Keynes: OU Press.

A classic text with good coverage of all the major debates in the philosophy of science.

Hart, C. (2001). *Doing a Literature Review: Releasing the Social Science Research Imagination.* London: SAGE.

This is a popular text for students who have been asked to conduct their first literature review.

Hart, C. (2007). *Doing a Literature Search: A Comprehensive Guide for the Social Sciences.* London: SAGE.

This book is an excellent accompaniment to Hart's older book on literature reviewing.

Richards, G. (2002). *Putting Psychology in its Place: A Critical Historical Overview*, 2nd edn. London: Routledge.

Superb coverage of the history of psychology from the earliest days of the discipline through to the present day.

Sternberg, R.J. (2003). *The Psychologist's Companion: A Guide to Scientific Writing for Students and Researchers*, 4th edn. Cambridge: Cambridge University Press.

This book is aimed at psychologists who want to write about their research, but is worth the investment if you plan to become a psychologist. It covers everything from planning a study to writing it up and submitting it for publication. See chapter two for literature searching advice.

Williams, M. & May, T. (1996). *Introduction to the Philosophy of Social Research.* London: UCL Press.

The name says it all – an excellent introduction to the philosophy of social research which will take you much further than you need in the first year of a psychology degree. In fact this one should last you all the way to your third year and beyond.

2 Variables: definitions and measurement

- This chapter explains why we need to define variables explicitly in psychology.

- It begins by introducing the varieties of variables that you may encounter.

- It then covers differences between independent and dependent variables.

- Finally, this chapter will introduce you to important issues in the measurement of variables.

INTRODUCTION

As mentioned in Chapter 1, a variable is simply something that *varies* (hence **variable**) in some way that we seek to measure. In psychology (and particularly quantitative research in psychology) we need to be very explicit about what it is we are measuring. Woolly definitions are no good here as they result in poor quality research with inconsistency about the exact focus of the investigation. We want to produce high quality research and so we need to make sure that we are very clear about what it is that we are measuring.

Variables can be any number of things, such as a person's height or weight, attitudes towards fox-hunting or the latest 'boyband', self-esteem or anxiety and so on. As stated earlier, really anything that varies that we choose to measure can be a variable. You will already be familiar with measuring many variables such as height, weight and age. There are standard units of measurement for these variables (metres, kilograms and years respectively) and we all understand how to measure these variables and what the results mean. However, some other variables (such as self-esteem and anxiety) that you are very likely to encounter in psychology are much harder to measure accurately, and furthermore there is often considerable disagreement over the best way to measure them. Measures that are not easily measured are called **constructs**. Constructs are unobservable variables, and therefore variables that have to be measured indirectly.

2.1 Operationalising variables

When we try to explicitly define and then measure variables, or constructs, we say that we are **operationalising** variables. Try to define some of your own variables and see how you get on – it is not as easy as it seems (Box 2.1).

Box 2.1

Activity box | **Operationalising variables**

- Try to write your own definitions of the following constructs:
  1 Self-esteem
  2 Anxiety
  3 Love
- How did you find it? The last one, in particular, is not easy. Now try to think through how you could measure these constructs. What variables do you need to explicitly define and how would you measure them?
- Yes, that was even harder. We guarantee that by the end of this book, if you stick with it, you will be considerably better at being able to define and measure constructs.

We all have common-sense understandings of self-esteem, anxiety and love so there must be some mutual understanding of these constructs. What we need to do in psychology is draw out these common understandings (and also quite possibly elements that are not commonly understood) and make them explicit so we can measure them. So, how would we measure self-esteem? Well, there are a number of standardised tests (such as the Rosenberg Self-Esteem Inventory) for self-esteem that are in widespread use in psychological research. The most commonly used version of the Rosenberg Self-Esteem Inventory consists of ten statements (including statements such as 'I like myself'). Responses to these statements are measured using a four-point scale (a **Likert scale**) recording how much you agree or disagree with the statement (1 = I disagree very much, 2 = I disagree, 3 = I agree and 4 = I agree very much). This test is considered to be a **valid** and **reliable** measure of self-esteem (these concepts are discussed in detail in the next chapter) and has been tested on a wide variety of populations. It is these qualities that enable us to state that the test has been **standardised**. Tests of these kinds are available to measure many psychological constructs and are widely used in psychological research (and clinical settings). However, sometimes we have to create our own scales (see Chapter 5), and we do this by defining our variables and operationalising their measurement. The important point, however, is that we need to be clear, unambiguous and explicit about what it is we are measuring.

2.2	Independent and dependent variables

When we carry out experiments (and often in survey research as well) we need to distinguish between two kinds of variables: **independent** and **dependent variables**. Very simply, the independent variable (or **IV** for short) is that which we (the experimenters) manipulate in order to measure an effect in the dependent variable (or **DV**). The IV is completely under our control while the DV is not under our control (in fact it is the data). Let us suppose we have an experiment designed to investigate children's memory for numbers. We design the experiment so the children are assigned to two **conditions** ('conditions' is simply the technical term used in experimental design for the groups that participants are assigned to where they experience different manipulations by the experimenter). In the first condition, children are simply left alone for ten minutes to remember a list of ten five-digit numbers (let us call this the 'unassisted learning condition'). In the second condition, children are taught the numbers (by a teacher) in the same ten-minute period with a particular memory technique of story-telling association (let us call this the 'assisted learning condition'). After the ten minutes children are tested (using a pencil and paper test) on their recall of the numbers. In this study the IV is the learning method (whether children are in the assisted or unassisted conditions) and the DV is the children's recall of the numbers (our data on their success).

In experimental design (and indeed in most scientific research) the central process is to ascertain the relationship between the IV (or IVs – plural – we often have multiple independent variables) and the DV (or occasionally multiple DVs). Traditionally, we would try to keep all other relevant variables constant while we manipulate the IV (or IVs) in order to measure the effect on the DV. This is why we frequently carry out experiments in a laboratory setting (see Chapter 6 on experimental design). Have a go at distinguishing between the independent and dependent variables in Box 2.2.

Box 2.2

Activity box	IVs and DVs

Which are the independent variables (IVs) and dependent variables (DVs) in each of the statements below?

- Attitudes to condom use are influenced by health promotion campaigns.
- As your age increases your IQ decreases.
- Women are better drivers than men.
- John's behaviour when at a football match is much more violent than when at home with his family.
- People with a 'type A' personality are more likely to smoke.

Talk to your tutor if you struggle to identify the IVs and DVs in the statements above.

Constant versus random error

As we stated above, when we conduct experiments in psychology we try to measure the effect of our IV (or IVs) on our DV. However, there are a number of other factors (or **extraneous variables** – sometimes called **nuisance variables**) that may get in the way of us accurately measuring the relationship. These other variables may be categorised as producing either **constant error** or **random error** according to the effect that they have on the findings. Constant error occurs when we have a systematic effect of some extraneous variable on one (or more) of our experimental conditions. That is, the extraneous variable is affecting the relationship between our IV and DV in one (or more) condition more than the other (or others) in a constant manner. Obviously, constant error seriously damages what we can say about our results, because we may actually be measuring an effect that is not really present (and is really simply the result of constant error from an extraneous variable).

One of the key issues in experimental design is how we minimise (and if at all possible, eliminate) constant error. Let us imagine a natural experiment concerned with measuring the effect of lecturing style on student learning. The IV is style of lecture (traditional versus interactive) and the DV is success in a multiple-choice test about the material presented in the lecture. Students are selected for one or the other condition on the basis of where they sit in the lecture theatre. So, students who sit at the front of the lecture theatre are given the interactive lecture, while the other students who sat at the back are taken to another room and given the traditional lecture. There is a danger here of constant error from an extraneous variable. It is quite likely that where students sit in a lecture theatre is not random. For instance, we might suspect that students who elect to sit at the front of a lecture theatre are more motivated to learn than those who sit at the back. This may therefore mean that any effect we find on account of the IV is directly affected by a constant error (motivation for learning among the students). If we were trying to minimise the effect of error in this piece of research we might want to allocate students to experimental conditions in a more random manner than where they elect to sit. Indeed, **randomisation** of participants is a key technique used in experimental design to minimise the effect of constant error on an experiment.

Random error presents the researcher with quite a different problem to constant error. Although in many cases we can eliminate (or at the very least, minimise) constant error through good experimental design, it is often not possible to eliminate random error despite our best efforts. This does not mean that we should not try to eliminate random error; just that we should be realistic about what we can control in an experiment. Random error is, very simply, where we have an effect from an extraneous variable on our measurement of the relationship between the IV and DV that is random (and therefore, unlike constant error, *not* constant towards one condition more than another). If we study the performance of mice in solving mazes we might encounter the problem of random error. In animal studies of this kind psychologists frequently use food to reinforce correct behaviour. Mice are therefore kept hungry before the maze-solving exercise and receive a food reward for successful completion (the food acts as the motivation to complete the task as quickly as possible). However, even with mice randomly assigned to experimental conditions (such as maze in darkness versus maze in daylight – the IV – to investigate the effect of visual perception on maze-solving ability), we might still have some mice who are more strongly motivated by food than others. This is an individual difference that we cannot control for. However, this random error should contribute to unpredictable error in our measurement of the DV (the success of mice in completing the mazes) because we have randomly assigned mice to the two conditions. We would expect a roughly equal mix of hungry and not-so-hungry mice in the two conditions because they were randomly assigned.

As you can see above, random error *obscures the effect* we are interested in identifying in our experiment whereas constant error *biases (or distorts)* our results. Ideally we would have neither type of error but research can never be perfectly controlled. We must try to minimise both and be particularly alert to the possibility of constant error, which may produce findings that are biased and unreliable.

Confounding variables

When we have a biased result due to constant error from an extraneous variable we say that our findings have been **confounded**. Confounding occurs when a real effect between the IV (or IVs) and the DV is biased or distorted (and sometimes obscured completely) by another (often unexpected) variable. If we had expected an effect from this variable then we would have either included it in our study as another IV or controlled for its effect through the careful design of our study. However, no matter how careful we are, we may sometimes discover the effect of a **confounding variable** during the course of our research.

Confounding variables can act on the relationship between an IV (or IVs) and a DV in a number of different ways. They can result in (1) an effect being observed in the DV apparently on the basis of the IV when in fact there was no effect produced by the IV at all, or (2) their action can obscure a real effect between an IV (or IVs) and DV. Imagine that we are interested in consumer behaviour and particularly ice cream consumption. We, being very naive psychologists, search for variables that seem to have an effect on ice cream consumption and discover a very strong effect for shorts-wearing in men. That is, as the wearing of shorts (among men and to a lesser extent women) (our IV) increases so does the consumption of ice cream (our DV). We have found an effect – Eureka! We contact the major ice cream manufacturers immediately and state with certainty that if they want to increase ice cream consumption they must try to increase the number of people wearing shorts. But as we are sure you know, we would be mistaken if we thought that the wearing of shorts increased the amount of ice cream consumption, and very stupid in contacting the ice cream manufacturers on the basis of this very poor quality research. The relationship we have measured between the IV and DV is in this case caused by a third (**confounding**) variable – hot weather! Although this is an obvious example that shows the effect of a confounding variable, the history of psychology is littered with examples of people getting it wrong because of the effect of confounding variables. So, beware – the solution to this problem is careful planning of your study, good design and vigilance when conducting your analysis.

2.4	Levels of measurement

Accuracy of measurement, very generally, is an important issue in all quantitative social science research. However, the specific topic of measurement *scales* (or levels of measurement) is thought to be crucial by some writers. It is worth being familiar with the basic issues and aware of why some consider an understanding of measurement levels crucial to psychological research.

Four measurement levels (that all psychological phenomena can be measured on – from a quantitative perspective at least) have been identified in the literature on statistics. The distinction between these four types of scales is considered important for what they enable us to do with our data when conducting statistical analyses. The argument is that we can use certain statistics only with certain types of data (that is, data measured at a particular level – **nominal**, **ordinal**, **interval** or **ratio**). In essence, higher levels of measurement (interval and ratio) give greater amounts of information about our data and therefore whatever it is that we have tried to measure. This in turn enables us to use a wider variety of statistical tests (tests that rely on this extra information to work correctly) than if we had used lower levels of measurement (such as the nominal and ordinal levels).

Nominal

Nominal-level scales are really best understood not as scales but as a way of labelling categories of data. Variables such as 'sex' or 'ethnicity' are nominal-level variables. In fact, categorical data (see Section 2.5 below) are often measured at the nominal level for we merely assign category labels at this level of measurement. At this level of measurement we assign numbers to meaningful categories (that are *mutually exclusive* – items in categories cannot be placed in more than one category) in order to count membership of that category. So, for instance, we may give the value of 1 to women in our study and 2 to men when collecting data. This does not mean that women are half men – just that when we have a value of 1 it represents a woman and a value of 2 represents a man in our study. Other examples of nominal-level data are:

■ Number of voters supporting each political party in a general election campaign:

Labour	Conservative	Liberal Democrat
10,236	2333	7667

or

■ Number of people in our study subscribing to different religious beliefs:

Protestant	Muslim	Atheist
122	56	47

Ordinal

Ordinal-level scales are the simplest true scale in which phenomena (people, objects or events of some kind) are ordered along some continuum. At this level of measurement phenomena are ranked or ordered along some dimension of meaning. We will know who came first, second or third in a test but not how much higher the score was of the person in first place over the person in second place. That is, we do not gather information at this level of measurement about the distances between positions. The ordinal level of measurement gives us more information about our data than the nominal level for it tells us about the order of the individual values. An example of the ordinal level of measurement would be as follows:

■ results of a 100 m run (position only and not times):

1st place	2nd place	3rd place
Jane	Jenny	Joanna

Interval

With an interval-level scale we have a measurement scale where the differences between items on the scale really mean something. When we measure temperature (in Celsius or Fahrenheit) we measure it at the interval level. A difference between 10 degrees and 20 degrees Celsius in terms of its value is the same in quantity as the difference between 70 and 80 degrees. That is, a ten-point difference has the same meaning anywhere along the scale. As you can see, interval scales have intervals equal in amount across the entire scale. We do need to be a little bit careful here. While the measuring system we use is interval (that is, the mercury in the thermometer changes by an equal amount for each equal unit of change in temperature), we cannot say that 20 degrees Celsius is twice as hot as 10 degrees Celsius. For us to make this claim about the level of measurement we would need to be measuring the phenomenon at the ratio level where we have a true zero point.

This is the most common form of measurement used in psychological research, although it is worth noting that many people argue that much of what psychologists treat as interval-level data is in fact ordinal data. Many of the scales used in psychological research, such as scales of self-esteem, anxiety, depression and so on, or five-point (or seven-point) Likert scales (more about these later) of a person's attitude to fox-hunting (how much they agree or disagree with it), are assumed to be interval. That is, we assume that the difference between scores on the scale is equal. So, when we have one person who marks that they 'strongly agree' with fox-hunting (and score 1 on our scale) and another who marks that they 'agree' (and score 2 on our scale) we assume their scores are the same distance apart as the two people who mark that they 'strongly disagree' (and score 4 on our scale) and 'disagree' (and score 3 on our scale) with fox-hunting. In truth we cannot know this from our simple five-point scale of attitudes towards fox-hunting, and the criticism of psychological research of this kind is valid. However, psychologists respond very simply by stating that the scales they use consist of, at least, approximately equal intervals and are meaningful measures of the phenomenon being studied. Another distinction has been proposed at this level of measurement to help deal with this problem – the **plastic interval** level of measurement (Wright, 1976, cited in Coolican, 1994). However, we do not believe that this approach really solves the problem of measurement for psychological scales but merely serves to introduce another category of measurement, which is not in widespread use and has no implications for the method of statistical analysis employed by psychologists. There are no tests employed by psychologists that are specifically appropriate for a plastic interval level of measurement (only tests at the nominal, ordinal or interval level). It is generally considered acceptable in psychology to treat ordinal data as interval; if there are at least five (Johnson & Creech, 1993), and preferably at least seven, points on the scale (Miles & Banyard, 2007).

Ratio

Ratio scales, like interval scales, have intervals of equal amounts but also, unlike the interval level, have a *true* zero point. This results in a scale where the relative proportions on the scale make sense when compared with each other. This is, not surprisingly, the 'gold standard' of levels of measurement and also, rather ironically, very rarely found in psychological measurement. Time is perhaps the best example of ratio-level measurement. With time there is the possibility of a zero point – where we have no time to measure (unlike temperature measured in Celsius or Fahrenheit where zero does not mean that there is no temperature to measure). The distinction between interval and ratio levels of measurement will rarely be of concern to you as a student of psychology (or indeed later on as a professional psychologist or researcher). When choosing statistical tests it is generally considered appropriate to treat both interval and ratio levels of measurement in the same way. However, the distinctions between nominal, ordinal and interval levels of measurement are believed by some to have important implications for the statistical tests you are able to conduct on your data (although see our discussion of levels of measurement below).

The need for common sense in psychological research

Why do we (rather controversially) believe that a concern with measurement levels is overstated among some (though not all – Howell, 2001, is a notable exception) writers on research methods in psychology? Indeed, some authors structure their books on research methods entirely around levels of measurement and position all other material on method and statistics in relation to this. We think this is missing the point about why measurement levels matter. It would be very easy for us to be very prescriptive about levels of measurement and issue reams of rules to follow. But this is not the answer to the problem of measurement in the social sciences (and would merely complicate issues for students wanting to learn how to be good researchers). What we need (when measuring variables) is common sense and understanding and not lists of rules about which test is needed in which circumstance.

The central issue we need to understand when considering measurement in the social sciences is the meaning of the numbers that we collect. It is useful to draw a distinction (in our minds) between the numbers themselves, which we collect in the course of some investigation and then subject to statistical tests, and the objects to which they refer. We can pretty much quantify and count anything we wish but that does not guarantee that it means very much psychologically speaking. Statistical tests enable us to carry out mathematical manipulations of numbers but they do not have any consideration of the meaning of these numbers built into their procedures. This is where we (as psychologists) come in when we interpret what the numbers mean when the tests are carried out. Without our interpretations the statistics we end up with are meaningless. What we need to do when we carry out a statistical test is ascertain whether the results are related in any meaningful way to the phenomena we have investigated. So, when we claim to have measured self-esteem using a questionnaire containing seven-point Likert scales (see Chapter 5), we need to acknowledge that the numbers are only surrogates for the underlying construct we are trying to measure. As noted by Miles & Banyard (2007), 'almost no data in psychology are *really* measured on a *truly* continuous scale' (p. 138). We can treat the data as interval (continuous) and perform statistical procedures, because we have a substantive theory that self-esteem exists as a continuous quantity. The greater the number of points on the scale, the greater the correspondence between the data and the construct (Johnson & Creech, 1993). It is important to perform tests that are appropriate for the level of measurement of the data, but you should consider the role of substantive psychological theory in deciding what that level is.

2.5	Categorical and continuous variables

Variables can be distinguished from each other in a number of ways (one of the most important was given above – the distinction between independent and dependent variables). We can also discriminate between **discrete** (or **categorical**)

variables, such as sex or social class, and **continuous variables**, such as age or anxiety score. Discrete variables are those that take on only a limited (or discrete) number of values (sex is male or female, social class may be A, B, etc.). This is in contrast to continuous variables which can have (in theory at least) any value between the lowest and highest points on the scale. That is, there is no limit to the subdivision of the scale. Age can be measured to the nearest year (most commonly) but also (to a finer level) in years and months or (finer still) years, months and days or years, months, days, hours. You get the idea – we can keep subdividing a continuous scale into finer and finer units of measurement.

All the scales mentioned above (and also all IVs and DVs) can be divided into two categories according to whether they are discrete or continuous variables. Nominal-level data, as stated above, can only be discrete whereas ordinal may be discrete or continuous (although strictly speaking it cannot be truly continuous as ordinal scales will usually have 0.5 as the smallest unit of measurement). As you might expect, interval and ratio scales can be either discrete or continuous. This distinction becomes particularly important when we want to carry out statistical analyses on our data, for some tests are appropriate for discrete variables while others are appropriate for continuous variables. We will return to this distinction again in Part 2 when we explore the statistical analysis of quantitative research data.

Further reading

We would not recommend a great deal of further reading on the topics raised in this chapter. For most students there is a real danger in getting bogged down in detail that may obscure the bigger (and much more important) picture. However, there are a couple of texts that include comprehensive coverage of, for instance, the measurement of data.

Black, T. R. (1999). *Doing Quantitative Research in the Social Sciences: An Integrated Approach to Research Design, Measurement and Statistics*. London: Sage.

This book also provides comprehensive coverage of the definition and measurement of variables.

Pashler, H., Yantis, S., Medin, D., Gallistel, R. & Wixted, J. (2002). *Stevens' Handbook of Experimental Psychology*, 3rd edn. New York: John Wiley & Sons.

A classic book on experimental psychology with considerable information on the issues raised in this chapter.

3 Reliability, validity, sampling and groups

- This chapter begins by explaining the concepts of reliability and validity.

- It then covers sampling, sampling bias and methods of sampling.

- Finally, this chapter will introduce you to the use of control and placebo groups in experimental research.

INTRODUCTION

As you saw in the previous chapter, psychological research requires us to be very precise in the ways we measure variables. Without precision we cannot guarantee the quality of the findings we produce. This chapter introduces you to some more technical issues in research. Two concepts that are central to any understanding of whether our findings are of worth or not are **reliability** and **validity**. These two watchwords are first introduced in this chapter, but covered in greater depth in Chapter 5 because they are central to the topic of questionnaire design. This chapter then covers the important, but sadly often neglected, topic of **replication**. We then move on to look at how we select participants for our studies, that is, how we **sample**. Finally, in this chapter we look at the benefits that can be gained through the use of **control** and **placebo groups**.

3.1   Reliability

Reliability concerns the stability of what we are measuring. That is, do we get the same result from our test (or study) on more than one occasion or was the result a freak instance (and therefore fairly meaningless if we are trying to say something general about human nature)? We want our results to be rigorous and this can be partly achieved through us gathering data that are reliable. So, for example, imagine we wish to produce a test of attitudes towards animal welfare. We give this test to our 'guinea pig', John, and he scores high (positive) on attitudes towards animal welfare. We then give John the same test on another occasion (several weeks later) and find he scores very low (negative) on attitudes towards animal welfare. So, what happened here? Well, very simply, our test is probably not reliable. We have tested it with the same person (so a comparable situation) on two occasions (this is a way of measuring **test–retest reliability**, which is discussed in Chapter 5) and found the test produced different results. This is not good enough if we are trying to produce a rigorous test of attitudes towards animal welfare. We want our measures to be reliable and provide similar results on different but comparable occasions.

3.2 Validity

Validity is another key element that should concern us when we are trying to carry out rigorous research. In short, validity is about whether a test (or measure of any kind) is really measuring the thing we intended it to measure. In chemistry or physics it is often the case that the item being measured exists in the world in a simple physical way (even if we need very sophisticated devices to see or measure it). However, psychological phenomena are not like these physical phenomena. Psychologists *assume* that people have 'attitudes' or 'personality traits' on the basis of our theories and evidence from studies of the way people behave in the world. However, we cannot ever really know if we are *really* measuring an attitude or personality trait in the same way as we know we are measuring wind speed or an electrical current since we cannot gather direct physical evidence for attitudes or personality traits.[1] In spite of this obvious limitation, psychologists have attempted to develop measures of psychological phenomena that are as valid as possible. Like reliability, there are several forms of validity that we should take into account when developing or testing measures of psychological phenomena. All types of validity have limitations, of course, and should be considered as ways of *increasing*, not proving, the *validity* of our measures. No measure is perfect, and there are no guarantees. These

---

[1] We will discuss this much more in Part 3 on qualitative approaches to data analysis. However, many qualitative approaches are not modelled on the natural sciences at all for the simple reason that (they argue) people's psychology is not like molecules or atoms in that it is not a measurable object extended in the world that is perpetually unchanging. Instead researchers from these perspectives argue that we can know about people (and their psychology) only in interactions between people or through language as that is the only information about our psychology that is publicly available to us all. We can never 'go inside' people's heads to find an attitude or personality trait (we could, of course, go inside to find some neurochemical pathways or anatomical structure). The other major factor that makes some researchers question an approach based on the natural sciences concerns human agency (the capacity, that we appear to have at least, to act in the world). Molecules and atoms do not make decisions and do not therefore have the potential to be different when placed in identical situations: human beings do and are often contradictory. We only need to observe other people to see this element of human nature in action.

issues are discussed in more detail in Chapter 5, in relation to questionnaires and psychometric tests. One type of validity is worth mentioning here, because it is relevant to psychological studies in general: ecological validity.

Ecological validity

Ecological validity is being increasingly examined in psychological studies. This is because a great deal of psychological research has been modelled on the natural sciences and therefore conducted in laboratories. Psychologists carry out rigorous studies in laboratories in an attempt to minimise the effect of extraneous variables. The worry with this approach is that these studies may lack ecological validity. That is, we may question whether the results gathered in a laboratory about some psychological phenomenon will generalise to other settings or places. Would our participants behave in the same way outside the laboratory as they do when subjected to a study within a laboratory setting? There is increasing concern that many of the findings produced through laboratory studies may lack ecological validity and therefore not reflect the natural behaviour of human beings at all. So, for instance, Asch's study of conformity, which we referred to in Chapter 1, was a laboratory-based study, which may have some limitations on account of its ecological validity. The participants were all strangers and were not given the opportunity to discuss their thoughts about the line lengths with each other. How often are you in a situation like that? We may seek to replicate Asch's study among an established group (such as friends in a lecture theatre) and allow people the possibility of discussion in an attempt to improve the ecological validity. What effect do you think this would have on the findings of the study? However, while many laboratory studies do suffer problems on account of a lack of ecological validity, it is important to be both realistic and thoughtful about the implications of this problem for research from this perspective. It is all too easy to criticise laboratory studies in this way but we do not think that this means all findings from laboratory-based research are just plain wrong! We have gained (and will continue to gain) considerable knowledge about human nature from laboratory-based research in spite of the limitations to this kind of work. All research in the social sciences suffers from some problems. What we need, if we wish to be good, effective and rigorous psychologists, is an awareness of these limitations and knowledge of how best to minimise their effects.

3.3   The role of replication in the social sciences

Replication is an important aspect of a traditional scientific approach to research in the social sciences. It is, however, often neglected because of the demand to produce new and novel findings. However, replication is important and worthy of attention. In order to establish the reliability and validity of research findings we need to be able to repeat a study exactly and find the same results as the original researcher. This is why you are instructed to produce research reports in a particular format (with all that detail). Other researchers need to be able to read a research report and carry out the same study themselves (that is, replicate it). As well as establishing whether findings are reliable and, to some extent, valid, replication also protects the discipline against fake (or fraudulent) findings. While this is uncommon, there are some notorious cases of psychologists inventing their results!

3.4 Populations and samples

Within a traditional scientific approach to psychology we often wish to generalise findings from a **sample** of people (a smaller subset) to the **population** from which they came. It is obviously impractical (if not impossible) in many cases to carry out research on every person within a particular population. We therefore need to be able to select a smaller number of participants for our research who are representative of the population as a whole. So, if we wish to carry out research on the phenomenon of the 'white van man' we cannot send a questionnaire (or interview) to every man who drives a white van in the United Kingdom (let alone every man who drives a white van in the rest of the world). What we need to do is select a smaller number of men who drive white vans as our sample. If our sample is a good one we would expect it to be representative of the population as a whole (all 'white van men'). The findings from our study of 'white van men' should tell us something about the whole population of 'white van men'. This is not as easy as it seems for we are always at risk of generating biased (or inaccurate) findings if our sample is not truly representative.

3.5 The problem of sampling bias

As mentioned above, we need our sample to be representative of the population from which it was drawn. If we studied only student samples in psychology we might well end up believing that most people stay up late, enjoy drinking and study hard. We need to be aware of the possibility of sampling bias when choosing who we are going to select from our population to study in our research. A great deal of research in the social sciences has been conducted with **convenience** samples (more on these below) which often comprise students. People who volunteer for social science research (and students in particular) have been found, in many ways, to be unrepresentative of the wider population. This is clearly a worry if we attempt to generalise our findings beyond our sample to the population. The principal way of minimising sampling bias is to employ one of the many sampling strategies recognised in the social sciences.

3.6	Methods of sampling

The first thing that is needed for all sampling to be effective is to clearly define the population of interest. All key variables that are used to define and mark the population of interest must be known and clearly defined. Once the population is clearly defined we then use an appropriate sampling strategy to draw our sample participants from the population of interest. Most of the strategies below (with the notable exception of convenience sampling) are ideals which are very difficult (if not impossible in some cases) to achieve in day-to-day real world research.

Random

This is generally considered to be the 'gold standard' for sampling. With **random sampling** each member of the population being studied has an equal chance of being selected for the sample. Furthermore, the selection of each participant from the population is independent of the selection of any other participant. There are a number of different methods for carrying out random sampling but it often involves potential participants being given a number (1 to N, where N is the total number of participants in the population). Then random number tables (or some other method of random number generation – e.g. through a calculator or computer) are used to generate numbers between 1 and N and those numbers selected become our sample participants. Random sampling is a particularly effective and unbiased method of sampling but, like all methods, cannot completely eliminate the sampling error that always occurs when we take a sample from a population (more of this in Chapter 6). Furthermore, random sampling is often an impossible ideal when we do not have access to the total population of interest.

Systematic

Systematic sampling is often used as a substitute for random sampling whereby we draw the sample from the population at fixed intervals from the list. So, if we had a list of addresses from the electoral roll for Sheffield we might decide to select every tenth address to make up our sample (which will receive our questionnaire). This approach is much simpler and easier to achieve than true random sampling. The main disadvantage of this approach is that there may exist some periodic function of our sample. If we decided to select the first ten members of a class of schoolchildren from a range of schools we might find that boys' names are always listed first. If this were the case our sample would probably consist of boys. Similarly, if we selected the first people to respond to a request for help with our research we might be selecting people who demonstrate particularly high levels of sociability or compliance. We must be careful with this approach to sampling that we do not accidentally introduce bias into our study (and it is easily done, for it is difficult to think of every possible factor that may influence our findings in advance of carrying out a study).

Stratified

Stratified sampling may be random or systematic and introduces an extra element into the process of sampling by ensuring that groups (or strata) within the population are each sampled randomly or to a particular level. We might, for instance, wish to carry out a survey of all first year students at the University of Imaginarytown about attitudes to a new university-wide compulsory course in IT and study skills. We cannot afford (in terms of time or money) to send a questionnaire to all first year students so we decide to randomly sample from the population (to a total of 10 per cent). However, we realise that simple random sampling may result in biased findings if, for instance, more students respond from the faculties of arts and humanities than from the faculties of science and engineering. This is where we might choose to use random stratified sampling. With this sampling technique we randomly sample from each faculty in the university until we have a final sample that reflects the proportions of students that we have in each faculty in the university. So, for instance, if we have 1000 students in the faculty of science and 500 in engineering we would want (if we were sampling 10 per cent of all university students) to randomly sample 100 students from the science faculty and 50 from the engineering faculty. This would mean that our final sample would be randomly generated in proportion to the number of students in each university faculty. Of course, university faculty is just one example of how we might stratify a sample. We might choose to stratify according to sex or age, social class and so on (the list is endless).

Cluster

There are times when we may wish to sample entire groups of people rather than individuals for our research. One common example of this is when psychologists carry out research in educational settings (especially schools). It is often most appropriate to sample entire classes from schools (for a variety of practical and ethical reasons). Sampling of natural groups (such as classes of students or schoolchildren) rather than individuals is called **cluster sampling**. Like the previous methods of sampling, care needs to be taken when sampling clusters to make sure those clusters are representative of the population. At the simplest level a researcher may just sample one cluster (a class of schoolchildren from one school). Here there is considerable danger in generalising from one's results to other classes and schools in the area and beyond. At the other extreme a researcher may randomly sample classes across age ranges and stratified by geographical region from the entire population of schools in the United Kingdom.

Stage

Stage sampling entails breaking down the sampling process into a number of stages. So, for instance, we may (in stage one) randomly sample a number of classes of children from schools in the United Kingdom. Then (in stage two) we may randomly sample a number of children from those classes that we have sampled. This approach would be called multi-stage cluster sampling (and you could even throw in a 'random' there if you liked and have 'multi-stage random cluster sampling'). Multi-stage designs are often particularly useful in very large studies. It is often (practically) impossible to randomly sample individuals from very large populations (for instance, all children from all schools in the United Kingdom). But if we wish to have a large sample that is representative of a very large population (such as all children in school in the United Kingdom) then multi-stage sampling may be the answer. So, for instance, if we wish to generate a sample of children that is representative of all children in school in the United Kingdom (a very ambitious thing to do!) we could begin by getting lists of all schools in the United Kingdom. We could then randomly sample from this list of schools (stage one), taking care to stratify our sample appropriately (e.g. by geographical region). Then we could contact those schools and get lists of all classes and randomly sample from those class lists (stage two) – again using appropriate stratification techniques. And finally in stage three we could get lists of children who belong to those classes and randomly sample from them. This would provide us with a random sample that (to a certain extent at least) would be representative of the total population of schoolchildren in the United Kingdom. We should point out that this particular example is not terribly realistic (as various aspects of the research process would intervene along the way to make things much more difficult and messy). Furthermore, this grand random multi-stage sampling strategy would be enormously expensive in terms of both time and resources.

Opportunity (or convenience)

This is, unfortunately, one of the commonest sampling strategies used by researchers in the social sciences today. Very simply, it entails us recruiting participants in any way possible (or convenient). So, we may recruit students in lecture theatres or people from the office block across the road. We may advertise and take all those that volunteer. This approach is clearly not ideal as we have little idea about whether our sample is representative of the population of interest to us in our research. However, **opportunity** sampling may be the only approach possible in some circumstances and we may have to tolerate the potential biases that ensue from this strategy. A lot of research in the social sciences is poorly funded (if funded at all) and conducted under extreme time pressure and may therefore necessitate a simple recruitment strategy. We might only have the resources available to recruit students in lecture theatres to our research. This may still be acceptable if we believe this strategy will introduce minimal (or irrelevant) bias to our findings. What we need to do if we use this approach is be sceptical of our findings and keep a careful watch on whether they seem to be valid and reliable.

Snowball

Snowball sampling is a very common sampling strategy that is often no more than convenience sampling under another name. However, there are times when snowball sampling is an appropriate (sometimes necessary) and strategic form of sampling. With this sampling technique the researcher will make contact with a small number of potential participants whom they wish to recruit to the research study. They will then use these initial contacts to recruit further participants (by recruiting friends and then friends of friends until the sample is sufficiently large). This strategy may be the most appropriate sampling strategy with some research studies. For instance, if you wish to study street gangs or drug users, access to these populations will be particularly difficult unless you are already a member of the group, and it is highly unlikely that you will be able to recruit many participants using the usual sampling strategies. However, if you can establish contact with just one or two gang members (or drug users) you can then use snowball sampling to recruit a sufficiently large sample. You would ask your initial participant to recruit fellow gang members (or drug users) to the study on your behalf. You can then ask this second set of participants to recruit some of their friends and so on until you have a large enough sample for your study.

The obvious problem with snowball sampling is that members of the sample are unlikely to be representative of the population. However, this depends on what we consider the population in our study. If we are interested only in the experience of a particular gang or members within this gang then it may be appropriate to recruit using a snowball strategy. This is more often the case with qualitative research concerned with understanding the experience of a (often small) number of people.

3.7   Sample sizes

So, the sixty-four million dollar question – does size really matter? Well, in general yes, the larger the sample size the better. This is simply because larger samples have less sampling error (we will return to sampling error in Part 2 – for now, take it on trust that the larger the sample size, the greater the precision of the sample in representing the population from which it was drawn). However, with all research there is a trade-off between size of sample and time and cost. With small sample sizes (50, 100, 150) precision increases significantly as the sample size increases and it is worth making every attempt to recruit as many participants as practically possible. However, once a sample gets above 1000 or so then there is less to be gained from significant increases in size. Sample error (and therefore precision) will continue to increase above 1000 but at a less rapid rate than below this figure. It is also important to remember that it is *absolute*, rather than *relative*, sample size that is important. Therefore, a national sample of 1000 children in the United Kingdom is as valid a sample as a national sample of 1000 children in the United States, despite the much larger population of children in the United States.

There are a number of additional factors that should be borne in mind when attempting to decide on the most appropriate sample size for your study. Firstly, it is important to consider the *kind of analysis* that will be conducted on your data, for this will have an impact on the size of sample needed. Students commonly forget to consider this factor in calculating their sample size and then run into problems when the time comes for them to analyse their data. Very simply, you need larger samples the larger the number of variables you plan to include in your study. This is sometimes referred to as the ratio of cases to IVs. There is no simple figure we can give you, for the ratio of cases to IVs will vary depending on which statistical technique you use to analyse your data. Various writers have provided formulae for calculating these ratios and the minimum sample size needed for different forms of analysis. This is beyond the scope of this text but worth checking out if you are carrying out your own research and need to know the minimum sample size for particular forms of statistical analysis (see the Further reading at the end of this chapter for more details).

Another factor that needs to be taken into consideration when calculating what sample size is needed is the likely response rate for the study. You will often see or hear mention of response rates in social survey research. In any research you will find people deciding not to respond to your request for them to participate. So, whether you send out 1000 unsolicited questionnaires or stand on a street corner asking every passer-by to come into the laboratory, a number of people will not complete the questionnaire or will refuse to take part in your experiment. It is important to know how many people have refused to take part, for a very high refusal rate may produce concerns about the **representativeness** of your sample. Are you recruiting only a particular type of person? How can you trust your findings if you do not have data on 90 per cent of those you sent the questionnaire to or asked to take part? We therefore try to maximise the response rate (the proportion of those contacted that agreed to take part). However, not everyone we contact may be suitable for our study or able to take part, so we tend to calculate the percentage response rate as follows:

$$\frac{\text{Number of questionnaires completed and returned (or people agreeing to take part)}}{\text{Number of questionnaires sent (or people approached)} - \text{unsuitable or uncontactable members of the sample}} \times 100$$

So, for instance, if we sent out 1000 questionnaires and had 100 returned correctly completed, 10 returned but not completed correctly and 10 returned because the addressee was not known then we have a response rate of $[100/(1000-10-10)] \times 100$, or 10.2 per cent. This is obviously a very low response rate but it is not uncommon to have low response rates (around 25 per cent) with unsolicited self-completion questionnaires sent by post. As well as trying to maximise our response rate (more on this in Chapter 5) we may need to try to predict the response rate if we wish to recruit a particular number of participants to our study. So, if we are sending out an unsolicited self-completion questionnaire and we need a sample size of 500 for our analysis, then, if we expect a return rate of 25 per cent, we need to distribute 2000 questionnaires.

The final factor that will be briefly mentioned here that may impact on the size of sample needed concerns the heterogeneity of the population from which we draw our sample. When a population is very heterogeneous, such as a national population of schoolchildren, then we are going to need a larger sample from this population than if the population is fairly homogeneous. Conversely, if our sample is very similar and demonstrates little variation (homogeneous across a number of characteristics of interest) then we will have less need to recruit a larger sample. It is also worth adding a note of caution about very large samples. Very large samples increase the likelihood of getting significant results (for a variety of statistical reasons). Good, you may think. Well, not necessarily, as the results may be significant but of no importance or practical consequence. This issue is discussed further in Chapter 11. So, while size does matter, it is not everything!

3.8   Control and placebo groups

In experimental (and some quasi-experimental) research we may need to recruit participants and assign them to one of two groups: **experimental** or **control**. We do this so that we can make comparisons between two (or more) groups of participants. The **experimental group** would be that which was given some intervention or programme (whether a new drug, education programme or psychological intervention) while the **control group** would be a matched (on appropriate characteristics, such as age, social class, etc.) group who did not receive the intervention. It is important to predict accurately which variables are likely to be important when matching participants. These variables are often demographic characteristics (such as age, sex, ethnicity and social class) but may also be psychological variables (such as attitudes or personality traits). When we sample for experimental research of this kind we often recruit matched pairs of participants so that we can then randomly allocate them to either the experimental or control groups.

A variation on the control group is the placebo group. We may employ a placebo group if we are worried about the possibility of a **placebo effect**. This is where a person (or group of people) responds to some stimulus as if it were having an expected effect when in fact it should have no effect at all. The classic example of this, which is tried and tested, is when we assign participants to two groups and give one group alcohol and another group (the placebo group) a liquid that we tell them is alcohol (but in fact contains no alcohol at all). What you find is that the placebo group who received a pretend alcoholic drink act as if they have consumed alcohol. So, we employ placebo groups in many situations (such as trials for new drugs) in order to minimise the expectation effects. We will address the issue of experimental and control groups further in Chapter 6.

Further reading

Robson, C. (2002). *Real World Research*, 2nd edn. Oxford: Blackwell.

Contains further information on reliability and validity and, most notably, sampling strategies not covered here that are rarely, but occasionally, used in the social sciences.

Tabachnik, B. G. & Fidell, L. S. (2006). *Using Multivariate Statistics*, 5th edn. New York: HarperCollins.

This is an advanced text! We do not recommend it at the introductory level of your studies. We have included it here because it contains useful information on how to calculate the minimum sample sizes for statistical tests.

4 Collecting data 1: interviews and observation

- This chapter introduces two of the main methods of data collection in psychology.
- It begins by introducing types of interviews, techniques and purposes. This includes coverage of group discussion and repertory grid techniques.
- The chapter then moves on to cover types and methods of observation.

INTRODUCTION

Psychology is a discipline reliant upon empirical evidence. Without empirical evidence to support our ideas we have no reason to believe our arguments about people any more than those of any man or woman in the street. It is through the use of empirical data that psychology strives to achieve the status of a science. However, it requires real skill to collect data and this chapter will sensitise you to some of the issues you must address when you seek to collect data about some topic. Without knowledge of the appropriate techniques of data collection the quality of your results may be questioned. This chapter focuses on the use of interviews and observation to collect data. The following chapter is devoted to questionnaire design and psychometrics and the next chapter experimental (and quasi-experimental) design – the other main approaches to collecting data in psychology. It should be noted that these chapters address only issues of data collection and not analysis (which is dealt with in Parts 2 and 3).

4.1 Interviewing

With the increasing use of qualitative approaches in psychology the use of interviews to collect data has grown. Interviews have always been a valuable method of data collection in psychology, particularly social psychology. They are a flexible method that enables researchers to collect detailed conversational material for analysis. Most of us have some experience of interviewing through, for instance, job applications (see Box 4.1). However, while interviews appear straightforward, there are particular issues to bear in mind when using them to collect data for psychological research. The following two sections will examine some of the most important factors in research interviewing.

Box 4.1

Activity box | **Experiences of interviews**

- Spend some time thinking about the possible places where interviews may be used (we have already mentioned job applications).
- How do the different types of interview differ?
  - Was the interviewer very formal or informal?
  - Did they follow a set list of questions or make them up as they went along?
  - How much control over the interview did the interviewee have?
- Finally, list some reasons why you think different types of interview are used in different settings.
  - For instance, you could argue that an interview using a set list of questions means that everyone gets the same chance (in a job interview, for instance).

4.2 Types, purposes and structures of interviews

Types and purposes of interviews

Only a few types of interview are commonly used for psychological research, including clinical/therapeutic interviews and face-to-face or telephone research interviews (and, recently, Internet/e-mail interviews).

Research interviews

Research interviews are the most common type of interview that you will encounter as a student of psychology. Their main function is to gather data (generally in the form of audio-recorded speech) from the participants about a topic that you, the interviewer, decide to study. You will talk to your interviewee face to face or on the telephone and use a series of questions to try to gather information about the thoughts, feelings and beliefs that the interviewee has about a particular topic. Box 4.2 gives an example of a typical study using semi-structured interviews. It highlights the usefulness of semi-structured interviews to generate text-based data where participants are attempting to understand or construct meaning about an experience they have had.

Box 4.2	Study box

Reavey, P. & Gough, B. (2000) Dis/locating blame: Survivor's constructions of self and sexual abuse. *Sexualities*, **3** (3), 325-46.

This study used semi-structured interviews with women who self-identified as survivors of sexual abuse to explore the way in which the participants made meaning out of their experience. The study interviewed only five women but generated a large amount of textual data that was then analysed using discourse analysis (see Chapter 21). This study found that women drew on several different discourses (think of them as stories for now), including discourses concerning the participant's past as blameworthy and present as 'survivors'. The participants made sense of their differing (present) situations through the use of these discourses. The authors argue that the work has implications for therapeutic practice through an examination of the ways in which talk of 'psychological problems' can be integrated into therapeutic narratives.

Therapeutic interviews

Therapeutic interviews (unlike research interviews) do not have data collection as their main function. This type of interview is generally conducted by a clinical professional with training in counselling or psychotherapy. Their primary function is (not surprisingly) concerned with the effective psychotherapeutic treatment of the client (interviewee or participant) rather than with data collection. Professionals in these settings may, however, audio record (or even video record) sessions to generate data for analysis at a later date.

Recording data

There are obviously a variety of methods of recording data from interviews, including note taking, audio recording and video recording. Each is dealt with briefly below:

- *Note taking.* This approach to recording data in an interview is difficult, slow and highly selective. It is generally only used in psychology where the use of audio recorders is too distracting or where recording equipment is unavailable (for instance, if you were interviewing in the field with people who find modern technology disturbing).

- *Audio recording.* This is the most commonly used method of data collection in interviews. Good quality audio recording equipment is readily available and familiar to most people you are likely to interview. There is a danger that the use of audio recording equipment may inhibit responses but this is generally compensated for by the fact that you have a permanent record of all verbal information exchanged. Now, for some practical advice about audio-recording interviews. Firstly, make sure you are familiar with the operation of the equipment you are using. While you do not need to be a rocket scientist to operate a tape recorder or digital recorder, many of us have been in the embarrassing situation of not knowing which socket to plug the microphone into or where to find the eject button. Secondly, make sure your equipment is up to the task at hand. You will have to go through the recording many, many times when transcribing the data (that is, making a written record of exactly what was said – see Chapter 18) and this is not a pleasant task when you are straining to hear what is being said. Thirdly, take along spare tapes (unwrapped!) if using a tape recorder, batteries and if possible another microphone (it is always best to be prepared). Finally, do not switch the recorder off immediately you finish the interview. The number of times you finish an interview, switch the recorder off and then find people telling you the most fascinating stories is amazing. So, leave the recorder going until the very last moment! Trust us, it will be worth it.

- *Video recording.* If we ask a group of students which is the best method of recording data they will inevitably say video recording. While we are increasingly living in a visual world, with video recording equipment readily available, more often than not it is *not* the best method of recording data in an interview. Video recording is likely to dominate the setting and disturb your participants, and although it records all information, much of this is excessive and irrelevant. However, video recording can be particularly useful where you are conducting a group interview. Trying to work out who said what can be very difficult with just an audio recording.

Interview structures

Interviews used to collect data in psychological research are generally categorised as one of three types: unstructured, semi-structured and structured.

Unstructured interviewing

Unstructured interviews are characterised by their lack of a predetermined interview schedule. They are usually exploratory and most useful where little is known about the topic. They may be particularly appropriate for certain theoretical perspectives (such as ethnography or life-story research) or in a clinical setting (such as a therapy session).

Advantages	Disadvantages
■ Flexible	■ Unsystematic
■ Rich data	■ Difficult to analyse data
■ Relaxes interviewee	■ Strongly influenced by interpersonal
■ Should produce valid (meaningful) data	variables
	■ Not reliable

Semi-structured interviewing

Semi-structured interviews, unlike unstructured interviews, use a standardised interview schedule. The interview schedule consists of a number of pre-set questions in a mostly determined order. However, this type of interview is not completely reliant on the rigorous application of the schedule. If the interviewee wanders off the question then the interviewer would generally go with it rather than try to return immediately to the next question in the schedule. In addition, the questions that make up the schedule are usually open-ended to encourage the respondents to elaborate their views about the topic (see the section on creating a good interview schedule below). And to further focus attention on the interviewee and their views the interviewer generally says very little. This is the most common type of interview used in psychological research.

Advantages	Disadvantages
■ Can compare responses and analyse data more easily	■ Some loss of flexibility for interviewer
	■ Question wording may reduce richness
■ No topics missed	■ Less natural
■ Reduction of interpersonal bias	■ Coding responses still subject to bias
■ Respondents not constrained by fixed answers	■ Limits to generalisation

Structured interviewing

Structured interviews rely on the application of a fixed and ordered set of questions. The interviewer sticks to the precise schedule rigorously and will (politely!) keep the interviewee concentrated on the task at hand. There is also a set pattern provided for responses. In many ways this type of interview is more like a guided

Advantages	Disadvantages
■ Easy to administer	■ Respondent constrained
■ Easily replicated	■ Reduced richness
■ Generalisable results (if the sample is adequate)	■ Information may be distorted through poor question wording
■ Simple data analysis	■ Suffers from difficulties associated with questionnaires
■ Reduced bias	
■ Lower influence for interpersonal variables	
■ High reliability	

questionnaire. This type of interview is often used when you have a very complex questionnaire to administer or where your participants are unable to complete a questionnaire on their own (for instance, very young children).

| **4.3** | Interview techniques |

For an interview to be successful (i.e. enable you to collect the data you want) it is vital that the interviewer has knowledge of (and sensitivity to) the effect of interpersonal variables, knowledge of techniques needed for successful interviewing, a good interview schedule and plenty of practice.

Effect of interpersonal variables

It is important to be aware of the possible effects of interpersonal variables on an interview and the data you collect. Because interviews are generally conducted face to face, people being interviewed are particularly susceptible to the influence that your sex, ethnicity, use of language or formal role (as a researcher/academic/expert) may have on them. Furthermore, people often feel the need to present themselves to others who are perceived to be in positions of power (such as an academic) in as good a way as possible (the **social desirability effect**). This can be particularly problematic with some topics where you want to hear about the failures or difficulties people have experienced rather than just their successes.

The effect of interpersonal variables and social desirability can be minimised in a number of ways. For instance, the type of language you use will affect the way the interviewee responds to you. If you use unfamiliar language (for instance, formal academic terms) people may feel alienated and try to present themselves in a similarly formal manner. So, always try to use appropriate language in a research interview. Obviously, rapport is also vital for effective interviewing. It can address the impact of social desirability and other interpersonal effects.

While it is important to make efforts to minimise the effects of interpersonal factors when interviewing, they will always be present in some form. However, this is not as big a problem as it seems as most analysis of interview material relies on an awareness of the effect of the interviewer on the interviewee. When carrying out qualitative analyses particular attention is paid to the influence of the interviewer on the production of the data.

Techniques needed for successful interviewing

As mentioned above, it is important to make your respondents comfortable and attempt to generate rapport with them if you are to stand any chance of carrying out a successful research interview. The best interviews are those where you develop a relationship with the interviewee such that they feel comfortable, relaxed and able to tell you about even the most intimate aspects of their lives. But how do you achieve rapport in an interview?

■ *Use of appropriate language*. It is important that your participants feel comfortable if you are to establish rapport, and the use of appropriate language is an important factor in doing this. For instance, if you use very formal language and technical terms your participants may feel even more anxious and uncomfortable. It is often advisable to try to use the language that your interviewee would normally use (but do not fall into the trap of trying to speak in a way that is not natural for you as well – you will only look stupid and lose any credibility you may have had).

■ *Neutrality*. As in counselling, you should appear neutral in a research interview. This means that you do not judge an interviewee or look shocked (not even a raised eyebrow) – no matter what! This is easier said than done, and worth practising in role-play.

■ *Confidentiality*. Most of the time you will be able to assure your participants of confidentiality and you should tell them this. This should help generate a feeling of safety for your interviewee. However, do remember that if you guarantee your participants confidentiality then you must really maintain confidentiality – so keep that data safe and remove any identifying features from your written report/s (this is discussed in more detail in Chapter 25).

Successful interviewing also requires the use of effective listening skills. Many lessons can be learnt from client-centred counselling where the focus of attention is always on the client receiving therapy. Through the use of a variety of listening skills you will be able to communicate to the interviewee that you want them to talk and keep talking. A number of key skills are listed in Box 4.3.

Box 4.3

Information box

Key skills for successful interviewing

Give your respondent permission to speak

One of the first things many experienced interviewers do is share information (with the interviewee) at the start of the interview about the purpose and importance of the research and why the information they will receive from the interviewee is of value. However, it is also worth telling the interviewee about the process of the interview as well. That is, that you will not be saying much (because you are interested in hearing what your respondent has to say) and that you want them to tell you as much as they can, even if they do not think it is important or of value. In other words, you encourage them to elaborate stories from the outset by giving them permission to speak.

▶

Box 4.3 *Continued*

Learn when not to talk

It is important to leave gaps so that an interviewee is able to find space to think, compose their response and talk. This is easier said than done and another technique worth practising in role-play. One more thing – try not to make too much noise when encouraging your participant to keep talking; a nod of the head will generally have the same effect without producing incessant grunts (that you have to transcribe later – see Chapter 18) on your audio recording.

Be comfortable with silence

When people first start interviewing (and for that matter counselling) they often find it difficult to step outside the normal conversational rules that are vital for effective communication in everyday life. One of those unwritten rules for many people is to fill silent pauses (have you ever wondered why we have so many conversations about the weather?). However, when you are interviewing you need to allow silence (as long as the interviewee is comfortable with it) so that people have sufficient time to think about their responses (remember you are familiar with your interview schedule but your respondents are not).

Do not trivialise responses

Another important lesson from counselling here. It is important that all responses are treated with respect. If you look like you could not care less (or shocked and disgusted) this will be picked up by your interviewee. You must listen to everything that is said and treat everything said with appropriate respect. This is important for both ethical and practical reasons.

Do not dominate

Some people can appear a little forceful in conversation. It is important that you recognise these aspects of your personality and try to lessen their effect in an interview. So, when we interview we may need to think about slowing down and talking more softly so that we do not dominate the interview and inhibit the interviewee. Of course, if you are very quiet and softly spoken you may have to learn to speak up. And one more thing – try not to let the setting (including the recording device) intimidate your participants. Many people feel intimidated by universities (especially laboratory rooms in a university) and surprising numbers of people are anxious when there is a tape or digital recorder present. So, try to interview people in a setting where they feel comfortable and keep the audio recorder out of the way so people forget about it.

Box 4.3 *Continued*

Look interested!

There are a number of ways of looking interested even if you are not! Firstly, appropriate listening and responding demonstrate interest. Secondly, the use of appropriate non-verbal communication (leaning forward and nodding) also helps. However, there is no substitute for genuine interest, so always try to interview people about things you care about.

A good interview schedule

A good interview schedule is a key factor for successful interviewing. At its most basic it is nothing more than a list of questions that you will ask your participants. However, a well-constructed schedule will enable you to gather much more detailed information about a topic than a hastily constructed list of questions. Semi-structured interviews (the most common form used in psychology) rely on a good schedule. Unstructured interviews generally require a list of questions or topics but not really a schedule that you follow in the interview. Conversely, you cannot conduct a structured interview without a formal list of questions and responses to communicate to your participants (often looking more like a complicated questionnaire than an interview schedule).

The way questions are worded in an interview schedule is important (although less so than with a questionnaire as you are present to clarify issues if they arise). However, the rules for wording appropriate questions for an interview are pretty much the same as those for questionnaires (see the advice given in Chapter 5 for questionnaires). There are a few issues of particular importance for writing good interview questions in Box 4.4.

Box 4.4

Information box

Writing interview schedules

Avoid jargon

Use language your respondent (and you) will feel comfortable with. Try to avoid jargon or technical terms that are not widely used and understood.

Try to use open rather than closed questions

Open-ended questions enable the respondent to open up about their thoughts and feelings.

- Bad: Should the president resign?
- Good: What do you think the president should do now?

Box 4.4 *Continued*

Minimal encouragers/probes

These are single words or short phrases that encourage or reinforce the interviewee. They are very helpful in demonstrating that you are listening and encouraging your participant to keep talking.

- Examples include: 'I see', 'Go on', 'Yes', 'Hmm', 'Can you tell me more?', 'What happened next?'

Probes can also be used to encourage the elicitation of specific types of information.

- For example, *affect*: 'How did that make you feel?'
- Or to focus on *awareness*: 'What do you think about that?'

Funnelling

Start by eliciting the respondent's general views and then move on to more specific concerns. The respondent may answer the later questions when answering the first (in which case you move on) but listing the more detailed questions enables you to check out all possible responses. This approach enables you to gather the most detailed information possible in a way that is led by the interviewee.

- For example:
  1 What do you think of current government policies?
     (a) On health issues?
     (b) On welfare issues?
  2 Is there anything you would like to see changed?
  3 Are there any new health or welfare policies you think should be introduced?
     (a) Integrated service delivery?
     (b) New national service framework?

Practice

There is no substitute for plenty of practice if you wish to become proficient at interviewing. Although the advice given in this chapter will help you write a good schedule and teach you the basics of interviewing, you will only develop the key skills you need through practice (see Box 4.5).

Box 4.5

- In a group of three, role-play some interviews. One of you should be the interviewer, one the interviewee and one an observer. Each of you should write a short interview schedule about a particular topic. Once you have done this, swap schedules and offer constructive criticism (about more questions, question-wording, etc.) to each other.

- Now it is time to practise interviewing (three in total) with each of you in a different role in each interview. All three of you should concentrate on the skills and techniques outlined in this chapter and identify any problems you encounter (for instance, the strengths and weaknesses of the schedule, what do you need to practise and improve, etc.).

- Following this role-play you should next try out your skills on a friend (who is not a psychologist) or (better still) a member of your family. Pick a topic that your friend or family member could talk about (for instance, talk to a grandparent about their wartime experiences) and write an appropriate schedule. Find a time when you will not be disturbed and carry out the interview (you should ideally audio-record this so you can listen to how it went later). Try to avoid sensitive topics until you have had more practice and – most importantly – support from an experienced researcher.

4.4   Group discussions

Group discussions have become an increasingly popular and important method of data collection in psychology in recent years. There has been a long tradition of *focus group* research, most often conducted within a broadly positivist tradition and used primarily in market research. In focus group research the primary aim is normally to survey public opinion about products or services using both quantitative and qualitative analysis of group member responses to prompts and questions. Focus groups offer a number of advantages, the primary one being the collection of large amounts of data in a relatively short space of time. More recently, there has also been growth in the use of group discussions to collect data within more critical qualitative perspectives. This latter approach employs group discussions to collect data which may be more naturalistic than that from individual interviews and one in which interactions can be foregrounded. Whilst the growth of this alternative use of group discussions has been relatively recent, the focus on interaction and – in particular – group dynamics has a long history, primarily within psychoanalytically informed analyses. Effectively, we see a split here between a concern with focus groups on content (e.g. attitudes or beliefs about a product) and process (e.g. the way in which people take turns in conversation or how power is employed between people). Of course, this is a crude split as many researchers will be interested in both aspects when using group discussions to collect data. Indeed, an additional benefit from using group discussions is the ability to collect data which better reflects shared meanings – that is, collective or socially constructed understandings – rather than simply garnering data from individuals necessarily reflecting their individual viewpoints. As a result, group discussions have proved to be a particularly important method of data collection (along with the collection of truly naturally occurring talk) in discursive methodologies (see Chapter 21).

There are a number of issues to be considered when using group discussions to collect data which are distinct from those issues common to both individual interviews and group data collection and we will outline a few of these below.

Selecting participants

The choice of participants for a group discussion will of course be dependent on the research question but there are additional concerns. A group could be selected from a naturally occurring group, such as a group of work colleagues or family unit. In contrast, a researcher might decide to recruit participants who are unknown to each other but have some connection to the research topic (for instance, by constructing a group of people who have never met but who all have experience of living with a medical condition). Regardless, it is important to make sure that the focus of the group discussion has been planned in advance and the group facilitator well placed to ensure that the group members feel comfortable and able to contribute to the discussion that takes place. When using pre-existing groups it is important to be mindful of existing group relationships and the impact that these will have on the discussion that takes place. Families, for instance, will invariably have well-established modes of communication, which – if the focus is on understanding naturally occurring discussion in families – may be part of the aim of the research but if this is not the primary concern may lead to some members dominating whilst others are silenced. Conversely, groups of strangers may feel distinctly uncomfortable in a group discussion setting unless the facilitator acts to ensure that any tension is dealt with early on. There are a variety of methods for dealing with this, including the use of warm-up exercises and by outlining group rules.

Warm-up exercises and group rules

A useful technique for establishing a sense of rapport within groups is to use some simple warm-up exercises. This can also form part of the data collection process. For instance, it might be useful to have some index cards with statements about the topic being studied on them for people to sort into groups or order of importance. As they do this they can be asked to explain their reasoning to fellow members of the group. When using such exercises it is important to keep them brief so there is plenty of time for the discussion proper and also to ensure the recording device is turned on as they often generate valuable verbal data.

Establishing group rules is vital when conducting group discussion research and is likely to involve a balance between providing a set of rules and negotiating particular issues. At the most basic it would be usual to make clear to all participants that it is crucial to respect each other and ensure that all information will be kept confidential. This can sometimes create problems when working with established groups or with people who are likely to encounter each other in settings outside the research group. Consent must also be established and this needs to be done on both an individual basis as well as a group basis. A researcher should talk through the research aims with each individual group member before they participate in the group and then also address this with the group as a whole. There should also be an opportunity for individual debriefing should participants want it and here they should be given the opportunity to withdraw their consent. A further issue that warrants some discussion is the level of participation and disclosure of individual members as participants need to be advised to ensure that they feel comfortable sharing information with others.

The role of the group facilitator

Facilitating a group is quite a different process from conducting an individual interview, although there are similarities with regard to the need to keep the focus on the participants and their views and ensure they feel comfortable to articulate whatever they wish. Like interviews, it will be necessary at times to ask questions but with groups these may be either to individuals, to encourage them to speak, or to the group to keep them on topic or to develop their arguments further. A facilitator might ask if people agree or disagree with something someone has stated but, regardless, it is important to try to be inclusive and supportive when posing questions. A group setting can feel quite threatening and it is therefore particularly important that a facilitator ensures no one feels isolated or threatened by any questions asked. Occasionally one or more people may dominate and it may be appropriate to intervene to enable others to speak. This needs to be done tactfully by, for instance, thanking the person for their views and then asking others about their views on what has been said. Alternatively, it might be appropriate to target questions to individuals but here it is often best to do this to a number of people rather than just one person to avoid them feeling exposed. Finally, it is worth being aware of the tendency for people to direct their responses to the facilitator rather than each other and inadvertently produce what is in effect a series of public individual interviews. Turning the response towards others is a useful technique to encourage people to talk with each other in such situations.

Recording the group discussion

Group discussion will invariably be recorded like individual interviews but they pose additional problems which should be considered. First, it is important to limit the numbers of participants to a relatively small number (four or five is usual) as it can become difficult not only to deal with managing a larger group but also transcribing the voices of so many people. Another tip is to try if at all possible to ensure that people have different-sounding voices. This is not of course possible all the time but it can make transcription an awful lot easier! Finally, it is important to think through – in advance – how such data will be analysed. A number of methods rely primarily on individual interviews and it can be difficult to use or adapt these methods for group data. As in all research, think through the whole process before embarking on any data collection to ensure you are not left with data that you do not know how to analyse.

| 4.5 | Repertory grid techniques |

Repertory grid methods (often known as rep grids) developed within personal construct theory (see Butt & Burr, 2004, for an introduction), a theory developed by personality theorist George Kelly. They have become an important method independent of personal construct theory, and are used in a wide variety of applied situations from clinical settings to business. Rep grids are used idiographically (focusing on one person's outlook) and also nomothetically (concerned with finding patterns amongst people). Their idiographic use has been particularly valuable in clinical settings. The essence of rep grids is how people understand the meanings that define their perception of relationships to others (a person's repertory of role constructs). At the simplest level, a person would be asked to compare and contrast sets of three people (for instance, themselves, their mother, their father) on dimensions of meaning. This is done by asking people how they think two of the figures are alike and different from the third. A person might, for instance, describe themselves and their mother as loving and their father as distant and thus produce a dimension of meaning of loving versus distant. This dimension would then be considered a significant construct for the person in how they understand their social world. By asking participants to compare a number of triads (self, mother, father, sibling, liked other, disliked other, ideal self, etc.) it becomes possible to elicit a broad range of constructs that describe a person's outlook on life. These constructs can then be examined to form the basis of further interviewing (or indeed, psychotherapeutic interventions) or subject to quantitative analysis using SPSS or a variety of dedicated computer programs to identify patterns and/or categories of meaning.

A further step that is commonly used is to ask participants to rate or rank each element (e.g. people) on the constructs that have been elicited. This results in a grid in which the elements constitute the columns and the constructs the rows. Participants then rate each element (for instance, using a seven-point scale with 1 equivalent to one end of a construct and 7 the opposite end) against each construct. So, for instance, self might be one of the elements which the participant rates as 1 on the construct loving versus distant to indicate that they perceive themself to be a very loving person. Rep grids of this form can be almost any size, from a minimum of six constructs to hundreds. Most researchers would expect to have reached saturation point with about 15 to 20 constructs, however. Grids (matrices of elements against constructs) can then be subject to a number of quantitative analyses to discern patterns in individual grids and also across a number of grids. It is also possible to use some of the specialist grid software to elicit constructs directly rather than use paper and pen. Analyses may involve correlating particular elements (such as self and ideal self) to reveal valuable information for use in, for instance, psychotherapy or personal development programmes. In many research applications researchers will often employ complex statistical methods such as factor analysis or multidimensional scaling, which are beyond the scope of this text, to determine patterns within the data. Interested readers should be able to find more on this by reading the sources listed in the Further reading section below.

4.6 Observation

Observation has a long tradition within psychology, particularly developmental psychology where for many years researchers have observed children in order to (for instance) identify developmental milestones. However, observation is not the exclusive preserve of developmental psychology. Studies of human interaction, animal behaviour and so on have relied upon observation for the collection of their data. Furthermore, participant observation (which is discussed in detail below), where the observer participates in the setting being observed, has played an important part in sociological (and to a lesser extent psychological) research. This section will introduce you to the various types of observational method in common usage, from structured observation in a laboratory setting to full participant observation. You will also be exposed to the particular uses of observation and some of its strengths and weaknesses. Observation can be of great use in gathering descriptive information about some behaviour (such as children's play). However, it is often difficult to ascertain a causal relationship between variables (e.g. the effect of number of toys on amount of play engaged in) with observational studies. This is because naturalistic observation does not allow you to manipulate independent variables (e.g. the number of toys available in a nursery) and measure the effect on the dependent variable (amount of play). However, there have been some innovative studies that have addressed this issue. For instance, there have been studies where independent variables are manipulated (number of toys or space available for play) in an ecologically valid way (e.g. in a nursery attached to a psychology department).

Choosing what to observe

One of the first issues that you will encounter when deciding on observation as a method is the decision about what to observe. It is all too easy to decide to observe some children playing but you will quickly encounter problems without a little more thought about what you will focus your observation on. Are you going to observe one child or several children? Are you going to record their speech and non-verbal behaviour? How will you know when they are playing? Are all types of play the same? These are just a few of the issues that you would need to address before starting an observation of children's play. Many people find they have observed much of what was going on but found to their cost that none of it was relevant to the research question they wanted to address. You need to know what it is that you want to get from your observation and what you need to observe to do that. Good observation is often theoretically informed so you have some principles guiding the focus of your research.

| 4.7 | Structured and non-participant observation |

Structure

Observations, like interviews, vary in the degree of structure that is imposed. They range from the fully structured with formal observation schedules to the relatively unstructured form that is participant observation.

Fully structured laboratory (controlled) observation

Fully structured observation involves the collection of data in a systematic, structured manner. You would generally use some method of data collection and coding to maximise the reliability of material collected. Observers may use grid recording systems where they make a note of how often a particular behaviour occurs. This obviously requires the use of a coding system, which enables you to decide to which category a particular behaviour should belong (coding is discussed in more detail below). These methods can be complex and often require training so that an observer can appropriately categorise behaviour and use the coding system reliably. A classic example of structured observation comes from Ainsworth's (1979) studies of attachment and separation amongst children. In these studies Mary Ainsworth video recorded children when their mothers left and a stranger entered. From these video recordings Ainsworth was able to understand more about the attachment needs and styles of children. Very often these types of study are conducted in a laboratory setting.

When attempting to collect data systematically and reliably we often want to control the effect of extraneous variables on the behaviour or setting. Obviously this is much easier in a laboratory than out in the field. Furthermore, the reliability of our observations will be improved through the use of, for instance, video recording equipment. It is much easier to observe (and then code) a situation using video recording in a laboratory. A great deal of structured observation is conducted in a laboratory for these reasons.

Advantages	Disadvantages
■ Systematic collection of data ■ Permanent record of data kept (if using recording equipment) ■ Extraneous variables controlled ■ Setting can be kept constant ■ Replication possible ■ Observer bias should be minimised	■ May lack ecological validity (see below) ■ Behaviour may not be spontaneous or realistic ■ May not be possible (where participants would not cooperate) or ethical in some situations

Naturalistic field (uncontrolled) observation

Unlike laboratory-based observation, **naturalistic observation** involves the observer studying people in their natural environment. This type of 'field' research has a number of benefits over laboratory-based observation, including, for instance, greater **ecological validity**, but not without some costs! This type of observation involves the observer recording data through video recording or, more often, note taking while trying to remain unobtrusive.

One of the main problems with naturalistic observation is the danger of your presence affecting the (naturally occurring) behaviour of the participants. We all know what it is like when someone produces a camera – some play up to it while others run for the hills, but no one acts naturally again until the camera is put away! This is especially true of children. However, given enough time children (and adults) tend to forget the camera is present and return to behaving naturally. This is very important for naturalistic observation. The best observational studies repeatedly observe the participants so that they get used to the presence of the observer and observing equipment. It is hoped that over time people will forget about the presence of the observer and act naturally. One other method for limiting your effect on the people being observed is by assuming a role where observation (in some form) is expected. So, for instance, we expect people sitting in a street-side coffee bar to watch the world go by. By assuming a role of this kind you can blend into the background and limit the influence you have on the setting.

Advantages	Disadvantages
■ Greater ecological validity (see below) ■ Realistic, spontaneously occurring behaviour ■ Useful where it is not possible to observe participants in a laboratory ■ Behaviour should be less subject to the demand characteristics of the setting	■ More difficult to conduct ■ Difficult for observer to be unobtrusive ■ Extraneous variables poorly controlled ■ Greater potential for observer bias ■ Replication may be difficult ■ Use of recording equipment may be difficult

Ecological validity

One of the key distinctions between laboratory and non-laboratory (or naturalistic) settings is the degree of **ecological validity**. Ecological validity concerns the meaningfulness of data collected in settings where it would naturally (and spontaneously) occur. Obviously, most observation in a laboratory is low in ecological validity because the behaviour would not occur naturally or spontaneously. Most of us are unfamiliar with laboratory settings and tend to produce very little behaviour spontaneously without some manipulation by the experimenter. However, if we are observed playing sport or drinking with friends (naturalistic observation) we tend to act as we always do in that setting – naturally and spontaneously (unless influenced by the presence of the observer, of course).

So, why conduct observations in laboratories at all if your data lack ecological validity? Well, there are lots of good reasons. Firstly, although ecological validity is important and is undoubtedly reduced in a laboratory, it does not mean that the data have no validity at all. We always have to compromise when conducting research in psychology and it may be worth sacrificing some degree of ecological validity for the benefits of a laboratory setting. These benefits include the following.

The practicality of observing complex behaviour

It may not be possible to observe some types of behaviour in a setting other than the laboratory. Laboratories may have equipment available that is necessary for the study in question. Observation laboratories typically include two-way mirrors (where you can observe your participants without them knowing you are there – all they see is a mirror), which are particularly useful for observing children (adults tend to guess what is going on very quickly), and high quality audio and video recording equipment. There may also be other equipment available (such as experiment generator software and/or psycho-physiological measuring equipment – discussed in Chapter 6, on experimental design) that you want to use in conjunction with observation.

Control over the setting

There are many benefits to recording natural spontaneously occurring behaviour but we invariably have no control over the person or people we are observing and their environment. It is important to remember that we do not just collect descriptive data through observation. Sometimes we want to test a theory about human behaviour where observation is the most appropriate form of data collection. Without the ability to manipulate the setting (as is often the case with field observation) it may prove impossible to test our theory (see Smith & Cowie, 1988, for examples of experimental observations of children).

Recording data

Note taking

Taking notes is the most traditional way of recording observational data but it is a difficult and highly subjective method. There are, of course, times when it is not possible (or desirable) to use video recording and here note taking comes into its own. For instance, participant observation (where you are immersed and active in the setting) generally requires the use of note taking to record data. Audio or video recording would often prove too intrusive when collecting data in this way.

Video recording

It is perhaps not surprising to find that video recording is most often the method of choice for observational studies. Certainly observations of large numbers of participants are not really practical without video recording. In addition, when the observation is based in a laboratory it may be convenient (and no more obtrusive) to use video recording.

Coding

As discussed above, **coding** may be a useful and necessary technique for data collection when carrying out systematic structured observations. If we wish to collect data in a systematic way we need some predetermined framework to impose on the setting we are observing. Without a framework of this kind it would not be possible to collect complex data in a reliable, systematic way. Generally a coding frame consists of a number of predetermined codes (symbols or shorthand codes) which should be comprehensive enough to cover most behaviours you are interested in observing (but not so many that you are unable to apply them reliably). Observers then indicate (on a coding sheet) every time some type of behaviour occurs (codes enable observers to cluster similar types of behaviour together). Some systems are more elaborate and involve rating scales for each behaviour (so, for example, the severity of some violent encounter may be rated 1 (minimal violence) to 7 (maximum violence)). An example of a coding frame is given in Box 4.6.

Box 4.6

Information box

Coding frame for structured observation

An example (part) of a coding frame designed for observing play in children.

Verbal behaviour		Non-verbal behaviour	
ATT	– Demands attention	HAN	– Holds hand
WINF	– Wants information	SMI	– Smiles
GINF	– Gives information	LOOK	– Looks around
IMT	– Imitates other child	REA	– Reaches out hand

■ And so on until you have enough categories to cover all elements of the behaviour you wish to observe (and there are many more categories needed to observe children's play).

■ These codes could then be arranged in an observation grid so that you can place a mark in a box every time the behaviour occurs during the observation period. The data can then be analysed statistically.

In addition to a coding frame, structured observation often needs some method of data sampling. When it is not possible to record a setting, 'live' coding is necessary. Obviously this is much more difficult than coding data in your own time from video after the event (for one thing, you do not have a rewind button when coding 'live'). When coding 'live' it may not be possible for you to observe some event or behaviour continuously for several hours as you wish. In these cases you may find a sampling strategy useful where you observe only the setting when some behaviour occurs (such as a playground fight starting) or for repeated (short) periods of time. If you ever try 'live' coding you will quickly appreciate the need for a sampling strategy. Two of the commonest sampling strategies are discussed below.

Event sampling

Event sampling is where you observe only when a particular event (such as a playground fight) occurs. This is generally over a sustained period of time and may be particularly useful if you are interested in observing some specific behaviour or event. For example, you may be interested in observing the ways in which playground fights dissipate. Choosing to observe the playground when a fight breaks out (the event of interest) should enable you to do this effectively. However, if you are interested in how fights start event sampling may be problematic, as the fight will invariably have started before you begin observing it! In this case you may need to use time sampling instead.

Time sampling

Time sampling involves repeated observations (for short periods of time) over a longer period of time. So, for instance, you may observe a setting (making detailed observations) for 15 seconds every five minutes over a two-hour period. This would result in 360 seconds (or six minutes) of observation in total, produced from a series of 'snapshots' of the setting. If the behaviour is complex then this may be all you can manage in one sitting. Further two-hour observations can then be undertaken until you feel you have collected sufficient data. Time sampling is best used where you can expect the behaviour of interest to occur repeatedly (such as playground fights). However, it is important to be aware of the possible limitations of this method of sampling. It is possible to produce a very unrepresentative picture of a setting if the time period chosen for the observation is not appropriate (for instance, too short or infrequent).

Multiple observers and reliability

When observing 'live' it is often advisable to have at least two observers. With particularly complex behaviour or many people being observed, you may need very large numbers of observers (at least two people per person being observed). All observers should be trained to use the coding framework so that it is applied consistently to the setting. When you have a record of observation from at least two observers it becomes possible to check the inter-rater (or inter-observer) reliability of your observations.

Inter-rater reliability

Inter-rater reliability is a measure of the degree of agreement (or disagreement) between two observers of an event (it can also be used for judging agreement in areas other than observation). Obviously, if your observation is reliable (and the coding system is working well) you should find that both observers record pretty much the same information (that is, when we recorded a fight in the playground of moderate severity, so did you). If a structured observation has produced reliable data there should be high inter-rater reliability. Inter-rater reliability is measured by correlating the scores (see Chapter 12) recorded by both observers. Values of inter-rater reliability range from 0 to 1 (or between 0 and 100 per cent), where 0 indicates no agreement and 1 total agreement, with good inter-rater reliability generally above 0.8 (80 per cent). However, the level of agreement deemed satisfactory is dependent on what is being observed. There are some situations where relatively modest levels of reliability may be acceptable (but there must be good reasons). Inter-rater reliability may be low for many reasons, including observer bias (where observers are evaluating behaviour rather than simply recording when it occurs). Training is often useful for minimising observer bias. Through role-play and practice observers can be taught to avoid evaluating the events they are observing and instead concentrate on producing as accurate a written record of the situation as possible.

However, human beings are always likely to miss the odd thing even when it may appear obvious to others. How often have we shouted our dismay (and much more!) at a soccer referee when they appear to be blind to what is happening straight in front of them?

4.8	Participant observation

Participant observation is a method very familiar to sociologists and social anthropologists but somewhat less so to psychologists. However, psychologists have used participant observation as a particularly insightful form of observation. Social psychologists have found the method useful for gaining insights into the way people understand and operate in their own environments. Participant observation produces highly subjective but very meaningful data that often cannot be collected in any other way. So what is participant observation? Well, when carrying out most forms of observation the observer tries to be unobtrusive. Participant observation accepts that in many cases this may not be possible or desirable and encourages the observer to participate in whatever is being observed (see Box 4.7).

Box 4.7

Activity box	Participant observation

This activity is designed to sensitise you to some of the difficulties involved in participant observation. Upon first inspection, participant observation seems a relatively easy method of data collection. However, as you should discover when you carry out your own observation, it can be surprisingly difficult.

- Decide on a setting to observe involving your friends or family. This could be an evening out in the pub with friends or a family mealtime; it does not matter as long as you are in a familiar (and safe) setting where you can observe for an hour or two.

- Observe the goings on – who said what, when and to whom, in other words what interactions took place. Try to find discreet moments to make some notes on a pad throughout the observation period. And at the end of the observation session write down as much as you can remember.

- Debrief the people who were the focus of your study fully about your activities once you have finished. You will need to explain what you were doing and why. Furthermore, you need to allow people to withdraw from the study at this time if they so wish. This should be unlikely when observing friends and family. See the discussion on ethics at the end of this section and Chapter 25.

Box 4.7 *Continued*

■ When you have some spare time, write up your notes with a commentary where you should attempt some analysis of what went on. Finally, reflect on the process of carrying out the observation, the effect you had on the setting, how easy or (more likely) difficult it was and what you think of the quality of your notes, analysis and write-up.

One of the biggest difficulties with participant observation is recording the data. How can you make notes when participating in a setting? Furthermore, if you are pretending to be a member of the group (rather than a researcher), as is sometimes the case with participant observation, then you may not want to risk being found out by making notes. What often happens is that notes are made at the end of the day (in private). Obviously this produces highly subjective data. However, this is less of a problem than it first seems. Firstly, many people using this method are working within the qualitative tradition of research (as discussed in Chapter 1). Qualitative approaches recognise and accept the subjective nature of data and work with it rather than trying to reduce it. Secondly, most participant observation studies involve the immersion of the observer in a setting for long periods of time so that individual observations are not crucial to the findings. Instead, experience gained through participation (over time) leads to personal insight into the lives of the people being observed.

However, there are different types of participant observation. In some situations participant observation is barely different from naturalistic observation with only limited involvement of the observer. However, participant observation may also involve the complete immersion of an observer into a setting (often for extended periods of time) where they become more of a participant than an observer.

Types of participant observation – full participant observation to full observation

Patton (1980) describes several types of participant observation with varying degrees of participation.

Full participant observation

With full participant observation the researcher does not disclose their identity but instead pretends to be a full member of the group being observed. The aim is for the people being observed to take the researcher as a full and authentic member of the group. It is thought that the trust that comes from the belief that the researcher is 'one of us' should lead to greater disclosure and greater ecological validity. Obviously, the deception involved in full participant observation raises serious ethical concerns (discussed below).

Participant as observer

With this type of participant observation the researcher's identity is not secret but simply kept quiet. The main reason given for the researcher being present is not their role as observer but some role salient to the group. This type of observation may be useful for research about a setting where you are already a participant (e.g. your workplace) or where you can easily become a temporary member of that group (for instance, as a relief teacher in a school). Box 4.8 describes a participant observation similar to this where the researcher lives in the city they observe (there are also some similarities to the 'observer as participant' approach described below).

Box 4.8	Study box

Beattie, G. (1986). *Survivors of Steel City – A Portrait of Sheffield*. London: Chatto & Windus Ltd.

This book presents a predominantly observational study of the lives of people living in Sheffield in the 1980s. It consists of observation of people in their natural settings supplemented by informal interviews. The data generated are rich and alive with the experiences of the men and women of Sheffield struggling to survive in a city suffering from years of unemployment, poverty and neglect. However, what emerges are the ways in which people have creatively carved out valuable and worthwhile roles in their particular communities. The researcher is often a participant in the settings he chooses to observe. However, he keeps his distance and tries to present an account that prioritises the experiences of the people he meets. There are no simple results or conclusions with work of this kind but instead a graphic insight into a community, and the people within it, fighting for its survival.

Observer as participant

This approach recognises the central importance of the observer role but relies on group members accepting this and over time learning to trust the researcher. It is this development of trust that is thought to facilitate the sharing of intimate information. The researcher needs to manage their role carefully in this situation. It is important to engender trust and not interfere in the natural actions of the setting being observed.

Full observer

This is not really participant observation at all but naturalistic observation as described previously in this section.

The table below outlines some of the advantages and disadvantages of participant observation.

Advantages	Disadvantages
■ High ecological validity ■ Detailed, insightful data ■ Highly contextual data ■ Development of trust may produce information inaccessible by other means	■ Researcher needs to rely on memory ■ Highly subjective ■ May be unreplicable ■ May be difficult to generalise results ■ There may be problems and even dangers in maintaining cover if full participant

Ethics

As mentioned above, participant observation raises a number of important ethical issues that need to be addressed (these are also dealt with in more detail in Chapter 25). The most important concern with full participant observation is the use of **deception**. Wherever possible, psychological research tries to minimise deception and maximise **informed consent** (that is, where the participants are *fully* aware of the nature of the study and still choose to participate in it). Obviously full participant observation involves deception and does not involve informed consent. It is therefore vital that there are very strong grounds for using this particular method. Unless there are, it would be unethical to proceed. Another concern with this method is the effect that disclosing your identity will have on the people you have been observing. What harmful effects might this betrayal have on those involved? Some previous studies have demonstrated the utility of this approach in ways that might be argued to justify its use. Holdaway (1982) studied 'canteen cultures' in the police force and revealed the deeply entrenched racist attitudes there. This important information might not have been revealed through any other method. However, despite studies of this kind there are still some who argue that there is never a good enough reason for this level of deception and betrayal (Banister, 1994). Certainly, before you contemplate using undisclosed participant observation you should think very carefully about whether there are less invasive ways of gathering the data and always seek advice from more experienced researchers.

Further reading

Arksey, H. & Knight, P. (1999). *Interviewing for Social Scientists*. London: Sage.

Bakeman, R. & Gottman, J. M. (1997). *Observing Interaction*. Cambridge: Cambridge University Press.

Jorgensen, D. L. (1989). *Participant Observation – A Methodology for Human Studies*. Sage Applied Social Research Methods Series Vol. 15. London: Sage.

Kvale, S. (2007). *Doing Interviews*. London: Sage.

Neimeyer, R.A. & Neimeyer, G.J. (Eds.)(2002). *Advances in Personal Construct Psychology*. New York: Praeger.

http://www.pcp-net.org/

Further information on personal construct psychology and repertory grid methods (along with several other methods that have been derived from personal construct theory) can be found in this book and website.

Wengraf, T. (2001). *Qualitative Research Interviewing*. London: Sage.

The books listed above provide excellent further coverage on the topics of data collection outlined in this chapter and are well worth a look before you decide to collect your own data.

5

Collecting data 2: questionnaires and psychometric tests

- This chapter introduces you to further methods of data collection, including questionnaire design and measurement.

- The importance of using an existing questionnaire, where possible, is emphasised.

- The process of developing a new questionnaire, where necessary, is described.

- This chapter will also introduce you to the field of psychometrics and its two key watchwords: reliability and validity.

- A selection of 'ready-made' reliable and valid tests are described, which you might consider using in your research.

INTRODUCTION

Real skill is required to collect data and without knowledge of the appropriate techniques of data collection the quality of your results may be questioned. This chapter is devoted to questionnaire design and psychometrics. Questionnaires are useful for collecting data from numbers of people in a systematic way. They are particularly valuable for development, social and applied (e.g. health) psychology research. As previously noted in Chapter 4, these chapters address only issues of data collection and not analysis, which is dealt with in Parts 2 and 3.

5.1 Questionnaires

Questionnaires are a particularly valuable method of data collection as they allow you to collect data from large numbers of people. Questionnaires are useful if you want to know something about the incidence of some behaviour or the opinions, beliefs or attitudes of large numbers or groups of people. So, questionnaires could be used to discover the beliefs of students about environmental issues or attitudes towards hunting with dogs. They are also useful if you want to measure something that is not directly observable (a theoretical **construct**). As psychologists, we can rarely measure constructs such as 'depression' directly. It may be possible to measure the consequences of depression, by using a questionnaire where participants can self-report their symptoms. However, gathering data from large numbers of people may be at the expense of the amount of information or detail you can collect. But with good questionnaire design you should be able to maximise the quality of data collected without increasing the size of the questionnaire unnecessarily. The field of psychometrics is concerned with the development of good psychological questionnaires. A good questionnaire is one that has **reliability** and **validity**. These two features are described in more detail later on in this chapter.

Questionnaires are useful for more than just collecting large amounts of data. They are often used as a convenient way of collecting background data (age, sex, ethnicity, etc.) in studies of all kinds and in the form of psychometric tests used to assess, for instance, cognitive ability or personality traits. They are also used to measure the effect of some intervention or treatment (such as a short course of psychotherapy) on the well-being (in terms of, for instance, anxiety or depression) of participants.

■ Questionnaires can be used in all types of study design, including experiments.

■ The term 'survey' is used to describe a study design where the questionnaire is the primary focus.

■ Questions in questionnaires are often called questionnaire **items**, particularly in psychology. Personality scales and tests are said to contain 'items' rather than 'questions'. We use both terms interchangeably in this chapter.

■ The term **scale** is used to describe a set of items that measure something psychological or something which is not measurable directly (a **construct**). Several scales might be published as an **inventory**.

5.2   The first rule of questionnaire design: don't reinvent the wheel

It is important not to 'reinvent the wheel' by developing a new questionnaire or scale unnecessarily. If a reliable and valid questionnaire exists for the construct you are interested in, use it or improve it (reliability and validity are described below). There are three reasons why this is the most sensible strategy:

1 Creating a new questionnaire takes a long time.

2 You will be able to make sense of your results and interpret them in light of the existing literature.

3 Other researchers will understand what you have claimed to measure. You will find it far easier to defend your study if the questionnaire or test is widely respected in the field.

As discussed in Chapter 3 a great many questionnaires simply present old wine in new bottles. Psychologists are very good at creating 'jangles' for constructs – different labels for what are essentially the same thing. For example, many different personality tests all claim to measure traits such as 'negative emotionality' or 'trait negative affect'. These are all jangles for Neuroticism. The term 'jingle' refers to giving different constructs the same name, a less common but equally wasteful exercise. This warning applies to questionnaires and tests regardless of how you use them. If you are conducting a survey or an experiment, the same principle applies. It also applies when the test is an 'outcome' measure in an experiment. For example, if you conducted an experiment (Chapter 6) to evaluate the impact of an intervention on depression scores, it would be very unwise to design a new questionnaire to measure depression. Use an existing, validated measure (in this case, the General Health Questionnaire, Hospital Anxiety and Depression Scale, or the SF-36 MCS scale would be appropriate).

| 5.3 | General principles, types and structure of questionnaires |

If you have decided to study a topic where the constructs have not been defined, or explored, it may be necessary to design a new questionnaire. Be very careful if you claim to be studying a 'new' construct. Researchers frequently claim to have discovered a 'new intelligence', a new 'cognitive domain' or another 'personality trait'. It later turns out that they have produced a jangle for cognitive ability or one of the big five personality traits. Most differences in personality traits, for example, can be understood in relation to the big five framework. Most cognitive skills are already well researched, in the hierarchical model of cognitive ability. These are explained in more detail later in the chapter.

General principles

There are a variety of general principles that inform good questionnaire design. One of the first principles is that you should keep the questionnaire as short as possible. Questions should be included only if you have good reasons for their inclusion (it is no good putting in a question 'just in case'!). People will find any excuse for not completing a questionnaire. We have all been there – approached by someone in the street or sent a questionnaire in the post. Did you take the time to complete the questionnaire? It is important that you design a questionnaire that is quick and easy to complete unless there are very strong reasons for doing otherwise. Research invariably involves a trade-off between the parsimony (simplicity) of the method of data collection and the depth of information gathered. You need to think about this balance and make the appropriate decision about ease of completion versus depth of information.

Readability

Another principle of questionnaire design is to ensure that it is written in language appropriate for your respondents (this is dealt with in more detail below). Many researchers overestimate the reading ability of the general population. You can test the readability of your questionnaire in Microsoft Word, in the spell checking facility. First make sure that this option is switched on. Click on **Tools**, **Options**, **Spelling and Grammar**. Check that both **Check grammar with spelling** and **Show readability statistics** are both ticked, then click **OK**. Next time you run the spelling and grammar check (**Tools**, **Spelling and Grammar**), readability statistics are displayed at the end of the process.

- Passive sentences are difficult to read, and should be avoided.
- Flesch Reading Ease is a score from 0 to 100 (higher scores indicate text that is easier to read)
- Flesch–Kincaid Grade Level converts the score into a US school grade level. This should be as low as possible; preferably 7th (age 12–13) to 8th grade (age 13–14) at an absolute maximum.

As a general rule, because some participants may have low levels of reading ability, you should improve the readability of your questionnaire. This can be achieved easily by reducing the length of sentences, and reducing the number of syllables in the words. For example, the first sentence of this paragraph requires a grade level of 14, which is degree level! This can easily be reduced by changing the sentence to 'Some people are not good readers. You should make your questionnaire easier to read.' This has a grade level of 3 (age 8–9), which is far more acceptable.

Attach a Participant Information Sheet

All questionnaires should begin with a Participant Information Sheet which tells participants about the study. It should explain clearly what it is about and why people should spend the time to complete your questionnaire. It should explain who you are and give contact details in case your respondents wish to ask questions about the study. It is also important to inform your respondents about what you intend to do with the data and whether you can assure them of anonymity and/or confidentiality. In fact, you would need very strong justification for being unable to protect the confidentiality of your participants. One final purpose of the introductory statement is to 'sell' your project. You need to maximise participation so you should tell people why your work is important and why you need their help. If you will ask sensitive questions, warn people on the Information Sheet so that they can choose whether or not to provide *informed* consent.

Attach a consent form

Depending on your institution and the nature of your study, you may need to attach a separate consent form. A consent form records the date, name and signature of each participant, indicating that they have read the Participant Information Sheet and agree to take part in the study. Some researchers combine the Participant Information Sheet with the consent form. If you have a separate consent form, make sure that this is detached from the questionnaire and stored separately in a secure location. Names that can be linked to the questionnaire (e.g. by ID number) are a threat to anonymity. Talk this through with your tutor or contact your relevant ethics review committee for advice specific to your project.

Stages of design

There are a number of stages that you need to go through to carry out a questionnaire study. Obviously the first stage is to decide on a topic to research and then develop your research question(s). This should be followed by careful planning and design of your questionnaire. This will include making decisions about the range and type of questions to include (open versus closed questions) and careful thought about question wording. Following the design of your questionnaire (discussed in more detail below) you should always **pilot** your questionnaire.

All questionnaires should be piloted – that is, tested out on a small number of people – before being widely distributed. Piloting will enable you to 'iron out' the flaws in your questionnaire and make sure that you are asking the right questions and providing the appropriate response options. It is often a good idea to sit with your pilot participants while they complete the questionnaire so that you can get feedback about it as you go. If your participants need to ask you questions then you may need to do some more work on your questionnaire. Finally, you should always ask for detailed feedback after your participants have completed the questionnaire. Was it relevant? Was it easy to complete? Could they express their responses as they wanted to?

Once you have piloted your questionnaire you should make sure that you address all the problems raised by your pilot participants. Do not just write them off. There is no point in carrying out a pilot study unless you use it as a check on the quality of your questionnaire. Remember to pay attention to the layout of your questionnaire – it should be clear (and ideally aesthetically pleasing) to your participants. In addition, the layout should enable you, the researcher, to read the responses off the questionnaire easily and enter them into the appropriate analysis software package (see Chapter 9).

Following successful piloting and revision of the questionnaire you will want to administer your questionnaire. This is where you distribute your questionnaires to your participants. It is important to distribute your questionnaire to an appropriate sample that will enable you to meet your study aims (see the section on sampling below). After your respondents have completed the questionnaire you will need to collect the questionnaires and enter and analyse your data.

Question types

Open versus closed questions

Open-ended questions (see Box 5.1) often generate more detailed information than closed questions, but at a cost. They increase the size of questionnaires and have a dramatic effect on how long it takes to complete a questionnaire. There is also a danger that many people will not complete open-ended questions at all (in order to complete the questionnaire as quickly as possible), resulting in very patchy data. It is advisable to avoid using open-ended questions without good grounds for including them (just wanting to know more about a topic is rarely a good reason). Open-ended questions need to be focused so you avoid essay responses that you can do little with. Furthermore, you need to know what form of analysis you can use to interpret the data you collect (of course this is true for any type of question but especially true of open-ended questions). However, there *are* good reasons for using open-ended questions. They enable you to collect richer data than closed questions – akin to data collected through interviews. They also avoid the problem of imposing the researcher's structure on the respondents. One of the commonest criticisms of questionnaires comprising closed questions is that they limit possible responses. Indeed, in extreme cases you could collect data that have little or no real meaning to the participants – they could follow the structure you supply and routinely answer the questions without any thought.

Closed questions require very careful wording and thought about the appropriate type of response options. You need clear, unambiguous questions and response options that enable people to complete the questions quickly and easily. You do not want people to feel frustrated and confused because they cannot work out what the question is asking or how to respond appropriately. There are some obvious benefits to using closed questions. Perhaps the most important is that they enable you to collect reliable information that is easily analysed. They also make a questionnaire easy and quick to complete for your participants. Finally, they provide a reliable way of making people respond to the issues you are interested in by avoiding the danger of open-ended questions where people tell you much more than you need to know. There are many different types of response option, ranging from 'yes/no' responses to Likert scales (where you respond from 1 (strongly agree) to 7 (strongly disagree), for instance). Some are shown in Box 5.1 and this issue is discussed again in the 'Measuring attitudes' section.

Box 5.1

Information box

Examples of open-ended and closed questions

Open-ended questions

1 What do you think about the government policy on university tuition fees?

_____

_____

_____

2 Briefly state what you think are the reasons for eating organic produce.

_____

_____

_____

Closed questions (with differing response options)

3 Do you think hunting foxes with dogs should be banned?   Yes ☐ No ☐

4 Adoption of children should be more accessible (circle one number below):

Strongly agree   1   2   3   4   5   6   7   Strongly disagree

5 I think the Internet is (circle a number for each line below):

Good	1	2	3	4	5	6	7	Bad
Interesting	1	2	3	4	5	6	7	Uninteresting
Useful	1	2	4	5	5	6	7	Not useful
Strong	1	2	4	5	5	6	7	Weak
Active	1	2	4	5	5	6	7	Passive

5.4   Writing questions and measuring attitudes

Writing questions

One of the most crucial elements of questionnaire design is how you word the questions. Badly worded questions will frustrate and confuse your respondents. Furthermore, they may also result in you collecting information that is not valid. However, there are a number of well-known rules that should enable you to construct questions that are clear and effective.

Ask one question at a time

This might seem obvious but there is more to it than meets the eye. One of the commonest problems people encounter when first writing questions is keeping them simple. It is all too easy to make a question too complex. So, keep it simple and make sure you are not trying to do too much with each question (if it *can* be worded as two questions then it *should* be). Asking people if they agree that 'Fox and badger hunting should be banned' is asking two questions. Some people may have different views about each type of hunting. This might be an interesting phenomenon to study.

Avoid ambiguous questions

As before, you need to keep things simple, but this time so that you avoid ambiguous questions (questions that have more than one meaning). When we write questions we obviously know what we mean but it is surprising how often this can seem ambiguous to other people. The question 'Fox hunting should stop when the fox goes to ground' refers to the fox going underground. Some people might think that it refers to the fox stopping on the ground, or being killed on the ground. The best way to check this is to pilot your questionnaire thoroughly.

Avoid double negatives

When asking people if they agree with questionnaire items such as 'Fox hunting should not be banned', double negatives make the question more difficult to follow. If the response options ranged from 'agree' to 'disagree', people might hesitate as they try to work out if they are agreeing with the ban, or that there should *not* be a ban.

Tell respondents if your questions are going to be sensitive

Be careful how you ask questions about 'sensitive' topics – you do not want people to find your questions offensive or shocking. At best they may miss the question out (and missing data can be a real problem which should be avoided) and at worst you may receive complaints about the offensive nature of your questions. One technique for avoiding shocks and surprises is to work towards the more sensitive questions gradually, giving explanations and even warnings (if necessary) of why you need to ask these questions. Ideally, the Participant Information Sheet should warn participants what kind of questions will be asked. The 'foot in the door' technique, increasing the sensitivity of questions once people have started the study, is generally not ethically acceptable. People may feel obliged to finish something they agreed to complete. The worst possible approach is to try to slip a question about a sensitive issue in among other more innocuous questions in the hope people will not notice – believe us, they will!

Questions should be neutral rather than value-laden or leading

You should always try to keep your questions neutral rather than value-laden. We often let our own value systems slip into our work without realising it. However, when designing questionnaire items we must pay particular attention to this issue. In addition, try to avoid using emotive language (unless there is some theoretical reason to justify it, of course). An example of a question that is value-laden is, 'Do you agree that the terrible cruelty of fox hunting should be banned?' A better format is 'Fox hunting should be banned' accompanied by a Likert scale (strongly agree = 1 to strongly disagree = 5). An example of a leading question is, 'Would you generally refrain from buying battery farmed eggs?' It is clear from the word 'refrain' that the participant is being led toward a desired response. A better alternative is, 'How often do you buy battery farmed eggs?' (1 = not at all to 5 = once a week). The response options capture the full range of battery buying behaviour. The phrase 'How often' suggest to the respondent that it is acceptable to report that they do buy battery eggs.

Avoid technical terms or jargon

Whether you are carrying out an interview or writing a questionnaire, you should avoid technical terms or jargon. For example, 'Drag hunts are preferable to standard fox hunts' only makes sense to those who know what drag hunts are. In fact you should avoid any language that may alienate your respondents. What may be familiar to you may not be familiar to your respondents. So the bottom line is, keep it simple. If you need to include technical terms (e.g. what a unit of alcohol refers to), add a short explanation.

Control for response sets

Another problem that needs to be avoided when designing a questionnaire is the effect called **response bias** or **response sets**. These are consistent sources ('sets') of polluting information that can influence the questionnaire responses. There are two response sets that you should be concerned about.

Social desirability is where a respondent attempts to 'look good'. This may involve them providing answers that are honest, but positively biased (**self-deception**), or answers that portray them in the best possible way (**impression management**). This does not always involve people lying – it often happens without people being aware they are doing it. One strategy for dealing with such social desirability effects is to include a social desirability (sometimes called a 'lie') scale. A social desirability scale consists of a series of questions (included among your other questions) that if responded to consistently show someone acting in a 'saintly' way (for instance, that 'you never lose your temper' or 'you always say "thank you"') which is just not realistic. If you find participants responding in this 'saintly' way you would generally exclude them from your analysis. The Socially Desirable Response Set Five-Item Survey (SDRS-5) is a short measure that can be incorporated into your questionnaire as a measure of the strength of socially desirable responding (Hays *et al.*, 1989). Responses are presented as 'Definitely True' (1), 'Mostly True' (2), 'Don't know' (3), 'Mostly false' (4) and 'Definitely false' (5). Listed below are items from the SDRS-5:

- How much is each statement TRUE or FALSE for you?
    - I am always courteous even to people who are disagreeable (1 = 1 point).
    - There have been occasions when I took advantage of someone (5 = 1 point).
    - I sometimes try to get even rather than forgive and forget (5 = 1 point).
    - I sometimes feel resentful when I don't get my way (5 = 1 point).
    - No matter who I'm talking to, I'm always a good listener (1 = 1 point).

If you observe high scores on this scale (e.g. 5 points), consider removing the data from this participant.

Response acquiescence is the tendency to agree rather than disagree with statements (it is also worth noting that there is a similar but smaller tendency to consistently disagree with statements). The easiest way to tackle this problem is to make sure that your questions are not all positively (or negatively) worded. In the SDRS (see above), three of the questions refer to 'underside' behaviour, so people with response acquiescence would receive an approximately neutral score. By making your questions unpredictable (including a variety of response options if possible) you force your respondents to think about each question (or at the very least give the respondent who always responds positively (or negatively) a neutral score, rather than an extreme one).

Sampling

An appropriate sample is vital for carrying out good quality research (see Chapter 3). Box 5.2 should act as a reminder of some of the commonest types of sample.

Box 5.2

Information box

Sampling strategies

Random sampling

This type of sampling involves the selection of participants at random from a list of the population. This generally involves random selection by computer or through the use of random number tables. This should give each person the same chance of being included in the sample.

▶

Box 5.2 *Continued*

Stratified random sampling

This involves dividing the population into a number of groups or strata where members of the group have some characteristic in common (e.g. strata for social class or sex). There is then random sampling from those strata in proportion to the number of people in the population as a whole.

Snowball sampling

Snowball sampling involves identifying one or more individuals from the population of interest (e.g. known drug users) and then using these participants as informants to identify further members of the group. These participants are then used to identify further participants and so on until you have enough people in your sample. This approach can be seen as a form of **purposive sampling**, which is useful when there are difficulties in identifying members of the population.

Convenience sampling

This is unfortunately one of the commonest approaches to sampling and probably the worst as it does not produce representative findings. In essence, convenience sampling involves choosing the nearest and most convenient persons to act as respondents. It is, however, sometimes the only possible sampling strategy and may be acceptable as long as its limitations are acknowledged.

Response rates

Unfortunately, many questionnaire surveys suffer because of low **response rates**. The response rate is the percentage of questionnaires completed and returned from those distributed. But what is a low response rate? Well, how long is a piece of string? It depends – on your topic, sample, questionnaire, survey design etc. Some journals will not accept studies that fail to reach a defined threshold for response rates (e.g. 70 per cent). It is sensible to compare your response rate with that of other similar studies. However, there are a number of ways of maximising your response rate (over and above the techniques discussed here on good questionnaire design), which can be summarised as follows (for a full review of methods which have proven effectiveness, see Edwards *et al.*, 2002):

- Keep your questionnaire as short as possible.
- Stick to a clear, relatively conservative layout.
- Include a pre-paid envelope with postal surveys.
- Send a reminder after one or two weeks have passed.
- Give advance warning – by a letter or postcard.
- Offer a small incentive if possible (e.g. entry to a prize draw).

We are aware that some of these methods have cost implications – use only those which are cost effective for the resources and time you have available.

Measuring attitudes

Attitude measurement generally relies on more careful measurement than an average questionnaire. This is because attitudes are often elusive, with people unaware that they possess them. Consequently, researchers interested in exploring someone's attitudes need to use particular approaches that are sensitive to this issue. Attitude scales do not usually use questions but a list of statements with which the respondent has to agree or disagree. An attitude scale generally consists of a list of such statements, all different but attempting to tap some consistent underlying attitude. Two of the most widely used forms of attitude scale are detailed below.

Likert scales

A **Likert scale** (Likert, 1932) is a five- (seven-, or sometimes more) point scale where respondents are able to express how much they agree or disagree with an attitude statement (see Box 5.1, question 4 for an example). There is more to developing a Likert scale than just assembling a list of statements about the attitude object. In order to develop a reliable scale you will need to carry out the following steps:

1 Produce an equal number of positive and negative statements about the attitude object. These constitute the scale items.

2 Ask the respondents to rate each scale item on the provided five- or seven-point response options (strongly agree to strongly disagree) according to how much they agree or disagree with the statements. However, some researchers prefer to use an even number of response options, so that participants tend away from responding 'unsure' or 'neither agree nor disagree' to many items.

3 Add up the scores on each item to give the respondent's overall attitude score (remembering to reverse the scale of negatively worded items – so that high scores are positive and low scores are negative responses).

4 Carry out an item analysis (see below) on the attitude statements in order to find those that discriminate most strongly between people with high attitude scores and those with low attitude scores.

5 Reject those items that are poor at discriminating between high scores and low scores but try to keep an equal balance of positive and negative items.

If you follow the five steps above, you should have a scale comprising items that directly (and indirectly) tap a person's attitude towards some behaviour or event of interest to you. It would also be advisable to determine the Cronbach alpha coefficient (see below) for the scale you have devised as a further check on its internal reliability.

Semantic differential scales

The **semantic differential scale** (Osgood *et al.*, 1957) is an alternative to the Likert scale that takes a more indirect approach to assessing a person's attitude towards some behaviour or event (see Box 5.1, question 5 for an example). It was designed to move beyond the arguably simplistic notion of an attitude as cognitive belief (as is generally assumed with Likert scales). Semantic differential scales rely on the ability of people to think in metaphors and express their attitudes by drawing parallels with other aspects of their experience. A semantic differential scale requires the respondent to indicate their thoughts and feelings towards the attitude object on a scale consisting of bipolar opposite adjectives. Once you have produced a scale with a number of suitable pairs of adjectives (from previous studies and pilot work), you can then assess the internal reliability by calculating a Cronbach alpha coefficient on the scores produced by a set of respondents. Semantic differential scales have been shown to have good reliability values and correlate well with other attitude scales (go to Box 5.3).

5.5 Psychometrics

Psychometrics is an area of psychology concerned with the quality of scales and items designed to measure psychological constructs (e.g. personality traits, cognitive ability). Quality is assessed using two criteria: reliability and validity. The importance of reliability and validity for measurement in psychology was initially discussed in Chapter 3. They are clearly very important when collecting data with questionnaires. Reliability concerns the internal properties of a scale (does it 'hang together'?). Validity concerns the external properties of a scale (does it correlate with other variables or other scales?). There are several different kinds of reliability and validity. Correlations are used to evaluate the strength of these criteria. Please see Chapter 12 to learn about correlations.

5.6 Reliability

Internal consistency

When developing a new scale, demonstrating internal consistency is one of the most important things to do. There are four ways to test internal consistency.

Split-half reliability

When we wish to calculate the split-half reliability we need to split the test items into two groups (for instance, even numbered items in one group and odd numbered items in the other group). We give a group of participants one set of questions (even numbered) on one occasion and then the same group of participants the other set of questions (odd numbered) some time later. We can then calculate the split-half reliability coefficient (r_a) by inserting the correlation coefficient (r) between the score obtained from the two sets of questions (gathered on two separate occasions) into the following formula:[1]

---

[1] Do not worry about this formula at the moment. We will be covering statistics in Part 2. You will learn how to use SPSS in Chapter 9 and correlation coefficients are described in Chapter 12.

Box 5.3

Activity box   **Design and critique a questionnaire**

1 In your pair, choose one of the following areas for investigation:

 a Safer sex behaviour

 b Gender

 c Health

2 In your pair, establish a specific research question involving one of these three topics which can be appropriately answered by a questionnaire. For example:

 a How does alcohol consumption affect the use of condoms in casual sex?

 b How does gender interact with friendship behaviours and understandings (level of intimacy, type of activities, topics of conversation, expectations, etc.)?

 c What is the relationship between attitudes towards smoking or drinking and carrying out these behaviours?

3 Decide on the sections that will make up the questionnaire and the order in which they will appear.

4 In your pair, try to design sample questions (about enough for two pages of A4) for the questionnaire which address the research question you have decided on. For example, you could use open-ended questions, fixed response questions, or Likert scales. Along with each question you design you should write down its pros and cons.

5 Each pair should now swap their questionnaire with another pair to critique it. You should also tell the other pair what your research question is. The other pair should critique the choice of question type and overall design.

6 Communicate your criticisms to the other pair constructively! Try to highlight weaknesses and strengths. But do not criticise unless you can suggest a better alternative! Each pair should then improve their questionnaire in line with the criticism (if it is valid).

$$r_a = \frac{2r}{1+r}$$

However, while the split-half method solves the problem of memory effects (as the participants do not get the same items on more than one occasion), it does not provide a solution to practice effects. Participants may still be able to learn how to respond to items by completing the test on more than one occasion. Furthermore, the allocation of items into two groups may, depending on the method in which they were allocated to the two groups, give different results. Finally, many tests comprise multiple subsets of items (or subscales) which may limit the possibility of splitting the items into two groups.

Inter-item reliability

This statistic is similar to split-half reliability. It is essentially the 'average' correlation between each and every pair of items.

Item-total reliability

Here, each item is correlated with a score comprising of the total of the other items. In a ten-item scale, scores 1 to 9 are summed, and item 10 is correlated with that score. This is repeated for every item, and the average correlation is calculated.

Alpha reliability

Alpha reliability (also called **Cronbach alpha** after its creator) is similar to split-half reliability except that the process is repeated for every random pair of splits! In practice, researchers tend to report only the alpha reliability score. Therefore, there is no need to report the three alternatives above. Unless you want to have a nervous breakdown, we strongly recommend not attempting to do this by hand! SPSS can calculate alpha reliability for you. Values of 0.70 or higher are considered acceptable. However, psychological scales that require more introspection (thinking inwardly about what response to give) than tests of skills are likely to have lower internal consistency. Values of 0.60 or higher are sometimes considered acceptable (Youngman, 1979).

If you wish to calculate a Cronbach alpha reliability test this is very easy using SPSS. You will need to read Chapters 9 and 10 to learn the basics of SPSS. You can then simply select **Analyze** from the top menu bar and then **Scale** and **Reliability Analysis**. You then use the Variable Picker button to move the variables you wish to check for reliability into the **Items** box. When requesting a Cronbach alpha with SPSS it is worth checking the box for '**Scale if item deleted**' (available in the **Statistics** box) as this will give you the alpha coefficient for the scale with items removed (so you can determine (and then remove) less reliable items and maximise the alpha coefficient). If you decide to remove poorly performing items, it is good practice to administer the new set of items to a new sample. This is often not feasible for small-scale research projects – another reason why using existing questionnaires is preferable. Questionnaire development may involve several amendments to items before it becomes a reliable scale or inventory.

Item analysis

Item analysis is a method of producing a questionnaire scale with higher internal reliability by identifying items that discriminate well between high attitude and low attitude scores. First, for each item calculate the correlation between each person's score on that item and their score on the test as a whole (the summed score of each item). Second, identify the top and bottom overall scores (10 per cent or 15 per cent generally) on the test. Third, calculate the total scores of these two groups of people for each item in the test. If these two (extreme) groups scored very differently on the item then it is highly discriminative – if not then it is low in discriminating between the two groups and should be discarded.

Test–retest reliability

This form of reliability is particularly important for scales designed to measure constructs that are supposed to be stable. If a test of Conscientiousness, a trait that is claimed to be stable, produces very different scores each time it is measured, then either (1) it can hardly be a reliable measure of that construct or (2) the construct itself is not stable. Test–retest reliability is less important for constructs that we expect to change over time, such as physical or mental health status. Values of 0.7 or higher are considered good, but become stronger evidence if the time between testing is extended. At least three months is required. The LBC1921 study (see Box 5.4) is unique in that the two measures of cognitive ability were recorded 66 years apart. Test–retest reliability, when demonstrated over a long period, can be interpreted as evidence that a construct is **stable**.

While the test–retest measure of reliability is an obvious way of determining whether we are getting consistent responses to our measure, there are a number of limitations. The principal problem is that we test the same participants twice. Participants may remember the test and simply repeat their earlier responses (rather than thinking about their individual responses to the test items). Furthermore, even if participants cannot remember individual items there may be a problem due to practice (a **practice effect**). If the participants have the opportunity to respond to the same test on two occasions they may learn *how to* respond to certain types of questions. This is particularly common with tests of cognitive ability where, for instance, participants often improve their scores on problem-solving questions given the opportunity to practise responding to these types of items. Memory and practice effects can both artificially inflate the correlation coefficient between the two tests, thus distorting our evaluation of the reliability of the test.

Inter-rater reliability

Scales designed to measure constructs such as personality traits can be said to have inter-rater reliability if two observers agree in the ratings they have given. That is, the two independent sets of ratings correlate highly. For example, suppose that a researcher thinks that personality traits can be observed in horses. They create a new personality trait scale that is designed to measure conscientiousness in horses. It might contain items such as 'Keeps a clean and tidy stable' or 'Grooms regularly'. If two horsekeepers rated a horse's behaviour independently on this scale, we would hope for inter-rater reliability – a high degree of correspondence between both sets of ratings.

Parallel forms reliability

Researchers often need to create a scale that closely resembles an existing scale. This method for evaluating the reliability of a test requires us to produce two equivalent versions of the same test. When creating a test (or measure) of something (whether it be a measure of attitudes, personality traits or anything else for that matter) it is commonplace to develop multiple items designed to measure the same thing. This enables test developers to create two versions of the same test. Many standard psychometric tests have alternative forms. By creating pairs of items when developing a test and then separating them, we can create two different versions of the test (based on equivalent items) and carry out an **alternate forms reliability** test. This involves us giving the two versions of the test to the same group of participants on two separate occasions. We can then calculate a correlation coefficient for the two tests on the same people. For example, the International Personality Item Pool provides a free version of the NEO-PI-R, a popular measure of the **Big Five** personality traits (see Box 5.5). This allows researchers and students, who may not have the resources available to pay for the proper NEO-PI-R, to use an equivalent test. The high correlation between both tests provides evidence of parallel forms reliability. This means we can be confident that both tests are essentially the same.

However, as you might have already guessed, this approach, although solving the problem of memory effects, does not solve the problem of practice effects. But if there are so many problems with us giving the test to the same group of participants, why don't we use two groups (matched for criteria, such as age, sex, etc.)? Well, we are afraid that there are as many, if not more, problems in establishing reliability with this approach. Firstly, we have the problem of knowing what variables are going to be key criteria in matching the groups. There might be age effects for attitudes towards animal welfare but we do not necessarily know this. Furthermore, we may find that other attributes (such as education, social class, religion and so on) also affect responses to our test. In fact, we can never really know exactly how to match our participants – we can only try our best using the knowledge and evidence available to us. It is therefore often, though not always, a better bet to carry out a reliability test using the same group of participants and attempt, as best we can, to lessen the effect of memory and practice on our evaluation of the test.

Box 5.4 Study box

An unreliable measure of 'cognitive styles'

Peterson, E. R., Deary, I. J., and Austin, E. J. (2003). The reliability of Riding's Cognitive Style Analysis test. *Personality and Individual Differences*, **34**, 881–91.

Unlike widely researched constructs such as personality traits and cognitive ability, the cognitive styles literature is in its infancy.

Cognitive styles, it is claimed, are preferred ways or 'styles' of thinking and learning. Different people might have different ways

Box 5.4 *Continued*

that they like to process information. For example, when learning something new, you might tend to use images rather than verbal information and prefer looking at the whole picture rather than analysing small details. There are few reliable and valid measures of 'cognitive style' available. The reliability of one of the few measures available, Riding's Cognitive Style Analysis (CSA) test, was called into question by researchers at the University of Edinburgh. They developed a computerised form of the test to use in their study because the original test did not provide data about the individual items, only a total score for each scale. Their new measure correlated highly with the original test (r = around 0.7)

and therefore had parallel forms reliability (and concurrent validity). The wholist-analytic dimension was fairly stable one week later (r = 0.6) but the verbal-imagery dimension was not (r = 0.5). We might wonder what the point of measuring a cognitive style is if it changes after just one week. Furthermore, while the wholist-analytic dimension had reasonable split-half reliability (r = 0.7), the verbal-imagery dimension did not (r = 0.4). This demonstrated that the original measure, claiming to be a reliable measure of cognitive styles, was not in fact reliable at all. The study showed that more work was needed to improve the psychometric qualities of measures of cognitive styles.

Before moving on, we need to emphasise that reliability is necessary, but not sufficient, to demonstrate validity (Kline, 2000). That is, a scale can be reliable but not valid. However, a scale cannot be valid if it is unreliable! Reliability is the bread, and validity the butter, of scale development. You can eat bread on its own, but not butter. A good test is comprised of good items, reliable and well validated.

| 5.7 | Validity |

Face validity

Face validity refers to what a scale 'looks' like. Do the items seem to measure the construct, or do they not seem sensible? Scales with poor face validity, even if they are reliable, may leave participants confused and suspicious. If you designed a set of tests to measure cognitive ability, the tests should look like they measure cognitive skills. Adding items such as 'What is your favourite colour?' or 'What are your hobbies and interests?' would threaten face validity. However, face validity is not necessarily desirable. Items which are face valid mean that participants know what you are trying to measure, and could 'fake good' their responses (see above on response sets). This has been a concern in occupational testing, where personality tests are sometimes used in selecting job applicants. In summary, face validity can enhance participants' acceptance of a scale, but it is not necessarily connected with other aspects of validity. Face validity is sometimes a red herring. The other types of validity, now described, are more important.

Content validity

Content validity is similar to face validity, but the items are judged to be appropriate by experts in the field. For example, you might consult a researcher with experience in the area of depression, if you wanted to develop a new test to measure depression. Have all the relevant symptoms been included? If you were developing a test based on a literature review of a construct, you would want to ensure that all the content is covered in the scale (content coverage). For example, forensic psychologists developed a scale to measure **sensational hobbies and interests**. Sensational interests have rather violent, macabre or strange content (e.g. weapons, fighting, mercenaries, black magic). The psychologists drew on the forensic literature, clinical experience, and conversations with their colleagues. A list of 19 sensational interests was developed (see Egan *et al.*, 2001), which they argued has good content coverage of the 'sensational interests' construct. The process of establishing content validity is quite subjective, but is often necessary to ensure that important items are not missed.

Criterion validity

Criterion validity is concerned with whether the test gives results in agreement with other measures of the same thing. There are two main types of criterion validity used by psychologists: **concurrent** and **predictive**.

Concurrent validity

Concurrent validity is shown by a high correlation between two tests, which are taken at the same time. It is essentially the same as parallel forms reliability. The problem with both is that the 'other' test is assumed to be the gold standard scale that actually measures the construct. There may not be a suitable alternative form which you can use. If there were, you might not need to develop a new scale in the first place! Concurrent validity is normally assessed when researchers need to create a new test for a specific reason (for example, see Box 5.4).

Predictive validity

Predictive validity is shown when a scale predicts another variable. The other variable is the 'criterion' variable. The criteria should be variables different from the construct which the scale is supposed to measure. For example, it would be inappropriate to claim that a scale measuring reasoning ability had predictive validity because it predicted memory skills. Reasoning and memory are closely connected because they are part of a more general construct, cognitive ability. When assessing or reporting predictive validity, it is important to check that the criteria are truly 'external' to the scale. It might be tempting to evaluate a measure of conscientiousness by asking someone how tidy their desk is (a criterion variable). However, if the scale contains items such as 'I like to tidy up' and 'I love order and regularity' then there is too much overlap between the scale and their criterion. The tidiness of someone's desk is not external to the scale content. Objectively measuring the tidiness of someone's desk might be better (at least the criterion is not part of the questionnaire), yet there is still too close a correspondence between the scale and the criterion. It can be difficult to think of criteria that are truly external. Personality trait researchers have focused on health behaviours and health outcomes, because they are external, important 'real-life' outcomes. For example, scales designed to measure the trait Conscientiousness have been shown to predict many different kinds of health behaviours, and health outcomes (Bogg & Roberts, 2004). If a conscientiousness scale predicts objectively measured health outcomes, then we know that it has predictive validity. Predictive validity does not mean that the validity is important. We can still ask, 'so what?' Does the construct have any applied implications? It may be possible to use research about a construct, for example, to improve health (Hagger-Johnson & Pollard Whiteman, 2008).

Ultimate validity

Ultimate validity is a term coined to describe the predictive validity for the ultimate real-life outcome – mortality (O'Toole & Stankov, 1992). Conscientiousness is predictive of all-cause mortality (deaths from any causes) and cause-specific mortality (deaths from specific causes). This is a truly external criterion. It doesn't explain why personality might be associated with age of death, but it clearly demonstrates that the scale is measuring something important.

Population validity

Although **population validity** is not commonly referred to in the research literature, it is still worthy of mention. This type of validity is commonly a problem in journalistic reporting (and especially among pop psychologists on radio or television) when, for instance, they make claims about all men on the basis of research on a particular group of men. There is a danger in simply believing that our findings on a small sample of people will generalise to all members of the population from which our sample came. We need to be cautious about making claims of this kind. Effective methods of sampling (discussed below) are one important way of trying to increase the population validity of a study and therefore its **generalisability**.

Construct validity

All of the forms of validity described above are used to demonstrate construct validity, also called the **nomological network**. This is a network of research evidence surrounding and supporting the validity of a construct. Originally, this term was used to describe 'the interlocking system of laws which constitute a theory as a nomological network' (Cronbach & Meehl, 1955: 290). Psychological theories and scales rarely reach the status of laws, so the term has instead been used to refer to a network of correlations which support (not 'prove') a construct. Where specific aspects of reliability and validity are like 'flowers', construct validity is a bouquet of flowers. Taken as a whole, confidence is gained in the existence of constructs such as 'personality traits' and 'cognitive ability' because a large network of studies has built up around them, supporting the validity of the construct. Construct validity is crucial to psychologists, because the constructs which they use are precisely that – constructs. They are variables we cannot observe directly, developed from theories and research studies. Reliability and validity are evaluated in the service of construct validity, the overall aim. Construct validity takes a long time, usually many years, to develop. In the short term, there are two ways to quickly evaluate the viability of a scale in terms of construct validity. Both evaluate the pattern of correlations with existing scales. Therefore, they assume that there is already a good measure of the construct available. These are now described.

Convergent validity

If a test has convergent validity, it should correlate with tests that measure the same construct, but also 'related constructs'. In the SF-36 (page 111), the Physical Component Summary correlates with other measures of physical health, and measures of health that are related to physical aspects of health. Therefore, it has convergent validity. The measures all converge on the 'physical' health construct.

Discriminant validity

If a test has discriminant validity, it should not correlate with tests that measure different constructs, nor with unrelated constructs. In the SF-36, the Physical Component Summary does not correlate highly with measures of mental health, nor with measures related to mental health, such as anxiety or depression. Therefore, it has discriminant validity – it can discriminate between physical and mental health measures.

Summary

It takes a lot longer to demonstrate validity than it takes to demonstrate reliability. No single research study can provide all of the necessary evidence that a scale has reached the 'gold standard' of construct validity. When developing your own scale, you are not expected to achieve construct validity on your own. When evaluating existing scales, you should consider the wider nomological network. Validity is comprised of several different pieces of evidence and should be considered as a whole. This may involve looking for separate reports in research papers, or looking at the test manual if the scale is from a published inventory.

| 5.8 | Psychometric tests |

Psychometric tests are **standardised** forms of questionnaires designed to measure particular traits or personality types. By standardised we mean they have been tested on large numbers of participants, had their reliability ascertained and norms established for particular groups of people. The items will often be published as a set of scales called an **inventory**. This enables other researchers to use these scales (with confidence) without having to pilot and test the reliability of the scale. Because the tests are standardised we can compare the responses/scores we get from each of our participants (or group) with those responses/scores established as the statistical norm for a particular group of people. It should be noted that there have been some doubts raised over the validity of many psychometric scales in widespread use. While we can be assured of their reliability, the same cannot be said for their validity. This is because each test is based on an underlying theory (of personality or intelligence, for instance) that may be subject to considerable criticism (see Gould, 1996, for further discussion of these issues).

Personality inventories

Research into personality traits fell out of favour during the 1970s. This was partly because of a misunderstanding that small correlations with behaviour proved that traits did not exist (see Matthews *et al.*, 2003, for a historical review and discussion of recent developments). However, it was partly because there were simply too many different measures of personality in the literature. After years of disagreement, most personality researchers have agreed on a set of five dimensions. These are sufficient to capture most of the variability in traits. Most other personality traits or personality types you will encounter in the literature fit into the big five as blends of more than one trait. For example, 'shyness' is a combination of low Extraversion and high Neuroticism. Psychoticism is a blend of low Conscientiousness and low Agreeableness. Older tests, such as the Eysenck Personality Inventory (EPI) and Minnesota Multiphasic Personality Inventory (MMPI), are used in occupational contexts but are increasingly considered out of date by personality researchers. The big five provides a shared framework for making sense of the different kinds of traits that can be measured. A choice of different big five measures is shown in Box 5.5.

Box 5.5

Big Five personality inventories

NEO-PI-R and NEO-FFI. These two inventories are the most popular in the psychological literature. The shorter NEO-FFI (120 items) provides Neuroticism, Extraversion, Openness to Experience, Agreeableness and Conscientiousness (the big five). The longer NEO-PI-R (240 items) adds facets to each of the five traits, providing more detail. For example, Conscientiousness can be divided into Competence, Order, Dutifulness, Achievement-Striving, Self-Discipline and Deliberation. Most constructs that you will encounter in the literature are simply blends of different traits and facets, and are available in the NEO-PI-R.

Costa, P. T., Jr., & McCrae, R. R. (1992). *NEO PI-R Professional Manual*. Odessa, FL: Psychological Assessment Resources, Inc.

The International Personality Item Pool (IPIP). This website provides free versions of the NEO-PI-R, NEO-FFI and many other tests. It also has a 50-item and 100-item big five measure available.

http://ipip.ori.org/ipip/

Mini-markers. Saucier's mini-markers are 40 adjectives that provide a robust big five structure. Respondents are asked to rate themselves on adjectives that describe their traits. The mini-markers work just as well as other inventories, and may save time.

Saucier, G. (1994). Mini-markers: A brief version of Goldberg's unipolar big-five markers. *Journal of Personality Assessment*, **63** (3), 506–16.

Very brief versions. Two very brief measures are also available, both of which contain just 10 items. These are not recommended if you need a detailed trait assessment, but perfect if you want to add the big five to a larger study:

Gosling, S. D., Rentfrow, P. J. & Swann, W. B., Jr. (2003). A very brief measure of the Big Five personality domains. *Journal of Research in Personality*, **37**, 504–28.

Rammstedt, B. & John, O. P. (2007). Measuring personality in one minute or less: A 10-item short version of the Big Five Inventory in English and German. *Journal of Research in Personality*, **41**, 203–12.

Cognitive ability tests

Cognitive ability tests are designed to measure quality of intellectual functioning. They are sometimes converted into a single summary score, called the intelligence quotient, or **IQ**. There are many different kinds of intellectual skills, such as speed of information processing, reasoning, vocabulary, logic and memory. On average, people who score highly on these tests tend to score highly on other tests. This led researchers to argue that a single, underlying aptitude drives cognitive ability (the general intelligence factor, or *g*). Administering tests of cognitive ability is relatively straightforward, but is time consuming. The application of these tests has attracted much criticism, particularly in the context of educational and occupational testing. The general factor can be identified in samples of people, but does not necessarily apply to the individual. It is important to avoid reductionism (in this case, reducing individual differences to one number only). Some people are good at mathematical skills, but poor at verbal reasoning, for example. The solution is to ensure that you measure both general and specific skills, and interpret scores with caution. It is also important to acknowledge other skills valued in society, such as artistic skill, musical ability or the ability to tell a good story. Many tests of cognitive ability encompass a rather narrow range of skills and may also lack cultural sensitivity and cross-cultural validity. However, be suspicious of claims that there are 'multiple intelligences'. Very often, tests designed to measure a 'new' kind of intelligence are later found to correlate with *g*, or to measure other aspects of the person, such as personality traits or cognitive styles. Cognitive ability research is regaining popularity because of its role in preventing cognitive decline, dementia and Alzheimer's disease (see Box 5.6).

Box 5.6	Study box

Preventing cognitive decline in the elderly

Deary, I. J., Whiteman, M. C., Starr, J. M., Whalley, L. J. & Fox, H. C. (2004). The impact of childhood intelligence on later life: Following up the Scottish Mental Surveys of 1932 and 1947. *Journal of Personality and Social Psychology*, **86** (1), 130-47.

Early cognitive decline is a precursor to debilitating illnesses such as Alzheimer's disease. But does cognitive ability during childhood predict cognitive decline in later life? This question was once unanswerable, because measures of cognitive ability in childhood are usually not recorded. Clinicians face a difficult task when faced with patients who think their memory is beginning to fail. How would they find out what it used to be like? Researchers at the University of Edinburgh realised that IQ data was available for a cohort of Scottish schoolchildren born in 1921. In 1932, every child in the country sat an IQ test. In 1997, they began locating those who were living in and around Edinburgh, then aged 76, to take part in a study. The study will be used to learn about the factors involved in cognitive ageing and the prevention of dementia and Alzheimer's disease. A **battery** of cognitive ability tests was administered, including:

Moray House. This test was the original cognitive ability measure taken in 1932. It includes 75 questions assessing different kinds of skills, including word classification, reasoning and arithmetic.

Logical memory. This is a scale from the Wechsler Memory Scale. Participants are asked to recall the contents of two stories, after a short time interval.

Raven's progressive matrices. This test is popular with psychologists because it measures non-verbal reasoning ability. The items are patterns and shapes, so there is no

▶

Box 5.6 *Continued*

confounding from verbal ability and language. It correlated with the Moray House test, originally administered in 1932, providing evidence of convergent validity.

The researchers found that those with higher cognitive ability scores in childhood were less likely to have dementia later in life. They also had better health status today. The results highlight the need to do more research into cognitive ability, its impact on health inequalities and the role of the education system in tackling them.

More information about the ongoing Lothian Birth Cohort Studies can be found at: **www.psy.ed.ac.uk/research/lbc/LBC.html**

Measures of mental and physical health status

It may be useful to measure mental and physical health outcomes, particularly if the aim of a study is to test a psychological intervention. If health has increased after the intervention, compared to a control group who didn't receive an intervention, this provides evidence for the effectiveness of the intervention. Mental health outcomes can be measured using the General Health Questionnaire (GHQ) or the Hospital Anxiety and Depression Scale (HADS). However, these scales concentrate on anxiety and depression. The SF-36 Health Outcome Survey (36 items) is particularly attractive because it provides a general mental component summary (MCS) score and physical component summary (PCS) score. In fact, it is becoming difficult to justify *not* using the SF-36 in quantitative health research. Eight subscales provide scores on different and important aspects of health: physical functioning, role physical, bodily pain, general health, energy vitality, social functioning, role emotional and mental health, It has been extensively validated and comes in shorter forms, such as the SF-8 (eight items long). The SF-36 questionnaire and scoring instructions are available from: **www.rand.org/health/surveys_tools/mos/**

Further reading

Deary, I. (2001). *Intelligence: A Very Short Introduction*. Oxford: Oxford University Press.

This book is a short overview of cognitive ability assessment, including a historical review and recent developments in the field.

Kline, P. (2000). *A Psychometrics Primer*. London: Free Association Books.

This book should belong on the shelf of any psychologist involved in test development.

Matthews, G., Deary, I. & Whiteman, M.C. (2003). *Personality Traits*, 2nd edn. Cambridge: Cambridge University Press.

A comprehensive introduction to the history of personality trait research, measurement strategies and unanswered questions.

Oppenheim, A. N. (2000). *Questionnaire Design, Interviewing and Attitude Measurement*. London: Continuum.

Sapsford, R. (2006). *Survey Research*. 2nd edn. London: Sage.

Sapsford (2006) and Oppenheim (2000) provide excellent further coverage on the topics of questionnaire design and psychometric testing outlined in this chapter and are well worth a look before you decide to collect your own data.

6 Collecting data 3: experimental and quasi-experimental designs

- This chapter introduces experimental methods for collecting data.

- It begins by introducing the importance of the experiment as a form of data collection in psychology.

- The strengths and weaknesses of different types of experiment are evaluated.

- We make particular reference to laboratory-based experiments, the most typical approach in psychology, and describe four:

  - sources of experimental error, and

  - solutions to reduce this error.

- Practical strategies for conducting and describing an experiment are provided. They include elimination of bias, reflexivity and a warning about making causal inferences.

INTRODUCTION

A considerable body of knowledge in psychology has been generated through the use of a range of experimental methods. We say 'range' because there are many different approaches to and types of experiments, which will be introduced in this chapter. As you might have guessed, psychology has imported the experimental method from the natural sciences in an attempt to provide findings that are as robust as those produced in the natural sciences. Although experimental methods have been the backbone of much research in psychology they have also been the subject of considerable criticism. Like all methods of data collection, experiments have their advantages and disadvantages and it is important to be aware of these when conducting research.

| **6.1** | The role of experiments in psychology |

As already mentioned, there is a considerable tradition of research in psychology which has embraced experimental methods. Several subsections of the discipline are heavily reliant on this approach to data collection: cognitive psychology, psycholinguistics and neuropsychology are good examples. However, all areas of psychology have, at some time or another, used experimental methods to advance knowledge.

From the earliest days of psychology it was believed that experimental methods were vital for the development of psychology as a science. Pavlov (1927) thought that 'experimental investigation … should lay a solid foundation for a future true science of psychology'. See Box 6.1 for an example of a classic experimental design used by Pavlov in his many studies of learning in dogs. Animal experimentation like that used by Pavlov is controversial, with many people arguing that it is an unwarranted form of cruelty. We address this issue further in Chapter 25 when we introduce some arguments about the ethics of conducting research on animals.

| **Box 6.1** | Study box |

Pavlov, I. P. (1927). *Conditioned Reflexes* (trans. G. V. Anrep). London: Oxford University Press.

Despite much early discussion, principally amongst philosophers, it was only in the early twentieth century that we had evidence for the idea of learning associations. Pavlov is famous for his studies on learning (or conditioning) in dogs. Here we describe a basic but classic Pavlovian study that demonstrates the use of experimental design in psychology (in this case with animals rather than humans). Pavlov started his research on classical conditioning in dogs when he spotted that dogs would immediately salivate the moment he put food in their mouths. He also noticed that a dog would begin salivating when presented with items associated with food (such as a dog bowl). At first Pavlov tried to imagine what the dog might be thinking in order to understand why the dog would salivate in anticipation of food. However, this was a fruitless exercise and Pavlov decided the only way to get objective information about this phenomenon was to run a series of experiments. In Pavlov's experiments he paired a variety of neutral stimuli with food under carefully controlled conditions. No other stimuli were presented to the dog in the laboratory and the saliva was collected through a device that diverted saliva from the mouth. After repeated pairing of the food with the neutral stimulus Pavlov discovered that presentation of the neutral stimulus alone would cause the dog to salivate. Pavlov used various neutral stimuli (aural and visual – from a simple tone to a drawn circle) and found that through pairing these with an unconditioned stimulus (the food) the neutral stimuli became conditioned stimuli, producing conditioned responses (salivation). While this experiment identified a simple learning effect (through linking an unconditioned stimulus with a neutral stimulus), Pavlov spent the next 30 years exploring this form of learning that we now term 'classical conditioning'. One experiment is rarely enough to truly explore and understand even seemingly quite simple phenomena such as classical conditioning.

Pavlov was using a simple form of experimental design with dogs in order to explore learning through conditioning. The important message from this study is the need for rigour and clarity when designing experiments. At first Pavlov tried to imagine what it must be like to be a dog and then, perhaps not surprisingly, found this to be of little use when attempting to understand how a dog came to salivate when presented with a dog bowl or other neutral stimuli. It was only through a series of carefully controlled experiments where he carefully manipulated the independent variables (IVs) that he began to understand the learning mechanisms at work. Whether we are experimenting on humans or other animals we need to be very careful that we design our research in such a way that we minimise the possibility of external influences. That is, we need designs that enable us to be sure that the effect we are measuring in our dependent variable (DV) (or variables) is the result of changes to our independent variable (IV) (or variables) and not from other, as yet unknown or unmeasured, variables. In essence, an experiment is where we have complete control over the IV and where we control for the effect of extraneous variables. Now go to Box 6.2 and have a first attempt at designing your own experiment. Don't worry that you haven't read the rest of this chapter yet; we will return to the exercise later.

Box 6.2

Activity box	Designing an experiment 1

- Think of a research question which might be appropriately addressed through the use of an experiment. It can be a fairly rough and ready idea at this stage (and do not worry about the ethics of it at the moment – you will not actually carry it out) but it does need to be something you could carry out in a laboratory.

- Examples include:

  What is the effect of alcohol on student learning?

  Does sugar increase attention in children?

  Does television violence lead to real life violence among adults?

- Remember to try to make your experiment as realistic as possible (it needs to be something you *could do*) and remember, *rigour* is the word of the day. Decide on your IV (or IVs) and your DV (revisit Chapter 2 if you cannot remember the difference). Then create an experiment that allows you (the experimenter) to manipulate the IV (or IVs) and measure an effect on the DV.

- Once you have designed your experiment, continue reading this chapter. We will come back to your experiment again at the end of the chapter.

6.2   Types of experiment

True experiments

True experiments are principally laboratory-based investigations with, ideally, experimental and control groups where participants are randomly assigned to two (or more) **conditions** in a double-blind manner. It is important to remember that while the true experiment is considered the 'gold standard' by many within the scientific community, it is not the only means of gathering data in scientific research. For instance, astronomy relies a great deal more on observation than experimentation and is still considered a science. Furthermore, the use of experiments in the social sciences has been subject to considerable criticism. We present the principal practical/technical criticisms (and responses to these criticisms) levelled at experiments below but leave the broader philosophical debate to Part 3.

One of the main criticisms of experiments concerns their lack of face validity. In the natural sciences the study of particular particles removed from their 'natural' environment rarely presents problems. However, the idea that we can treat human beings in the same manner is generally considered problematic. Considerable concern has been expressed at whether behaviour (and other psychological constructs) expressed in a laboratory setting will generalise beyond that very artificial setting. Although this is a valid criticism of some experiments, it is not a damning criticism of all experiments. First, it is possible to conceive of experiments where behaviour is tightly controlled but does occur naturally. Second, many experiments are conducted on topics where the artificial nature of the setting is irrelevant. All that matters is accurate measurement (a lot of psycho-physiological research would fall into this category). Third, as with any method of data collection, it is important that care is taken to establish the face validity of the constructs being studied within an experiment. Finally, empirical research outside the laboratory can be called upon to support or challenge experimental findings (and vice versa, of course). True experiments are most often conducted in the laboratory, particularly in psychology. Strategies for conducting laboratory experiments are described below. First, we introduce some of the more unusual experimental designs.

Advantages	Disadvantages
■ Accurate measurement of variables is possible	■ The variables may be very narrowly defined and therefore lack construct validity
■ All variables can be controlled (error can be minimised)	■ It may not be possible to generalise beyond the experimental setting due to lack of ecological validity
■ Can compare responses and analyse data easily	■ The artificial nature of the laboratory may produce artificial findings
■ Easy to replicate	

Quasi-experiments

One-group post-test only

This is a **quasi-experimental** design that should generally be avoided unless there is no choice. With this design a single experimental group is given an intervention and then a **post-test** (that is, a test given after an intervention of some kind). Post-tests without **pre-tests** are generally useless. Without initial baseline measures on a variable there is no way to determine change as a result of an intervention. The only time this might be (reasonably) legitimate is if the post-test is a well-established test with known values for the population being studied. Even then, however, we do not know whether this particular sample is representative of the larger population and whether any differences in value between the post-test and the population are due to the intervention or differences between the sample and the population. If there is no alternative it may be worth conducting research using this design but incorporation of pre-tests and a control group is highly recommended. Another option may be to adopt a case study methodology and abandon a quasi-experimental design altogether. With a case study design you would collect multiple sources of data (often qualitative as well as quantitative) over time. Furthermore, unlike a quasi-experimental design, there would also often be information available about the context of the study that would inform the meaning of any analysis conducted.

Post-test only, non-equivalent groups

This is similar to the previous design but with the addition of a **control group** that would not receive the intervention. Once again, as this is a quasi-experimental design we are unable to randomly allocate participants to the two conditions for some reason. Instead, the participants are already receiving the intervention and we 'add in' another group of people (as similar as possible to the experimental group) to our design.

The danger with this design is that we cannot know whether differences between the two conditions are due to the intervention or existing differences between the participants in the two groups. This design would be improved through the addition of pre-tests and ideally random allocation of participants to conditions.

Pre-test post-test, single groups

Here we have another design like the one-group post-test only design but with the addition of a pre-test (that is, a test administered to establish baseline values before an intervention is given) for the participants. This design is more widely used than either of the previous designs for it seems to be (intuitively at least) a sound design for measuring the impact of an intervention.

There are, however, a number of limitations to this design that are not immediately obvious. These include (1) history effects, (2) maturation effects and (3) statistical regression effects. **History effects** are those effects that occur over time due to other events apart from the intervention occurring between measures. So, for instance, if we carried out a study of an educational intervention designed to increase school attendance we might find that other events had an effect on our dependent variable. It is not difficult to imagine scenarios where this might occur. What if there was a staff pay award between the two test periods, which led to increased staff morale, leading in turn to increased student interest, leading in turn to increased attendance? Any change measured in our DV (school attendance) from pre-test to post-test may be the result of this history effect rather than our intervention (or a bit of both – but we do not know how much is due to history and how much is due to the intervention).

Maturation effects are a little like history effects in that time is the crucial factor, but maturation effects are not concerned with particular intervening events but rather changes in individuals (or groups) that occur (fairly naturally) over time. Imagine we had a study of a new treatment for depression. We test our participants with the Beck Depression Inventory at time 1 and then again at time 2 (some three months later) after they have received the new treatment. If we discover that people are less depressed at time 2 than they were at time 1 we might feel fairly happy that this is due to our treatment. However, it may just be that our participants' mood has improved over time (depression is invariably cyclical) or that just being in a research study leads to improved mood. This is where a control group can be particularly important.

Finally, effects due to **statistical regression** are where we might find an improvement in scores for random statistical reasons. We will not go into this much here but things will become clearer when we introduce regression in Chapter 15. In essence, this statistical effect becomes a particular problem when we select participants with extreme scores on a scale. This is quite likely in studies where we are interested in the effect of an intervention of some kind. We are likely to select participants with depressed moods, poor living standards, low school attendance and so on. We do not tend to select a random array of individuals but mostly individuals in need of the intervention being administered. Because scores on tests always tend to suffer from **regression to the mean** between pre- and post-tests we are likely to witness improved scores if they were initially low (and below the mean score) or reduced scores if they were initially high (and therefore above the mean score). This leads to false improvement (or not) in post-test scores.

Pre-test post-test non-equivalent groups

This design first entails the researcher setting up experimental and control groups on some basis other than random assignment. Then pre-tests are given to each group. The experimental group receives the intervention (with the control group receiving no intervention). Finally, post-tests are administered to both groups to look for change as a result of the intervention.

This design is obviously very close to that of a true experiment, with the exception of random allocation of participants to conditions. While this design is clearly more sophisticated and valid than those above, there is still the possibility of threats to validity due to the non-random allocation of participants to conditions.

As detailed above, there are a number of strategies that may be used to minimise participant effects (such as participant matching) and it is important that care is taken with this stage of the research process. Because no test is ever 100 per cent accurate, error will always creep into a study and any differences between participants in the conditions will increase the likelihood that the error is systematic rather than random. As long as care is taken with participant allocation to groups, this is a popular and reasonably valid alternative to the true experiment.

Interrupted time series

This design entails multiple observations (or tests) of participants over time with an intervention occurring at some point in this series of observations. That is, the intervention interrupts the series of observations (or tests) that have been occurring over time. This design is particularly popular in economics and increasingly so in some branches of psychology (e.g. developmental psychology). Generally it is recommended that there are at least 50 observations with this design. This is clearly a formidable task and one that should be well thought through before being started. It is still possible to employ this design even if it is not feasible to carry out 50 observations or tests (interrupted by the intervention). It is possible to carry out and analyse time series studies with five observations before the intervention and five after (Robson, 2002). The analysis of such short time series designs is controversial, however.

Generally, time series designs are best carried out where the data collection can be unobtrusive. It is somewhat unlikely (and probably inadvisable) to ask a participant to complete 50 psychological tests. However, it is quite sensible to carry out 50 observations of children's (or adults') behaviour in a natural setting (such as the playground) or analyse data collected for some other purpose. More complex time series designs (than the single series design discussed above) are also possible. You could, for instance, carry out a time series study with an experimental group and matched control group, with the experimental group receiving the intervention and the control no intervention.

Regression discontinuity

This design is actually quite simple, despite the technical-sounding name. Like a true experiment, it requires participants to be allocated to two or more groups (one experimental and another control). However, unlike the true experiment, allocation occurs on the basis of some principle, such as scores on a test. The simplest technique is to allocate participants to one group (the experimental group, for instance) who score below a cut-off point on a test and those above this score to the other group (the control group). So, for instance, participants (e.g. schoolchildren) may be allocated to an experimental group (to receive the intervention) if they score below a critical point on a test (e.g. of mathematical ability). Those scoring above the cut-off point receive no intervention and instead form the control group. Like the time series design, this research technique enables the collection of multiple sources of information over time.

Field experiments

In a great deal of social science research it is not possible or advisable to carry out true experiments in a laboratory setting. An alternative is to carry out your experiment in 'the field', that is, the natural environment of those being studied. This could mean carrying out experiments in universities, schools or hospitals. The experimenter would still manipulate the IV (or IVs) and measure change in the DV as in true experiments. The experimenter would also try to control for the influence of extraneous variables but this will obviously be much more difficult in a field setting than in the laboratory. What is not possible, however, is the random assignment of participants to conditions, and this is the difference between quasi-experiments and true experiments. In an attempt to produce findings that demonstrate greater validity, psychologists (particularly social psychologists) have been using more and more field experiments and fewer laboratory experiments. Milgram, famous for his laboratory studies on obedience, also conducted field studies where, for instance, he would ask people to give up their seat for him on subway trains. Our own students have explored the use of field experiments in a wide variety of ways (try to think through possible field experiments of your own). It is important that these experiments are ethical, and this is not as simple as you may think. There are many possible implications to seemingly innocuous field experiments that need to be considered before they are carried out. In Milgram's study, for instance, what if one of the passengers became violent and attacked the experimenter?

Advantages	Disadvantages
■ Greater face validity	■ Less controlled than true experiments
■ Greater ecological validity	■ Greater opportunity for experimental error
■ Often cheaper	■ May raise more ethical concerns than true experiments

Natural experiments

There are often instances where it is not necessary (or possible) for an experimenter to directly intervene and manipulate an IV but he or she is still able to measure the effect of IV change on a DV. Natural experiments are those situations where the experimenters do not directly control the setting and manipulate the IV themselves. For instance, a bus company may decide to introduce a driver awareness programme for its workers, which would enable you to measure the DV (fewer accidents). You will not have directly manipulated the IV yourself but you may be able to carry out a natural experiment all the same. There are many similar instances where a researcher may be able to access some intervention or programme in order to study their effect. **Evaluation research** (also called small-scale evaluation) is often concerned with this sort of work, especially where the effect of interest is the efficacy of the programme or intervention. This kind of research is becoming increasingly important, especially in the health and social services with efforts to increase evidence-based practice (see the Further reading list if you wish to read more about evaluation research).

Another type of natural experiment is where a researcher might measure differences in musical ability between boys and girls in a school setting. Here the IV is the sex of the child and is therefore not subject to direct manipulation by the experimenter. An experimenter can have no influence over these structural variables (age, sex, social class, etc.) and cannot therefore conduct a true or field experiment. However, it is still possible to conduct a quasi-experiment of this kind.

There are many limitations with these kinds of quasi-experimental design. They will be higher in ecological validity than a true experiment but there is less control over the variables. There is also less likelihood that an experimenter will be able to control extraneous variables as efficiently as in a laboratory setting. This may result in a poorly controlled experiment under the influence of confounding variables. Furthermore, where there is no control over the IV it will not be possible to randomly select or match participants to groups.

Advantages	Disadvantages
■ More naturalistic than a true experiment and therefore greater ecological validity ■ Less potential negative impact on participants ■ May be the only design possible	■ Less controlled than a true experiment ■ Less (or no) control over the IV (or IVs) ■ Greater chance of experimental error ■ Greater chance of confounding variables

More unusual experimental designs

Single case study

The **single case** design is a peculiar design that originated in the work of B. F. Skinner (1938, 1974). Skinner was the founder of the approach known as radical behaviourism. Both the theories of radical behaviourism and its methodology are controversial but it is important not to dismiss them out of hand. There is a tendency in modern psychology to dismiss now-unfashionable theories without really appreciating their subtleties. Indeed, we wonder whether many modern-day psychologists who routinely dismiss Skinner's or Freud's work have ever read any Skinner or Freud. And we do mean the original and not the often mystical (and sometimes grossly inaccurate) versions that get transmitted from generation to generation through textbooks. Putting Skinner's work to one side, the single case design is still intriguing and worthy of consideration.

Firstly, a single case design does not necessarily mean a single participant design, for it is possible to have a single case that consists of a class of students, or other distinct group. However, for Skinner the single case design has the focus at the level of the individual rather than the group. Skinner was particularly concerned with developing a theory and method that could explain findings at the level of the individual rather than the group and a method that does not require vast quantities of statistics to discern change. There are numerous types of single case designs depending on the research aim and topic. Detail about these designs is beyond the scope of this text, but we will outline two of the simplest approaches to single case designs below.

The A–B design

This is the simplest single case design. Here a participant is exposed to two conditions. The first (A) is the baseline condition and the second (B) is the treatment. Both conditions are periods of time in which a participant is measured (or observed) on a particular variable more than once. The investigator may plot the measurements (test scores or behavioural observations) and 'eyeball' the chart to see if there is a difference in scores between condition A and condition B. Ideally, the baseline condition is continued until it is stabilised and only then is the participant exposed to the treatment condition. This enables researchers to clearly identify whether the treatment has an impact on the scores or observations. In practice, baseline stability may well not be achieved. It is important to conduct an extended number of measures or observations if we want to be assured that changes are meaningful. There are a number of limitations to this design, however. The main problem is that there may well be an interaction between history and treatment. That is, any change that occurs may be because of 'natural' changes that occur over time rather than because of the impact of the treatment intervention.

The A–B–A design

This design is an improvement over the A–B design because of the inclusion of a **reversal phase**. The reversal phase is simply removal of the intervention condition (B) and return to the baseline condition (A). If a stable baseline condition is achieved, there is clear change upon exposure to the intervention and return to the stable baseline upon reversal, then the experimenter has very strong evidence for the effectiveness of the intervention. Unfortunately, there are many single case studies where this design is not feasible. If the intervention seeks permanent change (such as some learning strategies or medical interventions) then we would not expect (or want) a return to the baseline condition, and there may also be ethical objections to removal of treatment from someone given initial evidence of its effectiveness.

Entirely non-experimental approaches

Correlation studies

Studies that are described as 'non-experimental' generally refer to designs that rely on cross-sectional data from surveys or questionnaires. They are not experiments. The variables are not manipulated, so the researcher uses correlations and regression to study the associations between them. There may not be an 'independent' and 'dependent' variable. The term 'association' is used to emphasise that the correlation is not causal (see discussion of causality below). Non-experimental approaches are popular in descriptive epidemiology, the science behind public health research. They are also popular in health psychology, where the aims to describe the association between a set of psychosocial variables and health outcomes (e.g. health behaviours and health status). Chapter 5 provides information on how to design and use questionnaires.

| 6.3 | Identifying four sources of error in experiments |

Having discussed alternatives to experimental designs and unusual experimental designs, in this section we introduce some of the key aspects (or fundamentals) of good experimental design for true experiments (i.e. those conducted in a laboratory). These are the most popular type of experiment in psychology. Recall that the aim of an experiment is to reveal an association between an independent variable (a 'condition') and a dependent variable (or 'outcome'). The association with the dependent variable is called the **experimental effect**. The experimental effect is what we are interested in. If an effect exists, you want to be able to detect it. If the effect is large, we say it has a large **effect size**. Large effect sizes are fairly easily to detect, but many effects in psychology are small. Four sources of **error** make detecting an effect more difficult: sampling error, measurement error, assignment error and error variance. After we have described these sources of error, we will provide you with some solutions.

Sampling error

Sampling error occurs when your sample is not representative of the population you are trying to generalise the results to. It is reduced by choosing a sample that is representative (see Chapter 3). A great deal of research is conducted on psychology students, for convenience, who are clearly not representative of the general population. However, this is not necessarily problematic. Psychological and social phenomena (e.g. processes, mechanisms) frequently occur throughout the population. As such, they can be demonstrated in any sample. Researchers often wish to demonstrate simply that a phenomenon or mechanism *can* occur or can be demonstrated to occur (Greenberg, 1987). This does not require a representative sample of the population. For example, consider the **Stroop effect**. This is a term given to the phenomenon in which the time taken to name the colour of a word is delayed if the word refers to a different colour (see MacLeod, 1991). The written word *interferes* with the naming of the colour. For example, if the word 'blue' is printed in red ink, the word 'blue' interferes and causes delay in naming the colour of the ink (for a demonstration, see **www.apa.org/science/stroop.html**). The Stroop effect appears to be a universal phenomenon and does not require a sample that is representative of the population – students will suffice. The problem arises when you study variables that are influenced by characteristics of the student population. These include anything that is related to socioeconomic status, political views, parental background, ethnicity, and so on.

Measurement error

Measurement error occurs when the variable you are trying to measure is not measured precisely. We can rarely measure variables perfectly, but some variables are easier to measure than others. When good equipment is available, variables such as reaction time, grip strength, eye tracking movements, brain activity and blood pressure can be recorded. When the instrument provides an accurate measure, we say that it is reliable. However, many variables fluctuate and are therefore sensitive. Blood pressure may be raised when it is measured because the participant is anxious about having their blood pressure taken. For this reason, many researchers take two or more measures of blood pressure and use the lowest value as the 'true' measure. Psychological variables are far more difficult to measure. Many of the phenomena we are interested in are unobservable, or are **constructs** (see Chapter 5). We can sometimes observe their *effects*, and use these as a proxy for the construct (e.g. record symptoms of depression rather than depression itself). Typically, questionnaires are used to measure psychological constructs (e.g. attitudes, personality traits, self-reported health status). These bring many sources of error, especially if they are unreliable and/or not validated. Response sets (e.g. socially desirable responding) also introduce measurement error (see Chapter 5 for a discussion of how to address these problems).

Assignment error

Assignment error occurs when participants in each experimental condition (or treatment) are different in some way. For example, suppose you wanted to study the Mozart effect hypothesis. This was a hypothesis (see Jenkins, 2001, for a review) that listening to Mozart's music (IV) improves performance on a test of spatial reasoning (DV). You could recruit 25 participants and assign them to a Mozart condition. After that, you could then recruit another 25 participants and assign them to a control condition with no music (or something other than Mozart). This would not be appropriate because you have introduced assignment error. The first 25 participants to enrol in your study may differ from those enrolling later, in important ways (e.g. Aviv *et al.*, 2002; Stevens & Ash, 2001). Students who sign up early may have different personality traits and cognitive skills from those signing up later. They might be more likely to notice your recruitment poster, make a note, remember to contact you and remember to arrive at the correct time. You would have introduced unknown, unmeasured and confounding variables into the assignment. Administering the first condition to early participants could reduce the chance of detecting an experimental effect, or increase the chance of detecting an effect that is spurious.

Error variance in the data

When you have collected data, error variance will exist in the data set. Scores on the dependent variable (in the Mozart effect study, spatial reasoning scores) will vary from person to person. They will also vary between the two conditions

(Mozart vs. control) if there is an experimental effect. The experimental effect is revealed by **between-group variance** and is a *good* thing. If there was no variance between the groups, there would be no experimental effect. Between-group variance is described as **systematic** variance because it is introduced by the experiment itself. However, there will also be **within-group variance**. This is comprised of natural variation in the dependent variable – individual differences in performance. Within-groups variation introduces **unsystematic** error into the data. Unsystematic error is 'noisy' and we could lose the signal – the systematic error from the experimental effect. To summarise, between-group error variance reveals the experimental effect, but within-group variance threatens it. These issues are dealt with more fully in Chapter 11.

6.4 Four ways to reduce error in experiments

Sampling error addressed by an appropriate sampling strategy

Sampling error is removed by ensuring that your sample is representative of the population you want to generalise to. As explained above, psychological phenomena that are thought to be universal (e.g. the Stroop effect) do not require representative samples of the general population. Depending on what experimental effect you are interested in, you will need to decide on an appropriate sampling strategy. This may be governed by the nature of the independent variable and whether the experiment is conducted in the laboratory or naturalistically. It may also be governed by the need for matching.

Measurement error addressed by reliable and valid measures

Measures that are reliable and valid will reduce measurement error. Equipment that is in good working order, and administered more than once, can help reduce measurement error. When using self-reported measures, ensure that they have previously been demonstrated as reliable and valid measures of the construct you are trying to measure. If they haven't, you will need to demonstrate this yourself (see Chapter 5 for a discussion of reliability and validity). Response sets, such as socially desirable responding, can be removed by using a screening tool that identifies participants with unusually high scores on the set.

Assignment error addressed by randomisation

Assignment error is the easiest form of error to remove. The solution is simply to randomise participants into the two (or more) experimental conditions. This can be achieved by tossing a coin (not while the participants are present) or by generating a random sequence of 1s and 2s, in a spreadsheet, for example.

When you have small sample sizes, this strategy may produce unequal numbers of participants in each condition. Therefore, some researchers prefer to use other methods of randomisation.

Error variance addressed by independent vs. repeated measures approach

In addition to the broad meaning of experimental design (the whole process of sampling, measurement, assignment and data collection), the term experimental design is also used more specifically to refer to two approaches to collecting data in the experiment. The first is an **independent measures** design, where different participants are assigned to different conditions. The second is a **repeated measures** design, where participants take part in both conditions. In independent samples designs, the between-groups variance will provide an estimate of the experimental effect. However, there will be a large amount of within-group variance, making it more difficult to find an effect. One strategy is to select matched 'controls' for each participant, who are as similar as possible to their matched participant in the experimental condition. In repeated measures designs, the within-group variance is reduced, because each person acts as their own control and has experienced both conditions. The way in which independent measures and repeated measures data are analysed will be discussed in Chapter 11. In the section below, these designs are described in more detail. After that, some more unusual designs will be described that are useful in particular circumstances.

6.5	Types of experimental design

Independent samples

An **independent samples** design is simply any design where we have two (or more) groups of people assigned to each condition (rather than one group of people subjected to repeated conditions, for instance). A different group of people takes each experimental condition. So, imagine we wanted to conduct a study about the influence of alcohol on motor performance. We set up one laboratory with samples of clear alcohol and a test of motor control (say a driving simulator game) and another identical laboratory with samples of a clear liquid (with similar taste) that does not contain any alcohol and another identical driving game. We randomly allocate our student volunteers to either the experimental condition (exposure to alcohol) or the control condition (no alcohol) but never both. Our manipulation of alcohol quantity is the IV and success on the driving game the DV. This true experiment is an independent samples design, for the two groups of participants are assigned to separate conditions (alcohol or no alcohol).

The main difficulty with this design is that we need to make sure our participants are similar in the experimental and control conditions. Knowing what variables might be important to our study is the first difficulty. Do we think the age of our participants will affect our results? Or their social class, ethnicity or religious beliefs? As you can imagine, there is an inexhaustible supply of variables that *may* impact on our findings. While demographic variables are obvious factors, other more psychological or sociological variables may also need controlling. Once we have decided on the variables that may affect our study findings, we need to make sure that these factors are evenly balanced between our two (or more) groups. This is not a perfect science and there will always remain a risk that our groups are not similar on some key criterion that does matter to the topic being investigated. The other solution to the problem of independent samples is to randomly allocate participants to groups. As mentioned above, this is advantageous for it can account for extraneous variables that we did not know would affect our findings. However, you need sufficiently large samples to carry out randomisation and this technique is only possible where you can carry out true experiments.

Independent samples designs are most often used when (1) order effects are likely, (2) the IVs are not amenable to repeated measurement, (3) where people are not likely to experience two conditions in real life, and (4) most importantly, where the DV may be affected by repeated exposure of participants to conditions.

There is no universally agreed form of words to describe this design and you may also find it called an **independent groups** design, an **independent subjects** design or a **between-group** design.

Matched pairs

This design is a variation on the independent samples design where we make greater efforts to ensure there are no significant differences between participants in each of our conditions. With this design participants are paired up according to those criteria that are likely to impact on our DV. So rather than just trying to match our *groups* on variables such as age, sex and so on, we have a tighter control over the process by matching pairs of participants in our experimental and control groups. Participants are recruited to **matched pairs** and then randomly allocated to either the experimental or control conditions. By matching pairs of participants we should minimise the effect of individual differences among the participants (more than through group matching). Furthermore, because the design is an independent samples design we also avoid the problems of order effects that occur with repeated measures designs.

The most perfect matched pairs designs are those involving monozygotic (or identical) twins. Here we have participants who are as perfect a match as is realistically possible in the social sciences. Medical and social science researchers are particularly keen on studies involving monozygotic twins for it is the only situation where it is possible to control for genetics (as identical twins are genetically identical) and identify differences due to the environment alone.

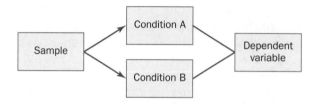

Figure 6.1 A parallel groups designs

Parallel groups

In a parallel groups design, a variation on independent samples design, participants are assigned to independent samples (see Fig. 6.1). One group is in condition A (e.g. Mozart), one in condition B (e.g. no music). Condition B is sometimes a control condition. There may also be two conditions (A and B; two different pieces of music), plus a control condition (C) where no 'treatment' is given. The results are analysed using statistical tests such as independent *t*-test or independent ANOVA (see Chapters 11 and 13).

Factorial

Participants are randomised into four conditions (see Fig. 6.2). One quarter do condition A, one quarter do condition B, one quarter do conditions A *and* B. The remaining quarter do not take part in either condition: they are in the control group. The strength of this factorial design is that it may reveal an interactive effect of receiving two treatments. If an intervention improves an outcome over and above the effect of the separate outcomes, it is considered to be interactive. Factorial designs are popular in health psychology, for this reason. Interventions to improve health need to be cost-effective. If two interventions are administered at the same time they can achieve more than two interventions administered separately and this will save on resources. Results from factorial designs are analysed using statistical tests such as independent ANOVA (see Chapter 13).

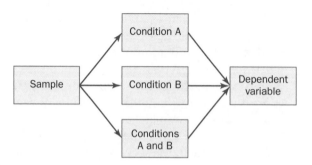

Figure 6.2 A factorial design

Repeated measures

Repeated measures designs are those where a participant is exposed to two or more conditions. There are obvious advantages over the independent samples designs but also some significant disadvantages. The obvious advantage is that you do not need to match participants in the two groups. With repeated measures you have a perfectly matched design. This is obviously very helpful when it is not possible to randomly assign participants to groups or where the variables needed for matching are unclear. The other obvious advantage is that you can recruit fewer participants than in an independent samples design. You get more data for your time/money with a repeated measures design!

The principal problem with a repeated measures design is that your participants get exposed to more than one condition and this may well result in an **order effect**, meaning that the order in which the conditions are presented changes the results. Strategies for detecting and controlling for order effects are discussed below. In summary, repeated measures designs are particularly useful when (1) order effects are not likely, (2) where the IVs are amenable to repeated measurement (demographic variables such as sex are not, of course), (3) where the design replicates experience in real life, and (4) most importantly, where individual differences between subjects are likely to impact on the DV.

Crossover design

Participants take part in condition A and condition B. However, the order in which they take part in each condition is randomised. Suppose we recruit 20 participants who take part in a Mozart condition, followed by a heavy metal condition. We find that our participants score (on average) better in the Mozart condition than in the heavy metal condition, on spatial reasoning. Assuming that the sample is representative of the population and the measure of spatial reasoning is reliable, can we conclude that the Mozart condition is superior? The answer is no – not with certainty in any case. This is because our participants may benefit from practicing on the spatial reasoning test. When they take the test for the second time, their score may improve. What we need to do here, to prevent this order effect, is **counterbalance** the administration of the tests (or any other experimental conditions for that matter). (See Fig 6.3.)

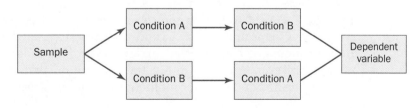

Figure 6.3 A crossover design

The principal method for counterbalancing in this case would be to split our sample of 20 into two groups of 10 (using random allocation) and expose each group to the conditions in a different order (this is the **ABBA** counterbalancing technique – no relation to the Swedish super-group). So, the first group would receive the Mozart condition first (A) and the heavy metal condition second (B). The second group would have this order reversed and receive the heavy metal condition first (B) and the Mozart condition second (A). So, you can see that one group has the sequence AB and the other group the sequence BA (hence ABBA). If both groups score higher in the Mozart condition we will have greater certainty about our initial finding that there is a stronger Mozart effect for Mozart music than for heavy metal music. If, however, we find that reversing the order (from AB to BA) results in higher scores on spatial reasoning, we may have discovered an **order effect** (another source of experimental error) rather than a true experimental effect.

In the health sciences, researchers usually include a **washout period** (a gap of time) between the conditions to ensure that the treatment (e.g. a new drug) does not persist into the second condition. In psychology, it may not be clear how long the 'washout' period should be. Listening to Mozart may continue to improve performance on the task during the heavy metal condition, or vice versa. How long should you wait until starting the second condition? There is rarely an immediately obvious answer to this question.

There are three limitations to counterbalancing that are worth noting. First, it is important to realise that counterbalancing does not remove order effects. It should highlight them and, if we are lucky, make the effects constant. It is then up to us to determine why we have an order effect and how we can minimise its impact on our research. Second, counterbalancing relies on the **assumption of symmetrical transfer**. That is, we assume that the effect of completing test (or condition) A followed by test B is just the reverse of having test (or condition) B followed by test A. This may not always be true. An order effect may occur in only one direction. Results from crossover designs are analysed using related *t*-test or repeated measures ANOVA (see Chapters 11 and 13). The presence of order effects can be controlled by including an additional **interaction** variable in the ANOVA (see Chapter 13) between the independent variable and the order of administration in your analysis (e.g. A first = 1, B first = 0). Third, counterbalancing can become very complex when we have more than two conditions. With two conditions we need just 2 groups. However, with three conditions (A, B and C) we need 6 different groups (to get all possible sequences: ABC, ACB, BAC, BCA, CAB, CBA); with four levels we would need 24 groups; with five levels 120 groups and so on! A Latin square design may be more appropriate here. In summary, counterbalancing can control for order effects and practice effects. However, you need to test the assumption that there is no crossover between the first and second condition, by including a washout period.

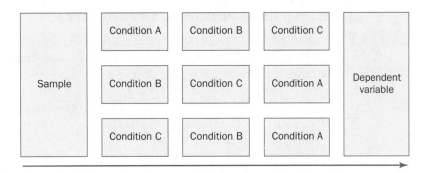

Figure 6.4 A Latin square design

Latin square

Latin square designs are used when there are several different treatments but the researchers want to capitalise on the advantages of having repeated measures. They are similar to crossover designs, but with a twist. For example, three participants do three conditions. A Latin square provides the order of conditions for each participant. One does A, B and then C. One does B, C and then A. One does C, B and then A (see Fig. 6.4). The effect of the 'row' and 'column' is removed in the analysis, leaving only the effect of condition. This design is popular in psycholinguistics, where experiments often use stimuli such as words or parts of sentences, which are 'conditions'. The design can be used to ensure that each participant sees each word only once. However, Latin square designs do not work when there are order effects.

6.6 Running an experiment

Most psychology experiments are laboratory based. This is because the laboratory offers us the best chance of minimising extraneous variables through strict control of the environment. The IV (or IVs) and DV can be precisely defined, controlled and measured in a laboratory. Use of the laboratory is especially important when we need to measure psychological or physiological functions at a very fine level. Psycho-physiological studies, for instance, where we wish to look at the effect of psychological stimuli (such as threatening words or images) on physiological functions (such as heart rate and respiration or even brain function), must be carried out in very carefully controlled conditions. However, even when we are not working with such a fine level of measurement, the laboratory enables us to eliminate the effects of extraneous variables and concentrate our attention on the effect of an IV on a DV. In this section, we introduce you to some of the 'nuts and bolts' of how to administer an experiment, once you have selected the most appropriate design.

Administration and demand characteristics

The effect of an experimenter's expectations or the participants' knowledge that an experiment is being carried out is called the **demand characteristics** of the experiment. If we find that the demand characteristics rather than the IV are affecting the participants' behaviour we have a threat to the reliability and validity of our findings. A particularly well-known example of a demand characteristic, known as the **Hawthorne effect**, occurred during research at an electric company plant designed to maximise morale and productivity[1]. What the experimenters found was that every intervention they tried (such as improved light, facilities, etc.) improved productivity. This was because the workers in the experimental condition knew they were in a special group and always tried to do their best. It was the demand characteristic (knowledge of being in an experimental group) that led to the changes in the DV (productivity) and not manipulation of the IVs (improved light and facilities). How do you think you could prevent this demand characteristic from happening in other studies?

Demand characteristics are a particular problem in studies where the participants are volunteers. In these situations it has been argued that the participants want to cooperate with the experimenter and enable them to achieve their experimental objectives. This may lead to participants trying to guess the true nature of an experiment in order to perform in the most appropriate manner for the experimenter! Just being aware that one is being experimented on is likely to alter behaviour. This may involve attempts to present oneself in the most socially desirable manner.

One way of minimising demand characteristics is to separate the participants from the expectations of the experimenter and limit their knowledge of the true nature of the experiment. We can do this through **double-blind** studies. **Single-blind** studies are where the participants are unaware of whether they have been assigned to the experimental or control condition. We can achieve this in pharmaceutical research through use of a placebo (very often a sugar pill) with the control group and a pharmacologically active pill with the experimental group. As both groups are taking a pill, neither will be aware of whether they are in the experimental group (with the real drug) or in the control group (with the placebo). However, there is still a potential problem in single-blind studies that concerns the demand characteristics of the experimenter. If the experimenter knows which group a participant belongs to they may (inadvertently) act differently with the two groups (and there is research evidence for this occurring). This is why we need **double-blind** studies. In double-blind studies not only are the participants unaware of which condition they are in (experimental or control) but so is the experimenter! In order to achieve this, allocation of participants may be carried out by an independent third party (who has nothing more to do with the participants after randomly allocating them to the two groups). Each participant will be given a unique ID code that can be decoded by the third party once the study is over and the results are being analysed. This elaborate procedure is an effective way of minimising any demand characteristics and is the 'gold standard' for experimental design. Some studies are described as **triple-blind**, meaning either that the statistician who analyses the

---

[1] The exact details of what took place during these studies is controversial with some writers challenging the accuracy of the story told of this work. Regardless, the effect exists and does therefore warrant consideration in experimental designs

data is unaware of the treatment conditions, or that any/all of the researchers involved in the study are not aware of the treatment conditions. Because this term is used inconsistently, it is important to find out what a researcher means if they describe their study as triple-blind.

Administration and experimenter bias

One form of **experimenter bias** has already been mentioned above when discussing the demand characteristics that may be produced through inadvertent verbal and non-verbal cues given off by the experimenter. However, there are other possible sources of experimenter bias. It is important to remember that experimenters are people with particular attitudes and beliefs, needs and motives. All of these factors are likely to influence a study. Researchers are motivated to research a particular topic for a reason and it is often a very personal reason. Without this motivation we would not have researchers working day and night for little pay in search of answers to their questions. Expecting researchers to be completely unbiased is asking too much of anyone and is terribly naive. We need to be aware of our motivations and biases and recognise any potential influence that these may have on our research. Furthermore, we need to be aware of demographic characteristics (such as age, sex, social class, ethnicity) that may influence our findings. However, it is difficult to know what impact these factors may have on our research for it is likely to be different with different research topics and different participants. In experimental research the aim is to minimise the impact of all of these variables through well-controlled studies. We will leave you to decide how well psychologists can really achieve this aim of objectivity.

Another approach to the experimental strategy of (attempting to) control the effect of the experimenter on the participants and topic is to recognise and then accept these effects. In most qualitative research this aspect of the relationship between the researcher, the participants and the topic of research is known as **reflexivity**. There is no attempt to remove this personal researcher effect for it is not believed to be possible (or indeed a good thing to do). Instead, qualitative researchers try to recognise their role in producing their research findings and make this explicit (and part of the analytic process). We talk more about this in Part 3.

6.7	Describing an experiment: a note about causality

Most researchers who use experiments subscribe to a positivist view of social science. At its most extreme, the positivist view is that: (1) objective facts can be gathered from direct experience or observation; (2) science enables us to gather facts that are value-free; (3) science is largely dependent on quantitative data; (4) the fundamental function of science is to develop universal causal laws; (5) cause is established through finding empirical evidence for events occurring together –

constant conjunctions; and (6) it is possible, and indeed desirable, to transfer techniques from the natural sciences to the social sciences (adapted from Robson, 2002: 30). Few researchers would subscribe to all of these views, particularly numbers 1 and 2, but many would agree that positivism is the best method available for studying psychological phenomena that we have available. Experiments are an extension of this stance. The important issue for us here concerns statement number 5 – the belief that cause is established through constant conjunction. This is simpler than it sounds. All this means is that when we state that one event *causes* another event, what we are really saying is that when one event occurs so does the other (there is a constant relationship between the two events). This idea is based on Hume's (1738/1888) argument that it is *only possible* to observe the 'constant conjunction' of events when attempting to establish causal relations. So, we know, for example, that if it is freezing weather outside this will *cause* water to freeze. What we actually observe is the constant co-occurrence of these two events (freezing weather and freezing water) and nothing more. The freezing weather occurs first and we can therefore conclude that it was the cause of the water freezing (providing we have eliminated other possible causes). In the standard positivist view of science this is all we need in order to establish a causal relationship – a constant occurrence of one event preceding another event.

With this traditional view of science, researchers look for a constant conjunction between two (or more) variables – invariably an IV (or IVs) and a DV. This has been the standard technique for establishing causal relationships within the natural sciences and has therefore been imported into the social sciences with the same aim. However, there has been concern expressed over this approach to establishing causal relationships. This is because it seems to be rather rare to establish a constant conjunction when people are included in the equation. It has been argued that psychology and the social sciences more generally have yet to produce any scientific laws, despite 100 years of research (Robson, 2002). This has resulted in calls from some for a radical alternative to the scientific method that has been imported from the natural sciences. We return to this argument again in Part 3.

However, if you do subscribe to a positivist view of psychology and wish to use experiments to establish causal relations, there are a number of factors you need to consider. Firstly, many people confuse **causality** with **correlation**. This is not surprising given the notion of constant conjunction discussed above. If we wish to establish causal relations then we need to design our study such that we can establish that our IV caused the change in the DV rather than just co-occurred with it. This generally requires longitudinal (rather than cross-sectional) designs that enable us to track changes in our DV over time. For it is only possible to establish a causal relationship if we know that an IV *temporally precedes*[1] a DV and that all other possible extraneous variables have been controlled. If we

---

[1] We have deliberately kept things simple here but like most philosophical issues it is not really that simple! There have been arguments in the philosophical literature that causality need not depend on temporal relationships where a cause always precedes an effect. Aristotle, for instance, argued that backwards causation was entirely feasible. Indeed, what constitutes causality between the constant conjunction of a pair of events is an ongoing issue in the philosophy of science. Guidance for further reading on this thorny issue is given at the end of this chapter.

only have a constant conjunction then we cannot know which event caused the other and all we know is that the events are correlated with each other.

In the social sciences, causality is very much a research design issue rather than something that can be achieved through techniques of data analysis. Many people make the mistake of assuming causal relationships when analysing their data when in truth they do not have sufficient information to make these claims. This problem is particularly relevant in non-experimental (correlational) designs, described above. Researchers address this by describing 'associations' rather than 'causes' and wait until a large network of evidence has been collected before attempting to explain the association in a causal way. This is very similar to the **nomological network** used by differential psychologists who study personality traits and cognitive abilities (see Chapter 5). No single study, especially if it is non-experimental, can provide evidence about causality. We must look at the nomological network as a whole, including substantive theory, multiple lines of evidence, and in some cases, biological plausibility.

6.8	Returning to the basics of design

Earlier in this chapter we asked you to design an experiment (in Box 6.2). Read Box 6.3 and see how you did at your first attempt at experimental design.

Box 6.3

Activity box	Designing an experiment 2

Now, in the light of the material on experimental design covered in this chapter, revisit the experiment you designed at the beginning (see Box 6.2) and see how rigorous you were:

- Did you take account of whether you had repeated or independent samples?
- Did you include an experimental and a control group?
- Did you carry out pre- and post-tests?
- How did you plan to recruit and allocate participants to groups?
- Can you think of any other threats to the validity and reliability of your experiment?
- What other designs might be appropriate for studying the topic you planned for your experiment?
- Given the same task again, how would you design your experiment and what would be different from last time?

As we are sure you will have realised, there is a lot more to experimental design than you might have first thought.

Further reading

Chalmers, A. (1999). *What is This Thing Called Science?* 3rd edn. Buckingham: OU Press.

As stated in Chapter 1, this is a classic now in its third edition. It contains an excellent discussion of the nature of scientific laws, causality and much more besides. Well worth reading.

Field, A. & Hole, G.J. (2002). *How to Design and Report Experiments*. London: Sage.

This text differs from many research design books because it includes several sections on how to write about the results of an experiment in the form of a report. If you need to design, run and report your findings, this book is a useful primer.

Franklin, R. D., Allison, D. B. & Gorman, B. S. (Eds) (1996). *Design and Analysis of Single Case Research*. Mahwah, NJ: Lawrence Erlbaum Associates.

Excellent coverage of both the design and analysis of single case designs.

Kerlinger, F. Kirk, R. E. (1995). *Experimental Design: Procedures for the Behavioral Sciences*, 3rd edn. Belmont, CA: Brooks/Cole.

Wide-ranging and detailed coverage of traditional experimental designs.

Robson, C. (2002). *Real World Research*, 2nd edn. Oxford: Blackwell.

An excellent general research methods resource with further coverage of a variety of experimental designs and suggestions for further reading. It is also a good starting point if you want more information on evaluation research.

Rosenthal, R. & Rosnow, R. (2007). *Essentials of Behavioral Research*, 3rd edn. London: McGraw-Hill.

A classic text, recently updated, aimed at quantitative researchers in psychology and the behavioural sciences. It provides good coverage of experimental techniques, research design and data analysis issues.

7 E-research

- This chapter introduces different kinds of e-research methods.

- A distinction is made between e-research where the topic is 'online' or 'offline'. Examples for each type are introduced and described.

- Ethical issues raised by e-research are considered, which arise because participants may not be aware of the researcher, or may not consider their activities to be public.

- Throughout the chapter, practical suggestions are offered and links to resources are given.

INTRODUCTION

The Internet is an umbrella term for all of the computers and servers that are connected together and able to communicate with each other. It covers e-mail, chat services and file transfer programs. The World Wide Web (WWW or the web) is only one part of the Internet, a method for obtaining information from the Internet. Typically, this involves web browsers and web pages.

The term 'e-research', strictly speaking, refers to research conducted on the Internet. It refers to every stage of the research process, from literature searching using web databases to the publication and dissemination of results using web-based journals. However, the term is often used to refer specifically to data *collection* methods using the Internet. This aspect of e-research has raised the most new possibilities (and pitfalls) for psychologists who conduct research. There are potentially as many different kinds of Internet methods of data collection as there are standard research methods. For example, questionnaires, interviews and psychological experiments can all be conducted online. Many different devices, not just computers, can be used to collect data using the Internet: mobile phones, touch-screen kiosks, digital television and devices that record levels of physical activity. We focus less on these kinds of devices and instead on the use of personal computers in particular, for two reasons. First, their usage depends on the make and model of equipment chosen. The instructions would depend on what

▶

you have available for your project. Second, most of these devices can be used for traditional methods of data collection (e.g. using an MP3 player to record an interview), and so are not particularly remarkable.

Links to three web research portals are shown in Box 7.1. Given that the collection of data on the web using personal computers is the most widespread e-research activity in psychology, this is the focus of this chapter.

Box 7.1

Information box

E-research portals

These three e-research portals can be used for two purposes: finding a study to take part in and advertising your own study. As well as traditional psychology research, we recommend taking part in as many different kinds of e-research as possible. This will give you a flavour of the different kinds of e-research that are currently under way, and prepare you for designing your own e-research study in the future.

- **Psychological Research on the Net** http://psych.hanover.edu/research/exponnet.html
- **The Web Experiment List** http://genpsylab-wexlist.unizh.ch/
- **Online Psychology Research (UK)** www.onlinepsychresearch.co.uk

---

7.1 Types of e-research

There are two types of e-research which we have called 'online' and 'offline' topics (see Table 7.1). Online topics are areas of research about the Internet itself. For example, studies of how people use chat services or how visitors behave when they visit a website. As a researcher conducting online research, you would be particularly interested in the Internet in and of itself. Offline topics are areas of research where the topic itself can be anything at all. The Internet is used merely for the purposes of collecting data. For example, an online personality questionnaire is an e-research study, but the topic itself (sources of variation in people's personality traits) is not about the Internet. Most of the e-research in psychology fits into this category, because the research question is not about the Internet itself. Many psychologists use the Internet as a means to an end – a convenient way to collect data about a topic they are interested in. There are eleven examples that follow (five online and six offline methods). However, there may be situations in which the online/offline distinction is less clear cut. For example, if a researcher studies an online support group for a particular disease, the role of the Internet in providing that support might be important to consider. Do people value the online nature of the group? How is the support group organised? Here, the disease and the online support network are both possible foci for study.

Table 7.1 Online and offline e-research

Web-based research	Examples
Online topics	**Type 1** Chat behaviour Online behaviour Website visitor statistics Online game analysis Online interventions
Offline topics	**Type 2** Online questionnaire Online experiment Online interview Online focus groups Consensus research Content analysis

7.2   A warning – what is the population?

Before embarking on web-based data collection, it is important to think about what your sample will represent. What is the population? Although Internet users are *becoming* more similar to the general population, there is evidence that Internet use is still higher among those with higher levels of socioeconomic status. You cannot assume that your web-based questionnaire, for example, is a random sample. It is not the same as stopping people in the street, or random number dialling for telephone interviews (and indeed, even here the sample is not likely to be truly random unless you take steps to avoid factors that may result in particular people being more likely to take part than others). The experience, motivation and interest that frequent Internet users bring to your study topic may well differ from what exists among infrequent or non-users. It will almost certainly differ in those who found your study and were interested enough in the topic to take part! Having said that, a great deal of psychological research is still based on psychology students, who are also different from the general population (Kimmel, 1996; Sieber & Saks, 1989). In some cases, web-based data collection is a better alternative to relying on undergraduate volunteers. For instance, you may be better able to access 'hidden populations' such as people from marginalised groups. Whatever you decide, remember to define the sampling frame appropriately. This might be easier if you focus on a specific online 'community' rather than the *general* population. There are many different kinds of communities to be found: on listservs, discussion boards, chat rooms, websites (e.g. Facebook) and within fantasy game arenas (e.g. Second Life). Linking your research topic to an online community may provide a better fit between the research question, the sampling frame and the population of interest.

7.3   E-research and online topics

Chat behaviour

Researchers specifically interested in communication using the Internet have considered the role of Internet technologies in the communication process. Chat can be incorporated within a website (e.g. Facebook) but is traditionally done using a chat service (e.g. MSN) with or without a web camera (webcam). Research questions centre around how the technology influences the communication process (see Box 7.2). What are the effects of text on information exchange and empathy? Does having a webcam make a difference? What kinds of emoticons (symbols used to represent emotions) are used? What kind of abbreviations are used? In studies of e-mail behaviour, the 'network' of e-mails that connect people in the workplace can be used to describe key decision makers and power structures within an occupational setting. Clearly, when participants know they are taking part in a research study of this nature, behaviour may change and this threatens validity.

Box 7.2

Activity box   **Designing a study of Internet chat**

This exercise is designed to sensitise you to the importance of choosing Internet technologies carefully, so that they match the research question.

1 Find a partner for this exercise if you can, then pick one of these three topics:

Anonymity and self-disclosure

Memory

Personality traits

2 In your pair, establish a quantitative research question involving one of these three topics which can be appropriately answered by a questionnaire. For example:

Do people disclose less information about themselves when a webcam is present?

Box 7.2 *Continued*

Do abbreviations and emoticons improve memory of the conversation several hours later?

Can features of chat text provide clues about the writer's personality traits?

3 Describe a research design that can answer your research question. Say something about the following:

What is the independent variable?

What is the dependent variable? How will you measure/record it?

What is the sampling frame? Will participants know each other, or be strangers?

Which Internet technologies will you use?

Online behaviour

What people *do* online, rather than what they say, is the domain of studies into online behaviour. These concern the information-seeking and browsing behaviour of one person, rather than the interactive communication that chat involves. This does not mean that websites are not interactive, only that the focus is on how a person responds to the web pages they see. Research into specific websites themselves is discussed below under 'website visitor statistics'. Online behaviour studies include research into the frequency of Internet use, including personal problems that may arise such as compulsive use, addiction, gambling and surfing for leisure on paid work time. An example is shown in Box 7.3.

Box 7.3	Study box

Internet addiction and loneliness

van den Eijnden, R. J., Meerkerk, G.-J., Vermulst, A. A., Spijkerman, R. & Engels, R. C. (2008). Online communication, compulsive Internet use, and psychosocial well-being among adolescents: a longitudinal study. *Developmental Psychology*, **44** (3), 655–65.

Does Internet use decrease social well-being, or does poor social well-being lead to increased Internet use? This tricky question of causality was evaluated by Dutch researchers interested in the role of the Internet in psychosocial well-being. 'Compulsive' Internet use was a construct defined by several indicators: information-seeking, surfing, gaming, pornography, downloading, e-mail, chatting and instant messaging. Young people who took part in more of these activities tended to take part in more of the others. Chatting, instant messaging and downloading were particularly strong indicators of compulsive use. The authors found that instant messaging was especially predictive of later depressive feelings and loneliness. The results show that the Internet is not necessarily a tool for reducing social isolation and increasing well-being. The Internet can become compulsive, and lead to psychosocial problems. The study also highlights the strength of *longitudinal* e-research designs.

Website visitor statistics

The behaviour of visitors to a website is very important in the commercial world. It can tell researchers how to market their products more effectively. What pictures do people like to click on? What links are most popular? How many times do people return to a site? Research of this nature tends to focus on one website; a site which has the same design for all visitors. The assumption is usually that the most popular links and popular pages can be identified by counting the number of visits to that page. However, as a psychologist, you may want to consider this approach from a different perspective. You could randomise visitors to a website into one of two conditions. You could then compare the effect of different layouts, pictures or text on important dependent variables. For example, does using pictures improve memory for the content of a website better than words? Does having fewer pages increase visitor satisfaction with a site? Does the attractiveness of the site really matter, or is ease of use more important? Carefully designed experiments can be combined with user visitor statistics to provide high quality data about web behaviour. However, there may be ethical issues if you want to create a website purely for the purposes of research (see below).

Online game analysis

Online gaming is interesting because it may reflect psychological and social processes that occur in everyday life in addition to the fact that it is clearly an important activity for very many people, especially younger people. Emotions run high during games. A virtual ball-tossing game can be used in **functional magnetic resonance imaging** (fMRI) studies. The fMRI technique allows us to visually inspect what happens to brain activity when we are deliberately excluded from the action (Eisenberger *et al.*, 2003). This has provided important insights about how the brain processes emotional pain. When we are socially ostracised, there is a strong similarity to how the brain processes physical pain. When we play games, they often involve constructs such as trust, altruism and competitiveness. This need not involve a real person. Consider, for example, the **Prisoner's Dilemma**. This has been turned into a game which you can play online (see **www.open2.net/trust/dilemma/dilemma_game.htm**). You are asked to imagine that you and an accomplice have been arrested for a crime. There is only enough evidence to convict you of a minor offence. You agreed in advance that you would not confess, but the police offer you a quick release if you provide evidence to convict your colleague. The problem is, they might do the same thing and you would both end up in jail. It quickly emerges that the best thing to do is to trust the other person, stick to your original agreement and keep quiet. A computer gaming study where this situation was simulated provided evidence that trusting your colleague is the best thing to do. It is called the **Tit for Tat** strategy. Research into gaming strategies has provided fascinating insights about how trust and cooperation may have evolved throughout human history (see Ridley, 1997, for more about the relationship between evolution, games and trust in humans). Evolutionary psychologists call this phenomenon **reciprocal altruism** and have noticed that it occurs in many different situations. Games, then, are useful to researchers because they may reveal psychological processes that have important implications for understanding real-life outcomes.

Online interventions

E-research can be used to administer interventions and evaluate their effectiveness. For example, you could design a randomised controlled trial (see Chapter 6) to evaluate the effect of providing tailored feedback on a web questionnaire to students on their unhealthy behaviours (see Box 7.4 for an example). You could e-mail the students several months later and ask them to complete the questionnaire again. If behaviours were more unhealthy in the control group several months later, then you could conclude that the Internet-mediated intervention had been successful. The combination of web questionnaire and e-mail reminders is a useful way to deploy longitudinal research designs for psychological topics. Frequently, the topics do not concern the Internet itself. The next section introduces web-based research for 'offline' topics.

Box 7.4	Study box

Web-based interventions for alcohol use

Bewick, B. M., Trusler, K., Barkham, M., Hill, A. J., Cahill, J. & Mulhern, B. (2008). The effectiveness of web-based interventions designed to decrease alcohol consumption – a systematic review. *Preventive Medicine*, **47** (1), 17-26.

Social norm theory predicts that we are more likely to change an unhealthy behaviour if we think that our peers have more healthy levels of that behaviour. It is common for young people to think that levels of alcohol consumption are higher among their peers than the actual level of consumption. This might lessen the impact of health promotion campaigns designed to reduce problem drinking. Providing information to students about their levels of drinking, *compared to their peers*, could prove a powerful technique for reducing high and dangerously high levels of alcohol consumption on campus. Researchers at the Leeds Institute of Health Sciences developed a web-based questionnaire that doubled as an intervention for problem drinking (www.unitcheck.co.uk). Students at the University of Leeds reported their alcohol consumption. After being stratified by sex, age, year of study and drinking patterns, the students were divided into two conditions. Half were placed in the 'intervention' condition, where tailored feedback was provided. The feedback was automatic, providing information on how the student's level of drinking compared with the group average (other students). The other half were placed in the control condition. After 12 weeks, there was a small reduction in the mean units of alcohol reported in the intervention condition (about 1 less unit per drinking occasion). This is a small but clinically significant effect. It is particularly interesting that most students thought that receiving feedback on peer norms would not change their drinking

Box 7.4 *Continued*

(94 per cent), yet it did have an encouraging impact. The results show that e-research can be a useful tool for interventions that change behaviour, at the same time as collecting data for research. The method could be used to intervene with other unhealthy behaviours and with other populations in the future.

7.4 E-research and offline topics

Online questionnaire

Online questionnaires are the most common form of e-research study in psychology. If you take a look at the web research portals (Box 7.1), you will see that the vast majority of e-research studies involve an online questionnaire of some description. Social and personality psychologists find them particularly useful because they often rely on questionnaire items (see Chapter 5) to measure the constructs they are interested in. There are clear advantages to conducting web questionnaires (see Gosling *et al.*, 2004; Rhodes *et al.*, 2003; Whitehead, 2007):

- Larger sample sizes.
- Access to 'hard to reach' communities.
- Low costs after initial start-up cost.
- Reduced missing data.
- Export directly to Excel or SPSS.
- The link (URL) can be circulated on e-mail lists.

However, these advantages need to be balanced against the weaknesses. Many of these weaknesses apply to e-research in general and were discussed earlier in the chapter:

- Participant fatigue. With the proliferation of web studies, people may become more frustrated with questionnaires and groan at the thought of filling in yet another online survey. Unsolicited e-mails from commercial companies may have lowered trust in online research – and online researchers.
- Within-study drop-out. It is easy to abandon a lengthy web questionnaire if it becomes too boring. If you have the functionality to record information that is already submitted before people drop out, how will you handle this? Assume withdrawal from the study, or attempt to model the data as partially missing?
- Multiple and mischievous submissions. How will you detect random or lazy responding, or duplicate questionnaires?
- Representativeness. What is the population you have sampled, if you have defined a sampling frame at all (Rhodes *et al.*, 2003)? How will you report this when you write up the results?

- High levels of socio-economic status. Participants who have Internet access, can follow your instructions and are interested in online research may have higher levels of socio-economic status. This may introduce sampling bias into your study.

- Loss of control by the researcher. This is discussed further in the ethics section below.

Creating a web questionnaire is relatively straightforward. It is becoming easier, because there are many 'off the shelf' websites that provide questionnaire creation services (see Box 7.5). These often charge a fee, but this is often worth the additional expense because of the time saved. If you know how to create a web questionnaire from scratch, great, but not everyone has this expertise.

Box 7.5

Information box

Online questionnaire tools: Free or fee?

Remember: without encryption technology, questionnaire data sent through the Internet is not necessarily secure or anonymous. If in doubt, seek advice.

Free generators

Do it yourself The 'cheapest' way to make an online questionnaire is to write one yourself. If you know how write HTML code, upload web pages using FTP, set permissions on remote directories and have working knowledge of MySQL and PHP, this is probably the best option. You will need web space and may need to have MySQL or PHP enabled features. Web design training courses may be available at your university or college, and there are plenty of books available on web design. However, the old saying goes, 'The cheapest is dearest in the end'. The time taken to learn how to make an online questionnaire from scratch may cancel out any savings you make by not paying for an 'off the shelf' package.

SurveyWiz (http://psych.fullerton.edu/mbirnbaum/programs/surveyWiz.htm). This is a 'quick and dirty' questionnaire generator. Responses can be text boxes or radio buttons (options where one response must be selected). It is free, making it highly attractive as a research tool. As with designing your own questionnaire from scratch, it helps to have HTML experience. A help page is provided, and a JavaScript that can randomise participants into two conditions (http://psych.fullerton.edu/mbirnbaum/programs/RandomAss.txt).

Fee-based generators

You will have to pay for the services below, but unless you have enough web design experience to create your own questionnaire from scratch, it is probably worth it. It is important to balance the time you will save by using an 'off the shelf' service like Survey Monkey against the time you will lose by having to learn how to make your own.

Box 7.5 *Continued*

Survey Monkey (www.surveymonkey.com). Survey Monkey is perhaps the most popular fee-based questionnaire generator and one we recommend highly. The features are very easy to use. You can change the appearance of the questionnaire. Results can be exported in a variety of formats, so that you can analyse the data in Excel or SPSS. Check the feature highlights on the website to learn more.

PHPQ (www.chumpsoft.cm/products/phpq). Chumpsoft have developed a powerful tool, but one which requires a little more experience with web design. PHPQ questionnaires look great – and participants will prefer the interface to more 'bog standard' HTML questionnaires. Try the online demonstration and see for yourself.

Qualtrix (www.qualtrix.com). Another popular tool; Qualtrix has several online tutorials and sources of information and support. It is popular with many psychologists conducting online questionnaires. It handles a wide range of response types (e.g. sliding scales, matrices and multimedia). Complex forms of randomisation (e.g. randomisation of questions only within a certain block of questions) are available. **Question piping** (when questions are automatically filled based on previous answers), **branching** (diverting respondents into a relevant question based on a response) and **skipping** (not displaying irrelevant questions) are useful features.

University-hosted questionnaire tools. Many universities provide their own questionnaire generators and online hosting services. Check with your tutor and computing support team to find out if one is available wherever you are. Virtual learning environments (e.g. WebCT, Blackboard) can incorporate questionnaires, a useful way to target students, depending on what is available to you.

Online experiment

It is relatively straightforward to write a program to produce a study that randomises participants into two or more conditions. You may want to compare responses to two different pieces of text, two questionnaires or two pictures. For example, a JavaScript program used in conjunction with SurveyWiz can allocate participants at the point of entry to the study. Similar features may be available for other tools. A set of guidelines is available for conducting web experiments (see Reips, 2002). It is important to acknowledge the loss of control over the experiment if you conduct it online. How do you know that the participant is following the instructions properly, or even that the participant is not six people having a jolly good laugh? One type of web experiment has been enormously successful and has managed to address many of these issues by carefully designed methods (see Box 7.6).

| Box 7.6 | Study box |

Back, M. D., Schmukle, S. C. & Egloff, B. (2008). How extraverted is **honey.bunny77@ hotmail.de**? Inferring personality from e-mail addresses. *Journal of Research in Personality*, **42** (4), 1116–22.

How extraverted do you think someone with the e-mail address **honey.bunny77@hotmail.de** might be? Is **thefascinatingking@gmx.net** probably rather narcissistic? When we choose an e-mail address, it presents a 'thin slice' of who we are, to people whom we often haven't met. When you think about it, there is a surprising amount of personal choice involved when you create an e-mail address. You can use your own name or a fantasy name. You can choose 'Yahoo' or 'Hotmail' or many other e-mail providers. You can often reveal your gender and other demographic variables. You can add underscores, hyphens and other symbols. You might think that stereotypically sociable people would choose e-mail addresses that sound extraverted, and that a sample of people who were shown the e-mail address would agree. Researchers at the University of Leipzig tested this assumption, by measuring the personality traits of 599 young people (mostly

female) and recording their e-mail address. Participants in the study were asked to guess the big five personality traits (see Chapter 5) of the person whose e-mail address they were shown. There were two findings. First, people tended to *agree* on the personality characteristic that the address invoked. That is, there was a high level of inter-rater reliability (see Chapter 5). Second, there was only a weak level of *accuracy* in the judgements. In other words, there were low levels of self- and rater-reliability. With the exception of Openness to Experience, most of the correlations between actual traits and traits estimated from the e-mail addresses were low. Having said that, the authors note that this finding is striking, given that e-mail addresses are such a 'thin slice' of a person. It is surprising that any correlation at all can be detected from such little information about a person. Clearly, e-mail addresses 'contain a kernel of truth' about personality traits.

The Implicit Association Test

Project Implicit is a large web-based project (**https://implicit.harvard.edu/implicit/**) designed to study implicit attitudes. The researchers describe implicit attitudes as 'thoughts and feelings that exist either outside of conscious awareness or outside of conscious control'. The experiment can measure, quite cleverly, how people subconsciously evaluate two different groups. You can take part in a study yourself to learn about your own subconscious prejudices – the study is as useful as a tool for self-reflection as it is for research. For each stigmatised group (e.g. gay and lesbian people) there are four stimulus categories: gay people, straight people, good phrases, bad phrases. The respondent first has to decide whether the stimulus is gay (e.g. the word 'gay' or a picture of 'man and man'), straight (e.g. the word 'straight' or a picture of a 'man and woman'), good (e.g. 'joyful', 'beautiful') or bad (e.g. 'agony', 'terrible'). The 'e' and 'i' keys of the keyboard are used for each response option. Next, the stimuli are mixed and paired with two response options (e.g. gay or good, straight or bad). Finally, the response options are reversed (e.g. gay or bad, straight or good). The dependent variable is reaction time. Implicit bias occurs when the respondent is quicker to classify straight when it is paired with 'good' and gay when it is paired with 'bad'. For example, a respondent with an implicit bias against gay people might be quick to pair 'gay' with 'bad', even if that person denied negative attitudes towards gay people in a self-reported questionnaire. The IAT shows how easily 'bad' concepts can be linked with stigmatised groups, even among participants who claim not to have prejudices. Research into stigma will benefit from the IAT test because much of it involves poorly defined constructs, convenience samples and cross-sectional data. The IAT, in contrast, has a tightly defined construct (implicit bias as measured by reaction time), a diverse range of participants, and can incorporate complex research designs. You may want to adapt the IAT for your own research question. One way to address stigma is to first consider the possibility of our own, implicit biases against stigmatised groups, and try to change them.

Online interviews

The Internet offers great potential for qualitative research and online interviews are one of three potential ways in which it may be utilised. Whilst there are undoubted advantages to using the Internet which will be discussed below, there are also some significant difficulties and indeed potential problems that need to be acknowledged. Indeed, it is worth sounding a word of caution as many new researchers can get caught up in the excitement of new technology and lose sight of the aim of psychological research in the process. So beware the lure of new technology! In the following section we will first outline some of the benefits of using the Internet for interviews (and indeed qualitative research more generally, as the comments apply regardless of the method used), then move on to the practicalities of conducting interviews in this way and end with some discussion of potential problems and limitations.

Perhaps the principal advantage in using the Internet for qualitative research is the possibility of broadening access to participants. The Internet enables researchers to access participants from people who are geographically distant and so is particularly valuable for cross-cultural research. More than this, though, is the possibility of gaining access to populations that are traditionally hard to reach through conventional methods, such as people with mobility difficulties, mothers at home with children or people with agoraphobia, for instance. A further advantage may occur if we want to study 'sensitive topics' where people might be embarrassed to speak in a face-to-face context. It is quite clear that for some people it is easier to discuss sensitive issues (such as some sexual or emotional problems) online than when communicating face to face with another person. Finally, the Internet may also provide us with access to participants engaged in dangerous or politically sensitive activities. This is a highly complex and difficult area, raising many legal and ethical issues, and one that is unlikely to be suitable for student projects, but some issues – such as terrorism, for instance – may be more amenable to research via the Internet. This is all in addition to the possibility of research that directly addresses

Internet-mediated activities (such as membership of online support groups), of course, which has proven to be a rich area of research in recent years.

An additional benefit of using the Internet for qualitative research is the ability to reduce transcription bias and indeed also the practical difficulties of transcription itself (see Chapter 18). There are many discussions and debates about transcription and the methods by which the spoken words are 'translated' into written text, such that using written text directly may be one way of minimising some of the difficulties. An Internet interview or discussion is in itself a verbatim account of the exchange with no loss in conversational features within the particular context of the exchange. That is, whilst there is clearly a loss of some key features of conversation (discussed further below), in online research these are known in advance with all parties working within the limits of the communicative medium (rather than the researcher deciding which elements are most important when deciding what to transcribe and analyse). The practical advantages of having a 'ready made' transcript to analyse should also not be underestimated. Transcription is a very time-consuming business and given the inevitable resource pressures on the research process this may be one way of maximising research output within any given research context.

So, how might we go about conducting interviews using the Internet? Well, there are a number of options. First, we might conduct an e-mail exchange with our participants. This has a number of advantages and disadvantages. First, large numbers of people have access to e-mail and can find the time to enter into an e-mail exchange with a researcher. There is time for people to consider the questions and write a response which they feel best represents their views. The researcher also has the benefit of time to consider their responses and adapt their questions accordingly to maximise the quality of information being elicited. However, e-mail exchanges lack the immediacy of real-time chat (either in face-to-face conversation or using Internet Relay Chat services) and can therefore produce rather stilted exchanges. The ability to formulate and edit responses can lead to the production of material that is more akin to a formal exchange (or indeed production of a formal position statement) than a casual and frank exchange of views about a topic of interest. It can also take a very great deal of time to collect data. Decisions need to be made about whether to supply a number of questions at one time, balancing the danger of overloading participants (such that they drop out or fail to write very much) with the need to speed up the collection of data. People will rarely wish to commit to an overly long exchange which may go on for weeks, months or even years (though they sometimes do, of course!). An alternative is to conduct interviews in real time using IRC. This has the advantage of enabling the collection of data that is (arguably) much more naturalistic. The immediacy also means that data collection can be conducted within a relatively short period of time. There are practical difficulties, however, as all parties need access to suitable hardware (broadband is pretty much essential) and software and have the requisite knowledge to use it! People also need adequate typing abilities to be able to sustain real-time chat well enough for data collection. This clearly limits access, which is rather unfortunate given that the argument often made in favour of using the Internet is widened access. The important thing is that this is a judgement call and the researcher needs to weigh up the pros and cons of using these methods of data collection with the aims of their research project. It is vital that the research aims are not compromised (by, for instance, limiting studies only to people wealthy and able enough to use IRC), whatever method of data collection is used.

There are a number of theoretical concerns about using the Internet for data collection in qualitative research that we will also touch upon here. The first is the nature of the data that is collected. There have been complex discussions about the loss of the body in computer-mediated data collection and this remains an area that will be increasingly discussed and researched in future. For some qualitative researchers aspects of non-verbal (embodied) communication are vital in order to fully understand the world of another person and there are fears that this information will be lost with qualitative data analysis using the Internet (see Langdridge, 2007, for a discussion of these issues in relation to phenomenological psychology). Researchers may also be concerned about the loss of extra-linguistic information from the exchange. Discourse analysts (see Chapter 21), for instance, are particularly interested in the finer details of conversation and whilst it is perfectly possible to analyse e-mail or IRC exchanges using discourse analysis, it is quite a different process (with quite different outcomes) from analysing face-to-face conversation.

If you want to use the Internet to facilitate data collection for qualitative research of any kind you would be well advised to discuss this with your tutor and/or look to some of the guidance that can be found in the texts listed in the Further reading section below.

Online discussion (focus) groups

Many of the issues relevant to conducting group discussions raised in Chapter 4 are, of course, relevant here but there are a few things that are specific to conducting discussion online that will be briefly addressed. First, there are practical issues to consider, such as the availability of suitable conferencing software (and the ability of the participants to use the software) along with the need to manage the research process so that people all come online at the same time to participate. However, perhaps the most significant issue is the danger of a loss of control of the setting when conducting discussion groups online. In face-to-face settings, discussion groups require considerable expertise to manage to ensure that speakers feel safe, are able to contribute fairly and so on. This is even more difficult online as there are fewer ways of communicating and indeed controlling the situation. There is often a sense of depersonalisation online (and indeed, even if not, often very different etiquettes in operation), so it can all very easily get out of hand. What is most important is to stress the ground rules at the start and ensure that everyone complies with them throughout the discussion itself. Moderating such a discussion is quite a skilled business and it is essential to practise this before you collect your data for real. For instance, people may start multiple discussions, ignoring the postings of some people and only responding to others. This will need to be actively managed in order to collect data that makes sense and also to ensure that people do not feel disenfranchised. Without verbal cues it is also difficult to know how people are feeling so it is worth checking every now and again. Some people might be slower at typing than others or happy to read and only post occasionally, but they may equally be upset by something that has been written and feel very aggrieved. You would likely see this in how they present themselves physically in a face-to-face group but it is not so easy when online.

The level of disclosure may also vary a great deal in online discussions and needs to be managed very carefully. The permissive atmosphere (resulting from the feeling of anonymity) may encourage inappropriate disclosure that others find difficult and the person later regrets. The possibility of follow-up contact (via the telephone, e-mail or private IRC) is essential to ensure that people do not suffer as a result of their participation.

Online discussion groups can provide an excellent means of data collection but need to be handled very carefully and so should not be seen as 'an easy option' by any means. Whilst it may seem more difficult to recruit people to attend face-to-face discussion groups, the relative ease of managing the group and ensuring the collection of good quality data may outweigh the difficulties. The driving force should be the research question, as always, and the decision about method of data collection dependent on the research aims, whilst recognising that practicalities (especially concerning the availability of resources, not least the time of the researcher) are a fact of all research!

Participant observation

Participant observation has been discussed in Chapter 4 and whether face to face or online is only rarely a suitable method of data collection for an undergraduate student. The practical and ethical demands are such that normally only experienced researchers or students studying for higher research degrees (with support) will be able to conduct research employing this method of data collection. It is, however, a particularly valuable way of collecting data in some circumstances (how else might we come to know about virtual communities, for instance?) and one which offers the potential for really rich data which cannot be gathered through other methods – like interviewing – alone (see Box 7.7).

Box 7.7 **Study box**

Boellstorff, T. (2008). *Coming of Age in Second Life: An Anthropologist Explores the Virtually Human*. Princeton: Princeton University Press.

Whilst this study has been conducted by a social anthropologist rather than a psychologist, it is an excellent example of both the value of online participant observation and also the complexity of conducting such research. Boellstorff conducted more than two years of participant observation within Second Life. Second Life is a 3D virtual world (see

Box 7.7 *Continued*

secondlife.com), the most popular of its kind with a huge number of users. In Second Life people construct avatars (3D images of their virtual selves) and form relationships, create communities, buy property or build homes, go to bars and so on, pretty much everything that one might expect in 'First Life'! This book documents the first sustained study of this world, using ethnography and, in particular, participant observation to collect data. To this end, Boellstorff created an avatar for himself (Tom Bukowski) and spent two years living in Second Life, meeting and talking with other people and exploring all realms of this fasci-nating other world. This is not a 'mere game' given that for many people Second Life is as important (if not more important) for them than 'real life' and in this book there are discussions of meanings of selfhood, intimacy and community – amongst many other things – among the people living in this alternative world. In the process, the very notions of 'real' and 'virtual' are challenged: the nature of what we understand as 'real' and what we understand as 'virtual' is thus called into question by this fascinating technologically mediated development in ways of living.

Consensus research

A feature of modern life is that many decisions are taken following a group discussion over e-mail. For example, a committee representing a particular area of expertise in psychology might be asked to agree a 'consensus statement' which represents their view on the current situation for a given topic. If you have ever participated in something similar (e.g. a student project that involved group work), you may appreciate how difficult reaching a consensus can be. There are many factors to consider – personal views, professional views, how to explain key concepts to outside audiences and managing conflict within the group. Consensus research is becoming an increasingly popular topic to study these kinds of processes. It is not only interesting, but since e-mail records can be analysed, it is possible to find out *how* these decisions are reached. This is usually done qualitatively (e.g. using the text) but e-mails can be represented quantitatively (e.g. by finding out who the 'central players' in the e-mail exchange were, how many e-mails were sent, who they were sent to). E-research into consensus statements by e-mail is best described as a mixed method (see Chapter 24).

Content analysis

The content analysis of web pages and other Internet material is similar to the content analysis of traditional media, such as newspaper reports. The technique is still a valid approach to research, not only useful for studying information of historic value. Many disciplines use content analysis to study a wide range of topics. For example, health scientists may be concerned about the quality of information about genetic screening available online. Historians may want to study the history of the content of popular web pages, as in the Internet history project. Psychologists interested in the content of the Internet are more likely to be concerned with psychological aspects of that content, for example the ways in which people describe their lives, their identities and their hobbies and interests. Qualitative researchers may be particularly interested in discourse – how text is used to construct meaning and communicate with an audience in the online context. Forensic psychologists may be interested in how and why people might advertise violent hobbies and interests on their profiles or blogs. Content analysis offers many research possibilities for psychologists and is likely to become increasingly popular in the future.

Content analysis of discussion boards

Researchers have analysed the content of discussion boards, including those within online communities and support networks. The analysis of discussion boards as an alternative to online interviews appears, at face value, to be a wise strategy. Online communities and support groups (e.g. for life-threatening illnesses) are a potentially rich source of data. You can gain insights that would be very difficult to obtain via traditional means, and there is no need to arrange a face-to-face interview for every member of the group. However, there are several practical and ethical issues raised by this approach (see Box 7.8 and the section on ethics below).

Box 7.8

Information box:

Researching online communities

The purpose of this box is to encourage you to think about the range of issues you should consider before conducting research into an online community. They are reproduced from Eysenback & Till (2001):

Intrusiveness. Discuss to what degree the research conducted is intrusive ('passive' analysis of Internet postings versus active involvement in the community by participating in communications).

Perceived privacy. Discuss (preferably in consultation with members of the community) the level of perceived privacy of the community (Is it a closed group requiring registration? What is the membership size? What are the group norms?).

Vulnerability. Discuss how vulnerable the community is: for example, a mailing list for victims of sexual abuse or people living with AIDS will be a highly vulnerable community and so any research needs to be conducted with care.

Potential harm. As a result of the above considerations, discuss whether the intrusion of the researcher or publication of results has the potential to harm individuals or the community as a whole.

▶

Box 7.8 *Continued*

Informed consent. Discuss whether informed consent is required or can be waived (If it is required how will it be obtained?).

Confidentiality. How can the anonymity of participants be protected (if verbatim quotes are given originators can be identified easily using search engines, thus informed consent is always required).

Intellectual property rights. In some cases, participants may not seek anonymity, but publicity, so that use of postings without attribution may not be appropriate.

7.5 Ethical issues in e-research

The ethical issues raised by e-research are determined by two factors. First, are the participants aware that they are being studied, or unaware? Second, are the participants identifiable, or anonymous? Depending on the answer to these questions, four situations arise. These are shown in Table 7.2, adapted from the British Psychological Society (2007) guidelines on the ethics of Internet research (these are available to download: see the list of further reading at the end of this chapter). In traditional observational research, it is only ethically acceptable to observe people in a situation that would normally involve being observed by strangers. For example, it would be acceptable to observe how many people drop litter in a street, without their knowledge. However, the British Psychological Society (2006) guidelines (for psychology in general) remind researchers to consider 'local cultural values and of the possibility of intruding upon the privacy of individuals who, even while in a normally public space, may believe they are unobserved'. The Internet has its own sets of cultural values, depending on the online community. There is also disagreement among researchers about the extent to which online discussion boards are 'public' – probably because these boards are so different from each other. Online environments, such as Facebook, can be perceived as a private setting, but users may not be aware of the privacy implications of sharing information online.

Table 7.2 Typology of four types of IMR studies and examples of ten ethical issues raised (British Psychology Society, 2007)

	Identifiable	Anonymous
Recruited	Verifying identity Informed consent Withdrawal	Levels of control Monitoring the consequences of research
	Data protection	Protecting participants and researchers
Unaware	Deception (including lurking, cutting and pasting extracts)	Understanding of public and private space Debriefing

Recruited and identifiable participants

Recruiting participants for an Internet-mediated study, in which participants can be identified, removes anonymity, which can be unethical. This can be addressed if participants give informed consent and know that they can be identified. However, they still have the right to withdraw and request that their data are removed. This is more difficult for qualitative research taken from people's online postings. Once written up into a research report, the extract cannot be removed and could identify the participant. Search engines such as Google can easily identify the location of a snippet of text. It may be possible to find the name, e-mail address and place of work of a person whose online quote is pasted into a research study. This is even more fraught when the participant has not given consent, discussed below.

Unaware and identifiable participants: the unethical fishbowl?

This type of study is only recommended in extremely unusual cases. If the participant can be identified from the data collected, but they are unaware that their data is being used for research, then the following criteria should apply. First, their 'data' are already publicly available. Historians frequently use data about people and then write about them. You might be interested in particular people, their writing, how they present themselves, case studies (e.g. in forensic psychology). This might include a web page, blog or diary. This is not as clear cut as it may seem. Many blogs, for example, are accessible to all and therefore public. Some, however, cannot be read until the user joins an online group. It may be easy for anyone to join that group, but is the blog now public? What if the group is a support group for a life-threatening illness? How would you feel if you were seeking support online, and then discovered that your postings were being cut-and-pasted into a researcher's project? Eysenbach & Till (2001) cited a quote from a participant who decided to leave an online support group after finding out that researchers had been **lurking** (observing without participating as a member) on the boards: 'When I joined this, I thought it would be a support group, not a fishbowl for a bunch of guinea pigs. I certainly don't feel at this point that it is a safe environment, as a support group is supposed to be, and I will not open myself up to be dissected by students or scientists.' Remember: lurking can cause distress, and damage online communities.

Recruited and anonymous participants

This is arguably the most straightforward design, ethically speaking. Participants are aware that they are taking part in research, will provide informed consent and the data will be anonymised. As long as the data is truly anonymised, this is fine. However, the loss of control over the study environment may cause problems. If your study causes mild distress, normally addressed by debriefing participants after the study, how can you ensure that participants receive the debriefing? In a focus group, laboratory experiment or interview, you can use human interaction to judge whether people are finding the study difficult to manage and discuss issues with them during or afterwards. This is more difficult to do online. There are ways in which this can be addressed. For example, provide a list of sources of information and support at the beginning or end (or preferably both) of the study. If interviewing online, can participants contact you later? How would you handle a situation in which someone wrote 'I feel really upset, I can't cope with this' and then signed off, before receiving any debriefing information or sources of support?

There are also some technical issues here. How will you deal with people taking part more than once? As mentioned above in the section on online questionnaires, multiple and mischievous submissions can be difficult to detect. Recording the Internet Protocol (IP) address of the computer that sent the data submission is one option. However, this removes anonymity and does not always work. IP addresses can be shared by several people and are not always available.

Unaware and anonymous participants

Examples here include monitoring of user behaviour when visiting a website. What links do they click on? What do they type in the search box? Commercial websites use all of this information. Facebook has tailored advertisements based on personal details. Some researchers have created websites and discussion boards purely for the purposes of observing visitors' behaviour. This raises ethical issues. The status of the participant might change during the course of the study. They might be unaware and anonymous to begin with, and then provide informed consent to take part in a study, in which they are recruited and identifiable.

The purpose of the typology is to make sure that you have thought about the issues raised by Internet-mediated research, even if your study doesn't fit neatly into one box. Many researchers are not familiar with web technology, particularly how easy it is to identify people from surprisingly little information. This extends to data protection laws, discussed briefly in the next section.

Security

Internet-mediated data collection is often *less* secure than traditional paper-and-pencil alternatives. It is important to understand that data transmission is not automatically secure when transmitted online. In fact, it can often be less secure than postal questionnaires, for example. E-mail might feel like a conversation between two people, but e-mails are like sending postcards without envelopes. The e-mail passes through many different computers before it reaches the recipient, and is stored by universities, hosting companies etc. E-mails can be read by other people, even if they are not supposed to. Partners, friends, flatmates, colleagues, family members – they can all potentially go into the 'sent items' folder and find e-mails. This raises issues if you decide to write to participants by e-mail about a sensitive research topic (e.g. attitudes to and current feelings about divorce). What might happen if their partner sees it? Questionnaire data could be intercepted by someone else, unless 128-bit encrypted. When collecting data such as e-mail addresses, dates of birth, etc. it may not be appropriate to use a standard web questionnaire method.

Legal requirements

In addition to the many sets of guidelines available for ethical online research, you must ensure that you meet any current legal requirements for processing of data in your country. This applies to standard research, but is discussed here because additional issues are raised by the Internet data collection mode. Ethical guidelines, while there is some overlap with legal requirements, do not necessarily cover the Data Protection Act (relevant to readers in the UK). You need to make sure that wherever you are, you have addressed ethical and legal issues. For example, in the UK the Data Protection Act requires that separate consent should be obtained if a questionnaire asks about sensitive topics. Sensitive data can mean different things to different people. In the Data Protection Act, the following topics are defined as sensitive:

- Racial or ethnic origin
- Political opinions
- Religious or other beliefs
- Trade union membership
- Physical or mental health condition
- Sex life
- Criminal proceedings or convictions

This definition is not included in many sets of ethical guidelines. It is permissible to process these kinds of data if consent has been provided – but it must be in addition to informed consent, where the Data Protection Act applies. In practice, this means you must ask for informed consent and then ask for a separate statement about the sensitive topics. In the UK, for example, researchers are required to lodge a notification of their research with the Information Commissioner, although many universities will have lodged university-wide notifications (you can check at **www.esd.informationcommissioner.gov.uk/esd/search.asp**). The use of discussion board material is perhaps the most ethically sensitive area.

Obtaining informed consent for an online study

If you provide a simple 'I agree' or 'I consent' button at the bottom of the Participant Information Sheet, how can you be sure that they have really read the instructions? The bottom line is that you can't. However, it may be possible to build in a screening tool that ensures that the instructions have been read. The example below illustrates a consent form for a study requiring that participants agree to five criteria: they are healthy volunteers, resident in the UK, willing to participate, have read the Participant Information Sheet and understand that they can leave the study at any time. In brackets are numerical codes given to the responses. In this example, a script was written which prevented the study from opening unless the sum of the responses was five.

I have a long-term illness, health problem or disability, which limits my daily activities or the work I can do

Yes(0)   No(1)

I live in the United Kingdom (UK)

No(0)   Yes(1)

I would like to participate in this study

Yes(1)   No(0)

I have read the Participant Information Sheet

No(0)   Yes(1)

I understand that I can leave the study at any time by e-mailing the researcher

Yes(1)   No(0)

This does not guarantee that the inclusion criteria for the study have been met and that the statements really apply, but at least the statements have to be read. We can have more confidence that people have consented, even if they opt out of reading the Participant Information Sheet, rather than have clicked the agree button by accident and didn't realise what they were supposed to read. Multiple statements of informed consent may be obtained when a study is divided into several sections. If demographic information is collected first, researchers will know the characteristics of participants who leave the study at an early section. However, it is not generally ethical to stagger the sections so that their sensitivity increases over time (see Chapter 5). This can be considered a form of deception/pressure and may exploit the willingness of participants to complete a study which they have started. This can be addressed by providing examples in the Participant Information Sheet of the kinds of questions that will be asked. Additional guidelines should also be provided on the Participant Information Sheet for web questionnaires as follows:

- Provide contact details (e.g. e-mail address) at the beginning and end of the study.
- State who the data controller is (e.g. the university department where you are based).
- State whether any third parties will have access to the data.
- Provide a link to a relevant set of ethical guidelines (e.g. BPS; see Chapter 25).
- Provide examples of the kinds of questions that will be asked, especially sensitive questions.
- Provide an estimate of how long the study will take, if known (there may be cost implications of staying online for long periods).

- Explain what will happen to the data.

- Clarify whether the data will leave a permanent traceable record (web hosting companies will store data and databases).

- In the statement about risks and benefits of taking part, remind participants that nothing online is fully confidential, e.g. 'no computer transmission can be perfectly secure, but reasonable efforts will be made to protect the security of your data'.

- Provide a link to any software or plug-ins that are needed for the study and provide the minimum necessary technological requirements on the part of the user. Ideally, these should be free.

Further reading

Birnbaum, M. H. (2004). Human research and data collection via the internet. *Annual Review of Psychology*, **55**, pp. 803–32.

This book is written by the author of SurveyWiz.

British Psychological Society ethical guidelines

www.bps.org.uk/the-society/code-of-conduct/code-of-conduct_home.cfm

This web page contains both the BPS Code of Ethics and Conduct (2006) and the BPS report 'Conducting Research on the Internet: Guidelines for ethical practice in psychological research online' (2007). See also Chapter 25.

Joinson, A.N. (2002). *Understanding the Psychology of Internet Behaviour: Virtual Worlds, Real Lives*. Basingstoke: Palgrave.

A fascinating book for those interested in the psychology of online behaviour *per se*, rather than the role of the Internet in research.

Joinson, A.N., McKenna K., Postmes, T. & Reips, U. (Eds) (2007). *Oxford Handbook of Internet Psychology*. Oxford: Oxford University Press.

A large volume containing contributions from the leading e-researchers in psychology.

Mann, C. & Stewart, F. (2002). *Internet Communication and Qualitative Research: A Handbook for Researching Online*. London: Sage.

A little dated now but still an excellent text covering many of the major issues in conducting qualitative e-research.

Reips, U. & Bosnjak, M. (Eds) (2001). *Dimensions of Internet Science*. Lengerich, Germany: Pabst Science Publishers.

This book contains advice on how to design and conduct an online experiment, with particular reference to decision making, cognitive psychology, personality psychology and evolutionary psychology.

Resources

www.websm.org

This website is a popular resource for e-researchers, with an emphasis on survey methods.

Part 2

Analysing quantitative data

8 Fundamentals of statistics

9 Entering and manipulating data

10 Graphical representation and descriptive statistics

11 Bivariate analysis 1: exploring differences between variables

12 Bivariate analysis 2: exploring relationships between variables

13 Analysis of variance (ANOVA)

14 Multivariate analysis of variance (MANOVA)

15 Regression
   ■ Statistical test flowchart

16 Introducing R and R commander

8 Fundamentals of statistics

- This chapter begins by addressing mathematics anxiety and then introduces some of the basic principles of statistics.

- It describes the difference between descriptive and inferential statistics.

- The chapter covers measures of central tendency and dispersion.

- It then moves on to cover probability, the normal distribution and z-scores.

- Finally, this chapter will introduce you to Type I and Type II errors, statistical power, and differences between parametric and non-parametric tests.

INTRODUCTION

We think it is probably worth spending a little time addressing any mathematics anxiety that you may be feeling before we move on to explore the topic of statistics in detail. While it is undoubtedly true that the topic of statistics is one of the least popular elements of a psychology degree, it is an essential element and one that is within your capabilities. If you are that rare individual who loves maths then you can probably skip this section and move on to Section 8.1. However, if you have unwelcome memories of learning mathematics at school looming into consciousness as we approach the thorny issue of statistics, then stick with us.

First, some research on mathematics anxiety. There is considerable evidence that mathematics performance is significantly affected by anxiety (Ashcraft & Faust, 1994). Anxiety about your mathematics ability will produce poorer performance at mathematics tasks. And this is one of the major problems for any teacher of statistics. Early negative experiences of mathematics (often at school) can leave a student with a lack of confidence that makes any future learning of statistics more difficult than it need be (Monteil *et al.*, 1996). If your confidence can be increased then learning will become easier and your mathematics ability will

▶

improve by leaps and bounds. So, we need to increase your confidence and this can only happen if you engage with statistics with enthusiasm and an open mind. Belief in your own ability is the key to success!

Now let us explore your experience and feelings about mathematics (and hence statistics) a little more (see Box 8.1). We hope that if we *work together* you will find that statistics really are quite straightforward. We will endeavour to keep our presentation of statistical information clear and simple so you can try to read and engage with the material. We will try to use real-world examples wherever possible and you will try to apply these statistical ideas to your own experience wherever possible. And finally, we guarantee that if you put in the effort to understand this material you will be able to conquer any fear you may have. You may never find statistics to be your favourite aspect of psychology, but we are sure that you will be able to learn enough to tackle this essential aspect of the discipline with confidence.

Box 8.1

Activity box **Exploring statistics anxiety**

- Spend some time thinking about your experiences of being taught mathematics at school.
  - What was your worst moment?
  - What was your best moment?
  - What do you think was the main difference between the best and worst moments?
- Do you think your memories of being taught mathematics have influenced your feelings about mathematics in general?
  - For instance, do you now approach all maths topics with some fear and trepidation?
  - Do you avoid engaging with mathematics at all (in daily life and in education)?
- Do you have a strategy for dealing with your mathematics anxiety?
  - For instance, is your strategy to avoid maths completely?
  - If you avoid maths, how will that help you when you must complete a course in statistics to gain a degree in psychology?
- Try to think through alternative strategies for dealing with your mathematics anxiety and instigate a plan to carry out an alternative strategy that you feel comfortable with and that will enable you to maximise your success at statistics. Remember, the key to success is commitment to learn. If you put in the effort you will succeed.

8.1 Descriptive and inferential statistics

Quantitative research is designed to generate numbers and this is the reason we need both **descriptive** and **inferential statistics**. The first thing we need to do with our data is to summarise some basic features of the numbers that make up our set of data. Just re-presenting the numbers generated in our study is rarely enough. We need to do some work on the data so that we can understand what they mean in more detail. **Descriptive statistics** are usually the first stage in any quantitative analysis and concern the range of techniques that enable us to summarise our data ('descriptive statistics' are sometimes called 'summary statistics' for this reason). The most fundamental and important descriptive statistics are those concerned with identifying the central tendency (or typical value such as the average) of a set of numbers and those concerned with how the remaining numbers are distributed (how much they vary) around this central (or typical) value. Both of these issues are explored in detail below.

Inferential statistics are those ways of exploring data that enable us to move beyond a simple description of individual variables to making inferences about the *likelihood* of our findings occurring. We are particularly concerned with identifying whether our findings (relationships or differences between one or more variables) are more or less likely to have occurred than by chance alone. Or, what are the *probabilities* (likelihood) that the relationships/differences occurring between variables within our data set are **significant** (and therefore of interest to us in the social sciences) and not just the result of 'meaningless' chance relationships/differences that occur with all variables?

8.2 Measures of central tendency and dispersion

The arithmetic mean

This is certainly the most important measure of central tendency and also the most familiar. In fact the **arithmetic mean** (most often just 'mean' will do) is what we normally call the average. Very simply, the mean is the result of adding up all the numbers in our set and dividing by the total number of values.

So if six people took 6, 8, 10, 15, 20 and 7 seconds to solve a simple maths problem (a series of additions and subtractions), we would need to add up all six numbers and divide by six as there are six values in this set of numbers (as below):

$$\frac{(6 + 8 + 10 + 15 + 20 + 7)}{6} = \frac{66}{6} = 11 \text{ seconds}$$

So, the mean of this set of numbers is 11 seconds. This gives us some idea of the central tendency among this set of numbers, or the most typical value. The mathematical symbol used to represent the mean is: $\bar{X}$. This symbol is called 'X bar' (the 'X' of this is pretty obvious and 'bar' is what we call the line over the top of a symbol). The mathematical formula for calculating the mean is as follows:

$$\bar{X} = \frac{\Sigma X}{N}$$

Do not panic as the maths appears. Remember our deal: we will explain these things and you must stick with it. All this formula tells us is what we already know about calculating the mean (or $\bar{X}$) of a set of numbers. That is, we simply (1) add up all the values, and (2) divide by the total number of values in the set of numbers.

So, in order to calculate $\bar{X}$ (the mean) the formula tells us to add up the numbers in our set of numbers (this is the part on top of the line):

$$\Sigma X$$

The sigma symbol (Σ) tells us to add up whatever follows it and in this case that is the symbol X which stands for all the numbers in our set of numbers. So, the top half of our formula tells us to add up all the numbers in our set. The bottom half of the formula has the italicised capital N symbol. This symbol represents the number of values in a set of scores (six in this case). And that is all there is to the formula. We replace specific numbers with symbols so that we can provide general instructions for different sets of numbers. You just need to follow the rules of the formula, insert your numbers in the appropriate part of the formula, add, subtract, multiply or divide as appropriate, and that is all there is to it.

We will try to keep formulae to a minimum in this book. These days there is little need for calculating statistics by hand (or with a calculator). Most people who work with statistics (including many psychologists) will have access to computer programs that do the mathematical work for them. However, it can often be useful to *know* how a statistical test works even if you will rarely have to carry it out by hand. Understanding some of the basic principles can be very helpful in getting a good general overview of what we are doing when we carry out statistical tests. Without some level of understanding of the mathematics involved in statistical tests there is a danger of you falling foul of GIGO – Garbage In Garbage Out. A computer program will do as you tell it and that is the case even if you are telling it to carry out tests that are totally inappropriate for your data. Computers only help with the mechanics – you need to take charge of the important task of deciding what test is needed in what circumstance and why, and then carrying out the vital task of interpreting what the results mean.

Advantages	Disadvantages
■ Mean is the basis for many powerful statistical tests ■ It is the most sensitive of the measures of central tendency covered here ■ It takes an exactly central position on an interval and continuous scale	■ Its sensitivity can also be a disadvantage as it is susceptible to extreme values (outliers)

We just want to explain why the sensitivity of the mean can be a disadvantage if we have extreme values (or **outliers**) among our data set. Imagine a seventh person completes our mathematics task. This person, like our previous six participants, is an undergraduate student. But this individual was recovering from a very heavy night on the town and was hung over. We did not know this but it clearly affected their performance on the mathematics task (as they could not concentrate) and they took 186 seconds to complete the task. If we include this score in our set of scores the mean becomes:

$$\frac{(66 + 186)}{7} = \frac{252}{7} = 36 \text{ seconds}$$

Thirty-six seconds is clearly not the best indicator of what is a typical value in our set of scores. After all, six of the scores are well below this value and only one is above it (and then this value is much higher). This is a danger when calculating a mean and a good reason why you should investigate the cause of extreme values in your data set (or use another measure of central tendency) should they exist. Extreme values in one direction (above or below the mean score) will distort the mean (although extreme values simultaneously above and below may cancel each other out) and reduce its utility as a measure of central tendency.

Median

The **median (Med)** is another measure of central tendency that does not suffer problems (like the mean) when there are extreme values in a set of data. The median is simply the central value of a set of numbers. With an odd number of values this is very easy. Using the data for the mathematics task above (seven items), the median is the fourth value along once the data have been put in numerical order:

$$6, 7, 8, 10, 15, 20, 186$$

So, in this case the median of our set of numbers is *10*. However, if there is an even number of values (e.g. without the 7th person added), we need to take the mean of the two central values (in this case 8 and 10) in order to calculate the median value for our set of numbers as follows:

$$6, 7, 8, 10, 15, 20$$

So, in this case the median is $\dfrac{8 + 10}{2} = 9$

The procedure for calculating the median value is as follows:

1 Find the median position or location (where N is the number of scores in our set of data):

$$\frac{N + 1}{2}$$

2 If N is odd then this will be a whole number:

$$\frac{7 + 1}{2} = 4$$

So, we know that in this circumstance (when the data are in numerical order) the median will be the fourth value along.

3 If N is even then the value is midway between two of the values in the set when numerically ordered:

$$\frac{6 + 1}{2} = 3.5$$

This tells us that in this circumstance the median is midway between the third and fourth values in the set of numbers (when they are in numerical order). Here we take the mean of the third and fourth numbers in our set and this gives us the median.

If there are a large number of values (or there are ties – equal values where the median falls) then the previous approach can be tedious and tricky. There is a formula that can be used instead which does not require us to order our set of numbers to calculate the median. However, we can honestly say that in all the years we have been carrying out the quantitative analysis of data we have never had to use this formula. A couple of clicks of the mouse will instruct a computer program to do this mathematical work for you. Quite frankly we cannot think of any reason for you needing to know about this arcane formula.

Advantages	Disadvantages
■ Easier to calculate than the mean (with small groups and no ties) ■ Unaffected by extreme values in one direction, therefore better with *skewed* data than the mean ■ Can be obtained when extreme values are unknown	■ Does not take into account the exact values of each item and is therefore less sensitive than the mean ■ If values are few can be unrepresentative

Finally, we want to explain why the median may be unrepresentative when the number of values in a data set are few. Imagine a set of data as follows:

6, 9, 11, 233, 234

In this case the median is 11, which does not tell us much about the central tendency of our set of data. We need to be careful in situations like these and avoid use of the median if at all possible.

Mode

We cannot calculate either a mean or a median if our data are on a nominal scale. However, we can say which category has the highest frequency count. This is the **mode** (or **Mo**), a useful measure of central tendency. The mode is the most frequently occurring value in a set of numbers.

So, what is the mode for the following set of numbers?

$$1, 1, 1, 2, 2, 2, 3, 3, 3, 4, 4, 4, 4, 5, 5, 5, 6, 6, 6, 7, 7, 8, 9$$

As we are sure you have already worked out, the mode is 4 for this set of numbers because this is the value that occurs most often (four times, in fact). All the other numbers in this set occur three times or fewer. Let us go back to the mathematics test data we used before:

$$6, 7, 8, 10, 15, 20, 186$$

With this set of data there is no modal value, for all the figures occur only once. In other circumstances we may find that we have more than one modal value. For instance, have a look at the following set of numbers and identify the mode:

$$1, 1, 2, 2, 2, 3, 3, 4, 4, 5, 5, 5, 6, 6$$

With this set of data there are in fact two modes (2 and 5) – the set of values is said to be **bi-modal**. There are occasions when the mode is a particularly useful measure of central tendency. When the data are distributed in the way seen above, with two modal values, the mean or median would give scores that were literally central for our set of numbers, when we might be interested in the fact that our distribution of numbers is actually U-shaped or bi-modal. A classic example of this sort of distribution occurs with measures of masculinity and femininity. For instance, if we asked 50 men and 50 women to complete a questionnaire which instructed them to rate themselves against traditionally masculine and feminine personality traits, we should not be surprised to discover that we are likely to get a bi-modal distribution of scores. We are likely to find men scoring themselves highly on masculine traits and women scoring themselves highly on feminine traits. If we took the mean or median for this set of scores we would have the impression that our typical person was androgynous with scores midway between the masculine and feminine traits. However, the mode may show us that we have a U-shaped distribution of scores, leading us to investigate why this might be the case.[1]

---

[1] Actually, more recent research indicates that traditional sex role distinctions are breaking down and people are likely to score highly on some masculine and some feminine traits and therefore be classed as androgynous. Furthermore, the whole concept of sex role has been seriously attacked (see *Men in Perspective* by Edley & Wetherell, 1995, for a very good introduction to these issues as they concern men).

Advantages	Disadvantages
■ Shows the most important value in a set ■ Unaffected by extreme values in one direction ■ Can be obtained when extreme values are unknown ■ More informative than mean or median when distribution is U-shaped, e.g. measures of masculinity/femininity	■ Does not take into account the exact value of each item like the mean ■ Not useful for small sets of data where several values occur equally frequently (1, 1, 2, 2, 3, 3, 4, 4) or for sets of data with no values occurring more than once

Levels of measurement and central tendency measures

As mentioned above, the three measures of central tendency described above have their respective merits and demerits. In addition, it is important to recognise that each of the measures is more or less appropriate for different levels of measurement (interval/ratio, ordinal or nominal), as outlined below:

■ *Interval/ratio*: at this level any of the three measures of central tendency may be used. However, the **mean** is the most sensitive measure at this level of measurement and should be the preferred choice unless there are other known reasons to reject it.

■ *Ordinal*: at this level the mean cannot be used but median and mode can both be used. The **median** is more sensitive than the mode and is generally the most appropriate measure of central tendency at this level.

■ *Nominal*: if data are in categories then you have no choice as only the **mode** can be used.

Recall from Chapter 2 that the distinction between ordinal and interval data is not always clear for psychological measures. Psychologists often treat ordinal data as though it were continuous, which is permissible if there are at least seven points on the scale (Miles & Banyard, 2007).

Measures of dispersion

Without knowledge of spread (dispersion), a mean or any measure of central tendency can be very misleading. Consider these two sets of numbers:

120, 130, 140, 150, 160

10, 40, 150, 200, 300

Both sets of numbers have a mean of 140 but the second set of numbers varies around this figure much more than the first set. In other words, they demonstrate greater **dispersion** around the measure of central tendency (in this case the mean). Dispersion is a measure of how much or how little the rest of the values tend to vary around the central tendency or central value in a set of numbers. Measures of dispersion provide the other crucial piece of information needed to describe a set of numbers and there are a variety of techniques (detailed below) that may be used, each with their pros and cons.

Range

This is the simplest measure of dispersion. The range is the distance between the highest and lowest values in a set of numbers. Look at the following scores:

$$22, 25, 30, 42, 88, 102$$

The range is 102 minus 22, which equals 80. The procedure for calculating the range is therefore very simple: (1) find the top value of the set of numbers, (2) find the bottom value of the set and (3) subtract the bottom score from the top score.

Advantages	Disadvantages
■ Easy to calculate ■ Includes extreme values	■ Distorted by extreme values ■ Relies on the two extreme values in the set of numbers and is therefore unrepresentative of the distribution of values between the extremes

The main disadvantage of the range is that it relies on two values alone (the highest and lowest) and these values are the most extreme values in the set of numbers (by definition). If these numbers are statistical outliers (and therefore outside the normal range we would expect for our data) then the value of the range is likely to be unrepresentative of the general pattern of dispersion in the data. Furthermore, the range does not tell us whether or not the values are closely grouped around the mean – it only gives us a gross estimate of the spread of numbers in the data set.

Semi-interquartile range

This deals with the last disadvantage of the range and is a more sophisticated range statistic. This measure of dispersion concentrates on the distance between the two values which cut off the top and bottom 25 per cent of scores. If your data are arranged in ascending numerical order, the first quartile (Q_1) (which is also the 25th percentile) is the point where the lowest quarter of scores are cut off and the third quartile (Q_3) (which is also the 75th percentile) is where the lowest three-quarters of scores are cut off (or the highest quarter). So, if we have the following set of data:

1, 2, 3, 4, 5, 6, | 7, 8, 9, 10, 11, 12, 13, 14, 15, 16, 17, 18, | 19, 20, 21, 22, 23, 24

Q_1 Q_3

Then, as you can see, the first and third quartiles cut off the bottom and top 25 per cent of scores, or the bottom and top quarter of scores (which is the bottom and top six scores in this case as there are 24 scores in total). In order to calculate values for Q_1 and Q_3 in this case we have to take the mean of the scores either side (just like the median). If the set of numbers is even (like the case above with 24 numbers in the set) the quartiles will occur between scores (like the median). If the set of numbers is odd they will fall exactly on two numbers in the set. In the case above, the value of the first quartile is therefore:

$$\frac{6 + 7}{2} = 6.5$$

The value of the third quartile is 18 plus 19 divided by 2 which equals 18.5 (mean = 18.5). The distance between these two scores is:

$$18.5 - 6.5 = 12$$

Therefore the interquartile range for this set of data is 12. The **semi-interquartile range** is half of this value (hence 'semi') and is therefore 6. The formula for the semi-interquartile range is:

$$\frac{Q_3 - Q_1}{2}$$

And therefore the procedure for calculating the semi-interquartile range is as follows:

1 Find the 1st quartile (Q_1) and the 3rd quartile (Q_3).
2 Subtract Q_1 from Q_3.
3 Divide the result of 2 above by 2.

This measure of dispersion is most commonly used when the measure of central tendency being used is the median. Indeed, the median can also be called the second quartile (Q_2), for it will fall exactly halfway along a set of data with 50 per cent of the values above it and 50 per cent below it:

The median for this set of data is the mean of the values either side of the line dissecting the data (12 and 13) which equals 12.5.

Advantages	Disadvantages
■ Easy to calculate ■ Representative of the central 50 per cent of values in the data set ■ More robust to problems caused by outliers	■ Still relies on just two values and therefore does not provide a measure of dispersion based on all values in a set of data

Mean deviation

This is not really used as a measure of dispersion any more (the standard deviation – see below – has replaced it). However, we think it is worth including it here to help you understand a little more about the principles underlying different measures of dispersion in general and to prepare you for the slightly more complicated statistics (variance and standard deviation) that follow.

The **deviation** (x) of a score is the difference between it and the mean for the set of scores from which it was extracted. The formula is:

$$x = X - \bar{X}$$

The symbols should be familiar by now. X stands for a score in our set of data and $\bar{X}$ is the value of the mean for the set of data. So if we look at the following set of scores:

$$22, 25, 30, 42, 87, 100$$

the mean is 51 and each deviation is as follows:

$$22 - 51 = -29$$
$$25 - 51 = -26$$
$$30 - 51 = -21$$
$$42 - 51 = -9$$
$$87 - 51 = 36$$
$$100 - 51 = 49$$

As you can see, some values are negative and some positive, as we would expect when we subtract the mean from any set of scores. You might think that a good measure of dispersion would be simply to take the average of this set of deviations. This would provide a measure of dispersion based on all values in our set of data rather than just two (like the range and semi-interquartile range). However, if you simply take the average of a set of deviations you will get a value of zero. If you do not believe us, add up the deviations above and see what happens (and if you are still sceptical then make up your own set of data and try it again). The problem is caused by the fact that the mean is exactly central in a set of data and the negative deviation scores cancel out the positive deviation scores, in any set of data. What we need to do is to get rid of the negative signs and just examine the *absolute* values of our deviation scores, and this is exactly what we do when we calculate the mean deviation (MD). The formula for the mean deviation is as follows:

$$MD = \frac{\Sigma |X - \bar{X}|}{N}$$

As before, N is the number of scores, Σ is the instruction to add up all the values that follow, $|X - \bar{X}|$ means take the *absolute* value (that is, lose the minus sign or always take the smaller value from the larger value) of the difference between the scores and the mean. Therefore, if we wish to calculate the mean deviation of our set of data above we first obtain the deviation scores for our values (as above) and then remove the minus signs, resulting in the following:

$$|X - \bar{X}| = 29, 26, 21, 9, 36, 49$$

$$\Sigma|X - \bar{X}| = 170$$

Therefore the mean deviation (MD) is 170 divided by 6 (170/6) which equals 28.33. As we stated earlier, the mean deviation has the advantage of including all values (unlike the range and semi-interquartile range). However, it is very rarely used and has largely been superseded by the standard deviation (see below).

Variance and standard deviation

Variance

An alternative way of removing the minus signs from a set of deviation scores is to *square* (that is, multiply scores by themselves) the values. Squared deviations are always positive because a minus times a minus is always a plus. If we square deviation scores and then add these up ($\Sigma(X - \bar{X})^2$) and divide by the number of values in the set (N) we get the **variance**:

$$\text{Variance} = \frac{\Sigma(X - \bar{X})^2}{N}$$

where: X is the individual score,

$\bar{X}$ is the mean score,

$X - \bar{X}$ is the deviation (sometimes known as d),

$(X - \bar{X})^2$ is the squared deviation,

Σ is the instruction 'take the sum of' (or add up),

$\Sigma(X - \bar{X})^2$ therefore means take the sum of the squared deviations,

N is the total number of scores in the data set.

This formula gives the variance of the set of scores in front of us. This is fine if we just wish to describe the distribution of scores in a particular sample or if we have data on an entire population. However, more often than not we want to describe our sample and then infer that this is representative of the population from which our sample came. This means that we want any statistics (such as the mean and variance) to be appropriate for the population as well as the sample. In other words, we want any statistics carried out on our sample to gen-eralise to the population. So, why are we telling you this now? Well, statisticians 'have shown' that an adjustment should be made to the formula given above for the variance of a set of scores when we want to generalise from a sample to a population. An unbiased estimate of the variance of a population is given by the following formula:

$$\text{Variance} = \frac{\Sigma (X - \bar{X})^2}{N - 1}$$

As you can see, we now have $N-1$ on the bottom line (the denominator) of the equation. This is referred to as the **degrees of freedom**. This formula is the standard one used to calculate the variance of a sample (for we nearly always wish to generalise to the population from a sample and we almost never have access to an entire population). The 'degrees of freedom' in this case is the number of deviations from the mean that are free to vary. This is one less than the total number of scores in a set of numbers because the last value is fixed by the need for the total average deviation to be zero (as we saw earlier). As you can see, our measure of dispersion is affected by (and in this case divided by) the number of things free to vary in our sample. There are other reasons (mathematically speaking) for using $N-1$ in place of N but these are unnecessary for understanding the principles underlying measures of dispersion and well beyond the scope of this book.

Standard deviation

A disadvantage of using variance as a measure of dispersion is that it produces large values in squared units due to our squaring the deviations. We can restore the values to the correct units by simply taking the square root (as the opposite of taking the square) of the variance. The square root of the variance is called the **standard deviation (SD** or **s.d.**) and is the most common measure of dispersion used in psychology.

$$SD = \sqrt{\frac{\sum (X - \bar{X})^2}{N - 1}}$$

You will invariably see the mean and standard deviation paired together as the principal descriptive statistics of a set of data. This measure is particularly popular because of its links to the normal distribution (which will be introduced below) and the numerous statistics associated with this distribution.

Advantages	Disadvantages
■ Like the mean, it forms the basis of many more complicated statistics ■ Takes account of all values in a data set ■ Is the most sensitive of the measures of dispersion covered here	■ A bit complicated to calculate by hand! (but very easy with computer software)

If you need to calculate the standard deviation by hand there is an easier version of the formula:

$$SD = \sqrt{\frac{\sum X^2 - \frac{(\sum X)^2}{N}}{N - 1}}$$

This formula is just a mathematical transformation of the previous formula and produces exactly the same results (test it out if you do not believe us). Just be careful not to mix up ΣX^2 – which means square the scores first and then add them together – with $(\Sigma X)^2$ – which means add together the scores first and then square the result. However, most people use statistics software on personal computers to calculate these statistics. This is a lot simpler and certainly more reliable than calculating statistics by hand.

Finally, just for a bit of interest in this section and to show why these statistics are important in pretty much all research, we have included Box 8.2. This outlines a nice study which looked at the experience of donor insemination treatment for fertility problems and along the way used some of the descriptive statistics outlined above (the mean and standard deviation) to inform the reader about the sample characteristics and results of the research.

Box 8.2	Study box

Salter-Ling, N., Hunter, M. & Glover, L. (2000). Donor insemination: Exploring the experience of treatment and intention to tell. *Journal of Reproductive and Infant Psychology*, **19** (3), 175-86.

This study was designed to explore the experience of men and women undergoing donor insemination treatment (DI). Donor insemination is a treatment for fertility difficulties in the male partner through use of donated sperm from another party. The study investigated perceived levels of distress, mood, adjustment to infertility and the intention to tell any child conceived of their origins. This study, in common with most research reports, used descriptive statistics to describe the important characteristics of the sample. Mean and standard deviation scores were given for age, duration of treatment and education. Furthermore, mean and standard deviation scores were given for the scales used to measure distress, mood and adjustment to infertility. So, for instance, the mean score for women was higher (mean = 8.17, SD = 2.60) than that of the men (mean = 6.20, SD = 3.05) on the scale measuring distress due to infertility. However, as we are sure you have already noticed, the variation around the mean was greater for men (higher standard deviation) than that for women on the scale. For information, the study also found high levels of anxiety and high scores on the infertility adjustment scale for men and women, highlighting how difficult it is to cope with infertility and then treatment. Interestingly, those who planned to tell children of their origins experienced lower levels of distress than those who did not intend to tell their children.

8.3	Probability

Now we go further into the realm of mathematics, but once again with the aim of understanding enough so that we can read and carry out our own research using statistics in an appropriate way. Many of the concepts in this section on probability will be already familiar. Remember, confidence is everything here. Engage with this material afresh and draw on your own knowledge and experience wherever possible.

There are three types of probability that are identified by mathematicians and philosophers alike. The three types of probability are: **subjective probability**, **logical** (or mathematical) **probability** and **empirical probability**. We will address each in turn below. But let us spend some time exploring your existing knowledge of probability. We are sure you make probability judgements on a daily basis. When choosing clothes in the morning, do you look outside in order to see whether you will need cool or warm clothes? And do you then make judgements about how likely it is that the weather will improve or get worse during the day? And make judgements about how likely it is that it will rain and you will need your umbrella? Yes – we all do and we all therefore engage in making probability judgements. In the case of the weather we often get it wrong but we will still try to gather empirical information (from direct observation and weather forecasts) in order to make predictions based on the likelihood of the weather turning out one way or another. There are numerous other examples. If you bet (on the horses or dogs) then we are sure you know a lot about probability (unless you enjoy losing). When you 'question spot' preparing for exams you are making decisions about the likelihood of the topics you have revised turning up in an exam on the basis of how often they have appeared in the past.

Subjective probability

Much of what we have discussed above falls under the description of **subjective probability**. Predicting the likelihood (or unlikelihood) of events in everyday life is the stuff of subjective probability. If you make predictions about the likelihood of your football team winning on Saturday you are making subjective predictions, for we cannot *know* whether the team will win or not. These probability predictions are ways of dealing with everyday doubt that we encounter, enabling us to exert some more control over our worlds. However, these predictions are subjective and are therefore described as *subjective* probability judgements.

Logical (or mathematical) probability

Logical (or mathematical) **probability** concerns those predictions that draw on formal mathematical theory. Much of this stems from studies of games of chance such as poker or bridge. With games such as these we need to know things such as (1) how likely it is that our hand of cards would occur and (2) what is the likelihood that the card we need will be dealt from the pack. With this approach to probability we examine the ratio of the number of favourable cases (our prediction) to the total number of equally likely cases. So, if we wanted to predict the logical probability that the first card drawn from a (well-shuffled) pack of 52 (excluding jokers) cards would be an ace, we would need to know the number of aces in the pack (4) and the total number of cards in the pack (52). The probability of drawing an ace from the pack is therefore 4 in 52, which is equivalent to 1 in 13. We have 1 chance in 13 of drawing an ace as our first card from the pack. See Box 8.3 for more on the probability of poker.

Box 8.3

Activity box | **Probability and the art of poker**

- In the most common form of poker five cards are dealt to each player. With a 52-card deck there are a maximum of 2,598,960 different possible hands that can be dealt. The order of winning hands is determined by the probability of their occurring, with the highest scoring hands being those that are least likely and the lowest scoring hands those that are more likely.

- The highest hand of cards that can be dealt in poker is the *royal flush*. With this hand you have the ace, king, queen, jack and ten of one suit. As there are four suits of cards (clubs, diamonds, hearts and spades) there is a 4 in 2,598,960 (or 1 in 649,740) chance of drawing a royal flush. As you might expect, you are not going to draw the highest hand very often.

- However, the lowest scoring hand is one containing only *one pair* (two cards of equal value). The chance of getting a pair is 1 in 2.36 and therefore quite likely.

- The chance of getting *four of a kind* is a little less than 1 in 4000. As you might expect, this hand is higher than a pair but lower than a royal flush.

Empirical probability

What if we want to know how likely it is that a lecturer will swear during a lecture. You will need to use empirical probability. With **empirical probability** the probability of an event (such as a lecturer swearing in a lecture) is estimated by the ratio of the number of times the event has occurred to the total number of trials (in this case the total number of lectures they have given):

$$p = \frac{\text{number of lecturers where a lecturer has sworn}}{\text{total number of lecturers so far}}$$

The probability of an event occurring is generally given the symbol p.

With this approach to probability we make estimates for the likelihood of future events based on what we know about these events from the past. We are making an estimate in this case because we are making a judgement on the basis of a sample from a larger number of possible trials.

Calculating probabilities

The probability of events occurring is measured on a scale from 0 (never happens) to 1 (always happens). In practice, probability values will inevitably fall somewhere between these values and have values larger than 0 but less than 1. Now let us see how much knowledge of probability you already have. Go to Box 8.4 and have a go at answering the questions about the probability of certain events occurring. Do not worry if you struggle or get some wrong as we have not told you how to calculate probability values yet!

Box 8.4	
Activity box	Calculating probabilities

Give the following a value (between 0 and 1) for how likely you think it is that these things will happen or not:

1 Your football team will win on Saturday.

2 You will win a million pounds on the lottery at some time in the next ten years.

3 You will think about your family within the next hour.

4 A coin tossed fairly will come down showing heads.

5 Two coins tossed fairly will both come down showing tails.

So here we go with the answers to the questions above:

1 Only a guess (*subjective probability*) – maybe 0.5 (50 per cent chance), but it will probably depend on who you support.

2 Again no definite answers here as it depends on how you play – but it is very low, about 1 in 14 million ($\approx 0.71^{-8}$)

3 Who knows? But you have been primed now so we think it will be about 0.75 (75 per cent chance).

4 With this and the next question we can offer some answers based on *logical* or *mathematical probability* rather than *subjective probability*. The answer to this question is 0.5 (there is a 50 per cent chance).

5 And here the answer is 0.25 (a 25 per cent chance). If you got this right then you can already calculate probability.

So how did you find the questions in Box 8.4? We hope you found a few questions okay, for several only involve making educated guesses with subjective probability – there is no magic formula for these sorts of judgements. Questions

4 and 5 were somewhat different, however, and require knowledge (which some of you may already have) of how to calculate probability values. So how should we calculate the answers to the coin-tossing questions in Box 8.4? Well, it is quite simple. With a single coin there are only two possible outcomes (heads or tails). There is therefore one chance in two that it will be a tail or one chance in two that it will be a head. This is the starting point. One of these outcomes will be our prediction (heads or tails). There is therefore one chance in two that a coin will come down heads (and the same for tails for that matter). The mathematical way of representing this calculation will be familiar to you (from above) and is as follows:

$$p = \frac{\text{number of ways desired outcomes can occur}}{\text{total number of outcomes possible}}$$

Remember p = the probability of an event occurring. Therefore if we predict that a coin will fall down heads we have:

$$p = \frac{1}{2}$$

Therefore, the probability of a coin coming down heads is 0.5. There are a number of rules for calculating probability when we combine events which tell us how to carry out our calculations. The two most important rules are the 'or' rule and the 'and' rule (see Box 8.5).

Box 8.5

Information box

Calculating probability

Probability calculation 1: the 'or' rule

The probability of event A *or* event B happening is $p(A) + p(B)$ where $p(A/B)$ is the probability of an event occurring.

If we want to calculate the probability that a coin will come down *either* heads *or* tails we need to calculate the probability of each event occurring and add them together. The probability of a coin coming down heads is 0.5 and the probability of a coin coming down tails is 0.5. Therefore, the probability of a coin coming down heads or tails is 1.0. As you might expect, this is higher than a coin coming down heads and furthermore demonstrates that we are certain to get a head or tail (ignoring possibilities of coins on their sides for now).

Probability calculation 2: the 'and' rule

The probability of event A *and* event B happening is $p(A) \times p(B)$ where $p(A/B)$ is the probability of an event occurring.

▶

Box 8.5 *Continued*

Go back to question 5 in Box 8.4. How do we calculate the probability that two coins will *both* come down tails? Well, as you can see, we need to multiply the probability of each event occurring by the other. So, the probability of a coin coming down tails is 0.5 (as shown previously). We therefore need to multiply 0.5 by 0.5, which gives us a value of 0.25, and this is the probability of both coins coming down tails. As you can see, this is less likely than one coin coming down tails, as you might expect.

If you want further proof that the 'or' rule given above is correct, look below where we have listed all possible coin-tossing outcomes (with one fair coin):

1st toss	2nd toss
H	H
H	T
T	H
T	T

As you can see, we have two heads coming down on the first toss, a head and a tail on the second toss, a tail and a head on the third toss, and two tails on the fourth toss. There are four possible outcomes and only one of these (the one with two tails) is the correct one. So, the probability of getting two tails is 1 in 4, or:

$$p = 1/4 = 0.25$$

8.4 Levels of significance

Statistical inference and probability

So what does all this discussion of coin tossing, games of cards and probability have to do with the study of statistics? Well, an understanding of probability is crucial for how we identify the effect of an IV on a DV. The guiding principle for making statistical inferences and eliminating the effect of random error is given in Box 8.6. The approach is quite simple but the reverse of what you might expect.

Box 8.6

Information box

Statistical inference and probability

How do we identify the effect of an IV on a DV (from Robson, 1994: 28)?

1 Estimate how probable it is that the random error itself could produce the changes in the dependent variable observed.

▶

Box 8.6 *Continued*

If

2 it seems unlikely that random error by itself could produce these changes

then

3 we decide that it is the independent variable that is having an effect on the dependent variable.

This argument is very important as it underpins much that will come later, so you need to make sure you understand what is going on here.

As you can see from Box 8.6, we do not start by trying to predict the likelihood that change in our dependent variable was caused by our independent variable, as you might expect. Instead, we first look at how likely it is that random error was the cause of the effect observed in the dependent variable. So, we first calculate the probability of the effect occurring through random error and only if this is not likely do we conclude that the effect was probably caused by our independent variable.

How do we decide if random error was the likely cause of the effect we are measuring on our dependent variable? Well, traditionally we look for a significance of 0.05 (the **5 per cent significance level**) or 0.01 (the **1 per cent significance level** – sometimes called 'highly significant'). With a 5 per cent significance level, 5 out of 100 (1 in 20) times the effect we are observing is due to random error and not the independent variable. Therefore, there is a 19 out of 20 chance that our independent variable was the cause of the effect. Similarly, with a 1 per cent significance level, 1 in 100 times the effect we are measuring is caused by random error and not the IV. Therefore, if we obtain a probability of *less than* 0.05 (e.g. 0.04 or 0.01) we say we have a significant effect of our independent variable (IV) on our dependent variable (DV). This is because it is unlikely that the effect we have measured is caused by random error (the chance that it is caused by random error is in fact less than 1 in 20). It is worth remembering, however, that there is nothing magical about these levels of significance. They are actually *arbitrary* cut-off points. They have been determined through years of research but they are not cast-iron guarantees that we do indeed have an experimental effect (and not one that is the result of random error). Do not fall foul of the temptation to believe any finding that is significant at the 5 per cent level and ignore any finding that is not significant at this level. Many psychologists will only consider findings that are significant at the 5 per cent level and will also treat such findings very seriously even if they make little sense. Remember to examine your findings in the context of previous research and theory, and consider how large and how important the results are (see Chapter 6).

Type I and Type II errors

What the above means is that there is only a 1 in 20 chance that we are making a **Type I error** (α) when we have a 0.05 level of significance. A Type I error is where we decide the IV had an effect on the DV when it did not and was caused by random error instead.

There is also the possibility of making a **Type II error** (β) when calculating the statistical significance of events. This is where we conclude that the IV has no effect on the DV when in fact it really is responsible for the change in the dependent variable. This may occur, for instance, if we set our significance level too high (e.g. 0.0001). With such a high level of significance we avoid the risk of a Type I error (where we infer an effect that is really the result of random error) but risk a Type II error instead. As you can see, we need to find a balance between these risks. Too low a level of significance and we risk a Type I error, and too high a level and we risk a Type II error. There is no perfect solution but social scientists generally agree that finding a relationship at the 0.05 level of significance is the best way of balancing these two positions.

8.5	The normal distribution

A measurement value of a continuous variable (such as a person's height or weight) is really the value that falls within a **class interval** rather than an exact measure, because we can always subdivide (in terms of measurement) a continuous variable. So, if someone is measured at 175 cm, what we are really saying is that they are closer to 175 cm than 174 or 176 cm. Technically we are saying that they are in the height class interval 174.5–175.5 cm. This is because we can always measure things (if they are continuous rather than categorical) at a finer level of measurement. If we are measuring the height of people to the nearest centimetre we are really placing people in class intervals 1 cm wide. But we could measure in fractions of centimetres (to two decimal places, for instance) or measure in millimetres and so measure height with greater accuracy than to the nearest centimetre. But it does not need to stop there – we could measure height to 10 decimal places, 100 decimal places and so on. There is no limit (theoretically speaking) to how fine we can actually measure things such as height (though in practice we encounter limits all the time – with how sophisticated our measuring equipment is, for instance). Now, if we measure a large enough random sample of people on height (or psychological variables such as IQ) – or on any number of continuous variables, for that matter – at a fine enough level we get what we call a **normal distribution** of scores. This distribution becomes increasingly apparent the finer the level of measurement and the larger the sample and is called the normal distribution because it is one of the commonest (and most useful – mathematically speaking) possible distributions of scores that we will encounter.

The distribution of scores on a continuous variable in these cases is not therefore random but demonstrates a particular pattern or distribution. What we tend to see if we collect enough data on height is that, for instance, most people are of a similar height (around 177 cm for men and 164 cm for women – falling somewhere in the middle of our distribution of scores). We would find only a very few people who are very short or very tall (at the edges of our distribution). The data are therefore **normally distributed**. If we were to plot the data on a graph (like a histogram) we would find we get a curve that closely approximates to an established mathematical curve known as the **Gaussian distribution**. This is why the normal distribution curve is sometimes (though rarely in the social sciences) called the **Gaussian distribution curve**. This curve can be produced mathematically through a very complex formula (not one we are going to reproduce here or one that needs concern you!). The **normal distribution curve** (see Fig. 8.1) demonstrates a number of important properties that enable us to make predictions about the likely spread of our data which form the basis for how we carry out tests of statistical inference.

As you can see, in Fig. 8.1 we have a normal distribution curve overlaid on a histogram (not much more than a fancy bar chart – this is covered in Chapter 10) of scores between 1 and 19. With finer measurement our bars would become finer and greater in number until they approximated to the normal distribution curve completely (and the bars would seem to disappear under the line of the curve). In the case above we only have 39 pieces of data that are roughly normally distributed. The mean of this set of data is 9.5 and this is where the normal distribution curve peaks. As you can see, it tails off at the edges because there are fewer occurrences at this level. Most scores occur in the middle of the distribution (as we would expect with many continuous variables – such as height, weight or IQ) with fewer scores at the extreme ends of the distribution (left and right). Similarly, if we got 100 people (randomly sampled) to fill in an IQ test we would

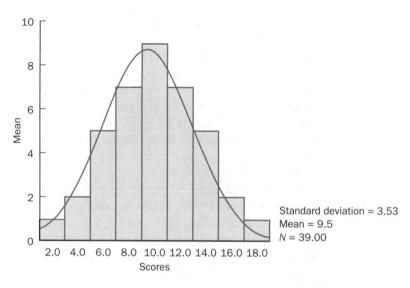

Figure 8.1 Example of a normal distribution curve overlaid on a histogram

expect to see a distribution of scores very similar to that shown in Fig. 8.1. Most people would score around the mean with an IQ of 100. A few would do poorly on the test and score towards 55 while a few people would do very well and score towards 145. What we would get if we drew this set of frequency data as a graph (like the one in Fig. 8.1) is a normal distribution curve.

It is important to remember that *not all* continuous data will be normally distributed. Much that we collect will be and psychologists nearly always try to maximise the chances of the data being normally distributed because many of the statistical tests that we wish to use require the data to be distributed in this manner. If our data are not normally distributed (and do not approximate to this bell-shaped curve) then we may need to use a particular type of statistics called **non-parametric statistics** (more of this below) rather than the more common (and generally more powerful and convenient) statistics known as **parametric statistics**. The alternative is to attempt to transform our data so that they do appear to be normally distributed. Guidance is given on computer transformations of data in Chapter 9. In order to achieve this we need to carry out some mathematical procedure on our data. This may involve squaring our data or taking the root. Other common transformations include taking logarithms or taking the reciprocal (mathematical terms which you should try to put to one side for now).

Characteristics of the normal distribution curve

The normal distribution curve describes what we might expect of our data when we collect a large enough representative sample of scores. However, this is an ideal because we almost never collect all of the possible scores for an entire population but instead rely on samples. In these situations we need to make sure that our sample scores are pretty much normally distributed (unless we have good reason for knowing why they should not be distributed in such a way).

The normal distribution curve is a curve that is symmetrical about the mid-point of the horizontal axis. Furthermore, the point at which it is symmetrical is the point at which the mean, median and mode all fall. The asymptotes (tails) never quite meet the horizontal, and (very usefully for us) when we have a normal distribution curve it is known what area under the curve is contained between the mid-point (mean) and the point where one standard deviation falls. Therefore, using units of one standard deviation you can calculate any area under the curve. The only difference between normal distribution curves is where their mean and standard deviation scores fall. If distributions are **standardised** so that they have the same mean and standard deviations then they will also demonstrate exactly the same distribution shape (see Fig. 8.2).

As you can see in Fig. 8.2, the normal distribution curve is bell-shaped and symmetrical about the mean. That is, the left side of the line (indicating the mean) is identical to the right side of the line. Furthermore, as stated above, the median and mode also occur with the mean at the mid-point of the normal distribution curve. As the curve tails away to the right and left and gets close to the horizontal axis it continues to decrease and approach the axis *asymptotically*.

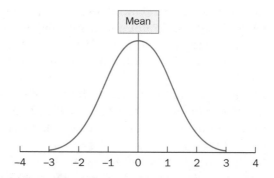

Figure 8.2 The normal distribution curve

That is, it keeps getting closer but never actually touches the horizontal axis. This is because there is a theoretical possibility (no matter how small) of getting values that are infinitely far away from the mean value in a set of scores.

So, the normal distribution curve is one where the mean, median and mode fall at the mid-point. However, there is another vital property of the normal distribution curve concerning the standard deviation. Because the normal distribution has known mathematical properties (known thanks to Gauss and others), we know that if scores are distributed in this standard way then the majority of scores will fall within one standard deviation of the mean (above and below). More precisely, we know that 68.26 per cent of scores will fall within one standard deviation of the mean (above and below). We also know that 95.44 per cent of scores will fall within two standard deviations (see Fig. 8.3) of the mean and 99.73 per cent within three standard deviations.

So we can now return to earlier discussions of IQ scores where the mean was 100. If we have a standard deviation of 15 then we know that 68.26 per cent of scores on our IQ test will be between 85 and 115. Furthermore, we know that 95.44 per cent will fall between 70 and 130 and 99.73 per cent between 55 and 145. As you can see, the probability that someone will score very highly (above 145) or very poorly (below 55) is very low (a probability of less than 0.0013, or 0.13 chance in 100, in fact).

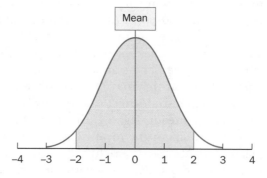

Figure 8.3 Standard deviations and the normal distribution

8.6 Understanding z-scores

If we wish to compare different people on a test or the same person on different tests we may well find it useful to standardise the scores. **Standard scores**, also known as **z-scores**, are produced by using the deviation from the mean in terms of standard deviation units. The formula is quite simple (and consists of familiar elements):

$$z = \frac{x}{\text{SD}}$$

where $x = |X - \bar{X}|$.

As well as standardising individual scores we can use this formula to transform all the scores in a distribution. In these circumstances we say that the distribution is standardised. Tables of the normal distribution are nearly always given in this standardised form. The table of critical values of the normal distribution is given in the Appendix. So, if we have a z-score of 0.5 then the proportion of the curve between this score and the mean (where the z-score = 0) is 0.1915. If the z-score is 1.0 then the area enclosed (under the curve) between the mean and the point at which z = 1.0 is 0.3413 (see Fig. 8.4).

About 34 per cent of the distribution lies between these points in the distribution. As you might expect, the area between z-scores of 1.0 and –1.0 is twice this (as the distribution is symmetrical). Therefore, 68.26 per cent (0.6826) of the distribution falls between z-scores of 1.0 and –1.0. This should be obvious, for this is the same as that given above with one standard deviation around (above and below) the mean. Remember, this table gives values for the standardised normal distribution, which produces predictable values of variation about the mean of a distribution of scores.

Another way of using the normal distribution table is to find the z-scores at which 95 per cent of the scores are contained. This will give us z-scores for a 5 per cent significance level (remember this is the standard for stating that we have a significant effect of an IV on a DV). Luckily, we already know what the z-scores

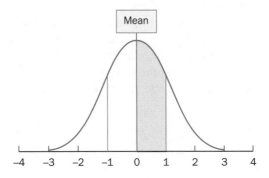

Figure 8.4 Area enclosed by the mean and z = 1.0

are to cover 95 per cent of the distribution. Look up a z-score of 1.96 in the table and you will see the table shows this is equivalent to a value of 0.4750. This indicates that 47.50 per cent of the distribution falls between 1.96 and the mean. Therefore, we know that 95 per cent (2 × 0.4750 = 0.95) is contained between z-scores of –1.96 and +1.96. And we therefore know that 5 per cent of the distribution of scores is beyond these limits. This is particularly useful, for when we have a z-score above 1.96 (positive or negative) we know that we have an effect for our IV on the DV at the 5 per cent level of significance.

What would the z-score need to be for us to have an effect at the 1 per cent level of significance? Have a go at working this out for yourself. If we want to calculate this score we have to round up our scores from the table, but you should find that z-scores of –2.57 and +2.57 contain a little under 99 per cent of the distribution (98.98 per cent, in fact). And a little over 99 per cent (99.02 per cent) is contained by –2.58 and +2.58. Either value would do but 2.58 would be the safer (and more cautious) choice for most purposes.

8.7   Standard error

Imagine we wished to give an IQ test to all students at university in the United Kingdom. We decide to take a sample of 1000 students (randomly selected from universities in the United Kingdom). We would probably expect to find the scores to be normally distributed around the mean (with some students scoring higher and others lower). Let us say that this sample has a mean of 120 (slightly higher than the national average). We then take another random sample of different students using the same sampling strategy. These students complete the same IQ test and once again we find the scores are normally distributed about the mean. However, we now find a mean of 119. If we took sample after sample it is quite likely that we would find all of our distributions to be normally distributed but with slightly different means every time. We would expect variation in mean scores from different samples just like we expect variation in raw scores. If we took enough samples we could produce a **sampling distribution of the means**. If we plotted all our mean scores we would expect to find a very tall and thin distribution as we would not expect a great deal of variation about the mean. In other words, we would expect the standard deviation of a set of mean scores to be considerably less than the standard deviation of a set of raw scores. The standard deviation of a set of means is called the **standard error**. There is a mathematical formula for the relationship between the standard error (SE) of the means and the standard deviation (SD) of the scores:

$$SE = \frac{SD}{\sqrt{N}}$$

where N is the size of the sample (1000 in this case).

8.8	Parametric versus non-parametric tests

As mentioned earlier, if we have data that are normally distributed we are generally able to use **parametric statistical tests**. These are the statistical tests most widely used and include tests such as the *t*-test (Chapter 11) and **analysis of variance** (ANOVA, Chapter 13). In many cases where data do violate the assumptions of parametric tests, we may still be able to use parametric tests, for many of them are extremely **robust** to violations of normality. However, we need to be careful that we do not employ a parametric test with data that are inappropriate since, even if we are able to calculate the test, we may well have findings that are meaningless. There are a number of assumptions that parametric tests rely on. One that should be familiar to you by now concerns the distribution of scores in the set of data. Parametric tests require the data to be pretty much normally distributed. We say pretty much, because data in psychology are rarely perfectly normally distributed and these tests are remarkably robust to violations of this particular assumption. Other assumptions will be addressed later, in Chapter 11, where we introduce some of the most commonly used parametric and non-parametric tests of difference.

One option mentioned earlier in this chapter, for dealing with data that are not normally distributed, is to employ data transformations (such as square or log transformations). These transformations simply require us to perform some mathematical manipulation of our data so that we can appropriately use parametric tests. With particular distributions of data particular mathematical transformations may result in normally distributed data. We will cover this further in Chapter 11, and Howell (in the Further reading section at the end of the chapter) provides superb coverage of this topic.

If, however, we have data that cannot or should not be transformed then we would probably employ a non-parametric statistical test. Some data may be distributed in such a fashion that they cannot be transformed into normally distributed data no matter what mathematical manipulation we try, and some data (such as rank score data) cannot be transformed in this way. Furthermore, there are many times when we may not wish to transform our data (it is controversial in some quarters) and instead choose to use a non-parametric test. There is considerable debate among statisticians and psychologists about the relative merits and demerits of parametric and non-parametric tests. Some statisticians claim we should always use non-parametric tests for they offer greater confidence in our findings if we do not know whether our data are appropriately distributed. They are also much simpler to calculate than parametric tests (this advantage is becoming much less important with the widespread use of statistics software) and can be used with all kinds of data that we are likely to collect. However, most psychologists tend to choose parametric tests in preference to non-parametric tests if the data allow it. This is because parametric tests are generally more **powerful** (see below) than the equivalent non-parametric test. So, for now, always use a parametric test if it is appropriate. If your data violate the assumptions needed to carry out a parametric test then consider transforming your data or employing a non-parametric test instead.

8.9	Statistical power

As we stated earlier, it is important to be aware of the risk of committing a Type I error (that is, finding an effect for an IV that is not there). There is another risk, that of being overcautious and committing a Type II error (not finding an effect when there was one present). A better approach than worrying about the risk of a Type II error is to talk in terms of **statistical power**. Power is defined as the probability of correctly rejecting a false null hypothesis and therefore finding an effect for the experimental hypothesis. Power equals one minus the probability of a Type II error (or mathematically, power = $1 - \beta$). This can be multiplied by 100 to express the value as a percentage (e.g. .80 × 100 = 80% power). Statistical power is affected by four things. They are (1) the probability of a Type I error, (2) the size of the effect, (3) the sample size and (4) the particular test being employed. We will quickly run through a few of these factors but will not engage with the mathematics of power calculations in this text. If you wish to explore these issues in more detail then we recommend you read the appropriate section in Howell (see Further reading below). The first factor should be rather obvious. If we increase the risk of a Type I error (α) then we decrease the probability of a Type II error (β) and therefore increase the statistical power of the test. The second factor is again fairly obvious. If we have an experimental design that will demonstrate a large effect, it will be easier to detect than one with a small effect. That is, the chances of finding a difference depend on how large the difference actually is. The third factor is perhaps the most important, and the one we can most easily manipulate to increase the power of a test. In brief, power is increased by increasing the sample size.

How many participants do you need?

There are formulae that enable us to calculate how large a sample size needs to be with a particular set of data and particular test to ensure a minimum level of statistical power (Howell provides details). A word of warning is needed here. While it is true that increasing the sample size increases the power of a test (and we want tests to be as powerful as possible), we always have to work within a particular resource limit. In reality, sample size for many projects is governed by time constraints, resources, and the number of volunteers that could be found. It is possible to calculate the sample size needed if you know the expected effect size and the level of alpha. When designing a fairly complicated experiment, with several variables, researchers often seek professional advice from a statistician or use particular software packages designed to tell them how much data they will need to collect. For students, this is often not practical. Support may not be available and software may be expensive or difficult to learn. When data has not been collected yet, calculating statistical power can be difficult. Using broad guidelines about sample size (rules of thumb) are no substitute for a proper sample size calculation. However, they do allow you to demonstrate that you have at least thought about statistical power, and can provide an approximate sample size to aim for.

Further reading

Howell, D. C. (2006). *Statistical Methods for Psychology*, International edn. Belmont, CA: Duxbury Press.

An excellent text that provides superb coverage of most statistical tests needed by psychologists and the mathematics behind such tests. Particularly notable for the good coverage of statistical transformations and statistical power calculations. This book will be recommended again and again but be warned – it does require you to engage with the mathematics underlying statistics in psychology and provides no information on the use of statistics software (such as SPSS) to carry out tests.

9 Entering and manipulating data

- This chapter begins by introducing the statistics software package SPSS.

- It then demonstrates how to enter and manipulate data within SPSS.

INTRODUCTION

This chapter, and the next six, introduce the use of the statistics package SPSS. In addition, these chapters provide further explanation and some mathematical detail (in boxes) of the particular statistical techniques being demonstrated. It is hoped that this combination should provide sufficient information for you to conduct your own statistical analyses while not overwhelming you with complex formulae. Suggestions are given at the end of Chapter 15 on further reading if you want to know more about the mathematical underpinnings of the techniques being demonstrated here or want to carry out techniques not covered here. However, the content in the next six chapters should provide enough for most undergraduate students beginning to get to grips with statistics and the analysis of data using SPSS.

SPSS (originally, though no longer, meaning Statistics Package for the Social Sciences) is an extremely powerful piece of statistics software marketed by SPSS Inc. SPSS has existed for over 30 years and is regularly updated with new versions. At the time we wrote this book, the highest version number available was 16.0. You may find that you only have access to a previous version (e.g. version 15). However, there were only minor changes made to SPSS between versions 15 and 16. The only markedly different feature added was the new **chart builder**, which replaced the need to have a separate menu option for every kind of chart (e.g. bars, scatterplots). You should be able to use any recent version reasonably confidently, once you have mastered the basics outlined in this chapter.

SPSS is the leading statistics package used by social scientists in the United Kingdom and United States. Most, if not all, psychology courses in the United Kingdom and United States will therefore include instruction in the use of this particular piece of software. It is not the only statistics software available, however, and there are some very good competitors (e.g. Mplus, SAS, STATA, R) that offer distinct advantages when conducting certain forms of analysis. The good news is that once you have learnt to use one package, learning to use others, should you need to, becomes simpler. The latest versions of SPSS run only on PCs (earlier versions ran on both PCs and Macintosh computers) and require a PC with Pentium processor running Windows (XP or Vista) with 512 MB of RAM and 450 MB of hard disk space. Most modern PCs fulfil these requirements easily and can therefore run SPSS without difficulty.

Statistics software such as SPSS has taken much of the hard work out of statistics by doing the maths for you. No longer do researchers have to sit with a calculator and work through formula after formula. Most statistical analyses now consist of just a few clicks of the computer mouse and out pop the results. This does not mean that your analysis is done entirely for you. The researcher still needs to get the data into the computer in an appropriate form, know which tests are appropriate for the data and interpret the often confusing results that are spewed out. In addition, some knowledge of the maths underlying statistical tests can protect the researcher from carrying out meaningless tests of their data. SPSS will occasionally issue a warning that the data are not appropriate for the test you ask it to carry out. However, more often it will not and if you do not know what you are doing you can produce results that are absolutely meaningless (Garbage In Garbage Out, or GIGO, is the key phrase here). So, the things all students need to learn about statistics are:

■ how to enter data appropriately in SPSS;
■ how to manipulate data in SPSS;
■ which tests are needed to analyse the data;
■ the assumptions of the tests being conducted (which may include understanding of the maths underpinning the statistic);
■ how to conduct tests using SPSS;
■ the meaning of results produced by SPSS.

This and the next six chapters address all six aspects of learning statistics using SPSS.

9.1 First steps with SPSS

There are essentially three stages in any analysis of data using a statistics package such as SPSS. You first of all need to get your data into the computer in an appropriate form. Then you need to click the appropriate buttons so that SPSS conducts the statistical test you want. Finally, you need to inspect and interpret the output (your results) produced by SPSS. Like any software package, there is quite a steep learning curve but, once you have mastered the basics, the operation becomes incredibly simple and any statistical test you wish to carry out is easily within your grasp.

The next six chapters include details of what 'buttons' you need to click to carry out the tasks you want. All commands given to the computer are through the keyboard or mouse. These days most software is designed to be operated principally through clicks of the mouse. SPSS is no different and once you have input your data (through the keyboard) you will find that most controls are simply a matter of clicking the mouse in the appropriate place. Command instructions in this text will be given in **bold**. If a list of command instructions is needed (for instance to carry out a particular statistical test in SPSS) then these will be given in a **command box**. Always remember that you cannot break the software. Yes, it can crash (seize up and stop working), but all software can do this. The worst that will happen is that you lose the analysis you were conducting. Once the computer is shut down and restarted things will return to normal. You need to have a spirit of adventure with SPSS and try things for yourself. This way you will gain confidence handling the software and be better able to tackle new problems when they head your way.

The first step is to open the software package so you can use it. With your PC (running the Windows operating system – which most do) switched on you should be faced with a screen something like Fig. 9.1 (your background may look different and you may have different icons on the screen but the basic format should be the same).

Now click (using the left mouse button unless told otherwise) on **Start** at the bottom left of the screen. This will produce a 'pop-up menu' where you should click on **Programs**. Here you will see 'SPSS for Windows' listed (providing you have SPSS installed on your computer). Click on these words and after a few seconds

Figure 9.1 Windows Start Screen reprinted by permission from Microsoft Corporation

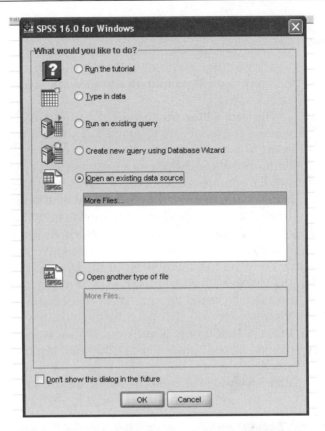

Figure 9.2 Initial SPSS dialogue box. SPSS screenshots reproduced courtesy of SPSS (UK) Ltd.

(and this can be quite a few seconds depending on the speed of your computer) SPSS should have opened on your computer (you may have another menu with 'SPSS 16.0 for Windows' listed – if so you should click on this to start the program). When installing the program you (or the person who installed the software if it was not you) may have chosen the option to have an icon (a small pictorial representation of the software) included on your desktop. If that is the case you do not need to use the **Start** button but can simply double-click (two clicks of the left mouse button, one immediately after the other) this icon and the program will start.

SPSS always starts with a dialogue box offering a number of options (unless you click in the box next to the phrase 'Don't show this dialog box in future'). The options are to **Run the tutorial**, **Type in data**, **Run an existing query**, **Create new query using Database Wizard**, **Open an existing data source** and **Open another type of file** (see Fig. 9.2).

If you wish to enter data from some research you have conducted then you should click next to **Type in data** (and you will see a black dot appear) and then click on **OK**. If you wish to open an existing data file, first click next to **Open an existing data source**, then click on the file you want to open in the list below and then click on **OK**. Alternatively, if you want to run the tutorial, click on that (you need not worry about the query aspect of SPSS). It is a very good idea to run the tutorial if you have time.

The Data Editor window

If you click on **Type in data** and then **OK** you will see the **Data Editor** window in SPSS (see Fig. 9.3).

The Data Editor window is the core of SPSS (along with the **Viewer** window where your results are displayed) as you can command the software from this point. There are other windows in SPSS (such as the **Syntax** window) but the Data Editor and Viewer windows are the two most important for you now. There is a list of menu options along the top (File, Edit, View, etc.), a row of command buttons beneath this menu bar (which we shall ignore for now) and a row of column labels (Name, Type, Width, etc.) beneath this. The data sheet proper is below these rows and looks like a spreadsheet with **cells** (boxes) where you can include information about your variables and cases and type in the data themselves.

There are two main views in the Data Editing window: the **Data View** and the **Variable View**. You can toggle (switch) between these two views by clicking on the tabs in the bottom left of the screen labelled **Data View** and **Variable View** (see Fig. 9.4). The tab is highlighted in white when selected (Variable View in Fig. 9.4). It is only when Variable View is selected that you will see the row of column labels (Name, Type, Width, etc.) displayed. For it is in this window that you define your variables (that is, give them a name, define what type they are, state how wide the columns should be and so on). When Data View is selected

Figure 9.3 The Data Editor window

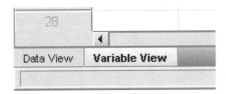

Figure 9.4 Switching between views

you get a screen where you can directly enter your data. Each *row* of cells *represents a case* which is normally one person (but may be the responses of a rat or pigeon instead). And each *column represents a variable* (the person's sex, age, responses to a questionnaire item and so on). On the other hand, when Variable View is selected each row represents a different variable and each column some attribute of that particular variable.

9.3   Defining variables

In SPSS you need to use the Variable View window to define your variables (see Fig. 9.5 for an example of a SPSS data sheet with defined variables). There are ten attributes that SPSS requires information on:

IRMDA_SPSS_Data.sav [DataSet1] - SPSS Data Editor

File   Edit   View   Data   Transform   Analyze   Graphs   Utilities   Add-ons   Window   Help

	Name	Type	Width	Decimals	Label	Values	Missing	Columns	Align	Measure
1	gender	Numeric	8	2	What is your g...	{1.00, male}...	6.00	8	Right	Ordinal
2	age	Numeric	8	2	What is your a...	None	None	8	Right	Scale
3	ethnic	Numeric	8	2	What is your et...	{1.00, Cauc...	None	8	Right	Ordinal
4	pathway	Numeric	8	2	Which pathway...	{1.00, Psyc...	None	8	Right	Ordinal
5	awaydiff	Numeric	8	2	Diff rating - livin...	{1.00, 1}...	6.00	8	Right	Ordinal
6	halldiff	Numeric	8	2	Diff rating - livin...	{1.00, 1}...	6.00	8	Right	Ordinal
7	citydiff	Numeric	8	2	Diff rating - livin...	{1.00, 1}...	6.00	8	Right	Ordinal
8	contdiff	Numeric	8	2	Diff rating - cont...	{1.00, 1}...	6.00	8	Right	Ordinal
9	workdiff	Numeric	8	2	Diff rating - wor...	{1.00, 1}...	6.00	8	Right	Ordinal
10	strucdif	Numeric	8	2	Diff rating - stru...	{1.00, 1}...	6.00	8	Right	Ordinal
11	socidiff	Numeric	8	2	Diff rating - ada...	{1.00, 1}...	6.00	8	Right	Ordinal
12	commdiff	Numeric	8	2	Diff ratings - oth...	{1.00, 1}...	6.00	8	Right	Ordinal
13	findiff	Numeric	8	2	Diff rating - fina...	{1.00, 1}...	6.00	8	Right	Ordinal
14	persdiff	Numeric	8	2	Diff rating - pers...	{1.00, 1}...	6.00	8	Right	Ordinal
15	family	Numeric	8	2	Family - have/w...	{1.00, Have ...	None	8	Right	Ordinal
16	ratefam	Numeric	8	2	How do you rat...	None	None	8	Right	Ordinal
17	friends	Numeric	8	2	Friends - have/...	{1.00, Have ...	None	8	Right	Ordinal
18	ratefrie	Numeric	8	2	How do you rat...	None	None	8	Right	Ordinal
19	doctor	Numeric	8	2	Doctor - Have/w...	{1.00, Have ...	None	8	Right	Ordinal
20	visitdoc	Numeric	8	2	Number of visit...	{1.00, Once...	None	8	Right	Scale
21	ratedoct	Numeric	8	2	How do you rat...	None	None	8	Right	Ordinal
22	tutors	Numeric	8	2	Tutors - have/w...	{1.00, Have ...	None	8	Right	Ordinal
23	ratetuto	Numeric	8	2	How do you rat...	None	None	8	Right	Ordinal
24	welfserv	Numeric	8	2	Welfare Service...	{1.00, Have ...	None	8	Right	Ordinal
25	ratewelf	Numeric	8	2	Welfare service...	None	None	8	Right	Ordinal
26	counsell	Numeric	8	2	Counselling - ...	{1.00, Have ...	None	8	Right	Ordinal
27	ratecoun	Numeric	8	2	Counselling - h...	None	None	8	Right	Ordinal
28	intcont	Numeric	8	2	Intention to con...	{1.00, Stron...	6.00	8	Right	Scale

Data View   **Variable View**

SPSS Processor is ready

Figure 9.5 The Variable View window

- Name
- Type
- Width
- Decimals
- Label
- Values
- Missing
- Columns
- Align
- Measure

Some of these are very important attributes but others are merely information about formatting your data (that is, how they will appear in SPSS). However, each of these will be discussed in turn below.

Name

Every variable must be given a name (although SPSS will provide default names). Names must be eight characters or fewer long and consist of letters or numbers (or both). They cannot contain punctuation or spaces. Just click on the cell and type the variable name in.

Type

If you click in a cell in the Type column a small grey box will appear on the right-hand side of the word (Numeric is the default). If you click on this grey box an options box will appear where you can define the type of variable that you wish to enter. Most of the time you can leave the default **Numeric** selected. If your variable should contain numbers then Numeric is the correct definition (you can change the required number of decimal places here too). If you wished to input words then you would select **String**. You probably will not need to use this feature, because most string data is coded as numeric before it is entered into SPSS. However, we have found it useful for storing data that sometimes contains letters, such as anonymous identifying codes (e.g. M01HA). There are a few more options, but these are rarely used in social science research.

Width

This tells the computer the maximum number of characters you will be entering in each cell. The default is eight, which is usually sufficient unless you plan to input extremely long numbers or string data.

Decimals

This attribute allows you to define the number of decimal places to be shown in each column of data. Clicking on the cell in the Variable View will bring up an up and down arrow which enables you to change the setting.

Label

You can use the label attribute to give your variables more meaningful names (there is only so much you can do with eight characters in the variable name!). Simply type further explanatory words/phrases into the appropriate cell.

Values

This attribute is designed to allow you to give labels to categorical data. So, for instance, if you had a variable 'sex' consisting of 'men' and 'women' you could attach a number to each category (1 = male and 2 = female). When you enter data you might enter 1 for male and 2 for female. Similarly, you may have a five-point scale in a questionnaire from 'strongly agree' to 'strongly disagree'. Each of the five response options can be labelled (as 1 = strongly agree, 2 = agree, 3 = unsure, 4 = disagree, 5 = strongly disagree). Clicking in a value cell brings up a small grey box, which enables you to define the values for your data.

Missing

It is important where you have missing data that this is indicated clearly within SPSS. So, for instance, if items were left unanswered in a questionnaire then instead of not entering any data at all, a specific value is given to indicate that the data are missing. It is common practice to use 9 or 99 as the missing value. However, this number must not be a value that could be scored on that variable. The **range plus one** technique involves assigning a missing data value that is one value higher than the highest possible score for that variable. For example, if the variable was a Likert scale ranging from 1 to 7, you could assign missing data as 8. It is easiest if you only have one value for missing data throughout your data. For this reason you may need to use a value such as –1 or 999 instead of 9 or 99. If you do not specify a value for missing data you will see a small black dot in the empty data cell where you did not enter data.

So, for instance, if you have a questionnaire that includes the age, sex and responses of participants to five-, seven- and nine-point Likert scales then you might choose 99 as your missing value (as long as you do not have any participants who are 99 years of age!). Every time you get a missing response to an item in your questionnaire you enter 99. Clicking on a cell (in variable view) brings up the small grey box which you can click on to bring up an options box where you can specify the missing value you want.

Columns

This attribute allows you to specify the width of a column that is to be displayed on screen (remember, the Width attribute concerns the *maximum* number of characters that may be input). Clicking on a cell brings up the up and down arrows where you can change the default setting for the width of a column displayed on the screen.

Align

You can align text within cells to the left, right or centre of the column. Clicking on a cell in the Align column brings up a drop-down menu with the three options that can be selected.

Measure

This attribute concerns the measurement level of the variable (see Chapter 2). There are three options available (on a drop-down menu when you click in a cell) in SPSS: nominal, ordinal and scale. These three options correspond to the measurement levels outlined in Chapter 2, as follows:

- **Scale**: data values are numeric values on an interval or ratio scale (e.g. age, income). Scale variables must be numeric.
- **Ordinal**: data values represent categories with some intrinsic order (e.g. strongly agree, agree, unsure, disagree, strongly disagree). Ordinal variables can be either string or numeric values that represent distinct categories (e.g. 1 = low, 2 = medium, 3 = high).
- **Nominal**: data values represent categories with no intrinsic order (e.g. sex or ethnicity). Nominal variables can be either string or numeric values that represent distinct categories (e.g. 1 = male, 2 = female).

9.4 Entering data

Once you have defined your variables in the Variable View window you can then proceed to enter your data using the Data View window. See Fig. 9.6 for an example of the Data View containing data that have been entered. Remember, each column in the Data View represents one of your variables while each row represents a case (one of your participants) – all the rows are numbered on the left by SPSS. All you need to do to enter your data is to click on a cell and type in the number you wish. This process can be speeded up by using the arrow keys to move around the data sheet (or the 'Tab' key to move from one cell to another to the right) instead of using the mouse.

	gender	age	ethnic	pathway	awaydiff	halldiff	citydiff	contdiff	workdiff	strucdif	socidiff	commdiff	findiff	persdiff
1	2.00	22.00	1.00	1.00	6.00	6.00		3.00	2.00	3.00	4.00	2.00	1.00	
2	2.00	21.00	1.00	3.00	3.00	3.00	2.00	3.00	4.00		2.00	5.00	2.00	3.00
3	2.00	20.00	1.00	1.00	2.00	3.00	1.00	3.00	3.00	2.00	2.00	1.00	1.00	2.00
4	2.00	19.00	1.00	1.00	3.00	2.00	4.00	2.00	2.00	3.00	2.00	2.00	1.00	2.00
5	1.00	19.00	1.00	1.00	6.00	6.00	6.00	4.00	4.00	2.00	1.00	1.00	1.00	2.00
6	2.00	19.00	1.00	1.00	2.00	5.00	1.00	2.00	4.00	1.00	1.00	5.00	1.00	2.00
7	2.00	20.00	1.00	1.00	6.00	6.00	6.00	3.00	3.00	2.00	1.00	2.00	2.00	3.00
8	1.00	18.00	1.00	4.00	2.00	3.00	3.00	2.00	3.00	4.00	1.00	2.00	2.00	5.00
9	2.00	22.00	1.00	1.00	6.00	6.00	6.00	3.00	2.00	4.00	2.00	2.00	1.00	2.00
10	2.00	19.00	1.00	1.00	6.00	6.00	2.00	3.00	3.00	2.00	2.00	3.00	2.00	3.00
11	2.00	18.00	1.00	1.00	6.00	6.00	6.00	3.00	3.00	4.00	2.00	4.00	2.00	3.00
12	2.00	32.00	1.00	4.00	6.00	6.00	6.00	2.00	2.00	2.00	6.00	1.00	1.00	1.00
13	2.00	42.00	1.00	1.00	6.00	6.00	6.00	2.00	2.00	4.00	6.00	1.00	1.00	1.00
14	2.00	20.00	1.00	3.00	3.00	3.00	3.00	3.00	3.00	2.00	2.00	4.00	1.00	2.00
15	2.00	20.00	3.00	3.00	6.00	6.00	6.00	3.00	1.00	4.00	6.00	1.00	1.00	1.00
16	2.00	18.00	1.00	1.00	2.00	3.00	1.00	4.00	3.00	1.00	3.00	5.00	4.00	2.00
17	2.00	19.00	1.00	1.00	6.00	6.00	6.00	4.00	3.00	3.00	2.00	3.00	2.00	3.00
18	2.00	22.00	1.00	3.00	3.00	3.00	6.00	3.00	2.00	2.00	2.00	2.00	1.00	3.00
19	1.00	23.00	1.00	3.00	4.00	3.00	2.00	2.00	2.00	3.00	2.00	4.00	4.00	3.00
20	2.00	18.00	1.00	1.00	6.00	6.00	6.00	3.00	3.00	4.00	5.00	4.00	4.00	3.00
21	1.00	33.00	6.00	6.00	6.00	6.00	4.00	3.00	4.00	2.00	2.00	4.00	2.00	4.00
22	2.00	18.00	1.00	1.00	2.00	5.00	4.00	3.00	3.00	3.00	1.00	4.00	4.00	1.00
23	2.00	19.00	2.00	3.00	6.00	6.00	6.00	2.00	2.00			6.00	6.00	6.00
24	2.00	29.00	1.00	3.00	6.00	6.00	4.00	3.00	3.00	3.00	6.00	2.00	1.00	3.00
25	2.00	28.00	1.00	5.00	6.00	6.00	6.00	3.00	1.00	3.00	5.00	1.00	3.00	1.00
26	2.00	18.00	1.00	1.00	2.00	4.00	2.00	3.00	4.00	4.00	3.00	5.00	4.00	3.00

Figure 9.6 The Data View window

9.5   Saving and opening data files

It is absolutely vital that you save your data regularly. If you do not you will regret it. Computers crash on a reasonably frequent basis and if this happens when you have not saved your data then you will lose that material. So, get into the habit of saving at every opportunity. It is very easy to save your data in SPSS. Just click on **File** at the top left of the screen and then select **Save** or **Save As** from this menu. This will bring up the usual Windows save option box. You can also save a file using the keyboard shortcut 'Ctrl + S' – hold down the 'Ctrl' and 'S' keys simultaneously. You should also be careful to back up your data, especially if the project is large. Floppy disks often corrupt (especially if old and well used) and you can lose all your data. Even memory sticks and hard disks can fail (though much less often than floppy disks) so make sure you have your data stored in more than one place.

9.6   Sorting and splitting files

When analysing your data you may well wish to manipulate your data in various ways. You may wish to select only women from your sample or modify a variable so it has only two categories instead of three, and so on. SPSS has a number of functions that enable you to manipulate your data. Many of these functions will seem decidedly dull at the moment but you will almost certainly need to come back to this section when you get into the process of data analysis proper.

Sorting data

When data are entered into SPSS it is not normally important which participants' data are entered first (all women and then all men, for instance). Most of the time it is acceptable to enter each participant's data in turn. However, you may wish to sort your data into some meaningful order and SPSS has a number of procedures to enable you to do this. So, for instance, let us say you wished to arrange your data with women first and men second. The instructions for this task are given in Box 9.1.

Box 9.1

Command box	Sorting data

1   Click on **Data** on the top menu bar.

2   Click on **Sort Cases** on the drop-down menu. This will bring up an 'options box' where you can select the variable/s you wish to sort your data by (see Fig. 9.7).

Figure 9.7 Sorting data

3   Click on the variable you want to sort your data by (gender is highlighted here) and then click on the **Variable Picker** button to the right (see Fig. 9.8) to select your variable. When you click on the Variable

Box 9.1 *Continued*

Picker button you will see the variable you selected appear in the empty white box on the right. If you want to remove this item then you just click on the Variable Picker button again (which is now pointing in the opposite direction).

Figure 9.8 The Variable Picker button

4   Decide whether you want to sort your data in ascending (by increasing numbers) or descending (decreasing numbers) order. Here we have men coded as 1 and women as 2 but we want women sorted first so we need to pick descending order. If we wanted men first we would pick ascending order. So, click on the descending order button and then **OK**. The data are now sorted into all women first and then all men in the data sheet.

Splitting files

SPSS allows you to split files into groups. This produces output in any subsequent analysis that is organised according to these groups. So, if you split your data into two groups for men and women all your statistics following this split will be presented separately for men and women. This is very useful if, for instance, you are interested in analysing the data separately for men and women but want to carry out the statistics commands only once. See Box 9.2 for information on conducting this operation.

Box 9.2

Command box	Splitting a file

1   Click on **Data** on the top menu bar.

2   Click on **Split File** on the drop-down menu. This will bring up an 'options box' where you can select the variable you wish to organise your output by and whether you wish to organise the output by groups or compare groups (try both selections and look at the differences in output).

3   Click on the variable you want to split your data by and then click on the **Variable Picker** button to the right to select your variable and then click **OK**. All your output will now be organised by the group you selected.

9.7 Selecting cases

An alternative to splitting a file so that all results are organised by the grouping variable is simply to select only those cases with particular values on a variable (so you could select only men, a value of 1, or only people scoring highly, values of 4 and 5 on a scale, for instance). The **Select Cases** function allows you to analyse a subgroup of cases. If you select cases SPSS will suppress those that you do not select. See Box 9.3 for details of how to select cases in SPSS.

Box 9.3

Command box | **Selecting cases**

1 Click on **Data** on the top menu bar.

Figure 9.9 Selecting cases 1

Box 9.3 *Continued*

2   Click on **Select Cases** on the drop-down menu. This will bring up an 'options box' (see Fig. 9.9) where you can choose on what basis to select your cases. Select the **If condition is satisfied** option and click on **If**. This will bring up another box where you can specify the grouping variable and the value (or values) that will be selected (see Fig. 9.10). In Fig. 9.10 you can see we have selected gender using the Variable Picker button and then selected the 'equals' symbol and the value 1. This means we have selected for gender = 1 (i.e. men in our sample).

Figure 9.10 Selecting cases 2

3   Click **Continue** to return to the previous option box (but now with gender = 1 specified) and then click **OK**. All your analyses will now be conducted on men only (as that was what we specified).

There are a number of points to make about selecting cases in SPSS. Firstly, there are a whole host of options to explore. You can select using logical operators (AND, OR, NOT) as well as simple mathematical functions (such as 'equals' or 'less than'). There is also a very extensive list of functions available as options in the 'Select Cases: If' window. These include functions such as **MEAN** (which will take the mean of the variables included) or **LN** (which will take the natural logarithm of the variable) and many more. Secondly, when using the **Select Cases** function it is important that you check that the **Unselected Cases Are Filtered** option is selected. The alternative is that unselected cases should be deleted. This can be dangerous, for if you permanently delete the unselected cases and then save your data you will lose those cases (that were not selected) permanently from your data file (unless you kept a back-up, of course). Thirdly, you must remember to switch the Select Cases function off when you want to analyse the whole data set again. It will stay on unless you return to **Data** and then **Select Cases** and click on the button next to **All cases** and then **OK**. Finally, you will see that there are four possible options for selecting cases. The **If** selection method (described above) is the most common method but you can also select a **Random sample of cases** or cases **Based on time or case range** (so the first 50 cases, for instance), or **Use filter variable** if you want to select cases where the value of the chosen variable is not zero (useful where you have 0 and 1 scores).

9.8	Recoding variables

It is often necessary to recode your variables to carry out particular forms of analysis. For instance, we sometimes need to collapse categories if there are too few responses on our existing categories. Or we might wish to reverse the values on a scale (so high values indicate a positive response). There are two main recoding options in SPSS. We can **recode** our variables into the **same variables** or **different variables**. The safest option is to recode your variables into different variables so you preserve your original values. See Box 9.4 for details of how to recode your variables.

Box 9.4

Command box	Recoding variables

1   Click on **Transform** on the top menu bar.

2   Click on **Recode** on the drop-down menu and either **Into Same Variables** or **Into Different Variables**. This will bring up an 'options box' (see Fig. 9.11).

3   Select which variable you wish to recode and use the **Variable Picker** button to move this into the white box ('intcont' here).

4   Type in a new name for the variable (if recoding into a different variable) to **Name** under the Output Variable section. You can also give more information about this variable under **Label**. Now click on **Change** and you will see the new variable name appear to the left in the white box.

▶

Box 9.4 *Continued*

Figure 9.11 Recoding into different variables

5   Click on **Old and New Values**. This brings up another options box where you can specify the old values and the new values (see Fig. 9.12). Here you input an old value (e.g. 1) on the left-hand side where it states **Old Value** and then the new value you want to recode it into on the right-hand side where it states **New Value** (e.g. 5). Then click **Add** to move the recode into the white box. You can include as many recodes for each variable as you want here.

Figure 9.12 Recoding old into new values

6   When you have included as many old and new values as you want, click on **Continue**. This returns you to the previous window where you can click **OK** to recode your data.

There are a number of other options you can select when recoding your data. You can choose to recode a range of data, which can be very useful if, for instance, you wish to recode a continuous variable such as age into a categorical variable (e.g. 'old' and 'young'). You can also choose to recode missing values if you wish. The option also exists to perform a **conditional recode**. This is where you specify that a variable should be recoded only <u>If</u> a particular condition is satisfied for that participant. You can perform a conditional recode by clicking on the <u>If</u> button.

9.9	Computing new variables

There are occasions when we need to calculate a new variable based on the values of existing variables. A common situation is where you need to take the mean of a number of existing variables to create a new overall variable. This is quite often necessary in questionnaire research where we have multiple items measuring one psychological concept. If you think back to Chapter 5, this is where we scale our data. It is a relatively simple matter to compute a new variable in SPSS. See Box 9.5 for instructions on computing new variables.

Box 9.5

Command box	Computing new variables

1 Click on <u>T</u>ransform on the top menu bar.

2 Click on **Compute...** on the drop-down menu. This will bring up an 'options box' (see Fig. 9.13) where you can choose what computational function you wish to perform on your variable(s). If you look at Fig. 9.13 you can see we have called the new variable 'Scale' (you have to type in your new variable name). We have also selected **Mean** from the mathematical functions available (select the function you want and use the **Variable Picker** button to move it to the white box). You can then select the variables you want to take the mean of (in this case 'ratecoun' and 'counsell').

3 Click **OK** to compute your new variable.

▶

Box 9.5 *Continued*

Figure 9.13 Computing new variables

You can obviously use the **Compute** function to carry out any number of mathematical functions. You can add or multiply variables together, take the logarithm and so on. The list is virtually endless. We would recommend you get your hands on a data set (SPSS has several that come free with the software or use the one provided on the Companion Website to this book) and just play around recoding and computing new variables – see what fun you can have!

Further reading

Kinnear, P.R. & Gray, C.D. (2008). *SPSS 16 Made Simple*. Hove: Psychology Press Ltd.

This book provides more detail on the functionality of SPSS version 16. It covers a wide range of statistical techniques.

10 Graphical representation and descriptive statistics

- This chapter begins by showing you how to use SPSS to produce descriptive statistics from your data.

- The chapter then demonstrates how to produce a variety of graphs and charts within SPSS, using the Chart Builder.

INTRODUCTION

The fundamentals of descriptive statistics have already been presented in Chapter 8 so there is no need for much discussion here. Instead, the focus in this chapter will be on demonstrating how easy it is to get any descriptive statistics you might want using SPSS. After demonstrating how to produce descriptive statistics in SPSS the chapter moves on to show how you can use SPSS to produce a wide variety of graphs and charts.

Graphical representation (showing your results in pictorial form) can be a very useful way of summarising your findings. Graphs are particularly good at giving an overview of the distribution and frequency of scores in a set of values. When shown how to produce graphs there is a tendency among students to overuse them, so be careful. Graphs may be aethestically pleasing but that does not mean they should be included in every results section you write! Tables are simpler and used more often and provide a particularly effective way of summarising one's results. A wide variety of graphs is used in the social sciences and this chapter will introduce some of the most important types. Different types of graphs fulfil different needs. For instance, a bar chart or histogram may be the most effective way of describing the distribution of scores where the data are categorical. However, if you want to look at whether there is an association between two variables you will probably want to produce a scattergram instead. In each of the sections below the major use of the particular graph will be explained and then detail will be given on how to produce that graph using SPSS.

▶

The data being used in this and some of the following chapters stem from some basic research conducted on student attrition (drop-out) at a fictional university.[1] The study was designed to survey first year university students and identify their views about the course they were on, any problems they might be facing (personal, financial, etc.), what they felt about the pastoral tutor system, and how these factors impacted on whether they intended to continue with the course or not. A self-completion questionnaire was constructed consisting of a series of five-point Likert scales designed to measure these factors. In addition, the questionnaire collected information about age, sex, ethnicity, course as well as their motivation to study (by using a newly devised test with scores from 0 to 60 – low scores indicate poor motivation while high scores indicate high motivation). From a total of 150 students in the year, 120 students returned their questionnaires (a good return rate of 80 per cent).

10.1   Descriptive statistics

There are a number of ways of obtaining descriptive statistics within SPSS. They are, for instance, often available when requesting inferential statistics. This is because it is always important to look at descriptive statistics first, in any kind of analysis. There are, however, some specific commands designed to produce 'stand-alone' descriptive statistics within SPSS, which will be covered here.

Frequency distributions, measures of central tendency and dispersion

The **Frequencies** command produces frequency tables which show the number of cases with a particular score on each variable selected and also other descriptive statistics if the appropriate options are selected. See Box 10.1 for information on obtaining descriptive statistics using the **Frequencies** command.

Box 10.1

Command box   Obtaining frequencies

1   Click on **Analyze** on the top menu bar.

2   Click on **Descriptive Statistics**.

---

[1] The study and data are fictional but based on some research conducted in our department on this issue.

Box 10.1 *Continued*

3   Click on **Frequencies** (see Fig. 10.1). This will produce the **Frequencies** dialogue box (see Fig. 10.2).

Figure 10.1 Obtaining frequencies output

Figure 10.2 Frequencies dialogue box

Box 10.1 *Continued*

4 Select the variable (or variables – you can select as many as you like) you want descriptive statistics for by highlighting the name of the variable (e.g. 'age' and 'gender') and using the **Variable Picker** button to move it into the **Variable(s)** box.

5 Click on the **Statistics** button to open the **Frequencies: Statistics** dialogue box (see Fig. 10.3). We have selected statistics for **Central Tendency** (mean, median) and **Dispersion** (standard deviation, minimum and maximum values). These are only meaningful for continuous variables (e.g. age), so remember to ignore these values for categorical variables (e.g. gender).

Figure 10.3 Frequencies: Statistics dialogue box

6 Once you have selected what statistics you want, click **Continue** to return to the **Frequencies** dialogue box.

7 Click **OK** to action your commands.

Once step 7 has been completed SPSS will produce the **Viewer** window which displays your results (see Fig. 10.4). You can alter the way the output appears in this window by clicking on the **Format** button in the **Frequencies** dialogue box. Try changing these settings to see which output format you prefer.

There are two parts to the Viewer window. The left-hand window acts in a fairly typical way to allow you to navigate your way through your output. If you click on a heading or subheading SPSS will take you to that part of the output in

→ **Frequencies**

Statistics

		What is your age?	What is your gender?
N	Valid	119	120
	Missing	1	0
Mean		22.9580	1.7417
Median		19.0000	2.0000
Std. Deviation		8.11715	.43955
Minimum		18.00	1.00
Maximum		52.00	2.00

Figure 10.4 The Viewer window

the right-hand window (where your results are displayed in a series of tables). The first table (titled 'Statistics') is (not surprisingly) where the statistics selected are displayed. The table starts by providing information about the number of cases (N), including details of any that are missing. These values are followed by values for the mean, median, standard deviation, minimum and maximum (if we had selected other options such as the mode, these too would appear here). For continuous variables, we want to know *how much* of a quantity exists. We can see that the mean age is 22.96 (SD = 8.12), ranging from 18 to 52. Measures of central tendency (e.g. mean, median) and dispersion (e.g. standard deviation) are not meaningful for categorical variables. It is not meaningful to say that the mean gender is 1.74. This illustrates an important learning point for using SPSS. It is an unthinking machine, automatically performing tasks that you ask it to perform. You must decide which variables are categorical and which are continuous, and interpret results accordingly. For categorical variables, the Frequency Table is the most relevant part of the output (see Fig. 10.5). It shows the proportion of men (N = 31, 25.8%) and women (N = 89, 74.2%) in the sample. For categorical variables, we want to know *how many* exist in each category.

What is your gender?

		Frequency	Percent	Valid Percent	Cumulative Percent
Valid	male	31	25.8	25.8	25.8
	female	89	74.2	74.2	100.0
	Total	120	100.0	100.0	

Figure 10.5 Statistics output table for age

Exploring your data

Although the method described above is the simplest way of getting SPSS to produce descriptive information about your data set, there is another, more sophisticated, procedure which is worth knowing about. The **Explore** procedure will provide a range of descriptive statistics and enable you to split your data set very easily according to scores on another variable (so you could split the data into men and women, for instance).

There are some important reasons for exploring your data before you carry out any further statistical tests. The first reason for this initial stage is, rather obviously, to describe your data (through descriptive statistics and possibly also graphs). However, there are other reasons for exploring your data before carrying out inferential statistics (where you compare one variable with another). The exploration stage involves screening your data to look for **outliers** (values outside the expected range), checking any assumptions required for the tests you want to conduct (whether the data are normally distributed, for instance) and characterising differences among subpopulations (groups of cases – men and women, for instance). Data screening may show that you have unusual values, extreme values, gaps in the data or other unexpected values. If you discover a problem you can attempt to rectify it before conducting any further tests which may be distorted by the unusual value(s). Very often extreme values (outliers) are due to mistakes when entering the data but sometimes they may be a spurious value given by a participant. If you discover an unusual value then you will need to go back to your data and try to identify the cause. If it was due to an error in data entry then that is easily corrected. However, if it was due to a strange response from a participant then you will need to think carefully about the reasons for this and whether you would be better off excluding this particular case from any further analysis. Exploring the data can also help to determine whether the statistical techniques that you are considering for data analysis are appropriate. Exploration may indicate that you need to transform the data if the technique requires a normal distribution. Or, it may be that you need to use non-parametric tests. See Box 10.2 for information about using the **Explore** command.

Box 10.2

Command box	Exploring your data

1 Click on **Analyze** on the top menu bar.

2 Click on **Descriptive Statistics**.

3 Click on **Explore**. This will bring up the **Explore** dialogue box (see Fig. 10.6). Here you can select which variables you wish to get descriptive statistics for (and graphs too) by moving variables (using the **Variable Picker**) into the **Dependent List** box (age is included in the figure). And if you want to get descriptive statistics separately for different groups (such as men and women) you can move the grouping variable (gender in this case) into the **Factor List** box.

▶

Box 10.2 *Continued*

Figure 10.6 Explore dialogue box

4   Click **OK** and the Viewer window will open with your output.

Finally, it is worth noting that you can produce charts and/or plots (different words, but graphs, charts and plots are all ways of graphically representing your data) when requesting descriptive statistics using both the **Frequencies** and **Explore** commands. If you want to produce graphical output you only need to click on the **Charts** button in the **Frequencies** dialogue box or **Plots** button in the **Explore** dialogue box. There are a number of options available but the choices are still quite limited. If you want a wider choice of graphs then you will be better using the **Graphs** function (described below).

10.2   Simple and complex bar charts

Simple **bar charts** are ideal for displaying frequency (the number of times something occurs) data for categorical variables. See Box 10.3 for details of the procedure.

Box 10.3

| Command box | Obtaining a simple bar chart |

1   Click on **Graphs** on the top menu bar.

2   Click on **Chart Builder** (see Fig. 10.7). This will bring up the **Chart Builder** dialogue box (see. Fig. 10.8). A reminder box appears, telling you that you should have declared the level of measurement for your variables before using the Chart Builder. Tick the **Don't show this dialog again** box and then **OK** to cancel this message (see Fig. 10.8).

Figure 10.7 Obtaining the Chart Builder

Figure 10.8 Chart Builder dialogue box

Box 10.3 *Continued*

3   In the Gallery area, there are different kinds of charts listed, alongside their corresponding buttons. For a simple bar chart, click on the **Simple Bar** button (see Fig. 10.9) and drag it to the preview area. This will create a chart preview (see Fig. 10.10).

Figure 10.9 Simple Bar button

Figure 10.10 Simple Bar dialogue box (1)

4   Click on the variable that you want to use (e.g. 'what is your ethnic origin'), and drag it to the **X-Axis?** box on the chart preview (see Fig. 10.11). There is no Y-Axis variable in this example, because we are interested in describing the frequencies for one variable, not the relationship between two variables.

5   Click **OK** and the Viewer window will open with your chart (see Fig. 10.12).

Box 10.3 *Continued*

Figure 10.11 Simple Bar dialogue box (2)

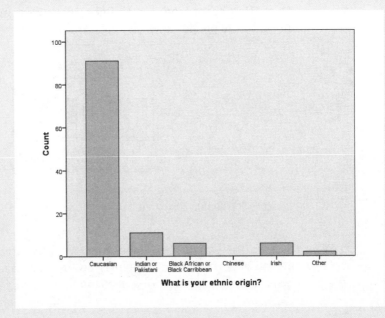

Figure 10.12 Output for simple bar chart

10.3   Histograms

Histograms are a special type of bar chart where all categories must be represented, columns will be of equal width per equal category interval, columns only represent frequencies and, finally, column areas are proportional to frequency. The most significant difference, however, between a bar chart and a histogram is that a bar chart must display discrete variables (such as sex or ethnicity) while a histogram can display continuous variables (usually on the *x*-axis, the horizontal axis) split into class intervals or discrete variables. Columns in a histogram represent the number of values found in the particular class interval. Frequencies are shown on the *y*-axis (the vertical axis). See Box 10.4 for instructions on obtaining a histogram.

BOX 10.4

Command box   **Obtaining a histogram**

1   Click on **Graphs** on the top menu bar.

2   Click on **Chart Builder** (see Fig. 10.7). This will bring up the **Chart Builder** dialogue box (see Fig. 10.8).

3   Select **Histogram** from the Gallery, then drag the **Simple Histogram** button to the preview area (see Fig. 10.13).

Figure 10.13 Simple Histogram button

4   Click on the variable you require (e.g. 'motivation to study'), and drag this to the **X-Axis?** box in the preview area (see Fig. 10.14). It is not necessary to define a Y-Axis for a histogram.

Box 10.4 *Continued*

Figure 10.14 Simple Histogram dialogue box

5   Click on **OK** and the Viewer window will create your histogram (see Fig. 10.15).

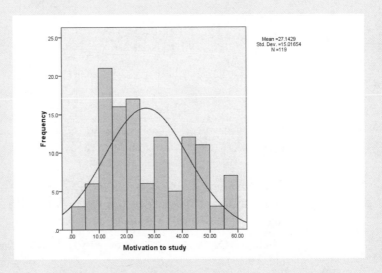

Figure 10.15 Output for simple histogram

10.4 | Pie charts

You are probably familiar with **pie charts** from school. They offer another way of presenting categorical data. They are not widely used in research, because percentages can be presented in the text of a report without the need for a visual illustration. However, there are occasional situations in which they might be useful. See Box 10.5 for instructions on obtaining a pie chart.

Box 10.5

Command box	Obtaining a pie chart

1   Click on **Graphs** on the top menu bar.

2   Click on **Chart Builder** (see Fig. 10.7). This will bring up the **Chart Builder** dialogue box (see Fig. 10.8).

3   Select **Pie/Polar** from the Gallery, then drag the **Pie Chart** button to the preview area (see Fig. 10.16).

Figure 10.16 Pie Chart button

4   Click on the variable you require (e.g. 'what is your ethnic origin'), and drag this to the **X-Axis?** box in the preview area (see Fig. 10.14). It is not necessary to define a Y-Axis for a pie chart.

5   Click on **OK** and the Viewer window will create your pie chart (see Fig. 10.17).

Box 10.5 *Continued*

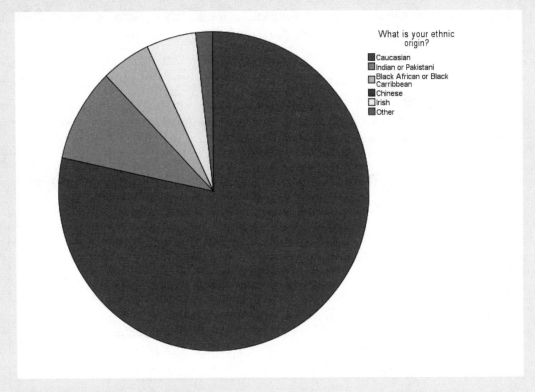

Figure 10.17 Output for pie chart

<table><tr><td>**10.5**</td><td>Boxplots</td></tr></table>

Boxplots (or 'box and whisker' plots) are summary plots based on the median, quartiles and extreme values rather than on means and standard deviations. The box element of the plot represents the interquartile range that contains 50 per cent of the values. The whiskers are the lines that extend from the box to the highest and lowest values, excluding outliers. The dark line across the box produced by SPSS shows the median value in the set of values. Boxplots are particularly useful ways of summarising experimental data and identifying outliers. See Box 10.6 for instructions about obtaining boxplots.

Box 10.6

Command box	Obtaining a simple boxplot

1   Click on **Graphs** on the top menu bar.

2   Click on **Chart Builder** (see Fig. 10.7). This will bring up the **Chart Builder** dialogue box (see Fig. 10.8).

3   Select **Boxplot** from the Gallery, then drag the **Simple Boxplot** button to the preview area (see Fig. 10.18).

Figure 10.18 Simple Boxplot button

4   Click on the categorical variable that you would like to use as a comparison (e.g. 'gender') and drag this to the **X-Axis?** box in the preview area.

5   Click on a continuous variable (e.g. 'diff rating – workload') and drag this to the **Y-Axis?** box in the preview area (see Fig. 10.18).

Box 10.6 *Continued*

6   Click on **OK** and the Viewer window will create your boxplot (see Fig. 10.19).

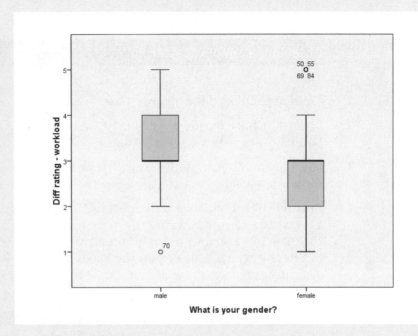

Figure 10.19 Output for simple boxplot

| **10.6** | Scattergrams |

Researchers are very often interested in the degree of relationship between two or more variables. For example, there is likely to be a relationship between a measure of children's maths or reading ability and age. As their age increases their ability to read and do maths will generally increase too. As long as we use appropriate tests for maths and reading ability we should find a strong association between age and maths ability and age and reading ability. This is what we call **correlation**. A high correlation coefficient between variables indicates a high degree of association (as one increases in value, so does the other, or as one decreases, so does the other) while a low correlation coefficient indicates a low degree of association between the two variables. We talk more about correlation and the different ways of calculating correlation coefficients that enable us to determine the degree of association between variables in Chapter 12. An easy way of examining the relationship between two variables is to plot a **scattergram** (sometimes called a scatterplot). So, for instance, if we wanted to examine the relationship between age and motivation to study in our data we might plot a scattergram for these two variables (see Box 10.7).

Box 10.7

| Command box | Obtaining a simple scatterplot |

1   Click on **Graphs** on the top menu bar.

2   Click on **Chart Builder** (see Fig. 10.7). This will bring up the **Chart Builder** dialogue box (see Fig. 10.8).

3   Select **Scatter/Dot** from the Gallery. Drag the **Simple Scatter** button to the preview area.

4   Drag one of the variables to the **X-Axis?** box (e.g. 'age') and one to the **Y-Axis?** box (e.g. 'motivation to study'), in the preview area (see Fig. 10.20). In our example, it doesn't matter which variable is placed on the X-Axis and which is placed on the Y-axis. If one of your variables is a dependent ('outcome') variable, it should be placed on the Y-axis.

Figure 10.20 Simple Scatter dialogue box

Box 10.7 *Continued*

5   Click on **OK** and the Viewer window will create your scatterplot (two equivalent scatterplots are shown in Figs 10.21 and 10.22).

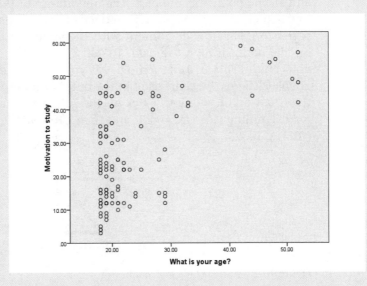

Figure 10.21 Output for simple scatter (1)

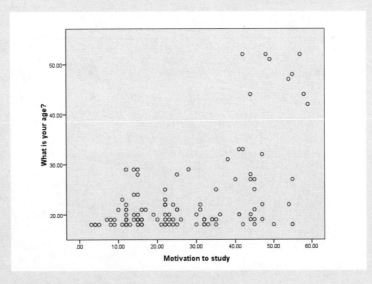

Figure 10.22 Output for simple scatter (2)

As you can see, in the output there is a positive correlation (association) between age and motivation to study. As age increases, so does the score on the measure of motivation for study. An important option available with scatterplots is the possibility of plotting what is known as a **regression line** onto the chart itself. This is a line of best fit which minimises the distance between itself and all the points on the plot. The importance of this line will become clearer in Chapter 15 when you are introduced to the statistical technique known as regression. For now be content with the ability to plot a line that shows the middle path through the data. To add a regression line you will need to edit your chart. This is quite simple. All you need to do to edit any chart is to double-click on the chart itself in the output Viewer window. This will open up the Chart Editor window. Click on the **Add Fit Line at Total** button to add a regression line (see Fig. 10.23) and then **Close** to view the updated scatterplot (see Fig. 10.24).

Figure 10.23 Add Fit Line at Total button

Figure 10.24 Chart Editor

10.7 Editing charts

We have already introduced the Chart Editing functions above but there are many more options available. Just remember that if you want to edit a chart you need to double-click on it in the output Viewer window to bring up the Chart Editor window. Once in this window most modifications can be made by selecting the element of the chart you want to change (e.g. the *x*- or *y*-axis, the title, bars on a bar chart, a slice of a pie chart) and then clicking on the relevant button (there is a row of button options at the top of the screen – see Fig. 10.25). Once you have made your choice of modification you will usually need to select **Apply** to action your command.

Figure 10.25 Chart Editor button

If you want to know what a button does in SPSS, just move your mouse pointer over any one of them and hold it there for a second or two. A pop-up label will appear which tells you what that particular button will do. You can change the title, colours of pie slices or bars in a bar chart. You can change the styles of lines on the chart or fill patterns. You can add text to your chart or swap your axes over (so the *x* becomes the *y* and vice versa). The important thing to remember is that you cannot cause any damage, so get a chart into the Chart Editor and play around. If you want further information about manipulating your chart then consult the online help available in SPSS by clicking **Help**.

11

Bivariate analysis 1: exploring differences between variables

- This chapter begins by explaining the fundamentals of inferential statistics and specifically bivariate difference of means tests (*t*-tests and their non-parametric equivalents).

- It then demonstrates how to carry out bivariate parametric and non-parametric tests of difference by hand and using SPSS.

INTRODUCTION

This chapter and the following three chapters introduce the reader to **inferential statistics**. If you remember from Chapter 8, these are statistics concerned with understanding differences or relationships between variables and whether these differences or relationships are more or less likely to have occurred by chance alone. That is, do we have a difference or relationship where it is highly probable that the difference or relationship occurred for interesting psychological reasons rather than by chance? This chapter and the following chapter refer to **bivariate analysis**, which simply means the analysis of two variables.

This chapter covers a number of tests designed to identify whether any difference between two sets of scores is statistically significant. That is, the tests identify whether the difference between the two means is sufficiently different from no difference that it is unlikely (improbable) that the samples came from the same population. Which particular test of difference is needed will depend on your data.

11.1   Theoretical issues in inferential statistics

How significant are significance tests?

Before going any further it is worth warning you of the (almost certainly) mistaken belief that a significant result (where the probability that the result occurred by chance is less than 1 in 20 – $p < 0.05$) is necessarily meaningful. This error is understandable. It is almost impossible to publish quantitative research where the results do not demonstrate significant effects (differences or relationships). Psychological research is driven by the need to obtain and then publish significant results. The danger with relying solely on statistical significance when evaluating your results is that significance tells us nothing about the size or importance of the effect. Don't get us wrong: significance is important in identifying differences or relationships between variables that are unlikely to have been caused by chance, but significance results should be supplemented by some measure of **effect size**. This is because statistical significance is not related to the size or importance of a difference or relationship. As you increase a sample size the likelihood of getting significant results increases (the test becomes more sensitive). So, calls to increase the sample size in a study might well improve the likelihood of finding a significant effect but not one that is large or important. Despite views to the contrary, significant findings obtained with a small sample are more likely to be robust than those obtained with a large sample.

Measuring effect sizes

If you wish to measure effect sizes there are two main approaches. With studies concerned with the relationships between variables (covered in the next chapter and Chapter 15, on regression), effect sizes are demonstrated through the **proportion of variance** explained (the r^2 value). However, with tests of difference, such as those covered in this chapter, it is possible to calculate effect sizes for mean differences (with independent groups). This measure of effect size is usually referred to as d and requires you to:

1 find the mean sample standard deviation (by adding the SD of group 1 to the SD of group 2 and dividing the total by two);

2 find the value of d – the effect size (by subtracting the mean of group 1 from group 2, ignoring any signs, and dividing by the mean SD obtained in (1) above).

Cohen (1988) suggests that $d = 0.2$ (and above) indicates a small effect size, $d = 0.5$ (and above) a medium effect size and $d = 0.8$ (and above) a large effect size. Essentially the effect size tells us about the degree of overlap between our sample score distributions. The higher the effect size, the less overlap there is between the two distributions of scores. Means and standard deviations needed for the calculation given above can, of course, be calculated by SPSS.

Parametric versus non-parametric tests

The basic distinction between **parametric** and **non-parametric tests** has already been introduced in Chapter 8. In general, if the data are categorical or nominal level (i.e. frequencies) then it is only possible to use non-parametric tests. If the data are non-categorical then it is possible to use either a parametric or non-parametric test, and you, the researcher, must decide which is more appropriate. The decision about which to use is dependent on a number of factors: (1) the level of measurement, (2) the distribution of population scores and

(3) any differences in the variance of the variables. Generally, it is thought appropriate to use parametric tests when the level of measurement is interval or ratio level, the distribution of scores is normal, and the variances of both variables are equal. Remember that the reason for the need for data to fulfil these requirements is because parametric tests are based on the assumption that we know certain features of the population from which the sample is drawn. Non-parametric tests (sometimes called distribution-free tests) do not depend on assumptions about the form of the distribution of the sampled populations.

There is some argument, however, about the need for data to meet these three conditions in order for parametric tests to be conducted. The first condition (level of measurement) is routinely ignored in psychological research. Many tests used in psychology employ Likert scales, which are, strictly speaking, measured at the ordinal level. According to the criteria above, this would mean that we should only use non-parametric tests when analysing Likert (and other similar) scales. However, the importance of levels of measurement is overstated in research methods texts (as we discussed in Chapter 2). We, the researchers, might know what our scores indicate but the tests do not and it is therefore common practice to treat ordinal-level data (such as Likert scales on questionnaires) as if they are interval level and subject them to parametric tests. As far as the second and third conditions are concerned, a number of studies have tested these assumptions and found that parametric tests (such as the *t*-test) are remarkably **robust** to violations of normality and unequal variances. One exception is where both the size of samples and the differences in variances are unequal or where both distributions of scores are non-normal (Bryman & Cramer, 1997). Data that are not normally distributed can, of course, be transformed. It is common practice in some areas of psychology to transform one's data by computing logarithm scores for the values or taking the reciprocal ($1/N$). If you wish to do this you will need to use the **Compute** command in SPSS (described in Chapter 9) – Howell (2001) provides more detail on transforming data.

Ideally, your data should be normally distributed, with your variables having pretty much equal variances for parametric tests. You will also need data measured at the ordinal level, at the very least, and ideally measured at the interval or ratio level. However, minor variations from this standard will probably not cause too many problems. If in doubt, run parametric and non-parametric tests on your data and see if you get different results. If you do and you have reason to believe that your data do not fulfil the three conditions detailed above then you are probably safest reporting the non-parametric test results.

11.2   Introducing the *t*-test

The *t*-test (sometimes called Student's *t*-test) is one of the most widely known and used tests in psychological research. This is a parametric test designed to test for difference between two mean scores. There are two versions of the test. The **related** (or paired samples or correlated) *t*-test is used when the two sets of scores come from a single sample of people (or when the correlation coefficient between the two sets of scores is high). The **independent groups** (or unrelated) *t*-test is used when the two sets of scores come from two different samples of people. So, if you test the same group of participants twice (say, you give a test of attention in the morning and then again in the afternoon to look for an effect due to time of day) you will need to use the related *t*-test. If you have two different groups of people, however, you will need to use the independent groups *t*-test.

Theoretical background

If we have mean scores for two conditions A and B (these could be experimental conditions or two different questionnaire items) and we want to know whether there is a significant difference between these sets of scores then two factors will influence our decision. Firstly, there is the size of difference between the means, and secondly, there is the amount of variability (variance) in the sets of scores. The bigger the difference in means, the greater will be our confidence that the effect is due to a real psychological difference rather than chance. However, the greater the variability in scores, the lower will be our confidence. The *t*-test takes account of both factors:

$$t = \frac{\text{difference in means}}{\text{standard error of the difference in means}}$$

If you remember, the standard error is the name given to the standard deviation of the mean. In this case, this is extended to indicate the standard error of the difference in two means. If two samples are drawn from a single population and means calculated, there will almost always be some difference in the mean scores. If we took repeated pairs of samples and calculated their means and then noted the difference we could plot these differences. This would give us the sampling distribution of the difference in means (similar to the sampling distribution of means described in Chapter 8). This distribution of scores will look like a flattened normal distribution and is the *t*-distribution. The larger the sample size, however, the closer the *t*-distribution gets to the normal distribution. Thankfully, there is no need to sample scores repeatedly to build up sampling distributions to conduct statistical tests. Instead, we rely on statistical theory about the population and sample to derive formulae that enable us to calculate a *t*-test.

Fig. 11.1 shows the sampling distribution of *t* (a flattened-looking normal distribution) and the line indicates the observed differences in means between two groups. This difference in means is unlikely to have occurred by chance if the samples have been drawn from the same population. It is therefore much more likely that this difference in means is a significant difference between the two values. We need to decide on a significance level and check our difference value against this value. The conventional significance value is 5 per cent (remember, this is the probability of making a Type I error – deciding there was an effect when this is not the case – 1 in 20 for 5 per cent and 1 in 100 for 1 per cent). If you look at Fig. 11.1 again you can see that the two tails of the distribution are shaded. These are the top and bottom 5 per cent of the distribution. Any value of *t* falling into the top or bottom 5 per cent of the distribution indicates a significant (at the

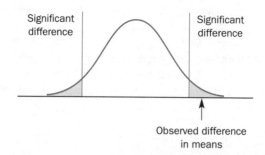

Figure 11.1 Observed difference in means on the sampling distribution of means

5 per cent level) difference between the two mean scores. All you need to do to assess the significance of a difference in means is to calculate the value of t (by hand using a simple formula or using SPSS) and see if it exceeds the 5 per cent value (in a table of t values). If you use SPSS to calculate a t value it does this for you. One thing to remember about the t distribution is that it changes shape with different sample sizes and the 5 per cent value of t will therefore be different with different sample sizes. Fortunately the degrees of freedom in a study are related to sample size and are used to locate the appropriate 5 per cent value of t instead of sample size.

One- and two-tailed tests

One final consideration needs discussion before we move on to calculating t-tests: whether we need **one-** or **two-tailed tests**. There will be times when we can predict the direction of effect of our difference (that is, predict which mean score will be higher or lower). We may have theoretical grounds for expecting a particular difference or information from previous research. There may also be common-sense reasons for predicting direction. If, for instance, we tested a group of 18-year-old people against a group of 80-year-old people on reaction time we would have good grounds for believing that the reaction times of the younger people would be quicker than those of the older people. In these circumstances we would use a **one-tailed test**. However, there may be other times when we do not have any idea about the direction of the effect and in these circumstances we use a **two-tailed test**.

When we carry out a one-tailed test we are only dealing with one end (tail) of the distribution shown in Fig. 11.1. In this case the null hypothesis that there is no difference between the means is tested against a directional alternative hypothesis where one condition has a higher mean than the other (A higher than B or vice versa). We only decide there is a significant effect if the value of t falls at one end (the predicted end!) of the distribution. A two-tailed test is where we conclude there is a significant effect if the value of t falls at *either* end of the distribution. Here, the null hypothesis is tested against a non-directional alternative hypothesis which predicts that there is a difference of some kind between conditions A and B.

Predicting direction has an important effect on the interpretation of significance using values of *t*. When we have a one-tailed *t*-test the 5 per cent value becomes a 2.5 per cent value. This is because the 5 per cent value of *t* includes both ends of the distribution (2.5 per cent in each end). If we do not correct this and use the 10 per cent value of *t* (which gives us the 5 per cent value for one tail) with a one-tailed test then there is less likelihood of finding a significant effect (because we are judging *t* against a higher standard). If you are calculating a *t*-test by hand you will often need to look up the 10 per cent value of *t* for a one-tailed test at the 5 per cent level (but not in this book as we have included columns for one- and two-tailed tests). If you are using SPSS to calculate a *t*-test it will look up the appropriate value of *t* for you and report the significance. As you might have realised, a result may be significant with a one-tailed test when it is not significant with a two-tailed test. You must remember that any predictions of direction need to be made before the test is carried out and ideally should be grounded in established theory. It is bad practice to hunt around for significant results and then make up some **post hoc** (after the event) explanation for predicting direction.

11.3	Calculating an independent groups *t*-test

The formula and instructions for calculating an **independent groups *t*-test** by hand are given in Box 11.1. Instructions for obtaining an independent groups *t*-test using SPSS are given in Box 11.2. Both examples of the *t*-test given here (the calculation by hand and the one using SPSS) will use the same data (detailed in Box 11.1). Further information about interpreting the SPSS output is also given below.

Box 11.1

Stats box	Calculating an independent groups *t*-test

Formula for calculating an independent groups *t*-test

$$t = \frac{\bar{X}_A - \bar{X}_B}{\sqrt{\dfrac{\left[\sum X_A^2 - \dfrac{\left(\sum X_A\right)^2}{N_A}\right] + \left[\sum X_B^2 - \dfrac{\left(\sum X_B\right)^2}{N_B}\right]}{(N_A - 1) + (N_B - 1)} \times \left(\dfrac{1}{N_A} + \dfrac{1}{N_B}\right)}}$$

We know – it looks horrific! The trick with all formulae is to break them down into sections and tackle each section at a time. There are lots of discrete units in the formula above, most of which should be quite familiar to you. There are symbols for the mean, sigma (Σ – meaning add up the set of numbers) and *N* (the number of numbers in the set), and that is about it. If you treat all formulae as sets of instructions and tackle each element step by step, you will find them a breeze. If you still struggle, take heart from the fact that most of us now use SPSS to do the maths.

Box 11.1 *Continued*

Worked example

The data

Two groups of people were given a test for motivation to learn (scored 0 to 25). Group A comprised a group of teenagers with below-average exam results. Group B comprised a group of teenagers with above-average exam results. The researchers wanted to see if there was a significant difference in scores between the two groups on the motivation to learn test. The data were normally distributed and they therefore decided to calculate an independent groups *t*-test. They did not know whether there would be a significant difference between the two groups in any particular direction so calculated a two-tailed test.

Group A	Group B
12	20
10	11
8	18
14	12
17	22
11	24
12	17
9	23
11	19
15	13
	19
	23

Step by step procedure

1 Calculate all mathematical expressions first:

N_A = 10 (the number of scores in group A)
N_B = 12 (the number of scores in group B)
ΣX_A = 119 (all the scores in group A added up)
ΣX_B = 221 (all the scores in group B added up)
ΣX_A^2 = 1485 (each score in group A squared and then all of these added up)
ΣX_B^2 = 4287 (each score in group B squared and then all of these added up)

$$\bar{X}_A = \frac{\Sigma X_A}{N_A} = \frac{119}{10} = 11.9$$

$$\bar{X}_B = \frac{\Sigma X_B}{N_B} = \frac{221}{12} = 18.42$$

Box 11.1 *Continued*

2 Now simply 'plug' all these values into your formula:

$$t = \frac{11.9 - 18.42}{\sqrt{\dfrac{\left[1485 - \dfrac{(119)^2}{10}\right] + \left[4287 - \dfrac{(221)^2}{12}\right]}{(10-1) + (12-1)} \times \left(\dfrac{1}{10} + \dfrac{1}{12}\right)}}$$

3 Finally, get clicking on that calculator (remember to do it in stages and write the value for each section down on paper) and your *t* value will be revealed:

$$t = -4.03 \text{ (rounded up to two decimal places)}$$

4 Calculate the degrees of freedom (df = $N_A + N_B - 2$):

$$df = 20$$

5 Consult the table of *t* values (see the Appendix for statistical tables) and see if the value of *t* is larger than that given for df = 20 at the 5 per cent level (0.05). The 5 per cent value of *t* for a two-tailed test with 20 degrees of freedom is 2.086. The value here exceeds this (you should ignore the sign of *t*) and therefore indicates that there is a significant difference where $p < 0.05$. Looking at the 1 per cent (0.01) value of *t* (which is 2.845 for 20 df) the difference is significant at that level too.

6 Report your findings:

The mean score for motivation to learn for teenagers with above-average examination results (M = 18.42, SD = 4.44) is significantly higher ($t = -4.03$, df = 20, two-tailed $p < 0.01$) than that for teenagers with below-average examination results (M = 11.9, SD = 2.77).

Note: the formula for the standard deviation (SD) is given in Chapter 8.

Box 11.2

Command box Computing an independent groups *t*-test

1 Make sure your data are entered correctly. There should be a grouping variable to tell SPSS which group your data belong to in addition to your test variable (see Fig. 11.2).

2 Click on **Analyze** on the top menu bar.

3 Click on **Compare Means** on the drop-down menu.

Box 11.2 *Continued*

Figure 11.2 Data entered correctly for an independent groups *t*-test

4 Click on **Independent-Samples T Test**. This will bring up a dialogue box where you need to specify your **Test Variable** ('motlrn' in this case) and your **Grouping Variable** ('group' in this case) by using the **Variable Picker** button to move the appropriate variables into these boxes (see Fig. 11.3).

5 With your grouping variable in the **Grouping Variable** box highlighted click on **Define Groups**. This will bring up another dialogue box where you specify the two values for your grouping variable (1 and 2 in this case). Click **Continue** to return to the previous dialogue box. You will see the two question marks replaced by the values you entered.

6 Click **OK** to run your test. Your results will appear in the output viewer window.

Box 11.2 *Continued*

Figure 11.3 Independent-Samples *T*-test dialogue box

Interpreting your SPSS output

Two tables are produced for this test (see Figs 11.4 and 11.5). The first table (group statistics) reports the mean and standard deviation scores for the dependent variable (motlrn – motivation to learn). These values are given separately for your two groups (labelled 1 and 2 here instead of A and B). For group A (teenagers with below-average exam results) the mean is 11.9 and the SD is 2.77 (to two decimal places) while group B (teenagers with above-average exam results) has a mean of 18.42 (to two decimal places) and an SD of 4.44.

The second table (Fig. 11.5) contains your *t*-test output. The first thing to look at is the result of the **Levene's Test for Equality of Variances**. If this test is significant then your variances are unequal and you must examine the *t*, df and *p*

Group Statistics

	GROUP	N	Mean	Std. Deviation	Std. Error Mean
MOTLRN	1.00	10	11.9000	2.76687	.87496
	2.00	12	18.4167	4.44069	1.28192

Figure 11.4 Group statistics output table

Independent Samples Test

		Levene's Test for Equality of Variances		t-test for Equality of Means						
									95% Confidence Interval of the Difference	
		F	Sig.	t	df	Sig. (2-tailed)	Mean Difference	Std. Error Difference	Lower	Upper
MOTLRN	Equal variances assumed	2.331	.142	-4.026	20	.001	-6.5167	1.61864	-9.89308	-3.14
	Equal variances not assumed			-4.199	18.681	.001	-6.5167	1.55205	-9.76891	-3.26

Figure 11.5 Independent samples *t*-test output table

values for the row 'Equal variances not assumed'. If the Levene test is not signifi-cant then your variances are equal and you can examine the *t* and *p* values for the row labelled 'Equal variances assumed'. In the case of the data here, the Levene test is not significant ($p = 0.142$), so we can assume the variances are equal. The *t* value, therefore, is –4.03, df = 20 and $p = 0.001$. These results should be reported the same as those calculated by hand (see Box 11.1). SPSS gives exact significance values ($p = 0.001$) and it is perfectly acceptable to include these exact values in your results instead of writing $p < 0.01$. Note that when SPSS reports $p = .000$ this actually means $p < .001$ (only three decimal places are displayed). If you need to report a *t*-test result for unequal variances you should write some-thing like this before reporting your results in the normal way: 'Because the variances for the two groups were significantly unequal ($F = 9.11$, $p < 0.05$) a *t*-test for unequal variances was used.'

Note that there may be small differences in the results obtained using SPSS and those calculated by hand due to rounding.

| 11.4 | Calculating a related *t*-test |

The formula and instructions for calculating a **related *t*-test** by hand are given in Box 11.3. Instructions for obtaining a related *t*-test using SPSS are given in Box 11.4. Both examples of the *t*-test given here (the calculation by hand and the one using SPSS in Box 11.4) will use the same data (detailed in Box 11.3). Further information about interpreting the SPSS output is given below.

Box 11.3

| Stats box | Calculating a related *t*-test |

Formula for calculating a related *t*-test

$$t = \frac{\Sigma d}{\sqrt{\dfrac{N\Sigma d^2 - (\Sigma d)^2}{N-1}}}$$

There are several variations on this formula. They all do the same thing, so do not worry if you encounter differences from book to book (this one is probably the easiest to use).

Worked example

The data

The same group of people (a random sample of students) were given a test for attention (scored 0 to 25) twice: once in the morning and once in the afternoon. The researchers wanted to see if there was a significant difference between the morning and afternoon scores for attention (that is, whether attention differs according to the time of day). The data were normally distributed and the researchers therefore decided to calculate a related *t*-test. They did not know whether there would be a significant difference between the two conditions in any particular direction so calculated a two-tailed test.

Box 11.3 *Continued*

Condition A (morning)	Condition B (afternoon)
23	20
22	21
17	18
21	18
20	15

Step by step procedure

1   Calculate all mathematical expressions first:

Σd = 11 (sum of all the differences in scores between conditions A and B)*

$(\Sigma d)^2$ = 121 (the sum of all differences squared)

Σd^2 = 45 (differences are squared first and then added up)

N = 5 (the number of *pairs* of scores in your data set)

* Differences are simply obtained by subtracting one score (condition B, for instance) from the other score (condition A, for instance) for each person in the data set. The difference scores (*d*) for the set of scores given above are therefore: 3, 1, –1, 3 and 5.

2   Now simply 'plug' all these values into your formula:

$$t = \frac{11}{\sqrt{\left(\dfrac{(5 \times 45) - 121}{5 - 1}\right)}}$$

3   Finally, get clicking on that calculator (remember to do it in stages and write the value for each section down on paper) and your *t* value will be revealed:

$$t = 2.16 \text{ (to two decimal places)}$$

4   Calculate the degrees of freedom (df = *N* – 1) – remember, *N* is the number of *pairs of scores*:

$$df = 4$$

5   Consult the table of *t* values (see the Appendix for statistical tables) and see if the value of *t* is larger than that given for df = 4 at the 5 per cent level (0.05). The 5 per cent value of *t* for a two-tailed test with four degrees of freedom is 2.776. The value here is lower than this and therefore indicates that we *do not* have a significant difference between the two conditions.

6   Report your findings:

The mean scores for attention in the morning condition A (M = 20.6, SD = 2.30) and afternoon condition B (M = 18.4, SD = 2.30) did not differ significantly (*t* = 2.00, df = 4, two-tailed ns).

Note: ns stands for non-significant (you could write '*p* > 0.05' instead if you prefer).

Box 11.4

| Command box | Computing a related *t*-test |

1 Make sure your data are entered correctly (see Fig. 11.6). Data are entered like this because each case has two scores (so two variables per person, labelled 'morning' and 'afternoon' here, are needed).

Figure 11.6 Data entered correctly for a related *t*-test

2 Click on **Analyze** on the top menu bar.

3 Click on **Compare Means** on the drop-down menu.

4 Click on **Paired-Samples T-Test**. This will bring up a dialogue box where you can specify which pair of variables you wish to analyse (see Fig. 11.7). You need to highlight both variables to put them beside 'Variable 1' and 'Variable 2' in the **Current Selections** box. Once they are written there you can use the **Variable Picker** button to move them into the **Paired Variables** box.

5 Click on **OK** to run your test. The results will appear in the output viewer window.

Box 11.4 *Continued*

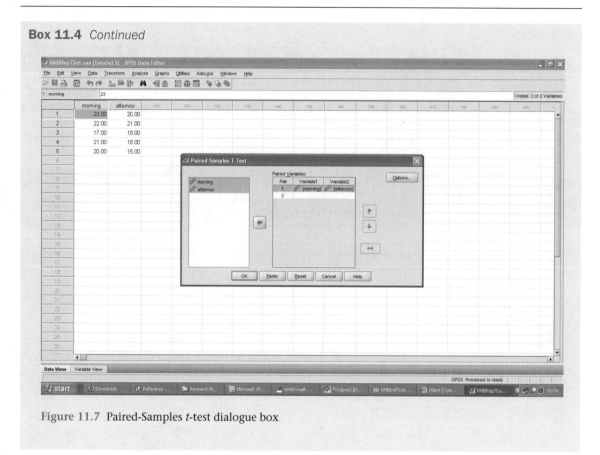

Figure 11.7 Paired-Samples *t*-test dialogue box

Interpreting your SPSS ouput

Three tables are produced for this test (see Figs 11.8–11.10). The first table ('paired samples statistics') reports the mean and standard deviation scores for the two variables ('morning' and 'afternoon'). The second test is the Pearson correlation coefficient (covered in the next chapter) for the two variables. This value should *ideally* be fairly large and significant (because we expect the two variables to be correlated – which is why we conducted a related *t*-test instead of an independent groups *t*-test). In this case the correlation coefficient is 0.51 (which is okay but not really large – values above 0.70 are generally considered large correlation coefficients) and not significant. It is still acceptable to report the results of the related *t*-test but thought should be given to carrying out an independent groups *t*-test instead (as the variables are not significantly correlated). The third

Paired Samples Statistics

		Mean	N	Std. Deviation	Std. Error Mean
Pair 1	morning	20.6000	5	2.30217	1.02956
	afternoo	18.4000	5	2.30217	1.02956

Figure 11.8 Paired samples statistics output table

Paired Samples Correlations

		N	Correlation	Sig.
Pair 1	morning & afternoo	5	.509	.381

Figure 11.9 Paired samples correlations output table

Paired Samples Test

		Paired Differences							
					95% Confidence Interval of the Difference				
		Mean	Std. Deviation	Std. Error Mean	Lower	Upper	t	df	Sig. (2-tailed)
Pair 1	morning - afternoo	2.20000	2.28035	1.01980	-.63143	5.03143	2.157	4	.097

Figure 11.10 Paired samples *t*-test output table

table shows the difference between the two mean scores along with the standard deviation and standard error. But most importantly, it also gives the value of *t*, the degrees of freedom and the two-tailed significance of *t*. As you can see, $t = 2.16$, df = 4, $p = 0.10$ (to two decimal places). Details on how to report this output are given in Box 11.3. SPSS gives exact significance values ($p = 0.097$) and it is perfectly acceptable to include these exact values in your results instead of writing $p > 0.05$ (or, if you have significant findings, $p < 0.05$ or $p < 0.01$).

Note that if we had predicted the direction of the effect and used a one-tailed test these findings would have been significant (simply divide the two-tailed *p* value given in the output by 2 to get the one-tailed *p* value: 0.097/2 = 0.0485). This case also highlights the danger of rounding up numbers too quickly as the rounded up figure of 0.1 divided by 2 equals 0.05 and our *p* value would have fallen exactly on the margins of significance (it should ideally be less than 0.05).

11.5 Introducing non-parametric tests of difference

The **Mann–Whitney *U*** and **Wilcoxon** tests are the non-parametric equivalents of the independent groups and related *t*-tests. The Mann–Whitney *U* is used when you have independent groups and the Wilcoxon with related samples. While *t*-tests are based on the mean, the Mann–Whitney *U* and Wilcoxon are based on ranks (and so require fewer assumptions about the distribution of scores to be met). Although non-parametric tests perform similar functions to the parametric equivalent they are not entirely performing the same function. *t*-tests are concerned with identifying a specific difference in the means of the population while the Mann–Whitney *U* and Wilcoxon tests are concerned with identifying whether the populations are the same or not. These tests are not as common as the *t*-test principally because the *t*-test is more **power efficient** (that is, it requires a lower sample size than the equivalent non-parametric test to identify a significant difference) and is very robust to violations of parametric assumptions. In general, the advice is to use a *t*-test unless your data are rank data or (with small data sets) if the data are obviously non-normal or there are large differences in variances between the two groups/conditions.

| 11.6 | Calculating a Mann–Whitney *U*-test |

The formula and instructions for calculating a Mann–Whitney *U*-test are given in Box 11.5. Instructions for obtaining a Mann–Whitney *U*-test using SPSS are given in Box 11.6. Both examples of the Mann–Whitney *U*-test given here (the calculation by hand and the one using SPSS) will use the same data (detailed in Box 11.5). Further information about interpreting the SPSS output is given below. The Mann–Whitney test involves the *U* statistic, which is based on the sum of the ranks of each group. The Mann–Whitney test is quite simple to calculate by hand but becomes laborious with large samples (it takes a long time to rank order a lot of data) and is generally calculated by hand only with small sample sizes.

Box 11.5

| Stats box | Calculating a Mann–Whitney *U*-test |

Formulae required to calculate a Mann–Whitney test

$$U = N_A N_B + \frac{N_A(N_A+1)}{2} - T$$

and

$$U' = N_A N_B - U$$

where *T* is the sum of the ranks for the smaller sample (group A if the samples are the same size).

Worked example

The data

Two groups of people (English students and mathematics students) were set the task of solving a crossword. The researchers wanted to see if there was a significant difference between English and maths students in the time taken to complete the crossword (timed in minutes). The data were not normally distributed and the researchers therefore decided to calculate a Mann–Whitney *U*-test. They predicted that English students would complete the task quicker than the maths students on the basis of their superior knowledge of the English language, so calculated a one-tailed test.

▶

Box 11.5 *Continued*

Group A (English)	Group B (maths)
15	33
20	45
22	14
10	24
30	33
	24

Step by step procedure

1   Rank the data (*taking both groups together*) giving the lowest score rank 1 and so on. Tied scores should be given the mean rank. For instance, if there are two scores of 12 tied for the 6th and 7th ranks then give both a rank of 6.5. If you have three tied scores for 10th, 11th and 12th ranks then give all three scores a rank of 11. The test should not be carried out if there are a large number of tied scores. The ranks for this data are shown below:

Group A	Group B	Ranks (group A)	Ranks (group B)
15	33	3	9.5
20	45	4	11
22	14	5	2
10	24	1	6.5
30	33	8	9.5
	24		6.5

2   Find the sum of the ranks (*T*) for the smaller sample (group A here). If both are the same size take the sum of ranks of group A.

$$T = 21$$

3   Find *U* using the formula given above:

$$U = (5 \times 6) + \frac{(5 \times 6)}{2} - 21$$

Remember, N_A is the number of scores in the smaller sample (or, if both are the same size, the sample which was used to calculate *T*).

$$U = 24$$

4   Find *U'* using the formula given above:

$$U' = (5 \times 6) - 24$$

$$U' = 6$$

▶

Box 11.5 *Continued*

5   Look up the smaller of U and U' in the Mann–Whitney table in the Appendix. There is a significant difference between the two sets of scores if the smaller of U or U' is equal to or less than the value in the table. The value in the table for $N_A = 5$ and $N_B = 6$ for a one-tailed test is 5 and there is therefore no significant difference between the sets of scores.

6   Report your findings:

Using the Mann–Whitney U-test we found no significant difference between the English and maths students on the time taken to complete the test crossword ($U = 6$, one-tailed ns).

Note: the U used to determine significance is the smaller value (of U and U') and is the value reported in the output and used below to calculate a z-score.

Large sample sizes

It should be noted that this calculation for the Mann–Whitney test is only appropriate for small samples (where N is less than 20 in either set of scores). If the sample is larger than this then it is necessary to convert your Mann–Whitney result into a z-score. This is acceptable because the sampling distribution of the U statistic approaches the normal distribution when sample sizes are large (read Chapter 8 again if you are hazy about the normal distribution and z-scores). The easiest way to calculate a z-score from the results of a Mann–Whitney test is to first calculate the standard deviation (SD_U) of U using the formula below and to use this value in the formula below designed to calculate the z-score:

$$SD_U = \sqrt{\frac{N_A N_B (N_A + N_B + 1)}{12}}$$

$$z = \left(U - \frac{N_A N_B}{2} \right) \div SD_U$$

You can then look up this value of z against the values in the normal distribution table (see Appendix). For a two-tailed test z is significant at the 5 per cent level if it exceeds 1.96 and if it exceeds 1.64 for a one-tailed test.

Box 11.6

Command box	Computing a Mann–Whitney U-test

1   The data should be entered in the correct form. As this is an independent groups test this should be the same as the independent groups t-test (with a grouping variable and the dependent variable).

Box 11.6 *Continued*

2   Click on **Analyze** on the top menu bar.

3   Click on **Nonparametric Tests** on the drop-down menu.

4   Click on **2 Independent Samples**. This will bring up a dialogue box (see Fig. 11.11). The default test choice is the **Mann–Whitney**. You just need to move your dependent variable into the **Test Variable** box ('typestu' in this case) and your grouping variable into the **Grouping Variable** box (and then select **Define Groups** to put in the grouping numbers) just as you did with the independent groups *t*-test.

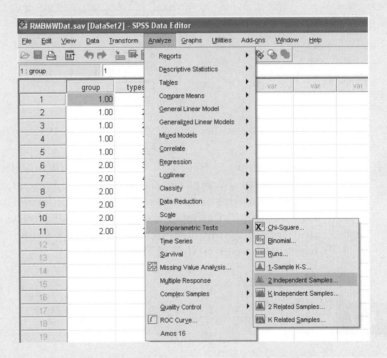

Figure 11.11 Non-parametric independent samples dialogue box.

5   Click **OK** to run your test. The results will appear in the output viewer window.

Interpreting your SPSS output

Two results tables are produced by SPSS (Figs 11.12 and 11.13). The first table gives information about the mean rank scores for the two groups and shows that the average rank for group 2 (maths students) is higher than the average rank for group 1 (English students). The scores for maths students are therefore higher than the scores for English students (which means, in this case, that maths students took longer to complete the task). The second table gives the

Mann–Whitney Test

Ranks

	gr...	N	Mean Rank	Sum of Ranks
typestu	1	5	4.20	21.00
	2	6	7.50	45.00
	Total	11		

Figure 11.12 Rank output table for the Mann–Whitney test

Test Statistics[b]

	typestu
Mann-Whitney U	6.000
Wilcoxon W	21.000
Z	-1.651
Asymp. Sig. (2-tailed)	.099
Exact Sig. [2*(1-tailed Sig.)]	.126[a]

a. Not corrected for ties.

b. Grouping Variable: group

Figure 11.13 Statistics output table for the Mann–Whitney test

Mann–Whitney U value ($U = 6.00$) and significance level ($p = 0.126$). This table also gives the z-score ($z = -1.651$) and its significance ($p = 0.099$). The z-score should be used when there are a number of ties in the data (as it corrects for this problem). In general, however, there will not be a great deal of difference (in terms of significance) between the two p values. Details on how to report this output are given in Box 11.5.

11.7	Calculating a Wilcoxon test

The formula and instructions for calculating a Wilcoxon test by hand are given in Box 11.7. Instructions for obtaining a Wilcoxon test using SPSS are given in Box 11.8. Both examples of the Wilcoxon test given here (the calculation by hand and the one using SPSS) will use the same data (detailed in Box 11.7). Further information about interpreting the SPSS output is given below. The Wilcoxon test is similar to another very simple test (not covered in this book but easily available using SPSS), the **sign test**. The sign test only takes into account the sign (positive or negative) of the difference between a pair of scores. The t-test additionally involves the actual size of the difference (and is therefore more power efficient). The Wilcoxon falls between the sign and t tests (in terms of power efficiency) by using the sign of the difference and the *order* of sizes of these differences. Hence, the Wilcoxon is a more powerful test than the sign test and should (nearly) always be used instead.

Box 11.7

Stats box	Calculating a Wilcoxon test

Worked example

The data

One group of people (a random sample of nurses) was scored (high scores indicating higher use of correct procedures) for success in using the correct manual handling procedures on a ward twice: once during their day shift and once again during their night shift. The researchers wanted to see if there was a significant difference in scores between the nurses' behaviour (using correct manual handling procedures) during the day and night shifts. The data were not normally distributed (as they were frequency scores) and the researchers therefore decided to calculate a Wilcoxon test. They did not know whether there would be a significant difference between the two conditions in any particular direction so calculated a two-tailed test.

Condition A (day)	Condition B (night)
6	5
5	14
4	9
5	18
5	3
7	12
3	9
2	17

Step by step procedure

1   Calculate the difference between each pair of scores (taking the sign into account).

2   Rank the difference scores (*ignoring the sign*) where the lowest difference value is ranked 1 (below).

Difference	Rank
−1	1
9	6
5	3.5
13	7
−2	2
5	3.5
6	5
15	8

▶

Box 11.7 *Continued*

3   Find the value of T (the sum of the ranks for differences with the *less frequent* sign):

$$T = 1 + 2 = 3$$

(there are only two minus signs and their ranks are 1 and 2)

4   Look up the value of T against the values given in the Wilcoxon table (in the Appendix). When $N = 8$, $T = 4$ for a two-tailed test. Our value is below this (values equal to or below the value given in the table are significant) and we therefore have found a significant difference in our sets of scores.

5   Report your findings:

There was a significant difference in scores for the frequency of correct manual handling behaviour between nurses on the day and night shifts (Wilcoxon $T = 3$, two-tailed $p < 0.05$). Examination of the distribution of scores reveals that there was significantly more use of correct manual handling procedures during the night shift than during the day shift.

Large sample sizes

It should be noted that this calculation for the Wilcoxon test is appropriate only for small samples (where there are fewer than 25 pairs of scores). If the sample is larger than this then it is necessary to convert your Wilcoxon result into a z-score. This is acceptable because, like the Mann–Whitney U, the sampling distribution of the T statistic approaches the normal distribution when sample sizes are large (read Chapter 8 again if you are hazy about the normal distribution and z-scores). The easiest way to calculate a z-score from the results of a Wilcoxon test is to first calculate the standard deviation (SD_T) of T using the formula below and to use this value in the formula below designed to calculate the z-score:

$$SD_T = \sqrt{\frac{N(N+1)(2N+1)}{24}}$$

$$z = \left(T - \frac{N(N+1)}{4}\right) \div SD_T$$

The decision about whether z is significant is identical to that given above for the Mann–Whitney test with large sample sizes.

Box 11.8

Command box	Computing a Wilcoxon test

1   The data should be entered in the correct form. As this is a related test this should be the same as the related *t*-test (as two variable columns).

2   Click on **Analyze** on the top menu bar.

3   Click on **Nonparametric Tests** on the drop-down menu.

4   Click on **2 Related Samples**. This will bring up a dialogue box (see Fig. 11.14). The default test choice is the **Wilcoxon**. You just need to move your two variables into the **Test Pair** box just as you did with the related *t*-test.

Figure 11.14 Related-Samples dialogue box

5   Click **OK** to run your test. The results will appear in the output viewer window.

Interpreting your SPSS output

SPSS produces two output tables (Figs 11.15 and 11.16). The first table tells how many negative and positive ranks (and how many ties) we had in our data. It also gives us the values of the mean ranks for our two variables (day and night shifts). The second table reports the *z*-score and its significance for the test. SPSS does not use tables of critical values for the Wilcoxon test. Instead it automatically calculates the *z*-score (as was shown above in Box 11.7). As you can see, $z = -2.103$ and is significant ($p = 0.035$). Details of how to report your results are given in Box 11.7. Instead of reporting the value of T you will need to report the *z*-score when using SPSS.

Wilcoxon Signed Ranks Test

Ranks

		N	Mean Rank	Sum of Ranks
night - day	Negative Ranks	2[a]	1.50	3.00
	Positive Ranks	6[b]	5.50	33.00
	Ties	0[c]		
	Total	8		

a. night < day

b. night > day

c. night = day

Figure 11.15 Rank output table for the Wilcoxon test

Test Statistics[b]

	night - day
Z	-2.103[a]
Asymp. Sig. (2-tailed)	.035

a. Based on negative ranks.

b. Wilcoxon Signed Ranks Test

Figure 11.16 Statistics output table for the Wilcoxon test

12 Bivariate analysis 2: exploring relationships between variables

- This chapter begins by explaining the fundamentals of bivariate relationship tests (chi-square and correlation coefficients – Spearman and Pearson).

- It then demonstrates how to carry out these bivariate tests of relationships by hand and using SPSS.

INTRODUCTION

This chapter introduces you to tests of relationships between two (or more) variables. There are two major types of test of association introduced here. The first, χ^2 (**chi-square** – pronounced 'ky square') is a test of association for categorical data where we have frequency counts. **Correlation coefficients** (such as the Spearman and Pearson correlation coefficients), on the other hand, are designed to measure the relationship between pairs of continuous variables.

But what does it mean when we say two variables are related? Well, first it is important to stress that the search for relationships is not that different from the search for differences. If, for instance, we find that women do worse at tests of mechanical ability than men we would also expect to find a relationship (association) between men and scores on tests of mechanical ability. So, although we have split tests of difference from tests of association this is not a distinction cast in stone. In essence, tests of relationships are concerned with identifying patterns of relationships between two (or more) variables. If there is a relationship between two variables then the variation of scores in one variable is patterned and not randomly distributed in relation to the variation of scores in the other variable. So, for instance, we might expect to find a relationship (correlation) between social class and income: the higher one's social class, the higher one's income. So, income is not randomly distributed across social class (the likelihood of someone in a low social class having a high income is not the same as someone in a high social class). Instead, there is a pattern between the two variables that we can measure: income increases the higher the social class (or decreases the lower the social class). This chapter is concerned with detailing some of those measures of relationships between variables and includes information on measures of association for categorical (χ^2) and continuous variables (Spearman and Pearson correlation coefficients).

The **chi-square test** is a test of association suitable for use with frequency data, that is, when data are in the form of counts. So, if we counted the number of students working (counts for 'working' versus 'not-working') and looked at the impact of this on examination success (in terms of 'pass' versus 'fail') then we would have appropriate data for a chi-square test. The test is not, however, suitable for use with continuous variables unless those continuous variables are turned into categorical variables. If, for instance, we measured our participants' ages by asking people to write a number on a questionnaire, we would have a continuous variable unsuitable for use in a chi-square test. We could, if we wished, convert age into a series of categories (18–21, 21–25, etc., or young, middle-aged, older) where each category includes the information about how many (frequency) people belong in that particular category. The problem with conversions of this kind is that we lose valuable information about our distribution of scores. In general, we want to maximise statistical power and therefore preserve as much information as possible about our data. We would therefore normally only convert a continuous variable into a categorical variable if it were necessary to test a particular hypothesis.

Theoretical background

The basis for calculating chi-square is really very simple. The easiest way of understanding this statistic is to look at some data (pass/fail rates in a test of mechanical ability separated for equal numbers of men and women) in a table:

	Men	Women	Totals
Pass	23	14	37
Fail	7	11	18
Totals	30	25	55

This table shows that 23 out of 30 men passed the test on mechanics and 14 out of 25 women passed the same test. Seven out of the 30 men failed and 11 out of 25 women failed. Therefore, the proportion of men passing the test (23 out of 30 or 77 per cent) is greater than the proportion of women passing the same test (14 out of 25 or 56 per cent). The chi-square test provides us with a way of determining how unlikely it is to get such a difference in proportions as that shown here. That is, is the difference in proportions significant and are the two variables (gender and success/failure in the test of mechanics) significantly related? Or, more accurately, does membership of one category (e.g. men) tend to be associated with membership of another category (e.g. pass)?

It is quite easy to work out what frequencies we should *expect* in each of the four cells if there was *no association* at all. Thirty-seven out of 55 people (67.27 per cent) pass the test in total and, if there were no association, we would expect this *proportion* of men and this *proportion* of women to pass the test. This is very easy to calculate: we simply multiply this proportion as a fraction ($37 \div 55 = 0.6727$) by the total number of men ($N = 30$) to calculate the expected frequency for men passing (and by the total number of women, $N = 25$, for the expected frequency of women passing).

> Expected number of men passing the test = $0.6727 \times 30 = 20.18$
> Expected number of women passing the test = $0.6727 \times 25 = 16.82$

We can use the same method to work out the expected frequencies for the other two cells in the table (men and women failing the test). The general formula for calculating the expected frequency of a cell is:

$$\text{Expected frequency } (E) = \frac{\text{row total} \times \text{column total}}{\text{overall total}}$$

The final table of expected frequencies, where there is no association, for these data is shown below:

	Men	Women	Totals
Pass	20.18	16.82	37
Fail	9.82	8.18	18
Totals	30	25	55

It is now simply a case of using the formula for chi-square (given in Box 12.1 below) to compare the **observed frequencies** (*O*) we obtained in our research with those **expected frequencies** (*E*) we have just calculated. If there is a sufficiently large difference between *O* and *E* we should find the value of chi-square larger and therefore significant.

It is important to note at this stage that chi-square is *only appropriate* when the observations made to generate the frequencies are *independent* of each other. That is, each observation must qualify for *one cell only* in the frequency table. It is not appropriate to use chi-square when you have a repeated measures design with pairs of scores.

Degrees of freedom

There are a few other important things that you should know about chi-square before you attempt to calculate this statistic. Firstly, although the example given above concerns a **2 × 2 contingency table** (a table of frequencies with two columns and two rows), chi-square can be calculated for larger frequency tables using exactly the same method. Expected cell frequencies are calculated and then compared against the observed distribution using the chi-square statistic.

The only extra information needed concerns the **degrees of freedom** (df) of the table being analysed. With a 2 × 2 table there is only one degree of freedom (this is because when one of the expected frequencies has been calculated the rest can be found by subtraction from the column and row totals – the totals being fixed). If you have a larger table you will need to use a formula for calculating degrees of freedom with chi-square:

$$df = (R - 1) \times (C - 1)$$

where R is the number of rows and C the number of columns.

Small samples

Finally, concerns have been raised over the use of chi-square with very small sample sizes. In general, the smaller the sample the worse the fit of the chi-square statistic to the continuous distribution against which it is measured. There are disagreements among statisticians about what counts as too small, however. The general guidance usually offered is to avoid using chi-square when more than 20 per cent of expected cells have values below 5. This would mean that we should not use chi-square on a 2 × 2 table if one or more of our cells had an *expected* (not observed) frequency below 5. However, if the total sample size is greater than 20 it seems to be accepted to use chi-square when one or two cells have expected frequencies below 5 (although the values should not be zero). If the sample size is below 20, however, there is a strong risk of a Type I error even if just one of the cells has an expected frequency below 5 and the chi-square statistic should not be used.

12.2   Calculating chi-square

The formula and instructions for calculating chi-square by hand are given in Box 12.1. Instructions for obtaining chi-square using SPSS are given in Box 12.2. Both examples use the same data but the calculation by hand will use data already displayed in a contingency table while the calculation using SPSS will use data entered normally case by case. Further information about interpreting the SPSS output is also given below.

Box 12.1

Stats box	Calculating a chi-square test of association

Formula for calculating a chi-square statistic

$$\chi^2 = \sum \frac{(O - E)^2}{E}$$

Worked example

Let us return to the data on the success (or not) of men and women passing the test on mechanics and use that data here. Steps 1 and 2 have already been completed for this data.

Step by step procedure

1   Arrange your data in a contingency table with row and column totals.

2   Calculate the expected frequency (*E*) for each cell in your table using the formula:

$$Expected\ frequency\ (E) = \frac{row\ total \times column\ total}{overall\ total}$$

3   Create another table for the expected frequencies or put them into your original table as below:

	Men	Women	Totals
Pass	23	14	37
	20.18	16.82	
Fail	7	11	18
	9.82	8.18	
Totals	30	25	55

4   Calculate the difference between *O* and *E* for each cell:

A $(O - E) = 23 - 20.18$ =   2.82
B $(O - E) = 14 - 16.82$ =   −2.82
C $(O - E) = 7 - 9.82$ =   −2.82
D $(O - E) = 11 - 8.18$ =   2.82

5   Square each of these values to obtain $(O - E)^2$ for each cell:

A $(O - E)^2 = 7.95$
B $(O - E)^2 = 7.95$
C $(O - E)^2 = 7.95$
D $(O - E)^2 = 7.95$

▶

Box 12.1 *Continued*

6   Divide each of these values by the appropriate value of *E* for that cell:

A $7.95 \div 20.18$ $= 0.39$
B $7.95 \div 16.82$ $= 0.47$
C $7.95 \div 9.82$ $= 0.81$
D $7.95 \div 8.18$ $= 0.97$

7   Now it is simply a case of calculating chi-square using all three elements of the formula calculated above:

$$\chi^2 = 0.39 + 0.47 + 0.81 + 0.97 = 2.64 \text{ with 1 df}$$

8   Look up the value of chi-square for 1 df in the appropriate table (in the Appendix). Chi-square = 3.84 for 1 df. Our value is below this so there is not a significant association between gender and passing the test on mechanics.

9   Report your findings:

There was not a significant association between observed and expected frequencies for gender and performance (pass/fail) on the test of mechanics given (χ^2 2.64, df = 1, ns).

Note: some writers suggest the use of Yates's correction when calculating χ^2 with 2×2 contingency tables because of a danger of overestimating the value of χ^2 in this case. This correction very simply requires us to subtract 0.5 from the value of $(O - E)$ for each cell before squaring the value for all four cells. It is probably safest to use this correction when calculating χ^2 for 2×2 tables. The χ^2 formula with Yates's correction is given below:

$$\chi^2 = \sum \frac{[(O - E) - 0.5]^2}{E}$$

Box 12.2

Command box   **Computing a chi-square test of association**

1   Your data (RMBChiSquare.sav, available from the book's website) should be entered normally, with cases (each person) as rows and variables (gender and pass/fail on the test) as columns and not as a contingency table.

2   Click **D**escriptive Statistics on the top menu bar.

3   Click on **C**rosstabs. This will bring up a dialogue box (see Fig. 12.1). It is called 'crosstabs' because we are cross-tabulating our data (putting it in a table to compare cells).

▶

Box 12.2 *Continued*

Figure 12.1 Chi-square test dialogue box

4   Move your row and column variables ('gender' and 'test') into the **Row** and **Column** boxes respectively using the **Variable Picker** button.

5   Click on **Statistics** to bring up another dialogue box where you can choose **Chi-square** by clicking the box next to the name. Click **Continue** to return to the previous dialogue box.

6   If you want to see row and column frequencies (and percentages) you will need to click on **Cells** and then click on the boxes next to **Observed**, **Expected** and **Row**, **Column** and **Total** percentages, if you wish, in this dialogue box (see Fig. 12.2). Then click **Continue** to return to the previous dialogue box.

7   Click **OK** to run your test. The results will appear in the output viewer window as usual.

Interpreting your SPSS output

SPSS produces three output tables (Figs 12.3–12.5). The first table simply shows the number of cases used in the test (all 55 in this case as there was no missing data). The second table (Fig. 12.3) is a contingency table which shows the

Case Processing Summary

	Cases					
	Valid		Missing		Total	
	N	Percent	N	Percent	N	Percent
gender * test	55	100.0%	0	.0%	55	100.0%

Figure 12.2 Case processing output table

gender * test Crosstabulation

			test		
			1	2	Total
gender	1	Count	23	7	30
		Expected Count	20.2	9.8	30.0
		% within gender	76.7%	23.3%	100.0%
		% within test	62.2%	38.9%	54.5%
		% of Total	41.8%	12.7%	54.5%
	2	Count	14	11	25
		Expected Count	16.8	8.2	25.0
		% within gender	56.0%	44.0%	100.0%
		% within test	37.8%	61.1%	45.5%
		% of Total	25.5%	20.0%	45.5%
Total		Count	37	18	55
		Expected Count	37.0	18.0	55.0
		% within gender	67.3%	32.7%	100.0%
		% within test	100.0%	100.0%	100.0%
		% of Total	67.3%	32.7%	100.0%

Figure 12.3 Cross-tabulation output table

observed and expected frequencies (because we selected this option using **Cells**). The third table (Fig. 12.4) gives the chi-square statistic, the degrees of freedom and significance level as the first line ('Pearson Chi-Square'). So, the chi-square value is 2.65 (to two decimal places), df = 1 and $p = 0.10$ (to two decimal places) and so is non-significant. The line beneath this gives the value of chi-square when Yates's correction is applied (as you can see, the value of chi-square is lower and so the chances of significance less). This is the line we should use when reporting our data with a 2 × 2 table (i.e. two variables). The other line worthy of attention is the one reporting **Fisher's Exact Test**. This test is an alternative to chi-square (which does the same thing) that should be used if you have a 2 × 2 table with small expected frequencies (below 5). SPSS also includes information about the number of cells with frequencies below 5 underneath this table, and

Chi-Square Tests

	Value	df	Asymp. Sig. (2-sided)	Exact Sig. (2-sided)	Exact Sig. (1-sided)
Pearson Chi-Square	2.645[a]	1	.104		
Continuity Correction[b]	1.790	1	.181		
Likelihood Ratio	2.652	1	.103		
Fisher's Exact Test				.150	.091
Linear-by-Linear Association	2.597	1	.107		
N of Valid Cases	55				

a. 0 cells (.0%) have expected count less than 5. The minimum expected count is 8.18.

b. Computed only for a 2x2 table

Figure 12.4 Chi-square statistics output table

this information should be used to make the decision between reporting the chi-square or Fisher's exact test statistics (with a 2 × 2 table). Details of how to report chi-square results are given in Box 12.1.

12.3 Introducing correlation coefficients

The notion of correlation has already been introduced at the beginning of this chapter and in previous chapters (when discussing scattergrams, for instance) so will not need much further discussion here. Two ways of calculating correlation coefficients are covered here. The first is **Spearman's Rho**, or rank-order correlation coefficient (normally just called 'Spearman's correlation coefficient'), which is suitable for non-parametric data. The second is **Pearson's Product–Moment Correlation Coefficient** (normally just called 'Pearson's correlation coefficient'), which is suitable for parametric data and is generally considered more powerful.

Theoretical background

A **correlation coefficient** (such as Pearson's or Spearman's) is a *descriptive* measure of the relatedness of two variables. We can, however, test correlation coefficients for significance by comparing them against tables of critical values. The strength of a correlation coefficient is expressed on a scale from -1 to $+1$ where -1 indicates a perfect negative correlation and $+1$ a perfect positive correlation. A value of 0 means there is no relationship between the two variables. Generally, correlation coefficients above 0.8 (positive and negative) are thought to represent strong relationships between variables. A correlation simply tells us about the pattern of the relationship between the two variables. A *positive* correlation tells us that as one variable increases (income, for instance) so does the other (age, for instance). A *negative* correlation, on the other hand, tells us that as one variable increases (age, for instance) the other variable decreases (memory test scores, for instance). The sign indicates the direction of the relationship while the number indicates the strength.

An important concept with correlation is the **coefficient of determination**. This is a measure of the amount of variation in one variable that is accounted for by the other. The coefficient of determination is simply the square of Pearson's correlation coefficient (r) multiplied by 100 (to give us the percentage of variation accounted for) and is therefore known as r^2. If we have a large correlation coefficient of 0.8, for instance, we can say that one variable accounts for $(0.8 \times 0.8) = 0.64 \times 100 = 64$ per cent of the variation in the other. A slightly lower correlation that may still be significant, of 0.6, means that only 36 per cent of the variance in one variable is accounted for by the other (as we are only talking about correlation and not causality it does not matter which way round we put our variables). In other words, 64 per cent of the variance in one variable is due to variables other than the one we measured! We therefore have to be cautious when interpreting correlation coefficients. Their absolute size matters: significance is not everything here! A small or moderate correlation coefficient may well be significant (especially with large sample sizes) but only explain a tiny amount of the variance.

It is generally a good idea to plot a scattergram (see Chapter 10) of the variables under investigation before computing a correlation coefficient. A scattergram enables us to visually inspect the relationship between two variables and check that the relationship is **linear**. The correlation coefficients being described here determine the strength of linear relationships. It is possible, however, to get relationships between variables that are not linear. Curvilinear relationships (see Fig. 12.5) are not unknown in psychology. If we used a linear technique with such data our results would be spurious (we are most likely not to find a relationship when one really does exist).

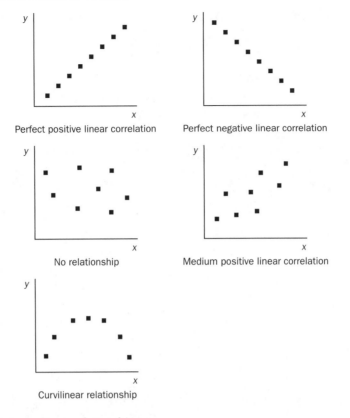

Figure 12.5 Linear and non-linear relationships

| **12.4** | Calculating correlation coefficients |

The formula and instructions for calculating a Spearman correlation coefficient by hand are given in Box 12.3. The formula and instructions for calculating a Pearson correlation coefficient by hand are given in Box 12.4. Instructions for obtaining both correlation coefficients using SPSS are given in Box 12.5. All examples of the correlation tests given here (the two calculations by hand and the one using SPSS) will use the same data (detailed in Box 12.3). Further information about interpreting the SPSS output is also given below.

Box 12.3

| Stats box | Calculating a Spearman correlation coefficient |

Formula for calculating a Spearman correlation coefficient

$$\rho = 1 - \frac{6 \sum d^2}{N(N^2 - 1)}$$

▶

Box 12.3 *Continued*

Worked example

We have collected scores on a standardised test of creativity for maths and music students and, on the basis of previous research, want to know if there is a relationship between the scores.

Data

Maths	Music
2	4
4	1
5	4
7	6
8	7
9	7
5	6
8	6
9	9
7	8

Step by step procedure

1   Begin by setting out the columns of scores you need to calculate the component parts of the formula (ranks for each group of scores *separately*, difference between ranks and squares of these difference scores):

Rank A	Rank B	d	d^2
1	2.5	−1.5	2.25
2	1	1	1
3.5	2.5	1	1
5.5	5	0.5	0.25
7.5	7.5	0	0
9.5	7.5	2	4
3.5	5	−1.5	2.25
7.5	5	2.5	6.25
9.5	10	−0.5	0.25
5.5	9	−3.5	12.25

2   Calculate $\sum d^2$ from your data = 29.5.

3   Simply insert these numbers into the formula:

$$\rho = 1 - \frac{6 \times 29.5}{10(100 - 1)}$$

4   Spearman's ρ (rho) therefore equals 0.82 and indicates a strong positive correlation between maths and music students on the test of creativity.

Box 12.3 *Continued*

5   This value can be compared against those in the table of critical values (see the Appendix) to assess its significance. The critical values for ρ at $p < 0.05$ and $p < 0.01$ are 0.648 and 0.794 respectively. Our value is above both of these values and is therefore significant at $p < 0.01$.

6   Report your findings:

There is a statistically significant positive correlation between maths and music students on the test of creativity ($\rho = 0.82$, $p < 0.01$).

Note: both the Spearman and Pearson correlation coefficients can be calculated only for *pairs of scores*.

Box 12.4

Stats box — **Calculating a Pearson correlation coefficient**

Formula for calculating a Pearson correlation coefficient

$$r = \frac{N\Sigma(XY) - \Sigma X \Sigma Y}{\sqrt{[N\Sigma X^2 - (\Sigma X)^2][N\Sigma Y^2 - (\Sigma Y)^2]}}$$

There are variations on this formula so you may see it written differently. This is clearly a little more complex than the formulae for the Spearman correlation coefficient. However, do not worry too much about formulae such as this: it really is quite straightforward if you break it down into its component parts.

Worked example

We will use the same data here as we did for the Spearman correlation coefficient (ρ) and see what result we get.

Step by step procedure

1   Begin by setting out your columns in order to calculate the elements of the formula you need (XY, which just means $X \times Y$, and X^2 and Y^2, where X represents the scores in group A – maths students – and Y the scores in group B – music students):

XY	X^2	Y^2
8	4	16
4	16	1
20	25	16
42	49	36
56	64	49
63	81	49
30	25	36
48	64	36
81	81	81
56	49	64

Box 12.4 *Continued*

2   Use these scores to calculate the other elements of the formula needed:

$$\Sigma X \quad = 64$$
$$\Sigma Y \quad = 58$$
$$\Sigma XY \quad = 408$$
$$\Sigma X^2 \quad = 458$$
$$\Sigma Y^2 \quad = 384$$

3   Now insert these figures into your formula and get working on that calculator:

$$r = \frac{(10 \times 408) - (64 \times 58)}{\sqrt{[(10 \times 458) - (64 \times 64)] \times [(10 \times 384) - (58 \times 58)]}}$$

4   Pearson's *r* therefore equals 0.77 (to two decimal places) and indicates a fairly strong correlation between maths and music students on the test of creativity.

5   This value can be compared against those in the table of critical values (see the Appendix) to assess its significance. The critical values for *r* at $p < 0.05$ and $p < 0.01$ are 0.632 and 0.765 respectively. Our value is above both of these values and is therefore significant at $p < 0.01$.

6   Report your findings:

There is a statistically significant positive correlation between maths and music students on the test of creativity ($r = 0.77$, $p < 0.01$).

Note: both the Spearman and Pearson correlation coefficients can only be calculated for *pairs of scores*.

Box 12.5

Command box	Computing Spearman and Pearson correlation coefficients

1   Your data (RMBCorLatDat.sav, available from the book's website) should be entered normally.

2   Click on **Analyze** on the top menu bar.

3   Click on **Correlate** and then click on **Bivariate**. This will bring up a dialogue box (see Fig. 12.6) where you can specify which variables you want to correlate with each other using the **Variable Picker** button to move them into the **Variables** box. Note you can include more than two variables in the Variables box (it will just calculate a series of bivariate correlations on your variables).

Box 12.5 *Continued*

Figure 12.6 Correlation dialogue box

4 Select whether you want a **Pearson** or **Spearman** (or both!) correlation coefficient by clicking in the box next to their name in the **Correlation Coefficients** section.

5 Click **OK** to run your command. Your results will appear in the output viewer window as usual.

Interpreting your SPSS output

SPSS produces one table for each correlation coefficient (so you will have only one table in your output if you only selected Pearson or Spearman). Here, we selected both so you could see the output from both tests (see Figs. 12.7 and 12.8). The first table (Fig. 12.7) shows the result of the Pearson calculation. The Pearson correlation coefficient ($r = 0.767$) is given along with its significance ($p = 0.01$). The second table (Fig. 12.8) shows the result of the Spearman calculation. The Spearman correlation coefficient ($p = 0.816$) is given along with its significance ($p = 0.004$). Both tables also include N (the number of cases in the data set). Details on how to report your findings are given in the two statistics boxes on calculating correlations by hand.

Correlations

		Music students	Maths students
Music students	Pearson Correlation	1.000	.767**
	Sig. (2-tailed)		.010
	N	10.000	10
Maths students	Pearson Correlation	.767**	1.000
	Sig. (2-tailed)	.010	
	N	10	10.000

**. Correlation is significant at the 0.01 level (2-tailed).

Figure 12.7 Pearson correlation coefficient output

Correlations

			Music students	Maths students
Spearman's rho	Music students	Correlation Coefficient	1.000	.816**
		Sig. (2-tailed)	.	.004
		N	10	10
	Maths students	Correlation Coefficient	.816**	1.000
		Sig. (2-tailed)	.004	.
		N	10	10

**. Correlation is significant at the 0.01 level (2-tailed).

Figure 12.8 Spearman correlation coefficient output

Analysis of variance (ANOVA)

- This chapter begins by explaining the fundamentals of the family of tests known as analysis of variance (or ANOVA).

- The chapter then demonstrates how to carry out independent and related one-way, two-way and mixed design ANOVAs using SPSS and provides information on planned and unplanned comparisons.

- Finally, information is given about non-parametric equivalents to ANOVA (the Kruskal–Wallis and Friedman tests).

INTRODUCTION

Up until now the tests (for differences and relationships) introduced have been for two variables only. The family of tests known as **ANOVA** allows us to go a step further and look for statistical differences between *two or more* variables. Back in Chapter 11 we introduced the *t*-test as a parametric test designed to examine the differences between two variables. As we are sure you will remember, the *t*-test works by comparing the means *and* the standard deviations of the two sets of scores. If the means and standard deviations are both very different then it is likely that they came from different populations and we conclude that the observed difference is significant. So why do we need another test of difference when we have the *t*-test? Surely we could just carry out a series of *t*-tests on two variables at a time until we had exhausted all possible combinations? Well, there is a problem with this strategy. First, and most importantly, is that repeated tests of data affect the probability of finding a difference (or relationship) by chance. A significance value of 0.05 indicates that there is a 1 in 20 probability that our finding occurred because of chance. If we did this test 20 times then we are *very likely* to get this finding by chance (at least once) and have a Type I error. We therefore need to be cautious about subjecting our data to repeated tests. The second problem with repeated tests is simply one of inconvenience. If there are a large number of variables then it becomes tedious and time consuming to carry out test after test on every possible combination of variables. For these reasons, the preferred option with more than two variables is to opt for an alternative to the *t*-test that can deal with several variables at the same time. The alternative when we have parametric data is the **Analysis of Variance** or **ANOVA**. ANOVA functions in a very similar way to a *t*-test. Like the *t*-test ANOVA compares the means of the variables being tested to see if they are sufficiently different that they are likely to have come from different populations. However, just as we found with the *t*-test, it is not enough just to examine mean differences. It is also necessary to include measures of variation in the calculation because high values for shared variation indicate that the two sets of scores are likely to have come from the same population even if the means are quite different.

13.1   Terminology and techniques

Theoretical background

ANOVA is a test designed to look at mean differences between groups and also look at the variation of scores within each set of data. The **variance ratio** (or ***F*-ratio**) is a statistic designed to identify significant differences between means (between-groups variation) and differences in scores within the groups (within-groups variation). The between-groups (or between-conditions in ANOVA speak) variation is that part concerned with examining the differences between means in the data. The within-groups variation is the variation in scores always obtained within any set of scores due to individual differences in responding and error (remember the discussion of measurement error earlier in the book). For this reason the within-groups variation is also known as the error variation. Strictly speaking, variation here refers to variance (a measure of dispersion), which was introduced in Chapter 8 (have another look now if you are hazy about this concept), and so the *F*-ratio is calculated as follows:

$$F = \frac{\text{between-conditions variance}}{\text{error variance}}$$

Thankfully, it is no longer necessary to calculate ANOVA by hand. While there is, arguably, some merit in working through the formulae for different types of ANOVA calculations, these are tedious and the results prone to error. SPSS will do all the mathematics for us and enable us to concentrate on the psychology. However, it is still important to understand what ANOVA is doing and what all the technical terms mean.

ANOVA designs

In ANOVA independent variables are referred to as **factors**, and factors can have several different **conditions**. So, for instance, if we are interested in the impact of age and social class on voting behaviour, voting behaviour is our **dependent variable** while age and social class are **factors**. Within each of these factors we might have a number of **conditions**. Social class is likely to consist of five conditions (classes A to E) while age might (if our data were categorical) consist of a number of age groups (18–25, 25–35, etc.) and so consist of a number of conditions too. It is important to recognise the differences between factors and conditions, for the number of factors determines the type of ANOVA you will need to calculate. There are different types of ANOVA for different types of data. With only one factor (which would have several conditions) we should calculate a **one-way analysis of variance**. There should be more than two conditions or it would be simpler to look for differences using a *t*-test, of course. A one-way ANOVA will give us information about the significance of difference between conditions on the one factor. If we had two factors we would calculate a **two-way analysis of variance**, three factors a three-way analysis of variance and so on. It is unusual to have tens of factors for it becomes almost impossible to understand what this means even if the computer will do the maths.

With SPSS you can choose to calculate **independent** (or **unrelated** or **between-subjects**) or **related** (or **within-subjects**) one-way ANOVAs, as well as independent or related two-way (or more) ANOVAs. SPSS uses the terms 'between-subjects' and 'within-subjects' in output tables. The independent one-way ANOVA is equivalent to an independent *t*-test but with three or more conditions. The related one-way ANOVA is equivalent to a related *t*-test but with three or more conditions. So, for instance, imagine you were interested in exploring the differences between three different after-school programmes on children's performances on end of year tests. Our dependent variable is the end of year test score and our factor is school programme. The school programme factor consists of three conditions (1 – literacy, 2 – numeracy, 3 – play). The three conditions are independent (or unrelated) as they consist of different children. Our data are therefore suitable for an unrelated one-way analysis of variance. Now imagine we want to look at the differences between the three school programmes and sex of child on their end of year test scores. Now we would need to carry out an unrelated two-way analysis of variance. The school programme is one factor (with three conditions) and sex of child is another factor (with two conditions, male/female).

Another example is that of the effectiveness of a new drug treatment regime designed to lower blood pressure. We have a study design where each person is assigned to condition A (standard drug treatment) for one month, condition B (new treatment regime) for one month and condition C (placebo) for one month. The conditions are given differently to different participants to minimise order effects but all participants receive all three treatments. Their blood pressure readings are recorded and the researchers want to know whether there is a significant difference in blood pressure readings between the three conditions. This calls for a repeated measures (or related) one-way analysis of variance. If we wanted to look at the impact of age and sex as well as the three treatment conditions we would need to carry out a **mixed design ANOVA**. This is because treatment condition is a repeated measure and age and sex are independent measures. A mixed design ANOVA is simply a cross between an independent ANOVA and a repeated measures ANOVA, which we use when we have unrelated and related scores in our data set. The possibilities are endless. However, be careful as very complex mixed designs can be a real headache when it comes to understanding what the statistics mean!

Planned and unplanned comparisons

As you know, a significant F-ratio tells us that the dependent variable varies with the levels of the factor. However, when we have a factor with three or more levels ANOVA does not tell us which means are significantly different from which other means. We therefore need to use other statistics to determine where exactly the significant difference occurs among the pairs of means. These statistics are used in making **planned** and **unplanned comparisons**. **Planned comparisons** are those decided on before the data were collected where the researcher predicts which means will differ significantly from each other. **Unplanned** (or **post-hoc**) **comparisons** are where differences between means are explored after the data have been collected. Unplanned comparisons, or more often post-hoc tests of significance, are commonly used with ANOVA designs. SPSS allows us to select post-hoc tests very easily when computing ANOVAs simply by clicking on the **Post Hoc** option button. Then it is a matter of selecting whichever tests are most appropriate for the data. There are ongoing debates over which comparison test is appropriate and Howell (2001) provides an excellent though typically complex discussion. In general, though, it is probably best to use the **Tukey HSD** (honestly significant difference) test or, if you want to be particularly conservative (cautious), the **Scheffé test** when conducting post-hoc comparisons of ANOVA results. The Scheffé test is also a better choice if you are not interested in differences between particular pairs of conditions but in the differences between sets of conditions (where combinations of conditions have been combined). If you have a *planned comparison* which you want to investigate you can still use the **Post Hoc** option with SPSS. However, you should choose the **Bonferroni test** instead of the Tukey HSD or Scheffé test in these circumstances.

It is important to note that SPSS will only produce post-hoc test statistics for between-subjects factors (the independent factors) and not within-subjects (repeated measure factors). If you have a repeated measure factor with three or more conditions then you will need to use multiple repeated measures t-tests (with the Bonferroni correction) as explained below. With mixed design ANOVA calculations SPSS will compute post-hoc statistics for the between-subjects factors but not the within-subjects factors.

An alternative way of identifying which pairs of means are significantly different is to use a series of t-tests after calculating the ANOVA. We know we told you about the problems of doing this at the start of this chapter, and those arguments still hold. The best option for multiple comparisons is to use the post-hoc tests described above. However, if you have repeated measures SPSS will not calculate these statistics so you will need to use *t*-tests to explore your data (if you have three or more conditions) following an ANOVA. There are also some other occasions when multiple *t*-tests may be appropriate (see Howell, 2001, for a discussion). It is important, however, that you employ the **Bonferroni correction** with these *t*-tests to reduce the likelihood of making a Type I error. If you are making comparisons among three conditions this simply requires you to multiply the (exact) significance level of your *t* statistic by 3 to get the real significance value. With more than three comparisons things are slightly more complicated. What the Bonferroni correction effectively does is share the significance level between the number of comparisons being made. So, with multiple comparisons (more than two *t*-tests) you will need to divide the overall significance by the number of comparisons being made. If you have four comparisons, for instance, you will need to find a significant value of *t* at the 1.25 per cent level instead of the 5 per cent level (5 ÷ 4 = 1.25). As we are sure you have realised, this makes it much less likely that your *t* value is significant, which is exactly what it is meant to do.

Mauchly's test of sphericity

There is one final issue that needs discussion before moving on to computing ANOVAs: **Mauchly's test of sphericity**. This is *only relevant* to repeated measures ANOVA calculations (the test statistic will only be output by SPSS when you have two or more levels of a repeated measures factor). This test is designed to determine whether your data meet certain assumptions (similar to the Levene test for equality of variance). Very simply, it tests the assumption that the correlations between all variables are roughly equal. If this statistic *is significant* then the assumptions have been *violated* and you should examine the results in the table of 'Tests of Within-Subjects Effects' for the **Greenhouse–Geisser** statistic instead of those you would normally use ('Sphericity Assumed') when interpreting the output of a repeated measures ANOVA.

13.2 Calculating a one-way ANOVA

A one-way ANOVA is the simplest type of ANOVA used when there is only one factor. There are two types of one-way ANOVA: the independent (or unrelated) one-way ANOVA and the repeated measures (or related) one-way ANOVA. They are computed in quite different ways in SPSS. Data for both are available from the book website (details of the data for the independent tests are given in Box 13.1, while details on the repeated measures and mixed design data are given in Box 13.2). Box 13.3 gives details of how to calculate an independent one-way ANOVA and Box 13.4 gives details of how to calculate a repeated measures ANOVA. Advice on interpreting the output for all tests is given below the command boxes.

There are two ways of computing an independent one-way ANOVA in SPSS. The simplest method is to select <u>A</u>nalyze, then **Compare <u>M</u>eans** and then **<u>One-</u>Way ANOVA**. This produces a dialogue box where the dependent variable and factor can be selected along with any post-hoc test you wish to conduct. Box 13.1, however, provides information about the slightly more complex method (using the **General Linear Model** command). We think this method should be preferred for a one-way ANOVA, because it can be used, no matter how many factors you have in your ANOVA model.

Box 13.1

Data box	Data used for independent ANOVA (one-way and two-way)

The data file being used here is called RMB_IND_ANOVA.SAV and is available from the book website. Fig. 13.1 shows how the data are entered in SPSS. It is the raw data from a study of the effect of three different educational interventions ('cond') on end of year performance (measured on an overall scholastic aptitude test scored 0 to 50) for young men and women (age 16) at school. The first condition (scored 1) is no active intervention (the control group) where pupils are allowed to chat to each other for an hour after school. Educational intervention A (scored 2) is a career guidance intervention where pupils are counselled about future careers. Educational intervention B (scored 3) is a motivational intervention where pupils are given motivational seminars to encourage achievement.

■ The dependent variable is performance on the end of year scholastic aptitude test ('test').

■ There are two factors that can be investigated: Factor 1 is the educational intervention ('cond'), which has three conditions (Control (1), A (2) or B (3)); Factor 2 is sex of pupil ('sex'), which has two conditions (1 or 2, where 1 = female pupils and 2 = male pupils).

Figure 13.1 Data being used for independent ANOVA computations

Box 13.2

| Data box | Data used for repeated measures ANOVA (one-way and mixed design) |

The data file being used here is called RMB_REPEAT_ANOVA.SAV and is available from the book website. Fig. 13.2 shows how the data are entered in SPSS. It is the raw data from a study of the effect of different quantities of alcohol on performance on a driving simulation task (test scored 0 to 100 with higher scores indicating better avoidance of hazards) for young men and women (age 18). Drink1 (scored 1) is consumption of one standard measure of alcohol. Drink2 (scored 2) is consumption of a further standard measure of alcohol. Drink3 (scored 3) is consumption of a third standard measure of alcohol.

- The dependent variable is performance on the driving simulator (with higher scores indicating better performance).

- There are two factors that can be investigated: Factor 1 is the impact of alcohol on performance, which has three conditions (Drink1 to Drink3, scored 1, 2 or 3), Factor 2 is sex of participant ('sex'), which has two conditions (1 or 2, where 1 = women and 2 = men).

Figure 13.2 Data being used for repeated measures ANOVA computations

Box 13.3

| Command box | Computing an independent one-way ANOVA |

1. Open the file RMB_IND_ANOVA.SAV (see Fig. 13.1). Click **Analyze** on the top menu bar.

2. Click on **General Linear Model** and then **Univariate**. This will bring up the **Univariate** ANOVA dialogue box (see Fig. 13.3). Univariate refers to the fact that we have only one dependent variable.

Figure 13.3 Univariate ANOVA dialogue box

3. Use the **Variable Picker** button to move the dependent variable ('test') into the **Dependent Variable** box.

4. Use the **Variable Picker** button to move the factor variable ('cond') into the **Fixed Factor(s)** box.

5. Click on the **Options** button to open a new dialogue box where you can select descriptive statistics by clicking on the box next to **Descriptive statistics** (see Fig. 13.4). Options for **Estimates of effect size** and **Observed power** are also available.

6. Click on the **Post Hoc** button to open a new dialogue box where you can select post-hoc tests for multiple comparisons. You need to move the variable you want post-hoc tests for into the **Post Hoc Test** box using the **Variable Picker** button and then select the tests you want (see Fig. 13.5).

Box 13.3 *Continued*

Figure 13.4 Univariate: Options ANOVA dialogue box

Figure 13.5 Univariate: Post Hoc ANOVA dialogue box

7 Click **OK** to run the ANOVA. Your results will appear in the output viewer window.

Interpreting your SPSS output for an independent one-way ANOVA

When descriptive statistics and post-hoc tests are selected, SPSS produces five tables in the output for an independent one-way ANOVA. Only three of these tables need attention, however (see Figs 13.6–13.8). The first table (Fig. 13.6) to look at is the table of descriptive statistics (if you selected this option) as this gives us the mean and standard deviation for each of the three conditions. The next table to look at is the 'Test of Between-Subjects Effects' (Fig. 13.7), which gives the F-ratio ($F = 8.026$) for our factor variable 'cond' along with the degrees of freedom (df = 2) and significance value ($p = 0.002$). As the significance value is below 0.05 we can say we have a significant difference between the means of the three conditions (the three educational interventions). This only tells us we have a significant difference but not among which pairs of conditions. In order to determine where exactly the difference(s) occur(s) (i.e. between which pair or pairs of variables) we need to look at the next table, 'Multiple Comparisons' (Fig. 13.8). This table will appear only if post-hoc tests were selected, of course. This table gives us the values for the Tukey HSD (the top half of the table) and Scheffé (the bottom half of the table) tests (as both were selected). The Tukey HSD is generally the test of choice and we shall look at that here (it is worth looking at the different results you get with different post-hoc tests, however). The left-hand column shows the result of comparing each group with every other group. As you can see, there is some repetition as Control is compared with Intervention A and then with Intervention B in the first row while Intervention A is compared with Control and Intervention B in the second row. The scores for each group are compared with the scores for every other (every possible combination will be covered). The second column ('Mean Difference (I–J)') shows the difference in means for each comparison. If you look at the first row of figures where Control is compared with Intervention A you can see the mean difference between these two conditions is –12.4 (that is, the mean of the Control condition minus the mean of the Intervention A condition).

Descriptive Statistics

Dependent Variable:test

cond	Mean	Std. Deviation	N
CONTROL	17.7000	4.73873	10
INTERVENTION A	30.1000	5.87745	10
INTERVENTION B	31.3000	12.44588	10
Total	26.3667	10.24016	30

Figure 13.6 ANOVA descriptive statistics output table

Tests of Between-Subjects Effects

Dependent Variable:test

Source	Type III Sum of Squares	df	Mean Square	F	Sig.	Partial Eta Squared	Noncent. Parameter	Observed Power[b]
Corrected Model	1133.867[a]	2	566.933	8.026	.002	.373	16.053	.934
Intercept	20856.033	1	20856.033	295.272	.000	.916	295.272	1.000
cond	1133.867	2	566.933	8.026	.002	.373	16.053	.934
Error	1907.100	27	70.633					
Total	23897.000	30						
Corrected Total	3040.967	29						

a. R Squared = .373 (Adjusted R Squared = .326)

b. Computed using alpha = .05

Figure 13.7 ANOVA test output table

Post Hoc Tests

cond

Multiple Comparisons

Dependent Variable:test

	(I) cond	(J) cond	Mean Difference (I-J)	Std. Error	Sig.	95% Confidence Interval Lower Bound	95% Confidence Interval Upper Bound
Tukey HSD	CONTROL	INTERVENTION A	-12.4000*	3.75855	.007	-21.7190	-3.0810
		INTERVENTION B	-13.6000*	3.75855	.003	-22.9190	-4.2810
	INTERVENTION A	CONTROL	12.4000*	3.75855	.007	3.0810	21.7190
		INTERVENTION B	-1.2000	3.75855	.945	-10.5190	8.1190
	INTERVENTION B	CONTROL	13.6000*	3.75855	.003	4.2810	22.9190
		INTERVENTION A	1.2000	3.75855	.945	-8.1190	10.5190
Scheffe	CONTROL	INTERVENTION A	-12.4000*	3.75855	.010	-22.1348	-2.6652
		INTERVENTION B	-13.6000*	3.75855	.005	-23.3348	-3.8652
	INTERVENTION A	CONTROL	12.4000*	3.75855	.010	2.6652	22.1348
		INTERVENTION B	-1.2000	3.75855	.950	-10.9348	8.5348
	INTERVENTION B	CONTROL	13.6000*	3.75855	.005	3.8652	23.3348
		INTERVENTION A	1.2000	3.75855	.950	-8.5348	10.9348

Based on observed means.
The error term is Mean Square(Error) = 70.633.

*. The mean difference is significant at the .05 level.

Figure 13.8 ANOVA multiple comparisons table

Therefore, the mean of the Intervention A condition was higher than that of the Control condition (by a value of 12.4 to be exact). If we move along the same row of figures we can see that this difference is significant ($p = 0.007$). By looking at the three tables together we can report the following:

1 An independent one-way ANOVA showed that there was a significant effect for the intervention programme on the end of year scholastic aptitude test ($F = 8.026$, df = 2, $p = 0.002$).

2 There is a significant difference ($p = 0.007$) between the means of Control condition (M = 17.7, SD = 4.74) and Intervention A (career guidance intervention) (M = 30.1, SD = 5.88), with pupils in Intervention A scoring higher on the test of scholastic aptitude than those in the Control group.

3 There is a significant difference ($p = 0.003$) between the means of Control condition (M = 17.7, SD = 4.74) and Intervention B (motivation intervention) (M = 31.3, SD = 12.45), with pupils in Intervention B scoring higher on the test of scholastic aptitude than those in the Control group.

4 There is not a significant difference ($p = 0.945$, ns) between the means of Intervention A (career guidance intervention) (M = 30.1, SD = 5.88) and Intervention B (motivation intervention) (M = 31.3, SD = 12.45).

Box 13.4

Command box	Computing a repeated measures one-way ANOVA

1 Open the file RMB_REPEAT_ANOVA.SAV (see Fig. 13.2). Click **Analyze** on the top menu bar.

2 Click on **General Linear Model** and then **Repeated Measures**. This will bring up an initial Repeated Measures ANOVA dialogue box, where you need to define your factors. You do this by typing in the number of levels (conditions) you have in each factor. In this case we only have one factor with three levels (1, 2 or 3 drinks) so we type in 3 in the **Number of Levels** box and click **Add** (see Fig. 13.9). Then click **Define** to open the **Repeated Measures** dialogue box.

3 You now need to move your repeated measures conditions (drink1, drink2 and drink3 here) into the **Within-Subjects Variables** box using the **Variable Picker** button. As they are moved across they will replace the underline and question mark already in the box (see Fig. 13.10, where 'drink1' and 'drink2' have already been moved across).

4 Click on the **Options** button to open a new dialogue box where you can select descriptive statistics by clicking on the box next to **Descriptive statistics**.

5 Click **OK** to run the ANOVA. Your results will appear in the output viewer window.

Box 13.4 *Continued*

Figure 13.9 Defining factors dialogue box

Figure 13.10 Repeated Measures ANOVA dialogue box

Interpreting your SPSS output for a repeated measures one-way ANOVA

SPSS produces more output for repeated measures ANOVA than with an independent ANOVA. However, you will need to look only at three of these tables (see Figs. 13.11–13.13). The first table to look at is the one with descriptive statistics of the data (the mean and standard deviation), for this tells us which condition has the highest score (Fig. 13.11). The second table to look at is the one labelled 'Mauchly's Test of Sphericity' (Fig. 13.12). If you remember, we explained that this test is needed with repeated measures ANOVA. If the test is significant then we need to examine the 'Greenhouse–Geisser' results instead of those where we have Sphericity Assumed. In this case the test is significant so we will need to examine the 'Greenhouse–Geisser' line of results (for Factor 1) in the table labelled 'Tests of Within-Subjects Effects' (Fig. 13.13). The F-ratio is 59.331 with df = 1.189 and a significance of $p = 0.001$ (although SPSS shows 0.000, this means $p < 001$). There is therefore a significant difference in the mean scores for the three conditions. In order to find out exactly where the difference(s) lie(s) with repeated measures ANOVA results it is necessary to compute a further set of related t-tests on the data (and then assess the significance using the Bonferroni correction). The results for these tests on the data are given in Fig. 13.14. All three differences are significant ($t = 2.23$, df = 19, $p = 00.038$; $t = 7.71$, df = 19, $p = 0.001$; $t = 8.11$, df = 19, $p = 0.01$) until the Bonferroni correction is applied (as there are three conditions, the values of p must be multiplied by 3). The first pair (between drink1 and drink2) is no longer significant ($p = 0.114$) while the second (drink1 and drink3) and third pairs (drink2 and drink3) remain significant ($p = 0.003$).

Descriptive Statistics

	Mean	Std. Deviation	N
drink1	82.8500	9.67512	20
drink2	81.1000	9.20469	20
drink3	64.5000	7.52889	20

Figure 13.11 ANOVA descriptive statistics output table

Mauchly's Test of Sphericity[b]

Measure:MEASURE_1

Within Subjects Effect	Mauchly's W	Approx. Chi-Square	df	Sig.	Epsilon[a]		
					Greenhouse-Geisser	Huynh-Feldt	Lower-bound
factor1	.318	20.649	2	.000	.594	.611	.500

Tests the null hypothesis that the error covariance matrix of the orthonormalized transformed dependent variables is proportional to an identity matrix.

a. May be used to adjust the degrees of freedom for the averaged tests of significance. Corrected tests are displayed in the Tests of Within-Subjects Effects table.

b. Design: Intercept
Within Subjects Design: factor1

Figure 13.12 Table of Mauchly's test of sphericity

Tests of Within-Subjects Effects

Measure:MEASURE_1

Source		Type III Sum of Squares	df	Mean Square	F	Sig.	Partial Eta Squared	Noncent. Parameter	Observed Power[a]
factor1	Sphericity Assumed	4102.300	2	2051.150	59.331	.000	.757	118.663	1.000
	Greenhouse-Geisser	4102.300	1.189	3450.976	59.331	.000	.757	70.529	1.000
	Huynh-Feldt	4102.300	1.223	3355.595	59.331	.000	.757	72.534	1.000
	Lower-bound	4102.300	1.000	4102.300	59.331	.000	.757	59.331	1.000
Error(factor1)	Sphericity Assumed	1313.700	38	34.571					
	Greenhouse-Geisser	1313.700	22.586	58.164					
	Huynh-Feldt	1313.700	23.228	56.557					
	Lower-bound	1313.700	19.000	69.142					

a. Computed using alpha = .05

Figure 13.13 Table of within-subjects effects

Paired Samples Statistics

		Mean	N	Std. Deviation	Std. Error Mean
Pair 1	drink1	82.8500	20	9.67512	2.16342
	drink2	81.1000	20	9.20469	2.05823
Pair 2	drink2	81.1000	20	9.20469	2.05823
	drink3	64.5000	20	7.52889	1.68351
Pair 3	drink1	82.8500	20	9.67512	2.16342
	drink3	64.5000	20	7.52889	1.68351

Paired Samples Correlations

		N	Correlation	Sig.
Pair 1	drink1 & drink2	20	.932	.000
Pair 2	drink2 & drink3	20	.352	.128
Pair 3	drink1 & drink3	20	.328	.157

Paired Samples Test

		Paired Differences							
					95% Confidence Interval of the Difference				
		Mean	Std. Deviation	Std. Error Mean	Lower	Upper	t	df	Sig. (2-tailed)
Pair 1	drink1 - drink2	1.75000	3.50751	.78430	.10843	3.39157	2.231	19	.038
Pair 2	drink2 - drink3	16.60000	9.62672	2.15260	12.09456	21.10544	7.712	19	.000
Pair 3	drink1 - drink3	18.35000	10.12176	2.26329	13.61287	23.08713	8.108	19	.000

Figure 13.14 Related *t*-test output

We can therefore report the following:

1 A repeated measures one-way ANOVA showed a significant effect for the three conditions ($F = 59.33$, df = 1.19, $p = 0.001$). As Mauchly's test of sphericity was significant the results are reported for Greenhouse–Geisser.

2 The means for performance on the driving simulator for the three conditions (1 to 3 drinks) were 82.85 (SD = 9.68), 81.10 (SD = 9.20) and 64.50 (SD = 7.53) respectively. Therefore, the amount of alcohol increased the more drivers failed to avoid hazards.

3 Three related *t*-tests were performed with Bonferroni correction).

13.3 Calculating a two-way ANOVA

A two-way ANOVA is very similar to a one-way ANOVA but with the inclusion of a second factor. For instance, using the example from the independent one-way ANOVA given above, we set out to test the condition (educational intervention) against test (the score on the scholastic aptitude test). Another variable is added with a two-way ANOVA so we might test the condition (educational intervention) *and* sex (sex of pupil) against test (the score on the scholastic aptitude test). The two-way ANOVA looks for an **interaction** between the factors in addition to the **main effects** for each factor on its own. We might find, for instance, that female pupils respond better to one of the educational interventions than the male pupils (when compared on test scores). The procedure for computing an independent two-way ANOVA with SPSS is almost identical to that used to compute an independent one-way ANOVA. And the procedure for computing a repeated measures two-way ANOVA with SPSS is almost identical to that used to compute a repeated measures one-way ANOVA. The only difference in both cases is that we need to specify an additional factor when defining our factors. This is done at the start with a repeated measures ANOVA (you just <u>**Add**</u> more than one factor in the initial dialogue box) and when selecting the <u>**Fixed Factor(s)**</u> with an independent ANOVA. Box 13.5 provides instructions for calculating an independent two-way ANOVA using the data described in Box 13.1 (including sex of pupil in addition to the condition factor).

Box 13.5

Command box	Computing a two-way ANOVA

1   Click on <u>**Analyze**</u> on the top menu bar.

2   Click on **General <u>L</u>inear Model** and then <u>**Univariate**</u>. This will bring up the **Univariate** ANOVA dialogue box.

3   Use the **Variable Picker** button to move the dependent variable ('test') into the <u>**Dependent Variable**</u> box.

4   Use the **Variable Picker** button to move the factor variable ('cond') into the <u>**Fixed Factor(s)**</u> box *and then* the other factor variable ('sex') into the <u>**Fixed Factor(s)**</u> box (see Fig. 13.15). This is the only procedural difference between a one-way and two-way ANOVA calculation using SPSS.

▶

Box 13.5 *Continued*

Figure 13.15 Univariate ANOVA dialogue box for two-way ANOVA

5   Click on the **Plots** button to open the **Univariate: Profile Plots** dialogue box. Move the factor variable ('cond') to the **Horizontal Axis** box and the other factor variable ('sex') to the **Separate Lines** box (see Fig. 13.16).

Figure 13.16 Univariate ANOVA profile plots box for two-way ANOVA

Box 13.5 *Continued*

6   Click on the **Post Hoc** button to open a new dialogue box where you can select post-hoc tests for multiple comparisons. You need to move the variable you want post-hoc tests for into the **Post Hoc Test** box using the **Variable Picker** button and then select the tests you want.

7   Click on the **Options** button to open a new dialogue box where you can select descriptive statistics by clicking on the box next to **Descriptive statistics**.

8   Click **OK** to run the ANOVA. Your results will appear in the output viewer window.

Interpreting your SPSS output for a two-way ANOVA

SPSS produces a similar set of tables for the independent two-way ANOVA as it does for the independent one-way ANOVA. Three tables are shown here (Figs 13.17–13.19). The first is the 'Descriptive Statistics' table (Fig. 13.17), which shows the means and standard deviations for every combination of sex and condition. The next table, labelled 'Tests of Between-Subjects Effects' (Fig. 13.18), like before, provides information on the main effects of the factors but also the interaction between the factors. The F-ratio for the factor 'cond' (educational intervention) is 23.771, which has 2 degrees of freedom and is significant ($p = 0.001$). This is expected, as condition was significant in the one-way ANOVA (we need to examine the multiple comparison test to determine where the differences lie but they should be similar to those we had before). The F-ratio for 'sex' (sex of pupil) is 15.409 (df = 1) and is also significant ($p = 0.001$). If we look back at Fig. 13.17 we can see that female pupils have a higher mean (M = 29.87, SD = 10.47) than male pupils (M = 22.87, SD = 9.01). So, we can see there are significant differences in scores on the test between the three conditions and between the two sexes. The final part of Fig. 13.18 that we need to

Descriptive Statistics

Dependent Variable: test

sex	cond	Mean	Std. Deviation	N
WOMEN	CONTROL	20.2000	4.14729	5
	INTERVENTION A	27.2000	2.28035	5
	INTERVENTION B	42.2000	6.76018	5
	Total	29.8667	10.47355	15
MEN	CONTROL	15.2000	4.20714	5
	INTERVENTION A	33.0000	7.17635	5
	INTERVENTION B	20.4000	2.40832	5
	Total	22.8667	9.01480	15
Total	CONTROL	17.7000	4.73873	10
	INTERVENTION A	30.1000	5.87745	10
	INTERVENTION B	31.3000	12.44588	10
	Total	26.3667	10.24016	30

Figure 13.17 ANOVA descriptive statistics output table

Tests of Between-Subjects Effects

Dependent Variable:test

Source	Type III Sum of Squares	df	Mean Square	F	Sig.
Corrected Model	2468.567[a]	5	493.713	20.701	.000
Intercept	20856.033	1	20856.033	874.467	.000
sex	367.500	1	367.500	15.409	.001
cond	1133.867	2	566.933	23.771	.000
sex * cond	967.200	2	483.600	20.277	.000
Error	572.400	24	23.850		
Total	23897.000	30			
Corrected Total	3040.967	29			

a. R Squared = .812 (Adjusted R Squared = .773)

Figure 13.18 ANOVA test output table

Multiple Comparisons

Dependent Variable:test

	(I) cond	(J) cond	Mean Difference (I-J)	Std. Error	Sig.	95% Confidence Interval	
						Lower Bound	Upper Bound
Tukey HSD	CONTROL	INTERVENTION A	-12.4000*	2.18403	.000	-17.8542	-6.9458
		INTERVENTION B	-13.6000*	2.18403	.000	-19.0542	-8.1458
	INTERVENTION A	CONTROL	12.4000*	2.18403	.000	6.9458	17.8542
		INTERVENTION B	-1.2000	2.18403	.848	-6.6542	4.2542
	INTERVENTION B	CONTROL	13.6000*	2.18403	.000	8.1458	19.0542
		INTERVENTION A	1.2000	2.18403	.848	-4.2542	6.6542
Scheffe	CONTROL	INTERVENTION A	-12.4000*	2.18403	.000	-18.0976	-6.7024
		INTERVENTION B	-13.6000*	2.18403	.000	-19.2976	-7.9024
	INTERVENTION A	CONTROL	12.4000*	2.18403	.000	6.7024	18.0976
		INTERVENTION B	-1.2000	2.18403	.861	-6.8976	4.4976
	INTERVENTION B	CONTROL	13.6000*	2.18403	.000	7.9024	19.2976
		INTERVENTION A	1.2000	2.18403	.861	-4.4976	6.8976

Based on observed means.
The error term is Mean Square(Error) = 23.850.

*. The mean difference is significant at the .05 level.

Figure 13.19 ANOVA multiple comparisons table

examine concerns the interaction between condition and sex. If you look at the line beginning sex*cond you can see there is an *F*-ratio of 20.277 (df = 2) which is also highly significant (*p* < 0.001).

In order to make sense of your interaction you will probably find the interaction graph helpful. This is a line graph showing the interaction between your factors (see Fig. 13.20). Female pupils in general had higher scores on the test than male pupils (the main effect for 'sex' described above). The three different conditions also produce different test results (the main effect for 'condition' described above) with the control condition producing lower test scores than either intervention. But as you can see, there is a clear interaction in this case. Female pupils in the second intervention (B) got a higher test score than male pupils but male pupils in the first intervention (A) got a higher test score than female pupils. Clearly, male pupils have responded best (in terms of test scores) to the career guidance intervention while female pupils have responded best to the motivational seminar intervention.

Profile Plots

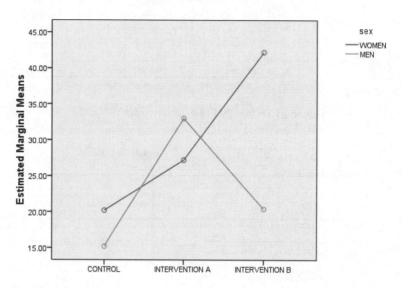

Figure 13.20 Interaction graph

The results should be reported in a similar way to those for an independent one-way ANOVA. However, it is also common practice with two-way ANOVAs to include an ANOVA summary table in a results section which includes information on the sums of squares, degrees of freedom, mean square, F-ratio and probability for the factors, interaction and error (information obtained from the 'Tests of Between-Subjects Effects' table).

13.4   Calculating a mixed design ANOVA

It is not a very great leap now to use SPSS to compute a mixed design ANOVA (where you have one or more repeated measures factors and one or more independent factors). The procedure is almost identical to a repeated measures ANOVA with one additional step (the inclusion of the independent factor in the Between-Subjects Factor(s) box) in the Repeated Measures dialogue box (Box 13.6). The only other difference is the option to select post-hoc tests for the independent factors (if they have three or more conditions). Otherwise the procedure is the same. The output is also very similar to that produced for a repeated measures ANOVA. The example below uses the repeated measures data described in Box 13.2 but this time including the independent factor 'sex' (sex of participant).

Box 13.6

Command box	Computing a mixed design ANOVA

1 Click on **Analyze** on the top menu bar.

2 Click on **General Linear Model** and then **Repeated Measures**. This will bring up an initial Repeated Measures ANOVA dialogue box, where you need to define your factors. You do this by typing in the number of levels (conditions) you have in each factor. In this case we only have one factor with three levels (1, 2 or 3 drinks) so we type in 3 in the **Number of Levels** box and click **Add** as before. Then click **Define** to open the Repeated Measures dialogue box.

3 You now need to move your repeated measures conditions (drink1, drink2 and drink3 here) into the **Within-Subjects Variables** box using the **Variable Picker** button as before.

4 You will also need to move your independent factor (sex) into the **Between-Subjects Factor(s)** box using the **Variable Picker** button.

5 Click on the **Options** button to open a new dialogue box where you can select descriptive statistics by clicking on the box next to **Descriptive statistics**.

6 If you have an independent factor with more than two conditions you may also want to click on **Post Hoc** to select post-hoc multiple comparisons. In this case the factor (sex) only has two conditions so this is unnecessary.

7 Click **OK** to run the ANOVA. Your results will appear in the output viewer window.

Interpreting your SPSS output for a mixed design ANOVA

The results produced are very similar to those given in repeated and independent ANOVA computations so we won't spend too much time on them here. Figs 13.21–13.25 show the important tables. Four of the five tables should be very familiar by now. As with any test, examine the descriptive statistics first (see Fig. 13.21). Remember that you will need to check whether Mauchly's test of sphericity (see Fig. 13.22) is significant in order to decide which line of the output in the 'Within-Subjects Effects' table to examine. In this case the test is significant so once again it is necessary to look at the Greenhouse–Geisser row in the 'Within-Subjects Effects' table (Fig. 13.23) to determine the significance of the repeated measures factor (number of drinks consumed). The 'Within-Subjects Contrasts' table is the only new table (Fig. 13.24). However, this simply shows the interaction ('FACTOR1*SEX') where you should generally examine the row for linear (rather than quadratic) contrasts. Details of the interaction (between the two factors) and effect of the independent factor (sex of participant) are given in the 'Within-Subjects Contrasts' and 'Between-Subjects Effects' tables (Figs 13.24 and 13.25).

Descriptive Statistics

	sex	Mean	Std. Deviation	N
drink1	1	84.3000	8.05605	10
	2	81.4000	11.31567	10
	Total	82.8500	9.67512	20
drink2	1	82.8000	7.98332	10
	2	79.4000	10.42646	10
	Total	81.1000	9.20469	20
drink3	1	67.5000	6.24055	10
	2	61.5000	7.79245	10
	Total	64.5000	7.52889	20

Figure 13.21 ANOVA descriptive statistics output table

Mauchly's Test of Sphericity[b]

Measure:MEASURE_1

Within Subjects Effect	Mauchly's W	Approx. Chi-Square	df	Sig.	Greenhouse-Geisser	Huynh-Feldt	Lower-bound
					Epsilon[a]		
factor1	.323	19.213	2	.000	.596	.650	.500

Tests the null hypothesis that the error covariance matrix of the orthonormalized transformed dependent variables is proportional to an identity matrix.

a. May be used to adjust the degrees of freedom for the averaged tests of significance. Corrected tests are displayed in the Tests of Within-Subjects Effects table.

b. Design: Intercept + sex
   Within Subjects Design: factor1

Figure 13.22 Mauchly's test of sphericity

Tests of Within-Subjects Effects

Measure:MEASURE_1

Source		Type III Sum of Squares	df	Mean Square	F	Sig.	Partial Eta Squared	Noncent. Parameter	Observed Power[a]
factor1	Sphericity Assumed	4102.300	2	2051.150	57.419	.000	.761	114.839	1.000
	Greenhouse-Geisser	4102.300	1.193	3439.836	57.419	.000	.761	68.478	1.000
	Huynh-Feldt	4102.300	1.300	3155.315	57.419	.000	.761	74.652	1.000
	Lower-bound	4102.300	1.000	4102.300	57.419	.000	.761	57.419	1.000
factor1 * sex	Sphericity Assumed	27.700	2	13.850	.388	.681	.021	.775	.108
	Greenhouse-Geisser	27.700	1.193	23.227	.388	.577	.021	.462	.094
	Huynh-Feldt	27.700	1.300	21.306	.388	.594	.021	.504	.096
	Lower-bound	27.700	1.000	27.700	.388	.541	.021	.388	.091
Error(factor1)	Sphericity Assumed	1286.000	36	35.722					
	Greenhouse-Geisser	1286.000	21.467	59.907					
	Huynh-Feldt	1286.000	23.402	54.952					
	Lower-bound	1286.000	18.000	71.444					

a. Computed using alpha = .05

Figure 13.23 Tests of within-subjects effects table

Tests of Within-Subjects Contrasts

Measure:MEASURE_1

Source	factor1	Type III Sum of Squares	df	Mean Square	F	Sig.	Partial Eta Squared	Noncent. Parameter	Observed Power[a]
factor1	Linear	3367.225	1	3367.225	63.850	.000	.780	63.850	1.000
	Quadratic	735.075	1	735.075	39.291	.000	.686	39.291	1.000
factor1 * sex	Linear	24.025	1	24.025	.456	.508	.025	.456	.098
	Quadratic	3.675	1	3.675	.196	.663	.011	.196	.070
Error(factor1)	Linear	949.250	18	52.736					
	Quadratic	336.750	18	18.708					

a. Computed using alpha = .05

Figure 13.24 Tests of within-subjects contrasts table

Tests of Between-Subjects Effects

Measure:MEASURE_1
Transformed Variable:Average

Source	Type III Sum of Squares	df	Mean Square	F	Sig.	Partial Eta Squared	Noncent. Parameter	Observed Power[a]
Intercept	347929.350	1	347929.350	2159.934	.000	.992	2159.934	1.000
sex	252.150	1	252.150	1.565	.227	.080	1.565	.220
Error	2899.500	18	161.083					

a. Computed using alpha = .05

Figure 13.25 Between-subjects effects table

13.5   Non-parametric alternatives – Kruskal–Wallis and Friedman

There are non-parametric equivalents to independent and repeated measures one-way ANOVAs. They are not commonly used (principally because ANOVA tests are remarkably robust to violations) but are still worth mentioning, albeit briefly. They are most often used with rank order data. The **Kruskal–Wallis** test is the non-parametric equivalent of the independent one-way ANOVA and the **Friedman** test is the non-parametric equivalent of the repeated measures one-way ANOVA. The procedures for computing these tests using SPSS are very similar to the procedures for calculating Mann–Whitney and Wilcoxon tests (given in Chapter 11). Instructions for calculating these tests using SPSS are given in Box 13.7.

Box 13.7

Command box   **Computing Kruskal–Wallis and Friedman tests**

1   Click **Analyze** on the top menu bar.

2   Click **Nonparametric Tests** and then **K Independent Samples** for the Kruskal–Wallis *or* K Related **Samples** for the Friedman tests. This will bring up a dialogue box where the variables to be tested can be specified.

3a   With **K Independent Samples** you will need to specify your grouping variable as you do with an independent *t*-test, the only difference being the greater number of groups (you define a range here rather than specify values for the two groups). You will also need to move your dependent variable into the **Test Variable List** box using the **Variable Picker** button.

3b   With **K Related Samples** you will need to highlight all of your repeated measures conditions and move them into the **Test Variables** box using the **Variable Picker** button.

4   Click **OK** to run the test. The output will appear in the output viewer window.

Interpreting your output for Kruskal–Wallis and Friedman tests

The output from both tests is very similar and very simple to understand. Each test produces two output tables. The first table (labelled 'Ranks') provides information about the mean rank scores for the conditions, while the second table (labelled 'Test Statistics') reports the value of chi-square (the statistic computed in these tests), its degrees of freedom and significance. The output from these tests should be reported in the same format as that for the Mann–Whitney and Wilcoxon tests described in Chapter 11.

14 Multivariate analysis of variance (MANOVA)

- This chapter introduces multivariate analysis of variance (MANOVA).

- It provides examples of when it would be appropriate to use MANOVA.

- Alternative strategies are described for situations where MANOVA might not be appropriate.

- An introduction to MANOVA is provided, with a worked example.

- A discriminant function analysis is used to supplement the results with a visual approach to the data.

INTRODUCTION

Multivariate statistics are required when there is more than one dependent variable in the study. This book concentrates on univariate statistics, where there is one dependent variable. Multivariate techniques are difficult to learn and require further study. Why, then, have we decided to include a chapter about MANOVA? The short answer is: because many of our students have asked us to. Although MANOVA is considered an advanced technique, many students discover that they will need, sooner or later, to consider more than one dependent variable in their research. We wanted to include MANOVA for this reason, but also so that we could alert you to some of the alternatives available. The first part of this chapter explains when it is appropriate to use MANOVA, and what alternatives are available when it is not appropriate. The second part runs through a worked example. Finally, discriminant function analysis is used to supplement and amplify the MANOVA results by displaying the results visually.

14.1   When would you use MANOVA?

There are usually three scenarios in which our students decide that they want to run a MANOVA. First, it can happen because students have designed a study where there are two dependent variables, chosen because they are substantively important, relevant to a theory, or identified in a literature review. There will normally be strong reasons for considering both variables. A second scenario is more unfortunate (and more common) – the study was badly designed. The decision about which variable should be the dependent variable was not thought through at the design stage, so several variables have to be shoehorned into the results. A third scenario in which we are often asked about MANOVA is when the study was non-experimental, such as a cross-sectional questionnaire study. Students often become confused about which variables are 'independent variables' and which are 'dependent variables'. In each of these three scenarios, MANOVA is not necessarily the answer.

Alternatives to MANOVA

There are several alternatives which you should consider using, if you have several dependent variables in your data. Think carefully about your research question, research design, and the data.

Factor analysis

If you have a large set of dependent variables, you can reduce them into a more manageable set of variables using factor analysis. Factor analysis is a 'data reduction' technique, popular with researchers who develop new questionnaires to measure psychological constructs (Chapter 5). A statistic called an **eigenvalue** describes the largest dimension of variance in the data, and then the next largest dimension, until most of the variance has been described. For example, suppose you administered the Youth Self Report scale in a study of antisocial behaviour among adolescents (e.g. Adalbjarnardottir & Rafnsson, 2002). This scale has 112 items, such as 'I disobey at school', 'I get into many fights', 'I destroy things belonging to others'. It would be unwise to treat these as 112 dependent variables. Instead, they could be factor analyzed to determine whether a single dimension of variation exists among each item. Then, Cronbach alpha (see Chapter 5) could be used to demonstrate that when treated as a single scale, there is sufficient alpha reliability. Adalbjarnardottir & Rafnsson (2002) treated the scale as a single variable, and found that it had excellent reliability ($\alpha = .89$). A full discussion of factor analysis is beyond the scope of this book. If you want to learn more about factor analysis, see Field (2005, Chapter 15).

Correlation and regression

If your study was non-experimental, it is often not appropriate to declare your variables 'independent' or 'dependent'. Students often tell us: 'I have a data set from a questionnaire study with lots of variables. I don't know how to analyse them. Someone told me that I should use MANOVA'. Here, we would recommend regression instead (see Chapter 15). There may be substantive variables that you want to treat as *outcomes*, or dependent in the sense that you want to see what predicts scores on a substantive variable (e.g. depression), but the independent variables are usually continuous (e.g. age, attitudes, anxiety) rather than categorical (e.g. control = 0, treatment = 1). In these situations, correlation and regression are appropriate techniques. You must be careful not to imply that the independent (or predictor) variables *cause* the dependent variable. The word 'associated' is more appropriate because it implies less strong assumptions about *how* they are associated.

In a situation where you have several substantive 'outcome' variables, you may need to perform separate multiple regressions or factor analyse the variables into a smaller number first (see above). If the variables are very similar, consider combining them into a 'total score' or dropping some of them. For example, if you have scores on four cognitive tests (verbal reasoning, quantitative reasoning, abstract visual reasoning, short-term memory) you can legitimately combine them into a single, composite measure. This is because prior research indicates that there appears to be one dimension of variation among cognitive tests – they do not measure substantially different skills (Deary & Batty, 2007). Put differently, people who have high scores on one of these tests tend to have high scores on the other tests. MANOVA may not be necessary here, because the tests can be treated as a single dependent variable (cognitive ability score).

Canonical correlation

If you want to find out whether a set of independent variables (e.g. personality traits) predict a set of dependent variables (e.g. unhealthy behaviours), then canonical correlation may be useful. If the dependent variables are highly correlated, then regression is probably more appropriate. You may want to consider dropping all but one of the variables, or combining them into a summary score. If, however, the variables are clearly quite different (e.g. smoking, alcohol, inactivity, high fat diet) then you have a strong rationale for using canonical correlation. Using eigenvalues (see above), canonical correlation produces two factors which maximise the scores on both sets of variables (independent and dependent). It looks for the highest correlation between the factors as far as is possible.

ANOVA

If you have conducted an experiment and there really are several dependent variables then this is the most difficult scenario to manage. It may be practical to treat each dependent variable separately, conducting univariate analyses (e.g. *t*-test, ANOVA, regression) on each one. However, you need to remember that this increases the likelihood of obtaining significant results by chance (Type I error) and is therefore more dangerous (see Chapters 8 and 13). MANOVA is the best strategy for ensuring that the Type I error rate is reduced, because it performs the whole analysis in one fell swoop. You do not capitalise on chance. However, if you are conducting research as part of a student project or learning exercise, it may be worth consulting your tutor to find out if MANOVA is taught at your level of study. MANOVA is not a requirement for many 'early level' psychology courses. Support may not be available, and tutors and/or supervisors may not have the expertise to help you if you get stuck. It may be acceptable to present separate ANOVAs for your purposes. We have found that some students misunderstood what was required of them in a research project and struggled on their own with MANOVA when all we really required was ANOVA. However, at some levels of study, and at some institutions, MANOVA may be a technique you are expected to learn, and expected to use. In the published literature, it would certainly not be acceptable to rely on the performance of several ANOVAs to analyse multivariate data sets.

14.2   Introduction to MANOVA

There are two main advantages of using MANOVA. First, it can model two dependent variables at the same time. Second, MANOVA can acknowledge and model the correlation between the dependent variables. In psychological research, it is often the case that the 'outcome' (dependent) variables we are interested in are related. It is rare for two outcome variables to be completely independent. For example, we may want to look at the impact of an educational intervention on students' exam marks, and on their coursework marks. Selected at random, half of students receive a free textbook, and the other half do not. We predict that marks will be higher, on both outcomes, for those who received the free book. The outcomes are probably correlated because (on average) students who get better marks in exams get better marks in coursework. However, exams and coursework are not the same outcome. For this reason, we may predict that our intervention has a different effect for each outcome. Lots of different scenarios could occur. The book could raise exam scores, but not coursework scores. It could raise coursework scores, but not exam scores. It could raise exam scores substantially, but raise coursework scores slightly. It could even lower exam scores (e.g. if it contained information that was distracting, irrelevant or confusing) while raising coursework scores (e.g. if it was particularly relevant for the coursework). Furthermore, there may be different effects on a composite of coursework and exam scores – some kind of general attainment score, which underlies both outcomes. In summary, MANOVA has two key strengths. It reduces the Type I error rate and acknowledges the correlation between dependent variables.

| **14.3** | Calculating a MANOVA |

A fictitious data set is used as an example. Data for this example are available from the book website (details of the data are given in Box 14.1). Box 14.2 gives details of how to calculate a MANOVA. Advice on interpreting the output for the MANOVA is provided below the command boxes. The primary research question was, 'does jogging or counselling improve scores on physical and mental health?' This seemingly simple question masks several secondary research questions, which complicate the interpretation of results. Which type of health is changed (physical *or* mental health)? If scores on health are changed, we want to know the direction of that change (increase or decrease). We also want to know the effect size (by how much are they changed). And because physical and mental are both dependent variables, and may be correlated, the size of this correlation is also part of the research question. MANOVA treats the dependent variables as a 'composite variable', creating a new combined physical and mental health variable. Do jogging or counselling predict the composite variable (physical *and* mental health)? Formally defined, the question here is 'what linear combination of physical and mental health scores best differentiates the counselling and jogging treatment groups?' Finally, as with many of the statistical tests described in this book, we want to know if the effects could have occurred by chance.

Box 14.1

| Data box | Data used for MANOVA |

The data file is called rmb-manova.sav and is available from the book website. Figure 14.1 shows how the data are entered in SPSS. It is the raw data from a fictitious experiment conducted to compare two different treatments (jogging and counselling) on two health outcomes (physical health and mental health). There were 15 participants assigned to each intervention, and 15 assigned to a control group with no intervention (45 in total). This is an independent measures design. The aim of the experiment was to see if jogging or counselling improved physical and/or mental health status.

Physical health is not the same as mental health, so they are two separate dependent variables. This does not mean that they are completely separate variables. Often, physical and mental health are correlated. People who have better physical health may tend to report better mental health, and vice versa. Physical and mental health status can be measured using the physical component summary (PCS) and mental component summary (MCS) scores from The SF-36 Health Outcome Survey. The SF-36 is a standardised, validated questionnaire designing to measure different aspects of health status (see Chapter 5). We know that the SF-36 can measure health because a large amount of previous research has demonstrated its reliability and validity.

Box 14.1 *Continued*

Figure 14.1 Data being used for the MANOVA

Box 14.2

Command box	Computing a MANOVA

1   Click on **Analyze** on the top menu bar.

2   Click on **General Linear Model** and then **Multivariate** (see Fig. 14.2). This will bring up the **Multivariate** dialogue box (see Fig. 14.3). Multivariate refers to the fact that we have more than one dependent variable.

3   Use the **Variable Picker** button to move the dependent variables ('PCS' and 'MCS') into the **Dependent Variable** box (see Fig. 14.4).

4   Use the **Variable Picker** button to move the factor variable ('cond') into the **Fixed Factor(s)** box (see Fig. 14.4).

5   Click on the **Contrasts** button to open the **Multivariate: Contrasts** dialogue box. Under **Change Contrast**, change **Contrast**, using the drop-down menu, to **Simple** and the **Reference Category** to 'First' (see Fig. 14.5). This will compare the control group (0) with the other two groups (1 and 2, jogging and counselling). Click on **Continue** to return to the **Multivariate** dialogue box.

▶

Box 14.2 *Continued*

Figure 14.2 Obtaining MANOVA

Figure 14.3 General linear model: Multivariate dialogue box (1)

Box 14.2 *Continued*

Figure 14.4 General linear model: Multivariate dialogue box (2)

Figure 14.5 Multivariate: Contrasts dialogue box

6   Click on the **Plots** button to open the **Multivariate: Plots** dialogue box.
     Use the **Variable Picker** button to move 'cond' into the **Horizontal Axis**
     box, then click on **Add** to move this to the **Plots** box. Click on **Continue**
     to return to the **Multivariate** dialogue box.

7   Click on the **Options** button to open the **Multivariate: Options** dialogue
     box. Use the **Variable Picker** button to move 'group' to the **Display**
     Means for: box. Under **Display**, select the following boxes: **Descriptive**
     statistics, **Estimates of effect size**, **Observed power**, **Homogeneity tests**.
     Other options may be relevant, depending on your research design.

8   Click **OK** to run the MANOVA. Your results will appear in the output
     viewer window.

Descriptive Statistics

	cond	Mean	Std. Deviation	N
SF-36 Physical Component Summary	No treatment (control group)	51.67	11.069	15
	Jogging	68.47	13.303	15
	Counselling	53.47	13.303	15
	Total	57.87	14.478	45
SF-36 Mental Component Summary	No treatment (control group)	48.47	13.303	15
	Jogging	61.67	11.069	15
	Counselling	71.67	11.069	15
	Total	60.60	15.054	45

Figure 14.6 Descriptive statistics

Interpreting your SPSS output for a MANOVA

Descriptive statistics

The first thing to inspect, as with any set of results, is the descriptive statistics (see Fig. 14.6). These are extremely useful for checking the accuracy of the data, and screening for potential errors. We should expect to see a sample size of 45, comprised of 15 in each of the three groups. Next, we can inspect the means and standard deviations in each group for the PCS and MCS. You can see that, in the control group, the PCS has a mean of 51.67, the MCS has a mean of 48.47 and the standard deviations are approximately 11. This is approximately what you would expect to find in a sample of the general population. The SF-36 scores are designed to have a mean of 50 and a standard deviation of 10 (this form of standardisation is called a *t*-score). Given that no intervention has taken place in this group, this is consistent with expectations. We can see that the jogging treatment has increased mean scores for both dependent variables (68.47 for PCS, 61.67 for MCS). This suggests that jogging has improved physical and mental health, but more so for physical health. Finally, we can see that counselling has a very slight impact on improved PCS scores (mean 53.47) but a large impact on MCS scores (mean 71.67). Standard deviations look very similar in all conditions, for all variables. We cannot interpret these statistics as significant at this stage, but they are useful as a preliminary step, and give an indication of the strength and direction of the experimental effect.

Box's test for equality of covariance matrices

MANOVA refers to **matrices** (the plural of matrix), which are grids of numbers, arranged in rows and columns. Because there are two dependent variables, the calculations are performed on matrices rather than on single numbers. Technically, single numbers are also matrices, 1 row by 1 column, but they are rarely called matrices. A column matrix (2 rows by 1 column) is used to do the calculations. Each group (jogging, counselling, control) has its own matrix. Ideally, we would expect these matrices to be different in some way. If they were the same, then there would be little point in conducting a MANOVA. Box's test is a test that the matrices are significantly equal (see Fig. 14.7). This test is about 'sameness', but we want the matrices to be significantly different. If the matrices

Box's Test of Equality of Covariance Matrices[a]

Box's M	1.705
F	.265
df1	6.000
df2	43964.308
Sig.	.953

Tests the null hypothesis that the observed covariance matrices of the dependent variables are equal across groups.

a. Design: Intercept + cond

Figure 14.7 Box's test

were the same, there would be no point in performing a MANOVA. For this reason, the p value for Box's test should be greater than .05 ($p > .05$). In our data, the value is 0.95, which is much larger that this. This very high value has occurred because the data are fictional, and the differences between groups have been designed purposely that way. The value of 0.95 is unlikely to occur in a real data set. When working with your own data, look for a value of .05 or higher.

Multivariate tests

The results we are interested in are the 'cond', the second row in the multivariate tests output box (see Fig. 14.8). There are four different tests (Pillai's Trace, Wilk's Lambda, Hotelling's Trace, Roy's Largest Root), which are different ways of testing the statistical significance of the eigenvalues. The technical detail behind these tests is beyond the scope of this book. The important thing to note is that they are all highly significant. The 'Sig.' column shows p values of .000 for each test. Remember that $p = .000$ in SPSS actually means $p < .001$. In other words, the probability that the eigenvalues from our data are actually this size, if null hypothesis was true, is very small indeed. The choice of test has no impact on whether the results are significant. When working with your own data, you may find that some tests are significant, and some are not. We will take Pillai's Trace, because it is the most conservative estimate.

Multivariate Tests[d]

Effect		Value	F	Hypothesis df	Error df	Sig.	Partial Eta Squared	Noncent. Parameter	Observed Power[b]
Intercept	Pillai's Trace	.971	6.911E2	2.000	41.000	.000	.971	1382.131	1.000
	Wilks' Lambda	.029	6.911E2	2.000	41.000	.000	.971	1382.131	1.000
	Hotelling's Trace	33.711	6.911E2	2.000	41.000	.000	.971	1382.131	1.000
	Roy's Largest Root	33.711	6.911E2	2.000	41.000	.000	.971	1382.131	1.000
cond	Pillai's Trace	.754	12.698	4.000	84.000	.000	.377	50.793	1.000
	Wilks' Lambda	.375	12.956[a]	4.000	82.000	.000	.387	51.823	1.000
	Hotelling's Trace	1.320	13.196	4.000	80.000	.000	.398	52.782	1.000
	Roy's Largest Root	.962	20.206[c]	2.000	42.000	.000	.490	40.412	1.000

a. Exact statistic

b. Computed using alpha = .05

c. The statistic is an upper bound on F that yields a lower bound on the significance level.

d. Design: Intercept + cond

Figure 14.8 Multivariate tests

■ Conclusion 1: Using Pillai's Trace, there was a significant effect of the intervention on the dependent variables ($F = 12.70$, df $= 4$, $p < .001$).

Levene's test

Levene's test corresponds broadly to the homogeneity of variance test in ANOVA (see Chapter 13). For repeated measures designs, Bartlett's test of sphericity corresponds to Mauchly's test of sphericity. We are looking for a non-significant value here, because the test is that the variances are *different* in each condition. The statistic is non-significant both for PCS ($p = .88$) and for MCS ($p = .85$), which means that the assumption of equal variances is tenable (see Fig. 14.9). Again, the values are artificially high and are often lower when working with real data. The significance value should be .05 or higher in your data.

Levene's Test of Equality of Error Variances[a]

	F	df1	df2	Sig.
SF-36 Physical Component Summary	.131	2	42	.878
SF-36 Mental Component Summary	.162	2	42	.851

Tests the null hypothesis that the error variance of the dependent variable is equal across groups.

a. Design: Intercept + cond

Figure 14.9 Levene's test

Effect size

The **effect size** is more interesting than the multivariate tests. It is provided in the 'Partial Eta Squared' column of the Tests of Between-Subjects Effects table (see Fig. 14.10). For each condition, it tells you how big the experimental effect was (here, how effective the interventions were). An Eta Squared of .01 is considered small, .06 medium and .14 large (Cohen, 1988). Partial Eta Squared may overestimate the effect size, particularly when you have a small sample size. Unfortunately, SPSS does not provide Eta Squared so we have to use Partial Eta Squared as an approximate guide. The values are .28 for PCS and .41 for MCS, indicating that the experimental effect was very large.

■ Conclusion 2: Partial Eta Squared values for PCS (.28) and MCS (.41) indicated a large effect size for the experimental conditions.

Statistical power

The standard acceptable threshold for statistical power in most psychology journals is 80% (see Chapter 8 for an introduction to statistical power). You can see that our data set has good statistical power, because the power value is greater than 80% in the Observed power column of the 'Tests of Between-Subjects Effects' column (see Fig. 14.10). Power values in SPSS output are expressed as a proportion of 1, so you can multiply the values to obtain a percentage ($.943 \times 100 = 94.3\%$ for PCS, $.998 \times 100 = 99.8\%$ for MCS). If your study is underpowered, then this value will be lower. You may need to increase your sample size to improve statistical power. However, power also depends on the effect size. Larger effect sizes are easier to detect with smaller sample sizes (see Chapter 8). Because our effect size was so large, the power is very high.

The size of the correlation between the dependent variables can influence the results of the MANOVA. In our example, the PCS and MCS were substantially correlated ($r = .39$). The SF-36 was designed to produce uncorrelated PCS and MCS scores, but in practice researchers often find that they are correlated (e.g. Farivar *et al.*, 2007). Whatever your choice of dependent variable, you may find that they are more correlated than you expected them to be. Therefore, it is important to consider the implications of this correlation for your results. The correlation between your dependent variables will influence the statistical power of your study. In our example, the most conservative estimate of power is 94.3%.

■ Conclusion 3: The power of the MANOVA was 94.3% for PCS and 99.8% for MCS.

Between-subjects effects

The multivariate tests (see Fig. 14.8) confirmed that the experimental effect was significant. However, it did not tell us *which* dependent variables were significant. In the Tests of Between-Subjects Effects (see Fig. 14.10), the row labelled 'cond' (condition) shows us that PCS is highly significant ($F = 8.04$, 2 df, $p < .001$) and so is MCS ($F = 14.44$, 2 df, $p < .001$)

Tests of Between-Subjects Effects									
Source	Dependent Variable	Type III Sum of Squares	df	Mean Square	F	Sig.	Partial Eta Squared	Noncent. Parameter	Observed Power[b]
Corrected Model	SF-36 Physical Component Summary	2552.400[a]	2	1276.200	8.035	.001	.277	16.070	.943
	SF-36 Mental Component Summary	4062.400[c]	2	2031.200	14.439	.000	.407	28.878	.998
Intercept	SF-36 Physical Component Summary	150684.800	1	150684.800	948.726	.000	.958	948.726	1.000
	SF-36 Mental Component Summary	165256.200	1	165256.200	1174.728	.000	.965	1174.728	1.000
cond	SF-36 Physical Component Summary	2552.400	2	1276.200	8.035	.001	.277	16.070	.943
	SF-36 Mental Component Summary	4062.400	2	2031.200	14.439	.000	.407	28.878	.998
Error	SF-36 Physical Component Summary	6670.800	42	158.829					
	SF-36 Mental Component Summary	5908.400	42	140.676					
Total	SF-36 Physical Component Summary	159908.000	45						
	SF-36 Mental Component Summary	175227.000	45						
Corrected Total	SF-36 Physical Component Summary	9223.200	44						
	SF-36 Mental Component Summary	9970.800	44						

a. R Squared = .277 (Adjusted R Squared = .242)
b. Computed using alpha = .05
c. R Squared = .407 (Adjusted R Squared = .379)

Figure 14.10 Tests of between-subjects effects

■ Conclusion 4: The experimental effect was highly significant for both outcomes: PCS ($F = 8.04$, 2 df, $p < .001$) and MCS ($F = 14.44$, 2 df, $p < .001$).

Custom hypothesis tests

Because we planned some contrasts in advance, we can also look at which *conditions* had significant effects, for both PCS and MCS. In an intervention study such as this one, finding out which condition was most effective is part of the reason for conducting a MANOVA in the first place. *Which* intervention was most effective? For *which* outcome? The control group was used as the reference group, which makes sense because the aim of the study was to compare counselling with no intervention, and jogging with no intervention. In the Contrast Results output (see Fig. 14.11), level 1 (control) is compared with level 2 (jogging), and level 1 is separately compared with level 3 (counselling). Don't worry that we coded the conditions with different numbers (0 was control, 1 was jogging, 2 was counselling). SPSS will use the number 1 to identify the reference for the contrast. Both outcomes, the two experiment conditions (jogging and counselling), are compared to the control condition. Three of the comparisons are significant, and one is non-significant. For jogging (Level 2 vs. Level 1), the row labelled Sig. provides the probability that the value in the Contrast Estimate (the increase in PCS and MCS scores) is true, given a null hypothesis that the value is 0 (no change). We can see that jogging has increased PCS scores by 16.80 ($p < .001$) and MCS scores by 13.2 ($p < .004$). Both of these increases are highly significant. For counselling (Level 3 vs. Level 1) the story is different.

Custom Hypothesis Tests

Contrast Results (K Matrix)

		Dependent Variable	
		SF-36 Physical Component Summary	SF-36 Mental Component Summary
cond Simple Contrast[a]			
Level 2 vs. Level 1	Contrast Estimate	16.800	13.200
	Hypothesized Value	0	0
	Difference (Estimate - Hypothesized)	16.800	13.200
	Std. Error	4.602	4.331
	Sig.	.001	.004
	95% Confidence Interval for Difference — Lower Bound	7.513	4.460
	Upper Bound	26.087	21.940
Level 3 vs. Level 1	Contrast Estimate	1.800	23.200
	Hypothesized Value	0	0
	Difference (Estimate - Hypothesized)	1.800	23.200
	Std. Error	4.602	4.331
	Sig.	.698	.000
	95% Confidence Interval for Difference — Lower Bound	-7.487	14.460
	Upper Bound	11.087	31.940

a. Reference category = 1

Figure 14.11 Contrast results

Counselling has raised PCS scores only by 1.80 points ($p = .698$) which is not a significant increase. In contrast, it has raised MCS scores by 23.20 points which is highly significant ($p < .001$).

■ Conclusion 5: Compared to the control group, jogging significantly increased both PCS and MCS scores. Counselling, compared to the control group, increased PCS scores but the increase was not statistically significant. It did raise MCS scores and this was highly significant.

The MANOVA plots

It is unfortunate that the MANOVA plots are printed last in the SPSS output. They are usually the second thing we look at (after descriptive statistics) when running a MANOVA. With a visual display of the data, a picture is worth a thousand words. As can be seen in Figs. 14.12 and 14.13, the results of the experiment are crystal clear. There is a clear impact on MCS scores from jogging, and more so from counselling. PCS scores are only slightly increased by counselling, and are substantially increased from jogging. These plots convey most of the information described in the results, and are a useful accompaniment to the statistics. Another visual technique is available that can help you understand more about what is happening to the dependent variables: discriminant function analysis.

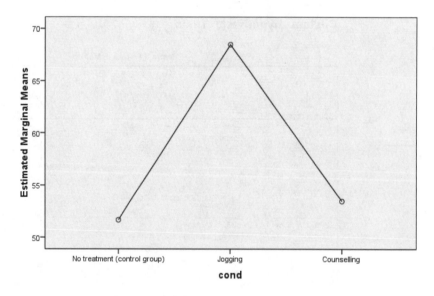

Estimated Marginal Means of SF-36 Physical Component Summary

Figure 14.12 MANOVA plot for PCS

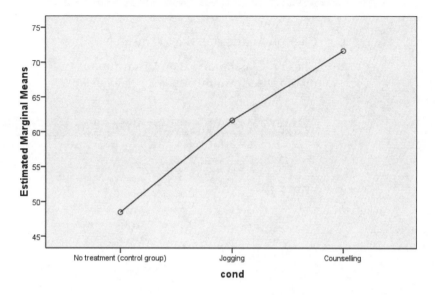

Figure 14.13 MANOVA plot for MCS

14.4 Running a discriminant function analysis

Using MANOVA, we have discovered a difference in physical and mental health between the three groups of the experiment. However, we also want to know the *directions* and *dimensions* along which these differences can be detected (Tatsuoka, 1971). What is the *nature* of the relationship? How can it be characterised and described? We didn't just find that the conditions influenced physical and mental health separately – we also found that the conditions influenced physical *and* mental health together. There are two dependent variables here, which may co-vary (correlate). The fact that physical and mental health are correlated means that their relationship with the independent variable (the experimental conditions: jogging, counselling and control) is not going to be simple! We need to explore how the conditions are related to the co-variance in the dependent variables, variance comprised of both the physical and mental health data. Discriminant function analysis (Box 14.3) is one way to do that.

Box 14.3

| Command box | Running a discriminant function analysis to supplement MANOVA |

1   Click on **Analyze** on the top menu bar.

2   Click on **Classify** and then **Discriminant** (see Fig. 14.14). This will bring up the **Discriminant Analysis** dialogue box.

Figure 14.14 Obtaining discriminant function analysis

3   Use the **Variable Picker** button to move the grouping variables ('cond') into the **Grouping Variable** box.

4   Click on the **Define Range** button and enter the lowest and highest value for the 'cond' variable. In our example, 0 is the lowest and 2 is the highest, because there are three conditions in the experiment (see Fig. 14.15)

5   Use the **Variable Picker** button to move the dependent variables (here, treated as independent variables) into the **Independents** box. Discriminant function analysis calls the variables independent variables, because they predict the discriminant functions. This does not change our interpretation of the MANOVA, so don't worry about this.

Box 14.3 *Continued*

Figure 14.15 Discriminant function analysis dialogue box

6   Click on the **Classify** button to open a new dialogue box where you can select a combined plot by clicking on **Combined-groups** (see Fig. 14.16). Click on the **Summary** table option and then click on **Continue** to return to the Discriminant Analysis dialogue box.

Figure 14.16 Classify dialogue box

7   The default setting is to analyse both the 'Independents' simultaneously, so you can leave this option selected and click on **OK** to run the analysis. Your results will appear in the output viewer window.

Interpreting discriminant functions

The purpose of discriminant function analysis is to find the 'directions and dimensions' that best characterise and maximise the differences between the three groups and a composite of the dependent variables. The focus shifts from the effect of the independent variables to the relationship between the dependent variables (PCS and MCS). **Discriminant functions** are dimensions (also called variates, factors or latent variables) that capture the largest amount of variance in all of the scores. The term **variate** should not be confused with the terms **variable** or **variance**. For this reason, we prefer the term **discriminant function**. Eigenvalues are used to calculate what percentage of variance each dimension can account for. We can see from the Eigenvalues table in the output that the first discriminant function is large – it accounts for 72.9 per cent of the variance in the PCS and MCS scores (see Fig. 14.17). The second discriminant function accounts for 27.1 per cent of the variance. The Wilk's Lambda table (see Fig. 14.18) is simply a test that both these eigenvalues are significant (both are $p < .001$).

Analysis 1

Summary of Canonical Discriminant Functions

Eigenvalues

Function	Eigenvalue	% of Variance	Cumulative %	Canonical Correlation
1	.962[a]	72.9	72.9	.700
2	.357[a]	27.1	100.0	.513

a. First 2 canonical discriminant functions were used in the analysis.

Figure 14.17 Eigenvalues output

Wilks' Lambda

Test of Function(s)	Wilks' Lambda	Chi-square	df	Sig.
1 through 2	.375	40.654	4	.000
2	.737	12.680	1	.000

Figure 14.18 Wilks' Lambda output

The structure matrix

The structure matrix (see Fig. 14.19) allows us to interpret what the discriminant functions are comprised of. It is quite easy to interpret, because it presents the correlation between each variable and the two functions, which can be between 0 and 1. Clearly, the first function is comprised mostly of variance from the MCS ($r = .74$) and PCS scores, which contribute negatively to the variate ($r = -.20$). The second is a mixture of PCS ($r = .98$) and MCS ($r = .67$), but mostly PCS. It looks like there are two underlying dimensions that characterise our data.

Structure Matrix

	Function	
	1	2
SF-36 Mental Component Summary	.739*	.674
SF-36 Physical Component Summary	-.204	.979*

Pooled within-groups correlations between discriminating variables and standardized canonical discriminant functions
Variables ordered by absolute size of correlation within function.

*. Largest absolute correlation between each variable and any discriminant function

Figure 14.19 Structure matrix output

Most of the variance in the data was on MCS. However, there was a second, unmeasured dimension on which people varied. It was comprised of a blend of MCS and PCS variance. The intervention did not simply target PCS and MCS separately. It targeted two, more complex, components of health. Discriminant functions are not always interpretable. In our example, they are fairly easy to interpret as psychologically meaningful and sensible dimensions. This was because we knew, in advance, that the PCS and MCS both measured different components of health and that they were correlated. We knew, from the results of the MANOVA, that the experiment effects were most pronounced for MCS. Therefore, it is unsurprising that the first discriminant function captured mental health and the second discriminant function captured a composite of physical and mental health variance. With real data, however, you may find that the discriminant functions are not immediately meaningful. However, discriminant functions that do not seem intuitive can later turn out to have great scientific importance (Tatsuoka, 1971: 191). Do not dismiss them out of hand if they do not tell a clear story straightaway.

The combined groups plot

Visual techniques for displaying data are often the most powerful. The combined groups plot makes the story clearer for our example (see Fig. 14.20). The first thing to look at in this plot is the discriminant functions. The first function is plotted on the *x*-axis and the second is plotted on the *y*-axis. Different colours, which appear in Fig. 14.20 as different shades of grey, are used to identify which condition of the experiment the participant belonged to (jogging, counselling or the control condition). The 'centroid' is the average score for each condition on each of the discriminant functions. Each participant's score on the functions is displayed. Next, look at the *direction* in which the groups appear on each discriminant function, and at the *distance* between them. The direction of the first function runs from control, to jogging, to counselling. This variate captures the variance in mental health, and amplifies the insights we gained from the MANOVA. Counselling raised mental health the most, followed by jogging, followed by the control. The direction of the second function runs from control to counselling, to jogging. This reflects the (non-significant) slight increase in physical health we saw from jogging in the MANOVA. However, we learn here that the second variate isn't just variance from physical health. It is

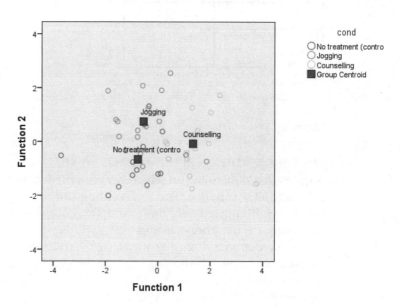

Figure 14.20 Combined groups plot

an unmeasured combination of 'left over' mental health variance *and* physical health variance. Jogging is tapping some general health construct, made up of the remaining 12 per cent of the variance left over from the first variate. So, it looks like jogging is good for some underlying 'physical and mental, but mostly physical' construct. Counselling, on the other hand, is good for mental health, and outperforms jogging. Another way to describe our findings is that jogging had an impact on the *covariance* (the shared variance) between PCS and MCS. By combining MANOVA with discriminant function analysis, we can explore subtle complexities such as this. MANOVA alone may not provide a full understanding of how the dependent variables are related, and how the independent variables influence their relationship. Visual techniques for exploring data are always a useful supplement to statistical tests. Hopefully, this introduction has sparked your interest in multivariate statistics. A word of warning, however: multivariate analysis rarely runs smoothly! A well-designed research question, with carefully planned methods, can often be analysed using univariate techniques. If you can use a simpler model, then that is what you should do.

Further reading

Field, A. P. (2005). *Discovering Statistics Using SPSS*, 2nd edn. London: Sage.

Chapter 14 is an excellent introduction to MANOVA and discriminant function analysis. You can even learn how to do one by hand! If you are interested in factor analysis, there is a separate chapter devoted to that (Chapter 15).

Tabachnik, B. G. & Fidell, L. S. (2006). *Using Multivariate Statistics*, 5th edn. Needham Heights, MA: Allyn and Bacon.

This book covers a wide range of multivariate techniques, but has separate chapters devoted to MANOVA canonical correlation, and discriminant function analysis. The book is very advanced, but extremely popular with quantitative researchers.

15 Regression

- This chapter begins by explaining the fundamentals of linear regression (simple and multiple).

- The chapter then demonstrates how to carry out multiple regression using SPSS.

- Finally, information is given about further reading on other statistical tests not covered in this book.

INTRODUCTION

We have already covered correlation (Chapter 12) and **regression** is really just an extension of correlation where the relationship between two or more variables is used for prediction rather than description. Very simply, when we have two variables that are related we can use the value of a score on one (or more) variables to predict the value of a score on the other variable. This is not perfect unless of course the relationship (correlation) between the two variables is perfect ($r = +$ or -1.0). In reality, a correlation will never be perfect so there will always be some error that we cannot account for but, in general, the stronger the relationship between the two variables (the higher the correlation), the better the prediction of one from the other. This is really all there is to regression. **Simple regression** is where we have only one independent and one dependent variable and **multiple regression** is where we have two or more independent variables and one dependent variable.

Regression (multiple regression to be precise) is most commonly used in survey research where the scores on a number of independent variables (measured using questionnaire scales) are used to predict some outcome variable (also measured using a questionnaire scale). For instance, the theory of reasoned action (Ajzen & Fishbein, 1980; Fishbein & Ajzen, 1975) is one of the most important theories in attitude-behaviour research. It provides a theoretical account of the way in which attitudes, subjective norms and behavioural intentions can be used to predict behaviour. According to the theory of reasoned action (TRA), behavioural intentions, which are the immediate antecedents to behaviour, are determined by attitudes and subjective norms. Attitudes refer to a person's positive or negative judgement of their performing the behaviour (e.g. 'For me, using contraception with my partner would be good/bad').

The second determinant of intention is the person's subjective norm which refers to perceptions of 'social pressure' to perform a given behaviour (e.g. 'Most people who are important to me think I should use contraception with my partner'). Therefore, it can be seen that behaviour is a function of behavioural intentions, which are a function of attitudes and subjective norms. So, if we have information about people's attitudes towards buying 'green' products and their subjective norm (what they think other people think they should do) about 'green' products then we should be able to *predict* their intentions to buy 'green' products and ultimately their actual behaviour. If someone scores high on a measure of positive attitudes to 'green' products and high on a measure of subjective norms (i.e. they think their partner, family and friends think they should buy 'green') then they should also score high on a measure of intentions to buy 'green'. This should, in turn, if the theory is correct, lead to them buying 'green' products.

If we want to examine relationships such as these (between attitudes, subjective norms, intentions and ultimately behaviour) then multiple regression is the statistical test of choice. It will enable us to determine the predictive power of the independent variables (intentions, attitudes and norms) on the dependent variable (behaviour). That is, it will enable us to say how much of the variance in our dependent variable is explained by our independent variables, and also the strength of the relationships between each IV and the DV. Regression, like ANOVA, enables us to examine the variance in the scores we observe (in our DV) that is accounted for by the scores on the variables that we have identified (our IVs). However, we do not generally manipulate the IVs with regression (as we would with ANOVA) but rather measure the 'naturally' occurring scores on these variables and see whether it enables us to predict scores on the dependent variable.

15.1 Terminology and techniques

Theoretical background

In Chapter 10 we explained how it was possible to fit a **regression line** to a scattergram. This line is the **line of best fit** – the line that most accurately represents the relationship between the two variables by minimising the distance between it and the points around it. There is only one line that minimises all the deviations of points on a scattergram. Some points will be above the line, others below it and some directly on it. The position of this line can be calculated mathematically by hand or using SPSS (as we did in Chapter 10). Regression uses this line of best fit to make predictions about values on a dependent variable from knowledge of scores on the independent variable (or a number of independent variables in the case of **multiple regression**).

You may remember from school that there is an equation for a straight line:

$$y = a + bx + e$$

In this equation y represents the dependent variable and x the independent variable. The value of a and b come from aspects of the line of best fit itself: a is the intercept (the point at which the line cuts the vertical axis), b is the slope of the line of best fit (the rate at which changes in scores on x affect scores on y). The slope of a line of best fit is also known as the **regression coefficient**. The e in the equation represents the **error** – the variance in y that cannot be explained by the other terms in the regression equation. Remember, the stronger the correlation between two variables the more the points on a scattergram fall on the regression line (there is less deviation about the line) and the lower the value of e (the error or unexplained deviation about the line of best fit).

Multiple regression is an extension of this principle where we have more than one independent variable (more than one x in the equation above) but still only one dependent variable (y). In reality, most people using regression to examine the relationships between variables (and predict one from another) use multiple regression (with two or more independent variables). There are two main reasons for this. The first is that simple linear regression between two variables (one IV and one DV) is no different from a Pearson correlation coefficient, so it makes most sense to calculate the correlation coefficient. Secondly, it is highly likely that we will want to have more than one predictor variable (IV) when trying to predict some aspect of human behaviour. We are complex creatures and it is highly unlikely that even the simplest of behaviours is predictable on the basis of only one other variable. We therefore need to have multiple independent variables (called **predictor variables** in multiple regression) to examine their impact on our dependent variable (called the **criterion variable** in multiple regression) and this leads us to use multiple regression. The equation for a simple linear regression between two variables (one predictor and one criterion) is extended for multiple regression to account for the influence of the additional predictor variables:

$$y = a + b_1x_1 + b_2x_2 + \dots + b_nx_n + e$$

Do not worry about this equation too much. It just shows how multiple regression is based on the same principles as simple regression. That is, the fundamental equation used to calculate the line of best fit is extended in multiple regression by including more measures of predictor variables (x_n – where n is the number of predictor variables) and more regression coefficients (b_n) for more and more predictor variables. Thankfully, the widespread use of computers means there is no longer any need to calculate these equations by hand. SPSS will do all the maths for us so we can concentrate on understanding what our findings mean.

Assumptions

■ The regression theory and techniques being discussed in this chapter concern linear regression. Simple and multiple regression are suitable when seeking to identify linear (straight-line) relationships between variables. If you are hazy about the difference between linear and non-linear relationships you should return to Chapter 12 where this is discussed in more detail (as it relates to correlation).

■ The criterion variable (dependent variable) must be continuous and measured at the interval or ratio level (although, as we discussed earlier in this section of the book, ordinal-level variables – such as Likert scales – are commonly used without the world ending!).

■ The predictor variables can be measured at the nominal, ordinal, interval or ratio levels. However, a *nominal-level* predictor variable *can only* be used if you have only two categories, which are coded 0 and 1 (rather than 1 and 2 or 3 and 4, etc.). This is what is known as **dummy coding**. Otherwise, anything goes!

■ It is important to have a large enough sample size when using multiple regression. Tabachnik & Fidell (2006) offer the following 'rules of thumb' for calculating how many cases are needed for **simultaneous** or **hierarchical multiple regression** (see below): $N \geq 50 + 8m$ (where m is the number of IVs) for testing the overall relationship and $N \geq 104 + m$ (where m is the number of IVs) for testing individual pathways. Therefore, if you have five IVs (predictor variables) you will need a sample size of 90 to test the overall relationship (between all five IVs and the DV) and a sample size of 109 to test individual pathways. As you will normally want to test the overall effect *and* individual pathways you should choose the higher value for your minimum sample size. If your data are not normally distributed (and appropriate transformations not undertaken) you will need even more cases, and if you wish to use **stepwise multiple regression** (see below) you will need even more cases (about 40 cases per IV are needed here).

Regression terms

There are several types of multiple regression (mentioned in passing above when discussing sample sizes) and a number of specialist terms that need to be understood before we explain how to calculate multiple regression. Important terminology is introduced first before the various types of multiple regression are discussed.

The **coefficient of determination** (r^2) was introduced in Chapter 12 when discussing the meaning of a correlation coefficient. This idea is a key one in multiple regression. The value of r^2 is the proportion of variance in the criterion variable which is accounted for by the predictor variables in the model being tested. This is really a measure of how good the predictor variables are in predicting the criterion variable (how much variance is explained and also by implication how much is left unexplained by the predictor variables). In general, we would report the **adjusted r^2** as this includes a correction for the number of predictor variables and participants. So, if we have an adjusted r^2 of 0.63 then we can say that our predictor variables have explained 63 per cent of the variance in our criterion variable.

The **beta value** (β) was introduced above when discussing the regression equation: the value of b (when standardised) is the beta value. The beta value is therefore a standardised measure of the strength of the relationship between a particular predictor variable and the criterion variable (very similar to a correlation coefficient, in fact). As the value is standardised, beta values will be between -1.0 and $+1.0$, with higher values indicating stronger relationships between the independent and dependent variables.

The most straightforward way of using multiple regression is the **simultaneous** method (called **Enter** in SPSS) where all predictor variables are entered into the regression equation simultaneously. That is, the relative contribution of each variable (in explained variance in the criterion variable) is assessed at the same time. An extension of this method is **hierarchical multiple regression** where the researcher specifies a precise relationship between the variables by entering them in a particular order. The contribution of each variable is assessed as it is entered, so the order in which the variables are entered is important. Hierarchical multiple regression is usually used where a researcher wishes to test a particular theory or has evidence from previous research for the relationships being ordered in a particular fashion. A further form of multiple regression is **stepwise multiple regression** where you let the computer determine the contribution of each variable (statistically); if a variable is not significant the computer will drop the variable. Stepwise multiple regression might be used, for instance, with more exploratory work when you have a number of predictor variables whose individual effect is unknown or when you want to find the smallest number of predictors among a set. Stepwise multiple regression is controversial, however, and should therefore only be used with caution (and a large sample size). In general, unless you have a particular theoretical model in mind, you should use simultaneous multiple regression (which is explained below).

Multicollinearity

One final consideration that should be mentioned is **multicollinearity**. This is something we know only too well as it came to haunt one of us during the final stages of our PhDs. It is quite likely that you will find your predictor variables are not only correlated with your criterion variable but also with each other. This is generally not a problem. However, if the correlations between predictor variables rises above a certain level you may have a problem with multicollinearity. Multicollinearity can cause a variety of problems and should be avoided at all costs in multiple regression analyses. You should therefore always compute the bivariate correlations between all your predictor and criterion variables before conducting multiple regression. This will enable you to examine the relationships between pairs of variables to see if there is a problem. If you have a correlation in excess of 0.90 then there is a *statistical problem* that *must* be addressed (Tabachnik & Fidell, 2006). Correlations above 0.70 indicate that there *might* be a problem and so should be investigated further (Tabachnik & Fidell, 2006). When there is a correlation above 0.90 then you will almost certainly have to delete one of the variables or, if it is theoretically sound, combine the two variables. When you have correlations in excess of 0.70 you should request 'collinearity diagnostics' within SPSS which will enable you to determine if there really is a problem. The 'collinearity diagnostics' will provide a variety of information about your data which you can use to identify any problems. If you have a conditioning index greater than 30 and at least two variance proportions greater than 0.50 (found in the 'Collinearity Diagnostics' table output in SPSS when collinearity diagnostics are selected – see below) then there is a problem with multicollinearity (Tabachnik & Fidell, 2006). If you find a problem then you need to proceed with caution and be careful when interpreting your findings. In general, the best solution is to delete or combine variables.

15.2   Calculating multiple regression using SPSS

The data being used here were described earlier (in Chapter 10) on student attrition (drop-out) at a fictional university. Suppose the study was a survey of 120 first year university students designed to identify their views about the course they were on, any problems they might be facing (personal, financial, etc.) and how these constructs impacted on whether they intended to continue with the course or not. A self-completion questionnaire was used to collect the data. It consisted of a series of five-point Likert scales used to measure the constructs. In addition, the questionnaire collected information about age, sex, ethnicity and course as well as the student's motivation to study. We will use the data here to demonstrate a multiple regression analysis. Specifically, we will look at predicting intentions to continue with the course from the information we have on ten other variables (where students have difficulties with the course, finance, living away from home, etc.). Our sample size is a little small for ten predictor variables ($N \geq 114$ and $N \geq 130$) but we should be okay using simultaneous entry multiple regression (the calculations given earlier for sample size are 'rules of thumb' – minor violations should be fine). Box 15.1 gives instructions for calculating multiple regression using SPSS.

Box 15.1

Command box | **Computing multiple regression**

1   Click on **Analyze** on the top menu bar.

2   Click on **Regression** and then **Linear** on the drop-down menus. This will bring up the **Linear Regression** dialogue box (see Fig. 15.1).

▶

Box 15.1 *Continued*

Figure 15.1 Linear Regression dialogue box

3   Move your criterion variable (dependent variable) into the **Dependent** box and your predictor variables (independent variables) into the **Independent(s)** box using the **Variable Picker** button.

4   Collinearity diagnostics can be obtained by clicking on **Statistics** and then clicking the box next to **Collinearity Diagnostics** in the dialogue box that appears.

5   Click **OK** to run the test. Your results will appear in the output viewer window.

Interpreting your SPSS output

The information you need to interpret your output is given in three tables (Figs 15.2–15.4). The first table (Fig. 15.2), labelled 'Model Summary', gives us the adjusted r^2, which is 0.564 in this case. Therefore, our predictor variables explain 56.4 per cent of the variance in the criterion variable. The second table (Fig. 15.3) gives the overall significance of our regression equation. This table is labelled 'ANOVA' because SPSS calculates regression and ANOVA in similar ways (using the general linear model), but do not worry about this or call your test an ANOVA – it is not, it is a regression. You do, however, need a significant value for the F-ratio (as you would with an ANOVA). If the F is not significant then your model does not fit your data (your regression equation is not significant) and you cannot go on to interpret any more of the output. The final table is the one labelled 'Coefficients' (Fig. 15.4) which gives information about the strengths of each particular relationship between the predictor variables and the criterion variable. The table gives values for standardised beta coefficients along with the t-value and significance for each beta coefficient. In this case only two predictors are

Model Summary

Mode l	R	R Square	Adjusted R Square	Std. Error of the Estimate
1	.812ª	.659	.564	.88367

a. Predictors: (Constant), Diff rating - personal problems, Diff rating - content of course, Diff rating - adapting to social life, Diff rating - financially coping, Diff rating - structure of course, Diff rating - living in city, Diff rating - living in halls or housing, Diff ratings - other commitments , Diff rating - living away from home, Diff rating - workload

Figure 15.2 Regression summary output table

ANOVAᵇ

Model		Sum of Squares	df	Mean Square	F	Sig.
1	Regression	54.314	10	5.431	6.956	.000ª
	Residual	28.112	36	.781		
	Total	82.426	46			

a. Predictors: (Constant), Diff rating - personal problems, Diff rating - content of course, Diff rating - adapting to social life, Diff rating - financially coping, Diff rating - structure of course, Diff rating - living in city, Diff rating - living in halls or housing, Diff ratings - other commitments , Diff rating - living away from home, Diff rating - workload

b. Dependent Variable: Intention to continue with course

Figure 15.3 Regression ANOVA output table

Coefficientsª

Model		Unstandardized Coefficients		Standardized Coefficients	t	Sig.
		B	Std. Error	Beta		
1	(Constant)	8.533	1.259		6.780	.000
	Diff rating - living away from home	-.405	.220	-.248	-1.843	.074
	Diff rating - living in halls or housing	-.289	.208	-.206	-1.389	.173
	Diff rating - living in city	.295	.164	.250	1.796	.081
	Diff rating - content of course	-.209	.228	-.120	-.920	.364
	Diff rating - workload	.069	.293	.042	.234	.816
	Diff rating - structure of course	-.200	.179	-.134	-1.119	.271
	Diff rating - adapting to social life	-.210	.157	-.153	-1.335	.190
	Diff ratings - other commitments	-.281	.134	-.284	-2.105	.042
	Diff rating - financially coping	-.222	.142	-.210	-1.568	.126
	Diff rating - personal problems	-.626	.117	-.551	-5.349	.000

a. Dependent Variable: Intention to continue with course

Figure 15.4 Regression coefficients output table

significantly related to the criterion variable: Difficulty rating – personal problems ($\beta = -0.551$, $t = -5.349$, $p = 0.001$) and Difficulty rating – other commitments ($\beta = -0.284$, $t = -2.105$, $p = 0.042$). All the other predictor variables are non-significant and do not therefore contribute to the variance explained in the criterion variable (intention to continue with the course). We can therefore report that using a simultaneous entry multiple regression we found a significant model ($F = 6.956$, df $= 10$, $p = 0.001$) of the relationships between ratings of difficulties and intention to continue with the course. There were two significant variables, difficulty due to personal problems ($\beta = -0.551$, $t = -5.349$, $p = 0.001$) and difficulty due to other commitments ($\beta = -0.284$, $t = -2.105$, $p = 0.042$), that were negatively related to the intention to continue with the course. The two strongest predictors of students leaving the course are difficulties due to personal problems and other commitments (principally work).[1]

Further reading on statistics

There are a number of books worth consulting if you want more information about statistics and their calculation.

Field, A. (2005). *Discovering Statistics Using SPSS for Windows*, 2nd edn. London: Sage.

Another cracking book with a great deal of information on more advanced statistical tests. If you want to know about partial correlation, logistic regression, more detail on complex ANOVA techniques, analysis of covariance, multivariate analysis of variance and factor analysis then this is the book for you. It also includes coverage of the calculation of these statistics using SPSS.

Howell, D. C. (2001). *Statistical Methods for Psychology*, 5th edn. Belmont, CA: Duxbury Press.

An excellent, though complex, book, providing detail of the mathematics behind a very wide range of statistical techniques. There is further information about the mathematics behind tests covered in this book as well as comprehensive information on power calculations, post-hoc tests, the general linear model and much more besides. It can be heavy going and there is no coverage of SPSS.

Tabachnik, B. G. & Fidell, L. S. (2006). *Using Multivariate Statistics*, 5th edn. New York: HarperCollins.

If you want to know something (anything almost!) about multivariate statistics then this is the book for you. It contains coverage of data screening, multiple regression (including logistic regression), canonical correlation, multiway frequency analysis, analysis of covariance, multivariate analysis of variance and covariance, profile analysis, discriminant function analysis, factor analysis and structural equation modelling. Remember these are advanced statistical techniques and this book is not for the faint-hearted.

---

[1] Although these data are entirely fictional, these were the two main reasons we found in our study for students leaving our courses. In a sense it is a reassuring finding as we know that, to a great extent, these factors are out of our control and those factors that are within our control are not significant in the decisions of students to leave our courses.

Statistical test flowchart

Which test now?

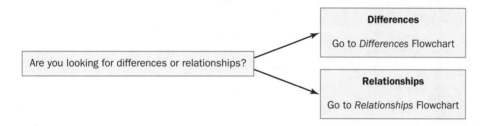

Are you looking for differences or relationships?

Differences

Go to *Differences* Flowchart

Relationships

Go to *Relationships* Flowchart

Differences flowchart

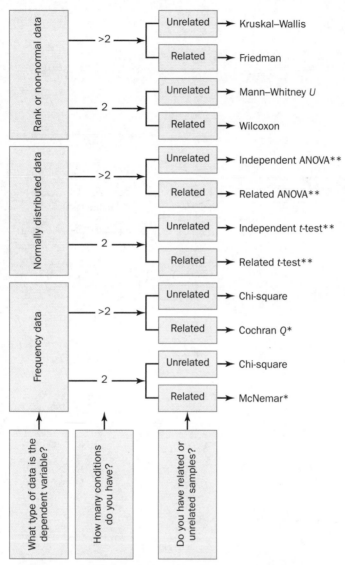

* These tests are not covered in this book but are available through non-parametric statistics in SPSS.

** If you have two or more dependent variables, you will need to use MANOVA. For one categorical predictor, use MANOVA (see Chapter 14 for an example). For two or more predictors, use factorial ANOVA. For a mixture of two or more categorical and continous predictors, use ANCOVA. These two tests are not covered in this book (see Tabachnik & Fidell, 2006, chapter 7, for more information about these techniques).

Relationships flowchart

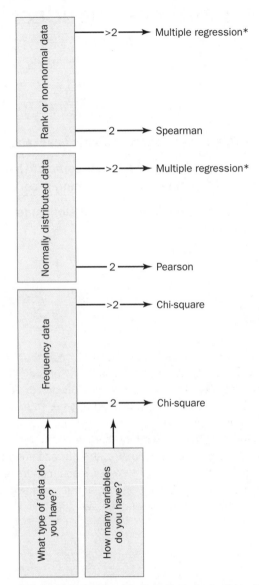

>2 ⟶ Multiple regression*

Rank or non-normal data

2 ⟶ Spearman

>2 ⟶ Multiple regression*

Normally distributed data

2 ⟶ Pearson

>2 ⟶ Chi-square

Frequency data

2 ⟶ Chi-square

What type of data do you have?

How many variables do you have?

* Note: Multiple regression is suitable for testing relationships with multiple IVs but only one DV.

16 Introducing R and R commander

- This chapter introduces R, an open source statistics package.

- The chapter then demonstrates how to carry out some of the techniques introduced in the previous chapters, using R code.

- Equivalent 'point and click' solutions are provided alongside, in boxes, to use with the R commander.

INTRODUCTION

Although many universities have site licences for SPSS, what if you want to run analyses at home, away from the university, or on your laptop? One of the disadvantages of using commercial statistical software is the cost involved. R is an alternative package and is free. The R project was developed in order to encourage 'open source' statistical programming. Open source means that the code is made freely available for use and modification. This means that there is no licence, and no costs involved for you. It is becoming increasingly popular, both with researchers and students, for this reason. We should warn you that we do not recommend R unless you are really keen to use it – the learning curve is steep, and if you have SPSS available, it may suffice for most purposes at your level of study.

16.1 What is R?

R is a statistical software package. Like SPSS, it has a **graphical user interface** (GUI, pronounced 'gooey'). Unlike SPSS, R does not come with convenient 'click and point' menus. It is possible to install 'click and point' menus, using the R commander, which is described later in this chapter. However, you would normally give R instructions in a programming language, called **R code** or **R syntax**. R has six key advantages:

1 It is free.

2 It is three programs in one. R can do statistical tests, high quality graphics, and work as a calculator.

3 R works on many platforms (e.g. Windows, Mac, Unix, Linux).

4 You can modify R code to suit your needs. The code is highly extensible, so you are not restricted by the examples provided.

5 There is a large, friendly community of R users. Online support groups and discussion lists may help you solve problems with your R code. This ethos often accompanies 'open source' projects.

6 Learning R is a way to develop programming skills, even if you already have some working knowledge.

There are also three disadvantages:

1 The learning curve is very steep. Programming R code (syntax is not intuitive for many people, and some students find it frustrating. However, it can be worth the extra effort, particularly if you plan to do quantitative research in the long term.

2 Although R has no licence, it is only *really* free if you have the time to learn how to use it! Learning R code is difficult, and may involve several hours of tweaking **snippets** (pieces) of code, taken from the help files, books, and examples found online.

3 R code might be highly extensible, but this means that examples you encounter online might be too complex or contain unnecessary information.

In practice, researchers tend to use more than one statistical package. R is growing in popularity, and even if you use SPSS, you can learn to use both. Instructions showing how to install R can be found in Box 16.1.

Box 16.1

Activity box   **Installing R**

If you are working at university, check with your computing support team. It may already be available, or they may need to install it for you. Many people have not heard about R yet. If you encounter resistance on the grounds of cost, remember to emphasise that there is no licence.

1 Go to the R website (http://cran.r-project.org)

2 Under **Download and Install R**, click on the appropriate platform (e.g. **Windows**) (see Fig. 16.1).

3 Click on **Base**, which refers to the base R package.

Box 16.1 *Continued*

Figure 16.1 Finding the appropriate platform on the R website

4 Click on the setup file. The name of the file will change, depending on the latest version of R that has been released. For example, R-2.7.1-win32.exe is the setup file for version 2.7.1. This number will change regularly, because R is updated frequently. The file will end in .exe (executable file) (see Fig. 16.2). **Run** the file to begin installation.

Figure 16.2 Downloading the R program file from the R website

5 Start R, by clicking on the program icon in your Windows **Start** menu (see Fig. 16.3).

Box 16.1 *Continued*

Figure 16.3 Starting R in the Windows Start menu

6 Set your local CRAN by clicking on **Packages, Set CRAN mirror** (see Fig. 16.4). CRAN stands for Comprehensive R Archive Network. Specify your nearest location to the network (e.g. **UK, Bristol**) from the list. You should do this each time you start R.

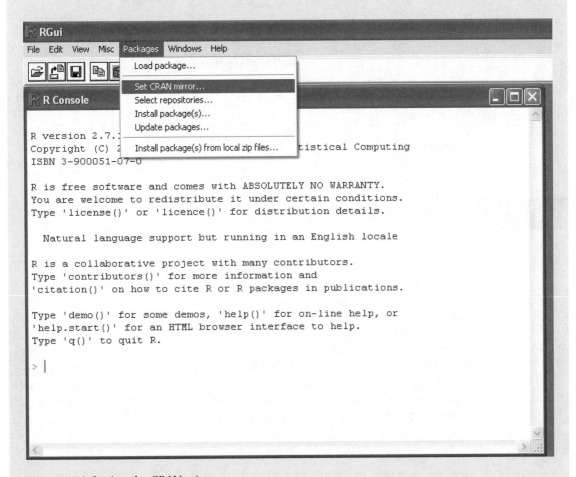

Figure 16.4 Setting the CRAN mirror

Box 16.1 *Continued*

7 Next, set your local working directory by clicking on **File**, **Change dir** (see Fig. 16.5). Choose the folder on your PC which you would like to work from. This tells R where you will store your data and where it should save your R code. You should do this each time you start R.

Figure 16.5 Setting the working directory

16.2   Installing new R libraries

Libraries are packages which are added to the base R package in order to run specific functions. The base package contains pre-installed functions. Functions are things you need to perform tests and models. For example, the **lm()** function fits a linear model to your variables. The **lm()** function is normally available in the R base package, but other functions (e.g. **showData**) are only found in 'add on' libraries. Researchers use different libraries, depending on what they need. For example, the psych package is popular with psychologists. Teachers and students who prefer the 'point and click' features of statistical software can use the **Rcmdr** (R commander) library, which we use below. To install a library, go to **Packages** then **Install package(s)**.

16.3   The R commander

Like SPSS, R has a GUI, called the R GUI. However, this does not contain 'click and point' menus and dialogue boxes. The R commander was developed by John Fox to address this limitation. Aimed at students and teachers, it provides a bridge between programming in R and the 'point and click' approach taken by SPSS. If you don't want to learn to write syntax in R, or you find it difficult, then R commander has a number of useful features:

- Like R itself, the R commander library is free.
- The R commander is easy to use, works on any machine, and is adaptable.
- It is deliberately designed 'to make it relatively difficult to do unreasonable things'!
- It looks and feels like other popular packages (e.g. SPSS).
- When you run a task in R commander, you can see what the R syntax would have looked like, if you had written it yourself. This will help you to learn how to write in R syntax.

Instructions on how to install R commander can be found in Box 16.2.

Box 16.2

Command box   **Introduction to R commander (Rcmdr)**

This command box assumes you have installed R, set the local CRAN, and set your working directory (see Box 16.1). The data (irmda.csv) is available from the book website. This box is only intended as an introduction to Rcmdr. Further information is available from the Rcmdr help files, which are provided when you install the package.

1   Go to **Packages** > **Install package(s)**.

2   Select the **Rcmdr** package and **Install** (see Fig. 16.6).

   If you are prompted with the message 'The following packages used by Rcmdr are missing...Install these packages?' click on **Yes**, then **OK**. The relevant packages should now install themselves automatically. This may take a long time, depending on what libraries have already been installed.

3   Normally, you would type **require Rcmdr** to start Rcmdr (see Fig. 16.7). However, the first time Rcmdr is installed it should start automatically.

Box 16.2 *Continued*

Figure 16.6 Installing the Rcmdr library

4   When Rcmdr has opened, select and import the **irmda.csv** data set by clicking on **Import data, from text file or clipboard** (see Fig. 16.8).

5   Give the data set a name (e.g. 'data'), specify the missing data indicator (9999) and the field separator (a comma) (see Fig. 16.9).

6   Tell Rcmdr which variables are factors (categorical variables). Click on **Data, Manage variables in active data set**, then **Convert numeric variables to factors** (see Fig. 16.10). Highlight the relevant variables, check that **Supply level names** is selected, then provide names for each level of the factor when prompted.

Box 16.2 *Continued*

Figure 16.7 Starting Rcmdr

Figure 16.8 Importing a data file

Box 16.2 *Continued*

Figure 16.9 Naming the data file, specifying a missing data indicator, and specifying the field separator

Figure 16.10 Specifying which variables are categorical

Box 16.2 *Continued*

7 To summarise continuous variables, click on **Statistics**, **Summaries**, **Numerical summaries** (see Fig. 16.11).

Figure 16.11 Summarising continuous variables

8 To summarise factors, click on **Statistics**, **Summaries**, **Frequency distributions** (see Fig. 16.12).

Figure 16.12 Summarising categorical variables

Box 16.2 *Continued*

Rcmdr menus

The Rcmdr menus are very similar to SPSS. The statistical tests used subsequently in this chapter will have a box showing you where to find the equivalent function in Rcmdr, for each piece of code. These descriptions of each menu are taken from 'Getting Started with the Rcmdr':

File: Menu items for loading and saving log/script files; setting options; and exiting.

Edit: Menu items (Cut, Copy, Paste, etc.) for editing the contents of the log/script and output windows. Right clicking in the script or output window also brings up an edit 'context' menu.

Data: Submenus containing menu items for reading and manipulating data.

Statistics: Submenus containing menu items for a variety of basic statistical analyses.

Graphs: Menu items for creating simple statistical graphs.

Models: Menu items for obtaining numerical summaries, hypothesis tests, diagnostics, and graphs for a linear or generalised linear model, and for adding diagnostic quantities, such as residuals, to the data set.

16.4 Importing data into R

It is possible to enter data directly into R (see below), but you may want to import some data. Data can be stored in a variety of formats, indicated by the file extension. For example, SPSS files end with .sav. When using R it is useful to use the comma separated values format (.csv). You can create these files in Microsoft Excel, by saving a spreadsheet in .csv format. We have provided, on the book website, all of the data sets used in this book, in .csv format. They are the same as the .sav versions used for the SPSS chapters.

Normally, the format of the data is to have one row per person, and one variable per column. Variable names are included at the top of each column: the header. This is called the **wide** data format. Repeated measures designs often have one observation per person, which means that a **long** format is required. A snippet of code is provided below that converts between both formats. Missing data can be represented by the letters **NA**, or by a numerical code (e.g. **9999**). However, you must tell R how missing data are coded in your data file, preferably as soon as you import any data (see Box 16.3).

Box 16.3

Activity box	Importing data into R

Please note: These snippets of code are for R, not Rcmdr. You can download them from the book's website (www.pearsoned.co.uk/langdridge). The hash symbol (#) means that the line is ignored by R.

- `data <- read.table(file.choose())` #browse for a data file
- `data <- read.table("file.csv", header=TRUE, sep=",")` # this
  # means that the file is file.csv, variable names are included
  # in the header, and the data are separated by commas
- `data <- read.table("file.csv", header=TRUE, sep=",",`
  `na.strings="9999")` # this tells R that it should replace
  # 9999 (or any value you have chosen) in your data, into NA
  # (missing data)
- `datafilename <- http://wps.pearsoned.co.uk/.../indanova.csv`
  # **http://www.pearsoned.co.uk/langdridge** # this imports a file
  # from the Internet
- `attach(data)` # this attaches the data to R, so that vari-
  # ables can be recognised simply by using their names
- `names(data)` # this prints a list of all the variables
  # available
- `fix(data)` # shows the data for checking purposes. You can
  # also edit data here.

16.5	Getting started with R code

Rather than learning the entire R programming language, many people prefer to learn a few basics and then modify snippets of existing R code to suit their particular problem. It is often a good idea to find a piece of code that does approximately the same as what you want, and then change it. This is the strategy adopted by the R help manuals (R help). R help shows a basic example, and more complex examples, for each package and function. Try starting with a simple example and then gradually change it until it does what you want. The R user community might be able to make some helpful suggestions if you get stuck (see the list of further R resources at the end of this chapter).

```
help() # starts the online help manuals
help.start() # provides help in a browser format
```

16.6 Making comments

Note that anything beginning with a hash symbol is ignored. This useful feature allows you to note comments about the code, which are not processed by R. You can add your own notes, which might help you remember what the code means in the future.

```
x <- 5 # this is a comment, ignored by R
```

16.7 Basic R commands

You will need a few basic commands in order to get started. Don't worry if these seem obscure, you can come back to them later. It is not always necessary to understand everything in a piece of R code. The > symbol indicates that R is ready and waiting for your instructions.

```
1+3 # addition
6-5 # subtraction
6*7 # multiplication
12/3 # division
sqrt(64) # square root
x<-5 # creates a variable called x with the value 5. The
# symbols <- (no spacing) are used to assign values to
# variables
y<-rnorm(500,100,15) # generates a variable called y with a
# normal distribution, 500 values, mean of 100, standard
# deviation of 15
ls() # lists all the objects you have created
library(help=base) # complete list of functions in the R
# base package. Use help() for more information on any one of
# these e.g. help(sum)
```

Remember that assignment does not use the equals sign (=). In this context, <- does not mean 'less than' and/or 'minus'. It is also worth nothing that if your code is longer than one line, the + symbol will appear, but this does not refer to addition. This means that R is waiting for the next part of the code. Press escape if this happens and you do not want it.

```
y<-rnorm(500,100
+ ,15) # the + symbol connects the two pieces of code
# together
```

16.8   Vectors

Vectors are sets of values that have been declared a group, and given a name. When there is only one value, the vector is called a scalar. We can group values together as vectors using the **concatenation** function. Concatenation simply means to link together, or to bind. When you are using small sets of data this function is quite useful. You can create small data sets by putting vectors together:

```
x <-c("1,2,3") #creates a vector called x containing the
# numbers 1,2,3
y <-2 #creates a vector only containing the number 2. This
# is a scalar.
```

If you prefer, enter the values one at a time:

```
x<-scan() #type in each number, then press enter. Press
# enter twice to finish the vector.
```

More often, you will want to import full data sets, and use the variable names to name your vectors (see below), using the **attach()** function.

BOX 16.4

Information box

Important vector functions

Here are some important functions. Among other things, they provide measures of central tendency and dispersion for your variables. Descriptive statistics were described in Chapters 8 and 10. Replace x and y with the vectors (variables) you are interested in:

- `max(x)` # maximum of x
- `min(x)` # minimum of x
- `sum(x)` # sum of all x values
- `mean(x)` # mean of x
- `median(x)` # median of x
- `range(x)` # range of x
- `var(x)` # variance of x
- `cor(x,y)` # correlation between x and y
- `quartile(x)` # gives the quartiles of x: 0%, 25%, 50%, 75%
  # and 100%
- `help(vector)` # help on vectors

16.9   Large and small numbers

R, like hand calculators, has a notation for displaying very small or very large numbers.

```
3.4e-2 # imagine that the decimal point should be moved two
# places to the left
3.4e3 # three places to the right i.e. 3400
```

16.10   Save your code

Working with R code (and SPSS syntax) will save you time in the long run, if you decide to use R. Rarely do researchers run an analysis once and only once. Steps have to be checked, repeated and modified. This is especially true if you are learning a new method. It may be easier to 'click and point' using menus and buttons (an option available using Rcmdr), but if you have to repeat this process, it can get frustrating. By saving R code, you can simply re-run what you have done before.

```
savehistory(file = ".someRcode") #save the history and
# provide a file name
```

or go to **File** > **Save History** (see Fig. 16.13) in the R GUI. You can also copy and paste R code into Notepad, and save it there. Table 16.1 shows how use Rcmdr menus to save your code.

Figure 16.13 Saving your work

Table 16.1 Using Rcmdr menus to save syntax, output or the R workspace

```
File - Open script file
|- Save script
|- Save script as
|- Save output
|- Save output as
|- Save R workspace
|- Save R workspace as
|- Exit - from Commander
|- from Commander and R
```

16.11 Creating and saving a data frame

When you have created vectors or variables, you can change them into a **data frame** (the data set which R is working from at a given time). This can be exported as a .csv file.

```
x <- rnorm(100,50,10) # random variable with a mean of 50, #
# standard deviation of 10
y <- rnorm(100,60,10) # random variable with a higher mean
z <- sample(c(0,1), 100, replace = TRUE) # random zeros and
# ones
new<-data.frame(x,y,z) # create a data frame containing x, y
# and z.
fix(new) # check the data set
write.table(new, file = "mydata.csv", sep = ",", col.names =
NA) # export the data frame. This will be stored in your # #
# working directory.
help(data.frame) # help with data frames
help(write.table) # help data tables
```

16.12 Graphs

In Chapter 10 you learned how to produce different kinds of graphs in SPSS. Here, the R code to produce the same graphs is provided. It is also available from the book website, remember that a bar chart is used to display discrete variables (such as sex or ethnicity) while a histogram can display continuous variables (usually on the *x*-axis, the horizontal axis) split into intervals or discrete variables. The gap in between the bars on a bar chart reinforces the fact that the variable is not continuous.

Univariate graphs

```
data <- read.table("irmda.csv",header=TRUE, na ="9999",
sep=",")
attach(data)
names(data)
gender<-factor(gender)
ethnic<-factor(ethnic)
hist(motstud) #histogram of motivation to study
pie(table(Dataset$ethnic), labels=levels(Dataset$ethnic),
main="ethnic", col=rainbow(length(levels(Dataset$ethnic))))
# pie chart for ethnicity
```

Multivariate graphs

When there are two variables, the type of graph depends on the dependent variable. If the dependent variable is continuous then scatterplots are appropriate. If it is categorical (such as sex or ethnicity) then a box-and-whisker or bar chart, for each level of the dependent variable, is appropriate. In the example dataset 'irmda.csv', age and motivation to study are continuous variables (interval level of measurement). Intentions to continue studying is, strictly speaking, an ordinal variable. The distance between 1 and 2 might not be the same as the distance between 3 and 4. Recall from Chapter 2 that it is common for psychologists to treat ordinal data as if it were truly interval.

```
boxplot(motstud) # boxplot for motivation to continue
# studying
boxplot(motstud ~gender, ylab="Intentions to continue
studying", xlab="Gender") # with labels
boxplot(motstud ~ethnic, ylab="Intentions to continue
studying", xlab="Ethnicity")# notice the impact small
# numbers from some ethnic groups
plot(age,motstud, col="blue") #scatterplot of age and
# motstud, using the correlation approach, with some colour
plot(motstud~age) #this method uses a tilde symbol, and the
# dependent variable goes first. This is the regression,
# formula-based approach. Conceptually, this is used when
# researchers are trying to predict the dependent variable
# from the independent variable. It is exactly the same when
# there are two variables, but since we often work with more
# than two variables you may want to adopt this technique.
plot(age,motstud,col="blue",xlab="Independent variable
(age)",ylab="Dependent variable (motivation)") #label the
# axes
abline(lm(motstud~age), col=as.numeric(gender)) # use the
# linear model function to add a line of best fit
```

```
plot(age,motstud,col=as.numeric(gender)) #use separate
# colors for each gender
plot(age,motstud,pch=as.numeric(ethnic)) #different symbols
# for ethnicities
```

Unlike SPSS, which produces graphs in one fell swoop, R encourages you to start with a basic graph and then add features piece by piece. This piecemeal approach may encourage you to ask more precise questions about which features of your data you want to display.

```
demo(graphics) # this will show some of the kinds of graphs
# you can produce in R. Hit "Return" or "Enter" to start the
# demo, and again for each graph.
```

You may prefer to produce simple graphs in Rcmdr (Table 16.2):

Table 16.2 Using Rcmdr menus to produce simple graphs

Graphs
|- Histogram
|- Boxplot
|- Scatterplot
|- Plot of means
|- Bar graph
|- Pie chart
| |- Save graph to file

Displaying more than one graph

The `mfrow` function is used to specify how many rows and graphs you need in the graph window, when you plan to present more than one graph. An example is shown below (see repeated measures ANOVA, below). The number of rows is specified first, then the number of graphs.

```
par(mfrow=c(1,1)) #This is the default setting (1 row and 1
# graph per row)
par(mfrow=c(1,2)) #1 row, 2 graphs
par(mfrow=c(2,3)) #2 rows, 3 graphs
```

16.13   Independent *t*-test

The `t.test()` function is used to perform both the **independent** and the **related *t*-tests**. When working with small data sets, you can simply enter the data yourself using the concatenate function. Next, combine the two vectors into a data frame:

```
group <-c(12,10,8,14,17,11,12,9,11,15,NA,NA) # note the two
# missing values
motlrn <-c(20,11,18,12,22,24,17,23,19,13,19,23)
data<-data.frame(group, motlrn) # create a data frame
summary(data) # summarise the data frame
boxplot(data) # show a boxplot to visualise the difference
# in means
t.test(group, motlrn, paired=FALSE) # the two groups are not
# paired
```

Alternatively, you can import the data directly, from an external file:

```
data <- read.table("indtdat.csv", header=TRUE, sep=",",
na.strings="9999")
attach(data) # remember that you need to attach the data
t.test(group1,group2,paired=FALSE)
```

The output is shown in the R console. If you have read Chapter 11, this output should be fairly self-explanatory. It provides the *t* value, degrees of freedom, and the exact *p* value. The 95 per cent confidence interval for the *t* value is also shown along with the mean value for each group. Boxplots are a very useful way to visually display the difference between the means.

16.14   Related *t*-test

For a **related *t*-test**, simply change `paired=FALSE` to `paired=TRUE`:

```
conditionA<-c(23,22,17,21,20)
conditionB<-c(20,21,18,18,15)
t.test(group1,group2,paired=TRUE)
data <- read.table("reaptdat.csv", header=TRUE, sep=",")
attach(data)
t.test(group1,group2,paired=TRUE)
```

You can perform a related *t*-test in Rcmdr (Table 16.3).

Table 16.3 Using Rcmdr menus to perform a related *t*-test

Statistics – Summaries – Active data set
|- Means
| |- Independent-samples *t*-test
| |- Paired *t*-test

16.15 Mann–Whitney test

The **Mann–Whitney test** is performed in the `wilcox.test()` function, with paired set to FALSE.

```
groupA<-c(15,20,22,10,30)
groupB<-c(33,45,14,24,33,24)
wilcox.test(groupA, groupB, paired=FALSE)
```

16.16 Wilcoxon test

The **Wilcoxon test** is performed in the `wilcox.test()` function, with paired set to TRUE. The Rcmdr version is shown in Table 16.4.

```
day<-c(6,5,4,5,5,7,3,2)
night<-c(5,14,9,18,3,12,9,17)
wilcox.test(day, night, paired= TRUE)
data <- read.table("wilcox.csv", header=TRUE, sep=",")
attach(data)
wilcox.test(day, night, paired=TRUE)
```

Table 16.4 Using Rcmdr menus to perform a Wilcoxon test

Statistics – Summaries – Active data set
|- Nonparametric tests
| |- Two-sample Wilcoxon test
| |- Paired-samples Wilcoxon test

16.17 Chi square

The chi square test is performed on a special type of vector – a **table**. You can create the 2 × 2 table using the cell counts themselves or by importing a data file. Both methods are illustrated below.

```
table <- matrix(c(23,7,14,11), nrow = 2, ncol=2, byrow=TRUE)
# byrow means that R should assume that values are
# listed row by row (23 and 7, then 14 and 11)
table # print the table you have created
chi <- chisq.test(table) # performs a chi square test on the
# table
chi # prints the results
```

```
chi$expected # provides the expected counts, under the null
# hypothesis
data <- read.table("chisqdat.csv", header=TRUE, sep=",") #
raw data
attach(data)
chisq.test(table(data))
```

Rcmdr requires you to enter the cell counts yourself (Table 16.5).

Table 16.5 Using Rcmdr menus to perform a chi square test

Statistics – Summaries – Active data set
|- Contingency Tables
| |- Enter and analyze two-way table

16.18   Correlation and linear regression

Recall from Chapter 15 that a correlation is the same as a linear regression with only one independent variable. The tradition in R is to use cor(x,y) for a correlation and lm(y~x) for linear regression. The tilde symbol (~) simply means that we want to predict, rather than simply describe, the association between x and y. The dependent variable we are trying to predict is shown first (y~x). The size of the association should not change depending on the method you use because they are the same model. The difference in approach is a subtle conceptual difference – the size of the association is unchanged.

```
data <- read.table("corladat.csv", header=TRUE, sep=",") #
# load the correlation data set
attach(data)
names(data)
plot(music,maths) # exploratory scatterplot of music and
# maths
cor(music,maths) # simple pearson correlation between music
# and maths
cor.test(music, maths, method = "pearson") # pearson
# correlation
cor.test(music, maths, method = "spearman") # spearman
# correlation
cor.test(music, maths, method = "pearson", alternative =
"greater") # alternative hypothesis can be "two.sided",
# "greater" or "less". Greater means that you predict a
# positive association, less refers to a negative association.
# Use two.sided if you are not sure.
par(mfrow=c(2,2)) #sets plotting to a 2x2 format
regression <- lm(maths~music)
```

```
summary(regression)
anova(regression) # ANOVA table to test the significance of
# the regression line
plot(maths~music) # plot regression
abline(regression) # add line of best fit
assumptions <- lm(residuals(regression)~fitted(regression))
plot(residuals(regression)~fitted(regression))
abline(assumptions)
summary(assumptions)
```

Instructions for performing correlation and regression in Rcmdr are shown in Table 16.6.

Table 16.6 Using Rcmdr menus to perform correlation and regression.

Statistics |- Summaries | |- Correlation matrix | |- Correlation test
or
Statistics |- Fit models |- Linear regression

16.19   Multiple regression

The data set used in this example was introduced in Chapter 15. There are ten independent variables, and one dependent variable (intcont).

```
data <- read.table("irmda.csv", header=TRUE, sep=",",
na="9999") # load the correlation data set. Don't forget to
# tell R how to recognise missing data (9999). If you don't,
# it will treat 9999 as a real number
attach(data)
names(data)
multreg <- lm(intcont ~ awaydiff + halldiff + citydiff +
contdiff + workdiff + strucdif + socidiff + commdiff +
findiff + persdiff) # ten independent variables
lm(intcont~awaydiff + halldiff + awaydiff:halldiff) # if you
# want to include an interaction, use the colon
# (awaydiff:halldiff) or asterisk symbol (awaydiff*halldiff)
summary(multreg)
library(car) # load the car package. You will need to
# install this from the CRAN if it is not available
vif(lm(intcont ~ awaydiff + halldiff + citydiff + contdiff +
workdiff + strucdif + socidiff + commdiff + findiff +
persdiff)) # collinearity diagnostics. As a rule of thumb,
# the VIF values should not be greater than five.
```

See Table 16.6 for the equivalent Rcmdr instructions.

16.20   One-way ANOVA

ANOVA can be performed using a variety of R library packages (usually **lm** or **aov**). These libraries differ somewhat, and provide different output. Explore the **help(lm)** and **help(aov)** files to determine the code you need. Below, we show a simple example using each package. Post-hoc comparisons are not straightforward in R but Tukey's HSD can be obtained fairly easily.

```
data <- read.table("indanova.csv", header=TRUE, sep=",")
attach(data)
names(data)
cond <- factor(cond) # tell R that cond is a factor
boxplot(test~cond, xlab="Condition", ylab="Test Score") #
# explore the difference in means with a boxplot (see Fig.
# 16.14)
```

Method 1

```
anova <- lm(test~cond) # lm library method: dependent
# variable, tilde symbol, then factors (independent variables)
summary(anova) # print a summary of the results
```

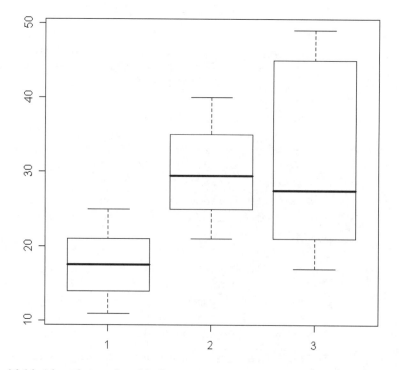

Figure 16.14 A boxplot produced in R

Method 2

```
anova<-aov(test~cond) # the ANOVA is performed with the aov
# library in this example
tukey<-TukeyHSD(anova, "iv", ordered=TRUE) # post-hoc tests
# (see Chapter 11)
summary(tukey)
plot(tukey) # if the confidence intervals run over zero,
# then there is a significant difference between the
# conditions (see Fig. 16.15)
```

Table 16.7 shows the Rcmdr menus that test for differences in means.

Table 16.7 Using Rcmdr menus to test for differences in means

Statistics
|- Means
| |- One-way ANOVA
| |- Multi-way ANOVA
|- Variances – Two-variances F-test
| |- Bartlett's test
| |- Levene's test
Models
- Select active model
|- Summarize model
|- Hypothesis tests – ANOVA table
|- Numerical diagnostics – Variance-inflation factors

Note. **MANOVA is not currently available in Rcmdr.**

Figure 16.15 A graphical representation of a Tukey post-hoc test

16.21   Two-way ANOVA

There are two methods of notation for introducing a second independent variable, or factor, in ANOVA terms (e.g. gender). The first spells out the full list of factors and the interaction (`test~cond+sex+sex:cond`). The second simplifies this arrangement by using the asterisk symbol (`test~cond*sex`). You may prefer to use the full version, to help you remember what variables have been included.

```
data <- read.table("indanova.csv", header=TRUE, sep=",")
attach(data)
names(data)
cond <- factor(cond) # turn cond into a factor
sex <- factor(sex) # turn sex into a factor
new<-data.frame(test,cond,sex)
par(mfrow=c(2,1)) #sets plotting to a 1x2 format
with(new, interaction.plot(cond, sex, test), xlab=F,
ylab=F)# explore using an interaction plot
barplot(tapply(test,list(sex,cond),mean),beside=T,col=rainbo
w(2), xlab="Condition", ylab="Mean test score") # the
# difference between the interaction plot and the bar plot is
# that the former assumes a continuous underlying variable.
# The smooth increase in test scores for men across the
# three conditions can help you interpret what is happening in
# the experiment. However, a bar plot is more accurate because
# the independent variables are categorical, not continuous
# (see Fig. 16.16).
labels<-c("Male", "Female") # create a vector with the label
# names to use in the key
legend(locator(1),labels,fill=rainbow(2)) # after this,
# click on the graph where you want the key to appear
```

Full notation

```
twowayanova <- aov(test~cond+sex+cond:sex)
summary(twowayanova) # check the output. Is the interaction
# term significant (p < .05)?
summary.lm(twowayanova) # the output provides extra, useful
# information. It shows which levels of the factors are
# significant, and the effect sizes.
```

Shortened notation

```
twowayanova <- aov(test~cond*sex) # should give the same
# results as above
```

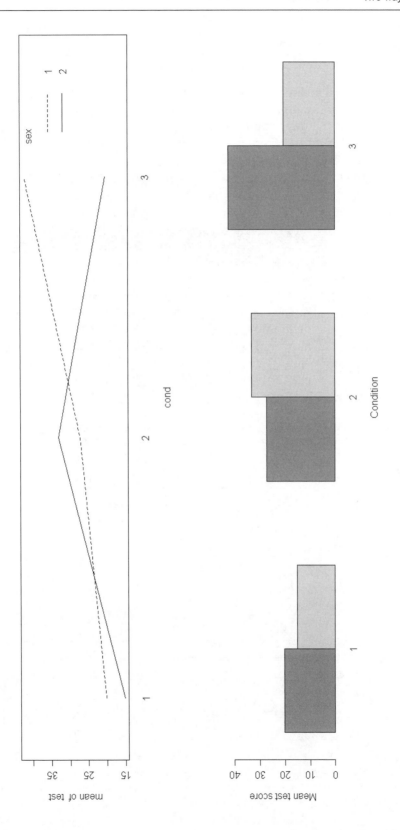

Figure 16.16 A line graph and bar graph of the same data, shown together

16.22   Repeated measures ANOVA

Repeated measures data can be stored in either wide or long format. Fig. 16.17 shows an example of wide format. There is one row per person and a score for each of the three conditions. Long format has one row per observation, so that each person has three rows of data (see Fig. 16.18). This may not be your preferred way of entering data, but repeated measures ANOVA in R uses long format. Therefore, it is useful to know how to **reshape** your data set from wide and long format (and back again).

RGui - [Data Editor]

R File   Windows   Edit   Help

	row.names	sex	time	score	id
1	1.1	1	1	89	1
2	1.2	1	2	88	1
3	1.3	1	3	70	1
4	2.1	1	1	90	2
5	2.2	1	2	92	2
6	2.3	1	3	76	2
7	3.1	1	1	67	3
8	3.2	1	2	68	3
9	3.3	1	3	65	3
10	4.1	1	1	95	4
11	4.2	1	2	90	4
12	4.3	1	3	71	4
13	5.1	1	1	78	5
14	5.2	1	2	74	5
15	5.3	1	3	69	5
16	6.1	1	1	88	6
17	6.2	1	2	83	6
18	6.3	1	3	72	6
19	7.1	1	1	84	7
20	7.2	1	2	89	7

Figure 16.17 Example of the format data

	sex	drink1	drink2	drink3
1	1	89	88	70
2	1	90	92	76
3	1	67	68	65
4	1	95	90	71
5	1	78	74	69
6	1	88	83	72
7	1	84	89	64
8	1	83	79	55
9	1	79	77	72
10	1	90	88	61
11	2	88	85	55
12	2	87	87	62
13	2	89	87	59
14	2	63	60	55
15	2	78	78	77
16	2	74	80	64
17	2	94	89	63
18	2	88	79	70
19	2	90	87	60
20	2	63	62	50

Figure 16.18 Example of the format data

16.23   Reshaping wide format data into long format

```
wide <- read.table("repeatanova.csv",header=TRUE,sep=",")
attach(wide)
fix(wide) # have a look at the wide format data
long <- reshape(wide, idvar="id", varying=list(2:4),
v.names="score", direction="long") # this tells R that you
# want to create a new variable, called id, to represent the
# participants in your data set, that the scores for each
# person are in columns 2 through 4, and that you want to
# create a new variable based on these, called score
attach(long)
```

```
long<-long[order(id),] # sort the file by id
write.table(long, file = "long.csv", sep = ",", col.names =
NA) # saves the long format data set in your working
# directory
fix(long) # have a look at the long format data for checking
# purposes
wideagain <- reshape(long, timevar="time", idvar="Subject",
direction="wide", v.names="score") # this converts long
# format back to wide format
```

This example will only work using long data format. If you have already attached the long data, you can proceed from interaction.plot. If you had any problems reshaping the data you can import the pre-prepared long data file instead.

```
long<-read.table("long.csv", header=T, sep=",")
attach(long)
names(long)
interaction.plot(time, factor(sex), score, ylab="Mean
score", xlab="Time", trace.label="group")
#Adapted from www.ats.ucla.edu/stat/R/seminars/
# Repeated_Measures/repeated_measures.htm
fligner.test(test~cond) # test for homogeneity of variances.
# If p < .05, the data do not meet this assumption and a
# correction may be required
repeatedaov <- aov(score ~ factor(sex)*factor(time) +
Error(factor(id)))
summary(repeatedaov) # you need to capitalize Error for this
# to work
# The example shows that the main effect of time is highly
# significant (p < 0.01), but that the main effect of sex and
# the interaction between sex and time are not. The lines for
# males and females are fairly close together, and are
# parallel, which illustrates these findings visually.
```

Finally, spread the word!

If you enjoy using R and want to encourage others to use it, tell your friends and colleagues. You can cite R in your reports and assignments using the information provided by this command:

```
citation() # this shows you how to cite R in your work
```

Further R resources

- Facebook group http://www.facebook.com/group.php?gid=4193309754
- Jiscmail discussion list for psychologists using R www.jiscmail.ac.uk/lists/psych-r.html
- R news http://cran.r-project.org/doc/Rnews
- Google group http://groups.google.com/group/The-R-Project-for-Statistical-Computing/
- Addicted to R http://addictedtor.free.r
- R mailing list http://www.r-project.org/mail.html

   The moderators of this list ask that you please reading the posting guide before posting a message to this list: http://www.r-project.org/posting-guide.html

- Quick R, for people already familiar with SPSS http://www.statmethods.net/index.html

Further reading

Crawley, M. (2005). *Statistics: An Introduction Using R*. London: John Wiley & Sons.

   A popular, short, introductory text.

Crawley, M. (2007). *The R Book*. London: Wiley.

   A hefty one, but well worth the investment if you plan to join the R community for the long haul. We strongly recommend this book. It covers a wide range of techniques and applications.

Everitt, B. & Hothorn, T. (2006). *A Handbook of Statistical Analyses Using R*. London: Chapman & Hall.

   Another large book, for the heavy R user.

Fox, J. (2002). *An R and S-PLUS Companion to Applied Regression*. London: Sage.

   An excellent book, focusing on regression in R.

Murrell, P. (2005). *R Graphics*. New York: Chapman and Hall.

   A book for those interested in the capabilities of R's graphics.

Venables, W. & Smith, D. (2002). *An Introduction to R*. Bristol: Network Theory Limited.

   A pocket-sized introduction to R.

Part 3

Analysing qualitative data

17 Fundamentals of qualitative research

18 Transcribing, coding and organising textual data

19 Phenomenological research methods

20 Grounded theory

21 Discourse analysis

22 Life story and narrative research

23 The use of computers in qualitative research

24 Mixed methods

17   Fundamentals of qualitative research

- This chapter begins by revisiting the discussion about qualitative and quantitative research methods and data analysis introduced in Chapter 1.

- Further links are made between qualitative epistemology and methodology.

- Finally, this chapter looks at the strengths, limitations and varieties of qualitative methods.

INTRODUCTION

This part of the book is concerned with demonstrating the use of qualitative methods in psychology. This particular chapter returns to some of the issues raised in Chapter 1 about philosophy, methodology and the differences between quantitative and qualitative methods. So, we need to revisit the philosophical assumptions that underpin the distinction between qualitative and quantitative research methods. However, before this, there is a brief reminder of some of the major issues already introduced.

If you remember, we discussed the question of 'what is science?' in Chapter 1. Everyday (or common-sense) understandings of science recognise it as the careful collection (through experience) of information about the world that enables us to establish facts and therefore build theories about the world. This accumulation of knowledge then enables us to control and change the world for the better. So scientific research, from this position, is the acquisition of knowledge based on experience that is objective. Chapter 1 also introduced the distinction between inductive and hypothetico-deductive approaches to research. Most quantitative research subscribes to the hypothetico-deductive approach that was advocated by the philosopher Karl Popper. In contrast, most qualitative research will embrace a more inductivist approach. That is, qualitative research will seek to avoid imposing a particular theoretical perspective on the questions being asked, data being collected and process of analysis.

Finally, Chapter 1 covered the basic distinction between qualitative and quantitative research. Quantitative research is that concerned with the quantification (counting) of phenomena while qualitative research is that concerned with the qualities of phenomena. Later in this chapter we revisit this distinction to draw out further distinctions and also discuss whether it continues to be an important way of categorising psychological research in the twenty-first century. However, we first wish to highlight some more philosophical concepts (and some more technical terms) that are important for understanding quantitative and qualitative research methods and the distinctions that may be drawn between them.

17.1   Philosophical underpinnings: the old paradigm

Epistemology

Epistemology is a philosophical term that is very commonly used, and although it sounds ferocious it has a very simple meaning. In short, epistemology concerns those questions we ask about our knowledge of some phenomenon. Or, in other words, epistemology is the branch of philosophy concerned with the varieties and validity of our knowledge of aspects of the world. Why do we need to know about this? Well, we need to know about epistemology because people (psychologists and philosophers) disagree (very profoundly) about what we can say *we know* about people. And these disagreements are key in understanding why some psychologists use quantitative methods modelled on the natural sciences to make truth claims about people and the world and others reject these completely. So, if you ever hear or read something where people are discussing the epistemological foundations of a theory or approach, they are talking about the philosophical assumptions concerning the question of what we can say we know about something. So, for instance, do we believe that our approach enables us to discover the truth of a real knowable world (the more traditional scientific approach – positivism, see below)? Or do we believe that our approach enables us *only* to identify some personally subjective, socially and historically contingent knowledge about a person's particular way of understanding the world (as we might expect in a phenomenological study, see Chapter 19)? But remember, these questions do not have certain answers. Psychologists disagree strongly about the knowledge claims we can make about our research and this is why the traditional scientific approach has come under fierce attack over the past 20 years or so.

Positivism

Positivism is a broad concept (often used together with empiricism to define a very traditional view of what science is – empiricism was covered in Chapter 1) that very simply means there is a simple, unproblematic relationship between our perception of the world and the world itself. If we are positivists we will believe that through systematic study of the world we can describe and explain what is really out there. Furthermore, the nature of the external world determines what we can say about it. There is ultimately some truth waiting to be discovered about the object of study. The goal of research for positivists is to provide objective knowledge about the world (or people living in the world if you are a psychologist); that is, knowledge that is impartial and unbiased. Once again, similar to developments in empiricism, understandings of positivism have moved on from this fundamental position. Very few psychologists today would class themselves in a very simple way as positivists, believing that our perception of people and events in the world is unproblematic (and unaffected by our preconceptions and presuppositions). However, psychologists may subscribe to some modified form of positivism (and similarly empiricism) and believe that there is a real, knowable world out there to investigate (albeit one understood through our perception of it). A great deal of research in biological and cognitive psychology (and in some developmental and social psychology) would be of this kind; its epistemological position is one based on a particular view of science that is positivist and empirical, principally using a hypothetico-deductive approach to knowledge acquisition. This type of research is invariably, though not necessarily, quantitative research. However, there is a growing body of research in social and developmental psychology which does not subscribe to positivism, or the hypothetico-deductive approach, but is more sceptical of what we can say we know about the world. This work tends to use inductive methods to generate descriptions of and theories about people and the world in which we live. This body of research is invariably, though not necessarily, qualitative research.

Criticism of the scientific approach

But what is wrong with the view outlined above? Surely psychology is *the* scientific study of people and should therefore use a scientific epistemology that emphasises the objective (empirical) collection of data through a hypothetico-deductive approach. Well, as we mentioned above, for many psychologists the discipline is just like this. But there is a growing group of people who think this approach is, at best, only one, and certainly not the only, way to understand human nature and, at worst, a fundamentally misguided way of carrying out research within psychology. And the principal factor underpinning these disagreements is the different beliefs about the epistemological assumptions underpinning the various methodologies.

What is wrong with the scientific approach to psychology? Well, there is not really the time or space to enter into this debate fully here. If you wish to read more about this, read some of the books listed in the Further reading section of this chapter. However, we will briefly run through a few of the criticisms levelled at positivist research (and also quantitative research more generally) to give you a feel for the arguments being made against the, still dominant, quantitative approach to social research. Perhaps the most important criticism concerns the notion that reality can be defined objectively and that there are psychological phenomena 'out there' that can be described and measured. This view is very difficult to justify. Most qualitative psychologists believe that psychological phenomena exist within (or between) the minds of people and are therefore always subject to interpretation. Furthermore, quantitative techniques of measurement invariably obscure this interpreted level of understanding through the imposition of highly structured tools onto the phenomena in question. At a more general level this problem arises because the social sciences and psychology in particular have attempted to use the natural sciences as a model of practice. Although natural sciences techniques have undoubtedly demonstrated their utility within that field, it is almost certainly the case that they are inappropriate for studying human nature. People are not passive phenomena waiting to be measured but active agents who change over time and who change their own worlds. Sodium from 50 years ago will still demonstrate the same qualities as sodium today, but people from 50 years ago are very unlikely to demonstrate the same qualities. In fact, the same person studied over only a very short time is likely to differ and change. Finally, the attempt of researchers within psychology to remain objective, one of the most important aims of positivist quantitative research, is flawed, for it is inevitable that the views of the researcher will influence the research process in any number of ways. The influence of the researcher and their views is apparent from the first question asked through to the interpretation of the findings found. Furthermore, many qualitative researchers would argue that not only is the attempt to remain objective flawed but it is also unnecessary. For it is only with recognition of the active involvement of the researcher in the research process that understanding can truly emerge.

Changing awareness of qualitative methods within psychology

While it is clearly the case that quantitative approaches to psychological research are still dominant within UK and US psychology, the criticisms from qualitative perspectives have had an impact. The desired change is more minor than many qualitative psychologists would wish but there is change, particularly in the United Kingdom and Continental Europe, nonetheless. Not only is there growth in qualitative research in Europe but there is also greater awareness and recognition of these perspectives among quantitative psychologists. Recent guidelines setting benchmarks for the discipline from the British Psychological Society and the Higher Education Council for England recognise the need for qualitative research methods to be taught alongside quantitative methods within an undergraduate psychology curriculum. Furthermore, although there are still differences of opinion, the arguments are no longer so vociferous and many more psychologists are using both quantitative and qualitative methods in their research programmes (see Chapter 24 on mixed methods). Whether the criticisms from qualitative researchers will ever impact fully is unknown, and for now at least the quantitative approach remains dominant, but at least it is a little more tolerant of qualitative approaches than before.

Philosophical underpinnings: the new paradigm

There are a number of philosophically and politically informed positions within the social sciences that have provided strong criticism of the positivist approach to research within psychology. We consider three of these below and present some of the implications of these positions for psychological research.

Social constructionism

Research from a socially constructed perspective is concerned with understanding the various ways in which people might construct their social reality. This approach has become more and more important in UK psychology since the 1980s. Unlike the traditional positivist approach, research from a social constructionist perspective recognises the fact that all experience is historically and socially contingent. That is, social phenomena are not simple unchanging events that we can measure but events that need to be understood in a specific way within particular social and historical conditions. Let us give you an example. Only a short time ago homosexuality was categorised within the psychological professions as a mental disorder. The diagnostic manuals (DSM and ICD) listed homosexuality alongside rape and paedophilia as a psychological problem in need of treatment and cure. Although not everyone accepts homosexuality within our society, things have changed. Homosexuality is no longer considered to be a disorder but just another aspect of sexual life in these late modern times. And people who are lesbian, gay and bisexual are, thankfully, no longer subjected to terrible treatments in an attempt to 'cure' them of their 'illness'. Changes such as these are important, for if one simply subscribed to a positivist view of psychology then how could this be explained? This is not simply a case of psychologists identifying a psychological phenomenon (homosexuality) and then measuring it, but something much more complex than that. This change has come about because times have changed (historical change) and with it attitudes within society (social change) such that homosexuality is no longer considered psychopathology. Social constructionists believe that all knowledge is like this, mediated by historical and social conditions, and that psychologists must recognise this within their research programmes and not simply believe that they are measuring things in a way that is neutral (or objective).

Feminism

The feminist critique is an important one that has had a tremendous impact on the discipline. Many of the problems with traditional positivist methodologies were highlighted and subjected to severe and sustained criticism by feminist scholars. First-wave feminists in the 1970s argued that women were either invisible or pathologised within the discipline. Psychological research either studied men exclusively or set out to draw comparisons between men and women where women would invariably be found to be inferior to men. Research of this kind served to maintain the status quo at that time when women were treated differently from men and given fewer opportunities. Feminist writers challenged both the epistemological and methodological foundations of this research in a way that was impossible to ignore. Psychological research was invariably conducted by men on men, or if women were involved they were found to be wanting in comparison to men. Feminist writers argued that this was not due to some inherent feminine weakness but to the bias of the researchers and their procedures.

A particularly useful and significant element to evolve from the feminist critique of positivist research has been the recognition of the role of the researcher within the research process. As we have already mentioned, quantitative positivist research attempts to limit the influence of the researcher through the use of particular methods. Feminist scholars argued that not only was this approach flawed but it was also unwise, for good research comes with a recognition of **reflexivity**, that is, the role of the researcher within the research process. Feminist research particularly, but also much qualitative research more generally, requires account to be taken of reflexivity within the analytic process. Here the researcher cannot remain hidden behind the mask of methodology but must instead 'come out' and be recognised for their role in producing the findings. This issue will be discussed again in some of the chapters that follow.

Queer theory

The criticism from queer theory is a new one for psychology and has yet to impact, but we believe it will, for it is a radical critique that problematises much within the discipline. Queer theory entails a conceptualisation of sexuality that sees sexual power embodied in different levels of social life (enforced through boundaries and binary divides such as masculine and feminine or men and women). What queer theorists are engaged in is the problematisation of sexual and gender categories (and all identities more generally). That is, no longer can we assume that sexual and gender categories such as 'masculine' and 'feminine' represent some underlying reality about the world. Instead they represent ways in which society may be categorised for various political aims. At its most extreme we see a willingness to interrogate areas not usually seen as the terrain of sexuality and the transgression of all conventional categorisations and the breaking of boundaries. So, what does this have to do with psychology? Well, very obviously it is tremendously important for how we understand the psychology of sex and gender. In combination with the feminist critique these categories become increasingly problematic and open to interpretation. But more broadly, queer theory provides a challenge to many of the, often very subtle, heterosexual assumptions that underpin knowledge within the discipline in much the same way as feminist theory offers a challenge to the many sexist assumptions that underpin knowledge. This critique is yet to impact on psychology but it will, and you are forewarned, so be prepared.

17.3   Revisiting the qualitative versus quantitative debate

How important is this divide – philosophically?

We have covered this issue a fair amount previously (in this chapter and Chapter 1). To summarise, there are distinct epistemological positions that can be taken by researchers within the social sciences. Philosophers have provided the foundation for these positions and continue to argue which is right and which is wrong (even when they do not believe we can ever know when something is right or wrong). Some psychologists believe (and argue) very strongly that their philosophical position is correct and that all others are wrong. One of the most vociferous debates of this kind in recent times in the United Kingdom came about with the arguments advanced by the discourse analysts (e.g. Potter & Wetherell, 1987). They argued very strongly that much previous research, and most especially positivist research, was fundamentally flawed. Instead of studying internal mental processes they argued that psychological research should be concerned with language use. This debate has not been resolved and so continues in UK psychology today, but it is no longer so vociferous. This is the strongest position taken and many others believe and advocate their own philosophical standpoint without expending too much energy arguing with others who may disagree. This has resulted in the proliferation of different methodologies within psychology and, some would argue, fragmentation of the discipline (Langdridge & Butt, 2004).

How important is this divide – practically?

The distinction between qualitative and quantitative research is clearly important on a practical level. By and large, the claims made about the world differ in quite dramatic ways and clearly the methods employed by quantitative and qualitative researchers are different. However, things are not totally clear cut, for some methods are used in quantitative and qualitative research. And furthermore, an increasing number of researchers are using both quantitative and qualitative methods together within the same research project (see Chapter 24). So while many qualitative methods developed within the context of a critique of quantitative methods, researchers are beginning to see the utility of a practical strategy to research where illumination of the topic under investigation becomes clearer with a multi-method approach. But how do we do this? Surely these approaches are so different, with different epistemologies, aims and methods, that they can never be combined? Well, firstly, people advocating a **pragmatic** approach to research would argue that the epistemological questions must be put to one side, for (i) the main concern is with what works, and (ii) these questions are never likely to be settled. So, we bracket off the philosophical questions – well, the philosophical debate at least – for we cannot forget the philosophical issues when it comes to the question of what our methods allow us to say about the world. What about the differing aims of quantitative and qualitative methods? Well, this divide is potentially one of the strengths of a multi-method approach, for with such a strategy we get the possibility of investigating a phenomenon where we ask different questions and get different answers. This gives us the possibility of **triangulation**, where multiple perspectives enable us to truly understand the phenomena of interest. Triangulation generally concerns the desire to gain multiple perspectives within a qualitative approach but it can also involve the use of multiple perspectives from different traditions (Flick, 2002). Quantitative research may tell us, for instance, how many people experience depression, while phenomenological qualitative research may help us understand what it is like to experience depression. By taking different perspectives and using different methods we get the possibility of greater understanding of the topic (see Chapter 24). This strategy seems to be growing within psychology, and most particularly within applied areas, but it remains controversial, for there are those who argue that the epistemological differences cannot and should not be ignored since they concern fundamental questions about the nature of the discipline.

How important is this divide – politically?

As you have probably guessed by now, the divide is clearly an important one politically. The very fact that some people call themselves quantitative and others qualitative means that the label matters. And in this case the label really does matter, for although things are changing, and there is growing acceptance of qualitative approaches, there are still arguments and issues on both sides. Very simply, the quantitative approach to psychology remains dominant and with this dominance come certain advantages. Firstly, quantitative research is more likely to get funded than qualitative research. Secondly, quantitative research is more likely to get published than qualitative research. This is important for academics, for career advancement is invariably dependent on securing funding and getting published. It is obviously also important for the discipline more generally, as qualitative research will remain sidelined if funding and publication rates do not increase.

17.4	Limitations of the new paradigm for the social sciences

Up until now we have been advocating qualitative methods and highlighting their advantages over quantitative methods, but it is important to recognise their limitations too. Imagine you wished to increase the number of people wearing condoms when having sex. This is important, for if we increase the number of condoms worn we will decrease sexually transmitted diseases such as HIV. Now imagine we carried out a discourse analysis of talk about condom use. Will this help us implement a new health education intervention (like a pamphlet promoting condom use) to increase condom use? Well, it might provide some insight, but as the concern with discourse analysis is language use we doubt whether it will provide us with simple answers that can quickly and easily be incorporated into a pamphlet we can distribute. Similarly, a phenomenological study may give us insights into the experience of negotiating condom use among a small number of people and these may be key insights that help with the pamphlet, but we cannot know whether they apply to more than the 12 people in our sample. So, while qualitative research may be helpful to some extent, a quantitative approach, where we sample a representative number of people and ask them about their attitudes towards using condoms, may well enable us to identify quickly and easily relevant variables that can be incorporated into our health education leaflet.

Now, we have given just one example, which arguably demonstrates the (practical) superiority of a quantitative approach in one specific situation, and therefore why, we believe, qualitative research cannot and should not be the only approach used by psychologists. However, there are as many other examples which, we believe, demonstrate the superiority of qualitative research and clearly demonstrate why quantitative research should not be the only approach. There are countless examples on both sides that demonstrate the utility of quantitative and qualitative methods in achieving some outcome. Whether a particular approach is useful will depend on the questions being asked and, as you might expect, there are many questions left to be asked by psychologists. It is for this reason that we believe qualitative and quantitative perspectives both have a part to play in improving our knowledge of human nature. There is clearly good and bad research from both perspectives but let us not let that cloud our judgement and obscure the possibility of a constructive future where both have an equally valued place.

17.5 Varieties of qualitative methods and analysis

Epistemology and methodology

We have talked about the debates concerning different epistemological positions and it is important to think about their impact on **methodology** and **methods** used. As Willig (2001) makes clear, it is important to clarify the differences between methodology and methods, for the link between epistemology is necessarily close with one (methodology) and not the other (methods). Methodology concerns the 'general approach to studying research topics' (Silverman, 1993: 1), while methods are the specific techniques used to carry out research within a general position. The methodological approach taken by a researcher will clearly be strongly influenced by their epistemological standpoint. If, for instance, you are sceptical about psychology as an objective scientific study of human nature then you are unlikely to locate yourself within the traditional quantitative paradigm. Instead you might embrace a more critical methodological position such as social constructionism. Here the link between your epistemological position and methodology is clear and necessary. However, there is not such a necessary relationship between your epistemological position and method. But your methodological position *will limit* the range of methods that are appropriate. It is unlikely, though not impossible, that a social constructionist would employ experimental methods. Similarly, a quantitative researcher using the hypothetico-deductive approach is unlikely to employ semi-structured interviews. So, although there are links between epistemology, methodology and method, these are *often important but not always necessary*.

Qualitative methodologies

There are many different epistemological and methodological positions and therefore, as you might expect, many different qualitative methods. This is one of the biggest problems for people new to qualitative research. Quantitative research is, by comparison, simple and clear cut. Everyone knows where they stand and what to do. Good quantitative research has certain common foundations, with only variations in, for instance, methods of data collection and techniques of statistical analysis. There are not fundamental differences in methods that determine the very nature of your research questions, design, methods of data collection and analysis. Well, qualitative research is not that simple and at first glance it will appear complicated and probably confused. However, once you move beyond this first impression, things are not as complicated as they look.

The first thing to recognise is the different approaches to qualitative research that you might encounter. Chapters 19 to 22 outline what we consider to be the most important theoretical approaches to qualitative research within psychology. However, there are (many) other approaches that you may encounter and we are sure some people will feel we have made some terrible omissions. The chapters include the following qualitative approaches: phenomenological research, grounded theory, discourse and narrative research. These can be divided at a very simple level into two groups:

1 those that emphasise meaning for the participants (phenomenology and grounded theory), and
2 those that concentrate on language use (discourse analysis).

Participants' understanding of their own experience is emphasised and prioritised with the first group of methods. The key factor underpinning the second is, however, recognition of the dynamic nature of language. Language does not simply describe the world but plays an active part in constructing the world. Discourse analysts are not concerned with understanding the experiences of participants, like the phenomenologists, but they might be concerned with how people construct meaning through language use. Things are complicated somewhat by narrative approaches to research (Chapter 22) as they effectively combine elements of both of the above, though with some narrative methods concentrating more on meaning and others on language use.

However, things are even more complex than this, for even within the particular approaches listed above there are further distinctions and sometimes sharp divisions. For instance, there is not one way of doing grounded theory but several and the two founders (Glaser and Strauss) each now occupy opposing positions about which is correct. Similarly, there is not one approach to narrative research, discourse analysis or phenomenology but many. Sometimes these differences are minor and have only a marginal impact on, for instance, an element of the analysis of data. However, some of these distinctions are major and profoundly alter the whole research process. In the chapters that follow we outline some of the divisions though not all. If you wish to know more about any particular perspective then it will be crucial that you read further about it. The chapters in this book provide only a brief introduction. If you wish to carry out research from any qualitative perspective it is important that you read more, much more.

Commonalities in qualitative research

Although there are many differences between the different theoretical perspectives, there are a number of similarities and common features that provide a distinction between qualitative research and quantitative research. Following Hammersley (1992) we outline some of the commonalities here. It is important to note, however, that none of these distinctions is cast in stone. Like much in the social sciences, there will always be exceptions that disprove the rule. So, it is important that you think through these distinctions rather than simply remember them. Firstly, as you already know, qualitative research is concerned with the qualities of phenomena and not their quantification. This does not mean that qualitative research is less precise than quantitative research, just that it has a different focus. Instead of looking for causal relationships, qualitative researchers will tend to prefer to describe or uncover the quality of the phenomenon being investigated. Secondly, and perhaps most importantly, qualitative research has a focus on meanings rather than on behaviour. Variables are unlikely to have a place in qualitative research. This is because the research will prioritise the experience of the participants (or the construction of meaning through language) and any attempt to define variables in advance of this inevitably entails imposing a particular way of seeing the world on a participant. Thirdly, as discussed above, qualitative research rejects the natural science model of scientific endeavour. Research will rarely employ a hypothetico-deductive approach wherein we seek, through the use of controlled settings, to test an explicitly formulated hypothesis and make predictions about the world. Qualitative research is concerned with identifying processes rather than with predicting outcomes. Fourthly and finally, qualitative research is almost always naturalistic. Qualitative researchers study people in their natural environments and seek to capture the richness of such settings. No attempt is made to control 'extraneous variables', for there can never be extraneous variables in qualitative research. The 'noise' is part and parcel of the phenomenon and to (attempt to) exclude it from an investigation is to lose the essential richness of a person's experience.

Further reading

Burr, V. (2003). *An Introduction to Social Constructionism*. 2nd edn. London: Routledge.

An excellent and very clear introduction to this topic. If you wish to grasp the emergence of this new approach to psychology then this book will be invaluable.

Denzin, N. K. & Lincoln, Y. S. (2005). *The Sage Handbook of Qualitative Research*. 3rd edn. London: Sage.

A mammoth and expensive book, so one to borrow from the library. It is extremely comprehensive and includes excellent material on reflexivity, feminism and a whole lot more.

Smith, J. A., Harré, R. & Langenhove, L. (1995). *Rethinking Psychology*. London: Sage.

Excellent coverage of many of the debates within psychology from a wide variety of qualitative positions. It is now a little dated but includes coverage of phenomenology, discursive and feminist approaches. The companion volume *Rethinking Methods in Psychology* is also excellent and worth reading.

18 Transcribing, coding and organising textual data

- This chapter begins by stressing the importance of transcription not only in terms of accuracy but also as part of the analytic process.
- Approaches to transcription are introduced.
- The chapter then moves on to consider first order, second order and third order coding as first stages in a thematic analysis of textual data.
- Finally, this chapter looks at ways of organising and presenting textual data.

INTRODUCTION

Once you have collected data through audio recordings of semi- or unstructured interviews, the next step in most qualitative research is to transcribe the material. Transcription is the process of turning the spoken word into written form. You may think this is a simple process but, like so much in the social sciences, it is a lot more involved than you may think. For a start, there are many different ways of transcribing and these vary from one methodological position to another. Secondly, transcription is hard work. Ask anyone who has had to transcribe just one or two interviews and they will confirm this! Qualitative research is not an easy option. You may not have several hundred questionnaires to code and enter into SPSS but transcription and analysis of qualitative data, in almost all cases, will take much longer. Finally, transcription is not simply a mechanical task, for properly understood it constitutes the first stage of analysis. There is more about this below.

It is worth noting that before the widespread use of audio recorders the only way to collect data from interviews or through participant observation was through field notes. As you might imagine, making written notes during an interview or during breaks in an observation is very difficult and will not produce a word-for-word record of what went on. Field notes should be as accurate as possible and record what was said by whom. They also offer the possibility of the researcher recording their impressions during an interview or observation. Field notes should be made at the time, or as soon after an interview or observation as possible, to maximise their reliability. However, you cannot expect field notes to be as accurate as a transcribed audio recording. But the inability to capture everything that was said word for word may not be as much of a problem within some research projects as you might think. Research seeking to understand what it is like to live a certain way that involves, for instance, longitudinal participant observation invariably involves an attempt by the researcher to enter the person's 'lifeworld' (see Ashworth, 2001) or way of perceiving the world. This means that it is less crucial to record every single spoken word for this is not crucial to understanding. Instead, understanding may come from immersion in the world and the development of empathy with the people you are studying. However, field notes are very rarely used in interviewing and really only remain as a method of data collection in participant observation (and even there researchers now often use Dictaphones to record their thoughts and observations).

Once you have some data in spoken, written or even visual form (we may analyse visual material as well as written material – more on this in Chapter 21 on discourse analysis), you will want to carry out some form of analysis. In most qualitative research the first stage would involve coding the data. Coding is the process of describing and understanding your data through the systematic categorisation of the data. Almost any thematic or discursive analysis begins with coding in an attempt to organise and manage the data. However, there will be differences in the process of coding depending on the methodology being employed. Many qualitative analyses are forms of thematic analysis where the aim of the analysis is to draw out themes of meaning. Sociologists (and some psychologists publishing in multidisciplinary journals) may report thematic analyses without too much regard for whether the methodological position of their work is grounded theory or phenomenology. Psychologists (and most certainly the editorial boards of psychology journals) tend to be much more concerned with methodological issues, especially in qualitative research, and therefore often need to justify their methods through reference to some methodological system such as grounded theory. In this chapter we explain different ways of coding textual data and then move on to discuss thematic analysis. In later chapters in this section of the book we cover other qualitative positions which have a number of similarities (analytically speaking) to thematic analysis, such as interpretative phenomenological analysis (IPA) and grounded theory.

18.1 Purposes and principles of transcription

As we stated above, there is a lot more to transcription than first appears. It is the first stage in a considerable amount of qualitative research and is a vital stage. Without good quality transcription your research will suffer. A transcript produced must be fit for purpose and the purpose will vary from one methodological position to another. A discourse analyst will want a much more detailed transcript than a phenomenologist. This is because the focus of a discourse analysis is with the micro-level organisation of language. A phenomenologist, on the other hand, will be much more concerned with more macro-level content. However, even a phenomenologist will want a clear and (very important!) accurate transcript. At the simplest level a transcript will record what was said by whom in a simple chronological order (see Box 18.1).

Box 18.1

Information box

Simple transcription – an example

Int: So, tell me what led you to feel this way.

Res: Well I don't know really. I guess it all began when I was younger and started to feel pressure from my parents to lose weight. I was big uh big boned you might say eh? But the pressure to lose weight and more uhm weight just got worse even so I felt ur no I mean it got worse no matter what I did. And then the names started you know piggy my little fat boy and stuff like that.

Int: And how did that make you feel?

Res: Err well uh it was awful. I cried myself to sleep and just wished I could be smaller.

Int: Smaller?

Res: Yea I jus jus wanted to disappear you know urm lose er become smaller and smaller so no one could see me and call me those names.

As you have probably guessed, 'Int' stands for interviewer and 'Res' for respondent. Very often a transcript will use names instead to identify the interviewer and respondent. They may be false names but using a name reminds us that there is a person here taking part in our research and not an unknown subject.

As you can see from Box 18.1, transcription at this level is simply the transformation of the spoken word that has been recorded into the written word verbatim (word for word). This needs to be done as accurately as possible and in most research this involves no attempt to 'correct' what was said: that is, grammar is not corrected, nor are any colloquialisms, mispronunciations and so on. The attempt is to reproduce in written form as accurately as possible exactly what was said. It is also usual practice to transcribe what both the interviewer and interviewee said, so prepare yourself for listening to yourself on the recording. The reason for this is that what the interviewer says is as important as what the interviewee says. Context is crucial in most qualitative research and the context for what an interviewee says includes the interviewer and their questions, comments and statements.

18.2   Systems of transcription

There is no universal system for transcription. The simple approach detailed above is adequate for much qualitative research but not all. Those approaches to research that focus on language and language use, such as discourse analysis, some forms of narrative analysis and conversation analysis (which is mentioned in Chapter 21), require a much more detailed level of transcription. But there are many different approaches to the analysis of language and different approaches tend to use different systems of transcription. Even within the same approach there are disagreements over which system of transcription to use.

What do we mean by 'system'? Well, when we said the approach detailed above was simple, that was not an understatement. While a verbatim record that focuses on the content of what was said may be adequate for a phenomenological analysis or grounded theory, it is most certainly not adequate for discourse or conversation analysis. This is because it does not record the conversation in sufficient detail. The important thing to remember is that spoken language not only involves verbal information but also the **prosodic** (phonological elements of spoken language such as intonation and stress), the **paralinguistic** (non-phonemic aspects of language, such as whether a word was said in a joking manner or seriously) and the **extralinguistic** (non-linguistic elements of speaking, such as gestures).

The very fine level of analysis in which a discourse or conversation analyst engages includes analysis of all these aspects of language, for they believe (and argue very strongly) that this information is *necessary* for understanding what is meant in an utterance (O'Connell & Kowal, 1995). This means that we need to include more information than simply verbal information in a transcript if we wish to conduct a linguistic analysis of this kind. Therefore we need a comprehensive system to record and code all this extra information into a written form. No system is perfect, however, and there are therefore arguments over which system is best and/or most appropriate for a particular form of analysis. One of the most widely used transcription systems is the Jefferson system. Gail Jefferson developed this system and a complete description can be found in Atkinson & Heritage (1984). See Box 18.2 for an example and very brief introduction to some features of this system.

Box 18.2

Information box

The Jefferson system of transcription

```
P:    well if you wanna the::n  ⌜ wot you mean
I:                              ⌞ yes
P:    is that I (0.5) can see ((sighs)) him
```

Box 18.2 *Continued*

I: (1.5) if <u>you</u> want to I guess =

P: = great I knew you would understand

What the symbols mean:

:   A colon indicates that a speaker has stretched the preceding vowel sound (the more colons the greater the stretch)

[ ]   Square brackets between lines of speech indicate overlapping talk

(2.0)   Numbers in brackets indicate a pause timed in tenths of a second

__   Underlining indicates speaker emphasis in a word

=   An equals sign means there is no gap between two utterances

... and there are many more symbols than this.

As you can see, this is a much more complex form of transcription that takes even longer to carry out than the simple transcription described previously. A great deal more detail is included that conversation and (many, if not all) discourse analysts believe is necessary to understand what is going on within a piece of talk. While the Jefferson system is widely used, there are many other systems that transcribe more information and are therefore even more complex (and at times almost unreadable). In addition, some authors have raised concerns over Jefferson's system (e.g. O'Connell & Kowal, 1995).

   The most important thing to remember about transcription is that the system employed must be fit for the purpose. If you wish to conduct a phenomenological analysis you will probably be satisfied with the simple system of transcription where only the verbal content of speech is recorded. The Jefferson system may well record more detail of what occurred in the speech being transcribed but it offers no benefit if that extra information is not going to be used in an analysis. On the other hand, if you wish to conduct most forms of discourse or conversation analysis it is vital that you use a comprehensive and very detailed system such as the Jefferson system or it will be impossible to carry out your analysis.

18.3   Transcription as analysis

We mentioned earlier that transcription could also be understood as the first stage of analysis and not just as a tedious and mechanical process necessary when gathering qualitative data. But why is this? One of the first elements of any qualitative analysis is becoming familiar with your data. It is vital that you get a feel for your data and one of the best ways of doing this is to transcribe the audio material yourself. When transcribing speech you are forced to listen to every detail in an attempt to get an accurate written record. No matter how hard you try, you are unlikely to listen this closely if you already have transcripts of your audio recording that someone else has produced.

Transcribing your own data also enables you to maintain a link between the raw data (your tapes or digital recording) and your transcript. It is important to maintain this link so that you do not rely on the transcripts too much and forget the audio recording. Information is missed with any transcript (no matter what system is used) and this information can only be recovered by listening to the recording. Sometimes we need to listen to a person to really understand what is going on and we will therefore need to return to the recording. Listening to the recording is also useful for reminding the researcher that the transcript belongs to a person (there is always the danger of forgetting this).

As you transcribe you can also begin the process of analysis more formally. When you are transcribing you should have a notepad handy so that you can make notes that occur to you. Notes of these kinds are called **memos** and are part of the data analysis strategy that stems from grounded theory (more about this in Chapter 20). In brief, a memo is a note to yourself from your reflection about the data. They are a useful way of beginning the process of theory development from the 'bottom up'. Later, when you are coding and categorising your data, your memos will provide information that may inform your analysis and theory development. Grounded theorists make memos as they code their data and it is a sensible thing to do during the process of transcription as well.

While we have stressed the value of transcription as a first stage in the analytic process, there are many researchers (ourselves included, we must confess) who get others (secretarial staff and research assistants) to transcribe their data for them. We have all done it ourselves once, for sure. The arguments above should be considered in context. The context in question, for us at least, is academic life. Academics these days rarely have the time available for this part of the research process. Pressure to carry out research and publish is immense and academics have found it necessary to employ strategies to maximise their output, and getting others to transcribe their data has increasingly become a necessary strategy. This is much more difficult for discourse and conversation analysts, for the complex system of transcription they use requires considerable expertise which is not widely available.

18.4 Coding qualitative data

Once you have a transcript you need to start the process of analysis proper and for thematic analysis this involves **coding**. Coding is very simply the process of assigning labels (or codes) to your textual data. Codes are usually applied to chunks of data. These chunks may be words, phrases, sentences or even paragraphs. The important thing to remember about coding is that it requires a human hand. The reason for human involvement is that coding entails the ascription of descriptors according to meaning in the text rather than simply because a word or phrase appears. So, you may have different words, phrases and sentences coded together and similar words, phrases and sentences coded differently (because of, for instance, the different contexts in which they appear). Coding is creative but it should also always be consistent and rigorous. There is no room for sloppiness here any more than in the statistical analysis of quantitative data.

In a thematic analysis three levels of codes are usually recognised (other forms of analysis such as discourse analysis will code data differently). These are **first**, **second** and **third level** (or **order**) **codes**, with the differences reflecting the differing levels of interpretation being applied to the text. Most people begin with a very basic descriptive level of coding and work upwards in a systematic manner towards a more interpretative level. However, not everyone goes through three levels and some people code once and then move on to the thematic analysis stage without multiple layers of codes.

First order coding

First order or descriptive-level coding is the most basic level of coding and the start of the analytic process where textual data are organised and categorised. Box 18.3 gives an example of this level of coding.

Box 18.3

Information box

First order descriptive coding

Whenever I feel down about my weight (WEIGHT) I make myself some comfort food (FUFC) or nip to the shops and buy crisps, biscuits or cake. I indulge myself (IMY) in this pleasure but then regret it afterwards (LREG).

Codes:

WEIGHT – Concern over weight

FUFC – Food used to provide comfort

IMY – Indulge myself with food when feeling down

LREG – Feel regret later after indulging in food

As you can see, this level of coding is very descriptive. There is minimal interpretation but it still requires care and thought. Guided practice is the best strategy for improving your ability to code effectively. If you look at the example, chunks of meaning are being coded ('feeling down about my weight' is coded as WEIGHT or concern over weight). Throughout the rest of the transcript you will look for further discussion of concern over the person's weight (if it occurs) and also code these chunks as WEIGHT. Similarly, any further mention of feeling regretful after indulging in food would be labelled LREG.

This is not a static process, however, for you may need to revise initial codes as you proceed through a transcript and/or as you move on to another transcript. In fact it is rare that your initial codes will be adequate for the task. You may find that a code such as WEIGHT is too crude to capture the meaning in the text adequately and it should therefore be understood in two ways (e.g. concern over weight because of others – WEIGHTO – versus concern over weight because of self – WEIGHTS). So, the initial code becomes subdivided. It is equally possible that you may need to combine codes if you realise that there is too much overlapping meaning. Nothing is cast in concrete. Your analysis must always be driven by your data and not by your desire to stick with your list of codes. Now have a go yourself (see Box 18.4).

Box 18.4

Activity box   **First order coding**

Make sure you have a partner for this exercise.

1 Individually read through an interview that you have transcribed or another piece of text that you have available (anything will do – you could use text from a newspaper, for instance), making short notes where appropriate ('memos') of ideas that occur to you about the meaning of the text.

2 Discuss your initial ideas with your partner and then write a short paragraph summary of these ideas.

3 Individually construct a small number of (first order) descriptive codes (four or five) which could be applied to the interview. At this level codes should simply describe what is going on in the text. Resist the temptation to explain – just describe what is there. This stage is all about categorising (or grouping) the text into units of meaning. Give a clear explanation of how each of the codes should be applied. Remember, try to create codes that apply to quite large chunks of text, i.e. represent some unit of meaning, value, action or activity. Chunks will probably be one or two sentences, though they may be shorter or longer than this.

4 Compare your descriptive codes with those of your partner. Compare them in terms of:

- agreement/disagreement;
- overlap of meaning (are they really about the same thing?);
- more general or less general (does one code incorporate several other codes as sub-codes?);
- separate concepts (no overlap at all);
- how clearly and unambiguously they are defined.

▶

Box 18.4 *Continued*

5 Make notes on the following:

- how easy or hard it was to make the codes unambiguous;

- problems you encountered in applying the codes to the transcripts;

- how well you think the codes capture the meaning of the interviews.

Second order coding

This level of coding entails somewhat more interpretation than first order coding. At this level these may be super-ordinate constructs that capture the overall meaning of some of the descriptive codes or they may be additional codes that reflect issues such as power, knowledge or conflict within the text (Box 18.5). You are now moving from the initial descriptive level of coding to a more interpretative level. However, you should resist the temptation to draw on grand psychological theories such as psychoanalysis. You still need to keep close to your data.

Box 18.5

Information box

Second order interpretative coding

Whenever I feel down about my weight I make myself some comfort food or nip to the shops and buy crisps, biscuits or cake (BODIMG). I indulge myself in this pleasure but then regret it afterwards (COPAREG).

Codes:

BODIMG – Participant often feels depressed about their body image and consequently indulges in comfort eating to alleviate distress. Feels they cannot control this situation.

COPAREG – Experiences cycle of pleasure and regret with food. Participant cannot break this cycle of pleasure and regret despite insight.

Third order coding

Here we are at a higher level of coding which may blur into the next stage, the thematic analysis. Codes at this level will be superordinate constructs that capture the overall meaning of some of your descriptive and interpretative codes. **Third order** (or **pattern**) coding involves moving from the initial descriptive level of coding to a more interpretative level of coding (Box 18.6). This is now the time to draw on psychological theories to aid your interpretation of the data. So think through relevant theoretical ideas that may inform the generation of themes of meaning within your text. Be careful, though, for your analysis must still be grounded in your data.

Box 18.6

Information box

Third order pattern coding

Whenever I feel down about my weight I make myself some comfort food or nip to the shops and buy crisps, biscuits or cake. I indulge myself in this pleasure but then regret it afterwards. (COABUSE)

Code for whole segment:

COABUSE – Cycle of abuse. The participant's relationship with food and their body is indicative of much of the way they relate to their own body. They feel alienated from their body, ashamed of it and abuse it in an attempt to exact some sense of control over their body and their emotions.

18.5   Thematic analysis

It is in fact only a short step from pattern coding to the next stage in a thematic analysis, which is to draw out the overarching themes in your data. Pattern coding sometimes results in this situation anyway, which is why some people do not recognise three distinct levels of coding. Once you have gone through the systematic process of coding your data, you will then want to draw out the higher-level concepts or themes. There will usually be only a few (often three or four) themes in a transcript on a particular topic and these will represent more general concepts within your analysis and subsume your lower-level codes. In a sense you were always building to this level of analysis. Look at the study described in Box 18.7 to get a feel for the level we are talking about.

Box 18.7   Study box

Grogan, S. & Richards, H. (2002) Body image: Focus groups with boys and men. *Men and Masculinities*, **4** (3), 219-32.

This study used focus groups with boys and young men to explore the way in which they understood issues such as body shape ideals, body esteem and so on. The study included focus groups of boys and men aged 8, 13, 16 and 19–25. The group facilitator encouraged

▶

Box 18.7 *Continued*

discussion about issues concerned with body image. The focus groups were tape-recorded and then transcribed. The data were then subjected to a thematic analysis. The themes represented the important overarching issues raised by the boys and men in the focus groups about body image. Themes included: *the importance of being muscular, fear of fat, being bothered or not with exercise, social pressure* and *power and self-confidence*. The theme *fear of fat*, for instance, concerned the beliefs that boys and men were responsible for being fat or not and demonstrated weakness if they were fat. In addition, it was accepted, even by those who felt themselves to be overweight, that blame and ridicule should be associated with being fat. Overall, the authors looked at these themes in relation to recent discussion about changes in attitudes to the male body and the increase in men being concerned with body image.

18.6 Organising and presenting the analysis of textual data

It is important to understand how to present a thematic analysis when reporting such work. Chapter 26 outlines the structure of quantitative and qualitative reports and journal articles but we would like to show how findings from a thematic analysis should be presented here. A thematic analysis will produce anything from a couple of themes to quite a number depending on the topic and size of project. How many themes are appropriate will depend on the data but it is unlikely that you will get into double figures. In published research, which we believe offers the best model for any report, you will see a fairly standard way of presenting findings from a thematic analysis. In the findings, analysis or results/discussion sections of a report, authors will generally structure the findings in terms of their themes. So, the authors of the study mentioned above in Box 18.7 started their results and discussion section (results and discussion sections are nearly always combined in qualitative research – more on this in Chapter 26) with a brief introduction and then went on to present their findings about *The Importance of Being Muscular*. This theme was used as a subheading and then followed with discussion of its meaning and quotes in support of the arguments. The authors then went on to discuss the other themes. See Box 18.8 for an example of what this section of a research paper (and any report of this kind) should look like.

Box 18.8

Presenting findings from a thematic analysis

Example (fictional and deliberately kept short).

Results/discussion

This study identified a number of themes arising in the context of young people's concern with their bodies. These included the following: Cycle of abuse, Re-visiting the past and The yo-yo experience.

Cycle of abuse

Several participants talked in ways that showed the relationship with food and their body is indicative of much of the way they relate to their own body. They often felt alienated from their own bodies, ashamed of them and sometimes abused them in an attempt to exact some sense of control.

Jayne: Whenever I feel down about my weight I make myself some comfort food or nip to the shops and buy crisps, biscuits or cake. I indulge myself in this pleasure but then regret it afterwards.

As you can see, Jayne demonstrates the classic cycle of excessive eating and consequent regret (Jones & Evans, 1999). Even though she demonstrates insight it is clear that this is something she sees as beyond her control.

Int: Tell me how you feel when you do this.

Fred: I know it is wrong but I cannot help myself I I really can't stop so I jus kinda take out all my frustration any way I can and I end up in a mess.

Fred is typical of many we interviewed when he talks about the frustration felt with these feelings of lack of control and regret [and so on ...]

Re-visiting the past

As discussed in previous research (Matthew & Milton, 2000), all participants talked of a time in the past when things were different [and so on ...]

As you can see from the example in Box 18.8, themes are presented and discussed in relation to previous literature on the topic. The example is fictional and somewhat short. In journal articles you will generally see more extensive discussion of each theme and greater use of quotes. Themes emerge from the data and are presented in a report in a systematic way, theme by theme. Each theme presents some discussion of its meaning along with data, in the form of quotes, in support of the arguments being made. Themes will generally consist of a number of arguments and also several quotes. The key issue with the presentation of findings is clarity. You need to express your findings clearly and succinctly so that readers can understand your statements and arguments. In addition, you need to convince readers of what you found and it is here that you need to present data (quotes) in support of your findings.

Further reading

Miles, M. B. & Huberman, A. M. (1994). *Qualitative Data Analysis: An Expanded Sourcebook,* 2nd edn. London: Sage.

This is a truly excellent book for understanding the practicalities of qualitative research. Very few books actually tell you how to conduct a qualitative analysis of data in as much detail as this book. There is detail on coding and analysis and a wealth of further information. Our only warning is to remember that while this book provides information about thematic analysis more generally, the authors also concentrate on their own particular methods for qualitative analysis (such as the use of matrices) grounded in the sociological tradition and which are only some amongst many methods used for the analysis of such data.

Phenomenological research methods

- This chapter begins by considering the fundamental assumptions that underpin all research from a phenomenological perspective.

- It then moves on to consider two different phenomenological approaches that are employed in psychological research.

- Finally, this chapter critically examines these two different approaches, drawing out the strengths and weaknesses of each and strengths and weaknesses of phenomenological perspectives more generally.

INTRODUCTION

This chapter is concerned with introducing an increasingly popular qualitative approach to research within psychology. Phenomenological approaches to research in psychology have their roots in phenomenological philosophy, which was initially developed by Edmund Husserl in the early part of the twentieth century. Phenomenological methods have been and continue to be used throughout the social and health sciences. They have been employed in psychological research for a considerable time in one form or another but it is only in recent years that we have witnessed a substantial rise in their profile within UK psychology. But what is phenomenology in this context? Very simply, it is the study of experience. The emphasis in all phenomenological investigations is the 'world in its appearing'; that is, people's perceptions of the world they inhabit. And phenomenological research in psychology aims to describe a person's perception of the world as it relates to aspects of their lived experience.

There is not simply one approach to the application of phenomenology within psychology, rather a family of approaches. Indeed, Moran (2000: 3), quoting the French philosopher Paul Ricoeur, remarks that phenomenology 'is the story of deviations from Husserl'. There are different emphases among the different approaches to phenomenology used in psychology depending on the philosophical underpinnings and methodological concerns. Some phenomenological psychologists draw principally on the philosophy of Husserl (e.g. the Duquesne School) whilst others are particularly interested in the application of ideas from the existential strand (that which is concerned with our embodied existence in the world) of phenomenological thought (e.g. Ashworth, 2000), while others may be more interested in hermeneutic phenomenology (that which is concerned with language and interpretation) (e.g. Langdridge, 2003, 2007). The existential strand draws on the philosophical work of such people as Heidegger, Sartre and Merleau-Ponty while the hermeneutic strand draws on the work of such people as Gadamer and Ricoeur. The distinctions between these different strands can be complex and difficult to understand. This chapter focuses on two of the most popular approaches to the application of phenomenological ideas to psychological research in the UK today: the Duquesne (pronounced DuKane) School – founded by Amedeo Giorgi and colleagues – and Interpretative Phenomenological Analysis (or IPA) – founded by Jonathan Smith. First, this chapter introduces some of the fundamentals that underpin all phenomenological research and then moves on to consider the methods and work of the Duquesne School and the methods and work of IPA.

19.1   The fundamentals of phenomenology: philosophical issues

This section will introduce some of the key philosophical issues in phenomenology. We will keep this as brief and simple as possible. However, these ideas *are* complex *and* counter-intuitive so can be very difficult to grasp (at least at first). They are not common sense and require you to suspend your everyday way of seeing the world and engage in an alternative way of seeing. However, it is important not to worry too much about these issues at this stage, for you can still conduct phenomenological research without engaging with the philosophy underpinning phenomenological approaches. Indeed, there are many researchers in the social sciences using phenomenological methods who know surprisingly little about the philosophy underpinning the approach they employ and advocate. We think phenomenological research is generally more rigorous, however, where the researchers have a good understanding of philosophical issues underpinning the approach they use, which is why we cover this material here.

Intentionality

Intentionality, in phenomenology, simply concerns the fact that our consciousness is always of something. The act of consciousness and the object of that act of consciousness are intentionally related. If 'I see', I see some object visually, whether it is another person or an ant; if 'I hear', I hear some sound, whether it is a voice or a musical note; if 'I think', I think of something, whether a philosophical principle or a state of affairs in my life. Every experience (or 'act of consciousness') is an experience 'of' (something). There is always a correlation between our experience and the object of that experience. Intention, as you might have guessed, is not used in the way we would use it usually (where we might intend to go to the gym), meaning a practical intention to do something. Instead, it is used in a specific way within phenomenology to refer to the mental processes involved in our conscious relations to objects.

So why does this matter? Isn't it obvious that consciousness is always 'of something', so why should we care? Well, the notion of intentionality goes right to the heart of a fundamental debate in philosophy. One of the dominant positions in the philosophy of mind over the past few hundred years has been a view of consciousness wherein consciousness exists within minds separate from the world. Here our consciousness is not 'of' something. This is very much a common-sense understanding within our culture. Most people believe that cognition must happen inside our heads and that we (as people) can be in touch only with our brain states. The problem then is how we know that there is more than just this intellectual perception; how we can know that our contact with the world is not just an illusion. If consciousness is something entirely inside our minds (our own private realm) how can we ever get 'outside' and enter the world (a public realm) we have in common with others? For phenomenologists, consciousness is not something that resides inside the person, a private domain that the individual tries to deliver to the public world. Instead, consciousness is always already turned out on the world through our intentional relationship with the world. It is a public thing and the mind and the world are necessarily and inseparably correlated with each other. The concept of intentionality is key to this alternative way of seeing. Phenomenologists do not recognise a simple distinction between subjects (people) and objects (things in the world) and therefore do not recognise a mind that is located within people. Instead, they argue that the focus of any investigation must be on that which is between people or between people and the world. The focus is therefore always the public realm of experience.

Idealism versus realism

Phenomenology also seeks to transcend the debate between the **idealists**, who very simply believe that everything we can say we know about the world is in the mind, and the **realists**, who believe that everything we can say we know about the world is in the world.

People who subscribe to idealism believe that what we perceive to be reality is in fact the product of our own minds. There is no real knowable world out there waiting to be perceived (as the realists would have us believe). This is not as mad a concept as it first seems. It does not mean that the world as we know it is not there at all, just that we can have no unmediated experience of it. Everything we can say we know about the world is mediated by our minds. There is not a straightforward relationship between the world (object) and us (subjects); everything is interpreted through the mind. A person's glass may be perceived as half empty or half full. The object (glass) is the same in both cases but the perception of it is mediated by a person's pessimism or optimism and all we have is the perception. Given this idealist position we can never know the 'true' nature of the world independent of our experience of it.

A realist, on the other hand, believes that we do have access to a real knowable world and that we can have unmediated access. This is the common-sense view that most people share about our knowledge of the world. There are different types of realist (as there are different types of idealist) but many realists in the social sciences believe that through the proper application of methods from the natural sciences we can access the world, describe and measure it. Explanation, causality and prediction are thought to be just as appropriate in the social sciences as they are in the natural sciences as we discover truths about the world. The phenomenological position transcends the debate between the realists and idealists and offers an alternative way of seeing things where the emphasis is on our experience or perception of the world. The important thing for phenomenologists is not whether there is a real world beyond our experience or whether it is all in our minds but what we actually have access to. And what we have access to is the shared public realm of experience. When a person perceives the world, that is all there is to interrogate. The focus of any phenomenological enquiry must be on the intentionality of some phenomenon. This may be the experience of grief or loss, the experience of illness or the experience of living under the threat of war. Intentionality can be of anything and the object of phenomenological enquiry is to describe the intentionality of the topic of interest. Furthermore, through repeated interrogation of multiple perceptions we can come to know something of the shared experience of that particular perception.

| **19.2** | The fundamentals of phenomenology: methodological issues |

Epoché

Phenomenological research is primarily concerned with **first-person accounts** of life experiences. A phenomenological investigation seeks to describe these accounts and arrive at an understanding of the meanings and essences (or fundamental structure) of experience. The **epoché** (pronounced ae-pockay) is a Greek word used by Husserl (1931) to mean the process by which we attempt to abstain from our presuppositions or those preconceived ideas we might have about the things we are investigating. This is sometimes referred to as **bracketing**. The core of epoché is doubt: not doubt about everything we say we know but doubt about the **natural attitude**, or the biases, of everyday knowledge. The aim of the epoché is to enable the researcher to describe the 'things themselves' and (attempt to) set aside our natural attitude, all those assumptions we have about the world around us. This is not an easy thing to do. The challenge is to let the things in our experience appear in our consciousness as if for the first time. This freshness of vision requires us to become aware of our presumptions and prejudices and then examine the object of consciousness from different perspectives. The ability to see phenomena from many different perspectives is crucial in uncovering the **essence** (or fundamental structure) of the phenomena.

How much we can truly bracket off our preconceptions is hotly debated within phenomenology. Critics of the phenomenological approach have challenged the possibility of ever achieving epoché. There are several different positions within phenomenology about this issue. The **transcendental phenomenologists** follow Husserl and argue that epoché is achievable and that it is possible to transcend one's own experience of the world to see it differently as another person might. The **existential phenomenologists** follow Heidegger, Sartre and Merleau-Ponty and believe that you should try to achieve epoché but that you can never truly bracket off all your presuppositions and achieve a 'god's eye view'. They stress the grounded and embodied nature of our being in the world. On the other hand, many **hermeneutic phenomenologists** who follow Heidegger, Gadamer and Ricoeur, employ a more reflexive notion of epoché, with the role of the researcher in co-constructing the findings more directly recognised within the research process. Note that these divisions are rather crude and that many people cross these camps and work differently within them. This has been simplified to emphasise the differences but, as always, this can lead to a false impression so please treat it as a distinction that is not hard and fast. The Duquesne School appears, at times, to subscribe to the transcendental position, while others working within phenomenological psychology (e.g. Ashworth, 2000) adopt a more existential position. IPA can be more readily located with the hermeneutic phenomenology camp. Whichever position is taken, the aim remains the same, which is to attempt to put aside one's preconceptions about the phenomenon being investigated and to emphasise experience through a return to the things themselves in their appearing to consciousness (see Langdridge, 2007 and 2008, for more on these distinctions).

Phenomenological reduction

The **psychological phenomenological reduction** continues the process initiated with the epoché. Once we have begun to see things as they appear, with our preconceptions bracketed off, we must now describe what we see, not just in terms of our perception but also in terms of our consciousness. Here we aim to capture and describe the total experience of consciousness in as much detail as possible. The task is to describe the general features of the phenomenon, excluding all elements that are not directly within our conscious experience. What this requires is repeated reflection on the phenomenon, examination and elucidation. All detail appearing to consciousness must be described, no matter how mundane it appears. The phenomenon should be examined from different angles until all possible ways of seeing are exhausted. One should examine minute details and then the whole, for part–whole relationships can help identify the essence of the phenomenon. The key to the reduction is repeated looking to uncover the layers of meaning inherent in the phenomenon being perceived. The rule of **horizontalisation** is crucial here. What this means is that we should not rush to produce vertical hierarchies of meaning, assuming that one thing is more important than another. We naturally tend to assume hierarchies of meaning in our everyday lives, but this must be suspended when engaged in the psychological phenomenological reduction. It is also crucial to engage in **verification**. This involves repeatedly checking the description against the phenomenon (often the transcript in research) to avoid moving beyond the 'things in their appearing'. It is very easy to fall back into the natural attitude and let our presuppositions influence our findings, so we must repeatedly verify our description by checking it against the data. Once the phenomenon has been exhaustively examined we would then seek to write a complete description of the experience. This process is about gaining a rich understanding of the nature and meaning of the phenomenon being investigated.

Imaginative variation

There is another stage that may be employed, following the psychological phenomenological reduction, to further elucidate meaning from an experience. **Imaginative variation** is the process of approaching the phenomenon being experienced from different perspectives through imaginatively varying features of the phenomenon. So, for instance, one might imagine the experience of watching *Eastenders* (or any other television soap opera) where the male characters are women and vice versa. How would this change the experience of watching the television show? It would almost certainly enable you to see the many gendered aspects of the experience of watching this particular television show. You might also imagine the show without the Queen Victoria pub. How would this affect the experience of watching the show? There would no longer be available the central revelatory point where characters can reveal private secrets to each other in a public space. This might reduce the excitement of the show as it is forced to reflect the more everyday (and mundane) experience we have where our private lives generally remain private. Alternatively, removal of the pub may simply mean that the launderette becomes more central in this role, highlighting the fact that revelation (or rather our experience of witnessing it) is a necessary and invariant property of the show.

As you can imagine, imaginative variation is potentially a very powerful technique for enabling us to uncover the layers of meaning and invariant properties of an experience. It does require practice to free oneself from the natural attitude and imagine other ways of being. Anything and everything is possible if only we are able to see.

This particular application of phenomenology to psychological research is sometimes referred to as **phenomenological psychology** and arose in the United States at Duquesne University in the late 1960s/early 1970s with the work of Amedeo Giorgi and colleagues. This approach was one of the earliest applications of phenomenological ideas to psychology (within a traditional psychology, rather than philosophy, setting). A considerable amount of empirical work has been conducted on a very wide range of topics, from the experience of being criminally victimised (Wertz, 1985) to feeling anxious (Fischer, 1974); from the structure of thinking in chess (Aanstoos, 1985) to the experience of learning (Colaizzi, 1971; Giorgi, 1985c). The approach is thought by some to be too descriptive and possibly also naive, with the apparent adherence to a transcendental phenomenological position. It is, however, one of the most well-formulated systems of phenomenological research in psychology and an approach that is founded on a clear (phenomenological) philosophical position.

Methods

The Duquesne School principally relies on two methods for data collection: written records of experiences and semi- or unstructured interviews. The main aim for data collection is to gain access to a **concrete description** of the experience of interest. So, participants are asked to remember an experience and either write a written account of this in as much detail as possible or recount the experience to another person within an interview. These concrete descriptions of experience enable the phenomenological psychologist to attempt to understand the essence of that experience for another person. Data are generally collected from a small number of participants, depending on the size of the research study. On average, studies of this kind being conducted by sole researchers tend to employ 6 to 12 participants. It is generally considered desirable for participants to vary in terms of their demographic characteristics (age, sex, ethnicity, etc.) as much as possible (Polkinghorne, 1989). It is argued that this provides a sufficiently wide range of perspectives to ascertain the invariant properties (or essence) that are common and also the individual (possibly unique) ways of seeing the phenomenon.

For Giorgi (1985c), a phenomenological psychological analysis involves four steps. The first step is to read the whole description of the experience (whether this is a written description or the transcript of an interview) in order to get a sense of the overall meaning. Second, the text is re-read from the beginning and an attempt is made to discern **meaning-units** within the text. Third, once the meaning-units have been discerned, the researcher attempts to express the psychological significance of each of them. Finally, the researcher attempts to synthesise all of the meaning-units so they can produce a structural summary of the experience in question. We will discuss each step in more detail below.

Overall meaning

This step is really very straightforward and simply requires a close reading of the text. It is important to read through the text several times and, we would argue, make memos of any thoughts and reflections that occur during the reading. The aim is to grasp the overall meaning of the experience being described for the participant. This should be done within the context of the epoché, where we attempt to bracket off our preconceptions and understand the meaning of the phenomenon for our participant(s). As we stated in the previous chapter, transcription can be a useful way of engaging with a text as it slows you down and forces reflection on meaning.

Identify meaning-units

It is now necessary to break the text down into smaller parts in order to discern meaning (essentially this is a form of coding like that described in the previous chapter). The particular method used by the Duquesne School requires that the researcher identify **meaning-units** within a psychological framework. The researcher must remain open to the text but has two horizons limiting their experience of the text. The first is the **psychological attitude** that they will adopt towards the text and the second concerns the **set** that the text is an example of. The reason for adopting a psychological attitude towards the text is obvious. The analysis is intended to be psychological and so requires this attitude of the researcher when engaged in the analytic process. Psychological phenomena are not simply found but created by psychologists engaged with the world (Giorgi, 1985a). If the researcher were instead interested in sociological meaning then they would need to adopt a sociological attitude. But what does it mean to adopt a psychological attitude towards the text? Well, this is the process of reflecting on changes in meaning within the text while working within the psychological framework of interest. This may mean a focus on perception or emotions or it may mean a more general focus on anything that appears psychologically relevant. Giorgi (1985b) acknowledges the difficulty in precisely articulating this process in a way that a novice could follow. This is a common problem in qualitative research where the best way to learn a method is to do it under supervision from someone experienced in the method. The **set** adopted is the attitude of the researcher towards the specific topic being investigated. So, although a phenomenological study requires a researcher to be open to the data and possibly discover things that were not expected, a researcher must still 'set' boundaries and investigate a specific topic, whether it is the experience of being a victim of crime or of being distrusted. So, two boundary conditions are established (the psychological attitude and the set adopted towards the data), but otherwise the process of discerning meaning-units must be conducted with as few preconceptions as possible with the aim of discovering the essence of the phenomenon being studied.

Giorgi (1985b) further makes it clear that, following Gurwitsch (1964), meaning-units should be understood as *constituents* and not *elements* of the whole. Constituents are parts of the whole which are context laden and whose meaning can only be understood within a particular context. Elements, on the other hand, are parts whose meaning can be understood pretty much independent of their context. A letter is a good example of an element, for the meaning of the letter 'b' is pretty much the same wherever it is found in a word or sentence. A word would be an example of a constituent, for the meaning of a word arises in the context of its relationship to other words within a sentence. Meaning-units should be understood as constituents according to this distinction.

At this stage the text is read for meaning and changes in meaning and through this the meaning-units are identified. The researcher should use the language of the participant to describe the meaning-unit, much as one would do when descriptively coding a piece of text. See Box 19.1 for an example of meaning-units and the next stage (below) of assessing their psychological significance.

Box 19.1

Information box

Meaning-units and psychological significance

The left-hand column represents the meaning-unit discerned from the transcript whilst the right-hand column represents the results of the next stage of analysis (below), where the phenomenon is understood more properly in terms of its psychological meaning for the set being investigated. The set being adopted in this study is the experience of mistrust. This is based on an interview with a woman telling the story of mistrusting her partner.

(1) CH states that she had been together with her boyfriend for a year when she first realised things were going stale and they were arguing more than usual.	(1) CH was in a relationship, which she thought was going stale.
(2) CH had started to spend more time with her partner in front of the TV and less time doing other things. They spent much less time engaging in activities than before.	(2) The relationship was perceived as stale due to the lack of activity and excitement.
(3) CH tried to talk to her partner about her feelings that they were stuck in a rut but this only caused more rows.	(3) CH thought talking through issues would help overcome these difficulties. CH felt that this did not help and only served to create more difficulties.

▶

Box 19.1 *Continued*

(4) For no apparent reason things seemed to improve. Over the space of a couple of months the rows became fewer and fewer and her partner seemed happier and more engaged with the relationship.

(4) With no clear explanation the relationship improved over the course of time.

(5) Then CH became suspicious of her partner. She noticed he was spending more time with his friends but thought that if that is what it takes to maintain the improved relationship then fair enough. However, CH still had a nagging doubt about the relationship. She thought that something was not quite right.

(5) Following a number of minor changes in her partner's behaviour CH became suspicious of him. At this time, however, she lived with the doubt and did nothing to confront these feelings.

(6) Upon reflection CH realised that her partner was paying more attention to his appearance, spending more time with friends. This led CH to ask more questions, leading her to notice the holes in the stories being told.

(6) CH began to put the minor changes together with her suspicion. This led to indirect confrontation enabling her to gather more information.

(7) CH kept a mental record of everything said so she could patch together her own story of events. She also talked to friends who were convinced her partner was having an affair. CH did not want to hear this at this time, however, which led to difficulties with her friends.

(7) CH then tested her beliefs with her friends. CH wanted to hear she was mistaken but found herself directly confronted with her fears. This led to confrontation with her friends as she denied the reality of the situation.

As you can see from Box 19.1, the analysis of meaning-units is very descriptive and remains very close in meaning (and language) to that of the participant. This is important, for when we say that a researcher works within a psychological attitude it does not mean that we import psychological theories into our analysis and 'see' the phenomenon in this particular way. Phenomenological research is instead much more concerned with understanding 'naive' ways of seeing, that is, understanding people's *everyday experiences*.

Assess psychological significance of meaning-units

This stage involves translating the participant's everyday expressions into psychological language while emphasising the phenomenon being investigated (see the right-hand column of Box 19.1 for an example). This process is achieved through reflection and imaginative variation (as described above). There will always be a tension between the concrete experience being described and the desire to produce a general category of meaning for the phenomenon. It is necessary to move away from individual idiosyncratic experiences and produce a more general elucidation of meaning for the phenomenon of interest. Here specific detail gives way to a more general understanding where the specific detail is not necessary for understanding the issue at hand. One must be careful, however, not to abstract too far and move beyond the data. Furthermore, while this stage concerns the translation of meaning-units into psychological language, this does not mean that one employs the psychological language of psychoanalysis, cognitivism or any other mainstream psychological perspective. The psychological language referred to here is one that is a mixture of common sense and phenomenology. If we translated meaning into psychoanalytic or cognitive language then we would be able to understand the phenomenon only in psychoanalytic or cognitive terms. The aim of phenomenological psychology is to describe the world in its appearing in everyday language, such that meaning can become apparent to anyone who cares to perceive it.

Synthesise meaning-units and present full structural description

The final stage is where one writes a full structural description of the phenomenon. This stems from (1) the process of identifying the invariant properties through (2) an analysis of meaning-units from a wide variety of participants' accounts of an experience and (3) their translation into a general psychological description. Here the researcher attempts to synthesise and integrate all of the insights gained about the phenomenon into one description. All aspects of the phenomenon discerned from the analysis must be taken into account in the production of the essential structural description. **Specific structural descriptions** can be produced for each participant's experience and then followed by a **general structural description** that captures the invariant properties of meaning that are common to all the specific structural descriptions. Indeed, both components can provide insight into the phenomenon of interest, one specific, rich and idiosyncratic that is faithful to the experience of the participant, the other more generalisable and/or accessible to others' experience. See Box 19.2 to get a real feel for the type of research conducted from this perspective.

Box 19.2	Study box

Wertz, F. J. (1985) Method and findings in a phenomenological psychological study of a complex life-event: Being criminally victimised. In A. Giorgi (Ed.) *Phenomenology and Psychological Research*. Pittsburgh, PA: Duquesne University Press.

This study sought to investigate the experience of being a victim of crime. It also aimed to further detail the way in which one might carry out a phenomenological study. Considerable detail of the method is provided and the paper provides an excellent example of phenomenological psychology research from the Duquesne School. The study was large for phenomenological research and involved a team of five people. Fifty interviews were conducted (in person or over the phone) with people who had been recent victims of crime. The study included a wide variety of participants in terms of type of crime experienced, age, sex and ethnicity in order to capture the full variability of the experience.

This book chapter focuses initially on one case, the case of a woman who was subject to a sexual assault. The analysis involves reducing her concrete description of the experience (immediately before, during and after) to meaning-units. Once this has been carried out the author presents an individual phenomenal description of the experience for this participant. This is a full account of the experience reconstructed from the interview in chronological order, mostly using the participant's own words. The author then presents a psychological structural description of the experience. This is a complex, detailed description of the phenomenon as experienced by this particular participant and includes detail on: *The 'before' of victimisation, The virtuality, nascence, and actuality of victimisation, The struggle against victimisation, The worlding of M's struggle against victimisation,* and *The new world 'after' victimisation.*

The author finally presents a general structural description, which captures the essence of the phenomenon of being a victim of crime. This description stems from a synthesis of all 50 individual phenomenal descriptions and provides insight into the general experience of being a victim of crime. This includes discussion of participants' worldviews before the crime, the struggle during the act of being subject to crime and the emergence of new meaning of *lost agency, lost community* and the *detrimental other.* The description then details the 'reality' of living 'after' being a victim of crime in which the crime was relived and the world seen as a crazy, unpredictable and scary place. Finally, successes in surpassing victimisation are described where people learn to make new and constructive sense of the experience. This is a long and detailed description which aims to capture the lived experience of being a victim of crime in graphic detail. It achieves this and is well worth reading in order to understand more about the impact of crime and also the phenomenological psychology method.

19.4   Searching for meaning: interpretative phenomenological analysis (IPA)

This approach to phenomenological research is more recent than the Duquesne School and emerged within UK psychology with the work of Jonathan Smith in the 1990s. This particular approach to qualitative research has grown in importance very quickly within the United Kingdom, though it has yet to impact on psychology within the United States. It was initially presented as a way of moving beyond the divide between quantitative social cognitive approaches and discursive approaches to health psychology in a way that enables researchers to 'unravel the meanings contained in … accounts through a process of interpretative engagement with the texts' (Smith, 1997: 189). Since this time it has been applied to a wide variety of topics in both social and health psychology.

It should be noted that whilst this method has become particularly popular in the UK, there are other similar approaches to phenomenological psychology which are popular elsewhere and warrant attention. The approaches of Max van Manen (1990) and Dahlberg *et al.* (2008), in particular, are similar in practice to IPA and should certainly be considered by the interested student of phenomenology. Whilst IPA is well formulated and clearly gaining widespread acceptance, it is only one of a family of methods, an approach to phenomenology stemming from the hermeneutic tradition (see Langdridge, 2007 and 2008, for more on this).

The approach is different from the Duquesne School in a number of ways. It (i) is explicitly more 'interpretative', (ii) aims to build psychological theory and (iii) engages with traditional social/health psychology theory and research much more readily than the Duquesne School. The approach is clearly informed by phenomenology but there has been some controversy about (i) how phenomenological the approach really is and (ii) how different it is from grounded theory and/or any standard thematic analysis. However, it is a clearly formulated and rapidly growing approach to research within UK psychology that has had a real impact on social and health psychology research and therefore is included here. We will return to these issues in more detail at the end of this chapter.

Method

Research using interpretative phenomenological analysis (IPA) tends to rely on data from standard semi-structured interviews. Unlike the Duquesne School, the interviews do not strictly focus on concrete description of an experience and may incorporate questions about a person's attitudes, beliefs and general reflections about the topic in question. The aim is to enable the participant to give as much detail as possible about their experience and enable the researcher to enter their life world as much as possible. Data may also be collected using diaries or other forms of writing. Like the Duquesne School the approach is **idiographic**, where each case is analysed individually before making any attempt to generalise beyond the individual. There are five stages of analysis: reading the case for overall meaning, identifying themes of meaning, structuring the themes extracted, producing a summary table of themes and arriving at a thematic integration of all cases. We will discuss each step in more detail below.

1 *Reading for meaning.* As stated above, IPA is idiographic and works from analyses of individual cases upwards to more general statements. One therefore begins with a case and works through the four steps outlined here repeatedly before attempting to integrate meaning across cases. Like the Duquesne

School, the first stage of an IPA is to read and then re-read the transcript, making notes, or **memos** as they are called in grounded theory, about one's thoughts, reflections and observations about the meaning of the text. These comments are traditionally recorded in the left-hand margin of the transcript.

2 *Identifying themes*. This second stage is pretty much the same as the stage of drawing out patterns and themes in a thematic analysis (described in the previous chapter). Here an attempt is made to draw out patterns of meaning in the text and record these initial themes in the right-hand margin of the transcript. Unlike the Duquesne School, it is not necessary to code each meaning-unit or use the language of the participants. Instead, chunks of meaning are coded as themes and psychological language may be used to capture the conceptual meaning inherent in the text. It is important that the coder remains open-minded at this stage and does not try to *impose* meaning on the text. IPA recognises that identifying themes is a negotiated process between coder and text where the coder needs to resist imposing their worldview on the text. The aim is to see the world through the participant's eyes and bracket off one's own preconceptions as much as is possible.

3 *Structuring themes*. This stage of the analysis entails the researcher listing the themes identified in the previous stage and attempting to look for relations between them. Through an engagement with the themes the researcher will structure them into clusters and hierarchies of meaning, if appropriate. Some themes will naturally appear to form clusters while others will appear superordinate or subordinate to others. Clusters of themes will also need to be labelled in a way that captures the overall meaning of the cluster. Some themes will also disappear at this stage, either because they become subsumed within other themes/clusters or because they appear irrelevant to the topic being investigated. The researcher will need to check their clusters of themes with the data (the transcript and possibly also the audio recording itself) to ensure that they are not moving too far beyond the data. There is a very real danger with phenomenological analyses of this kind that the researcher begins to theorise too quickly, moving beyond the data and therefore failing to truly grasp the meaning of the experience for the participant.

4 *Producing a summary table*. Here the researcher produces a summary table of the themes and clusters along with quotations to illustrate each theme and cluster. Some themes may disappear at this stage if they do not appear relevant or they appear marginal and/or too idiosyncratic. This is clearly a judgement call and one that must be carried out carefully. It is generally better to be over-inclusive (and remove themes later when integrating cases) than to lose important units of meaning. See Box 19.3 for an (abbreviated) example of a summary table.

5 *Integrating cases*. Once a researcher has completed the first four steps of their analysis for each case they may now attempt to integrate their findings and produce a table of master themes (and constituent themes) for the entire data set. Alternatively, some researchers complete the process described above for their first case and then seek to apply their summary table clusters and themes to their second case. They would then modify the clusters and

themes accordingly and proceed to their third case, modify as necessary and go on to the next, and so on until all cases were considered. Regardless of which strategy is used, this stage involves the researcher seeking to produce a summary table of master themes – or superordinate themes (with the subsidiary constituent themes) – that capture the meaning of the phenomenon for all participants. Each master theme will consist of one or more constituent themes (themes capturing lower levels of meaning) and will be supported by quotes from a number of participants. A summary table should be produced which lists these master themes along with the constituent themes and details of quotes (from a number of participants) in support of the themes that have been discerned. The number of master and constituent themes will vary from topic to topic and study to study.

Box 19.3

Information box

Example summary table

Low self-esteem
Poor body image   '... I hate what I have become ...'   p. 4, line 5
                  '... I have grown tired of living like this ...' p. 7, line 4
Excessive eating 'All I do is eat but that makes it better ...' p. 14, line 12
Feeling worthless
Low motivation   'I find it difficult to get going ...'   p. 2, line 22
                  'I am tired all the time.'   p. 1, line 23
Low social support 'I don't feel able to talk to anyone.'   p. 20, line 2
Unemployment   'I just wish I had a job ...'   p. 21, line 16

As you can see above, we have one cluster (*Low self-esteem*) with a number of subsidiary themes (*Poor body image*, *Excessive eating* and *Feeling worthless*). One of these subsidiary themes also has three further subsidiary themes (*Low motivation*, *Low social support* and *Unemployment*). An analysis will normally involve several clusters of meaning with a number of subsidiary themes. There is no limit to the number of clusters or levels of hierarchies that one may find (we have one cluster and a three tier hierarchy here).

The quotes presented here are abridged and you would expect to find many more and much longer quotes in a full IPA supporting the themes that have been found.

Finally, this work would be written up in a format similar to that of a standard thematic analysis. A 'Results/Discussion' or 'Findings' section of a journal article or book chapter would be structured generally by master theme (one after the other), with constituent themes discussed in relation to the extant literature within each master theme. Direct quotes from the participants would be used to provide evidence in support of the analysis being presented throughout the 'Findings' section (as discussed in the previous chapter). See Box 19.4 to get more of a feel for the type of research we are talking about.

Box 19.4   Study box

Flowers, P. & Buston, K. (2001). 'I was terrified of being different': Exploring gay men's accounts of growing up in a heterosexist society. *Journal of Adolescence*, **24**, 751–65.

This study demonstrates the application of interpretative phenomenological analysis (IPA) to an important topic: the experience of growing up as a young gay man in a heterosexist society (one that assumes people are heterosexual). Twenty semi-structured interviews were conducted with men (average age = 27 years) in the United Kingdom. Study participants were recruited through snowballing, where initial contact with key informants led to other gay men through social and sexual networks. Questions were asked about the men's thoughts and feelings about being gay, including the following: 'What does being gay mean to you?', 'How did you know you were gay?', 'When did you realise you were attracted to the same sex?' and so on. Themes that emerged from the analysis of the transcribed interviews included the following: *defined by difference, self-reflection and inner conflict, feelings of alienation and isolation, living a lie, disclosure* and *wholeness and integrity*. The men in this study talk of how they felt different from those around them in school and the home. This realisation of their sexual identity was strongly linked to feelings of alienation and isolation from their social networks. The expectation that all men were heterosexual, combined with homophobia, led the men to struggle with their sexual identity and internalise these negative beliefs about themselves. Many of the men tried to 'live a lie', assume the 'default position' and pass as straight. This option appeared to offer some a way of managing their gay identity but not without profound difficulties. The process of 'coming out' or telling others of their sexual feelings was of great importance for the men in this study. By telling, the men felt they were accepting and confirming their sexual identity. That is, they came to see themselves as others saw them, as gay men. This paper very successfully highlights the very real nature of growing up as a gay man in a heterosexist society. Subtlety and detail of experience are emphasised as the men recount their life stories. Implications for understandings of 'coming out' and school policy are discussed in relation to the findings.

19.5   Strengths, limitations and debates

Phenomenological approaches provide a welcome alternative to traditional (invariably quantitative) methods in psychology that impose a particular theoretical position on their participants. Phenomenological approaches offer a psychology that truly captures the rich lived experience of people engaged in life in its many varied forms. The Duquesne School and IPA offer two different ways of carrying out research, both of which emphasise the participant's world-views and enable us to capture something of the 'essence' of the phenomenon of interest.

Criticisms of phenomenological approaches generally have focused on three issues: the over-simplistic (or naive) view of language, the emphasis on description and the problem of bracketing. We will very briefly discuss each of these criticisms below, although interested readers are recommended to check out the suggestions for further reading and investigate these debates further themselves (Langdridge, 2008, discusses many of these issues in detail). Many of these debates are based on complex philosophical arguments so do not worry too much about the detail at the moment.

Firstly, critics of phenomenology have argued that there is an assumption among researchers that the participant's language reflects the reality of their lived experience. This is a problem for, as you will see in the chapter on discourse analysis, it can be argued that language does not merely reflect one's 'reality' but actually constructs that 'reality'. That is, language does not simply provide a mirror on our experience of the world and furnish us with direct accounts of that experience. Instead, language is functional and any talk about an experience enables us to investigate the talk about that experience but not the experience itself. As you might expect, phenomenologists would argue very strongly that there is more to our experience of the world than language. We are embodied creatures existing in space and time with agency (Ashworth, 2000), and psychology needs to retain this aspect of human nature to remain truly psychological (see Burr, 2002, for further discussion of these issues). However, even if one believes there is more to human nature than language, phenomenological approaches can still be criticised for lacking a sufficiently sophisticated view of language use (see Langdridge, 2003, 2007 and 2008 for more on this and the possibility of a narrative approach to phenomenology in providing a solution).

The second criticism levelled at phenomenological approaches is one that (to a great extent) splits the Duquesne School and IPA. IPA emerged as an alternative to the Duquesne School partly because Jonathan Smith felt the approach advocated by the Duquesne School was *too* descriptive (hence the 'interpretative' in interpretative phenomenological analysis). More generally, the descriptive quality of phenomenological research has been a problem for a number of people within psychology. This is not surprising when you remember that one of the principal aims of traditional quantitative approaches is to explain and predict on the basis of research. Phenomenological psychologists (and most particularly the Duquesne School) claim that their research, with its emphasis on describing 'things in their appearing', is truly the science of human nature and that the emphasis within more traditional quantitative psychology on importing techniques from the natural sciences is misguided. Still, for many psychologists there is a belief that the discipline must do more than describe if it is to have an impact on society.

The third criticism is perhaps the easiest to counter. Critics of phenomenology have (rightly) argued that it is impossible to bracket off all preconceptions and truly see the world from someone else's perspective. This is of course correct, but it was phenomenological philosophers who first made this point. Heidegger and Merleau-Ponty (two of the founding figures of the existential school of phenomenology) made this point some time ago and most phenomenologists recognise the impossibility of truly achieving epoché. Instead, most phenomenologists believe that it is important to *attempt* to bracket off our preconceptions, rather than impose our way of seeing the world on our participants, even if this can never fully be achieved.

Finally, it is important to return to some of the criticisms that have been levelled against IPA more specifically (Willig, 2001). While the Duquesne School is clearly attuned with phenomenological philosophy and identifiable as a distinct method of analysis, IPA is more of a problem. Willig (2001) raises the question of how phenomenological IPA really is. As Willig points out, Smith (1996) argued that IPA is concerned with *cognition*. This invokes a Cartesian conception of mind with the aim of research being the explication of these internal processes. This is clearly not in accordance with the notion of *intentionality*, the foundation of all phenomenology, which emphasises the fact that consciousness is not something internal to a person but something that occurs between people. As Willig (2001: 65) quite correctly states, 'it could be argued that genuinely phenomenological research should not study people's cognitions; instead, it should aim to understand lived experience'. While there are doubts about the phenomenological nature of IPA, in practice IPA researchers often adhere to similar principles to researchers from the Duquesne School. Also, very recently, there has been excellent work grounding IPA more clearly within the phenomenological philosophical literature and this is a very welcome addition (see Larkin *et al.*, 2006).

The second criticism raised about IPA by Willig (2001) concerns the perceived similarity between IPA and the subjectivist version of grounded theory. We would argue that IPA actually bears even more similarity to a standard thematic analysis, as practised in sociology, than grounded theory. There are clear similarities in method between IPA and grounded theory (and IPA and thematic analysis) and Willig therefore asks why should anyone use IPA when grounded theory is much more established as a method. She provides two answers to this question herself. The first is that IPA, unlike grounded theory or thematic analysis, is first and foremost psychological and therefore provides a systematic method that psychologists can use to carry out 'phenomenologically informed' social research. The second is that there is so much debate about which version of grounded theory to use that researchers may simply prefer to use a method that enables them to achieve similar outcomes without needing to engage in such debates and controversies. We think these two answers are good reasons for understanding the popularity of IPA but we think there is another. IPA has been positioned not in opposition to mainstream social psychology but as an adjunct. Psychologists working within this perspective will therefore have less need to justify their work than psychologists from other qualitative perspectives, for many of the arguments in favour of this work have already been made and need not be remade every time one produces new work. One final point worth making here is the way in which IPA is reaching almost hegemonic status in the UK, with many students unaware that there are alternative approaches to phenomenological psychological research. As has been pointed out in this chapter, there are indeed other approaches (such as the Duquesne School, as well as the work of van Manen, 1990, and Dahlberg *et al.*, 2008, amongst others), many of which are much more widely used and known outside the UK, and readers interested in phenomenology are well advised to make the effort to examine these approaches in addition to IPA so they can make a fully informed decision about the most appropriate member of the phenomenological family with which to conduct their research.

Further reading

Giorgi, A. (Ed.) (1985). *Phenomenology and Psychological Research*. Pittsburg, PA: Duquesne University Press.

A clear and accessible introduction to this particular approach to phenomenological research in psychology.

Ihde, D. (1986). *Experimental Phenomenology: An Introduction*. Albany, NY: SUNY Press.

A short but superb introduction to the fundamentals of phenomenology. Don Ihde uses a series of thought experiments primarily concerned with visual perception to demonstrate some of the principal epistemological and methodological concepts in the field.

Langdridge, D. (2007). *Phenomenological Psychology: Theory, Research and Method*. Harlow: Pearson Education.

A detailed introduction to both the philosophy and method of a wide range of phenomenological approaches. Guidance is given on the practicalities of carrying out research as well as discussion of key issues and debates in the field.

Smith, J. A., Jarman, M. & Osborne, M. (1999). Doing interpretative phenomenological analysis. In M. Murray & K. Chamberlain (Eds) *Qualitative Health Psychology: Theories and Methods*. London: Sage.

A clear statement of the application of IPA (as applied to health).

20 Grounded theory

- This chapter begins by considering the background to and fundamental assumptions of grounded theory.

- It then moves on to consider the different approaches to grounded theory that are in use today.

- The chapter then provides detail on some of the key methods used when carrying out research from this perspective.

- Finally, it critically examines the strengths and weaknesses of the different approaches to grounded theory.

INTRODUCTION

We have mentioned **grounded theory** in passing a number of times in this section of the book but have yet to explain what it is. In short, grounded theory is the systematic collection and analysis of (predominantly qualitative) data with the aim of generating theory. Grounded theory has a relatively long history in the social sciences, beginning properly[1] in 1967 with the publication of *The Discovery of Grounded Theory: Strategies for Qualitative Research* by Barney Glaser and Anselm Strauss. Grounded theory emerged within sociology (Glaser and Strauss are both sociologists) and is a well-established qualitative method, but it has yet to have the same impact within psychology. However, grounded theory is used by psychologists and it is likely to increase in popularity with the growth of interest in qualitative methods.

---

[1] We say 'properly' because Glaser and Strauss wrote *Awareness of Dying* in 1964, which was arguably the start of their writing about grounded theory. Their 1967 text, however, represented the first full expression of this research method.

20.1 Introducing grounded theory

Grounded theory has a number of distinguishing characteristics (Charmaz, 1995). These include: (1) the integrated nature of data collection and analysis; (2) coding and analysis driven by the data; (3) the development of theories to explain findings; (4) memo-making – or the writing of analytic notes when coding; (5) theoretical sampling of participants – that is, sampling is purposive rather than representative; and (6) delay of the literature review. We will return to these points later in this chapter, but two are particularly worthy of note now. Grounded theory is notably different from most other qualitative methods in that no attempt is made to separate data collection from analysis. These two aspects of the research process must be integrated in grounded theory. One collects data from a case and immediately begins the process of analysis rather than collecting data from all participants before the process of analysis begins. Grounded theory is also distinctive in its emphasis on the development of theory from empirical findings. Grounded theorists are particularly resistant to the separation of empirical findings and theory development (Charmaz, 1995).

There is considerable debate and many differences today among grounded theorists about the philosophical assumptions underpinning the method and to some extent about how the method should be used. Grounded theorists range from the interpretative to the positivist, and leading theorists have argued that this demonstrates the wide-ranging utility of the method (Charmaz, 1995). However, others (Willig, 2001) have noted that the many debates within the field may serve to undermine the popularity of the method if researchers must engage with these debates and position themselves before being able to get on with the business of research itself. For now, however, we will put these debates to one side and attempt to present some of the fundamental aspects of this method about which most, even if not all, grounded theorists would agree. We will return to the variations and debates at the end of this chapter.

20.2 Collecting data

As stated above, grounded theory is unusual in the way that data collection is connected to analysis. The interwoven nature of data collection and analysis means that one's analysis will inform and shape one's data collection. The key issue is that emerging themes from the data will result in more focused data collection around these themes. A significant benefit of this approach is in reducing the likelihood of amassing huge quantities of data that may be unfocused or even irrelevant to the topic of interest. The aim in the early stages of data collection and analysis is to remain open to the meaning in the data. In a way that is similar to phenomenological research, grounded theorists look for emergent themes in their data rather than imposing preconceived ideas or theories about the topic onto their data. Sampling is, like much qualitative research, often purposive wherein participants (or other sources of data) are chosen because they represent a particular category of person or experience. So, for instance, a researcher may be interested in exploring the experience of living with a terminal illness. In this case participants will be those in this situation. However, because grounded theorists aim to develop concepts and theory at a general as well as a substantive level, it is desirable, if feasible, that a sample includes a wide variety of people. So, while all participants may be experiencing terminal illness, the illnesses they face may well be very different and demographic characteristics (age, sex, ethnicity, etc.) may well vary quite considerably.

While other qualitative methods may also search for meaning in data, and some may even integrate data collection and analysis, grounded theory is distinct with regard to the explicit focus on generating theory from rich, detailed descriptions. Grounded theorists do not believe that it is enough to describe the 'things in their appearing' – qualitative research *must* contribute to theory generation. This aspect of the grounded theory method will be discussed in greater detail later in this chapter.

Theoretical sampling

Following memo-writing (see below) one may engage in **theoretical sampling**. This entails going back and collecting more data (from further interviews or collection of further documentation, etc.) in order to clarify concepts and develop the emerging theory. Sampling at this stage is not aiming to increase the representativeness of the sample but to enable further theory development. By this stage, the researcher should have already got well under way with the analysis and developed their categories. Theoretical sampling enables the researcher to flesh out these categories and through the **comparative method** (more on this below) better define their categories. Sampling may focus on particular individuals for further discussion of their stories or it may range across people (and/or other sources of data), focusing instead on a particular issue or theoretical concern. It is generally thought that this analytic strategy should be conducted later in the data collection/analysis process (Charmaz, 1995) because of the risk of closing down the analysis and imposing theoretical concepts on the data too early. Theoretical sampling enables further memo-writing and more sophisticated development of theory.

20.3	The dynamic nature of meaning making

Grounded theory analyses aim to be dynamic rather than static and have a particular concern with action and meaning. This processual approach, with the emphasis on what people are doing, enables the researcher to develop 'thick description' (Geertz, 1973). Thick (or rich) description is the starting aim of an analysis but not the end-point (which is substantive and then general theory development). However, at present many grounded theory studies work at this level of description without much theory development (Charmaz, 1995). Glaser & Strauss (1967) talk of meaning being 'discovered' in the data and that with sufficiently careful engagement a skilled researcher should be able to uncover these layers of meaning as if they resided in the world waiting to be uncovered. Many later writers, however, consider meaning to be constructed through an interaction between the researcher and that which is researched (e.g. Charmaz, 1995, 2006). Here meaning is not 'discovered' but created (socially constructed) through the research process between researcher and researched. In the past, issues of reflexivity have generally been under-theorised in grounded theory research (more on this later when discussing the limitations of research from this perspective).

While stories may be discovered by researchers it is also often the case that considerable effort be required to uncover the layers of meaning about the topic in question. Researchers may need to immerse themselves in the setting for considerable lengths of time even to know what questions to ask, let alone what answers to expect. It is generally recommended that researchers collect the data themselves (rather than employing research assistants) wherever possible. In grounded theory, more than most methods, the interwoven nature of data collection and analysis means that a separation of these two processes seems artificial. It is also thought that grounded theorists should transcribe their own data. Once again, this may not be possible, but if a researcher can afford the time then this is an excellent way of listening to one's data and starting to look for meaning. Finally, it is important to question those 'taken for granted assumptions' that we all have about the world. Instead of attempting to bracket these off, a grounded theorist should interrogate meaning with questions that enable clarification. Participants can be questioned again and again (if they are willing!) in order to clarify language and concepts. Even seemingly obvious concepts must be treated with care, for subtleties can often be masked through neglect at this stage. See Box 20.1 for an example of a grounded theory study that uses qualitative and quantitative approaches and a modified form of grounded theory.

Box 20.1	Study box

Henwood, K. & Pidgeon, N. (2001). Talk about woods and trees: Threat of urbanization, stability, and biodiversity. *Journal of Environmental Psychology*, **21**, 125-47.

This study sought to investigate the importance and value of woods and trees to people especially as they relate to local and cultural environments. Most previous research attempting to ascertain the importance of woods and trees to people has been quantitative and subject to criticism for its over-emphasis on economic factors. Instead, this study used mixed methods to explore the symbolic value of woods and trees to people living in North Wales. A stakeholder panel was established comprising 14 people invited from a wide range of stakeholder positions within the community. Second, five community focus groups were held one month after the initial stakeholder panel meeting. Twenty-nine people

Box 20.1 *Continued*

participated in this section of the research (groups comprised anything from 4 to 7 members). A variety of methods were used to elicit data, including discussion of photographs, mapping and grid exercises, ranking exercises and semi- and unstructured discussion. The paper presents the quantitative analysis of two of the structured tasks completed and a grounded theory analysis of the general discussions of the groups. As in a lot of grounded theory research being conducted today, the researchers were not able to combine the data collection and analysis phases. Instead, the analysis was conducted following completion of the focus groups. Three theoretical themes emerged from the analysis of the data: *The*

Threat of Urbanization, Stability and Familiarity and *Biodiversity*. The study highlighted the fact that trees, woods and forests are important to people at personal, local, community, cultural and global levels. For instance, trees, woods and forests are often important to people as settings for the recall of valued personal and family memories. In addition, woodland areas not only fulfilled immediate local needs (such as walking the dog) but 'higher-level' symbolic needs where they represented the 'goodness of nature' and so on. The authors discuss the need to consider the symbolic ways in which trees are important, in addition to economic analyses, when implementing environmental policy.

20.4   Coding

Coding is pretty much common to all qualitative research and grounded theory is no exception. Once data have been collected, analysis begins with systematic coding of the data. Coding is inductive (like phenomenological approaches, see Chapter 19) rather than deductive. Pre-existing codes are not created and then tested against the data. Instead, the researcher carefully examines the data for meaning and codes are constructed that are *grounded* in the data.

Line by line coding

Grounded theory generally employs **line by line coding**. This is, as you might have guessed, a process that involves the researcher going through the text line by line and attempting to code each line of text. This particular coding strategy is recommended for it is argued that it forces the researcher to remain close to the text. Categorisation is located in the text and the researcher is prevented from more global theorising arising from their preconceptions or theoretical interests. Here, unlike the descriptive coding of Giorgi's phenomenological psychology, researchers may engage with social science theory and concepts. However, care must be taken to make sure that these concepts and theories really do work with the data being analysed. If there is any tension it is better to use more neutral concepts and/or reserve any links with the discipline until later when reviewing the literature. The aim is for theory to emerge from the data, which is why one would generally delay the literature review until later in the analysis (rather than before collecting the data, as is usual). It is thought that reviewing the literature before data collection will necessarily lead researchers to interpret their data in particular ways which may not be truly grounded in the data. Charmaz (1995: 38) suggests some basic questions to ask of the data, which may help the process of coding:

- What is going on?
- What are people doing?
- What is the person saying?
- What do these actions and statements take for granted?
- How do structure and context serve to support, maintain, impede or change these actions and statements?

Codes need to be short and specific (remember you will have a code for every line of data you collect) and should be recorded against every line of data. Codes will merge into one another as a line of text will not necessarily represent a discrete unit of meaning. Line by line coding will also likely lead to the need for further data collection. As a researcher uncovers meaning in the text new questions will emerge as ideas about theory develop and these will require returning to your participants and following up these leads. See Box 20.2 for an example of line by line coding. The text comes from a study of young gay men and their expectations about parenthood.

Box 20.2

Information box

Line by line coding

Interview transcript	Code
They're … they're really proud of me actually. Really, really proud and that's why they've … I think that's why they've been so nice since I've moved back cos if I'd fucked around for eight months, being on the dole, not done much and dossed about 'oohh what am I going to do now' and not sorted out university they wouldn't have wanted me back. Errr but cos I've gone out I've proved … that I can … you see that was one of the main consensus about me going to university was that I had to prove that I could manage my own money.	Perception of parental pride and values. Linked with improved relationship between parents and son. Just 'fucked around'. Started to question the future. Perception that parental acceptance is tied to particular life choice (university). Desire to prove worth to parents. Management of money had previously been an issue and was now linked to acting responsibly and gaining parental recognition and respect.

Focused coding and categories

Focused coding is where one takes codes derived from line by line coding that keep appearing and then applies them to larger chunks of text. This approach is clearly less inductive than line by line coding and therefore much more selective. This coding technique will follow line by line coding when the researcher has identified which codes are most important analytically and best categorise the data. The codes are selected and then applied to larger sections of the text. At the same time as codes are applied, further information may be discerned which further refine these codes. Coding in grounded theory (or any other qualitative method for that matter) should always be dynamic, never simply mechanical. As higher-level codes are applied they will be modified, refined or fleshed out so that they better capture meaning in the text and, in the case of grounded theory, enable more sophisticated theory development. Focused coding enables researchers to identify broader **categories** of meaning and then test them against other data. A **category** is an overarching unit of analysis which may subsume other codes and themes that emerge from the data. Categories are more conceptual elements representing greater theoretical sophistication while always being tied to the data. Categories differ from codes in that they do more work (conceptually and analytically speaking). They do not simply describe the data. Categories may be named using a participant's words or may be written in more technical language. As the analysis proceeds, variations within and between categories will emerge which will further deepen the meaning of the category.

Constant comparative method

This is a key process in grounded theory for the development of **categories** and **theory**. The **constant comparative method** involves the researcher looking for similarities and then differences within and between categories (a constant comparison of meaning regarding specific topics). A researcher will have identified some phenomenon that is common in terms of meaning (a category) from their initial coding – based on similarities. They would then look for differences within that category which may result in subcategories, the revision of this particular category, or the development of separate categories.

This approach is considered particularly important in grounded theory for it is believed to prevent the development of grand overarching categories and theories. Categories (and later theories) are developed from the data (bottom up) but then later, when compared with other data, may be broken down into smaller units of meaning. The aim is to systematically develop categories and relationships between categories through constant comparative analysis so that all similarities and differences emerging from the data are adequately captured in the final analysis.

A further aspect of this coding process is **negative case analysis**. Once a category has been defined, researchers are encouraged to attempt to find a case that does not fit this category. This is an active attempt to produce an analysis that captures the full complexity of meaning across an entire data set where individual variations and differences are not ignored. If negative cases are discovered then the researcher will need to refine or change their categories so that these cases fit their coding.

20.5	Memo writing

Memo writing is a key element in the transition from coding to theory development. However, memo writing should begin from the first moment of analysis and continue to the very end. Memos are written notes from reflections on the data, which represent the development of theories about the topic. Memos can take any form. They are notes to yourself about any thoughts regarding the development of theory. They may include detail on coding or categories that have emerged from the analysis, comments on the relationships between categories, relationships between your knowledge of the topic and the data and so on. Memos should always be treated as preliminary: nothing written here is cast in stone. As one begins to write up the analysis, memos should be checked again with the data. The constant comparative method is important here too. The researcher should constantly compare one participant's views or beliefs with another or one particular experience with another. Information may also be compared from one moment to another over time. Memos should be dated so that there is a temporal record of theoretical developments and should also include information about their precise link with the data (i.e. transcript, paragraph and line numbers). Finally, memos enable the researcher to determine which categories are most important and further structure the analysis.

20.6	Theory development

So, grounded theory is a method that aims to develop theory, but what is meant by theory? Strauss & Corbin (1994: 278) define theory as follows: 'Theory consists of *plausible* relationships proposed among *concepts* and *sets of concepts*'. To be honest, this does not seem terribly helpful, for surely all qualitative research is concerned with understanding relationships between concepts (and sets of concepts) in the data. So, how is grounded theory different from phenomenological psychology, which does not have, as a principal aim, the development of theory? We think it is more a matter of levels of conceptual abstraction. An approach such as Duquesne School phenomenological psychology aims to stay very close to the data, focusing on rich description. A level of abstraction from this position occurs when the analyst produces the essential description. Grounded theory, like IPA, goes further and aims to produce a more interpretive level of understanding (located in the data) that is more conceptually abstract than that produced by descriptive phenomenological psychology. We think the distinction is a difficult one to grasp unless you have read work from these different perspectives. See Box 20.3 for some guidance on reading which may help you grasp these distinctions between description and interpretation.

Box 20.3

Activity box   Understanding theory development

As we mentioned in the main text, you really need to read empirical research from the different perspectives to fully grasp the often (apparently) subtle distinctions when they are described in books such as this. In reality, the practice and outcomes of different qualitative approaches can be quite marked.

Two works are listed below which we recommend you get hold of (either through your own library if they stock the books or through inter-library loan if they do not). We have already briefly summarised one of these papers in Box 19.2. Not only are these works good examples of their respective methods but they are also interesting to read!

The first paper is a classic phenomenological psychology study (about being the victim of crime). This is a fairly long book chapter written some time ago. When you read this chapter, engage in a process of virtual constant comparative analysis and compare and contrast what is being described with the method outlined in this chapter. Then read the second book (if you cannot find the time, just read some of it). Once again, compare the outcomes of a grounded theory study as described in this book with those outcomes produced by phenomenological psychology. As we are sure you will see, the level of conceptual abstraction (theory development) is very different.

Wertz, F. J. (1985). Method and findings in a phenomenological psychological study of a complex life-event: Being criminally victimised. In A. Giorgi (Ed.) *Phenomenology and Psychological Research*. Pittsburgh, PA: Duquesne University Press.

Strauss, A. & Glaser, B. (1970). *Anguish: A Case History of a Dying Trajectory*. San Francisco: Sociology Press.

Higher-order theory

Not only should grounded theory studies produce theories about particular topics but, according to the founders, it should also produce more **general theories** that move beyond the substantive boundaries of the particular topic being investigated. Here Glaser & Strauss (1967: 79) make the point:

Since **substantive theory** is grounded in research on one particular substantive area (work, juvenile delinquency, medical education, mental health) it might be taken to apply only to that specific area. A theory at such a conceptual level, however, may have important general implications and relevance, and become almost automatically a springboard or stepping stone to the development of a grounded formal [or as is more usually said, '**general**'] theory ... Substantive theory is a strategic link in the formulation and generation of grounded formal theory. We believe that although formal theory can be generated directly from the data, it is more desirable, and usually necessary, to start the formal theory from a substantive one.

[Bold emphasis added.]

So, as you can see, here we have a programme for qualitative work that leads to general theory. There are, of course, dangers with this process. As theories become more general and therefore necessarily more abstract, there is a real danger that they will become less and less grounded in the data. However, if researchers engage in constant comparative analysis even at this stage this danger should be circumvented. The constant comparisons between categories, substantive theories and general theories where they are constructed and deconstructed should minimise any risks of theory being developed that is *too far* beyond the data. This is a grand aspiration and one that, as yet, has not really been engaged with by researchers working from this perspective. As Kathy Charmaz (1995: 48) notes:

> Are most grounded theory works actually theory? No, not at this point. At present, most grounded theory researchers have aimed to develop rich conceptual analyses of lived experience and social worlds instead of intending to create substantive or formal theory.

For the time being at least, it seems as if one of the key aims of grounded theory method, theory development at both a substantive and a general level, is in its infancy. Maybe in time theory will develop, but we will have to wait and see.

20.7   Strengths, limitations and debates

As we mentioned at the beginning of this chapter, there has been considerable disagreement over the 'true' nature of the grounded theory method. One central dispute has centred on the need for grounded theory to be driven inductively by the data. The founders of grounded theory have different positions on this issue, reflecting their own histories. Barney Glaser (1992) has argued strongly that Strauss & Corbin's (1990) statement on grounded theory is too prescriptive and not sufficiently *grounded*. He believes that the methods outlined by Strauss and Corbin represent a break with the essence of grounded theory, as expounded in *Discovery*, with their concern with what Glaser described as forced conceptual description. The crux of the argument is that Strauss and Corbin believe that grounded theory must continue to develop from the original position expressed by Glaser & Strauss (1967) in *The Discovery of Grounded Theory*. Now, Glaser might not disagree with this argument, but he does disagree with the particular way in which Strauss and Corbin have developed the theory. He believes that they have moved too far from the inductive principles underpinning the original formulation of grounded theory towards a method that results in the imposition of the researcher's concerns on the data and, furthermore, one that is overly consumed with technical detail. The consequence of this division is that we now have two distinct types of grounded theory and continuing debate about the merits and demerits of each.

While the disagreements between Glaser and Strauss have clearly had most impact on the method, there are further variations (and debates) concerning the method to be found in the literature. We have already touched upon one earlier in the chapter: the distinction between *discovery* and *construction* of meaning. Another concerns the arguments between those using the *full version* and those using the *abbreviated version* of the theory. We will briefly outline both debates below.

The argument over discovery versus construction principally centres around the social constructionist reformulation of the theory by Kathy Charmaz (1990, 2006), although others have later stressed the need for more reflexive researcher engagement in grounded theory. In the original formulation of the theory Glaser and Strauss described a method that led to the *discovery* of *emerging* social facts. The role of the researcher in contributing to the construction of these social facts was underplayed or ignored. Charmaz (1990) argued that a social constructionist perspective is needed, where the researcher is understood to play a crucial role in the construction of categories of meaning and theories. Indeed, grounded theorists have been accused of positivism as a result of the desire, notable amongst Glaser and his followers, to produce a method which is rigidly empiricist and effectively codify qualitative research in a similar fashion to quantitative research.

The second major debate that is ongoing among grounded theorists concerns the use of either the *full version* or the *abbreviated version* of the method. As you might have thought by now, the full version of grounded theory is extremely involved. A researcher needs considerable time (and resources) to carry out a full grounded theory study. This has led to increasing numbers of people using grounded theory methods of analysis on pre-existing (or simply collected) interview transcripts or other textual material. The first stage in grounded theory research, where data collection and analysis merge, has been abandoned by many researchers. Instead, researchers collect all their data and then conduct an analysis, or use pre-existing textual materials, or both. This approach has become known as the *abbreviated version* of grounded theory. It has been argued that full grounded theory examines the social world from the 'outside in' (an **objectivist** position with the focus on social processes) while the abbreviated version operates 'from the inside out' (a **subjectivist** position with the focus on the world in its appearing for the participant) (see Charmaz, 1995: 30–1). As Willig (2001: 44) states:

It is, of course, possible to combine the two perspectives and to attempt to capture the lived experience of participants and to explain its quality in terms of wider social processes and their consequences. It could be argued that this would indeed be required in order to gain a full understanding of social psychological phenomena.

One of the most obvious limitations that can be (and has been) levelled against grounded theory is the same as that levelled against phenomenological approaches: the overly simplistic understanding of the function of language in interaction. As we stated when discussing the limitations of phenomenological methods, critics (particularly those from more discursive approaches, covered in Chapter 21) have argued that these methods assume that language merely describes the social world. So, when a participant tells you their day has been full of 'ups and downs' in an interview, this might be coded simply as it appears (they are expressing their feelings about the day in question). A discourse analyst, on the other hand, might venture another explanation based on what the participant was trying to do in that situation. They might have been trying to convince or persuade you of the horrors of their situation, for instance, rather than simply 'telling it like it is'. Grounded theorists would probably argue that, in the full version at least, a theorist never simply takes participants' statements as statements of fact but is always questioning their meaning within the wider social context. Through the repeated immersion in the setting that is required of the grounded theorist, they should become aware of the multi-layered meanings that might be expressed by participants and therefore engage critically with their material.

Another major concern with grounded theory is the apparent lack of concern over issues of reflexivity. There appears to be an assumption that the world is simply waiting to be discovered and that a good grounded theorist will be able to do just that if they employ their tools and techniques in the right way. Concerns have been expressed, as mentioned above, that a researcher does not, and cannot, *discover* the social world but must play a role in creating what they 'find'. It is therefore vital to adequately theorise the role of the researcher in producing the findings (*reflexivity*). Grounded theorists who do not engage with the social constructionist version of the theory have difficulty here for they end up having to espouse a kind of inductive positivism (where through careful, systematic observation of the social world we can find facts out there).

Finally, phenomenological psychologists may raise concerns over the aim to generate theory, especially general theory. Most grounded theory studies produce rich descriptions of the lived world of the participants in a way that many phenomenological psychologists would admire. While not engaging with the process of bracketing in quite the same way as phenomenological psychologists, grounded theorists do, through delay of the literature review, try to put their theoretical preconceptions to one side when engaging with a substantive research topic. However, the degree of conceptual abstraction required of grounded theorists when making the move from substantive to general theories will concern phenomenologists. Phenomenological psychologists would argue that grounded theorists end up *inappropriately* moving from a **human science**, with the principal aim being to describe the richness of our lived experiences, to a **natural science**, with the principal aim being prediction and control. For, while the aims and methods of the natural sciences have undoubtedly been useful in biology, physics and chemistry, they have not and cannot produce the same dividends when investigating human nature. For more on the distinction between natural and human sciences see Giorgi (1985b).

Further reading

Charmaz, K. (1995). Grounded theory. In J. A. Smith, R. Harré & L. Van Langenhove (Eds) *Rethinking Methods in Psychology*. London: Sage.

> An excellent introductory chapter on grounded theory method with plenty of examples from the author's own research on the experience of chronic illness.

Charmaz, K. (2006). *Constructing Grounded Theory: A Practical Guide Through Qualitative Analysis*. London: Sage.

> A very clear and practical book on the constructionist approach to grounded theory of Kathy Charmaz.

Corbin, J. & Strauss, A. (2008). *Basics of Qualitative Research*, 3rd edn. London: Sage.

> A detailed guide to the practicalities of grounded theory, following the approach of Strauss and Corbin (updated from the 2nd edition by Juliet Corbin alone following the death of Anselm Strauss in 1996).

Glaser, B. G. & Strauss, A. L. (1967). *The Discovery of Grounded Theory: Strategies for Qualitative Research*. Chicago: Aldine.

> The beginning of grounded theory and therefore a classic. There is information on the theoretical basis and clear guidance on carrying out research. It is well worth reading but should be located within a particular historical, political and disciplinary context. That is, the authors were presenting a radical alternative to current work in sociology, which necessitated a particularly polemical style.

Strauss, A. L. & Corbin, J. (1994). Grounded theory methodology. In N. K. Denzin & Y. S. Lincoln (Eds) *Handbook of Qualitative Research*. London: Sage.

> A very clear statement of the state of grounded theory 27 years on as perceived by two of the most significant figures in the field. There is very little information on how to carry out research from this perspective, however.

21 | Discourse analysis

- This chapter begins by outlining the background to discourse analysis and its growth in psychology.

- It then moves on to consider some of the different types of discourse analysis that are commonly employed in psychological research.

- The chapter then introduces two approaches to discourse analytic research in more detail: discursive psychology and Foucauldian discourse analysis.

- Finally, this chapter critically examines the strengths and weaknesses of these approaches and engages with some of the debates about the different strands of research from this perspective.

INTRODUCTION

Discourse analysis (DA) is a fairly new approach to research in psychology. We say 'approach' rather than 'method', for most discourse analysts consider DA to constitute a paradigm shift rather than simply another qualitative method (Potter & Wetherell, 1987), though this has been contested (more on this at the end of this chapter). So, what is meant by **discourse**? Well, it does vary among different approaches to discourse analysis. At the very least, discourse is all spoken and written communication, and discourse analysis is therefore concerned with analysing communicative utterances of these kinds. However, some approaches to discourse analysis (e.g. the Foucauldian approach) have a much wider conception of what constitutes the focus of their investigations. With this approach, discourse consists of spoken and written communication *and* all other forms of communication (from tarot cards and stained glass windows to bodies and gardens; Parker, 1992). Discourse analytic work is generally located within a **social constructionist** position. We outlined the basic idea behind this theoretical position in Chapter 17. In brief, social constructionist research is concerned with understanding the various ways in which people might construct their social reality. This is often through an understanding of the way in which language is used. If you remember, we used the example of homosexuality and the changing definitions of it as an example of the way in which a category, such as 'homosexuality', does not simply define the world as it is, but serves to impose a particular way of seeing on the world.

In this chapter we will outline some of the history and fundamental principles underpinning discourse analysis and then present a brief guide to the analysis of text from two different discourse analytic traditions. Wetherell (2001) identifies six approaches to 'discourse analysis': conversation analysis, discursive psychology, Foucauldian analyses, critical discourse analysis, interactional sociolinguistics and the ethnography of speaking, and Bakhtinian research. We will focus on just two of these: discursive psychology and Foucauldian discourse analyses. There are three reasons for this. First, and most importantly, these two approaches are the most widely used in psychology in the UK at the present time. Second, both approaches have a psychological focus (which is not necessarily the case with the remaining four). Finally, it would not be possible to do justice to all six traditions of discourse analytic research in one chapter (it is going to be hard enough with two!). However, if you are interested in learning about conversation analysis, critical discourse analysis, sociolinguistics or Bakhtinian research, then consult the two books by Wetherell *et al.* recommended at the end of this chapter.

21.1   The turn to language

Since 1985 we have witnessed the emergence of what has been heralded as a new paradigm for research (Harré & Gillet, 1994). Psychology has been, and continues to be, dominated by the cognitive paradigm since the 1970s. Cognitive psychology has impacted across the discipline and has formed the foundation of a considerable amount of research, not only in cognitive psychology itself but also in social and developmental psychology. Central to the cognitive approach is the concern with investigating mental processes (or cognitions). With this concern the computer model (that is, modelling human mental processes on the workings of computers) has been dominant for some time. From this perspective, a social psychologist attempting to understand attitudes towards nuclear disarmament, for instance, may ask people to express their attitude(s) (verbally or in a written form) and take this statement simply as representative of the attitude that they hold (strongly agree or strongly disagree, for instance). Language is held to be referential (it refers to things outside in the world or in our heads) and an attitude is a mental structure that is being referred to (and located somewhere in the brain). Discursive approaches to psychology challenge these 'common-sense' assumptions and represent a marked departure for the discipline in terms of both research aims and methodology (Harré & Gillet, 1994).

In the 1970s psychologists started to pay attention to the work of philosophers such as Wittgenstein and Foucault who, in radically different ways, emphasised the role of language in psychological understanding. Language was no longer seen as simply a way of talking about things in the world or as a way to talk about internal psychological states. Instead, it was argued that language (i) does things and (ii) serves to construct objects themselves. This is clearly a counter-intuitive idea – for how can language 'do things' or 'construct objects'? – and one that will take some effort to fully grasp. This new emphasis on the importance of language has been referred to as 'the turn to language'. The publication of *Discourse and Social Psychology* by Potter and Wetherell, in 1987, and *Changing the Subject: Psychology, Social Regulation and Subjectivity* by Henriques *et al.*, in 1984, has played an important part in the development and popularisation of this alternative approach to psychological research in the United Kingdom.

For discourse analysts, it is too simplistic to think that language simply describes our worlds ('inner' or 'outer'). What discourse analysts argue instead, in different ways, is (i) that discourse is **action-oriented** (language 'does things' such as persuade, justify, excuse and so on), and (ii) that discourse **constitutes subjectivity** (or 'selfhood') and power relations (that is, meaning about ourselves and the world can only be understood through language). We will focus on the discursive critique of the traditional concept of attitudes here to give you more of a feel for what we are talking about.

For a traditional (social cognitive) attitude researcher, a tick on a questionnaire indicating that someone agrees or disagrees with a statement is taken to provide information about an attitude (cognitive structure) that is inside their head. Language here, whether spoken or written, is taken to simply describe a cognitive state (an attitude towards something). Discourse analysts, by contrast, do not believe that language operates in this simple way. Instead, they argue that language is functional, it does things and is not simply descriptive (of some internal cognitive state). The social context (removed in most traditional attitude research) is essential for understanding what language is being used to do. A discourse analyst would look at what people are trying to do with their speech in a particular context. For instance, if we stated that 'fox-hunting is wrong' we might be trying to *persuade you* of this fact or show you how *kind we are* to animals, depending on the context. We are not neutrally describing some attitude about the world that is always consistent. We return to this important issue for DA below when discussing the influence of the philosopher John Austin on discursive psychology.

Traditional (cognitive social) approaches to attitudes have sought, through careful use of questionnaires and sometimes experimental research, to understand how people feel about objects and events in the social world. These researchers believe that when they measure a person's attitude towards an object or event then they have tapped how people feel about the object of thought. There is little doubt about the existence of the object of thought or about some 'internal' attitude that is held towards that object of thought (although it is worth noting that some have – to a certain extent – taken on board elements of the criticism from discourse analysts and argue that their work has a pragmatic focus instead of being wedded to an overly simplistic cognitivism). Discourse analysts, on the other hand, do not believe that things are so straightforward. They argue that *objects of thought do not exist independently of that thought* and that these thoughts are themselves constructed through language. So, for instance, if we investigate attitudes towards fox-hunting from a traditional social cognitive perspective we might find (from the use of questionnaires) that one person 'strongly disagrees' with fox-hunting while another 'strongly agrees' with fox-hunting. We have tapped their attitude towards fox-hunting. Discourse analysts, however, would argue that the object of the investigation (fox-hunting in this case) is itself socially constructed through language (and there are therefore multiple versions of this event). One person may see fox-hunting as 'a traditional way of controlling vermin' while another may see it as 'a cruel act against an innocent animal for fun'. The object of our attitude investigation is clearly not the same here. We do not have an agreement on what hunting actually *is*, so any study of attitudes (towards hunting) will fail to capture the essential differences between people on this topic. For discourse analysts, the differences between people stem not from their different attitudes towards an object or event, but from their differing versions of the object or event itself. This idea is taken up further below when we discuss the influence of the work of the philosopher Michel Foucault.

21.2	Approaches to the study of discourse

Theoretical divergences

Different strands of discursive research have different theoretical foundations. **Discursive psychology** has its roots in the later philosophy of Wittgenstein (1953) and Austin's (1962) speech act theory. **Foucauldian discourse analysis**, on the other hand, has its roots in the post-structuralist philosophy of Foucault (1970, 1971, 1972, 1977, 1978) and is indeed sometimes called **post-structuralist discourse analysi**s. Many of the theoretical differences between these two forms of DA are highly complex and require engaging with a considerable amount of philosophy. For now, this is not necessary, for when first working with discourse it is enough to recognise the fundamentals (as outlined in Section 21.1 above and in the introductions to each of the sections below) and the practical ways in which these two traditions of discursive research differ (discussed below). However, if now or later you do want to know more about the theoretical bases for these divergences in practice, then the further reading suggested at the end of this chapter will provide you with plenty of information to begin that journey.

Practical differences

There has been considerable debate over the differences between discursive psychology and Foucauldian discourse analysis (see Wetherell, 2001, and Willig, 2001, for more on this). The two forms of discourse analysis outlined in this chapter come from distinctly different philosophical traditions. This clearly impacts on the practice of these different methods. When this field of research emerged in the late 1980s in UK psychology both the theoretical and the practical distinctions seemed pretty clear, but this is no longer the case. Over recent years, new varieties of discourse analysis have emerged, while others have argued strongly for integration (e.g. Wetherell, 1998), and in practice many researchers have integrated ideas and techniques from different approaches. Indeed, even the term discursive psychology is not entirely clear as some use it to denote work with a more explicit theoretical background and focus (Potter, 2005) than others (e.g. Wetherell *et al.*, 2001a, 2001b).

The most significant distinction that has been drawn between discursive psychology and Foucauldian discourse analysis concerns the distinction between 'what people *do* with their talk and writing (**discourse practices**) and the sorts of **resources** that people draw on in the course of those practices' (Potter & Wetherell, 1995: 81). Discursive psychology has been primarily concerned with the action-oriented nature of language, that is, how people use language to do things (such as persuade, justify, excuse) – **discourse practices**. In contrast, Foucauldian discourse analysis has tended to focus on the way in which discourse constructs the social world, that is, the way in which discourse both allows and limits the possibilities available to people – understanding **discursive resources**. We will return to these differences and explore them in more detail when discussing the two different approaches to analysis below and again at the end of this chapter when discussing the debates about integrating these two approaches.

21.3 Discursive psychology

Discursive psychology is probably the most commonly used discourse analytic approach in psychological research in the UK today. This approach to the analysis of discourse was initially conceived and presented by Potter & Wetherell (1987) in *Discourse and Social Psychology*. In this book, Potter and Wetherell sought to challenge the cognitive approach to social psychology and offer a radical alternative derived from work on the philosophy of language by Wittgenstein and Austin. Their alternative was and is still controversial within the discipline but does represent the systematic expression of (arguably, see the discussion of this at the end of this chapter) an alternative paradigm for psychological research. This approach has been developed mostly within the United Kingdom to date. As we mentioned above, discursive psychology particularly draws on the work of the philosophers Wittgenstein and Austin, which we shall briefly cover here before moving on to consider some of the main issues in discursive psychology and how to carry out research from this perspective.

Wittgenstein – language games and private language

Wittgenstein was one of the most significant philosophers of the twentieth century. His ideas and writing are difficult, however, and have resulted in a considerable amount of controversy. In Wittgenstein's later work *Philosophical Investigations*, published in 1953, he put forward a number of powerful arguments about the nature of language which were to overturn the orthodox view of language that preceded his work. As we mentioned above, before Wittgenstein (and others – he was not alone in challenging the orthodox view of language) the orthodox view of language was that it simply offered a system of symbols that we can use to describe the world. Philosophers talked about language like mathematics, examining issues of reference (how language refers to objects in the world) and internal logic (the structure of language, how we put it together). Wittgenstein proposed an alternative conceptualisation where language was not a unified system (like mathematics) but a **toolkit**, where different elements of language have different practical functions. He developed this position further with the notion of the **language game**. Instead of language consisting of one unified structure, Wittgenstein argued that it was better understood as a series of **language games**, each with their own rules. So 'games', for Wittgenstein, include the process of describing appearances, making up a story or reporting an event. Each of these games has its own rules which are implicit. This crucial idea has filtered down into discursive psychology through the notion of the interpretative repertoire (Potter, 2001). The **interpretative repertoire** will be considered in more detail below but is 'the broadly discernable clusters of terms, descriptions and figures of speech often assembled around metaphors or vivid images ... the building-blocks used for manufacturing versions of actions, self and social structures in factual versions and performing particular actions' (Potter & Wetherell, 1995: 89). In other words, an analysis of the interpretative repertoires of language is the process of making explicit the implicit rules of language games.

Wittgenstein also, importantly, argued that emotions or thoughts are not events that happen inside our bodies, but rather conventionally agreed (public) linguistic terms that we learn to use. That is, for Wittgenstein, we have to learn how to use phrases such as 'I feel sad' – there is no (private) inner feeling of sadness that we feel, automatically label and then speak. We learn the external criteria of sadness (appearing sad) by seeing other people acting in this way and identifying the conditions surrounding this publicly observable state. We can never truly know what it is like for someone else to feel sad. We can never step into their mind and feel their sadness. A crucial part of Wittgenstein's arguments concerning the role of psychological terms like this was his critique of the concept of a **private language**. Wittgenstein argued that a private language was not possible and that language was always a public social event. The emphasis on the publicly observable nature of language (and the impossibility of accessing private language) has been taken on board by discursive psychologists (and other discourse analysts) and explains why their focus is so firmly on communication between people: for there cannot be access to anything inside people that is beyond language, such as cognitions or emotions. Instead, we must look at the way in which cognitions and emotions are constructed through language.

Austin – speech act theory

Austin's (1962) theory of speech acts has probably had more of a direct practical impact on the development of discursive psychology than Wittgenstein's arguments (even though they are a key part of its intellectual heritage) (Potter, 2001). Austin distinguished between the **performative** (utterances that do things) and **constative** (utterances that state things) elements of language. So, for instance, the sentence 'Keep off the grass' does not describe things but does something. It is not 'a description of the world which can be seen as true or false but an **act** with practical consequences' (Potter & Wetherell, 1987: 15). By contrast, a sentence that describes things (e.g. 'The door is blue') can be checked for its truth status and is what Austin referred to as a constative. Initially, Austin argued that sentences are either performative (actions) *or* constative (descriptions), but later in his general theory of speech acts his position shifted and he argued that *all* sentences consist of *both* elements. So, for instance, when a person say's 'I love you' they are not simply describing some (inner) state of love they feel towards you and then expressing it (a constative). Austin showed how even an apparently descriptive statement such as this is actually doing much more than just describing a state of affairs. By saying 'I love you', for instance, a person may be trying to 'reassure you' following their perception of some relationship difficulty, or they may be trying to 'convince you' of your central role in their life, or they may be trying to 'persuade you' to sleep with them (how cynical!), and so on. Austin recognised language as a practical human activity, which enables people to do things (from keeping people off newly laid grass to persuading someone else to sleep with them). Language, for Austin, like Wittgenstein, is intensely social. This directly relates to what is commonly referred to as the **action-oriented** nature of language in discursive psychology. Austin identified both the functional nature of language and how, for instance, the meaning of 'I love you' depends on a variety of *contextual issues* (which can be located in the text when carrying out an analysis). Analysing this action-oriented aspect of discourse is one of the central features of a discursive psychological analysis.

Discursive practice versus discursive resources

As we have already mentioned, discursive psychologists have tended to focus on practice while Foucauldian discourse analysts have focused on discursive resources. However, more recently there have been calls for a more integrated approach with a 'twin focus' (e.g. Wetherell, 2001) which is sometimes called **Critical Discourse Analysis (CDA)**. Though once again the meaning of this term is not always clear though in general it refers to discourse analytical work 'that primarily studies the way social power, abuse, dominance, and inequality are enacted, reproduced, and resisted by text and talk in the social and political context' (Van Dijk, 2001: 352). The explicitly political concern of CDA is in line with Foucauldian work but is controversial for discursive psychologists and others (such as **conversation analysts**) who have traditionally eschewed such an explicit political focus in their work.

It is also worth noting that the focus on discursive practice that has been so central to discursive psychology does not mean there must be a shift from investigating psychological issues to linguistic issues. Discursive psychology does not aim to improve our understanding of linguistics (though it may well inform this field) but instead to improve our understanding of social action. If discursive psychologists do attempt to investigate both practices and resources then discursive psychology should also improve our understanding of the construction of the self and the social world.

The emphasis on construction and content

Unlike a lot of traditional social psychology, the content of what people say is the principal focus of discursive psychology. In traditional social psychology what people say is taken to be indicative of something else (their attitudes, for instance). However, in discursive psychology the focus is on what is said and not on what is presumed to lie beneath this layer. In addition, discursive psychology does not address the object of language to exist in an unproblematic manner. These objects themselves are constructed through language. So, when investigating attitudes towards fox-hunting the aim is not to discern a person's attitude but instead to look at the ways in which people talk about fox-hunting – that is, what they are doing with their talk and how they construct their version of what fox-hunting is. Discursive psychology thus marks a break from traditional psychology through this focus on the construction and content of speech.

The importance of rhetoric, stake and accountability

Another feature of discursive psychology is the concern with the **argumentative nature of talk**. Billig (1991) has been a particularly important figure in highlighting the way in which people construct versions of the world which are designed to counter alternative versions. This **rhetorical view of language** emphasises the notion of people as *motivated language users* (in contrast to the traditional view of people as disinterested information processors). So, a person's expression of their attitude towards fox-hunting will be produced with an alternative position in mind (that of the pro-hunting lobby) and serves to counter an oppositional discursive position (Billig, 1991).

Another key idea in discursive psychology that is also concerned with the rhetorical nature of language is the notion of **stake and accountability** (Potter & Wetherell, 1995). Discursive psychologists have argued that people treat each other as agents who have a **stake** (or vested interest) in the activities in which they are engaged. So, for instance, someone might dismiss (**discount**) an expression of affection ('I love you') because it is merely an attempt to persuade them to sleep with another person, or they may discount criticism as the product of a nasty lecturer. Similarly, a person may position their talk in order to prevent such discounting. A scientist may, for instance, construct their talk as objective to prevent discounting of their expressed views on account of their political views or vested interests (Mulkay & Gilbert, 1982a, 1982b, 1983).

Finally, it is worth mentioning the notion of an **ideological dilemma**, a term coined by Billig and colleagues in 1988. This concept emerged through recognition of the often contradictory nature of everyday discourse. Discourses are used as flexible rhetorical resources in argumentation and consistency is not therefore to be expected. Contradictory discourses may be taken up and employed to win arguments (Edley & Wetherell, 2001) but this may result in what has been termed ideological dilemmas where a person espouses apparently contradictory views. So, for instance, a young mother in conversation might draw on a discourse about the intrinsic value of motherhood and childrearing for all women and later draw on an alternative discourse about the need for women to be able to work and bring up children in order to live satisfying lives. The ways in which people engage in such ideological dilemmas has been a fruitful area of research for discursive psychologists.

Doing discursive psychology

Potter & Wetherell (1987: 158–76) present ten stages for a discursive psychological analysis: *research questions, sample selection, collection of records and documents, interviews, transcription, coding, analysis, validation, the report* and *application*. We shall draw on these stages below to try to explain the process of carrying out discursive psychological research, but first it is worth mentioning some of the difficulties inherent in providing instruction for carrying out an analysis of this kind. Potter & Wetherell (1987: 168) describe discourse analysis to be 'like riding a bicycle compared to conducting experiments or analysing survey data which resemble baking cakes from a recipe. There is no mechanical procedure for producing findings from an archive of transcript.' And this is one of the principal difficulties in teaching discourse analysis. It is really best to learn by 'doing', and preferably by 'doing' discourse analysis with someone already experienced in the method. It is not impossible, however, to teach yourself discourse analysis; it will just require more reading and greater care. In the sections that follow we will try to detail some of the basics and provide suggestions for further reading that should allow the interested reader to make a start on this journey.

Asking appropriate questions

As we hope you realise by now, it is necessary for a discursive psychologist to ask different questions from those normally posed by traditional social psychologists. The topics that may be investigated are many and varied and the questions asked can be equally many and varied. However, the concern is with the way in which language is used and not what lies beyond language. There is no attempt to discern attitudes, beliefs, feelings or any other cognitive structure through talk. The focus is on the talk (or discourse) itself. How is it constructed and what function does it have?

Legitimate topics of investigations might include:

- the role of blaming and blame discounting in marital discord (from conversation recorded in a counselling setting);
- the construction of racist discourse in particular settings (e.g. a work setting);
- gendered discourse in teacher–pupil interactions;
- explanations given for wanting children (from interviews);
- investigation of medical repertoires of speech about patients with mental health problems; and so on.

The possibilities are endless but the focus is always on discourse. Any other questions are not the legitimate enterprise of a discursive psychologist.

Because of the time-consuming nature of transcription and analysis, and the focus on language and not on the people producing the language, samples are often quite small in discursive psychology. The size of the sample is not an issue for discursive psychologists (or discourse analysts in general, for that matter). Bigger is certainly not always better here![1] What is important is that the text that is analysed is adequate for making the claims an analyst may wish to make. Discourse analysts have analysed single pieces of text to good effect, highlighting important functions. Just increasing the size of the sample will not guarantee a more valid discourse analysis (in fact it may just increase the workload with no payoff in terms of validity). However, it might be necessary to have multiple sources of text to demonstrate the consistency and/or variability of a particular discursive device, structure or function. It is up to the analyst to detail their source of text and the reader to determine whether it is adequate for the research being presented.

Collecting data

Discursive psychologists (like most discourse analysts) prefer to use naturally occurring discourse rather than that produced through an intervention on the part of the analyst (by interviewing someone, for instance). This is because naturally occurring conversations (without the presence of the researcher or their equipment) are thought to be devoid of researcher influence (Webb *et al.*, 1996, cited in Potter & Wetherell, 1987). This is important, for it is argued that a researcher may get only a partial version of a person's world through an interview. Imagine you wished to research racist discourse in the workplace, for instance. Racism is generally frowned upon in our society and most people know that racism in the workplace may lead to disciplinary action if uncovered. It is therefore highly unlikely that people will freely express themselves when being interviewed by a researcher (even with the usual assurance of confidentiality). A discourse analyst would much prefer to get their hands on the tape recordings of job interviews or personal development review meetings so that

---

[1] But remember, this is often true of quantitative studies too. Sample size is just one factor among many others in any research study and increasing the size of a sample, even in a quantitative study, may not improve the work at all.

they can analyse naturally occurring discourse (which may demonstrate racism in all sorts of subtle or not so subtle ways). As well as the problems of people failing to tell the whole story in an interview, any discourse analysis of interview material must account for the nature of the interview setting in the analysis. This is likely therefore to limit the possibility of making claims about the talk beyond this particular setting.

Unfortunately, it can be very hard to get access to this naturally occurring material. We know it is all around us but tape recording it presents two problems: one practical and one ethical. The practical problem is obvious and is the most easily solved difficulty. Tape (and now digital) recording technology has improved so that recorders are small, portable devices that can be discreetly placed to capture natural, spontaneous conversation. Indeed, it is even possible to use miniature recording devices that are almost impossible to detect. The practical difficulties of recording natural conversation can clearly be overcome. However, the ethical problem is much greater. A discourse analyst would clearly prefer material recorded without the knowledge of the people engaged in conversation, for as soon as people are made aware of the presence of a recording device (even with the absence of the researcher), their conversation will change. But recording people's private conversations without their permission is unethical and an invasion of their privacy. Ethical research is extremely important to prevent the abuse of people by psychologists engaged in practice or research. What this often means is that discourse analysts are forced (i) to examine material that is already in the public domain (e.g. transcripts of public discussions or television discussion shows); (ii) to use material that is already being tape recorded for another purpose (such as counselling sessions or police interviews); or (iii) to use interviews to collect material (while recognising that this is sub-optimal).

In particular, interviews impose all sorts of constraints on people, which may lead to greater consistency in responding. Now, although this is normally desirable, discourse analysts are particularly interested in variation and want to explore the full range of accounting patterns that people normally employ. Remember that discursive psychologists are not attempting to understand people's psychological processes through language. They are interested in language itself and therefore need to access material that enables them to investigate the function of the discourse being employed. Of course, even in very tightly controlled interviews, variation will be apparent and discursive psychologists will find material to analyse. However, discursive psychologists have another technique for maximising variation in interviews. Unlike in the normal semi-structured interview, discursive psychologists may intervene much more and act in a confrontational way (Potter & Mulkay, 1985). This is not to say that you argue with your participant (though some do!), but an interviewer is much more likely to speak naturally themselves in such an interview. In addition, discursive psychologists may seek to explore the same issue on more than one occasion so that they can look for variation in the accounts given. Of course, given that the interviewer is playing an active part in an interview of this kind, their talk must be as much a part of the analysis as the participant's talk.

Analysis

The first stage of analysis is to produce a transcript of the interview or conversation (unless you are using material that is already transcribed). We discussed transcription in detail in Chapter 18 so will not say too much here. However, as we stated in Chapter 18, discursive psychologists often – though not always – use a reduced version of the Jefferson system (missing some of the detail but often including timed pauses, intonation symbols, etc.). This stage can take a very long time. It is generally thought that 1 hour of conversation will take about 20 hours to transcribe using the full Jefferson system and about 10 hours using the reduced Jefferson system (and we will warn you now that it takes even longer than this when you are just beginning).

Once you have a complete transcript (or transcripts), Potter & Wetherell (1987) recommend that you begin by coding your data. As you know, coding simply involves reducing your data into more manageable chunks on the basis of some criteria (like meaning-units in phenomenological psychology). Discursive psychologists code data according to the aim of the research. So, if the research is concerned with the way in which scientists talk about facts then any reference to facts in scientists' talk will be coded for inclusion in the next stage of analysis. This does not mean we simply go through and look for the word 'fact' (or 'facts') and include the sentence containing these words. Yes, we must look for these explicit references, but we must *also* look for implicit references to this issue (where people allude to the topic without using the word 'fact'). You need to be inclusive at this stage. If some text may be relevant (no matter how marginally) it should be included. It is also important to include sufficient text and not just a sentence – remember the context is crucial for discourse analysis. It is worth noting that this is not necessarily a simple one-stage process, for analysts may well return to their data and re-code it once the analysis is underway. Insights from the early stages of analysis may suggest other material (which was not initially included) that needs to be coded and included in the next stage of analysis.

Once this coding stage has been completed and the body of relevant materials extracted from the text, the next stage is the analysis proper. Discursive psychologists state that it is not possible (or appropriate) to describe in exact detail what steps an analyst should follow. Instead one must learn by reading other analyses and then having a go at the analysis. The important thing is to approach the text with the right philosophical attitude and so be ready to interrogate it appropriately. So, one must always remember the key issues mentioned above (the functional nature of language, rhetoric, stake and accountability and so on) when engaging in an analysis. It is, however, possible to offer some advice on how to analyse text from this perspective.

Potter & Wetherell (1987: 168) describe two phases:

> First, there is the search for pattern in the data. This pattern will be in the form of both variability: *differences* in either the content or form of accounts, and consistency: the identification of features *shared* by accounts. Second, there is the concern with function and consequence. The basic the-

oretical thrust of discourse analysis is the argument that people's talk fulfils many functions and has varying effects. The second phase of analysis consists of forming hypotheses about these functions and effects and searching for linguistic evidence.

So, analysis requires that we look at how the text constructs the object or event of interest. The analyst needs to look closely at the language used. What function does a particular word or phrase have for the object of meaning? So, when the anti-hunting lobby describes fox-hunting as 'a bloodthirsty spectacle' while the pro-hunting lobby describes it as 'a traditional country sport', different constructions have been set up. The first invokes a notion of backward cruelty towards animals while the latter invokes a notion of sporting tradition. These two **interpretative repertoires** (the 'tool kit' or resources of language) set up competing constructions of the event in question (fox-hunting). The anti-hunting repertoire concerns indulgence of base animal instincts at the cost of 'innocent' life, while the pro-hunting repertoire concerns the maintenance of tradition in the face of unwanted and unnecessary 'modernising' social change.

Writing it up

Like most qualitative reports, a discursive psychological report will be structured to include the usual **abstract**, **introduction** (which includes a review of the literature), **method** (including detail of the specific analytic method being employed), **analysis** or **findings** (which incorporates the discussion) and either a **conclusion** or **general discussion** and **references** sections. This stage of discourse analysis is crucially important, for as Potter & Wetherell (1987: 172) state, 'it constitutes part of the confirmation and validation procedures itself'. This is not unique to discursive psychology. Most qualitative research requires the report to include sufficient quotes to enable the reader to (i) be convinced of the findings, and (ii) be given the possibility of challenging the findings presented. In the case of discursive psychology extensive quotes will be included in any analysis/findings section. This stage operates as an essential validity check. The principal criterion for evaluating a discourse analysis is the **persuasiveness** of the account being given (as no claims to a realist notion of 'truth' are being made here). The findings must also be *coherent*, have *consequences* for the participants (that is, the participants should show an orientation to the issues being investigated by the analyst in the text itself), generate *new problems* for future investigation, and be *fruitful* (that is, it should make sense of the phenomena and generate new knowledge) (Potter & Wetherell, 1987). See Box 21.1 for an example of a discursive psychology study by Wiggins *et al.* (2001) on the construction of eating practices.

Box 21.1 Study box

Wiggins, S., Potter, J. & Wildsmith, A. (2001). Eating your words: Discursive psychology and the reconstruction of eating practices. *Journal of Health Psychology*, **6** (1), 5–15.

Previous research on eating has tended to focus on attitudes and behaviours towards food, especially when disordered. This paper discursively examined talk about eating practices using tape-recorded mealtime conversations of families at home. Fifteen hours of recorded mealtime conversations were obtained from three families. This was transcribed (using a basic system at first). Following this 'first pass' transcription, extracts that directly related to interaction about food were then re-transcribed using the Jefferson system. The analysis/discussion was divided into three parts: *constructing the object – food, constructing the individual – physiology* and *constructing the behaviour – refusing food*. Each of these topics concerned the way in which language is used to construct an aspect of eating: the food itself, a person's hunger, and eating 'restraint' respectively. As an example, look at the following excerpts of text (given in the paper to demonstrate the construction of food):

Extract 1: SKW/A1a/M1

1 *Sue*: >Come on< there was only a ↑tiny bit of (.) of

2 ↓<u>salm</u>on just ↑ ea:t <u>salm</u>on

3 *Chloe*: ↑N:<u>o</u> its fo:<u>ul</u>

4 (2.0)

5 *Emily*: I've eaten ↑ mine

6 *Sue*: Ye:ah ↑ you've eaten ↓ y<u>ou</u>rs

7 (1.0)

8 *Chloe*: I've been <u>try</u>:ing but (mine's inedible)

Wiggins *et al.* use this text to demonstrate the way in which food is constructed (rather than simply an agreed object in the world about which we might, for instance, measure people's attitudes – is it nice, horrible, etc.). The authors argue that this text demonstrates the interactional nature of eating – people do not simply consume food as individuals but engage with each other's actions. Line 3 is used as an example of how food is negatively constructed (as 'fo:ul') to provide *an account* for Chloe (the daughter) in resisting the offer made by Sue (the mother). So, they argue, not only is eating being negotiated but also 'the nature of the food *itself*' (p. 9). Line 5, where Emily (the other daughter) exclaims that she has eaten her salmon, serves to *undermine* the account given by Chloe. By stating that she has eaten the salmon, the salmon is being 'redefined' as edible (and therefore not 'fo:ul'). Support for this interpretation is given by the authors by looking at the following line (line 6) where Sue repeats the exclamation by Emily, suggesting that it supports her argument that the salmon is edible and should be eaten. The authors continue to explore the construction of eating practices with detailed discursive psychological analyses of more mealtime conversations throughout the paper. They conclude by arguing that this approach to eating research (concentrating on naturalistic conversations) highlights new avenues for research that have been ignored in traditional eating research which has focused on individual attitudes and beliefs.

| 21.4 | Foucauldian discourse analysis |

Michel Foucault, writing in a different tradition from Wittgenstein, also emphasised the importance of language in structuring our social worlds. Foucault's thought has influenced a great deal of research in the social sciences but has only influenced work in psychology relatively recently.

Foucault and discourse

Foucault was interested in the rules and practices that regulated discourse in different historical periods (Hall, 2001). **Discourse**, for Foucault, was more than simply passages of writing or speech that were put together. Foucault instead saw discourse as

> a group of statements which provide a language for talking about – a way of representing the knowledge about – a particular topic at a particular historical moment ... Discourse is about the production of knowledge through language. But ... since all social practices entail *meaning*, and meanings shape and influence what we do – our conduct – all practices have a discursive aspect (Hall, 1992: 291).

As you can see, this is a radical view which is not simply about language, but is a view where *all* social practices must be understood through their discursive construction. Discourse actually constructs the object or event itself. It both allows and limits the possibilities of understanding the object or event of interest. All meaning and meaningful practices are constructed through discourse (a social constructionist position). It is important to realise that although Foucault (and therefore Foucauldian discourse analysts) argues that all meanings and practices are constructed through discourse, this is not to say that there is nothing outside discourse. Foucault does not deny a material reality outside of discourse. However, he does believe that nothing can have *meaning* outside discourse (Hall, 2001). That is, we can only understand social practices through language; there is no way of thinking or understanding action that does not involve language and therefore discourse. Think back to the example we gave about homosexuality when discussing social constructionism in Chapter 17. Same-sex sexual behaviours have almost certainly always existed. However, it was only in the late nineteenth century that 'the homosexual' came into being (Weeks, 1981, 1985) – that is, an understanding of same-sex sexual behaviour was constructed, and a particular **subject** created ('the homosexual'), through particular discourses (predominantly medical, moral (religious) and legal). People did not talk of homosexuals before this time and also had different ways of understanding same-sex sexual behaviour. Practical consequences followed the production of 'the homosexual' in discourse. People now **positioned** as homosexuals (men and women who engaged in same-sex sexual behaviour) were subjected to the worst atrocities the medical and legal professions could throw at them. The medical discourse constructed the homosexual as 'sick' and in need of cure, while the legal discourse constructed the homosexual as 'bad' and in need of punishment. It is only relatively recently that we have witnessed an alternative discursive construction of sexuality which constructs same-sex sexual desire as 'lesbian, gay or bisexual' within a new, more liberal understanding of sexual diversity. With this changing discursive construction, lesbians, gay men and bisexuals now enjoy greater equality and access to the wider discursive community. As we are sure you can see, discourses (and subject positions within such discourses) both 'allow' and 'limit' ways of being. Exploring the discursive construction of objects or events in this historical way is one of the major aims of Foucauldian discourse analysis.

Another major issue in Foucault's writing was the link between **discourse** and **power** (Hall, 2001). Foucault was particularly concerned with the way in which knowledge could be put to work through discursive practices to regulate people's conduct. Knowledge is always part of a network of power relations as it is applied to the regulation of social conduct. This link between discourse, knowledge and power is important for moving Foucauldian discourse analysis from an intellectual exercise to something that has real implications for our social lives. Before Foucault, power was generally thought to operate in a direct, brutal, disciplinary way, being exerted by those in power onto those without power. Foucault, however, argued that knowledge was a form of power and also that power was involved in decisions about when and in what circumstances knowledge was applied or not. So, what we 'know' about something in a particular culture at a particular time (such as sexuality, criminality or mental health – three topics addressed by Foucault himself) determines our regulation and control of these matters. For instance, discursive constructions of sexuality in medical terms result in medical control over these matters, discursive constructions of sexuality in legal terms result in legal control, and so on. If we wish to study sexuality we must try to understand the relationships between these cultural and historical discursive constructions and power – that is, the ways in which power/knowledge serve to allow and limit certain social practices. This explicitly 'political' aspect of all Foucauldian work is one of the key distinguishing factors between Foucauldian discourse analysis and discursive psychology (though note the comment made earlier about attempts to bring the two forms together).

Doing Foucauldian discourse analysis

Many of the ideas outlined above on discursive psychology will also be relevant to conducting a Foucauldian discourse analysis. The sections on selection of material, sampling and so on are as relevant for this form of discourse analysis as they are for discursive psychology. The principal differences, of course, are the focus on **discourses** (and how these both allow and limit ways of speaking, or **subject positions**) and the explicit focus on **power and politics**. In addition, Foucauldian discourse analysts treat almost anything as discourse (discursive psychologists tend to concentrate on spoken and written text). So, you may see the analysis of images as well as text. Mundane objects (children's toothpaste tubes, for instance) may form the focus of analysis for what they say about the construction of meaning in the social world. There is no limit to what can be analysed. A more significant difference is the more 'macro-level' analysis conducted by Foucauldian analysts. There is rarely a concern with very 'micro-level' interactional issues around conversation that are the main focus of discursive psychology (see Box 21.1 for an example of the more micro-level analysis often conducted by discursive psychologists). Instead, Foucauldians seek to identify and describe discourses and then explore the ways in which they serve to **position** people. The other major difference between discursive psychology and Foucauldian discourse analysis concerns the explicit focus of the latter on matters of power and politics. We say more about this below but for now it is worth mentioning that Foucauldians invariably take an explicit political stance towards a topic and seek to use their analysis to undermine oppressive discourses. This has been the subject of considerable debate between the two schools of thought (see Burr, 2003; Parker, 1992; Wetherell, 2001, for more on this). Parker (1992) outlines 20 steps required for a Foucauldian analysis of discourse (see Box 21.2).

Box 21.2

Information box

Conducting Foucauldian discourse analysis

The 20 steps for Foucauldian discourse analysis (abridged slightly) from Parker (1992: 6–22):

1 Treating our objects of study as texts which are described, put into words.

2 Exploring connotations through some sort of free association, which is best done with other people.

3 Asking what objects are referred to, and describing them.

4 Talking about the talk as if it were an object, a discourse.

5 Specifying what types of person are talked about in this discourse, some of which may already have been identified as objects.

6 Speculating about what they can say in the discourse, what you could say if you identified with them.

7 Mapping a picture of the world this discourse presents.

8 Working out how a text using this discourse would deal with objections to the terminology.

9 Setting contrasting ways of speaking, discourses, against each other and looking at the different objects they constitute.

10 Identifying points where they overlap, where they constitute what look like the 'same' objects in different ways.

▶

Box 21.2 *Continued*

11 Referring to other texts to elaborate the discourse as it occurs, perhaps implicitly, and addresses different audiences.

12 Reflecting on the term used to describe the discourse, a matter which involves moral/political choices on the part of the analyst.

13 Looking at how and where the discourses emerged.

14 Describing how they have changed, and told a story, usually about how they refer to things which were always there to be discovered.

15 Identifying institutions which are reinforced when a discourse is used.

16 Identifying institutions that are attacked or subverted when a discourse appears.

17 Looking at which categories of person gain and lose from the employment of the discourse.

18 Looking at who would want to promote and who would want to dissolve the discourse.

19 Showing how a discourse connects with other discourses which sanction oppression.

20 Showing how the discourses allow dominant groups to tell their narratives about the past in order to justify the present, and prevent those who use subjugated discourses from making history.

It is important to remember, however, that this is just one way of doing a Foucauldian discourse analysis. You should use these steps as guidance; they are not cast in stone. Many people will take the 'essence' of these steps when conducting their analyses (see Box 21.3 below) rather than follow them mechanically. And other analysts may do things very differently while still adhering to the philosophy of Michel Foucault.

More detail on some of the most important steps listed above is given below.

Source: From I. Parker (1992) *Discourse Dynamics: Critical Analysis for Social and Individual Psychology*, London: Routledge, pp. 6–12. Reproduced with permission.

Discourse, the construction of objects and subjectivity

As we stated above, discourse constructs objects and subjects (or rather subject positions) for Foucauldian discourse analysts. This is therefore the starting point for all discourse analyses. Any discourse analysis must begin by examining elements of discourse in order to conjure up relevant associations. In addition, Foucauldians understand discourse as a coherent system of meanings – 'The statements in a discourse can be grouped, and given a certain coherence, insofar as they refer to the same topic' (Parker, 1992: 11). We need to draw on our own cultural knowledge to interpret meaning in discourses and, of course, different cultural positions will produce different readings of the discourse. There is clearly a good degree of similarity between this notion of discourse and the idea of interpretative repertoires in discursive psychology. They both concern an understanding of the discursive resources (in terms of recurrent terms that characterise objects and events) that are being drawn upon to produce meaning. Parker (1992), however, notes three differences. The first is the emphasis on grammatical constructions in discursive psychology. He cautions against this, for he argues this risks 'getting bogged down in formalism at the expense of content' (Parker, 1992: 11). Parker believes the concentration on the micro-level analysis of conversation (in terms of grammar and linguistic structure) actually impedes the main focus of discourse analysis, which is about content. Secondly, Parker believes that the reference to a 'limited range of terms' by discursive psychologists is limiting linguistic possibilities and suggesting that an analyst may actually achieve an understanding of 'the totality of meanings' (p. 11). Finally, Parker (curiously) criticises the use of the word 'repertoire' for having resonances with behaviourism.

So, if one of the present authors were to look at the poster on the wall in front of them they can immediately begin to engage in this initial process of Foucauldian analysis. The poster is from a 1944 'B' movie *Youth Runs Wild* with Bonita Granville, Kent Smith, Jean Brooks, Glenn Vernon and Tessa Brind. The poster includes two striking images: the first is a colour painting of two teenage girls and one teenage boy. The boy is between the two girls and looking at one who appears to be flirting with him while the other girl looks on angrily. The other image is a more stylised painting of two teenage girls (who may or may not be those in the main image) fighting, with the words 'It explodes in your face!' superimposed. So, what discourses does this 'text' conjure up? Well, it appears to bring up a discourse of teen sexuality, trouble and conflict. The very title of the film, *Youth Runs Wild*, suggests that we may be witnessing teenagers who are out of control or 'wild', indulging in 'animal' behaviour. This process of free association and questioning of the construction of objects is an essential first step in any Foucauldian discourse analysis.

The relationships between discourses

Discourses do not, of course, live in isolation. Every object or event can be constructed through any number of discourses in any number of ways. So, a person's construction of the abstract expressionist art of Mark Rothko (large canvases of blocks of colour and little else) may be different from that of a friend of theirs. One person may see moods expressed in the colour and quickly become drawn in and moved by the canvas. Their friend, on the other hand, may see another example of the 'art world con' where the art work demonstrates no unique ability, talent or even beauty. Still others might see discourses of money and wealth, privilege, indulgence, pretension and so on in the canvas. The possibilities are endless. By exploring these different discourses the analyst can identify the contrasting ways of talking about an object or event and the different subject positions (e.g. 'art lover' versus 'art sceptic') that these entail. If we return to the movie poster, we can see teenage sexuality being constructed in a particular way (as 'Exploding' and 'Wild'). The 'sensational' context of this discourse suggests that it is a subversive discourse in opposition to a normative discourse of 'chaste and responsible' teenage sexuality. These two discourses are clearly oppositional, constructing the same objects in radically different ways with radically different implications for social practices.

Discourses are also historically and culturally situated and a Foucauldian discourse analyst is likely to be interested in identifying the historical process by which a particular discourse arose. The analysis of the movie poster benefits from this kind of perspective. It is clearly located within a Western view of culture and sexuality (and this could be broken down further). It must also be seen within the particular historical contexts of the text (produced in 1944) and our reading (in 2008). It would be possible to explore the subversive notion of sexuality being produced in the poster within the context of life in 1944 when notions of sexuality were very different from today. The image of flirting on the poster was highly provocative, designed to inflame the cinemagoers of the time. The poster does not have that effect today, and now looks distinctly tame.

Discourse, politics and power

This last section concerns steps 15 onwards in Parker's (1992) 20 steps for analysis. He states that these steps are not necessary in an analysis but should be included, and most Foucauldians would agree. These last five steps in analysis concern the relationships between discourses and power and the ways in which discourses support institutions and reproduce power relations. As you can see, these steps require the analyst to take a political position. For instance, if we look at step 17, where we look at which categories of person gain and lose from the discourse, we cannot be neutral here. To evaluate gains and losses we must take a moral/political stance. Most Foucauldian discourse analysts do position themselves politically (as feminists or Marxists, for instance) and make this explicit in their analyses. There is no attempt to hide one's political leanings and (pretend to) deny their influence on the analysis. Foucauldians would generally argue that it is impossible to 'not be' political and to deny this is to risk producing an analysis that oppresses rather than emancipates. It is also worth noting that most Foucauldian discourse analysts appear to be left wing – it is not inconceivable for a discourse analyst (Foucauldian or otherwise), like any other person, to be right wing and therefore serve completely different political aims.

Now go to Box 21.3 and have a go at Foucauldian discourse analysis yourself and read Box 21.4 for an example of a study by Gillies (1999) on smoking, which employs a feminist version of Foucauldian discourse analysis.

Box 21.3

| Activity box | Analysing text using discursive psychology |

Now it is your turn to try your hand at analysing a piece of text from a discourse analytic perspective. The text is printed on the next page. It is from a flyer advertising a record label found in a CD (*Songbird* by Eva Cassidy).

It will be best to work with a friend/fellow student as you will be able to bounce ideas off each other (and it would be especially helpful to have access to someone well versed in discourse analysis).

Box 21.3 *Continued*

DIDGERIDOO RECORDS

Didgeridoo originated in 1980 in Sydney's Darlinghurst. Eighteen months later, the Hot record label started from the back of the shop. We've been releasing and distributing quality music ever since.

We're a dedicated bunch that spend our time turning people on to our catalogue of over 6000 titles:
Blues; Country; Electronic/Ambient; Folk; Latin; Jazz; Reggae; Rock & Pop; Roots/World; Soul; R'n'B; Hip-hop; and Soundtracks, Scores & Musicals.

We do this from both ends of the world.

Wherever you are, please contact us. We'd love to turn you on.

Source: Beyond the Sea Limited. Special thanks to Martin Jennings.

Once you have read through the text a few times, start the process of analysis (there is no need for coding here as the text is so short) by considering the function of the text. What are different sections trying to do? Break it down and explore the function of each section that you can differentiate.

Now, identify the ways in which the language is put together to achieve this function.

- Why do you think particular words/phrases were chosen?
- What ideas do these words/phrases evoke in you?
- How would different words/phrases work in place of the ones you have identified?
- What broader discourses do these words/phrases draw on?

We will give some help to get you going. The phrase 'Hot record label' appears important to us as it can be seen to be doing quite a lot of work in the text. What do you think – are we right? What ideas do the word 'Hot' evoke in you in this context? We know what it says to us – something that is 'happening', 'sexy' even. Why might this be used here? It seems to be an attempt to persuade the reader of the 'cool', 'street' nature of this particular record label. What if it said 'Cold' or 'Warm' – would this have the same effect? No, we don't think so. 'Hot' is a key word that invokes a particular discourse about music. This phrase (along with others that we leave for you to explore) seems to suggest a discourse of 'sexy, street music' which is at odds with the discourse of a commercialised record industry. Now you carry on exploring this text – see how you get on.

Box 21.4 Study box

Gillies, V. (1999). An analysis of the discursive positions of women smokers: Implications for practical interventions. In C. Willig (Ed.) *Applied Discourse Analysis: Social and Psychological Interventions*. Buckingham: Open University Press.

This study sought to use Foucauldian discourse analysis to investigate the way in which women construct the activity of cigarette smoking in order to inform health promotion strategies. The chapter begins by outlining the link between smoking and serious illness and the particular risks faced by women. Gillies then situates the research within the **critical realist** tradition of Foucauldian discourse analysis of Parker (1992). Semi-structured interviews were conducted with four working-class women who smoked. The interviews were transcribed (using the standard simple approach to transcription described in Chapter 18). The data were coded looking for references to smoking behaviour and cigarettes. This was then examined for recurrent patterns which demonstrated similarity in composition or content, and in terms of dissimilarity or contrasts. Finally, specific discursive constructions were identified: *discursive constructions used to explain and justify smoking, constructions of acceptable and unacceptable smoking, defusing health hazards* and the *medicinalisation of smoking*. So, for instance, the last discourse concerns the way in which respondents construct smoking as medicinal. Smoking was portrayed as relaxing and calming and particularly important in stressful situations. A medical discourse is invoked to warrant smoking as a necessary behaviour to deal with the stress experienced in their lives. The author argues that health promotion strategies need to engage with these discourses, and the resultant subject positions, if they are to improve their success. In particular, Gillies suggests that interventions could promote alternative subject positions where the body is promoted as a source of 'pleasure, strength and vitality' (p. 84) where the need for drugs (cigarettes) to deal with stress, for instance, is reduced.

21.5 Strengths, limitations and debates

As we mentioned earlier in this chapter, there have been calls for an integration between discourse analysis concerned with practices (mostly discursive psychology) and discourse analysis concerned with resources (mostly Foucauldian discourse analysis) (Billig, 1997a, 1997b; Wetherell, 1998, 2001). However, others have argued that there are clearly two distinct forms of analysis (discursive psychology and Foucauldian discourse analysis) coming from two quite distinct traditions (ethnomethodology – drawing on Wittgenstein, and speech act theory – versus post-structuralism – drawing predominantly on Foucault) (Parker, 1992; Potter, 1997). In a sense the manner of presentation in this chapter implies an allegiance on our part with separation. This is not true. We presented the material in two distinct sections so that we could enable the reader to understand the possibility of two forms before engaging in debates about integration (it would have been much harder to present an integrated approach and then try to tease out the two forms).

Wetherell (1998) argues that 'a division of labour' is counterproductive and that we should resist the break-up of discourse analysis into distinct camps. She instead argues that an eclectic approach that integrates both traditions of research must be superior for it allows the analyst to focus on both the discursive practices being employed and the wider social and institutional discursive resources being drawn upon. The focus on discursive practice within conversations enables an understanding of 'how speakers construct and negotiate meaning ... [whilst] ... a focus on discursive resources helps us to answer questions about why speakers draw on certain repertoires [or discourses] and not others' (Willig, 2001: 105, our words in square brackets). This debate has become even more acute between Critical Discourse Analysis (those forms of discursive analysis with an explicit focus on power and politics including some versions of discursive psychology/Foucauldian discourse analysis) and Conversation Analysis (CA) (which is another approach to the study of language with a particularly micro-level concern with conversational exchanges that is explicitly apolitical in practice) (Billig, 1999a, 1999b; Schegloff, 1997, 1999a, 1999b; Wetherell, 1998). The debate has become very heated but is worth exploring if the issue of politics in discursive research interests you (indeed, it also has resonance for wider issues in qualitative research more generally). If you are interested in knowing more about these arguments, the books by Wetherell *et al.* (2001a, 2001b) are a good starting point. Box 21.5 details a

Box 21.5	Study box

Edley, N. & Wetherell, M. (2001). Jekyll and Hyde: Men's constructions of feminism and feminists. *Feminism & Psychology*, **11** (4), 439-57.

This study employs an integrated approach to discourse analysis (incorporating aspects of both traditions – a close analysis of the function of the text and explicitly political examination of the discursive resources being drawn upon by the participants) to investigate the way in which men construct feminism and feminists. Data were obtained from several sources. Firstly, data were obtained from a series of group interviews with the researcher and three male students (aged 17–18 years). Each group was interviewed around eight times over a period of three months. The participants all came from white English backgrounds. Secondly, data were obtained from a set of 'one-off' small group discussions with over 60 men (aged 20–64 years). This set was predominantly, but not exclusively, white and, like the first sample, were all volunteers. The interviews included a wide range of questions about the men's lives, including three standard questions relevant to the present study about their views of feminism and feminists. The interviewer did not elaborate his own views about feminism in this case. The data were coded for references to feminism and feminists. Two competing interpretative repertoires were identified: a liberal feminist repertoire of feminism and a more complex, and negative, construction of extremist feminism, which positioned feminists as 'monstrous ogres or fiends'. The author then explores in detail the way in which these two repertoires were constructed and used, for instance, to argue about the 'true nature' of feminists and to position themselves simultaneously in favour of and against feminism and feminists.

study that demonstrates an integrated approach to discourse analysis by Nigel Edley and Margaret Wetherell.

One of the most significant criticisms that has been levelled at these two discursive approaches to psychological research concerns the perceived lack of 'a person' in this approach to psychology (see Burr, 2002; Butt & Langdridge, 2003). In an attempt to promote a truly social psychology, discursive psychology (Edwards, 1997; Harré & Gillett, 1994) and Foucauldian discourse analysis (Parker, 1992) have presented a radically non-cognitive account of the person in society. Recognising the ideological forces at work in the construction of the self (Potter & Wetherell, 1987), these approaches caution against any 'rush under the skull' to find the self. Rather than search for internal mechanisms which cause behaviour, they argue that we should concentrate on understanding linguistic practices – to produce a very different understanding of the self constructed through language (Potter & Wetherell, 1987). Discourse analysis does not concern itself with authorial intention but with the rhetorical force of the text, its impact, and the techniques used to produce meaning. It concentrates on what people are doing in their talk, and what resources they draw on in this exercise (Potter & Wetherell, 1995) rather than what the person behind the text intended. Madill & Doherty (1994) argue, however, that while discourse analysis (notably discursive psychology) has shifted the focus of enquiry away from personal intentions it still relies on an implicit model of the person as an active discourse user. Discursive psychology implicitly assumes an active language user who engages in discursive strategies to manage stake and accountability while never moving beyond the text to explicate this 'active language user'. The situation is different (and arguably better or worse) for Foucauldian discourse analysts, for the person is both passively constructed and positioned by discourse (with little room given for personal agency) or pretty much completely absent from an analysis. Whilst discourse analysis is still in a very healthy state, the growth of narrative approaches (see Chapter 22) reflect some of the dissatisfaction with the notion of agency and selfhood implicated in much discursive work.

Another criticism often levelled against discourse analysis is related to that above and concerns the question about what, if anything, exists outside discourse. Discourse analysts are agreed that discourse constructs the social world and that there is no meaning outside language. This has led to some psychologists (including some discourse analysts themselves) raising questions about the **extra-discursive** (that which is outside discourse). Ian Parker (1992: 28) adopts a **critical realist** position and argues that 'discourse analysis needs to attend to the conditions which make the meanings of texts possible'. The critical realist position is one that is being increasingly advocated by critical social psychologists wanting to recognise the importance of both the discursive and the extra-discursive. It is a philosophical position which recognises the way in which 'reality' is always mediated by language but acknowledges that our social reality so constructed is grounded in material structures beyond language. This is in stark contrast to Jonathan Potter and others who advocate a radical relativist position which does not accept any notion of reality at all that is extra-discursive (Edwards *et al.*, 1995). This debate is ongoing and has a long way to go yet.

Finally, it is worth mentioning an exchange between Martyn Hammersley (2003a, 2003b) and Jonathan Potter (2003a, 2003b) about whether discourse analysis (in its various forms) constitutes a paradigm shift or not. Hammersley argues that both conversation analysis and discourse analysis should not be considered as self-sufficient *paradigms* but rather as simply *methods* that may be used on their own or combined with others to study the social world. Whilst the details of the exchange are beyond the scope of this book, the debate is fascinating and important reading for those convinced (or otherwise) that discursive approaches truly represent a paradigm shift in psychology and the social sciences more generally.

Further reading

Burr, V. (2003). *Social Constructionism*, 2nd edn. Hove: Routledge.

An excellent introduction to social constructionism which explores much of the background to the different types of discourse analytic research being conducted today.

Kendall, G. & Wickham, G. (1999). *Using Foucault's Methods*. London: Sage.

This is a superb book for grasping the fundamentals of Foucault's thought and the implications for research in the social sciences. It is not tied to any particular form of discourse analysis (which may be a good thing or not depending on your perspective) and also engages with techniques from sociology, such as Actor Network Theory (which are likely to be unfamiliar to you, so be warned).

Parker, I. (1992). *Discourse Dynamics: Critical Analysis for Social and Individual Psychology*. London: Routledge.

Excellent coverage of theoretical and practical issues in Foucauldian discourse analytic research.

Potter, J. & Wetherell, M. (1987). *Discourse and Social Psychology: Beyond Attitudes and Behaviour*. London: Sage.

A recent classic that was, in part, responsible for popularising the discursive approach to social psychology. It is also an excellent read and a very good starting point for anyone wanting to understand more about this approach to research.

Wetherell, M., Taylor, S. & Yates, S. J. (2001). *Discourse as Data: A Guide for Analysis*. London: Sage.

An excellent book covering pretty much the entire range of discourse analytic methods that you would encounter in psychology. It is not a book for beginners but is well written and full of practical exercises and advice.

Wetherell, M., Taylor, S. & Yates, S. J. (2001). *Discourse Theory and Practice: A Reader*. London: Sage.

This is the companion book to *Discourse as Data*. Here the focus is on the theoretical underpinnings of the different traditions of discourse analytic research. The book includes some new writing from leading writers in the field as well as a collection of classic readings.

22 Life story and narrative research

- This chapter begins by outlining some of the history of life story research.

- It then moves on to consider the recent growth of interest in narrative research in psychology.

- The chapter then considers some of the ways in which narrative data may be collected and analysed.

- Finally, this chapter critically examines the strengths and weaknesses of this approach.

INTRODUCTION

Life story research has a long history within the ethnographic traditions of sociology and social anthropology and has recently started to impact on psychology, mainly through the growth of interest in narrative psychology (Sarbin, 1986). This chapter begins with a consideration of life story research, what it is, some of its history, and where it has been going over the past few years. We then move on to concentrate in depth on the life history approach and the recent interest in narrative research in psychology. This includes consideration of two broad approaches to narrative – 'small' and 'big', that is, those concerned with narrative practices and those concerned with narrative content – and some of the ways in which this data can be analysed. There are numerous approaches to narrative in the social sciences, health sciences and humanities and only a small amount of the work will be touched upon here, but we hope to introduce you to this rich approach to psychology and point you in the direction of possible sources of information should you wish to find more out about these methods.

<table>
<tr><td>**22.1**</td><td>The turn to narrative</td></tr>
</table>

Life story research is a relatively new approach to research within the social sciences that has become increasingly important over the past 20 years or so, although life stories have existed and been recorded and valued as a crucial aspect of differing culture(s) for many years before this (Plummer, 2001). This approach has principally arisen in sociology, oral history and social anthropology, with its sociological roots traceable to the early days of ethnography (notably the Chicago School of Sociology[1]) (Plummer, 2001). There have been some notable psychologists who have sought to study narratives of people's lives (e.g. Bruner, 1987; Mair, 1989) but it is only more recently that there has been sustained interest in this method within psychology with the growth of life story and narrative methods within the qualitative tradition (Atkinson & Delamont, 2006; Crossley, 2000). So, what is life story research? Well, very simply, life story research (sometimes called narrative or auto/biographical research) has traditionally been the attempt to investigate and understand the lives of people as told through their own stories (or narratives).

Bruner (1986) argued that there are two distinct forms of cognition: the paradigmatic (or logico-scientific) mode and the narrative mode. Psychology has been – and to a great extent, still is – concerned primarily with the former, searching for universal truths about human nature as if human beings were simply objects in the world to study. The narrative mode, however, is concerned with human life as a whole, expressed in the stories we tell of ourselves and others. That is, from this perspective human nature cannot be reduced to episodes but must rather be treated in its own terms through the stories we tell and narrative practices we engage in.

> If you want to know me, then you must know my story, for my story defines who I am. And if I want to know myself, to gain insight into the meaning of my own life, then I too must come to know my own story.
>
> (McAdams, 1993: 11).

There is not simply one approach to narrative research in psychology, however. You might not be surprised to hear that there are different approaches, the members of which disagree quite forcefully over the proper concern of narrative research. Broadly speaking, the older tradition has been with understanding content, what Bamberg (2006) terms 'big stories', whilst more recently there has been considerable growth in work on narrative practices, what Bamberg has

---

[1] The Chicago School of Sociology, which emerged in the 1920s and 1930s in Chicago, has played an important part in the history of the discipline. From the publication of Thomas & Znaniecki's (1958) *The Polish Peasant in Europe and America* (first published 1918–21; republished 1927), which presents an astonishingly detailed life story ethnography, the Chicago School has been recognised as the start of ethnographic and life story research as we know it today (Plummer, 2001).

referred to as 'small stories'. Narrative practices are 'the contexts in which narratives take place, what they consist of, their performances' (Bamberg, 2006: 139). That is, how selves and identities are produced in interactions, drawing on particular narratives. This territory dispute is rather unfortunate, for some writers have turned to narrative in order – at least, in part – to bring together narrative content and practice (e.g. Crossley, 2000 and Langdridge, 2007, 2008). Indeed, within psychology a number of researchers work with narratives to address the perceived limitations of such diverse approaches as phenomenology and discourse analysis (e.g. Crossley, 2000; Langdridge, 2007). Some of the differences represent different theoretical traditions in psychology, those coming from the discursive (and narratological) traditions being more interested in practice and form, whilst those coming from certain schools of sociology and phenomenology are more interested in content. There are researchers attempting to bring together both content and form but this has been contentious as either side can – and does – claim that insufficient attention has been paid to either content or practice. These debates are discussed further at the end of this chapter.

In the following sections (22.2 to 22.6) we focus predominantly on 'big story' narrative research as this is the older and dominant tradition (Atkinson & Delamont, 2006) and then turn, albeit briefly, to provide some information about methods of narrative practice and form, namely the approach of Riessman. Indeed, whilst there is this split, much of the information in the following sections has relevance to both approaches, though it is clearly much more focused on working with 'big' stories of individuals' lives.

22.2	Selecting informants

Unlike most quantitative research, the aim of selecting participants who are representative is not the key issue in life story research. Instead, the focus is on selecting a life, from the many millions available, that we wish to study. Should this be the great person (as we see in so much commercial biography), the marginal person or the common (or ordinary) person? Plummer (2001) argues that there are two main ways in which lives are selected for study: the **pragmatic** and the **formal** approach.

The **pragmatic** (or sometimes 'chance') approach is not really a strategy at all but more an observation of how many lives have been selected for research of this kind. Researchers have bumped into or got to know people whose stories they thought were worth telling. Plummer (2001) tells of how Bogdan met Jane Fry, a transsexual, when she came to speak at a group he attended. This resulted in what is now considered a classic life story: *Being Different: The Autobiography of Jane Fry* (Bogdan, 1974). Many other classic life story works have also been the result of chance encounters or the product of finding someone intriguing when interviewing participants in an ongoing study. Here there are no techniques for recruiting other than knowing that someone has something to say about a topic of interest. The issue is finding a **key informant** who has a story worth telling, who is articulate and, crucially, who is willing to devote a considerable amount of time to enable you to tell their story.

The **formal** approach is more strategic and requires a choice between recruiting the **great person**, **marginal person** or **common person**. The great person has been a common choice in commercial autobiography but much less so in sociological (or psychological) writing. In essence, the great person (Gandhi, Hitler, Luther, Mandela and so on) is someone who is exceptional in some way. Note that great does not necessarily equate with good here – witness Hitler. But these people have led exceptional, extraordinary lives, which may tell us something about the historical times in which they lived, and/or something about greatness itself, and/or something about difference and marginality. The **marginal person** has been the mainstay of life history work. Here, marginal is taken to mean someone who is living on the margins of two societies. The marginal societies may be 'male' and 'female' societies, as in the case of Jane Fry (Bogdan, 1974); or 'Poland' and 'Chicago' societies, as in the case of Wladek (Thomas & Znaniecki, 1958). What these people on the margins can offer is insight into a society which we 'take for granted'. Telling the stories of those on the margins enables us to open up and interrogate 'common-sense' assumptions about psychology and the social world.

The **common** (or **ordinary**) **person** can also be the topic of life story research. However, while it is perhaps not too difficult to identify the marginal or great lives, what is an ordinary life? Well, we guess this means any life that at least on the surface does not seem extraordinary in any way (whether marginal or great). Undoubtedly much will emerge during the course of charting the ordinary person's life that may be quite extraordinary. But many people live extraordinary lives in the most ordinary of circumstances and are well worthy of study for what they can tell us about 'everyday' life. See Box 22.1 for an example of a classic study by Harold Garfinkel (1967) of the extraordinary (marginal) life of Agnes, a hermaphrodite (that is, the rare condition of being born with both male and female sex characteristics).

Box 22.1	Study box

Garfinkel, H. (1967). Passing and the managed achievement of sex status in an 'intersexed' person part 1. In H. Garfinkel, *Studies in Ethnomethodology*. Englewood Cliffs, NJ: Prentice Hall.

This study sought to investigate the experience of living as an 'intersexed' person, that is, a person who has crossed the divide, in this case from male to female. It concerns the life of Agnes, who was born a hermaphrodite with predominantly male genitalia and was brought up for the first 17 years of her life as a man. At the age of 19 Agnes wished to undergo sex reassignment surgery so that she had the sexual characteristics of the woman she believed herself to be. This required the surgical removal of her penis and testes and construction of a vagina. This particular study was conducted in collaboration with

▶

Box 22.1 *Continued*

Robert Stoller (a psychiatrist) and Alexander Rosen (a psychologist), who were involved in the treatment of Agnes, and consisted of 35 hours of conversations between Garfinkel and Agnes.

This life history is specifically concerned with exploring the experience of crossing the sex divide and understanding the taken-for-granted assumptions that 'normals' have about their sex and sexual identity. The study as presented here does not therefore explore any other elements of Agnes's life. Garfinkel presents a mainly theoretical description of the experience of 'passing' as a woman when Agnes had the genitals of a man. Many interesting theoretical observations emerge in this study. At the time of this study there was considerable prejudice about transsexuality and Garfinkel observed the way in which Agnes positioned herself separately from transsexuality and homosexuality, instead arguing that she was a woman from birth who due to unfortunate environmental circumstances had been thought a man. For instance, Garfinkel reports how Agnes 'reconstructs' her past and present such that she is '120 per cent woman' and her boyfriend '120 per cent man'. He also describes the process of 'passing' where Agnes had to actively work (socially) to appear as a 'natural' woman while always risking detection. From this one exceptional life story Garfinkel manages to explore the many *taken for granted assumptions* about sex that would not be revealed through investigations with people fully (and 'naturally') immersed in their ascribed sex categories (male or female). It was only through the careful and systematic study of one person who had crossed this divide that Garfinkel could identify the boundary conditions for membership of each sex.

22.3	Collecting data

There are a number of sources of data that can be sought out in order to provide information about a person's life and/or data for narrative research. Pre-existing documentation or self-documentation is one possible source of information. Secondly, unstructured (or, more rarely, semi-structured) interviews are commonly used. Thirdly, participant observation (with accompanying unstructured interviews) may be another, and finally, amongst researchers more interested in narrative practice, naturally occurring conversations may be a valuable source of data. We will deal with each of these in turn below.

If the person you are investigating is a great person it is quite likely that there will be written (or audio or visual) documentation available about them. This can be a particularly valuable source of information and is the traditional starting point for commercial biographies. With some important figures, there will be too much information and the effort required in sifting through this may be considerable. In addition, it is important to be critically aware of the information that is available to you. You may only have access to certain material (other information that may be illuminating but controversial may have been destroyed or hidden in an archive or family record). And of the information that is available, much will be secondary material, written by others, about the person in question. Just think of the documentaries that have appeared about great people in recent years and think of the controversy that they evoke.

An alternative source of documentary material can come from a participant's own writing. It is possible to ask a participant to keep a diary if they do not already do so (some may have done this for a considerable time already). This can provide a remarkable insight into the day-to-day experiences of a person's life and also provide an invaluable starting point for further discussion. It is also possible to ask people to write concrete descriptions of their experiences (a very common method in phenomenological psychology) or to write their own biographies. These may end up as finished documents in a research report or the starting points for your own writing on these people's lives. This approach to data collection is obviously one that is collaborative. Indeed, there has been considerable debate in life history research about *ownership* of the material. If the researcher re-tells someone else's story, whose story is it? If it is not the researcher's property, what rights do they have in publishing and making a career on the back of it? There are some very complex and difficult ethical and moral debates that need to be seriously engaged with before conducting research of this kind.

A second major source of data comes from unstructured interviews (see Chapter 4). This is probably the commonest strategy for data collection (Plummer, 2001). Note here, though, that it is an unstructured or biographical (rather than the semi-structured) interview that is the norm. Life story research cannot be carried out by a researcher armed with a semi-structured interview protocol on an hour-long visit to a participant. A relationship needs to be built up, often over a considerable length of time, and many unstructured interviews may be needed to gather the richness of data needed to tell a life story. Obviously, studies try to shorten this process but the benefit of the unstructured interview is clear. This method does not impose the researcher's agenda on the participant but is designed to enable them to tell their story. The researcher adopts the position of interested observer, ready to question, interrogate, interpret, and even challenge, if necessary. It is not just a series of conversations, however, for this is about data collection, and the researcher still needs to prioritise the life world of the participant. See Box 22.2 for some advice on conducting biographical life story interviews.

Box 22.2

Information box

Life story interviews

We wrote about unstructured interviews in Chapter 4 but a little more guidance is probably needed, as they are not as straightforward to conduct as you might think.

First, unstructured life story interviews are not simply conversations as you might have with a friend. You may become a friend of your participant(s) but it is important to remember that this is still research and the focus is on telling the life story of the participant (and not you, unless you are writing your autobiography and you are the participant, of course!). You will therefore tend to stay in the background while your participant recounts their story.

▶

Box 22.2 *Continued*

Second, even more so than in semi-structured interviewing, it is important to give your participant 'permission to speak'. This will still seem a strange idea until you carry out your first interview and reach that moment where your participant has nothing more to say and you have nothing more to ask. The feelings of discomfort rise and we guarantee you will close the interview at that point (almost always too early).

One interview will not be sufficient! Although a considerable amount of qualitative psychology uses the 'one shot' interview, this will never be enough to capture a person's life story. You will need to talk repeatedly with your participant over a sustained period of time (this can be several years) to truly capture their story. This will produce an enormous amount of data (plenty of transcripts and other documentation) that will need organising and then analysing.

But where do you start if you do not have a series of questions to ask from a carefully constructed interview protocol? Below are a few starting points adapted from Plummer (2001: 124–5).

An opening instruction

(From McAdams, 1993: 256–64, cited in Plummer, 2001: 124)

You can begin your series of life story interviews with some instructions such as the following:

> I would like you to begin by thinking about your life as if it were a book. Each part of your life comprises a chapter in the book. Certainly the book is unfinished at this point; still, it probably contains a few interesting and well-defined chapters. Please divide your life into its major chapters, and briefly describe each chapter. You may have as many or as few chapters as you like, but I would suggest dividing it into at least two or three chapters, and at most seven or eight. Think of this as a general table of contents for your book. Give each chapter a name and describe the overall contents of each chapter. Discuss briefly what makes for a transition from one chapter to the next … Looking back over your entire life story with chapters, episodes and characters, can you discern a central theme, message or idea that runs throughout the text? What is the major theme of your life …?

Then you might choose to focus on different chapters in different interviews and explore the meaning for your participant of each chapter (period in their life). It is even possible to ask your participant to write down their chapters and headings (or you transcribe these) and then to use these as the focus of discussion in the interviews.

Key issues to explore

(Adapted from Atkinson, 1998).

There are a number of issues that structure most people's lives:

Box 22.2 *Continued*

- Birth and family of origin
- Cultural setting and traditions
- Education
- Work
- Love and relationships
- Friendships
- Family life
- Spirituality
- Major life themes – problems and successes
- Vision of the future.

Each of these topics can form the focus of an interview (or interviews) and further questions could be developed within each category to facilitate discussion.

A life narrative interview protocol

(From Gubrium, 1993: 189–90, cited in Plummer, 2001: 125.)

It is possible to construct an interview protocol designed to encourage the telling of a life story. The one below is probably very useful where time is limited and you cannot devote several years of your life to the life story of one participant. Using this interview protocol produces a more structured interview situation but one which still encourages the telling of a life story.

Life in general

1 Everyone has a life story. Tell me about your life, in about 20 minutes or so if you can. Begin wherever you like and include whatever you wish.

2 What were the most important turning points in your life?

3 Tell me about the happiest moments in your life.

4 What about the saddest points?

5 Who have been the most important people in your life?

6 Who are closest to you now?

7 What does your life look like from where you are now?

8 If you could live your life over, what would you do differently?

9 How do you explain what's happened to you over your life?

10 If you had the opportunity to write the story of your life, what would the chapters be about? Chapter 1? Chapter 2? ... What about the last chapter?

Self

1 How would you describe yourself when you were younger?
2 How would you describe yourself now?
3 Have you changed much over the years? How?
4 What is your philosophy of life? Overall, what is the meaning of life to you?

Another method of data collection that is commonly used by life story researchers is participant observation (see Chapter 5), the mainstay of ethnographic research in sociology. Participant observation can be a particularly tricky approach to data collection but one that, if carried out well, can be uniquely illuminating. Life story research rarely relies on participant observation alone. Unstructured interviews, and possibly also the collection of other documentation, will be used as well. This approach enables the researcher to **triangulate** their findings, that is, compare the findings from several different methods (see Section 22.4 below).

Finally, it is worth mentioning the use of naturally occurring conversations in narrative research. For those researchers most interested in 'small stories', that is, the practices and forms of narratives, naturally occurring data is often the most appropriate choice. In many ways, this follows the conventions of discourse analysis discussed in the previous chapter. The aim is to gather data in which micro-level analyses can be conducted on data which is natural and spontaneous using techniques from narrative and discourse analyses.

22.4   Triangulation

As mentioned above, **triangulation** is an important strategy that can be employed in any form of qualitative research, but one that is particularly valuable when investigating other people's lives. Triangulation enables one to see the life (or topic of interest) from differing perspectives. Strictly speaking, this form of triangulation is **data triangulation**, where one uses different methods to collect data on the same topic (Denzin, 1989). The aim with data triangulation is to attempt to transcend the particular limitations of any one method of data collection by engaging with a number of different methods. Here, when attempting to make sense of someone's life, analysis of unstructured interviews, participant observation and other documentary material may enable the researcher to tease out the many layers of meaning that one method alone might miss. Flick (2002: 227) argues that, contrary to popular opinion, 'Triangulation is less a strategy for validating results and procedures than an alternative to validation ... which increases scope, depth and consistency in methodological proceedings.' Triangulation is also discussed in Chapter 24

22.5   Analysing life story data

At the very simplest, one might simply reproduce a participant's story in its raw form. That is, a researcher might 'tell it like it is' in the participant's own words. In truth this rarely happens, as there is nearly always some editorial intervention in any storytelling. At the very least, a social science researcher would attempt to reconstruct a life story through editing. Repeated elements would be deleted and the story would be reconstructed into an appropriate narrative form. This may be a simple chronological structure or another appropriate narrative structure that best facilitates the telling. At this level there is little obvious analysis, as we understand analysis generally in psychology. But this does still constitute analysis. Organising and editing textual information is analysis. What is required of the researcher here is the ability to read, reflect and re-read the data (as is common in any qualitative analysis) to get a feel for the story being told. It is then the responsibility of the researcher to tell the story as truthfully as they can (that is, keeping close to the data). Researchers vary in the degree to which they comment and reflect on the story being told. Some writers add only minimal commentary – maybe just clarificatory remarks. This approach is controversial, however, with some writers arguing that it is not enough to simply re-present a story (Atkinson & Delamont, 2006). For researchers such as Atkinson and Delamont, research which simply re-presents a life story is uncritical and complicit in reproducing elements of a very modern culture of confessional. Instead, they argue that researchers have an obligation to do much more by working critically and analytically with the data they have collected, recognising the socially situated nature of its production and presentation. Narratives are not produced by an individual in a vacuum but are rather a product of the individual *in relation to* the social world in which they live.

With this in mind, other narrative researchers explicitly attempt to draw out important meanings and structures in narratives and develop links with extant theory and/or develop new theories. Issues such as **plot type** (see Elsbree, 1982 and Gergen & Gergen, 1986), **rhetorical structure** (Billig, 1997a, 1997b; see also Langdridge, 2007), **narrative coherence** and **tone** are frequently examined (see, for instance, McAdams, 1993). So, for instance, Elsbree (1982) has suggested that there are essentially only five types of plot: taking a journey, engaging in a contest, enduring suffering, pursuing consummation and establishing a home. Researchers may look at how these types of plot have been employed for certain rhetorical effects (see Chapter 21) and/or look at the way in which a tone of a narrative changes throughout the telling (so, someone may begin a story in a heroic manner only to end with a sense of tragedy or failure). Examining features such as narrative tone and rhetorical function may provide further information about the stories being told that are otherwise not revealed by simply concentrating on substantive content. The notion of a **canonical narrative** (Bruner, 1990) is also a particularly useful analytic tool, recognising the way in which narratives are as much a production of the social world as individual storyteller. Canonical narratives are stories which represent broader societal stories about how life should be lived. Researchers frequently draw on these concepts and many others pragmatically, depending on the aims of their research. If a researcher is interested in making links to theory, a life story may operate in a number of ways (Plummer, 2001: 159). It may be used:

- to challenge an extant theory or particular aspect of theory (similar to negative case evaluation in grounded theory – see Chapter 20);
- to illustrate or illuminate some aspect of an extant theory;
- to develop theory.

It is also worth noting that just because there is no generally agreed upon elaborate formal system of analysis, the analysis is no less valid. **Validity** is whether the method being used is actually tapping the issue it is supposed to be tapping. With this understanding there can be no doubt that the life story approach is very valid. A researcher telling a life story is as close to the data as it is possible to be. Greater use of (analytic) technique may make a method more **reliable** but not **valid**. However, as Plummer (2001: 155) states, when referring to concerns raised about the reliability of life story work: 'The problem, however, is really being tackled from the wrong end: validity should come first, reliability second. There is no point in being very precise about nothing!'

Some researchers have, however, employed other more systematic approaches to the analysis of life story data, some of which will be mentioned below (and see the method of Riessman discussed at the end of this chapter). Methods such as thematic analysis, phenomenological psychology, grounded theory and discourse analysis have all been used to analyse data collected in this way. The disadvantage of these methods is the tendency to break up stories by extracting themes. The essential narrative quality of a life may be lost when analysed in this way and as a consequence narrative researchers often modify the methods so that the inherent structure of stories is not lost.

Thematic analysis, phenomenological analysis, grounded theory and discourse analysis

Life story data, like any textual material, can be subjected to a thematic analysis, phenomenological analysis, grounded theory analysis or, indeed, discourse analysis. Some life story researchers employ these methods of analysis, in whole or in part, to assist their data analysis. As we mentioned above, the real tension concerns the tendency of these methods of analysis to reduce a story to thematic components, thereby losing the essential narrative structure of a beginning, middle and end. This may not be as problematic as it seems. First, some approaches within these traditions do not break up narratives (e.g. the phenomenological psychology of Giorgi – see Chapter 19). In phenomenological psychology, one of the analytic steps is to reconstruct the story that is told in chronological order. It does not require much adaptation to use this analytic method with entire life stories. It is also possible to adapt the other methods (thematic analysis, grounded theory and some versions of discourse analysis) to preserve the narrative structure. It is also worth noting that it is sometimes not appropriate or desirable to tell a story as traditionally conceived in the West, with a beginning, middle and end. Not all cultures understand stories in this chronological way (Riessman, 1993). Furthermore, a story that is told chronologically might actually lend itself (in terms of clarity or power) to being re-told in a more episodic way. The best way to grasp the application of these methods to the analysis of life stories is to read examples and then have a go yourself. We believe that academics (and most particularly psychologists) can be too precious about methods. So often, a study suffers through a kind of methodological dogmatism, where all too often valuable data are wasted because of the decision to employ only a particular method or technique of analysis (when others might further illuminate the material).

22.6	Writing a life story

We consider writing more generally in Chapter 26 but it is worth introducing some of the issues surrounding the presentation of life story material here. Traditionally, psychological research has been written up in a format similar to that in the natural sciences. The scientific laboratory write-up forms the model for publication in professional journals. The report is clearly structured, beginning with an 'Introduction', which reviews the literature and leads the reader to the explicitly stated hypotheses that will be tested. A 'Method' section follows, which details (in a prescribed form) the participants, procedure, materials, etc. that have been used in the study. We then have the 'Results' section, which presents the results of statistical tests, and finally the 'Discussion', where the author interprets his or her results and makes links back to theory and the extant literature. This format has served quantitative psychologists well and will no doubt continue to be the dominant form of presentation for this kind of research. It is, however, an entirely inappropriate form for the presentation of life story analyses. How could one present someone's life in terms of methods, results and discussion? It makes no sense. Qualitative researchers, in general, have moved away from the standard scientific report format towards other, more appropriate formats. Life story researchers have, perhaps, travelled the furthest from the scientific report format.

There are many different ways of presenting life story research. One of the most ambitious (and rare) formats is to present the 'whole life' of the person from their birth to their death (or somewhere before this). The structure is chronological and charts a life with chapters devoted to periods of a person's history. The story may be told principally in the participant's own words or in the words of the researcher or some mix in between. It is rare to tell the story solely in the words of the researcher (though it has been done) and it is most common to mix the words of both parties. A more common approach will be to present some aspect of a person's life – their struggle with anorexia, their experience of living as a transsexual and so on. Here, depending on the length of the report (i.e. whether a journal article or book), a story will be written that is much more tightly focused. The level of interpretation given will depend on the aims and theoretical stance of the author. Some authors are content to edit and maybe comment but little more, preferring to let their participant tell their own story in their own words. Others may want to link the life story with previous literature and theory and play a much more important part in the writing. The participant's own words may well become secondary and used (as one might with a thematic or discourse analysis) to support and illuminate the statements and arguments of the author.

Ethical issues

Whatever presentation method is chosen, the life story method raises a number of ethical issues. First, there is the question of anonymity. If one writes a life story (even a focused story) then it is very difficult to obscure that person's identity and enable them to remain anonymous (as is typical in social science research). Changing a person's name to protect their anonymity is probably insufficient when so much detail of their life is being publicly revealed. Real care must be taken and these issues must be discussed and negotiated at the beginning of any research relationship. They must also be revisited before any report becomes public, for aspects of a person's life may have emerged unexpectedly through the course of the study which they would rather have remained private.

Life story research also raises the thorny issue we touched upon earlier of who owns the material that is generated. This is a complex issue that requires considerable care. There are legal data protection issues to be aware of as well as the ethical/moral arguments about ownership of such personal material.

Finally, there are issues concerning the relationship between researcher and participant. Social science research becomes most personal (and *potentially* least professional) with life story research. It is inevitable that people will form genuine friendships with 'participants' when they spend so much time together. However, it is important to remember that the relationship is not an equal one. In psychotherapy, for instance, a client and therapist may become attached over the years but the therapist must always be mindful of the professional nature of their relationship and not allow their personal feelings to interfere in any way. This is not easy and is something that is widely discussed in the therapeutic community. Therapists have support through supervision where they can discuss these issues. The same is probably advisable for researchers engaged in life story research. We would recommend all life story researchers to work with another experienced researcher who can act as their supervisor. Difficult issues that arise in the relationship between researcher and participant can then be discussed with the co-worker. This arrangement may also prove to be valuable with data analysis, when another perspective can be particularly valuable. The best way to get a feel for life story work is to tell and then analyse a life story yourself. The safest method is to tell your own story (see Box 22.3).

Box 22.3

Activity box   Telling your story

- Write or amend an interview protocol, like that given in Box 22.2, to ask yourself questions to prompt you telling your own story. Get a recording device and make time to ask yourself the questions in your interview protocol. Try to take the task seriously and answer each question as fully as possible.
- Transcribe the recording and then create a follow-up interview protocol designed to explore those issues raised in the first interview in more depth. Once again ask yourself the questions and record the interview. You can repeat this procedure as many times as you like until you feel you have exhausted your story (or yourself!).

Box 22.3 *Continued*

- Try to write your own life story. Use a simple chronological structure using quotes (from yourself) throughout your report. See what links you can make to ideas and theories in the psychology literature. Add a reflexive section into your report and reflect on the procedure and difficulties in telling a life story.

22.7   Narrative practice and form

In the following section we briefly discuss one of the most popular approaches to narrative research that focuses more closely on narrative form than content (though the distinction is not hard and fast, as Riessman herself stresses the importance of both content and form). This approach is now well established and widely used and so warrants attention. There are very many different approaches to working with narrative practice and structure (see, for instance, Taylor, 2006, for an approach which builds directly on discursive psychology), and so it is important to recognise that this is not *the* approach to 'small story' – that is, practice or form focused – narrative analysis but one of many. There is no one thing that can be described as narrative analysis (Manning & Cullum-Swan, 1994); there are many different techniques and methods.

Riessman's (1993) method of narrative analysis

Riessman's approach to narrative analysis is distinct from the more traditional life story research through its concern with language use. For narrative analysts, like Riessman, discourse analysts, some phenomenologists (e.g. hermeneutical/narrative – see Langdridge, 2003, 2007) and indeed grounded theorists (e.g. Charmaz, 2006), language does not simply describe a person's reality. Instead, language functions to construct the world and must be recognised as a medium replete with rhetorical functions. Riessman (1993: 21), referring to Halliday (1973), recognises that 'language has three analytically distinct but interdependent functions', all of which are needed if one is to fully grasp the meaning in the text. The three functions are: (1) the ideational function – content of the speech in terms of meaning, (2) interpersonal function – the role of relationships between speakers in language use, and (3) textual function – syntax and semantics of language. There is no doubt that life story research has been dominated by the first view of language as a way of communicating information. The structural and interpersonal components have been of less concern, though researchers are becoming increasingly interested in these factors (though unfortunately often at the expense of content!). Riessman (1993: 21) argues that narrative analysis 'provides methods for examining, and relating, meaning at all three levels'.

So, how do you carry out a narrative analysis as proposed by Riessman (1993)? Well, there is not enough space to go into detail here but we will try to give you a flavour of the approach, and if you want to know more then consult the recommended reading by Riessman at the end of the chapter. Once a story has been collected (recorded), the first key stage in analysis for Riessman is transcription. She suggests roughly transcribing the material first to get a feel for the stories being told. At this point the analyst needs to identify narrative segments of the talk. Much of the talk will be question and answer exchanges in semi-structured interviews and will not therefore form the focus of analysis. However, unstructured interviewing is more likely to facilitate the telling of stories that can be subjected to a narrative analysis. As Riessman (1993) points out, it may be no easy task to identify where a story begins and ends. Once the segment has been chosen the analyst must re-transcribe the material in much more detail (some 'small story' narrative analysts will use the Jefferson system of transcription discussed in Chapter 18) into numbered lines of text which detail all the pauses, breaks, overlaps and so on of the talk.

Next, Riessman (1993) employs Labov's (1972, 1982) framework to examine the structure of the narratives. This framework suggests that every clause has a function which may be any of the following: to provide an abstract for what will follow (A), to orient the listener (O), to carry on the action (CA), to evaluate meaning (E) and to resolve the action (R). Each line is coded A, O, CA, E or R depending on its function (see Riessman, 1993: 59 for an example of this kind of coding). This analysis enables the reader to identify the specific functional purpose of clauses of text, which are normally not attended to when the text is read. Riessman (1993) does point out that this framework may not be appropriate for all narratives.

At this point, Riessman offers a number of techniques for analysing the text further. These include reduction of the text to a core narrative and analysis of the poetic structures in the story. The first approach is similar to techniques used in phenomenological psychology where one reconstructs the story that is told. The second technique is quite different and requires the analyst to attend to the (poetic) linguistic structures of talk (the speaking practices). The text is organised into lines, stanzas (series of lines of text on a single topic that have a parallel structure and sound as if they go together) and parts and then organised into metaphors. This finally results in a pictorial representation of these units of meaning. The key issue for Riessman (1993) is that there are many acceptable forms of narrative analysis and researchers must be (i) mindful of the constitutive nature of language and (ii) use a method of analysis that is appropriate to the text being analysed. Good advice indeed.

22.8 Strengths, limitations and debates

Narrative research builds on our common-sense understanding that the stories we tell of our lives are important in the making of selves and identities. This particularly modern (perhaps, postmodern) reflection has led to increasing interest in life story and narrative research and indeed increasing acceptance of the value of this approach in both research and also notably psychotherapeutic practice. As such, there is no doubt that this is a real growth area in research and will probably continue to be so for some time to come.

In UK psychology, interest in narrative has also grown greatly, at least in part as a result of researchers finding themselves frustrated by other qualitative methods. Discursive psychologists have, for instance, found 'the loss of a subject' problematic (see Chapter 21) whilst phenomenological psychologists have wanted an approach which takes the construction of meaning through language more seriously (see Chapter 19). Perhaps because of the different research traditions of people working in life story and narrative research, there is considerable disagreement over quite what narrative research is, or indeed, should be! This is a serious problem for those of us who would want this approach to grow, as students (and indeed academics) will find themselves frustrated by technical debates and arguments and an apparent lack of consensus about the methods to be employed.

The debates about the differences between work on narrative content and practice has echoes of debates between discourse analysts and other qualitative researchers (see, for instance, Potter & Hepburn, 2005). The desire to privilege one method over another can sometimes appear to have the feel of religious zealotry, rather than reasoned academic debate. And the danger of narrative research being bogged down in such debates is perhaps its biggest weakness. There is a tendency for 'small story' researchers to argue that all narrative research needs to engage with the micro-level features of storytelling (often using techniques for discourse and conversation analysis), with narrative practice itself (see, for instance, Bamberg, 2006). For a defence see Freeman (2006), who makes a convincing case for the value of both big and small story research in narrative research.

These arguments undoubtedly reflect the personal as well as professional interests of the researchers involved and readers would be advised to reflect on this when examining such debates. There is no simple truth here, or indeed anywhere else in academic argument, but rather a series of positions in academic debate, positions which should certainly be taken seriously but not simply supported or rejected without thinking through the implications for the research process and findings as a whole. What is most important is that we produce findings that make a difference, and technical debates can and do sometimes distract us from the most important issues in psychology. This has and will undoubtedly continue to happen with narrative approaches, phenomenology, grounded theory and discourse analysis alike. It is difficult to avoid being drawn into an argument when someone launches an attack and, as long as we take care not *only* to engage in argument, then perhaps this is healthy for our discipline: certainly better than simple stalemate. These debates are present in and between pretty much every theory and method (qualitative *and* quantitative) in psychology and there is little doubt that they will continue.

Further reading

Langdridge, D. (2007). *Phenomenological Psychology: Theory, Research and Method*. Harlow: Pearson Education.

> Whilst this book is clearly concerned principally with phenomenology (Chapter 19), it also discusses the turn to narrative in phenomenology and introduces an approach to narrative analysis which draws on elements from both the phenomenological and discursive perspectives.

McAdams, D. (1993). *The Stories We Live by: Personal Myths and the Making of the Self*. New York: The Guilford Press.

> An important and detailed examination of life story research and the importance of storytelling for understanding selves and identities.

Plummer, K. (2001). *Documents of Life 2: An Invitation to a Critical Humanism*. London: Sage.

> A superb book on the life story method by one of the leading sociologists in the field. This book is both comprehensive and eminently readable.

Riessman, C. K. (1993). *Narrative Analysis*. Sage Qualitative Research Methods Series 30. London: Sage.

> An excellent concise summary of one particular approach to narrative analysis. The text discusses the history of narrative research and positions narrative research in relation to ethnography and the Chicago School. It also provides a good level of detail on the specific methods of narrative analysis that the author advocates.

23 The use of computers in qualitative research

- This chapter begins by discussing the growth in the use of computers in qualitative research.

- It then moves on to consider how computers might be used and the ways in which this impacts on qualitative research.

- The reader is then introduced to one of the most widely used packages for the qualitative analysis of data: NVivo.

- Finally, this chapter discusses some of the debates about the use of computers in the qualitative analysis of data.

INTRODUCTION

There has been a rapid growth in the use of computers in all kinds of social research. This growth has been invaluable for many reasons. How many of us could imagine life without a computer and software? PCs and Macintosh computers equipped with word processing, spreadsheet and database software packages are widely available and widely used by researchers in the social sciences. Furthermore, quantitative research involving complex statistical calculations is no longer the province of the mathematical expert with a supercomputer on hand. The widespread availability of statistics packages such as SPSS has transformed this important element of social research in the most dramatic way. It is possible to calculate even very complicated statistics with just a few clicks of a mouse button. In the past these statistics would have required considerable mathematical ability even if they were possible to calculate at all without the use of very complex computer equipment. Things are somewhat different when we consider the impact of computers on the qualitative analysis of data. It is only relatively recently that specialist software for the analysis of qualitative data has begun to be employed in this field.

Qualitative researchers have tended to use word processing software to produce neat transcripts but then manual photocopy, cut and paste techniques when engaged in data analysis itself. In recent years software has emerged that is specifically designed to help with this stage of analysis. **Qualitative Data Analysis**

460

(QDA) software, also called **Computer-aided Qualitative Data Analysis Software (CAQDAS)**, has been greeted with mixed feelings. Some researchers see QDA software as greatly helpful in removing some of the difficulties in analysing data and potentially valuable in improving the rigour of qualitative analyses, whereas others see this software as potentially damaging the practice of qualitative analysis itself with the imposition of a new hegemony. Whether these beliefs for and against the use of QDA software are warranted is the subject of considerable debate. However, the most important thing to remember about *all* QDA software is that, unlike statistics software like SPSS, it *will not* do the analysis for you. As Flick (2002: 251) states, 'QDA software is more like a wordprocessor, which does not write the text but makes it somewhat easier to write a text.' QDA software simply assists in the mechanical processes involved in qualitative data analysis, thereby making life easier (once you have mastered the use of the software in the first place).

There are numerous software packages available for QDA. In fact, the situation is very similar to that in the early days of statistics software, before a very few packages (such as SPSS and SAS) became dominant and effectively the 'industry standard'. Different packages have advantages and disadvantages and are more or less appropriate depending on the type of analysis you wish to conduct. We will mention a few packages in this chapter (and introduce one in more detail) but you are advised to consult the suggestions for further reading if you want more thorough overviews of the range of packages available. The package that we intend to introduce in more detail here is **NVivo**. This is the most recent incarnation of a line of QDA software that started over fifteen years ago with NUD•IST. NVivo is one of the most popular software packages for qualitative analysis and continues to be developed and marketed by QSR. We will introduce some of the basics of NVivo here because 'NVivo is better at supporting the kind of research that most social scientists are involved in. It is not so much that different techniques are used but rather the differences in scale and situation' (Gibbs, 2002: xxiii). Although we will introduce some of the basics of NVivo in this chapter in order to give you a feel for what this software can do, there is not space in one short chapter for a thorough introduction that will enable you to carry out analyses using this software. However, suggestions for further reading will be given at the end of the chapter that will provide the necessary information should you wish to use NVivo in the analysis of your qualitative data. The manufacturers, QSR, themselves provide extensive guidance on the use of the software through guides and tutorials.

23.1   Use of computers in qualitative research

As we stated above, most specialist computer software used in qualitative research has been developed for the analysis of data. There are, however, a number of other processes for which computers and software may be used. Flick (2002) identifies 14 possible processes that may involve the use of computers: making field notes, transcribing, editing, coding, storage and retrieval of data, search and retrieval of data, connecting data segments to other segments (linking), memo writing, content analysis, displaying data, verification of conclusions, theory building, producing graphical representations of data and writing reports. Most of these activities can, of course, be carried out using standard word processing software. However, a certain number of these processes (such as coding, search and retrieval of data segments, displaying data/producing graphical representations and theory building) are laborious, if possible at all, with standard word processing software. QDA software has been developed to fulfil these more specialised functions more effectively and more efficiently.

Many researchers will no doubt continue to use their tried and trusted methods of qualitative analysis, using manual techniques of photocopying, highlighting, cutting and pasting, and wonder what all the fuss is about. After all, the software does not do that much – the researcher still does the analysis. So, why is there so much interest in these new developments? Well, we have no doubt that at least some of the interest is the general interest that people have in new technology. We are as guilty of being fascinated by new gadgets and gizmos as the next person. A new software package will therefore be intrinsically interesting to a number of people who simply like new technology. However, there are more significant reasons for the growing interest in using computers in qualitative analysis. The first and most significant gain with QDA software is speed (Seale, 2000). Managing one's data manually (from coding to searching and retrieving) is time consuming and QDA software can help speed this process up. This benefit is not one that will be immediately obvious, however, for it takes time to learn to use a new software package. Efficiency benefits will clearly be more important for larger and more complex projects rather than very small-scale research. Indeed, if you only intend to carry out the odd small-scale qualitative research project it is probably a false economy to buy and learn to use a piece of QDA software. The second gain thought to come from the use of QDA software is an increase in the rigour or quality of qualitative research (Seale, 2000). QDA software enables (and may impose) greater consistency in analytic procedures and also greater transparency in the analytic process itself (which may be important when working in teams). Finally, QDA software should make the management of qualitative data easier. Manual analyses require considerable thought about data management strategies (with everyone reinventing the wheel). QDA software provides a *regular* data management framework, which should make the process of data management easier and more consistent.

23.2 Qualitative analysis software

There are many different software packages available for QDA. Different programs serve different purposes and have been categorised in a number of types (Seale, 2000; Flick, 2002), including:

■ word processors (enabling a researcher to write, edit and search texts to a limited degree);

■ text retrieval programs (enabling a researcher to search, summarise and list texts and segments thereof);

■ code-and-retrieve programs (enabling a researcher to apply codes to segments of text and retrieve and/or list segments where codes were applied);

- code-based theory building (as above but also including features that support theory building – such as allowing relations to be described between codes along with subcategories, etc.).

Word processing software will be sufficient for many small-scale projects. However, text retrieval and coding software, once mastered, will enable greater speed and efficiency in QDA. Which package you should pick will depend on a number of factors (from Flick, 2002), including the following:

- How much knowledge do you have of computers and software?
- What type of study is being conducted?
  - Data source (one or many)?
  - Type of data (case or comparative study, structured or open data)?
  - Text or other visual data?
  - How big is the data set?
  - How big is the research project?
- What kind of analysis is planned?
  - Exploratory on confirmatory?
  - Simple or multiple-layered coding?
  - Fixed coding or evolving categories?
  - Very fine grained or more general?
- How much time do you have (to learn the software and do the analysis)?
- What can you afford?

All of these questions will have an influence on the appropriate choice of software. Further suggestions for readings which detail the merits and demerits ofrsoftware packages on the market are given in the Further reading section. It is unlikely, at least in the short term, that we will have one package that meets the very different needs of qualitative researchers. Different qualitative researchers engage in very different forms of analysis and therefore place different demands on the software. We think it will be some time yet before QDA software is dominated by one or two packages, as is the case in social science statistics software. However, some early market leaders are emerging and NVivo is one of them, on which we provide more detail below.

23.3   Introducing NVivo

NVivo is now in version 8.0 and represents one of the most well-developed QDA software packages around. However, version 2.0 of NVivo has sold widely and is still frequently used so we will provide some information about this version as well as the latest version here. The manufacturers continue to support both versions. NVivo 2.0 is only available for PCs and requires a minimum of a Pentium

100 MHz (400 MHz recommended) with 32 Mb of RAM (128 Mb recommended) and 40 Mb of hard disk space running Windows Me, 2000 or XP. If you are a Macintosh user then the only option is to run PC emulator software or use version 4 of NUD•IST (now called N4 Classic by QSR, the software developers). NVivo 8.0 also runs only on PCs and is much more demanding on hardware, requiring as a minimum a 1.2GHz Pentium processor or compatible, with 512 Mb of RAM, 1024 by 768 screen resolution, Microsoft Windows 2000 (Professional Service Pack 4) and 1 Gb of hard disk space.

In this chapter we are going to give you just a flavour of both versions 2.0 and 8.0 of NVivo so you can understand what this software does and therefore understand what QDA software does more generally. This is not a comprehensive introduction to the software, as that would require much more space than is available here and, to be honest, would be somewhat of a waste given the excellent help and tutorials already available for the software through the manufacturer's website. We begin with version 2.0, but some of the information is also applicable for the latest version (all of the functions in v. 2.0 are available in v. 8.0 even if the process for using them is slightly different). Some of the obvious differences between the two versions will then be pointed out, but if you want a more thorough introduction there are several options. The book by Graham Gibbs (2002) provides a very comprehensive overview of version 2.0 of the package and is a 'must buy' if you are really serious about using it. Further information and very good online tutorials for both versions can also be downloaded from the QSR website for free (**www.qsrinternational.com**) with excellent resources available for version 8.0. Upgrades to existing software and NVivo 8.0 can also be purchased directly through the site.

23.4   Getting started with NVivo 2.0

Starting a project

NVivo enables researchers to do two things. It helps with the storage and manipulation of text-based data and it enables a researcher to code their data (although it is worth knowing that codes are called **nodes** in NVivo). NVivo will also enable a researcher to search their data, link segments together and create models (including hierarchical tree diagrams of node structures). Finally, NVivo will assist in the preparation of results. NVivo keeps everything together in a **project**. Therefore, the first stage in using NVivo is to create a new project. The program is started like any other in Windows by double-clicking the icon or selecting the program from the **Start:Programs** menu at the bottom of the screen. The first thing you will see when starting NVivo is the **Launch Pad** (see Fig. 23.1).

There are four options available within the launch pad: you can create a new project, open an existing project, work through a tutorial or exit NVivo. If you click on **Create a Project** the New Project Wizard will open. Choose the **Typical** option (and not custom) and click **Next**. This will take you to another window

Figure 23.1 The Launch Pad

where you can give your project a name and a description. Once you have done this you should click **Next** again. This will produce yet another window where you can click **Finish** if everything looks okay (with your title, description, etc.). This opens the **Project Pad** window (see Fig. 23.2).

Figure 23.2 The Project Pad

Importing a file

You are now starting to use the program properly. This window enables you to create, browse, edit or explore your document(s) if you click on **Documents** or **Nodes**. You can type in text or import it into NVivo – it must be in a rich text format (.rtf), which you can do when you save a document in almost any word processing software. If you click on **Create a Document** then you can import a file or type data in directly. Most people will transcribe interviews directly into their normal word processor and therefore import these documents (in .rtf format, remember) into NVivo when it comes to carrying out their analysis. If you wish to import data you should click on this setting in the window that comes up when you clicked on **Create a Document** and then click **Next**. This will enable you to select a file on your computer. You will then be given some

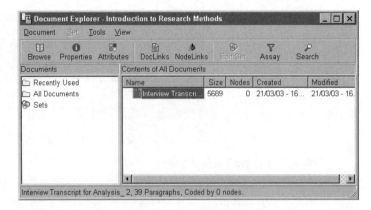

Figure 23.3 Document Explorer

naming options and you then click on **Finish**. You should see the rich text format document you selected being imported into NVivo. If you wish to take a look at your data you should click on **Explore Documents**. This will open the **Document Explorer** window (see Fig. 23.3).

Then click on the file you wish to open (it will be highlighted), and click on the **Browse** button over to the left near the top of this window. You should see the document you imported (see Fig. 23.4).

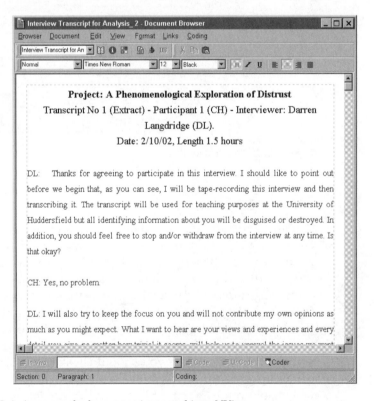

Figure 23.4 An example document imported into NVivo

Coding in NVivo

Now that we have shown you how to get a document into NVivo we can have a go at coding our data. While you are browsing your document you can begin coding *in vivo* (in the text as you read through it rather than using a predetermined coding framework). All you need do is drag your mouse over the text you think should be coded and then click on the **In-Vivo** button down at the bottom left of the screen. In the document browser window click **View** (on the menu bar at the top) and select **coding stripes** and you will see colour-coded tags over on the right-hand side of your screen every time you create a new code (remember, called a **node** in NVivo). When you have some text highlighted and you click on the **In-Vivo** button a new node will appear with a label of the text highlighted (you can change the label, if you wish, to whatever you want). With the coding stripes function selected you should see your new node appear on the right of the screen (see Fig. 23.5 for an example).

If you click on **Coder** just to the right of the **In-Vivo** function you will be able to see the details of your nodes (remember, think 'codes') in another window (see Fig. 23.6). The nodes produced here are **free nodes**. NVivo distinguishes between three types of node: **free nodes**, **tree nodes** and **case nodes**. **Free nodes** are the simplest and are shown in a list. **Tree nodes**, however, are

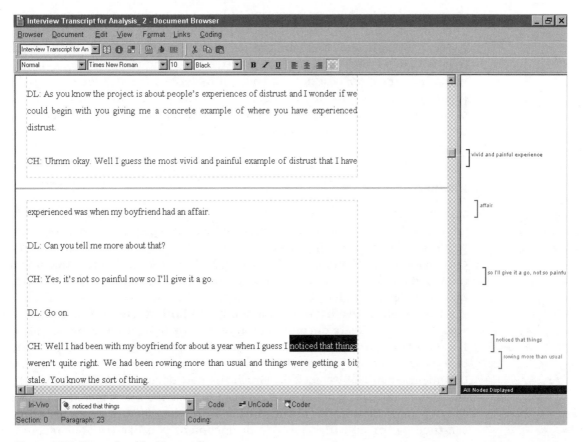

Figure 23.5 Example of In-Vivo coding

Figure 23.6 The Coder

more sophisticated and can be organised into a hierarchy (so you can code 1st, 2nd and 3rd order if you wish). **Case nodes** are used when you want to organise codes about particular cases (and can refer to all text for a case). It is important to note that free nodes can be made into tree nodes and vice versa. So, although we have a very simple list here we could, if we wished, arrange these free nodes into a hierarchical structure by making them tree nodes. All we need to do to change the nodes and create a structure is to drag and drop the free nodes onto the tree node symbol. We can then create a hierarchical structure.

Memos

Writing memos as you read and code your data is an important step in grounded theory and many other forms of thematic analysis. NVivo is designed to support this function. If you wish to write memos you need to create a memo document. From the **Project Pad** you will need to click on **Create a Document** (as we did above to import or create a new data file). This will give you the same options as before (see Fig. 23.7).

As you can see, we have the **Make a new blank document** radio button selected and the **Create document as a memo** box ticked (the top radio button **Locate and import readable external text file(s)** is selected when importing a data file from a word processor). If we click on **Next** we can then name this new document. Finally, if we click on **Finish** the new document will appear in the **Document Explorer** window where we can **Browse** the file. A memo or memos can now be written in this document file as the data file is coded. This memo can then be linked with any node or document you like (so your memo is directly linked with the appropriate node in the text you are analysing).

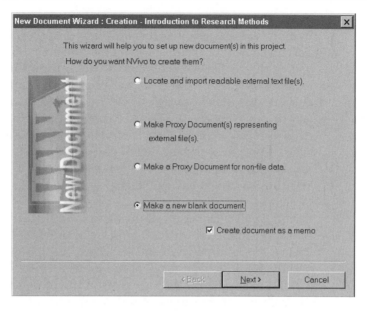

Figure 23.7 Options window produced when creating a document

Saving your project

It is important to save your data regularly (as you should do with any piece of software) and this is especially true when analysing data. NVivo itself does regular automatic saves of your project. You can, however, change the automatic default from the standard 15 minutes to something shorter (by selecting **Tools** and then **Options** from the **Project Pad** menu bar) and risk fewer losses should your computer crash. Never keep only one copy of your project – always back up your files. It is quite possible to experience disk failure and if your only saved project is stored on that disk you will lose all your work.

23.5   NVivo version 8.0

As you might expect, NVivo 8.0 can do all the same things as version 2.0 as well as a lot more. The main interface has been changed somewhat and it offers considerably more features and flexibility. It is, however, complex and requires some effort to master. NVivo 8.0 allows the user to work with pictures, photos, and audio and video files, which is a useful development for researchers interested in visual techniques and indeed for qualitative researchers more generally who wish to work directly with digital audio files when analysing data. This version also allows users to work with PDF files in addition to Microsoft Word, rich text and plain text files. And when Word documents are imported the formatting is preserved, which can save a considerable amount of time and effort. There are also very sophisticated organising and modelling features to further facilitate the analytic process.

Fig. 23.8 shows the **NVivo Workspace**. As you can see, this is rather different from the earlier version as it is now modelled on the Microsoft desktop format. There are a series of toolbars along the top as you might expect to find in Word and on the left is what is termed the **Navigation View** (see Fig. 23.9). The navigation view enables you to access all parts of a project, from **sources** (internal and external files from text to video), **nodes** (where you can code content as was shown with NVivo 2.0) and **models** (where you can construct static or dynamic visual representations of your data) to **classifications** (where you can classify cases – for instance, your participants – setting up attributes like age or sex, as well as relationships between cases, such as married to or brother of). Selecting a folder in navigation view (e.g. sources) shows the contents in what is termed the **list view** (see Fig. 23.10, which shows a list of interviews undertaken). If you click on one of the items in the list view (e.g. Anna), the interview that was conducted with her appears in the **detail view** pane below (see Fig. 23.11). As we hope you can see, whilst the command format and process is slightly different the essence of the software is the same. It is a way of organising and manipulating data to assist in the process of qualitative analysis. You can code in a huge variety of ways, construct interactive models, search sets of data, link data items together and much, much more.

Figure 23.8 NVivo Workspace

Figure 23.9 The Navigation View

Interviews							
Name	Nodes	References	Created On	Created By	Modified On	Modified By
Anna	98	190	16/02/2006 00:22	KMC	28/10/2007 10:07	MWO
Bernadette	111	161	16/02/2006 00:22	KMC	21/08/2007 08:31	KMC
Cross Cultural Solutions - Dh	31	74	22/08/2007 08:21	KMC	21/02/2008 05:22	SMB
Fredric	102	175	16/02/2006 00:22	KMC	21/08/2007 08:31	KMC
Grace	71	80	16/02/2006 00:22	KMC	21/08/2007 08:31	KMC
Ken	48	56	16/02/2006 00:22	KMC	21/08/2007 08:31	KMC
Mary	89	132	16/02/2006 00:22	KMC	21/08/2007 08:31	KMC
Nick	40	49	16/02/2006 00:22	KMC	21/08/2007 08:31	KMC
Peter	21	32	21/08/2007 08:35	KMC	27/10/2007 06:05	KMC
Phoebe	59	78	16/02/2006 00:22	KMC	21/08/2007 08:31	KMC
Sunil	44	54	16/02/2006 00:22	KMC	21/08/2007 08:31	KMC

Figure 23.10 The List View

Interviews

Name		Nodes	References	Created On	Created By	Modified On	Modified By
Anna		98	190	16/02/2006 00:22	KMC	28/10/2007 10:07	MWO
Bernadette		111	161	16/02/2006 00:22	KMC	21/08/2007 08:31	KMC
Cross Cultural Solutions - D		31	74	22/08/2007 08:21	KMC	21/02/2008 05:22	SMB
Fredric		102	175	16/02/2006 00:22	KMC	21/08/2007 08:31	KMC
Grace		71	80	16/02/2006 00:22	KMC	21/08/2007 08:31	KMC
Ken		48	56	16/02/2006 00:22	KMC	21/08/2007 08:31	KMC
Mary		89	132	16/02/2006 00:22	KMC	21/08/2007 08:31	KMC
Nick		40	49	16/02/2006 00:22	KMC	21/08/2007 08:31	KMC

Anna

Q.1 Current use of time

In an "ordinary" week, how do you currently spend your time?
(What takes most time, how much time spent on work, family, leisure etc...?)
I am still studying so an ordinary week for me is mainly spent studying and working part time. I send about 32 hours a week at work, 6 contact hours at university, and I spend my weekends and evenings studying. I also play Netball and attend a Yoga class of an evening once a week.

Q.1a Feelings about current time use?

(How do you feel about your time use now? Does it fit with your goals? Are there other things you'd like to fit in?)
Look, it's as effective as it can possibly be given my current commitments. I do wish I had more leisure time to spend with my friends and family and my partner. I also wish I had time to take dancing classes and learn a second language, but these things will need to wait until I have completed my course.

Q.2 Time use ten years on

Figure 23.11 The Detail View pane

There is no doubt that software like NVivo can be very valuable in a number of situations. Large-scale projects with multiple researchers will no doubt find the input of time required to learn how to use the software well worthwhile for the structure it will provide. Whether it is worth spending the time learning to use the software for an undergraduate project is another matter. If you have access to the software and particularly enjoy learning how to use new software packages then you might want to give it a go. However, in most circumstances it is probably best left until you undertake much bigger projects when it will truly repay the investment of time and effort.

Running a tutorial

That is about as far as we can go in the space available here but there is much more to learn about both versions of NVivo. The best strategy if you wish to learn more is to go to the QSR website and read the introductory guides and, if you have access to NVivo itself, run one or more of the tutorials available within NVivo itself (these are also available online for NVivo 8.0 and they are excellent). There are a variety of tutorial options, which will enable you to really get to grips with this particular software package. And there is no substitute for hands-on experience. You cannot break a program (although it may crash) so get stuck in there and give it a go!

23.6   Controversies and debates

Concerns have been raised about the impact of QDA software on qualitative research from the very start. Most of the dominant programs have developed broadly within a grounded theory perspective with a concentration on coding and retrieval of data. There has been much less software developed from other theoretical perspectives (such as phenomenology or discourse analysis). This means that people outside grounded theory either ignore QDA software or attempt to use it (with some difficulties) to assist their work (see, for instance, MacMillan, 2005). The dominance of some packages has also arguably influenced the very nature of qualitative analysis itself. NVivo, for instance, supports the development of hierarchical tree diagrams for codes and there has been a growth in the use of tree diagrams among these software users (Flick, 2002). Others fear that researchers may become increasingly distanced from their data and drawn into pseudo-scientific analyses. It is undoubtedly the case that the potential exists for QDA software to realise all of these fears, but this is not necessarily the case. QDA software will do what we want it to do. If it does not, then the option exists to create software that better fulfils our needs ourselves or stick with the old, tried and trusted methods of analysis.

Further reading

Flick, U. (2002). *An Introduction to Qualitative Research*, 2nd edn. London: Sage.

Contains a good chapter (Chapter 20) which debates the merits and demerits of using computers for QDA. It also provides some useful references for further reading.

Gibbs, G. R. (2002). *Qualitative Data Analysis: Explorations with NVivo*. Buckingham: Open University Press.

Excellent coverage of the NVivo version 2.0 QDA package. If you want to learn how to use this version of NVivo then this is the book for you. For information about NVivo 8.0 you are best advised to visit the QSR website (**www.qsrinternational.com**) where you will find excellent guidance on using the software and also other sources of information on how to use it.

24 Mixed methods

- The chapter considers the use of mixed methods in psychological research.

- It begins by defining mixed methods. They have existed for many years, but have only recently become popular in psychology.

- Four models of mixed methods are defined: preparation, generalisation, profoundisation and triangulation. These represent different ways to combine separate 'unblended' quantitative and qualitative methods.

- Triangulation is further divided into validity, complementarity and trigonometry models.

- Finally, an example of a fully 'blended' method is presented (Q-method).

INTRODUCTION

There has recently been increasing interest in the use of mixed methods. Psychologists have traditionally been poor at combining quantitative and qualitative methods: part of the difficulty partly lies in the way research methods are taught. Quantitative and qualitative techniques are often treated as quite separate approaches to research and indeed students are often encouraged to 'go narrow' early on in their careers, and join one of the two 'camps'. Whilst there are certainly arguments to support such specialisation, methods are not personality types. It is arguable that there should be no such thing as a 'qualitative researcher' or 'quantitative researcher', only a researcher who uses a method (or combination of methods) for a particular purpose.

The purpose of this chapter is to introduce you to a range of approaches to mixing methods. We hope to play a small part in changing the way in which psychology students think about methods. By the end of the chapter we want you to:

■ Understand that methods do not necessarily map onto paradigms (even if they often do). It is not simply the case that quantitative (always) = empiricism and qualitative (always) = constructivism.
■ Describe four models of mixed methods.
■ Differentiate four different types of triangulation.
■ Move beyond a simple 'quantitative vs. qualitative' debate towards a deeper understanding of the strengths and weaknesses of each, and the strengths and weaknesses of combining each.
■ Note that what you call mixed methods (e.g. blended, mixed, multi-method, parallel, synergistic, qualiquantological, quasitative) is a red herring. Energy should not be wasted in debates about terminology – the study design and its match to the research question are more important. We suggest that you use the general term 'mixed methods research' and then clearly describe (1) the research design and (2) how it is appropriate to answer the research question. In other words, what has been mixed? Why has it been mixed?
■ Replace the 'quantitative vs. qualitative' debate with a deeper understanding of how and when each, or both, is appropriate to a research question.
■ Recognise that methods can converge, complement or contradict each other (Kelle, 2001).
■ Critically evaluate claims in the literature that 'mixed methods' have been used.

Quantification and qualification are not 'methods' in their own right. There are many types of quantitative method and many types of qualitative method. They are better described as families of methods. As described below, these families are more related than is usually admitted.

24.1   Similarities between methods

Quantitative and qualitative methods are better understood as families of methods, which are more related than is often admitted. For example, consider these similarities:

■ Both attempt to describe or explain psychological processes which cannot always be observed directly.
■ Both attempt to measure or record their *effects*.
■ Both produce data which is a simplified form of raw experience.
  ■ Quantitative data are numerical, qualitative data are words or codes.
■ Both allow data to be transformed/analysed in more than one way.
  ■ Researchers often have to make a choice about how they will model their data. For example, they could use ANOVA or regression; themes or discourses.
■ Both are designed to be understood by particular audiences.
  ■ Some research communities will only accept findings presented in a certain way.

With this last point in mind, it is worth reflecting on the audience for research findings. If researchers tend to adopt quantitative or qualitative methods, and they tend to read journals that publish quantitative or qualitative methods, will their research have restricted impact? Arguably, all researchers should be well versed in a variety of methods from both 'families'. Increasingly, psychologists communicate their findings to other disciplines, and to the general public. Audiences are generally more receptive to results that they can understand. Ironically, there is evidence that a mixture of quantitative and qualitative methods (particularly data that can be easily visualised) is often more effective.

It is common for these similarities to be ignored. A somewhat artificial war has been created between the two families of techniques, each complaining with equal hostility about the 'arid, statistical, formalistic positivism' and 'warm, pink, and fluffy qualitative approaches' (Coxon, 2005). These attitudes construct a false dichotomy. Quantitative and qualitative methods differ, but this does not necessarily mean that they cannot be used together in sound ways such that the findings are valid. Important differences are listed in Table 24.1, adapted from Coxon's 'more sensitive and useful distinctions' (Coxon, 2005).

Table 24.1 Differences between quantitative and qualitative methods in different parts of the research process

	Quantitative	Qualitative
Epistemology	Positivism	Constructionism
	Empiricism	Interpretivism
Paradigms	Representational	Speech as data
Data	Numbers	Words, themes, codes
Data collection	Closed, systematised	Open, elicited
Data analysis	Statistics e.g. general linear models	Semantic, content or thematic analysis

However, many of the distinctions in the table could be debated and there are many psychologists who would disagree very strongly with such distinctions. For instance, there are important exceptions even to what many would consider a fundamental distinction: the experiment (associated with positivism) and critical social psychological approaches (often associated with the constructionist paradigm). Methods do not necessarily map onto paradigms neatly. For example, Pratto *et al.* (2007) used an *experimental* design to illustrate how racism can often go unnoticed (discussed later in Box 24.2). Working creatively with different methods and paradigms can be fruitful. It can also expose researchers to new ideas, who would not normally read about concepts studied in the 'enemy camp'.

It is, however, worth sounding a note of caution here. Whilst there are undoubtedly benefits that can come from mixing methods, there are also many potential problems and pitfalls. Very often students (and academics alike) decide to mix methods on the basis of a simple desire to know more about a topic ('surely by using both quant and qual we will find out more!') without thinking through how the use of mixed methods will actually facilitate greater knowledge of the topic in question. What often results is a piece of work which does not demonstrate sufficient knowledge of either method, with findings that consequently offer very little in the way of a contribution to knowledge and may be open to considerable criticism. There are many occasions when it is better to use one method well and concentrate on producing findings which add to knowledge in an important way rather than superficial insights from multiple methods that are of limited value. Furthermore, it is worth mentioning that it is unlikely that any one person will be sufficiently skilled in a very wide range of methods to conduct mixed method research well alone (the number of people who are expert at experimental design and stats *and* discourse analysis is likely to be very low indeed!). This means that in practice what often happens with good mixed method research is that teams of people with different expertise come together to work on a project. This is rarely possible for students and as such you need to be aware of your limitations and work within your knowledge base. Remember the old adage about the 'jack of all trades who is master of none' and you shouldn't go too far wrong.

24.2	Four models of (sequenced) mixed methods

Mixed methods have been described as 'a new star in the social science sky' (Mayring *et al.*, 2007: 1). In this section, we extend this analogy and describe the mixing of methods in terms of how methods are used to 'stargaze'. We describe how quantitative and qualitative methods can be used to 'gaze' at different kinds of research designs. There is no single guide that can provide you with a full understanding of mixed methods. Methods can be combined in many interesting ways. However, there are four broad ways in which quantitative and qualitative approaches can be used to answer a research question (Mayring, 2001):

■ the model of preparation (qualitative > quantitative > results);

■ the model of generalization (qualitative > results > quantitative);

■ the model of profoundisation (quantitative > results > qualitative);

■ the model of triangulation (qualitative+quantitative > results).

Diagrams illustrating how methods are sequenced in these four models are shown below. We will also show how triangulation can be further divided into three types: validity, complementarity and trigonometry (Kelle, 2001). In practice, mixed methods research can rarely be 'pigeonholed' in this way. When you begin to read about mixed methods, and look at results from mixed methods studies, you are likely to notice how varied the different types of designs can be. The four types of methods, and the subdivision of triangulation, should not imply that there aren't other more interesting and useful ways to combine methods.

These models refer to *mixed* methods, not to single methods than are inherently a *mixture* of both quantitative and qualitative approaches. These are **blended** methods and are considered later in this chapter.

The model of preparation (qualitative > quantitative > results)

The preparation model is perhaps the most commonly used form of mixed method. Qualitative data are used to generate preliminary data, perhaps from focus groups or interviews. These are then used to design a questionnaire or other quantitative measure, one which captures the important aspects of the qualitative data (see Fig. 24.1). Crucially, qualitative data are used here only as a preliminary step. The results emerge out of (and the study ends with) the quantitative phase, and qualitative data are not prioritised or valued in their own right (see Box 24.1). In our stargazing analogy, the preparation model is comparable to an astronomer who takes an initial look at the night sky, a scoping exercise, and records all of the stars that they see. The qualitative component corresponds to the initial scoping exercises (a look at the night sky). The quantitative component is that list of stars that were observed with the telescope.

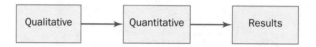

Figure 24.1 The model of preparation (adapted from Mayring, 2001)

Box 24.1 Study box

The preparation model: Designing a questionnaire

Qualitative component: Naithani, S., Gulliford, M. & Morgan, M. (2006). Patients' perceptions and experiences of continuity of care in diabetes. *Health Expectations*, **9** (2), 118-29. **Quantitative component:** Gulliford, M. C., Naithani, S. & Morgan, M. (2006). Measuring continuity of care in diabetes mellitus: An experience-based measure. *Annals of Family Medicine*, **4** (6), 548-55.

Continuity of care (receiving care from the same clinic or clinician throughout the course of an illness) is considered important in treatment of diabetes. However, an instrument to measure this aspect of care was not available. Researchers therefore decided to develop a new questionnaire. Qualitative interviews were used to identify four themes grounded in the experience of the patients themselves (longitudinal, flexible, relational, team/boundary continuity). The themes were drawn from patients' interviews, and wording agreed by the researchers. For example, to measure team continuity, patients mentioned that 'They share an agreed plan of treatment for my diabetes'. The questionnaire was then tested in telephone interviews at two time-points, 10 months apart, to demonstrate test–retest reliability (see Chapter 5).

Mixed methods can also be used to improve existing questionnaires, once they are developed. The Oxford Hip Score is an instrument designed to assess the quality of life in patients with hip problems (Wylde *et al.*, 2005). Monitoring routine assessment of hip scores in clinical settings, researchers found that many patients added 'unprompted, spontaneous annotations' to the questionnaires, which were treated as qualitative data. The annotations showed that patients found some items unclear,

▶

Box 24.1 *Continued*

wanted to explain pain more fully, found some items restrictive or irrelevant, and flagged that some questions had double meanings. Double meanings made some items difficult to answer, such as 'have you had any trouble getting in and out of a car or using public transport because of your hip?'. This data could be used to improve the questionnaire, providing an example of how the preparation model can be extended. Questionnaire development is ongoing, and although the quantitative component is emphasised, qualitative data can be used as preparation each time an instrument is revised.

The model of generalisation (qualitative > results > quantitative)

In the model of generalisation, priority is given to the qualitative component. Results emerge from the qualitative study and are supplemented by quantitative methods. The qualitative component is valued in its own right (see Fig. 24.2). The term 'generalisation' is used because the aim is typically to generalise the results of the qualitative phase to a larger sample size, or to test reliability by converting the qualitative data into quantitative data (e.g. by assigning numeric values to codes and themes). This should not be confused with the use of qualitative data to create questionnaires. In the preparation model, the qualitative data are merely pilot data and are not reported. In generalisation studies, the results emerge out of the qualitative phase. The emphasis is on interesting and important features of the data.

Applied to star gazing, the qualitative component would correspond to a constellation of stars. For example, a stargazer might spot that one constellation looks like a crab (cancer). The features of the constellations could be described, and meaning ascribed to their shapes (e.g. the signs of the Zodiac). The quantitative phase would add to this, perhaps by recording which stars comprised the constellation and what their features were. Like qualitative researchers, stargazers interested in constellations prioritise them more than the quantitative data. In the generalisation model, qualitative aspects are given higher value.

Focus groups are often used in market, media and political research. It is important to find out if new products, television shows and policies would be considered acceptable to a range of people. Any potential problems can be identified early on in the development process, by conducting focus groups. These can later be identified in larger surveys, perhaps general population samples. However, it in the views about acceptability which are most important. Quantitative research, in this context, is supplementary to the main focus of the investigation – the qualitative component. It might be useful to find out if a new policy would be considered unacceptable in the wider population, or if the

Figure 24.2 The model of generalisation (adapted from Mayring, 2001)

opinion was limited to one member of the focus group. The model here is generalisation. Can the qualitative results be generalised to a wider sample/population? Crucially, however, the qualitative results are the most important. They are used to identify *any* potential problems.

The model of profoundisation (quantitative > results > qualitative)

The model of profoundisation begins with quantitative methods, produces results, and then qualitative methods are used to enrich or tease out important aspects of the data (Fig. 24.3). This approach can be useful in exploring unusual aspects of data, outliers or contradictions, or to explain mechanisms and causal processes. It is increasingly popular to supplement randomised controlled trials (RCTs) of drug or psychological interventions in the health sciences, with qualitative interviews. Qualitative research is frequently used alongside randomised controlled trials, in order to gain a better understanding of why the trials sometimes fail. Trials often depend on achieving high levels of recruitment, informed consent and adherence to the treatment. For example, interviews were conducted with patients who had either enrolled in a trial or had refused to participate (Featherstone & Donovan, 2002). Because the quantitative component had already taken place (the randomised controlled trial), the qualitative component was used in a profoundisation model. The qualitative data enriched and expanded on aspects of the study that were not available from the quantitative component. The reasons why some patients refused to take part in the trial were revealed and the findings made more 'profound'. Although this is an interesting research topic in its own right, it is clear that the qualitative component was designed to service the larger study.

Quantitative data often contain anomalies that cannot be explained, such as outliers, or correlations that have the opposite sign to that expected. Having a large data set that covers all of the necessary variables does not mean that features of the data can all be understood. Furthermore, qualitative methods can often provide valuable insights into process that may sometimes be missing with the quantitative component. A certain percentage of the participants reported failing to use a condom when they have sex with their partner but 'why did they do this?' A qualitative component or follow-up study may be able to provide new and interesting insights into the process by which a decision was made such that the quantitative data are enriched further. Such qualitative elements may also lead to new avenues of research that may be tackled using either quantitative or qualitative methods (or of course both!). A stargazer might feel that they have had a good look at the night sky, and seen all of the stars and constellations that they wanted to see. However, they might have

Figure 24.3 The model of profoundisation (adapted from Mayring, 2001)

missed important features or wonder why a particular object moves so strangely in the night sky. A change of focus might be required in order to understand areas of empty space, unusual movement and stars which are brighter than expected. Are they black holes, or perhaps planets? Might there be another object influencing the phenomenon? Was a mistake made when the original map was created? These might be identified by focusing the telescope for a closer inspection (qualitative component) or using different instruments to look at things in a novel way, but are not immediately observable in the initial map (quantitative component). The change in focus supplements the quantitative component, but is not necessarily given higher priority.

The model of triangulation

The term 'triangulation' is perhaps the most frequently encountered term used to describe mixed methods. Here, it is used to describe a fourth model, in which both quantitative and qualitative methods are used, and the results emerge from both components (see Fig. 24.4). This is not the same as blended methods, which are discussed below. The two components are separate entities. The crucial difference between the triangulated model and the preparation, generalisation and profoundisation models is that the results emerge from the components simultaneously. There is no 'phase' in which either method is given priority. Equal value is placed on both components, chosen because they are needed to answer the research questions.

Maps of the night sky are a good analogy to method triangulation. They are meaningless unless both the stars and the constellations are identified. The map reader needs both phenomena to be identified. Ideally, the map would indicate where the constellation is, perhaps having picture drawings overlaid so that the map reader can see the shapes. A verbal description may also be required. Without both the map and the verbal description, the constellation would be difficult to identify. Incidentally, constellations can easily be identified by those who already know where to look – mirroring the role of the supervisor or experienced mixed methods researcher!

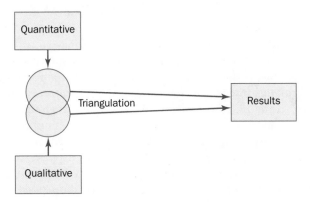

Figure 24.4 The model of triangulation (adapted from Mayring, 2001)

It is worth noting that triangulation does not only apply to methods. Triangulation is also used to describe other ways to combine wider features of research:

- *Triangulated data.* This is often used when describing sampling strategies. For example, a questionnaire designed to measure personality traits might be administered to people in several different countries. If the questionnaire is equally reliable in different countries, its cultural validity is enhanced. The data have been triangulated across more than one country to provide evidence of validity.

- *Triangulated researchers.* Researchers collaborate increasingly with people from disciplines outside their own. For example, a psychologist might work with a sociologist and a geographer to study the psychological impact of living in a socioeconomically deprived area. This is usually called interdisciplinary research. The research topic is triangulated across more than one discipline.

- *Triangulated theories.* Theories might be combined to provide a better tool for understanding complex psychological processes. For example, Pratto *et al.* (2007) combined norm theory with communication pragmatics to help explain a phenomenon called **implicit racism** (see Box 24.2).

- *Triangulated methods.* This is the form of triangulation we describe further below in this chapter. It refers to the combination of quantitative and qualitative methods in the research process.

What these four examples illustrate is that it is important to be clear about what you mean when you say that you have used 'triangulation'. What has been triangulated? Furthermore, be clear about what you think other researchers mean when they use this term. If it is not clear *what* has been triangulated, be suspicious! To complicate matters further, triangulation of methods comes in four forms.

Box 24.2	Study box

Triangulating theories to explain why race can go 'without saying'

Pratto, F., Korchmaros, J. D. and Hegarty, P. (2007). When race and gender go without saying. *Social Cognition*, **25** (2), 221-47.

Norm theory predicts that features of a social category (e.g. race or gender) become salient when the member of that category contrasts with the normative features of that category. For example, in the 1993 Miss Michigan contest, a contestant was described as 'the second Black to win the title...The first runner up was Erin Nance, 20, of Calhoun, GA'. Why do you think Nance's ethnicity is not mentioned? According to norm theory, this is because the normative features of the previous winners 'go without saying' (that is, she was white, within a population where being white was the norm). Features which are more typical of a social group are taken for granted.

Communication pragmatics provide an additional theoretical tool for understanding why this happens. Grice, a philosopher, argued that conversational maxims (rules) have evolved to facilitate speakers in establishing shared under-

Box 24.2 *Continued*

standing when in conversation. We are encouraged to say what we believe to be true (maxim of truth), say no more than is necessary (maxim of quantity), stick to the topic (maxim of relevance), and be clear (maxim of clarity). These maxims have been adopted in a theory called 'communication pragmatics'. When stereotypical features of categories are accepted as normative, there is no need to articulate them in conversations. Pratto *et al.* (2007) combined norm theory with communication pragmatics to design an experiment. For example, five fashion models were selected, one black woman and four white women. The hypothesis predicted that participants would tend to describe the black model as 'black woman' and the white models simply as 'women'.

Norm theory suggests that only atypical features of a category are salient. Communication pragmatics suggest that participants would be reluctant to provide more information than they thought was necessary, since most models in the group were white. Triangulating these two theories helped to provide an explanation of why features of people who are not minorities (in the above example, white contestants) 'go without saying' in many situations. Understanding these processes may help to understand how implicit racism and sexism occur in social interactions. There is privilege, the authors argue, in belonging to a group that is typically not 'marked' (as different) in a piece of conversation.

24.3   Four models of triangulated methods

Broadly speaking, there are four models of triangulation (see Fig. 24.5), adapted from Keele (2001).

Traditional model

Here, both methods (areas A and B) are required to obtain the relevant results (area C). This model is the prime reason for using mixed methods. Without the mix, it is not possible to gain any understanding of area C.

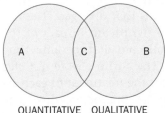

QUANTITATIVE   QUALITATIVE

Figure 24.5 A framework for thinking about models of triangulation (Keele, 2001).

Complementarity model

In this model, the two methods are used to supplement each other (area A + B + C). The aim of this model is to enhance complexity, by providing a larger picture than is available from each component alone. Here, the results are greater than the sum of the separate parts. We might term this an interactive or 'value-added' design. In this model, fully convergent findings are not desirable – we want more than that. The purpose is to extend understanding. It is therefore a move beyond validation. In fact, if exactly the same results emerged from each component there would be little point in designing a complementarity study. The results would suggest that either one of the methods was valid to use on its own.

Validity model

The two methods are used as a test of convergent validity for a construct. Area C is evidence of convergent validity (see Chapter 5). Here, the purpose of triangulation is one of mutual validity or to provide or enhance reliability. For example, both interviews and questionnaires are used to make a diagnosis of personality disorder. It is necessary to have both clinical information and structured instruments in order to obtain a complete understanding. Inter-rater reliability of qualitative data is a similar kind of exercise. The themes and codes generated by each rater are quantitative, but they are both working on the same qualitative data. The methods are combined to enhance validity, and the desired outcome is to get similar ratings from each researcher.

Divergent model

It is important to acknowledge that quantitative and qualitative methods may not agree. This model allows for situations where the two methods are contradictory (area A might not agree with area B). How would you handle triangulated research that produced divergent, rather than convergent, lines of evidence? This was the problem faced by Moffatt *et al.* (2006) who used a randomised controlled trial design at the same time as a qualitative, longitudinal study. The research question was, 'Does giving elderly patients advice on welfare rights improve their health?' The data were compared separately, producing a set of results that diverged. The randomised controlled trial (126 participants) found no significant impact of the intervention on outcomes. A qualitative study, collected at the same time (25 participants), found 'wide-ranging' impacts. The authors were not clear what this meant. They explored several options for the treatment of each component, which can be adapted if your triangulated design produces divergent results:

1 Treat as fundamentally different (might we need to accept that the two sets of results simply do not agree with each other?)

2 Explore the rigour of each component (was there a problem with one of them?)

3 Test its comparability (are they looking at the same phenomenon?)

4 Collect more data (more data might lead to convergence)

5 Re-evaluate the study design (was there some inherent incompatibility that led to the divergent findings?)

6 Compare the outcomes of the two components (if the study was concerned with a particular outcome measure, *how* was this different? Where did the difference occur – in the data, the coding of the data, or something else?)

You can use this 'six step' model if you are faced with divergent findings, in a triangulation design. (Go to Box 24.3 and Box 24.4.)

Box 24.3

Activity box   **Finding mixed methods in the literature**

The aim of this activity is to highlight how varied the reporting of mixed methods results is in the psychological literature.

1 Find three research studies in journal articles that claim to have used mixed methods [and triangulation] in their results. Pick a research topic that interests you. Use the literature searching guidelines (Chapter 1) to design an appropriate search strategy.

2 What was the research question?

3 What are the methods that have been mixed?

4 Which aspects of the data were quantitative?

5 Which aspects of the data were qualitative?

6 Why were mixed methods necessary to answer the research question?

7 Have the authors really addressed one question, or two or more questions?

8 Of the four types of mixed methods, which is the best description of the type of study?

9 Have the authors triangulated the method?

10 If so, what type of triangulation has been used? Could this have been described more clearly?

24.4   Blended or 'hybrid' methods

Some research designs are inherently mixed, and would not fit neatly into any of the models described above. We will call these **blended** methods. **Q-method** is an excellent example of a blended method. Themes, meanings, numbers and statistics cut across the method throughout its implementation. Q method is an old technique but one which is getting renewed interest and is growing in popularity. The second is multidimensional scaling, a powerful statistical technique for combining qualitative and quantitative data, representing them visually, and bringing in interesting extensions such as cluster analysis to further make sense of the data. Q method is chosen here for four reasons:

1 It is a versatile, robust and interesting method.
2 It is suitable for small-scale research projects (depending on the research question and time available).
3 It is not traditionally taught in psychology, but it should be. It can provide data that researchers would struggle to find in interviews or questionnaires, even when using both methods.

4 The hegemony of software developers is loosening (Coxon, 2005) and it is becoming easier to work with blended methods such as Q because software is becoming more flexible. Developers are increasingly responding to researchers' demands to include mixed method capabilities.

24.5   Q method

Billed as the 'systematic study of subjectivity' (van Excel & de Graaf, 2005: 1), **Q method** (also called Q sorting) is growing in popularity among social researchers. It is ideally suited to investigating topics that are inherently subjective and difficult to define (see Box 24.5). Psychologists frequently study exactly these kinds of phenomena: concepts which are difficult to grapple with, define, or one which is contested and/or has different meaning for different people (Watts & Stenner, 2005). Q method is a hybrid method, containing elements of interviewing, thematic analysis, correlations, factor analysis and multidimensional scaling. It is just as easy to do a bad Q study as it is to design a bad questionnaire or conduct a poor interview. Q method is best illustrated by demonstration, so we encourage you to try out a Q study online (see Box 24.6).

The Q-set

A great deal of time is spent developing a suitable Q-set. The Q-set contains a set of cards, each containing a statement about the topic. The statements follow the same guidelines as questionnaire items (see Chapter 5). For example, it is particularly important to write Q statements that do not contain more than one meaning (double-barrelled items: e.g. 'Whale culling and fox hunting should be banned') and double negatives (e.g. 'I would rather not stop walking to work'). You may want to conduct a pilot study, starting with a large number of cards and reducing this down to between 40 to 50 statements, but fewer or more statements are also used and considered acceptable (van Excel & de Graaf, 2005). Many researchers use 49 statements, because these can easily be arranged into a forced normal distribution (see Fig. 24.6).

Bryant, L. D., Green, J. M. & Hewison, J. (2006). Understandings of Down's syndrome: A Q methodological investigation. *Social Science & Medicine*, **63** (5), 1188-200.

How do parents' understandings of Down's syndrome influence their decision to undergo prenatal testing? This research question, developed by Bryant *et al.* (2006), is ideally suited to a blended mixed method technique. It enables the researchers to (1) take into account individual subjective ideas about Down's syndrome and (2) consider systematic or shared themes that appear repeatedly in the sample. Q method is an appropriate technique for both these aims: they require the systematic analysis of subjectivity. The Q-set was developed from many different sources, so that a full range of viewpoints can be sampled:

- Focus groups of nurses
- Interviews with clinicians
- Interviews with those who have lived experience of Down's syndrome

- Qualitative data from a previous study
- Publications on prenatal testing
- Magazines, newspapers and websites
- Information leaflets provided during screening.

The aim of Q is 'to study diversity of understanding rather than prevalence of understanding' (Bryant *et al.*, p. 1190). This is why most of the emphasis in Q method is placed at the design stage. We don't want to know what viewpoints exist in the general population: we want to capture the large range of different viewpoints. You should consult a similarly wide range of sources, appropriate to your topic, when designing your Q-set.

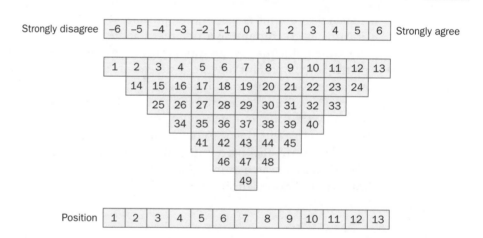

Figure 24.6 Q-grid for 49 Q statements, showing layout and numerical values assigned to each position

The P-set

The participants are a clearly defined sample (the P-set) who have been chosen because they represent a specific group, subculture or other important characteristic. Usually, the P-set have lived experience of the topic under investigation.

Their viewpoint, or perspective, on the topic is the qualitative element of the method. There are no guidelines on how to choose a sample size, but if you have a full range of views in your P-set, then it has been argued that 20 is sufficient to detect more than one viewpoint in the factor analysis. Usually, the P-set contains fewer people than the number of cards in the Q-set (van Excel & de Graaf, 2005).

The Q-grid

The Q-grid is a forced normal distribution (see Fig. 24.6). The grid is labelled 'disagree' at one end, and 'agree' at the other end. There are 49 cards, each of which is assigned by the participant into a box on the grid. Each position is given a numerical value according to its position (ranging from 1 to 13). The position is entered into SPSS as data, and this is then factor analysed. In the data file, there would be 49 rows (representing statements) and one column per person. It is the people who are factor analysed, not the variables. Other software programs for Q method are available, which have different approaches to the data.

Factor analysis

Factor analysis is a technique normally applied to variables for the purposes of data reduction. Psychologists use factor analysis to design questionnaires and psychological tests. They identify questionnaire items that 'hang together' into similar constructs, called factors. Some items 'load' (correlate) more highly with factors than others, and are therefore considered particularly good indicators of the underlying construct. For example, 'I am the life of the party' might load more highly onto a construct called Extraversion than an item 'I like parties' (you might like parties because you enjoy free food and drink, not because you are extraverted!). In Q-method, factor analysis is performed in a different way.

The participants (the R-set) are factor analysed, not the variables (the Q-set). This results in factors that define clusters of people. The clusters are prototypical points of view. For example, there might be three viewpoints in a Q-set about animal hunting – one in favour, one in favour for eating but not hunting for other reasons, and one against. Each person in the study will belong more strongly to one of these groups – they will 'load' or correlate highly with one, and less with the other two. The quantitative component of this mixed method is the correlations. Factor analysis can be conducted in SPSS, though the technicalities of the technique are beyond the scope of this text. If you want to learn more about factor analysis, see Field (2005, Chapter 15).

The assumption underlying this approach is that there are shared viewpoints – if everyone had a different viewpoint there would be no point in factor analysing the data because there would be no correlations between the rankings people provide for the statements (van Excel & de Graaf, 2005). The technique is popular as a critical method because it does not claim to divide people's psychological frameworks or social processes into different parts. Instead, it shows how people themselves connect and relate themes, according to their own subjective point of view (Watts & Stenner, 2005). However, the Q-set has been predefined by the researcher! It is therefore crucial to spend a lot of time developing a Q-set that includes a full range of concepts, views, opinions and ambiguities. The term for this is the 'opinion domain'. The aim, some argue, is not to be representative of the population, but to be '"broadly representative" of the relevant opinion domain' (Watts & Stenner, 2005). These might come from earlier qualitative interviews (your own or other published research), focus groups, media reports, theories, quantitative analyses, etc. It is not possible to embrace individuals' viewpoints if their defining views are not included in the Q-set. Once again, we see clear similarity with quantitative psychological measurement techniques.

Box 24.6

Activity box   **E-research for Q-method: Flash Q**

This exercise introduces you to the Flash Q, which you may want to consider using in your own research. If you decide to run a Flash Q study online, please ensure you have read the e-research chapter (Chapter 7) and understand the strengths, weaknesses and ethical issues for conducting research online.

Flash Q is ideally suited to small-scale projects and you may want to consider using it for your own Q study. It is free. Participants can be recruited online, which means that you may lose control over the research environment. Other issues raised by e-research are discussed in Chapter 7. You can also use Flash Q while you are present (e.g. a laptop connected to the Internet, Outlook required). You can source the software at this location: www.hackert.biz/flashq

The authors of Flash Q developed the tool to reduce the workload for the researcher, and for the participants themselves. It is extremely easy to use. The demonstration allows you to work through an example, before you start a design of your own.

1   Visit www.hackert.biz/flashq/demo/. Click on **Start demo**, **Continue**. Enter any code in the **User code** box, then click **Continue**.

2   The introduction begins, 'This study is about travel behaviour. We are interested in your attitude towards car and public transport as travel alternatives for middle-distance trips'. Click on **Continue**.

3   You are asked to divide the statements into three 'piles'. This would normally be done with cards on a table, with the researcher present, sorting into three piles. Online, participants must click and drag the cards on their own. Try sorting the 14 cards for yourself using the demo (see Fig. 24.7):

■ Statements you agree with

■ Statements you disagree with

■ The rest (neutral)

▶

Box 24.6 *Continued*

Figure 24.7 Flash Q: the initial sort

The second stage is to take the statements you most agree with, disagree with or feel neutral about. These are placed on the Q-grid, which has a normal distribution (see Fig. 24.8). The shape of the Q-grid is the same in every Q-sort study, but the number of cards may change and this determines the size of the grid. The three piles of cards are sorted onto this grid, providing participants with a way to think further about how they want to organise their viewpoints. Next, there is a chance to look over the grid and make changes if necessary. The time taken to do this may vary between participants. Finally, participants are asked to write about why they disagreed with, felt neutral about, or agreed with six of the statements.

The disadvantages of Flash Q mirror those of other Internet-mediated research (Chapter 7). What is the population? Unless you have clearly defined your sampling frame, how can the results represent the population you are interested in, or generalise to other members of that population? This weakness is not insurmountable. The Internet contains several clearly defined and 'hard to reach' groups. You might identify, for example, a support group for people who have had gastric bypass surgery. Members of an online group that requires membership, and has membership criteria, are ideally suited to this kind of study. If you advertise the study within a clearly defined group, those taking part may represent other members of the group, except if those who choose to take part differ in some way (a problem that applies to all research methods that require consent). A second weakness of Flash Q is that when the three piles are sorted, participants have to use a scroll bar to see the complete list of cards in each pile. Unless they have read the instructions carefully, they may simply place the statements they can immediately see onto the grid without much thought. Third, participants may rush the Q sort and take far less time than they would if you were present. Statements may not be reflected upon. The quality of the information you obtain may be reduced.

Box 24.6 *Continued*

You may want to consider a questionnaire as more appropriate for Internet research. See Chapter 7 for more issues about loss of control for the researcher in e-research designs.

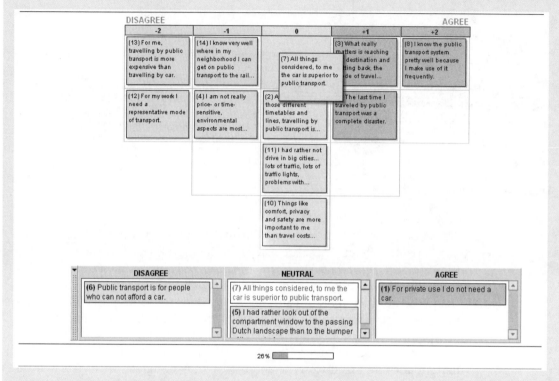

Figure 24.8 Flash Q: moving the cards into a forced normal distribution

Summary: Q method

- Q is first and foremost an exploratory technique. However, it may be useful to compare the results with another P-set.
- Most of the time spent preparing a Q study is in the writing of a good Q-set.
  - If you have limited time, try using an existing Q-set on another P-set.
  - Contact the authors of previous studies and ask if you can use their Q-set.
- Pilot your study before embarking on a full-scale version.
- Acknowledge the quantitative elements of the study. Do not ignore statistical issues involved in factor analysis – even if your reason for using Q method is to challenge empiricist epistemological thinking.

24.6	Other hybrid methods

Multidimensional scaling

Multidimensional scaling is a powerful (and complex) statistical technique that provides a 'map' of the variables in a data set and is another example of a blended method. Effectively, the product of the statistical analysis is a picture of the relationships between variables which can then be interpreted subjectively for meaning (or subject to further statistical analysis).The map is called the 'solution' because it is the map that best fits and represents the similarity or dissimilarity between each combination of variables. The closer the variables are in the map, the more similar they are. There is a direct relationship between correlations and the map. In fact, correlations are used to create the map. MDS is beyond the scope of this book. A key advantage of MDS is that it can be used with non-parametric data. If you have a set of rankings, for instance, it can use Spearman correlations to produce a map in which the 'distance' between the variables can still be represented without breaking any assumptions about having interval or ratio data, as is required for many statistical tests. The aim is to find a map that can be viewed in as few dimensions as possible, preferably two or three at a maximum. This method would require further reading if you decide to use it.

Summary: multidimensional scaling

- MDS can be used as an exploratory, descriptive tool.
- The solution is a 'map' of the similarities between variables.
- It encourages you not to rely on numbers when interpreting data.
- Visualisation is appealing because it conveys a lot of information at a glance.
- Clusters, similarities, differences, chains, and 'empty' regions can all be visually represented.
- More formal tests are available, but are not discussed here.
- Subjective interpretation alone is usually insufficient, particularly when the solution is not known in advance.

24.7	A final comment

In this chapter we have illustrated some of the benefits of mixed methods. It would not be responsible to claim that adopting them is easy, or would necessarily benefit you in your future career. There are clear benefits to 'going narrow' as researchers, which do have to be acknowledged. Working with familiar methods brings creature comforts.

- Expertise develops more deeply.
- Less new reading is required.
- Greater focus.
- Findings can be tailored to outlets more easily.
- It is easier to find the right supervision and support.
- It is clear which conferences you should attend.
- Single families of methods bring a sense of identity and social cohesion. Mixed methods can be lonely! Radical eclecticism may raise eyebrows.

Having said that, if you have even started to think about the range of possibilities for mixed methods in your future research, then this chapter has been successful. We want to emphasise that mixed methods are described in many different ways, and how they are described is ultimately not important. A great deal of energy is wasted by researchers who debate the name and type of mixed methodologies. Instead, focus on your research question, decide what, how (and if) you need to combine methods; then report the findings according to the GRAMMS criteria (O'Cathain *et al.*, 2008). Arguably, it is more important to ensure that your research question matches the methods you chose, no matter what they are and what you call them. And remember – mixed methods should not be used to answer more than one question separately. A study answering question 1 with method 1, and question 2 with method 2, is really two separate (single method) studies and should be treated as such. A true mixed method design works towards a single goal, or the understanding of a single concept, but requires more than one type of tool to do the job.

Further reading

Creswell, J. (2002). *Research Design: Qualitative, Quantitative, and Mixed Methods Approaches*, 2nd edn. London: Sage.

> If you are designing a mixed methods study, this book covers the main issues which you need to consider.

Creswell, J.W. & Plano Clark, V.L. (2006). *Designing and Conducting Mixed Methods Research*. London: Sage.

> The fact that this book is written by two experts in the mixed methods field is reflected in its content. A detailed description of four mixed methods studies, from start to finish, is included. You will gain an insight into how complicated, but how valuable, mixed methods can be.

Greene, J.C. (2007). *Mixed Methods in Social Inquiry*. San Francisco: Jossey Bass.

> This book is aimed at social researchers in the broadest sense, but gives an excellent flavour for the variety of mixed strategies available.

Plano Clark, V.L. & Creswell, J.W. (Eds) (2008). *The Mixed Methods Reader*. London: Sage.

This is an edited volume containing contributions from leading experts in the fast-growing mixed methods field. It is not focused exclusively on psychology, but that reflects the nature of mixed methods – disciplines are often mixed too.

Mayring, P., Huber, G. L. & Gurtler, L. (Eds) (2007). *Mixed Methodology in Psychological Research*. Rotterdam: Sense Publishers.

This edited book has separate chapters written by psychologists, offering their views on the current developments in mixed methods in psychology. The level of detail is quite heavy, but the chapters are accessible and a useful accompaniment to any of the more general mixed methods books in this list.

Todd, Z., Brigitte, N., McKeown, S. & Clarke, D. D. (Eds) (2004). *Mixing Methods in Psychology*. Hove: Psychology Press.

Chapter 6 of this edited volume is an excellent introduction to Q method, as applied to emotions.

Van Excel, N.J.A. & de Graaf, G. (2005). *Q-methodology: A sneak preview*. Retrieved 29/07/08 from http://www.qmethodology.net/index.php?page=1

This document is available online. It is a nice introduction to Q method and explains some of its underlying principles.

Resources: Q method

- www.qmethod.org
- listserv.kent.edu/archives/q-method.html
- www.qmethodology.net
- www.hackert.biz/flashq

Part

4

Ethics and reporting findings

25 The ethics and politics of psychological research

26 Reporting and presenting findings

The ethics and politics of psychological research

- This chapter begins by explaining why ethics are so important in psychological research.

- It then covers the fundamentals of ethics in psychological research, drawing on the guidelines produced by the British Psychological Society (BPS).

- Finally, this chapter discusses wider political issues in research.

INTRODUCTION

Now this is a chapter you may think you can skip. No! Ethics are an absolutely vital element for conducting psychological research in such a way that it does not harm other people. You might think 'I wouldn't deliberately harm anyone' and we are sure that is quite true, but research can impact negatively on people that you might not have thought about. And this is the reason for working through this chapter *before* conducting any research of your own! If you need persuading about the need for ethics, read about the history of psychology and you will quickly become aware of some of the atrocities that psychologists have committed, all in the name of scientific advancement. In the past, there were very different attitudes towards psychological research and much less consideration of ethics. This situation led to some astonishing studies being conducted that we now consider highly unethical. Research was often conducted with little or no consideration of the impact on the 'subjects' taking part (they were not 'participants'). Research was often at any cost and many people were harmed as a consequence.

Probably the most fundamental ethical principle is that researchers should treat their participants with respect. It is the responsibility of the researcher to ensure that no harm comes to their participants and this is a responsibility that must be taken seriously. After all, none of us (we hope) want harm to come to people who, by volunteering to take part in our research, are doing us a real favour! One way of emphasising this changed attitude to ethics is the change in term used for people taking part in research. People who were interviewed or experimented on were previously 'subjects', and this was a good description of their role – they were 'subjected' to the procedure (whether it was an interview or an experiment). The British Psychological Society (BPS), the governing body for psychology in the United Kingdom, now insists that researchers use the term 'participants' instead. This is because we should no longer be 'subjecting' people to our research. They should be 'participating' in the research. While this may seem a trivial change, it is an important first step. Changing the term we use for people helping us in our research encourages us to think about them as fellow human beings and therefore treat them with the respect they deserve.

A particularly contentious aspect of psychological research is that concerned with experimenting on animals. We have personal views about this form of research which we will put aside in this chapter. There are clear ethical guidelines about animal research which must *legally* be adhered to. This will no doubt satisfy a number of people that everything is being done to minimise harm to animals within the context of the need for such work. Others will feel differently, believing that there is a fundamental problem with this kind of research which no ethical guidelines can solve. This is a complex debate and there is not space to do it justice here. We will present the ethical guidelines for animal experimentation for your information later in the chapter and then leave this issue for you to debate among yourselves.

25.1 Ethical fundamentals

The ethical principles that researchers subscribe to today did not emerge out of thin air. They are the result of a very long tradition of philosophical work on ethics and morality. This work has been concerned with many different issues but particularly with understanding how and why we distinguish between actions that are right and those that are wrong. It is therefore important to learn (very briefly) about some of this philosophical work to improve our understanding of ethics and why we adhere to the principles that we do today. If you are interested in ethics and philosophical thinking about ethics then there are some suggestions for further reading at the end of this chapter.

Key issues in philosophical ethics

By and large, moral/ethical philosophers treat morality and ethics interchangeably (Singer, 1993). Ethics are generally understood as a system of moral principles and not as a distinct enterprise. Therefore, ethical principles stem from moral positions we take about issues and not from some 'independent' ethical way of thinking about our actions and effects. It is important to recognise that acting in a moral (ethical) way does not mean acting in a *necessarily* conservative fashion. When people speak of 'falling moral standards' they are invoking a particular view of morality (often a conservative one) and not a generally agreed view of morality. It is entirely possible to conceive of something like casual sex as moral *or* immoral and therefore increasing casual sex in our society as either a 'fall in moral standards' *or* a 'rise in moral standards'. These debates are grist to the mill for practical ethical philosophers and should remind us all that ethical guidelines are *guidelines* that should not be blindly followed but important principles that require careful thought and consideration.

There are two distinct schools of thought in philosophical ethics: **consequentialism** and **deontology**.[1] According to **consequentialism**, the rightness or wrongness of any act depends upon its consequences. It therefore follows that one should act in such a way as to bring about the best state of affairs (of goodness, happiness, well-being, etc.). The exact nature of the best state of affairs is, of course, open to debate. **Utilitarianism**, a particular subtype of consequentialist ethics, emphasises the role of pleasure or happiness as a consequence of our actions (Raphael, 1981). However, there is no reason why we should not seek to maximise many other factors (such as liberty, equality of opportunity, etc.) instead. According to **deontology**, however, there are certain acts that are right or wrong in themselves and not *necessarily* in terms of their consequences (Gillon, 1986). This is essentially a moral theory whereby certain acts must or must not be done regardless (to some extent) of the consequences of their performance or non-performance. There are, however, two well-established problems for deontological ethics. The first concerns the difficulty of how we know which acts are right or wrong *in themselves*, and the second concerns the difficulty of distinguishing between acts and omissions. If you want to know more about the debates between these two positions you should consult some of the further reading suggested at the end of this chapter.

These two philosophical positions clearly have implications for what we consider to be ethical research. One obvious example concerns the arguments about animal experimentation. A consequentialist may argue that the ends justify the means. That is, the immediate consequence of animal experimentation may be some suffering to the animals concerned, but the later consequence is the possibility of saving human lives, which justifies the earlier consequences. This consequentialist argument in favour of animal experimentation (you could equally make a consequentialist argument against animal experimentation) is itself predicated on a contentious deontological argument that human life is more important than animal life (and the animal suffering is therefore warranted by possible increases in human well-being). If, however, one does not accept this deontological presupposition, the consequentialist argument advanced above becomes more problematic. Peter Singer (1993) directly engages with these practical philosophical arguments and should be read if you want to understand more about these important ethical debates.

---

[1] Actually there are more than just two schools of thought. We know of four significant schools of thought (*consequentialism, deontology, intuitionism* and *Kantianism*) and there are probably many others. However, consequentialism and deontology are two of the most widely discussed in philosophical ethics and the most important for psychological ethics.

25.2   Confidentiality and anonymity

Confidentiality and **anonymity** are two of the most important ethical considerations in social science research. The BPS guidelines (details of these are given in the Further reading section at the end of this chapter) clearly state that information obtained about a participant during an investigation is confidential unless otherwise agreed in advance (subject to the requirements of legislation). That is, the fall-back position is one of confidentiality. No information given to a researcher by a participant should be revealed to another person (other than members of the research team, supervisors, etc.) unless prior agreement has been given by the participant. It is still important that researchers inform participants of the confidential nature of the relationship, for they are unlikely to be well versed in the BPS guidelines! Some research (often using questionnaires) may enable participants to remain anonymous. If this is the case then this should also be communicated clearly before people agree to take part. If, however, any identifying information is collected then the participants are not anonymous and this should be made clear. If confidentiality and/or anonymity cannot be guaranteed then the participants must be warned of this in advance of agreeing to participate. Many people may choose not to take part in a study where their personal information is not treated in a confidential manner. Participants have the right to expect that information they provide will be treated confidentially and, very importantly, if published, will not be identifiable as theirs.

25.3   Deception

Deception used to be commonplace in psychological research. This has changed in recent years. The BPS guidelines state that the withholding of information is unacceptable if participants are typically likely to object or show discomfort once debriefed. Furthermore, they state that participants should never be deliberately misled without extremely strong scientific (and this includes qualitative research) or medical justification. The fact that the guidelines use the word 'discomfort' demonstrates how much things have changed. 'Discomfort' is a very mild response which most of us feel at one time or another in our lives. However, it is our duty as researchers to minimise such unease and therefore to refrain from deceiving our participants about the true nature of the study without considerable justification. A distinction is made between providing deliberately false information and withholding some of the details of the study. The latter is considered more acceptable and is often necessary in experimental research. The former, however, requires considerable justification and the possible effects on a participant need to be considered carefully.

If a study does involve deception then the investigator has a special responsibility to: (i) ensure that participants are provided with sufficient information at the earliest stage (**debriefing**) and (ii) consult appropriately upon the way that the deception will be received. Debriefing is a vital part of any study involving deception. Investigators should normally provide participants with any necessary information to complete their understanding of the nature of the research as soon as possible after the deception occurred. This should be before the participants leave the research setting. So, if, for instance, you are carrying out an experiment where the true nature of the study needs to be hidden, you must make sure that all participants are informed about the real purpose of the study before they leave the laboratory. This debriefing should also be an *active intervention*. It is not enough to hand out a leaflet and let people wander off. You must make sure they have read the leaflet and are able to ask any questions they might wish about the true nature of the study. However, debriefing does not provide a justification for unethical aspects of an investigation – any deception must be justified on strong scientific or medical grounds.

Finally, if during an investigation you become aware of psychological or physical problems then the BPS guidelines state that you have a responsibility to inform the participant if you believe that by not doing so the participant's future may be endangered. We urge caution, however. If you discover some psychological or medical problem then it is very important that you consult with experienced colleagues/supervisors. How information of this kind is communicated is important and such matters must be handled with care and sensitivity. Care must also be taken if participants seek professional advice during an investigation. If the question falls outside your realm of *professional expertise* then you should *not offer an opinion* and the appropriate source of professional advice should be recommended instead.

| 25.4 | Discomfort and harm |

Researchers have a *primary* responsibility to protect participants from **physical** and **mental harm** during the investigation. It is not the responsibility of your participants to look after themselves. It is you who are exposing them to risk (however small) and it is therefore your responsibility to protect them from both physical and mental harm. The BPS guidelines state that, normally, the risk of harm must be no greater than in ordinary life. But what does this mean? Well, there is no easy answer, for some people may lead very risky lives while others do not. In general, all attempts are made to keep risk to an absolute minimum unless there are very strong scientific and/or medical grounds for doing otherwise. If there is risk associated with your study, participants should be informed of all risks and informed consent given (see below). In addition, it is important to make sure that you ask your participants about any factors that might create a risk, such as pre-existing medical or psychological conditions.

25.5	Consent

Consent is another particularly important ethical issue. The BPS guidelines are very clear that all participants should be informed sufficiently about a study that their consent to participate is properly informed. If a person consents without knowing the full nature of the research to which they are consenting then their consent is not informed and therefore not valid. This is why deception is so problematic. If participants are under 16 years old their consent should be given *plus* that of their guardian(s). This is important, for research involving children should not ride roughshod over their views even if, in law, they may not be able to give their consent (which is why we need the consent of their guardian(s)). Similarly, if you have adult participants who are unable to give informed consent then consent should be obtained from a family member or other party able to appreciate the impact of the research on the individual. It is important that researchers are aware of the fact that they are often in a position of authority (or perceived as such) which grants them influence over participants. This relationship must be treated with caution so that consent is not given under duress, however mild.

Participant observation

There may be particular ethical issues when conducting studies involving participant observation. Some sociologists have suggested that private locales ought to remain protected from the prying eyes of the social scientist and that it is unethical for a social scientist to deliberately misrepresent their identity for the purpose of entering a private domain to which they are not otherwise eligible. Furthermore, it has been argued that it is unethical for a social scientist to deliberately misrepresent the character of the research in which they are engaged. If we subscribed to this ethical position it would effectively mean the end of undisclosed participant observation for sociologists and psychologists. Needless to say, there are a number of researchers who recognise the particular ethical difficulties inherent in ethnographic research but still believe the ends (in terms of unique insight into others' lives) outweigh the means (uninvited intrusion often involving deception). These two positions involve complex arguments on both sides. If you are contemplating participant observation, it is crucial that you discuss the ethical issues early on with experienced colleagues/supervisors.

25.6	Non-participation and withdrawal

At the start of any investigation the investigators should make it clear to the participants that they have the **right to withdraw** from the study at any time. This is irrespective of whether any payment or other inducement has been given. Furthermore, participants do not have to give any explanation for their withdrawal from the study. This ethical principle is often particularly difficult for researchers. One of the hardest parts of many studies is recruitment. Until you have experienced the frustrations involved in recruiting participants you will not be able to appreciate the desperate desire to hang on to every one of them. Psychological researchers are human beings like anyone else and need to be careful that their desire to keep participants does not result in their minimising the opportunities for participants to withdraw from the study. In addition, there are genuine scientific concerns about participants withdrawing from research studies. If 'drop-out' is high a researcher might be concerned that there is some common element of the research or participants that leads them to drop out. This might have important implications for the study findings. So, while participants do not need to give an explanation for withdrawing from a study, the researcher is perfectly entitled to ask why they do not wish to continue. It is important that questions of this kind are not used to coerce participants into staying. Finally, participants have the right to withdraw *retrospectively* any consent given, and to require that their own data, including recordings, be destroyed. This can be particularly galling but recognises the fact that the data are the property of the participant and that we only have access to this material with their permission.

Observational studies

Naturalistic observation studies present particular problems for consent. If people are being observed in a natural setting, gaining consent may be problematic. It is always possible to ask people if they mind being observed, but researchers may worry about contaminating the naturalness of their observation (see also Chapter 7 for information about e-research and ethics). The general principle is that, unless those observed give their consent to being observed, observational research is only acceptable in situations where those being observed would expect to be observed by strangers. This is still not entirely clear cut, however. We will give you a real-life example. Many years ago, some students were given the task of observing a setting, making field notes and then writing up the study. They were told that this must be a public setting and that care must be taken not to intrude upon anyone's privacy. One particular group of students took this advice seriously but still ran into ethical difficulties. When they returned from their observation the tutors were rather surprised to find they had observed people in a porn cinema! Now, although you could argue that the cinema is a public place, we do not think it is a place where people expect to be observed (quite the opposite, in fact) and is therefore not an appropriate place for naturalistic observation. It is also important for researchers to pay particular attention to local cultural values and the privacy of individuals even if observing in a public place. In some cultures 'people watching' may be looked upon quite differently from how it is generally perceived in the United Kingdom.

506   Chapter 25 / The ethics and politics of psychological research

---

| 25.7 | Research with (non-human) animals |

As we stated above, research using (non-human) animals is controversial. More precisely, experimenting on animals is controversial. Fieldwork with animals is generally thought to be acceptable as long as disturbance is kept to an absolute minimum. There are arguments for and against psychological research which involves animal experimentation, and it is something that you need to think about for yourself. Animal experimentation is not commonly part of an under-graduate education in psychology any more, so you will not have to engage directly with the ethical guidelines on this matter unless you decide to go on to further study or research that uses animals. However, it is important that you understand the ethical issues involved in research with non-human animals so we have presented a summary of the major ethical principles in Box 25.1.

Box 25.1

Information box

Ethical guidelines for research with animals

Adapted from the BPS 'Guidelines for psychologists working with animals' (2007).

Legal issues

All researchers working with (non-human) animals must abide by British law designed to protect their welfare. Detailed guidance on animal experimenta-tion is given in the Animals (Scientific Procedures) Act (1986) published by HMSO. In addition, researchers engaged in fieldwork with animals must abide by legislation concerning endangered species.

Replacing the use of animals

There is an expectation that – where possible – alternative methods of research (and especially teaching) that use previous research or computer simulations instead of animals should be used. It is now commonplace to use computer simulations for students studying rat behaviour rather than run-ning rats through mazes yourself.

Choice of species

Appropriate species of animals should be chosen in such a way that suffering be minimised. Thought should be given to the level of sentience and the nat-ural history of the species. Knowledge of whether the animal has been bred in captivity is also important.

▶

Box 25.1 *Continued*

Number of animals

Researchers are legally required to use the smallest number of animals neces-sary to accomplish the goals of the research. Advice is also given about ways of reducing the number of animals used in such research.

Experimental procedures

- Deprivation and aversion techniques must be undertaken with care and with regard to the particular needs of different species. Alternatives should be used wherever possible.
- Animals should be housed in such a way that they are not subject to undue stress due to isolation or overcrowding.
- Staged encounters between predators and prey should be avoided wherever possible and natural encounters used instead.
- Proper care should be taken with surgical procedures such that stress and residual effects are minimised.
- Animals found to be suffering severe pain or distress should be humanely killed using an approved technique.

Fieldwork

Researchers studying free-living animals should minimise interference with individual animals and also the environment in which they live. Care should be taken with any procedure that requires removal (however short) of an animal from its environment.

Animal procurement

Animals used in experiments must only be purchased from Home Office approved establishments.

Housing and care

Researchers also have a responsibility of care for the conditions under which animals are kept. Animals must be kept in accordance with the regulations of the Animals (Scientific Procedures) Act (1986). Minimum requirements include: a degree of freedom of movement, food, water, and care appropriate to its health and well-being. Natural living conditions should be reproduced if at all possible.

Animals in psychology teaching

Students must not be required to carry out any experimental procedure that they consider ethically unacceptable and should be encouraged to form their own judgements about such matters. The use of live animals in teaching is prohibited unless the topic cannot be taught by any other means.

Box 25.1 *Continued*

The use of animals for therapeutic purposes

Animals may occasionally be used by psychologists as adjuncts to therapy. This may include the use of dogs or horses, for instance, to facilitate psychological development. In addition, animals (such as spiders or snakes) may be used for behavioural exposure in the treatment of phobias. In all cases, similar standards of care to those expected for experimental animals is required. Stress on the animal should also be minimised with it given the opportunity to retreat where appropriate.

Clinical assessment and treatment of animal behaviour

Some psychologists work with animals with disordered behaviours. Specific guidelines and a scheme for accreditation for this work have been drawn up through a collaboration of the BPS and Association for the Study of Animal Behaviour (ASAB).

Source: From The British Psychological Society (2007) *Guidelines for Psychologists Working with Animals*, Leicester, UK: BPS. Copyright © 2007 The British Psychological Society. Reproduced with permission.

25.8	Equal opportunities

Equality of opportunity is generally considered an essential factor in our educational and work lives. It is also important to consider equal opportunity issues in the context of psychological research. Feminist researchers have argued that there is considerable sexism in psychological research. Robson (2002), drawing on work by Eichler (1988), identifies seven sources of sexism in research: *androcentricity, overgeneralisation, gender insensitivity, double standards, sex appropriateness, familism* and *sexual dichotomism*. We will address these issues here but the interested reader should use Robson (2002) as a starting point for further reading on this issue.

Androcentricity simply means viewing the world from a male perspective. This is a particular problem with psychological research. There has been a long tradition of developing and testing instruments on men and then assuming they will be appropriate for use with women. In addition, when comparisons are made, the male response is generally assumed to be the normal position and the female response abnormal. **Overgeneralisation** is similar and is where one studies only one sex and then generalises to the other. Care needs to be taken to avoid such sexism in research. **Gender insensitivity** is where one ignores sex as a possible variable. **Double standards** is a description for the process of treating identical behaviour by men and women differently. **Sex appropriateness** is a particular form of double standard where some behaviour (or belief, etc.) is assumed to be a female (or male) activity. So, for instance, a researcher might assume that only men are interested in casual sex. **Familism** is the tendency to treat the family as the smallest unit of analysis. This can be a particular problem for women where an individual woman's behaviour, beliefs or views are obscured with the family as the unit of analysis. Finally, **sexual dichotomism** is where men and women are treated as two entirely separate groups with no overlap at all. Some of these sources of bias are *possible* but not *necessary* sources of sexism. For instance, it may be appropriate in some cases to treat the family as the smallest unit of analysis.

In addition, researchers need to be aware of equal opportunity issues regarding age, social class, ethnicity and culture, religion, sexuality, dis/ability and so on. There are many assumptions made that serve to exclude people who are older, working class, black, gay and so on that are very subtle. It is only if we all pay attention to these issues that psychology will be able to move beyond its somewhat controversial history and transform itself into a discipline for and about *all people* and not just the privileged few.

25.9	Politics and psychological research

There has been a tradition of positivist research (which is invariably quantitative) conducted by psychologists who have assumed it is objective and therefore 'value free' or immune from politics. Thankfully, this is changing, at least in part due to the influence of qualitative research which often engages a great deal with political questions in one way or another. The very idea of 'value free' science is now largely discredited. This view has been critiqued to such an extent by philosophers of science that it is no longer tenable. The choice of a research topic, formulation of research questions, choice of methods and so on all involve value judgements of some kind. If we decide to research drug use or anorexia or attitudes to nuclear weaponry or more apparently mundane topics then we are making decisions based on a value system (our own). Similarly, the way we formulate research questions and choose some methods over others depends on the particular value system we wish to buy into. Therefore, if all research involves value judgements to some degree then it must necessarily be political. Hammersley (1995) argues that there are four ways in which values are involved in social research:

1 The very fundamental commitment to advancing knowledge is political. The fact that we prefer knowledge to ignorance immediately invokes a particular value system.

2 The need for resources in research is dependent on political decisions. Decisions about the allocation of resources are political (see Langdridge, 2006). Health psychology is an increasingly popular area of research partly because resources are increasingly being allocated to this topic. Resources are allocated to this area (and not others) for various political reasons.

3 All research relies on presuppositions reflecting the values of the researcher. The choice of topic, questions asked, etc. will be founded on these presuppositions. The presuppositions themselves will depend on the biography of the researcher and may include demographic variables such as their sex, age,

social class, ethnicity, etc., as well as their experience of education, family life and so on.

4 Social research will always have effects on people's lives. Participants will be directly affected by research through their involvement, while others may be affected through the consequences of the research findings. How findings are presented will depend on the researcher's value system.

It is therefore important that we are *critically aware* of our own value systems and the influence that they have on our work. Ignorance is no defence!

25.10	Evaluation research

Evaluation research is concerned with the evaluation of the worth or merit of an intervention of some kind. It is becoming an increasingly important form of social research as education, health and social care organisations are recognising the merit of evaluating their programmes or interventions. Evaluation research uses the standard techniques of social science research but in applied settings. So, for instance, evaluation research may involve the evaluation of an after-school homework programme to see whether it improves educational achievement, or the evaluation of the use of counselling in doctors' surgeries to reduce attendance of 'heart sink' patients, and so on. This type of research invariably raises significant ethical and political issues, which require particularly sensitive handling from the investigator. One of the unique aspects of evaluation research is the need to engage group skills, management ability, political dexterity and sensitivity to multiple stakeholders (any persons with an interest in the research). A considerable amount has been written about this form of research and the particular demands that it places on researchers (see Further reading).

25.11	The need for balance

While this chapter has been concerned with emphasising the need for ethics in psychological research, this last section offers a few words of caution about the proliferation of what we can only call an 'ethics industry'. In recent years, we have witnessed increasing concern about ethical issues and the growth of ethics committees. Ethics committees (university, health trust and so on) now routinely assess research proposals before allowing research to be conducted. This is clearly a sensible precaution that is designed to serve the needs of the public and protect them from harm. However, many researchers are worried about a growth in conservatism (in research) as a result of the growth of the 'ethics industry'. More and more researchers are having to deal with often spurious 'ethical concerns' that do nothing more than prevent good quality and important research. The *fear of harm* is often out of proportion to any *real risk*. Researchers are having to fight overly conservative ethics committees where almost any piece of research involving people raises 'ethical concerns'. This is clearly nonsense and represents a real risk to academic freedom and the future generation of knowledge. Human beings must be treated with respect but do not need to be treated with 'kid gloves', and as long as 'sensitive' topics are treated with care there should be *no* 'no go areas'. Ethical issues are important and must be accounted for but they must not be used to stifle research.

Further reading

Robson, C. (2002). *Real World Research*, 2nd edn. Oxford: Blackwell.

> This book contains a chapter on evaluation research which will provide an excellent starting point if you are interested in finding out more about evaluation research. In addition, there is further discussion of ethical issues and feminist criticism of social science research. It also provides guidance on further reading.

Singer, P. (1993). *Practical Ethics*, 2nd edn. Cambridge: Cambridge University Press.

> This is a fascinating book containing some extraordinary and controversial ethical arguments. Peter Singer is a leading, but very controversial, ethical philosopher who writes with great clarity and depth of argument. This book engages with a considerable range of practical ethical issues, including arguments about animal rights, abortion, euthanasia, the environment and much more besides. The arguments are always strong and demand attention but do not always make comfortable reading. Give it a go – you will not be able to forget it.

The British Psychological Society Ethical Principles for Conducting Research with Human Participants. [currently being revised]

The British Psychological Society Code of Ethics and Conduct (2006).

The British Psychological Society Guidelines for Psychologists Working with Animals (2007).

The British Psychological Society Report of the Working Party on Conducting Research on the Internet (2007).

> These guidelines are all available from the BPS website (**www.bps.org.uk**). The first document is currently being revised but is the main source of information for students and academics on research ethics. The second document includes details of a code of conduct for professional psychologists, and the third document the latest details of ethical principles for working with humans and animals. The final document includes the most recent guidelines produced for conducting research using the Internet. All of the above guidelines are clear and concise and an essential source of information on this important topic.

26 Reporting and presenting findings

- This chapter begins by outlining the standard scientific report style.
- The chapter then moves on to consider modified structures for qualitative research reports.
- Finally, information is provided about writing research proposals and writing for publication.

INTRODUCTION

This chapter concerns the ways in which we might write and present research findings. It provides detail about writing and presenting research reports (lab or fieldwork write-ups) as well as writing for publication. There are standard ways in which research is reported and it is important to familiarise yourself with these formats. There is a (pretty much) standard format for presenting quantitative research. Things are somewhat different when it comes to qualitative research. There are quite a few variations in format, as one might expect when thinking of the different qualitative methods employed by psychologists. In general, however, there are a number of common elements in all research reports and these will be emphasised here. The best way to get a feel for different styles of presentation is to read, read, read! If you read journal articles and book chapters you will see the subtle (and not so subtle) differences in presentation style and format.

26.1 The standard scientific report style

Format

The standard format for presenting quantitative research is given in Box 26.1. These are broken down in more detail, section by section, below.

Box 26.1

Information box

The standard scientific report format

The following headings are normally included in a standard quantitative report:

Title

Abstract

Introduction

Method:

   Participants

   Apparatus/materials

   Procedure

Results

Discussion

References

Appendices

Title

This should be concise, informative and include all the main variables in the research being reported.

Abstract

This is a brief summary (around 100–150 words but sometimes longer). It comes at the beginning of the report and includes brief details of the main findings and conclusions. It is important that the abstract is sufficiently detailed that the interested reader can fully grasp the nature of the study and therefore know whether it is worth reading on. Structured abstracts are becoming increasingly common. These will typically include a series of headings with one or two sentences for each heading. Common headings for a structured abstract include *Objectives, Design, Methods, Results* and *Conclusions,* though these do vary from journal to journal.

Introduction

Start with the general psychological subject area. Discuss theory and research which is relevant to the research topic – this is your **literature review**. The literature review is a vital component of all research reports and further detail on writing this section is given below. In essence, this section of a report requires that you move from the general area to the particular hypotheses to be tested via a coherent and logical argument. This section of a report should end with a statement of the specific hypotheses being tested or research questions. These may be incorporated into the last paragraph rather than listed separately.

Literature reviews (see Chapter 1 for information about searching the literature) usually form part of the introduction to a journal article or research report. Literature refers to the body of knowledge about a topic (in the form of journal articles, books, etc.). Literature reviews critically examine existing materials in a subject area and function to:

- situate research within a theoretical context;
- give an up-to-date discussion of current material and relevant research.

A literature review critically summarises and evaluates existing research findings. Reviews should highlight relationships between different material in the form of similarities and differences. It should also show how previous material relates to original research. It is useful to ask the following questions when writing a review:

- What do we already know?
- What are the main concepts?
- What are the relationships between these concepts?
- What are the existing theories?
- Where are the gaps in existing understanding?
- What views need to be tested further?
- What evidence is lacking?
- Why study the research problem?
- What contribution will the present study make?
- What research designs or methods are appropriate/inappropriate and why?

But what does it mean to critically analyse the literature? This involves giving considered and justified examination of the methods, findings and interpretations of the data. When critically evaluating a piece of research you need to go beyond description by giving opinions (based on psychological knowledge and not your own personal opinions) and evaluations. It is important that you do not take everything at face value but instead you must question and explore the literature. This can be done by relating different types of material to each other, look for similarities, differences and contradictions. You should also be explicit about underlying theories and values in the work you are reviewing.

When you write a review, write with a purpose. Look at previous reviews (in journal articles and book chapters) for ideas about structure and style. Always write a plan as this will provide you with a structure to work from. In essence, this involves you deciding what you are going to say before you decide how to say it and providing a brief map for your writing. You should also seek to structure your review in a logical way – generally *not* by author – tell a story as you would in an essay. That is, group similar information together and show the relationship between the work of different researchers, highlighting similarities and differences. Indicate the position of the work in the history of the research area and start with general and then move to more specific issues. You will need to include enough description to let the reader know what you are talking about but it is not necessary to detail every aspect of every study you are considering in your review, especially if it does not add anything more to the reader's understanding of the topic.

Method

- **Participants**. This subsection would generally include the following information about your participants: age, sex, social class, ethnicity, religion, whether they were volunteers, their naivety (whether they are psychology students, for instance). This section will also sometimes include some detail of the research design if it involves assigning participants to different groups.

- **Apparatus/materials**. You need to give enough detail here for a replication to be possible. It is important therefore that you give details of any technical equipment used (e.g. heart monitors), instruments, scales and psychometric tests (e.g. the IPIP). You do not need to provide information about everyday equipment (such as PCs or pencil and paper) unless there is something special or unique about these items. When providing information about any instruments or tests used you should also include information about the reason for choosing this particular instrument/test and their reliability/validity if it has been verified previously. Put technical details in an appendix if necessary.

- **Procedure**. In this subsection you describe what happened from start to finish in sufficient detail for someone to replicate your study. You should include any standardised instructions here or put them in an appendix if they are very extensive. If you are in doubt about this section, test it on a friend and see if they know what you did!

Results

Present descriptive statistics first, then inferential statistics in this section. Numbers on their own are not sufficient. You should provide some *brief* commentary on the tests used and results found. This commentary should not, however, pre-empt your discussion, where you interpret and discuss the meaning of your results. Tables and graphs are very useful ways of summarising the data and should be used where appropriate. Any raw data or mathematical working that needs to be seen (and most will not) should go in an appendix and not the results section.

Discussion

This section is where you interpret and discuss the meaning of your results. Firstly, summarise (one or two paragraphs) what you have found and then move on to relate your findings to the hypotheses (or research questions) and then to other relevant literature on the topic. This is the moment where your findings are related to the literature you reviewed in your introduction. It is also generally appropriate to evaluate your method and suggest possible improvements and future studies. If there are limitations to your research, remember to frame your criticism positively – do not just stick the boot in or you will undermine your own research.

References

Throughout your reports (and essays for that matter) you must support statements with evidence (and therefore a reference – Author (Year)). It is *vital* that you list *all* those authors you refer to in the main body of your report in a full reference list at the end of the report. You must use the correct format. Further information is given on the need for referencing and referencing style below.

Appendices

Do not overdo these – we do not need to see everything. However, you may want appendices for any questionnaires you have designed, raw data (if necessary), or working out for statistical tests (if necessary). Traditionally, appendices were numbered using Roman numerals. This is generally no longer the case and they are now numbered 1, 2, 3, etc.

Referencing

Referencing is citing or documenting your sources. The literature is used to provide *evidence* for the statements made in a literature review. It is important to use a consistent referencing system (there are quite a few different systems) to show what information or ideas you have used in your writing. If you are studying at a university you will be provided with details of the 'in-house' referencing style, and if you wish to write for publication all journals (and book editors) provide details of their expectations. Most requirements in psychology will be similar to those detailed here. But why is referencing so important in psychology? The following are just a few reasons:

- It shows you are familiar with the literature.
- It enhances the credibility of your writing.
- It gives credit to other people for their work.
- It helps other people find literature you have used.

You should reference all information and ideas from existing work that you use in your writing. This is whether you use your own words or an extract from the source (a quote). You would not generally reference general knowledge in a field or your own ideas and research. The best approach is, if in doubt, then *reference!* Forgetting to reference may lead to suspicion of plagiarism (cheating through copying or passing off someone else's work as your own) and this is treated very seriously now by all universities and will lead to disciplinary action.

There are two components to referencing, which vary according to the referencing system being used. Firstly, you would have an in-text reference to show which piece of information belongs to another writer. This should include the author's name and date of publication and is used to find the full bibliographic information, which is listed in the 'References' section of your report. Your reference list contains this full bibliographic information at the end of the piece of work. A reference list should include details of all authors cited in the main text listed in alphabetical order. This list will provide enough information to enable a reader to locate the references you cite in the main text in support of your arguments. It is very important to use a consistent system and make sure your in-text references and reference list match! See Box 26.2 for some examples.

Box 26.2

Information box

Referencing

For example ...

Intoxicated people are more likely to commit an aggressive act (Pernanen, 1991) and use illicit drugs (Plant, Plant, Peck & Setters, 1989) than sober people. Research by Goldman, Brown and Christiansen (1987) on outcome expectancies may help explain why people are more likely to participate in risky activities when they are intoxicated relative to when they are sober.

References

Goldman, M. S., Brown, S. A. & Christiansen, B. A. (1987). Expectancy theory: Thinking about drinking. In H.T. Blane and L.E. Leonard (Eds) *Psychological Theories of Drinking and Alcoholism*, New York: Guilford Press, pp. 181–226.

Pernanen, K. (1991). *Alcohol in Human Violence*. New York: Guilford Press.

Plant, M. L., Plant, M. A., Peck, D. F. & Setters, J. (1989). The sex industry, alcohol, and illicit drugs: Implications for the spread of HIV infection, *British Journal of Addictions*, **84**, pp. 53–9.

Quotes, where you use exact words from a source, must also be referenced. When you reference a quotation you must include page numbers for the quotation in addition to the author's surname and year. Quotes should be used sparingly to illustrate key points or when the words themselves are important. It is always better to rephrase rather than quote wherever possible. Long quotes should be indented and separated from your words in the text. Short quotes should be put in quotation marks (' ') and integrated into the text. For examples (first a short quote in the text and then a longer quote), see Box 26.3, and look at Box 26.4 for further information on problems you might encounter when referencing sources.

Box 26.3

Information box

Quotations

An example of a short quote embedded in the text (page number after the colon with the year – page numbers may also be written as (p. 43) in brackets after the quote):

> According to Tiffany (1990: 43), controlled processing is necessary in situations in which 'stimuli [and] responses are sufficiently variable ... to prevent the development of automatic response'. This is an important finding.

An example of a longer quote which is separated from the text and indented:

> The de-centering involved in achieving an understanding of different perspectives is seen as part of the maturation process, but Merleau-Ponty (1962) points out that the primitive position of humankind is one that assumes that we are all participants in the same world (and hence not as vulnerable to the FAE). Our relationship to our own body pre-figures our relation to that of the other:

> > Between my consciousness and my body as I experience it, between this phenomenal body of mine and that of the other as I see it from the outside, there exists an internal relation which causes the other to appear as the completion of the system. The other can be evident to me because I am not transparent to myself and because my subjectivity draws its body in its wake. (Merleau-Ponty, 1962: 352)

> For Merleau-Ponty, it is what goes on *between* two people, rather than inside either of them, that is primary.

Box 26.4

Possible problems when referencing

There are many possible problems that you might encounter when referencing. Do not worry too much about this, for these can catch us all out! Just make sure you can reference books and journal articles appropriately and then look up how to reference more unusual materials when you need to. Some possible problems include the following:

- No author listed (you may need to use the name of the article and year instead of the author in this case).
- Too many authors listed (this is where you can use the phrase '*et al.*' – which means 'and others' in Latin – after the surname of the first author to save writing down every name when using this reference).
- Bibliographic information missing (include what you can and note information missing).
- An unusual type of reference (these can catch us all out – consult a book on referencing or other work which has referenced similar material).

Perhaps the most common 'unusual' reference you are likely to encounter is when referencing websites. There is no fully agreed standard here but we give an example below which includes most detail considered important.

Neimeyer, R.A. (2004). The Internet Encyclopaedia of Personal Construct Psychology: Repertory grid methods [WWW page]. URL http://www.pcp-net.org/encyclopaedia/repgrid-methods.html (visited 29 July 2008).

More possible problems (solutions in brackets)

- Using information referenced or quoted from someone else (Smith, 1991, cited in Brown, 1991).
- Your idea has already been published by someone else (see also Brown, 1991).
- You want to use an adapted version of someone else's work (adapted from Brown, 1991).

26.2   Writing up qualitative research

A great deal of the advice given above about the standard scientific report also applies to qualitative research reports. So, we would expect a qualitative research report to include a review of the literature and be properly referenced. The purpose of both of these is exactly the same. The review operates to locate the current research within the wider knowledge base about the topic, while references are used to provide evidence in support of the statements and arguments being made.

However, there are some differences between qualitative research reports and the standard scientific report. The most common format for the presentation of qualitative research is the **modified scientific report**. This format uses some of the categories of a scientific report but with modifications. If you are in doubt about how to present your qualitative findings then this format is the safest. This format is shown in Box 26.5.

Box 26.5

Information box

Presenting qualitative research

The modified scientific report is the most common way of presenting qualitative research in psychology. Many of the sections are the same as the standard scientific report. It is worth noting, however, that although the sections may have the same heading label the content may well look quite different.

Title
Abstract
Introduction
Method:
    Participants
    Theoretical background
    Analytic strategy
Results/Discussion or Findings
References
Appendices

A few words are needed about the various sections included in a qualitative report. Firstly, the **title** and **abstract** are likely to be similar to those found in a standard scientific report. The only difference is that the abstract will (probably) never be formally structured in a qualitative research report. The **introduction** in a qualitative report should, like a quantitative report, include a thorough review of the literature. This should outline the major issues regarding the topic of interest. However, unlike a quantitative report, the introduction would not end with a statement of the hypotheses (because there will not be any). It may end with some broad research questions, but even these are not always necessary with qualitative research.

The **method** section will also be quite different. There will be information about the participants, as you would find in a quantitative report, but this may be presented quite differently. Most qualitative research published in mainstream psychology journals will feature a **participants** subsection in the method section that is very similar to the section in a scientific report. It will include quantitative measures of how many participants, ages, sex, etc. However, some reports will present this section differently. One increasingly popular option, if there are very few participants, is to include brief biographical statements for each participant in this section. This clearly moves away from the tendency to describe the participants as a homogeneous mass and recognises the unique contribution of each participant to the research. There is quite a lot of variation in the remaining subsections of the method section. What subsections are included here will depend on the particular qualitative method being reported. However, there will generally be some information about the **theoretical background** to the method (often included as a **methodology section**). This section will report the epistemological assumptions underpinning the method and probably also some information about any debates in the field. There may also be a section on the **analytic strategy** (sometimes called **coding strategy**), although this is increasingly included within a section on methodology. This subsection includes detail about the practicalities involved in the analysis of the data. The theoretical and analytic sections are quite often combined into one subsection of the method section.

This leaves the results and discussion sections. These are nearly always combined in qualitative research reports. This section may be called **results/discussion** or **findings** or **analysis** – it is really a matter of tradition (regarding the qualitative method and journal) and personal preference. The reason for this merger between results and discussion is obvious. In qualitative research the analysis of data invariably includes interpretation *and* discussion of meaning. It is therefore only appropriate that these two sections merge into one. There may also be a short **conclusion** section, which summarises the study, highlights any limitations and provides suggestions for future research. The **references** and **appendices** are the same as with the traditional scientific report.

While the modified scientific structure is probably the most common way of reporting qualitative research, it is not the only way. There are a number of other strategies that may be more appropriate. Three possible options are:

1 **Narrative structure** – a straightforward account of the study told as a story (with a beginning, middle and end). Life story research is frequently reported in this manner.

2 **Chronological structure** – a time-ordered account of the study. This may be used with diary research or research involving repeat interviews.

3 **Theory-generating structure** – theoretical arguments, often derived from the data, are used to structure the report.

Reflexivity

We mentioned **reflexivity** (the role of the researcher in the production of the findings) in Part 3 of this book. It is, however, worth returning to this important topic again here. Qualitative reports are increasingly including discussions of reflexivity. This operates both at a theoretical level (and is therefore most often discussed in the **theoretical background** subsection of the **method** section) and at a practical level. Writers are now including personal reflexive statements so the reader can situate the researcher and understand more of their role in producing the findings being presented. These reflexive statements often take the form of a brief biography of the author as it relates to the topic of study or the reporting of a diary kept by the author during the project. This is quite a move away from the traditional approach to presenting research, where the author is apparently invisible. It is also often appropriate to include a reflexive statement in a qualitative dissertation and PhD, and we are seeing this used to good effect more and more.

26.3 Writing skills

There are a number of suggestions that can be made to improve your writing and this is what we attempt here. First of all, make sure your report (and any essays you write) is presented to a high standard. All work should be word processed and spell checked. With the widespread use of word processing software there really is no excuse to present work in a shoddy fashion. All word processing software includes spell checkers and grammar checkers. Spell checking your work is an absolute must! Errors will always slip through the net. Constant recurring spelling errors, however, can seriously damage the perceived quality of your work. Grammar checking features are not quite as helpful as spelling checking features (principally because English grammar is so complex). However, if you do have problems with grammar then run through your work with a grammar checker. However, do not just accept all the suggestions made. The software is not perfect, so assess the problem it raises and accept or refuse the suggestion. We find that grammar checkers are most useful in reminding us to use shorter sentences.

There are two options when using spelling and grammar checking features. You can click to use them at the end of your work when it is (nearly) finished and do one final check on spelling and grammar, or you can have them on while you write, highlighting errors as you go along. We do both! We think constant correction is a useful way of learning to correct spelling as you write. It is true that this can interrupt the flow of writing, but with practice you will actually improve your spelling (which is a valuable transferable skill). However, even with the spelling check switched on while writing it is still possible to miss something, so go through your text again at the end. If the spell checker makes a strange suggestion, override it or look the word up in a dictionary. There is no room for complacency if you want to produce really good work. One final tip – make sure you have the spell checker checking for UK English and not US English. There will be a variety of language options and programs can sometimes switch to US English when you are not looking! We tend to leave any grammar checking to the end or we end up with a manuscript covered in green highlights.

The next way of improving your writing is to redraft your work. It is very rare that a first draft will be acceptable for anyone. We never produce anything in a first draft that is acceptable for publication. It is a necessary part of writing to read your work through and redraft it. This should be done several times so that the final work is as polished as it can be. We know it can be hard to read your own work through. We both remember the battle we had to make ourselves read through the answers in exams. But it is worth it and you might be pleasantly surprised at some of the things you write. It is worth reading a piece of work through at two levels. It is important to begin reading your work at a micro level first. Is everything spelt correctly? Do all your sentences make sense? Is every line grammatically correct? Is each paragraph clear and does each paragraph have a reason for being there? The work will need reading through several times at this level and then be redrafted accordingly. The next level of reading and redrafting is more global, where you read your work through to assess overall flow and narrative coherence. Are you addressing the question (that was set or that you set yourself) and does the work tell a good story from beginning to end? We go through several iterations at this level with the focus on **narrative smoothing** – the process of producing a good story that reads well by ironing out any difficulties or inconsistencies in the text.

The final writing tip concerns the need to think about who you are writing for and what you are trying to say. If you are writing an assignment as an undergraduate then your tasks will probably be to (i) answer the question(s) that have been set or produce a piece of work in the required format (like a lab write-up), and (ii) demonstrate that you have met the appropriate assessment criteria. Whether the assessment criteria are explicitly stated or not, you will need to demonstrate your knowledge of the particular area you are writing about. This means you will need to show that you understand the reasons for using a particular method or that you know what particular terms mean. That is, you must show that you know what you are talking about and that you are not just parroting appropriate answers or following a predetermined format. If you are writing for publication in a professional or academic journal then there is much less need to show that you know what you are talking about. While this aspect of writing is still present, there will be many more areas of common knowledge that will not require spelling out (more on this below).

The next thing to think about when writing is to think about what you are trying to say. Write plans (of headings and subheadings) for all work you present and redraft these until you have a structure that tells the story you wish to tell. Then take these headings and write a first draft of your work. Every paragraph you write should make a point – otherwise why is it there? But remember not to try to pack too much into a paragraph – if the topic has changed then think about having a new paragraph. Similarly, think about what work is being done by the sentences you write – make every one count. What is most important is that you keep your writing clear and simple. Many students think that they have to write in complex sentences and use fancy words. This is not true. Good writing is clear and straightforward. The aim of writing is communication, so make sure that when you write the reader knows where you are going and what you are trying to say.

26.4	Presenting research – writing for publication

Finally, it is worth spending a few moments on presenting research findings. There are many possible audiences for academic writing. University lecturers/researchers most often present their findings by writing academic books (textbooks or monographs) and/or journal articles. This, of course, constitutes the literature in the field (which is reviewed) and represents the latest knowledge on a particular topic. Although most undergraduates will not publish books or write in academic journals, it is not impossible to do so. Sometimes students produce outstanding dissertations that are worthy of publication and we have even known the odd undergraduate essay to be published in an academic journal. The best way of learning to write for academic publications is to read books and articles and try to write in these styles. If your dissertation work is of a very high standard then your supervisor is likely to suggest working with you to publish it. This way you will receive direct guidance on writing for publication.

However, while academics most often aim to publish in academic journals and books, there are other ways of disseminating one's research. The other major outlet for research is at academic conferences where research is presented as oral papers or posters. Conferences consist of a series of oral paper presentations (anything from 15 to 30 minutes, but sometimes longer) of research to one's peers. There will be the opportunity for questions and things can sometimes get quite lively if the research is controversial! However, the aim is to disseminate research findings and get feedback from one's peers that may help when attempting to publish it. Also, as all academics know, conferences are great fun and a way of meeting up with old friends. Poster presentations are an alternative way of presenting findings at a conference. Research is presented as large (often A0) posters and the author(s) will normally stand by their posters to chat and answer questions at set times during the conference.

Although oral presentations, posters and publications in academic books and journals are the main outlets for research, there are many other ways of disseminating findings. It is possible to present psychological research in newspapers, magazines and other written media (newsletters, etc.). Others present research on radio or television. The possibilities are endless. The key with disseminating research in these forms is to develop an appropriate **voice**. It is unlikely that the normal academic way of writing will be appropriate for these outlets. A much more upbeat 'pop' form will be needed to bring the discipline alive and satisfy the commercial demands of newspapers, magazines, radio and television. Some academics do this very well while others steer clear. If you are interested in writing then get involved with your student newspaper (write a column) or try writing for a professional newsletter. The more you write, the better your writing will become. So, get out there and give it a go – no one gets anywhere waiting for the world to come to them!

Further reading

Silverman, D. (2004). *Doing Qualitative Research: A Practical Handbook,* 2nd edn. London: Sage.

This is not only an excellent book on the practicalities of carrying out qualitative research but also a valuable resource on writing, particularly for Masters and PhD students. There are a series of sections offering advice on writing research dissertations (at BA/BSc level as well as MA and PhD level). These sections also include suggestions for further reading on writing research reports and publishing.

Appendix: Tables of critical values for statistical tests

Table A1. Chi-square   527

Table A2. Mann–Whitney U   528

Table A3. Normal distribution   529

Table A4. Pearson correlation coefficient   530

Table A5. Spearman correlation coefficient   531

Table A6. T-test   532

Table A7. Wilcoxon   533

Table A1 – Critical values of chi-square (one-tailed test)

df	0.10	0.05	0.025	0.01	0.005
1	2.706	3.841	5.024	6.635	7.879
2	4.605	5.991	7.378	9.210	10.597
3	6.251	7.815	9.348	11.345	12.838
4	7.779	9.488	11.143	13.277	14.860
5	9.236	11.070	12.833	15.086	16.750
6	10.645	12.592	14.449	16.812	18.548
7	12.017	14.067	16.013	18.475	20.278
8	13.362	15.507	17.535	20.090	21.955
9	14.684	16.919	19.023	21.666	23.589
10	15.987	18.307	20.483	23.209	25.188
11	17.275	19.675	21.920	24.725	26.757
12	18.549	21.026	23.337	26.217	28.300
13	19.812	22.362	24.736	27.688	29.819
14	21.064	23.685	26.119	29.141	31.319
15	22.307	24.996	27.488	30.578	32.801
16	23.542	26.296	28.845	32.000	34.267
17	24.769	27.587	30.191	33.409	35.718
18	25.989	28.869	31.526	34.805	37.156
19	27.204	30.144	32.852	36.191	38.582
20	28.412	31.410	34.170	37.566	39.997
21	29.615	32.671	35.479	38.932	41.401
22	30.813	33.924	36.781	40.289	42.796
23	32.007	35.172	38.076	41.638	44.181
24	33.196	36.415	39.364	42.980	45.559
25	34.382	37.652	40.646	44.314	46.928
26	35.563	38.885	41.923	45.642	48.290
27	36.741	40.113	43.195	46.963	49.645
28	37.916	41.337	44.461	48.278	50.993
29	39.087	42.557	45.722	49.588	52.336
30	40.256	43.773	46.979	50.892	53.672
40	51.805	55.758	59.342	63.691	66.766
50	63.167	67.505	71.420	76.154	79.490
60	74.397	79.082	83.298	88.379	91.952
70	85.527	90.531	95.023	100.425	104.215
80	96.578	101.879	106.629	112.329	116.321
90	107.565	113.145	118.136	124.116	128.299
100	118.498	124.342	129.561	135.807	140.169

Table A2 – Critical values for the Mann–Whitney U-test: 5% level of significance

N_B	1	2	3	4	5	6	7	8	9	10	11	12	13	14	15	16	17	18	19	20
N_A																				
1	–	–	–	–	–	–	–	–	–	–	–	–	–	–	–	–	–	–	–	–
2	–	–	–	–	–	–	–	0	0	0	0	1	1	1	1	1	2	2	2	2
3	–	–	–	–	0	1	1	2	2	3	3	4	4	5	5	6	6	7	7	8
4	–	–	–	–	–	–	3	4	4	5	6	7	8	9	10	11	11	12	13	13
5	–	0	1	2	2	3	5	6	7	8	9	10	12	13	14	15	17	18	19	20
6	–	–	–	–	–	5	6	8	10	11	13	14	16	17	19	21	22	24	25	27
7	–	–	–	–	–	–	8	10	12	14	16	18	20	22	24	26	28	30	32	34
8	–	–	–	–	–	–	–	13	15	17	19	22	24	26	29	31	34	36	38	41
9	–	–	–	–	–	–	–	–	17	20	23	26	28	31	34	37	39	42	45	48
10	–	–	–	–	–	–	–	–	–	23	26	29	33	36	39	42	45	48	52	55
11	–	–	–	–	–	–	–	–	–	–	30	33	37	40	44	47	51	55	58	62
12	–	–	–	–	–	–	–	–	–	–	–	37	41	45	49	53	57	61	65	69
13	–	–	–	–	–	–	–	–	–	–	–	–	45	50	54	59	63	67	72	76
14	–	–	–	–	–	–	–	–	–	–	–	–	–	55	59	64	67	74	78	83
15	–	–	–	–	–	–	–	–	–	–	–	–	–	–	64	70	75	80	85	90
16	–	–	–	–	–	–	–	–	–	–	–	–	–	–	–	75	81	86	92	98
17	–	–	–	–	–	–	–	–	–	–	–	–	–	–	–	–	87	93	99	105
18	–	–	–	–	–	–	–	–	–	–	–	–	–	–	–	–	–	99	106	112
19	–	–	–	–	–	–	–	–	–	–	–	–	–	–	–	–	–	–	113	119
20	–	–	–	–	–	–	–	–	–	–	–	–	–	–	–	–	–	–	–	127

Table A3 – Critical values of the normal distribution

z	0.00	0.01	0.02	0.03	0.04	0.05	0.06	0.07	0.08	0.09
0.0	0.0000	0.0040	0.0080	0.0120	0.0160	0.0199	0.0239	0.0279	0.0319	0.0359
0.1	0.0398	0.0438	0.0478	0.0517	0.0557	0.0596	0.0636	0.0675	0.0714	0.0753
0.2	0.0793	0.0832	0.0871	0.0910	0.0948	0.0987	0.1026	0.1064	0.1103	0.1141
0.3	0.1179	0.1217	0.1255	0.1293	0.1331	0.1368	0.1406	0.1443	0.1480	0.1517
0.4	0.1554	0.1591	0.1628	0.1664	0.1700	0.1736	0.1772	0.1808	0.1844	0.1879
0.5	0.1915	0.1950	0.1985	0.2019	0.2054	0.2088	0.2123	0.2157	0.2190	0.2224
0.6	0.2257	0.2291	0.2324	0.2357	0.2389	0.2422	0.2454	0.2486	0.2517	0.2549
0.7	0.2580	0.2611	0.2642	0.2673	0.2704	0.2734	0.2764	0.2794	0.2823	0.2852
0.8	0.2881	0.2910	0.2939	0.2967	0.2995	0.3023	0.3051	0.3078	0.3106	0.3133
0.9	0.3159	0.3186	0.3212	0.3238	0.3264	0.3289	0.3315	0.3340	0.3365	0.3389
1.0	0.3413	0.3438	0.3461	0.3485	0.3508	0.3531	0.3554	0.3577	0.3599	0.3621
1.1	0.3643	0.3665	0.3686	0.3708	0.3729	0.3749	0.3770	0.3790	0.3810	0.3830
1.2	0.3849	0.3869	0.3888	0.3907	0.3925	0.3944	0.3962	0.3980	0.3997	0.4015
1.3	0.4032	0.4049	0.4066	0.4082	0.4099	0.4115	0.4131	0.4147	0.4162	0.4177
1.4	0.4192	0.4207	0.4222	0.4236	0.4251	0.4265	0.4279	0.4292	0.4306	0.4319
1.5	0.4332	0.4345	0.4357	0.4370	0.4382	0.4394	0.4406	0.4418	0.4429	0.4441
1.6	0.4452	0.4463	0.4474	0.4484	0.4495	0.4505	0.4515	0.4525	0.4535	0.4545
1.7	0.4554	0.4564	0.4573	0.4582	0.4591	0.4599	0.4608	0.4616	0.4625	0.4633
1.8	0.4641	0.4649	0.4656	0.4664	0.4671	0.4678	0.4686	0.4693	0.4699	0.4706
1.9	0.4713	0.4719	0.4726	0.4732	0.4738	0.4744	0.4750	0.4756	0.4761	0.4767
2.0	0.4772	0.4778	0.4783	0.4788	0.4793	0.4798	0.4803	0.4808	0.4812	0.4817
2.1	0.4821	0.4826	0.4830	0.4834	0.4838	0.4842	0.4846	0.4850	0.4854	0.4857
2.2	0.4861	0.4864	0.4868	0.4871	0.4875	0.4878	0.4881	0.4884	0.4887	0.4890
2.3	0.4893	0.4896	0.4898	0.4901	0.4904	0.4906	0.4909	0.4911	0.4913	0.4916
2.4	0.4918	0.4920	0.4922	0.4925	0.4927	0.4929	0.4931	0.4932	0.4934	0.4936
2.5	0.4938	0.4940	0.4941	0.4943	0.4945	0.4946	0.4948	0.4949	0.4951	0.4952
2.6	0.4953	0.4955	0.4956	0.4957	0.4959	0.4960	0.4961	0.4962	0.4963	0.4964
2.7	0.4965	0.4966	0.4967	0.4968	0.4969	0.4970	0.4971	0.4972	0.4973	0.4974
2.8	0.4974	0.4975	0.4976	0.4977	0.4977	0.4978	0.4979	0.4979	0.4980	0.4981
2.9	0.4981	0.4982	0.4982	0.4983	0.4984	0.4984	0.4985	0.4985	0.4986	0.4986
3.0	0.4987	0.4987	0.4987	0.4988	0.4988	0.4989	0.4989	0.4989	0.4990	0.4990

Table A4 – Critical values for the Pearson correlation coefficient

	One-tailed test			
	0.05	0.025	0.01	0.005
	Two-tailed test			
N	0.1	0.05	0.02	0.01
4	0.900	0.950	0.980	0.990
5	0.805	0.878	0.934	0.959
6	0.729	0.811	0.882	0.917
7	0.669	0.754	0.833	0.875
8	0.621	0.707	0.808	0.834
9	0.582	0.666	0.750	0.798
10	0.549	0.632	0.715	0.765
11	0.521	0.602	0.685	0.735
12	0.497	0.576	0.658	0.708
13	0.476	0.553	0.634	0.684
14	0.458	0.532	0.612	0.661
15	0.441	0.514	0.592	0.641
16	0.426	0.497	0.574	0.623
17	0.412	0.482	0.558	0.606
18	0.400	0.468	0.543	0.590
19	0.389	0.456	0.529	0.575
20	0.378	0.444	0.516	0.561
21	0.369	0.433	0.503	0.549
22	0.360	0.423	0.492	0.537
23	0.352	0.413	0.482	0.526
24	0.344	0.404	0.472	0.515
25	0.337	0.396	0.462	0.505
26	0.330	0.388	0.453	0.496
27	0.323	0.381	0.445	0.487
28	0.317	0.374	0.437	0.479
29	0.311	0.367	0.430	0.471
30	0.306	0.361	0.423	0.463
35	0.283	0.334	0.392	0.430
40	0.264	0.312	0.367	0.403
45	0.248	0.294	0.346	0.380
50	0.235	0.279	0.328	0.361
60	0.214	0.254	0.300	0.330
70	0.198	0.235	0.278	0.306
80	0.185	0.220	0.260	0.286
90	0.174	0.207	0.245	0.270
100	0.165	0.197	0.232	0.256
200	0.117	0.139	0.164	0.182
300	0.095	0.113	0.134	0.149
400	0.082	0.098	0.116	0.129
500	0.074	0.088	0.104	0.115
1000	0.052	0.062	0.074	0.081

Adapted from Howitt, D. and Cramer, D. (2000). *An Introduction to Statistics in Psychology*, 2nd edn. Harlow, UK: Prentice Hall.

Table A5 – Critical values of the Spearman correlation coefficient

	One-tailed test			
	0.05	0.025	0.01	0.005
	Two-tailed test			
N	0.1	0.05	0.02	0.01
5	0.900			
6	0.829	0.886	0.943	
7	0.714	0.786	0.893	
8	0.643	0.738	0.833	0.881
9	0.600	0.683	0.783	0.833
10	0.564	0.648	0.745	0.858
11	0.520	0.620	0.737	0.814
12	0.496	0.591	0.703	0.776
13	0.475	0.566	0.673	0.743
14	0.456	0.544	0.646	0.714
15	0.440	0.524	0.623	0.688
16	0.425	0.506	0.602	0.665
17	0.411	0.490	0.583	0.644
18	0.399	0.475	0.565	0.625
19	0.388	0.462	0.549	0.607
20	0.377	0.450	0.535	0.591
21	0.368	0.438	0.521	0.576
22	0.359	0.428	0.508	0.562
23	0.351	0.418	0.497	0.549
24	0.343	0.409	0.486	0.537
25	0.336	0.400	0.476	0.526
26	0.329	0.392	0.466	0.515
27	0.323	0.384	0.457	0.505
28	0.317	0.377	0.448	0.496
29	0.311	0.370	0.440	0.487
30	0.305	0.364	0.433	0.478
35	0.282	0.336	0.400	0.442
40	0.263	0.314	0.373	0.412
45	0.248	0.295	0.351	0.388
50	0.235	0.280	0.333	0.368
60	0.214	0.255	0.303	0.335
70	0.198	0.236	0.280	0.310
80	0.185	0.221	0.262	0.290
90	0.174	0.208	0.247	0.273
100	0.165	0.197	0.234	0.259
200	0.117	0.139	0.165	0.183
300	0.095	0.113	0.135	0.149
400	0.082	0.098	0.117	0.129
500	0.074	0.088	0.104	0.115
1000	0.052	0.062	0.074	0.081

Adapted from Howitt, D. and Cramer, D. (2000). *An Introduction to Statistics in Psychology*, 2nd edn. Harlow, UK: Prentice Hall.

Table A6 – Critical values for the *t*-test

	One-tailed significance			
	0.05	0.025	0.01	0.005
	Two-tailed significance			
df	0.1	0.05	0.02	0.01
2	2.920	4.303	6.965	9.925
3	2.353	3.182	4.541	5.841
4	2.132	2.776	3.747	4.604
5	2.015	2.571	3.365	4.032
6	1.943	2.447	3.365	3.708
7	1.895	2.365	2.998	3.500
8	1.860	2.306	2.897	3.355
9	1.833	2.262	2.821	3.250
10	1.813	2.228	2.764	3.169
11	1.796	2.201	2.718	3.106
12	1.782	2.179	2.681	3.055
13	1.771	2.160	2.650	3.012
14	1.761	2.145	2.625	2.977
15	1.753	2.132	2.603	2.947
16	1.746	2.120	2.583	2.921
17	1.740	2.110	2.567	2.898
18	1.734	2.101	2.552	2.878
19	1.729	2.093	2.539	2.861
20	1.725	2.086	2.528	2.845
21	1.721	2.080	2.518	2.831
22	1.717	2.074	2.508	2.819
23	1.714	2.069	2.500	2.807
24	1.711	2.064	2.492	2.797
25	1.708	2.064	2.485	2.787
26	1.706	2.055	2.479	2.779
27	1.703	2.052	2.473	2.771
28	1.701	2.048	2.467	2.763
29	1.699	2.045	2.462	2.756
30	1.697	2.042	2.457	2.750
35	1.690	2.030	2.438	2.724
40	1.684	2.021	2.423	2.704
45	1.679	2.014	2.412	2.690
50	1.676	2.009	2.403	2.678
55	1.673	2.004	2.396	2.668
60	1.671	2.000	2.090	2.660
65	1.669	1.997	2.385	2.654
70	1.667	1.994	2.381	2.648
75	1.665	1.992	2.377	2.643
80	1.664	1.990	2.374	2.639
85	1.663	1.988	2.371	2.635
90	1.662	1.987	2.369	2.632
95	1.661	1.985	2.366	2.629
100	1.660	1.984	2.364	2.626
200	1.653	1.972	2.345	2.601
300	1.650	1.968	2.339	2.592
400	1.649	1.966	2.336	2.588
500	1.648	1.965	2.334	2.586
1000	1.646	1.962	2.330	2.581
•	1.645	1.960	2.326	2.576

Table A7 – Critical values of the Wilcoxon Signed Rank Test

	One-tailed test		
	0.025	0.01	0.05
	Two-tailed test		
N	0.05	0.02	0.01
6	2	1	
7	4	2	
8	6	4	0
9	8	4	2
10	11	8	3
11	14	11	5
12	17	14	7
13	21	17	10
14	26	21	13
15	31	25	16
16	36	30	20
17	42	35	24
18	47	40	28
19	54	46	33
20	60	52	37
21	68	59	42
22	76	66	47
23	84	74	54
24	92	81	60
25	101	90	67

References

Aanstoos, C. M. (1985). The structure of thinking in chess. In A. Giorgi (Ed.) *Phenomenology and Psychological Research*. Pittsburgh, PA: Duquesne University Press.

Adair, J. G. & Vohra, N. (2003). The explosion of knowledge, references, and citations. Psychology's unique response to a crisis. *American Psychologist*, **58**, 15–23.

Adalbjarnardottir, S. & Rafnsson, F. D. (2002). Adolescent antisocial behavior and substance use: Longitudinal analyses. *Addictive Behaviors*, **27** (2), 227–40.

Ainsworth, M. D. S. (1979). Infant–mother attachment. *American Psychologist*, **34**, 932–7.

Ajzen, I. & Fishbein, M. (1980). *Understanding Attitudes and Predicting Behavior*. Englewood Cliffs, NJ: Prentice Hall.

Arksey, H. & Knight, P. (1999). *Interviewing for Social Scientists*. London: Sage.

Asch, S. E. (1951). Effects of group pressure upon the modification and distortion of judgements. In H. Guertzkow (Ed.) *Social Psychology*, 3rd edn. New York: Holt, Rhinehart & Winston.

Asch, S. E. (1952). *Social Psychology*. Englewood Cliffs, NJ: Prentice Hall.

Asch, S. E. (1956). Studies of independence and conformity: I. A minority of one against a unanimous majority. *Psychological Monographs*, **70** (9) (whole issue, no. 416).

Ashcraft, M. H. & Faust, M. W. (1994). Mathematics anxiety and mental arithmetic performance: An exploratory investigation. *Cognition and Emotion*, **8** (2), 97–125.

Ashworth, P. D. (2000). *Psychology and 'Human Nature'*. Hove: Psychology Press.

Ashworth, P. D. (2001). *Four cardinal features of existential-phenomenological psychology*. URL http://www.shu.ac.uk/services/lti/ltri/who/15244pp.htm (19/03/2003).

Atkinson, J. M. & Heritage, J. (Eds) (1984). *Structures of Social Action: Studies in Conversation Analysis*. Cambridge: Cambridge University Press.

Atkinson, P. (1998). *The Life Story Interview*. London: Sage.

Atkinson, P. & Delmont, S. (2006). Rescuing narrative from qualitative research. *Narrative Inquiry*, **16** (1), 164–72.

Atkinson, P. & Hammersley, M. (1994). Ethnography and participant observation. In N. K. Denzin & Y. S. Lincoln (Eds) *Handbook of Qualitative Research*. London: Sage.

Austin, J. L. (1962). *How To Do Things With Words*. Oxford: Clarendon Press.

Aveyard, H. (2007). *Doing a Literature Review*. Maidenhead: Open University Press.

Aviv, A. L., Zelenski, J. M., Rallo, L. & Larsen, R. J. (2002). Who comes when: Personality differences in early and later participation in a university subject pool. *Personality and Individual Differences*, **33** (3), 487–96.

Bakeman, R. & Gottman, J. M. (1997). *Observing Interaction*. Cambridge: Cambridge University Press.

Bamberg, M. (2006). Stories: Big or small: why do we care? *Narrative Inquiry*, **16** (1), 139–47.

Banister, P. (1994). Observation. In P. Banister, E. Burman, I. Parker, M. Taylor and C. Tindall (Eds) *Qualitative Methods in Psychology: A Research Guide*. Buckingham: Open University Press.

Billig, M. (1991). *Ideology and Opinions: Studies in Rhetorical Psychology*. London: Sage.

Billig, M. (1997a). *Arguing and Thinking: A Rhetorical Approach to Social Psychology*. Cambridge: Cambridge University Press.

Billig, M. (1997b). Rhetorical and discursive analysis: How families talk about the royal family. In N. Hayes (Ed.) *Doing Qualitative Analysis in Psychology*. Hove: Psychology Press.

Billig, M. (1999a). Whose terms? Whose ordinariness? Rhetoric and ideology in Conversation Analysis. *Discourse & Society*, **10** (4), 543–58.

Billig, M. (1999b). Conversation Analysis and the claims of naivety. *Discourse & Society*, **10** (4), 572–76.

Billig, M., Condor, S., Edwards, D., Gane, M., Middleton, D. J. & Radley, A. R. (1988). *Ideological Dilemmas: A Social Psychology of Everyday Thinking*. London: Sage.

Black, T. R. (1999). *Doing Quantitative Research in the Social Sciences: An Integrated Approach to Research Design, Measurement and Statistics*. London: Sage.

Bogdan, R. (1974). *Being Different: The Autobiography of Jane Fry*. London: Wiley.

Bogg, T. & Roberts, B. W. (2004). Conscientiousness and health-related behaviors: A meta-analysis of the leading behavioral contributors to mortality. *Psychological Bulletin*, **130** (6), 887–919.

Bruner, J. (1986). *Actual Minds, Possible Worlds*. Cambridge, MA: Harvard University Press.

Bruner, J. (1987). Life as narrative. *Social Research*, **54** (1), 11–32.

Bruner, J. (1990). *Acts of Meaning*. Cambridge, MA: Harvard University Press.

Bryman, A. & Cramer, D. (1997). *Quantitative Data Analysis with SPSS for Windows*. London: Routledge.

Burr, V. (1995). *An Introduction to Social Constructionism*. London: Routledge.

Burr, V. (2002). *The Person in Social Psychology*. Hove: Psychology Press.

Burr, V. (2003). *Social Constructionism*, 2nd edn. Hove: Routledge.

Butler, G. & McManus, F. (2000). *Psychology: A Very Short Introduction*. Oxford: Oxford University Press.

Butt, T. & Burr, V. (2004). *Invitation to Personal Construct Theory*, 2nd edn. Oxford: Wiley-Blackwell.

Butt, T. & Langdridge, D. (2003). The construction of self: The public reach into the private sphere. *Sociology*, **37** (3), 477–94.

Chalmers, A. F. (1999). *What Is This Thing Called Science?*, 3rd edn. Milton Keynes: Open University Press.

Charmaz, K. (1990). 'Discovering' chronic illness: Using grounded theory. *Social Science and Medicine*, **30**, 1161–72.

Charmaz, K. (1995). Grounded theory. In J. A. Smith, R. Harré & L. Van Langenhove (Eds) *Rethinking Methods in Psychology*. London: Sage.

Charmaz, K. (2006). *Constructing Grounded Theory: A Practical Guide Through Qualitative Analysis*. London: Sage.

Cohen, J. (1988). *Statistical Power Analysis for the Behavioral Sciences*, 2nd edn. New York: Academic Press.

Colaizzi, P. (1971). Analysis of the learner's perception of learning material at various stages of the learning process. In A. Giorgi, W. Fischer & R. von Eckartsberg (Eds) *Duquesne Studies in Phenomenological Psychology I*. Pittsburgh, PA: Duquesne University Press.

Coolican, H. (1994). *Research Methods and Statistics in Psychology*, 2nd edn. London: Hodder & Stoughton.

Corbin, J. & Strauss, A. (2008). *Basics of Qualitative Research*, 3rd edn. London: Sage.

Coxon, A. P. M. (2005). Integrating qualitative and quantitative data: What does the user need? *Forum: Qualitative Social Research*, **6** (2). Retrieved 29/07/08 from http://nbn-resolving.de/urn:nbn:de:0114-fqs0502402

Creswell, J. (2002). *Research Design: Qualitative, Quantitative, and Mixed Methods Approaches*, 2nd edn. London: Sage.

Creswell, J. W. & Plano Clark, V. L. (2006). *Designing and Conducting Mixed Methods Research*. London: Sage.

Cronbach, L. J. & Meehl, P. E. (1955). Construct validity in psychological tests. *Psychological Bulletin*, **55** (4), 281–302.

Crossley, M. (2000). *Introducing Narrative Psychology: Self, Trauma and the Construction of Meaning*. Buckingham: Open University Press.

Dahlberg, K., Dahlberg, H. & Nyström, M. (2008). *Reflective Lifeworld Research*. Lund, Sweden: Studentlitteratur.

Deary, I. (2001). *Intelligence: A Very Short Introduction*. Oxford: Oxford University Press.

Deary, I. J. & Batty, D. G. (2007). Cognitive epidemiology. *Journal of Epidemiology and Community Health*, **61** (5), 378–84.

Denzin, N. K. (1989). *Interpretive Biography*. London: Sage.

Docherty, M. & Smith, R. (1999). The case for structuring the discussion of scientific papers. *British Medical Journal*, **318** (7193), 1224–5.

Edley, N. & Wetherell, M. (1995). *Men in Perspective*. London: Prentice Hall.

Edley, N. & Wetherell, M. (2001). Jekyll and Hyde: Men's constructions of feminism and feminists. *Feminism & Psychology*, **11** (4), 439–57.

Edwards, D. (1997). *Discourse and Cognition*. London: Sage.

Edwards, D., Ashmore, M. & Potter, J. (1995). Death and furniture: The rhetoric, politics and theology of bottom line arguments against relativism. *History of the Human Sciences*, **8** (2), 25–49.

Edwards, P., Roberts, I., Clarke, M., Diguiseppi, C., Pratap, S., Wentz, R. & Kwan, I. (2002). Increasing response rates to postal questionnaires: Systematic review. *British Medical Journal*, **324**, 1183+.

Egan, V., Charlesworth, P., Richardson, C., Blair, M. & Mcmurran, M. (2001). Sensational interests and sensation seeking in mentally disordered offenders. *Personality and Individual Differences*, **30** (6), 995–1007.

Eichler, M. (1988). *Nonsexist Research Methods: A Practical Guide*. London: Unwin Hyman.

Eisenberger, N. I., Lieberman, M. D. & Williams, K. D. (2003). Does rejection hurt? An fMRI study of social exclusion. *Science*, **302**, 290–2.

Elsbree, L. (1982). *The Rituals of Life: Patterns in Narrative*. Port Washington, NY: Kennikat Press.

Eysenbach, G. & Till, J. E. (2001). Ethical issues in qualitative research on internet communities. *British Medical Journal*, **323** (7321), 1103–5.

Eysenck, H. J. & Eysenck, S. B. G. (1964). *The Eysenck Personality Inventory*. London: Hodder & Stoughton.

Farivar, S. S., Cunningham, W. E. & Hays, R. D. (2007). Correlated physical and mental summary scores for the SF-36 and SF-12 Health Survey, v.1. *Health and Quality of Life Outcomes*, **5**, 54+.

Featherstone, K. & Donovan, J. L. (2002). 'Why don't they just tell me straight, why allocate it?' The struggle to make sense of participating in a randomised controlled trial. *Social Science & Medicine*, **55** (5), 709–19.

Field, A. P. (2005). *Discovering Statistics Using SPSS*, 2nd edn. London: Sage.

Field, A. & Hole, G. J. (2002). *How to Design and Report Experiments*. London: Sage.

Fischer, W. F. (1974). On the phenomenological mode of researching 'being-anxious'. *Journal of Phenomenological Psychology*, **4** (2), 405–23.

Fishbein, M. & Ajzen, I. (1975). *Belief, Attitude, Intention and Behavior: An Introduction to Theory and Research*. Reading, MA: Addison-Wesley.

Flick, U. (2002). *An Introduction to Qualitative Research*, 2nd edn. London: Sage.

Foucault, M. (1970). *The Order of Things*. London: Tavistock.

Foucault, M. (1971). *Madness and Civilisation: A History of Insanity in the Age of Reason*. London: Tavistock.

Foucault, M. (1972). *The Archaeology of Knowledge*. London: Tavistock.

Foucault, M. (1977). *Discipline and Punish*. London: Tavistock.

Foucault, M. (1978). *The History of Sexuality*. Harmondsworth: Allen Lane/Penguin.

Franklin, R. D., Allison, D. B. & Gorman, B. S. (Eds) (1996). *Design and Analysis of Single Case Research*. Mahwah, NJ: Lawrence Erlbaum Associates.

Freeman, M. (2006). Life 'on holiday'? In defense of big stories. *Narrative Inquiry*, **16** (1), 131–8.

Garfinkel, H. (1967). Passing and the managed achievement of sex status in an 'intersexed' person part 1. In H. Garfinkel, *Studies in Ethnomethodology*. Englewood Cliffs, NJ: Prentice Hall.

Geertz, C. (1973). *The Interpretation of Cultures*. New York: Basic Books.

Gergen, K. J. & Gergen, M. (1986). Narrative form and the construction of psychological science. In T. Sarbin (Ed.) *Narrative Psychology: The Storied Nature of Human Conduct*. New York: Praeger.

Gibbs, G. R. (2002). *Qualitative Data Analysis: Explorations with NVivo*. Buckingham: Open University Press.

Gillies, V. (1999). An analysis of the discursive positions of women smokers: Implications for practical interventions. In C. Willig (Ed.) *Applied Discourse Analysis: Social and Psychological Interventions*. Buckingham: Open University Press.

Gillon, R. (1986). *Philosophical Medical Ethics*. Chichester: Wiley.

Giorgi, A. (Ed.) (1985a). *Phenomenology and Psychological Research*. Pittsburg, PA: Duquesne University Press.

Giorgi, A. (1985b). Sketch of a psychological phenomenological method. In A. Giorgi (Ed.) *Phenomenology and Psychological Research*. Pittsburgh, PA: Duquesne University Press.

Giorgi, A. (1985c). The phenomenological psychology of learning and the verbal learning tradition. In A. Giorgi (Ed.) *Phenomenology and Psychological Research*. Pittsburgh, PA: Duquesne University Press.

Glaser, B. G. (1992). *Emergence vs Forcing: Basics of Grounded Theory Analysis*. Mill Valley, CA: Sociology Press.

Glaser, B. G. & Strauss, A. L. (1964). *Awareness of Dying*. Chicago: Aldine.

Glaser, B. G. & Strauss, A. L. (1967). *The Discovery of Grounded Theory: Strategies for Qualitative Research*. Chicago: Aldine.

Gosling, S. D., Vazire, S., Srivastava, S. & John, O. P. (2004). Should we trust web-based studies? A comparative analysis of six preconceptions about internet questionnaires. *American Psychologist*, **59** (2), 93–104.

Gould, S. J. (1996). *The Mismeasure of Man*, 2nd edn. Harmondsworth: Penguin.

Greenberg, J. (1987). The college sophomore as guinea pig: Setting the record straight. *The Academy of Management Review*, **12** (1), 157–9.

Greene, J.C. (2007). *Mixed Methods in Social Inquiry*. San Francisco: Jossey Bass.

Gurwitsch, A. (1964). *The Field of Consciousness*. Pittsburgh, PA: Duquesne University Press (French original, 1957).

Hagger-Johnson, G. E. & Pollard Whiteman, M. C. (2008). Personality and health – So what? *The Psychologist*, **21** (7), 594–6.

Hall, S. (1992). The west and the rest. In S. Hall & B. Gieben (Eds) *Formations of Modernity*. Cambridge: Polity Press/The Open University.

Hall, S. (2001). Foucault: Power, knowledge and discourse. In M. Wetherell, S. Taylor & S. J. Yates (Eds) *Discourse Theory and Practice: A Reader*. London: Sage.

Halliday, M. A. K. (1973). *Explorations in the Functions of Language*. London: Edward Arnold.

Hammersley, M. (1992). *What's Wrong with Ethnography: Methodological Explorations*. London: Routledge.

Hammersley, M. (1995). *The Politics of Social Research*. London: Sage.

Hammersley, M. (2003a). Conversation analysis and discourse analysis: Methods or paradigms? *Discourse & Society*, **14** (6), 751–81.

Hammersley, M. (2003b). Doing the fine thing: A rejoinder to Jonathan Potter. *Discourse & Society*, **14** (6), 795–8.

Harré, R. & Gillet, G. (1994). *The Discursive Mind*. London: Sage.

Hart, C. (2001). *Doing a Literature Review: Releasing the Social Science Research Imagination*. London: Sage.

Hart, C. (2007). *Doing a Literature Search: A Comprehensive Guide for the Social Sciences*. London: Sage.

Hays, R. D., Hayashi, T. & Stewart, A. L. (1989). A five-item measure of socially desirable response set. *Educational and Psychological Measurement*, **49**, 629–36.

Henriques, J., Hollway, W., Urwin, C., Venn, C. & Walkerdine, V. (1984). *Changing the Subject: Psychology, Social Regulation and Subjectivity*. London: Methuen.

Holdaway, S. (1982). 'An inside job': A case study of covert research on the police. In M. Bulmer (Ed.) *Social Research Ethics*. Basingstoke: Macmillan.

Howell, D. C. (2001). *Statistical Methods for Psychology*, 5th edn. Belmont, CA: Wadsworth.

Hume, D. (1888). *A Treatise of Human Nature*. Oxford: Oxford University Press (first published 1738, London: John Noon).

Husserl, E. (1931). *Ideas* (trans. W. R. Boyce Gibson). London: George Allen & Unwin.

Jenkins, J. S. (2001). The Mozart effect. *Journal of the Royal Society of Medicine*, **94**, 170–2.

Johnson, D. R. & Creech, J. C. (1993). Ordinal measures in multiple indicator models: A simulation study of categorization error. *American Sociological Review*, **48** (3), 398–407.

Jorgensen, D. L. (1989). *Participant Observation – A Methodology for Human Studies*. Sage Applied Social Research Methods Series Vol. 15. London: Sage.

Kelle, U. (2001). Sociological explanations between micro and macro and the integration of qualitative and quantitative methods. *Forum: Qualitative Social Research,* **2** (1). Retrieved 29/07/08 from http://www.qualitative-research.net/fqs-texte/1-01/1-01kelle-e.htm.

Kerlinger, F. & Lee, H. (1999). *Foundations of Behavioural Research*, 4th edn. London: Thomson Learning.

Kimmel, A. J. (1996). *Ethical Issues in Behavioral Research: A Survey*. Cambridge: Wiley-Blackwell.

Kirk, R. E. (1995). *Experimental Design: Procedures for the Behavioral Sciences*, 3rd edn. Belmont, CA: Brooks/Cole.

Kline, P. (2000). *Psychometrics Primer*. London: Free Association Books.

Kvale, S. (2007). *Doing Interviews*. London: Sage.

Kuhn, T. (1970). *The Structure of Scientific Revolutions*, 2nd edn. Chicago: Chicago University Press.

Labov, W. (Ed.) (1972). The transformation of experience in narrative syntax. In W. Labov (Ed.) *Language in the Inner City: Studies in the Black English Vernacular*. Philadelphia: University of Pennsylvania Press.

Labov, W. (1982). Speech actions and reactions in personal narrative. In D. Tannen (Ed.) *Analyzing Discourse: Text and Talk*. Washington, DC: Georgetown University Press.

Langdridge, D. (2003). Hermeneutic phenomenology: Arguments for a new social psychology. *History and Philosophy of Psychology*, **5**, 30–45.

Langdridge, D. (2006). Ideology and utopia: Social psychology and the social imaginary of Paul Ricoeur. *Theory and Psychology*, **16** (5), 641–59.

Langdridge, D. (2007). *Phenomenological Psychology: Theory, Research and Method*. Harlow: Prentice Hall.

Langdridge, D. (2008) Phenomenology and critical social psychology: Directions and debates in theory and research. *Social and Personality Psychology Compass*, **2** (3), 1126–1142, doi: 10.1111/j.1751-9004.2008.00114.x

Langdridge, D. & Butt, T. (2004). The fundamental attribution error: A phenomenological critique. *British Journal of Social Psychology*, **43**(3), 357–69.

Larkin, M., Watts, S. & Clifton, E. (2006). Giving voice and making sense in interpretative phenomenological analysis. *Qualitative Research in Psychology*, **3**, 102–120.

Lewis, S. & Roberts, N. W. (2008). The literature search process: Protocols for Researchers. Retrieved 29/07/08 from http://www.library.nhs.uk/SpecialistLibraries/Download.aspx?resID=101405.

Likert, R. A. (1932). A technique for the measurement of attitudes. *Archives of Psychology*, **140**, 55.

MacLeod, C. (1991). Half a century of research on the Stroop effect: An integrative review. *Psychological Bulletin*, **109** (2), 163–203.

MacMillan, K. (2005). More than just coding? Evaluating CAQDAS in a Discourse Analysis of news texts. *Forum: Qualitative Social Research*, **6** (3), Art. 25, http://nbn-resolving.de/urn:nbn:de:0114-fqs0503257. [Retrieved 30/08/08]

Madill, A. & Doherty, K. (1994). 'So you did what you wanted then': Discourse analysis, personal agency, and psychotherapy. *Journal of Community & Applied Social Psychology*, **4**, 261–73.

Mair, M. (1989). *Beyond Psychology and Psychotherapy: A Poetics of Experience*. London: Routledge.

Manning, P. K. & Cullum-Swan, B. (1994). Narrative, content, and semiotic analysis. In N. K. Denzin & Y. S. Lincoln (Eds) *Handbook of Qualitative Research*. London: Sage.

Matthews, G., Deary, I. J. & Whiteman, M. C. (2003). *Personality Traits*, 2nd edn. Cambridge: Cambridge University Press.

Mayring, P. (2001). Combination and integration of qualitative and quantitative analysis. *Forum: Qualitative Social Research*, **2** (1). Accessed 29/07/08 from http://www.qualitative-research.net/fqs-texte/1-01/1-01mayring.d.htm.

Mayring, P., Huber, G. & Gurtler, L. (Eds) (2007). *Mixed Methodology in Psychological Research*. Rotterdam: Sense Publishers.

McAdams, D. (1993). *The Stories We Live by: Personal Myths and the Making of the Self*. New York: The Guilford Press.

Miles, J. & Banyard, P. (2007). *Understanding and Using Statistics in Psychology: A Practical Introduction*. London: Sage.

Moffatt, S., White, M., Mackintosh, J. & Howel, D. (2006). Using quantitative and qualitative data in health services research – what happens when mixed method findings conflict? *BMC Health Services Research*, **6**(28). See: http://www.pubmedcentral.nih.gov/picrender.fcgi?artid=1434735&blobtype=pdf

Monteil, J. M., Brunot, S. & Huguet, P. (1996). Cognitive performance and attention in the classroom: An interaction between past and present academic experiences. *Journal of Educational Psychology*, **88**, 242–8.

Moran, D. (2000). *Introduction to Phenomenology*. London: Routledge.

Moustakas, C. (1994). *Phenomenological Research Methods*. London: Sage.

Mulkay, M. & Gilbert, G. N. (1982a). Joking apart: Some recommendations concerning the analysis of scientific culture. *Social Studies of Science*, **12**, 585–615.

Mulkay, M. & Gilbert, G. N. (1982b). Accounting for error: How scientists construct their social world when they account for correct and incorrect belief. *Sociology*, **16**, 165–83.

Mulkay, M. & Gilbert, G. N. (1983). Scientists' theory talk. *Canadian Journal of Sociology*, **8**, 179–97.

Neimeyer, R. A. & Neimeyer, G. J. (Eds)(2002). *Advances in Personal Construct Psychology*. New York: Praeger.

O'Cathain, A., Murphy, E. & Nicholl, J. P. (2008). The quality of mixed methods studies in health services research. *Journal of Health Services Research and Policy*, **13**, 92–8.

O'Connell, D. C. & Kowal, S. (1995). Basic principles of transcription. In J. A. Smith, R. Harré & L. V. Langenhove (Eds) *Rethinking Methods in Psychology*. London: Sage.

O'Toole, B. I. & Stankov, L. (1992). Ultimate validity of psychological tests. *Personality and Individual Differences*, **13** (6), 699–716.

Oppenheim, A. N. (2000). *Questionnaire Design, Interviewing and Attitude Measurement*. London: Continuum.

Osgood, C. E., Suci, G. J. & Tannenbaum, P. H. (1957). *The Measurement of Meaning*. Urbana: University of Illinois.

Parker, I. (1992). *Discourse Dynamics: Critical Analysis for Social and Individual Psychology*. London: Routledge.

Pashler, H., Yantis, S., Medin, D., Gallistel, R. & Wixted, J. (2002). *Stevens' Handbook of Experimental Psychology*, 3rd edn. New York: John Wiley & Sons.

Patton, M. Q. (1980). *Qualitative Evaluation Methods*. London: Sage.

Pavlov, I. P. (1927). *Conditioned Reflexes* (trans. G. V. Anrep). London: Oxford University Press.

Plano Clark, V. L. & Creswell, J. W. (Eds) (2008). *The Mixed Methods Reader*. London: Sage.

Plummer, K. (2001). *Documents of Life 2: An Invitation to a Critical Humanism*. London: Sage.

Polkinghorne, D. E. (1989). Phenomenological research methods. In R. S. Valle & S. Halling (Eds) *Existential–Phenomenological Perspectives in Psychology: Exploring the Depths of Human Experience*. New York: Plenum Press.

Popper, K. R. (1963). *Conjectures and Refutations*. London: Routledge & Kegan Paul.

Potter, J. (1997). Discourse analysis as a way of analysing naturally occurring talk. In D. Silverman (Ed.) *Qualitative Research: Theory, Method and Practice*. London: Sage.

Potter, J. (2001). Wittgenstein and Austin. In M. Wetherell, S. Taylor & S. J. Yates (Eds) *Discourse Theory and Practice: A Reader*. London: Sage.

Potter, J. (2003a). Discursive psychology: Between method and paradigm. *Discourse & Society*, **14** (6), 783–94.

Potter, J. (2003b). Practical skepticism. *Discourse & Society*, **14** (6), 799–801.

Potter, J. (2005). Making psychology relevant. *Discourse & Society*, **16** (5), 739–47.

Potter, J. & Hepburn, A. (2005). Qualitative interviews in psychology: problems and possibilities. *Qualitative Research in Psychology*, *2* (4), 281–307.

Potter, J. & Mulkay, M. (1985). 'Scientists' interview talk: Interviews as a technique for revealing participants' interpretative practices. In M. Brenner, J. Brown & D. Cantor (Eds) *The Research Interview: Uses and Approaches*. New York: Academic Press.

Potter, J. & Wetherell, M. (1987). *Discourse and Social Psychology: Beyond Attitudes and Behaviour*. London: Sage.

Potter, J. & Wetherell, M. (1995). Discourse analysis. In J. A. Smith, R. Harré & L. Van Langenhove (Eds) *Rethinking Methods in Psychology*. London: Sage.

Pratto, F., Korchmaros, J. D. & Hegarty, P. (2007). When race and gender go without saying. *Social Cognition*, **25** (2), 221–47.

Raphael, D. D. (1981). *Moral Philosophy*. Oxford: Oxford University Press.

Reips, U. D. (2002). Standards for Internet-based experimenting. *Experimental Psychology*, **49** (4), 243–56.

Rhodes, S. D., Bowie, D. A. & Hergenrather, K. C. (2003). Collecting behavioural data using the World Wide Web: Considerations for researchers. *Journal of Epidemiology and Community Health*, **57** (1), 68–73.

Richards, G. (2002). *Putting Psychology in its Place: A Critical Historical Overview*, 2nd edn. London: Routledge.

Ridley, M. (1997). *The Origins of Virtue*. New York: Viking.

Riessman, C. K. (1993). *Narrative Analysis*. Sage Qualitative Research Methods Series 30. London: Sage.

Rist, R. C. (1975). Ethnographic techniques and the study of an urban school. *Urban Education*, **10**, 86–108.

Robson, C. (1994). *Experiment, Design and Statistics in Psychology*, 3rd edn. London: Penguin.

Robson, C. (2002). *Real World Research*, 2nd edn. Oxford: Blackwell.

Rosenthal, R. & Rosnow, R. (2007). *Essentials of Behavioral Research*, 3rd edn. London: McGraw Hill.

Sapsford, R. (2006). *Survey Research*, 2nd edn. London: Sage.

Sarbin, T. R. (1986). *Narrative Psychology: The Storied Nature of Human Conduct*. London: Praeger.

Schegloff, E.A. (1997). Whose text? Whose context? *Discourse & Society*, **8**, 165–87.

Schegloff, E.A. (1999a). Shegloff's texts as Billig's data: A critical reply. *Discourse & Society*, **10** (4), 558–72.

Schegloff, E.A. (1999b). Naivete vs sophistication or discipline vs self-indulgence: A rejoinder to Billig. *Discourse & Society*, **10** (4), 577–82.

Seale, C. (2000). Using computers to analyse qualitative data. In D. Silverman (Ed.) *Doing Qualitative Research: A Practical Handbook*. London: Sage.

Shenkin, S. D., Starr, J. M. & Deary, I. J. (2004). Birth weight and cognitive ability in childhood: A systematic review. *Psychological Bulletin*, **130**, 989–1013.

Sieber, J. E. & Saks, M. J. (1989). A census of subject pool characteristics and policies. *American Psychologist*, **44** (7), 1053–61.

Silverman, D. (1993). *Interpreting Qualitative Data: Methods for Analysing Talk, Text and Interaction*. London: Sage.

Silverman, D. (2004). *Doing Qualitative Research: A Practical Handbook*. 2nd edn. London: Sage.

Singer, P. (1993). *Practical Ethics*, 2nd edn. Cambridge: Cambridge University Press.

Skinner, B. F. (1938). *The Behavior of Organisms: An Experimental Analysis*. New York: Appleton.

Skinner, B. F. (1974). *About Behaviourism*. London: Cape.

Smith, J. A. (1996). Beyond the divide between cognition and discourse: Using interpretative phenomenological analysis in health psychology. *Psychology and Health*, **11**, 261–71.

Smith, J. A. (1997). Developing theory from case studies: Self-reconstruction and the transition to motherhood. In N. Hayes (Ed.) *Doing Qualitative Analysis in Psychology*. Hove: Psychology Press.

Smith, P. K. & Cowie, H. (1988). *Understanding Children's Development*. Oxford: Blackwell.

Sternberg, R.J. (2003). *The Psychologist's Companion: A Guide to Scientific Writing for Students and Researchers*, 4th edn. Cambridge: Cambridge University Press.

Stevens, C. D. & Ash, R. A. (2001). The conscientiousness of students in subject pools: Implications for 'laboratory' research. *Journal of Research in Personality*, **35** (1), 91–7.

Strauss, A. L. & Corbin, J. (1990). *Basics of Qualitative Research: Grounded Theory Procedures and Techniques*. Newbury Park, CA: Sage.

Strauss, A. L. & Corbin, J. (1994). Grounded theory methodology. In N. K. Denzin & Y. S. Lincoln (Eds) *Handbook of Qualitative Research*. London: Sage.

Tabachnik, B. G. & Fidell, L. S. (2006). *Using Multivariate Statistics*, 5th edn. New York: HarperCollins.

Tatsuoka, M. M. (1971). *Multivariate Analysis: Techniques for Education and Psychological Research*. New York: John Wiley.

Taylor, S. (2006). Narrative as construction and discursive resource. *Narrative Inquiry*, **16** (1), 94–102.

Thomas, W. I. & Znaniecki, F. (1958). *The Polish Peasant in Europe and America*. New York: Dover Publications (first published 1918–21; republished in 2 vols, 1927).

Todd, Z., Brigitte, N., McKeown, S. & Clarke, D. D. (Eds) (2004). *Mixing Methods in Psychology*. Hove: Psychology Press.

Van Dijk, T. A. (2001). Critical Discourse Analysis. In D. Tannen, D. Schiffrin & H. Hamilton (Eds), *Handbook of Discourse Analysis*. Oxford: Blackwell. Downloaded from http://www.discourses.org/download/articles/ [accessed 30/7/08].

Van Excel, N. J. A. & de Graaf, G. (2005). *Q-methodology: A Sneak Preview*. Retrieved 29/07/08 from http://www.qmethodology.net/index.php?page=1

van Manen, M. (1990). *Researching Lived Experience: Human Science for an Action Sensitive Pedagogy*. Albany, NY: SUNY Press.

Watts, S. & Stenner, P. (2005). Doing Q methodology: Theory, method and interpretation. *Qualitative Research in Psychology*, **2**, 67–91.

Weeks, J. (1981). *Sex, Politics and Society*. London: Longman.

Weeks, J. (1985). *Sexuality and its Discontents*. London: Routledge.

Wengraf, T. (2001). *Qualitative Research Interviewing*. London: Sage.

Wertz, F. J. (1985) Method and findings in a phenomenological psychological study of a complex life-event: Being criminally victimised. In A. Giorgi (Ed.) *Phenomenology and Psychological Research*. Pittsburgh, PA: Duquesne University Press.

Wetherell, M. (1998). Positioning and interpretative repertoires: Conversation analysis and post-structuralism in dialogue. *Discourse and Society*, **9** (3), 387–413.

Wetherell, M. (2001). Debates in discourse research. In M. Wetherell, S. Taylor & S. J. Yates (Eds) *Discourse Theory and Practice: A Reader*. London: Sage.

Wetherell, M., Taylor, S. & Yates, S. J. (2001a). *Discourse as Data: A Guide for Analysis*. London: Sage.

Wetherell, M., Taylor, S. & Yates, S. J. (2001b). *Discourse Theory and Practice: A Reader*. London: Sage.

Whitehead, L. C. (2007). Methodological and ethical issues in Internet-mediated research in the field of health: An integrated review of the literature. *Social Science and Medicine*, **65** (4), 782–91.

Wiggins, S., Potter, J. & Wildsmith, A. (2001). Eating your words: Discursive psychology and the reconstruction of eating practices. *Journal of Health Psychology*, **6** (1), 5–15.

Williams, M. & May, T. (1996). *Introduction to the Philosophy of Social Research*. London: UCL Press.

Willig, C. (2001). *Introducing Qualitative Research in Psychology: Adventures in Theory and Method*. Buckingham: Open University Press.

Wittgenstein, L. (1953). *Philosophical Investigations* (trans. G. E. M. Anscombe). Oxford: Blackwell.

Wylde, V., Learmonth, I. D. & Cavendish, V. J. (2005). The Oxford hip score: The patient's perspective. *Health and Quality of Life Outcomes*, **3** (66) http://www.hqlo.com/content/pdf/1477-7525-3-66.pdf

Youngman, M. B. (1979). *Analyzing Social and Educational Research Data*. New York: McGraw-Hill.

Index

Aanstoos, C.M. 392
ABBA counterbalancing 130
abstract 430, 513, 520
accountability 425–6
action-oriented discourse 420, 424
active intervention 503
Adair, J.G. 17
Adalbjarnardottir, S. 296
adjusted $r2$ 319–20
Ainsworth, M.D.S. 76
Ajzen, I. 316
alignment 200
analysis 38, 429–30, 521
analysis of variance (ANOVA) 189, 271–94, 297–8, 305, 322, 323
  between-subjects 273, 274, 275
  designs 273–4
  independent 128, 274, 275, 278–82
  interaction 130
  Kruskal–Wallis and Friedman tests 293–4
  Mauchly's test of sphericity 275
  mixed design 274, 277, 290–3
  one-way 273, 275, 277, 278–86, 350–1
  planned and unplanned comparisons 274–5
  related (within-subjects) 273, 275
  repeated measures 274, 275, 277, 282–6, 354–5
  theoretical background 272
  two-way 273, 275, 286–90, 352–3
  unrelated 273, 275
  see also multivariate analysis of variance
analytic strategy (coding strategy) 521
androcentricity 508
'and' rule 180–1
animal research 506–8
Animals (Scientific Procedures) Act (1986) 506, 507
anonymity 502
ANOVA *see* analysis of variance
apparatus/materials 515
appendices 516, 521
apples and oranges problem 31

argumentative nature of talk 425
arithmetic mean 165–7
Asch, S.E. –5, 52
Ashcraft, M.H. 163
Ash, R.A. 124
Ashworth, P.D. 374, 387, 390, 402
association 122
assumption of symmetrical transfer 130
Atkinson, J.M. 376
Atkinson, P. 444–5, 449, 452
attitudes 51, 98–100
audio recording 64
Austin, E.J. 103
Austin, J.L. 421, 422, 424
Aveyard, H. 17
Aviv, A.L. 124

Back, M.D. 147
Bacon, F. 6
balance, necessity for 510–11
Bamberg, M. 444–5, 458
Banister, P. 85
Banyard, P. 47, 48, 170
bar charts 216–19, 344, 353
Barkham, M. 143–4
Bartlett's test of sphericity 305
batteries 110
Batty, D.G . 297
Bayes, T. 11–12
Beattie, G. 84
behaviourism 7
beta coefficient 320, 322
between-groups design 127, 272
between-subjects effects 306–7
Bewick, B.M. 143–4
bias 44, 133
Big Five personality traits 103
Billig, M. 425, 426, 439, 440, 452
biological psychology 16

bivariate analysis: variables, differences between 230–54
  independent groups *t*-test 235–41
  inferential statistics, theoretical issues in 230–2
  Mann–Whitney *U*-test 246–50
  non-parametric tests of difference 245–6
  t-test 232–5, 241–5
  Wilcoxon test 250–4
bivariate analysis: variables, relationships between 255–70
  chi-square calculation 258–63
  chi-square test 256–8
  correlation coefficients 263–70
blended or 'hybrid' 'hybrid' methods 477, 486–7
Boellstorff, T. 151–2
Bogdan, R. 445–6
Bogg, T. 106
Bonferroni test 274, 275, 284, 286
Boolean operators 22
box-and-whisker charts 344
box plots 223–5, 350
Box's test for equality of covariance matrices 303–4
bracketing 389
branching 146
browsing 17
Bruner, J. 444, 452
Bryman, A. 232
Burr, V. 74, 402, 434, 441
Butt, T. 74, 367

Cahill, J. 143–4
canonical correlation 297
canonical narrative 452
cases, integration of 399–400
categories 411
causality 133–5
central tendency and dispersion, measures of 165–76,
      211–14
  arithmetic mean 165–7
  dispersion measures 170
  levels of measurement and central tendency measures
      170
  mean deviation 173–4
  median (Med) 167–8
  mode 169–70
  range 171
  semi-interquartile range 171–2
  standard deviation 175–6
  variance 174–5
Chalmers, A.E. 7–8, 12
Charmaz, K. 406, 407, 408, 410, 414–15, 456
charts, editing 229
Chicago School 444n
chi-square 255, 256–63, 347–8

chronological structure 521
clarity, maxim of 483
classical conditioning 114–15
classifications 470
class interval 183
code-and-retrieve programs 462–3
code-based theory building 463
coding 79–80, 409–12, 467–8
  constant comparative method 411–12
  focused 411
  line by line 409–10
  see also textual data: transcribing, coding and organising
coefficient:
  of determination 264, 319
  see also correlation coefficients
cognitive ability tests 109–11
cognitive psychology 7
'cognitive styles', unreliable measure of 103–4
Cohen, J. 305
Colaizzi, P. 392
collinearity diagnostics 321
columns 197, 200
combined groups plot 313–14
common person 446
common sense, necessity for 48
communication pragmatics 483
comparative method 407
complementarity 477, 484
computers and qualitative research 460–73
  controversies and debates 473
  qualitative analysis software 462–3
  see also e-research; NVivo
computing new variables 208–9
concatenation function 341
conclusion 430, 521
concrete description 392
conditions 42, 116, 273
confidentiality 67, 154, 502
conjunctions, constant 134
consensus research 152
consent 91, 504
  see also informed consent
consequentialism 501
constant comparative method 411–12
constantive elements of language 424
constituents 394
constructionist paradigm 476
construction of meaning 415, 425
constructs 40, 88, 89, 124
content 425
  analysis 152–4
contextual issues 424

control:
  groups 59, 117
  loss of 145
  for response sets 95–6
conversation analysts 424
Coolican, H. 47
Corbin, J. 412, 414–15
correlation 122–3, 134, 225, 264, 297, 3348–9
  see also correlation coefficients
correlation coefficients 255, 263–70
  Pearson 244, 255, 263–4, 265, 267–70
  Spearman 255, 263–4, 265–7, 268–70
Costa, P.T. 109
counterbalancing 129–30
covariance 314
Cowie, H. 78
Coxon, A.P.M. 476, 486
Cramer, D. 232
critical appraisal 33
Critical Discourse Analysis 424
critical realism 439, 441
Cronbach alpha 101–2, 296
Cronbach, L.J. 407
Crossley, M. 444, 445
crossover design 129–30
Cullum–Swan, B. 456
custom hypothesis tests 307–8
cut-off points, arbitrary 182

Dahlberg, K. 398, 404
Dary, I.J. 110–11
data 338, 476
  analysis 476
  exploring 216–17
  files, opening 201
  frame, creating and saving 343
  see also data collection; entering and manipulating
database selection 20–1
data collection 406–7, 427–8, 476
  life story and narrative research 447–51
  see also experimental and quasi-experimental designs;
    interviews and observation; questionnaires and
    psychometric tests
Data Protection Act 157
Deary, I.J. 103, 297
debriefing 503
deception 85, 502–3
decimals 199
de Graaf, G. 487, 489
degrees of freedom 175, 257–8
Delamont 444–5, 452
demarcation 10
Denzin, N.K. 451

deontology 501
dependent variables 42, 43–4, 45, 49
  analysis of variance (ANOVA) 273
  experimental and quasi-experimental designs 115,
    118, 120, 124, 126–7, 129, 131–2, 134
  fundamentals of statistics 181, 182–3, 187–8
  multivariate analysis of variance 317, 319
descriptions, general/specific structural 396
descriptive statistics 211–17, 303
  exploring data 216–17
  frequency distributions, measures of central tendency
    and dispersion 211–14
  see also graphical representation
design 37–8
designing research questions 19–20
designing search terms 21
differences flowchart 326
discomfort 502, 503
discounting 425
discourse analysis 418–42, 453
  Foucauldian 432–9
  language 419–21
  practical differences 421–2
  strengths, limitations and debates 439–42
  theoretical divergences 421
  see also discursive psychology
discovery of meaning 415
discriminant function analysis 309–14
discursive psychology 421, 422–31
  analysis 429–30
  construction and content, emphasis on 425
  data collection 427–8
  discursive practice vs. discursive resources 424–5
  language games and private language 423
  questions, appropriate 426–7
  rhetoric, stake and accountability 425–6
  speech act theory 424
  text analysis 437–8
  writing up 430–1
discursive resources 422
discussion boards 153–4
discussion groups, online 150–1
discussion section 454, 516, 521
dispersion 211–14
divergent model 484–5
Doherty, K. 441
Donovan, J.L. 480
double-blind studies 132
double negatives, avoidance of 94
double standards 508
dummy coding 319
Duquesne School 387, 392–8, 401–4, 412

editing 338
Edley, N. 169, 426, 440–1
Edwards, D. 97, 441
effect size 123, 231, 305
Egan, V. 105
Egloff, B. 147
Eichler, M. 508
eigenvalue 296, 312
Eisbree, L. 452
Eisenberger, N.I. 142
empiricism 8n
encouragers 70
Engels, R.C. 141
entering and manipulating data 192–209
    computing new variables 208–9
    Data Editor window 196–7
    entering data 200–1
    recording variables 206–8
    saving and opening data files 201
    selecting cases 204–6
    sorting data 202–3
    sorting and splitting files 201–2, 203
    SPSS 193–5
    variables, defining 197–200
epistemology 362, 369–70, 476
epoché 389–90
equal opportunities 508–9
e-research 137–59
    chat behaviour 140–1
    internet addiction and loneliness 141
    online behaviour 141
    online game analysis 142–3
    online interventions 143–4
    population, definition of 139–40
    for Q-method: Flash Q 490–2
    types 138–9
    website visitor statistics 142
    see also ethical issues; offline topics
error 123, 318
    assignment 124, 125–6
    constant 43–4
    measurement 124, 125
    random 43–4
    sampling 123, 125
    standard 188
    type I and type II 183, 190, 298
    unsystematic 125
    variance in data 124–5, 126
essence 390
ethical issues 85, 454–6, 499–511
    animal research 506–8
    balance, necessity for 510–11
    confidentiality and anonymity 502
    consent 504

deception 502–3
discomfort and harm 503
equal opportunities 508–9
ethical fundamentals 500–1
evaluation research 510
non-participation and withdrawal 504–5
see also ethical issues in e-research
ethical issues in e-research 154–9
    informed consent 157–9
    legal requirements 157
    recruited and anonymous participants 155–6
    recruited and identifiable participants 155
    security 156–7
    unaware and anonymous participants 156
    unaware and identifiable participants 155
evaluation research 120, 510
event sampling 80
existential phenomenologists 390
expected frequencies 257
experimental effect 123
experimental group 59
experimental and quasi-experimental designs 113–35
    A-B-A design 122
    A-B design 122
    administration and demand characteristics 132–3
    administration and experimenter bias 133
    assignment error 124, 125–6
    causality 133–5
    correlation studies 122–3
    design basics 135
    designing of experiment 115
    error variance in data 124–5, 126
    field experiments 120
    independent samples 126
    measurement error 124, 125
    natural experiments 120–1
    quasi-experiments 117–19
    repeated measures 129–31
    role of experiments 114–15
    sampling error 123, 125
    single case study experiments 121
    true experiments 116
extra-discursive factors 441
extraversion 18
Eysenbach, G. 153
Eysenck Personality Inventory 108

factor analysis 296, 489–92
factorial design 128
factors 273
falsifiability 10
familism 508
Farivar, S.S. 306
Faust, M.W. 163

Featherstone, K. 480
feminism 365–6
Fidell, L.S. 319–21
Field, A. 296, 489
file 338
findings 38, 430, 521
first-person accounts 389
Fischer, W.F. 392
Fishbein, M. 316
Fisher's Exact Test 263
five per cent significance level 182
Flash Q 490–2
Flesch–Kincaid Grade Level 90
Flesch Reading Ease 90
Flick, U. 451, 461, 462–3, 473
focus groups 71, 479–80
'foot in the door' technique 94
forced conceptual description 415
formal approach 445–6
format 338, 354, 355–6, 512–16
Foucault, M. 420, 421, 422, 424, 432–9, 441
Fox, H.C. 110–11
Fox, J. 333
F-ratio 274, 284, 288, 290, 322
Freeman, M. 458
frequency distributions 211–14
Freud, S. 6, 121
Friedman test 293–4
functional magnetic resonance imaging 142
funnelling 70

Garfinkel, H. 446–7
Gaussian distribution 184
Geertz, C. 407
gender insensitivity 508
general discussion 430
General Health Questionnaire 111
generalisability 106
generalisation model 479–80
general theories 413–14
generators 145–6
Gergen, K.J. 452
Gergen, M. 452
Gibbs, G.R. 461, 464
Gilbert, G.N. 425
Gillet, G. 419, 441
Gillies, V. 437, 439
Gillon, R. 501
Giorgi, A. 387, 392, 393–4, 409, 417, 453
Glaser, B.G. 371, 405, 408, 413–15
Glover, L. 176
gold standard 47, 54
Gosling, S.D. 109, 144

Gough, B. 63
Gould, S.J. 108
GRAMMS: Good Reporting of a Mixed Methods Study 486–7, 494
graphical representation 338, 343–5
    bar charts, simple and complex 216–19
    box plots 223–5
    charts, editing 229
    displaying more than one 345
    histograms 220–1
    multivariate 344–5
    pie charts 222–3
    scattergrams 225–8
    univariate 344
    see also descriptive statistics
graphical user interface 328, 333
great person 446
Greech, J.C. 47
Greenberg, J. 123
Greenhouse–Geisser statistic 275, 284, 285, 291
grey literature 25
grounded theory 405–17, 453
    abbreviated version 415
    coding 409–12
    data collection 406–7
    full version 415
    meaning making, dynamic nature of 407–9
    memo writing 412
    strengths, limitations and debates 414–17
    theoretical sampling 407
    theory development 412–14
groups 71–4
Gubrium 450
Gurwitsch, A. 394

Hagger–Johnson, G.E. 106
Halliday, M.A.K. 456
Hall, S. 432, 433
Hammersley, M. 371, 442, 509
harm 503
    potential 153
Harré, R. 419, 441
Hawthorne effect 132
Hays, R.D. 96
Heidegger 403
Henriques, J. 420
Hepburn 458
Heritage, J. 376
hermeneutic phenomenologists 390
higher-order theory 413–14
Hill, A.J. 143–4
histograms 220–1
history effects 117–18

Holdaway, S. 85
horizontalisation 390–1
Hospital Anxiety and Depression Scale 111
Hotelling's Trace 304
Howell, D.C. 48, 190, 232, 274–5
human science 416
Hume, D. 134
Hunter, M. 176
Husserl, E. 386–7, 389–90
hypotheses 12, 36
hypothetico-deductive method 12–13

idealism versus realism 388–9
ideational function 456
ideological dilemma 426
idiographic approach 398
imaginative variation 391
Implicit Association test 147–8
importing a file 465–6
impression management 95
independent groups design 127
independent measures design 126
independent subject design 127
independent variables 42, 43–4, 45, 49
    experimental and quasi-Experimental designs 115,
        120–1, 124, 127, 129, 131–2, 134
    fundamentals of statistics 181, 1182–3, 187–8
    multivariate analysis of variance 317, 319
induction 9, 11
inferential statistics, theoretical issues in 230–2
informants, selection of 445–7
Information Commissioner 157
informed consent 85, 90, 154, 157–9
intellectual property rights 154
intelligence quotient 109, 110
intentionality 387–8, 403
interaction 286
internal consistency 99
International Personality Item Pool 103, 109
interpersonal function 456
interpretative phenomenological analysis 387,
        397–404, 412–13
interpretative repertoire 423, 430
interrupted time series quasi-experiments 119
interval-level scales 46–7, 49
interval/ratio 170
interviews and observation 61–85
    ecological validity 78
    ethics 85
    group discussions 71–4
    interpersonal variables, effect of 66
    interviewing 62
    interview schedule 69–70

interview skills 71
multiple observers and reliability 81–2
naturalistic field (uncontrolled) observation 77
observation 75–6
participant observation 82–5
practice 70–1
recording data 63–4, 79–81
repertory grid techniques 74–5
research interviews 62–3
semi-structured interviewing 65, 69, 447
structured interviewing 65–6
structured observation 76–7
techniques for successful interviewing 66–9
therapeutic interviews 63
unstructured interviews 64–5, 69, 447–8, 451
interviews, online 148–50
introduction section 430, 454, 513–15, 520
intrusiveness 153
intuitionism 501n
inventory 88, 108
item analysis 101
items 88

jangles 18, 21, 89
jargon, avoidance of 69, 95
Jefferson, G. 376–7
Jefferson system of transcription 376–7, 429, 457
Jenkins, J.S. 124
jingles 18, 21, 89
John, O.P. 109
Johnson, D.R. 47
journals 25

Kantianism 501n
Kelle, U. 475, 477
Kelly, G. 74
key informant 446
key words, linkingmaxi together 21–2
Kimmel, A.J. 139
Kline, P. 104
Kowal, S. 376–7
Kruskal–Wallis test 293–4

label 199
Labov, W. 457
Langdridge, D. 150, 367, 387, 390, 398, 402, 441, 445,
        452, 456, 509
language 67, 376, 419–21, 423, 424
    see also discourse analysis
Larkin, M. 403
Latin square 131
LBC1921 study 102
Levene's Test for Equality of Variances 239, 305
Lewis, S. 22

life story and narrative research 443–58
    analysis of life story data 451–3
    data collection 447–51
    informants, selection of 445–7
    narrative practice and form 456–7
    strengths, limitations and debates 457–8
    triangulation 451
    writing a life story 454–6
likelihood 165
Likert scales 41, 48, 92, 95, 98–9, 232, 321
linear relationship 264–5
line of best fit 317–18
line graphs 353
list view 470
literature review 513–14
Loftus, E. 14
logical memory 110

McAdams, D. 444, 449, 452
McCrae, R.R. 109
MacDonald 35
MacLeod, C. 123
MacMillan, K. 473
Madill, A. 441
main effects 286
Mair, M. 444
manipulating data *see* entering and manipulating data
Manning, P.K. 456
Mann–Whitney *U*-test 245, 246–50, 252, 3347
MANOVA *see* multivariate analysis of variance
marginal person 446
matched pairs 127–8
Matthew 384
Matthews, G. 108
maturation effects 118
Mauchly's test of sphericity 275, 284, 285, 291, 292, 305
Mayring, P. 477, 478, 479, 480–1
mean deviation 170, 173–4
meaning making, dynamic nature of 407–9
meaning, overall 393
meaning-units 392–7
measurement level 200
median (Med) 167–8, 170
Meehl, P.E. 407
Meerkerk, G.-J. 141
memory, short term 18
memos 378, 399, 412, 468–9
mental component summary 111
mental harm 503
mental health status, measures of 111
Merleau-Ponty 403, 518
MeSH headings 21, 24

meta analysis 31
method 430, 515, 520–1
methodology 369–701
method section 454, 521
Miles, J. 47, 48, 170
Milgram 120
Milton 384
mind map 26
Mini-markers 109
Minnesota Multiphasic Personality Inventory 108
missing dat a 199
mixed methods 474–94
    blended or 'hybrid' methods 486–7
    generalisation model 479–80
    multidimensional scaling 493
    preparation model 478–9
    profoundisation model 480–1
    similarities between methods 475–7
    triangulation models 481–5
    see also Q method
mode 169–70
models 338, 470
modified scientific report 520
Moffatt, S. 484
Monteil, J.M. 163
Moran, D. 386
Moray House test 110, 111
Mozart effect hypothesis 124, 129, 130
Mulhern, B. 143–4
Mulkay, J. 428
Mulkay, M. 425
multicollinearity 320–1
multidimensional scaling 493
multiple regression 316, 317, 318, 319, 321–3, 349
    hierarchical 319, 320
    simultaneous 319
    stepwise 319, 320
multivariate analysis of variance (MANOVA) 295–314
    alternatives to 296–8
    calculation 299–309
    discriminant function analysis 309–14
    plots 308–9
mutual exclusivity 45

narrative coherence 452
narrative mode 444
narrative research *see* life story and narrative research
narrative review 17
narrative smoothing 523
narrative structure 521
natural attitude 389
natural science 417
negative case analysis 411

NEO-FFI 109
NEO-PI-R 103, 109
neutrality 67
Newton, I. 6
nodes 464, 467–8, 470
nominal-level scales 45–6, 49, 170, 200
non-parametric tests 185, 189, 231–2, 245–6
non-participation 504–5
normal distribution 183–6
notation 352–3
note taking 63, 79
numbers, large and small 342
NVivo 461, 463–4
NVivo 2.0 464–9
   coding 467–8
   importing a file 465–6
   memos 468–9
   saving project 469
   starting a project 464–5
NVivo 8.0 469–72

objectivist position 415
objects, construction of 435–6
observational studies 505
observed frequencies 257
O'Cathain, A. 486, 494
O'Connell, D.C. 376–7
offline topics 138–9, 144–54
   consensus research 152
   content analysis 152–4
   online discussion (focus) groups 1150–1
   online experiment 146–8
   online interviews 148–50
   online questionnaire 144–6
   participant observation 151–2
one-group post-test only quasi-experiments 117
one per cent significance level 182
one-tailed tests 234–5
online topics 138–9
operationalising concepts 36
order effect 129, 130
ordinal-level scales 46, 49, 170, 200
organising see textual data: transcribing, coding and
   organising
organising ideas 35
'or' rule 180
Osgood, C.E. 99
O'Toole, B.I. 106
outcome 89
outliers 167, 215
overgeneralisation 508
overviews 31
OVID 20, 22, 26–30

Palmer, J.C. 14
paradigmatic mode 444
paradigms 13, 476
parallel groups 128
parametric tests 185, 189, 231–2
Parker, I. 418, 434–7, 439, 441
Partial Eta Squared values 305
participant fatigue 144
Participant Information Sheet 90, 91, 94, 158
participant observation 151–2, 447, 451, 504
participants 515, 520
participant selection 72
pattern coding see third order
Patton, M.Q. 83
Pavlov, I.P. 114–15
Pearson correlation coefficient 244, 255, 262, 263–4,
   265, 267–70
performative elements of language 424
personality inventories 106–9
personality traits 51
persuasiveness 430
Peterson, E.R. 103
phenomenological research methods 37, 386–404, 453
   Duquesne School 392–7
   epoché 389–90
   idealism versus realism 388–9
   imaginative variation 391
   intentionality 387–8
   interpretative phenomenological analysis 397–401
   phenomenological reduction 390–1
PHPQ 146
Physical Component Summary 107, 111
physical harm 503
physical health status, measures of 111
PICO model 19–20, 24, 32, 34
pie charts 222–3
Pillai's Trace 304, 305
piloting 91
placebo groups 59
planned comparisons 274
planning research 16–38
   analysis 38
   choice of topic to write about 33–5
   controlled vocabulary 21
   critical appraisal 33
   database selection 20–1
   design 37–8
   designing research questions 19–20
   designing search terms 21
   findings 38
   hypotheses 36
   linking key words together 21–2
   meta analysis 31

overviews 31
psychological literature 17
reading narrative reviews 30–1
reading review articles 30
reading systematic reviews 31
sampling 37
searching for reading 17–18
searching the World Wide Web 26–30
theory 36
truncation symbols and wildcards 22–6
variables 36
writing reviews 32–3, 35
plastic interval level 47
plot type 452
Plummer, K. 444, 445, 448–9, 450, 452–3
politics 433, 437–9, 509–10
Polkinghorne, D.E. 392
Pollard Whiteman, M.C. 106
Popper, K. 7, 10, 11, 361
populations and samples 53, 139–40
positivism 362–3, 476
post-hoc tests 235, 274, 275
post-test only non-equivalent groups quasi-experiments 117
Potter, J. 367, 418, 420, 422, 423, 426–7, 428, 429–30, 439, 441, 442, 458
power 189, 190, 245, 305–6, 433, 437–9
practice 70–1, 102
pragmatics 367–8, 445
Pratto, F. 476, 482–3
pre-existing (self) documentation 447
preparation model 478–9
presenting findings *see* reporting and presenting findings
pre-test post-test non-equivalent groups quasi-experiments 118–19
pre-test post-test single groups quasi-experiments 117–18
Prisoner's Dilemma 42
privacy, perceived 153
probability 165, 176–81
    calculation 179–81
    empirical 178
    logical (mathematical) 177–8, 179
    and poker 178
    and statistical inference 181–2
    subjective 177, 179
probes 70
procedure 515
profoundisation model 480–1
project 464
prosodic (phonological) elements of language 376
P-set 488–9, 492
pseudo-science 10

PsychINFO 20, 21, 22, 24, 26–30
psychoanalytic theory 6–7
psychological attitude 393
psychological literature 17
psychological phenomenological reduction 390
PubMed 20, 21
p value 346

Q method 486, 487–92
    factor analysis 489–92
    P-set 488–9
    Q-grid 489
    Q-set 487–8, 489–90
QSR website 464, 472
qualitative analysis, fundamentals of 361–71
    changing awareness within psychology 364
    commonalities 371
    epistemology 362, 369–70
    feminism 365–6
    methodology 369–71
    new paradigm, limitations of for social sciences 368–9
    positivism 362–3
    qualitative versus quantitative debate 367–8
    queer theory 366
    scientific approach, criticism of 363–4
    social constructionism 365
Qualitative Data Analysis (QDA) software 461, 462, 463, 473
qualitative methods 15, 16, 37–8, 62, 476, 478
Qualtrix 146
quantitative methods 13–15, 16, 37–8, 361–4, 369–70, 476, 478
queer theory 366
questionnaire, online 144–6
questionnaires and psychometric tests 87–111
    attitudes, measurement of 98–100
    cognitive ability tests 109–11
    consent form 91
    control for response sets 95–6
    general principles of questionnaires 89
    mental and physical health status, measures of 111
    Participant Information Sheet 90
    personality inventories 106–9
    psychometrics 99
    questionnaires 87–9
    question types 92–3
    readability of questionnaires 90
    response rates 97–8
    sampling 96–7
    stages of design 91
    writing questions 93–5
    see also reliability; validity
questions:

appropriate 426–7
    open 69
    piping 146
quotations 518

Rafnsson, F.D. 296
Rammstedt, B. 109
randomised controlled trial 480
randomization 125–6
range 171
    plus one technique 199
Raphael, D.D. 501
ratio scales 47, 49
Raven's progressive matrices 110–11
R code/R syntax 328
reading:
    for meaning 398–9
    narrative reviews 30–1
    with purpose 35
    review articles 30
    systematic reviews 31
realism 388–9
Reavey, P. 63
reciprocal altruism 143
recording data 63–4, 79–81
recruited and anonymous participants 155–6
recruited and identifiable participants 155
references 430, 516–19, 521
reflexivity 133, 366, 416, 521–2
regression 297, 316–27
    assumptions 319
    coefficient 318
    differences flowchart 326
    discontinuity quasi-experiments 119
    linear 228, 317, 348–9
    multicollinearity 320–1
    relationships flowchart 327
    simple 316, 319
    statistical 118
    terms 319–20
    theoretical background 317–18
    to the mean 118
    see also multiple
Reips, U.D. 146
relationships flowchart 327
relevance, maxim of 483
reliability 41, 50–1, 99–4, 453
    alpha (Cronbach alpha) 101–2, 296
    alternate forms 103
    inter-item 101
    inter-rater 81–2, 102
    item-total 101
    parallel forms 103–4

split-half 99–102
    test-retest 51, 102
Rentfrow, P.J. 109
repeated measures 126, 129–31
repertory grid techniques 74–5
replication 38, 52–3
reporting and presenting findings 512–24
    writing for publication 524
    writing skills 522–3
    writing up qualitative research 519–22
    see also standard scientific report style
representativeness 58, 144
reshaping data 354
response 95, 96, 97–8
results section 454, 515, 521
reversal phase 122
review, remembering purpose of 35
reviews, systematic 17
revision 91
rhetoric 425–6
rhetorical structure 452
Rhodes, S.D. 144
Ricoeur, P. 386
Riding's Cognitive Style Analysis test 104
Ridley, M. 142
Riessman, C.K. 445, 453, 456–7
Rist, R.C. 15
Roberts, B.W. 106
Roberts, N.W. 22
Robson, C. 38, 119, 134, 181, 508
robustness 189, 232
role-play 71
Rosenberg Self-Esteem Inventory 41
rows 197
Roy's Largest Root 304
R and R commander 328–56
    basic R commands 340
    chi-square 347–8
    correlation and linear regression 348–9
    creating and saving data frame 343
    definition 328–9
    format, reshaping 355–6
    graphs 343–5
    importing data into R 338–9
    installation 329–32
    large and small numbers 342
    making comments 340
    Mann–Whitney test 347
    multiple regression 349
    one-way ANOVA 350–1
    R code 339
    R commander 333–8
    repeated measures ANOVA 354–5

saving codes 342–3
t-test 345–6
two-way ANOVA 352–3
vectors 341
Wilcoxon test 347

Saks, M.J. 139
Salter-Ling, N. 176
sampling 37, 53, 96–7
  bias 53
  convenience 53, 97
  distribution of the means 188
  independent 126
  multi-stage cluster 56
  random 96
  size 57–9, 190
  small 258
  snowball 97
  statified random 97
  theoretical 407
  see also sampling methods
sampling methods 54–7
  cluster 55
  opportunity (convenience) 56
  random 54
  snowball 57
  stage 56
  stratified 55
  systematic 54–5
SSarbin, T.R. 443
SAS 461
Saucier, G. 109
saving data files 201
saving projects 469
scale 88, 200
scattergrams 225–8
scatterplots 344
Scheffé test 274, 280
Schegloff, E.A. 440
Schmukle, S.C. 147
science, history of 6–13
  definition of science 7–9
  falsifiability 10
  hypothetico-deductive method 12–13
  induction 9
scientific approach, criticism of 363–4
Seale, C. 462
searching for reading 17–18
searching the World Wide Web 26–30
search string 21, 22, 24, 28
Second Life 151–2
security 156–7
selecting cases 204–6

self-deception 95
semantic differential scales 99
semi-interquartile range 171–2
sensational hobbies and interests 105
'sensitive' topics 94
sentences, passive 90
set 393
setting, control over 78
sex appropriateness 508
sexual dichotomism 508–9
SF-36 Health Outcome Survey 107, 111, 299, 306
Shenkin, S.D. 31
Sieber, J.E. 139
significance tests 165, 230–1
sign test 250
Silverman, D. 369
simultaneous method 320
Singer, P. 500, 501
single-blind studies 132
skimming 17
Skinner, B.F. 121
skipping 146
Smith 35
Smith, J.A. 387, 397–8, 402, 403
Smith, P.K. 78
snippets 329
ssociability 18
social bookmarking 25, 26
social constructionism 365, 418
social desirability 66, 95
social-economic status 145
Socially Desirable Response Set Five-Item Survey 95–6
social psychology 16
social sciences, methods in 16
sorting data 202–3
sorting and splitting files 201–2
sources 470
Spearman correlation coefficient 255, 263–4, 265–7, 268–70
speech act theory 424
Spijkerman, R. 141
SPSS 74, 101, 193–5
  analysis of variance (ANOVA) 273, 274, 275, 286, 290
  differences between variables 232, 234–5, 237, 241, 246, 250
  entering and manipulating data 192–3
  multivariate analysis of variance (MANOVA) 307, 308, 317, 318
  qualitative methods 461
  relationships between variables 258, 265
square 174
stable construct 102
stages of design 91

stake 425–6
standard deviations 175–6, 186, 188
standardisation 41, 108
standardised distributions 185
standard scientific report style 512–19
    format 512–16
    referencing 516–19
standard scores *see z* scores
Stankov, L. 106
Starr, J.M. 110–11
statistics 338
statistics, fundamentals of 163–90
    descriptive and inferential 165
    normal distribution 183–6
    parametric vs. non-parametric tests 1189
    power 190
    standard error 188
        statistical inference and pprobability 181–2
        statistics anxiety 164
    type I and type II errors 183
    z-scores 187–8
    see also central tendency and dispersion; probability
Stenner, P. 487, 490
Stevens, C.D. 124
Strauss, A.L. 371, 405, 408, 412, 413–15
Stroop effect 123, 125
structure matrix 312–13
subject creation 432
subjectivity 415, 420, 435–6
subject positioning 432, 433, 434
submissions, multiple and mischievous 144
substantive theory 414
summary tables 399, 400
survey 88
Survey Monkey 145–6
SurveyWiz 146
Swann, W.B. Jr 109
synonyms 24

Taachnik, B.G. 319–21
Tatsuoka, M.M. 309, 313
Taylor, S. 456
technical terms, avoidance of 95
text retrieval programs 462–3
textual data: transcribing, coding and organising
        373–85
    first order coding 379–81
    organising and presenting analysis 383–5
    second order coding 381
    thematic analysis 382–3, 384
    third order coding 381–2
    transcription as analysis 377–8

transcription, purposes and principles of 374–5
    transcription systems 376–7
textual function 456
thematic analysis 382–3, 384, 453
themes, identification of 399
themes, structuring of 399
theoretical background 521
theoretical construct 88
theories 12, 36
theory development 412–14
theory-generating structure 521
theory of reasoned action 316–17
Thomas, W.I. 444n, 446
Tiffany 518
Till, J.E. 153
time sampling 81
title 513, 520
Tit for Tat strategy 42
tone 452
toolkit 423
topic choice 33–5
traditional model 483
transcendental phenomenologists 390
transcribing *see* textual data: transcribing, coding and
        organising
triangulation 368, 451, 481–5
trigonometry 477
triple-blind studies 132–3
true zero point 47
truncation symbols 22–6
Trusler, K. 143–4
truth, maxim of 483
t-score 303
t-test 189, 232–5, 250, 275, 286
    dependent 345
    independent 128, 233, 235–41, 345–6
    multiple repeated 274
    related 232–3, 241–5, 346
Tukey HSD test 274, 280
Tukey post–hoc test 351
tutorials 472
t-value 322, 346
two-tailed tests 234–5, 252
two × two contingency table 257
type 198

unaware and anonymous participants 156
unaware and identifiable participants 155
University-hosted questionnaire tools 146
unplanned comparisons 274
utilitariansim 501

validity 41, 51–2, 99, 104–7, 453, 477, 484
  concurrent 105
  construct 106–7, 135
  content 105
  convergent 107
  criterion 105–6
  discriminant 107
  ecological 52, 77, 78
  face 104
  population 106
  predictive 105–6
  ultimate 106
values 199
  absolute 173
  bi-modal 169
  Partial Eta Squared 305
van den Eijnden, R.J. 141
Van Dijk, T.A. 424
Van Excel, N.J.A. 487, 489
van Manen, M. 398, 404
variables 36, 40–9, 312
  categorical and continuous 48–9
  common sense, necessity for 48
  confounding 44–5
  constant versus random error 43–4
  criterion (dependent) 105, 318, 319
  defining 197–200
  extraneous (nuisance) 43
  interpersonal 66
  interval-level scales 46–7
  names 198
  nominal-level scales 45–6, 319
  operationalising 41
  ordinal-level scales 46
  predictor 318, 319
  ratio scales 47
  recording 206–8
  see also bivariate analysis; dependent; independent
variance 174–5, 312
  between-group 125
  proportion 231
  ratio (F-ratio) 272
  systematic 125
  within-groups 125
variate 312
vectors 341
verification 391
Vermulst, A.A. 141

very brief versions 109
video recording 64, 79
'visual perception' 5
vocabulary, controlled 21
Vohra, N. 17
vulnerability 153

warm-up exercises 72–3
washout period 130
Watts, S. 487, 490
Webb 427
Web of Knowledge 20, 22
Wechsler Memory Scale 110
Weeks, J. 432
Wertz, F.J. 392, 397, 413
Wetherell, M. 169, 367, 418, 419, 420, 421–2, 423, 424, 426–7, 429–30, 434, 440–1
Whalley, L.J. 110–11
Whitehead, L.C. 144
Whiteman, M.C. 110–11
Wiggins, S. 430
Wilcoxon test 245, 250–4, 347
wildcards 22–6
Wilk's Lambda 304, 312
Willig, C. 369, 403, 406, 415–16, 421, 440
withdrawal 504–5
within-groups variation 272
within-study drop-out 144
Wittgenstein, L. 420, 421, 422, 423, 439
word of mouth 25
word processors 462–3
working memory 18, 21
World Wide Web 137
Wright 47
writing
  for publication 524
  with purpose 35
  reviews 32–3, 35
  skills 522–3
  up 430–1
  up qualitative research 519–22
Wylde, V. 478

Yates's correction 260, 262
Youngman, M.B. 101

Znaniecki, F. 444n, 446

z-score 187–8, 252, 253